The
CHICKAMAUGA
Campaign

Barren Victory: The Retreat into Chattanooga,
the Confederate Pursuit, and the Aftermath of the Battle,
September 21 to October 20, 1863

David A. Powell

SB

Savas Beatie
California

Library of Congress Control Number: 2016948567

ISBN: 978-1-61121-328-7

eISBN: 978-1-61121-329-4

05 04 03 02 01   5 4 3 2 1
First edition, first printing

SB

Published by
Savas Beatie LLC
989 Governor Drive, Suite 102
El Dorado Hills, CA 95762

Phone: 916-941-6896
(E-mail) sales@savasbeatie.com

05 04 03 02 01   5 4 3 2 1
First edition, first printing

Savas Beatie titles are available at special discounts for bulk purchases in the United States by corporations, institutions, and other organizations. For more details, please contact Special Sales, P.O. Box 4527, El Dorado Hills, CA 95762, or you may e-mail us at sales@savasbeatie.com, or visit our website at www.savasbeatie.com for additional information.

Proudly published, printed, and warehoused in the United States of America.

To my wife, Anne, my steadfast partner in this project;
I could not have done it without you.

Table of Contents

Preface

"... for the purpose of preserving and suitably marking for historical and professional military study the fields of some of the most remarkable maneuvers and most brilliant fighting in the war of the rebellion."

— *enabling legislation, Chickamauga and Chattanooga National Military Park, August 19, 1890*

The publication of *Barren Victory*, the third volume in *The Chickamauga Campaign* trilogy, brings to a close a project that has been with me for nearly two decades.

What began in 1997 as the research for a board game has now culminated in this final installment of (to steal a phrase from the late, great British science fiction author and humorist Douglas Adams) the increasingly inaccurately named The Chickamauga Campaign trilogy. The "inaccurate" part relates to the fact that I have written two additional books on Chickamauga: *The Maps of Chickamauga* (Savas Beatie, 2009), and a Confederate cavalry study entitled *Failure in the Saddle* (Savas Beatie, 2010). Both compliment this trilogy and quite rightly could be seen as additional volumes of one (very large) project.

Barren Victory is a data-driven study. It includes five narrative chapters that examine the final moments and longer-term repercussions of the campaign. The balance of the book—one might consider it the heart of this work—incorporates a great deal of additional information that until now cannot be found elsewhere. I compiled the numbers and loss data for each army from hundreds of sources. I believe this information is the most comprehensive statistical exploration of the forces engaged to date. The first two volumes provided some of this information, but *Barren Victory* expands that material into three different appendices, all fully sourced.

Barren Victory also includes a detailed bibliography. I once glossed over bibliographies, viewing them as the necessary but boring background to good scholarship. Necessary indeed they are. But boring? Not to me, at least not any longer. These days I peruse bibliographies to discover new materials, and in some cases even new repositories. The model of the genre, as far as I am concerned, is Dr. Richard A. Sauers's *The Gettysburg Campaign, June 3 - August 1, 1863* (Greenwood, 1982; the second edition was published in 2004). For space reasons, *Barren Victory's* bibliography lacks the annotations found in Dr. Sauer's work, but I have adopted one aspect I wish others would emulate: the identification of the regimental affiliation for each source, wherever possible, since that information is not always readily apparent at first glance. Regiments were the fundamental building blocks of both soldier life and army organization. Reading a soldier's service account without knowing his regimental affiliation omits invaluable context. I found this bit of data an immense help when cross-referencing my assembled material, and I suspect other readers will, too.

Acknowledgments

To plunder an oft-quoted line of poetry, "No man is an island." Who to thank? There are so many people. Foremost among them all is my wife of 31 years, Anne, whose patience with this labor has been unflagging. Writing with a full-time day job means filling up early morning hours, weekends, and seizing spare moments when they arise. It also means using limited vacation time to travel for research, for touring, speaking, and for supporting new books as they are released. Thank you, love, for putting up with everything.

Next in importance is my partner in cartography, David Friedrichs. Dave has been a part of this project since its inception, as evidenced by his work in *Maps of Chickamauga*; and his maps have graced every one of my books since. At last, Dave, we can move on.

Two men I have repeatedly thanked before, but who deserve mention again, are Jim Ogden and Glenn Robertson. I wish to thank Chickamauga-Chattanooga National Park Historian James H. Ogden, III for his indefatigable willingness to discuss any and all things Chickamauga over the years. Jim loves the park with a devotion that is second to none, and knows more about it, I suspect, than any other man alive. The other is the Dean of Chickamauga scholars, William Glenn Robertson. Formerly of the Combat Studies Institute, Dr. Robertson has also been willing to share his knowledge with me over the years, and has been nothing but generous in doing so. Glenn is writing his own great tome on the Chickamauga Campaign. I firmly believe that more good work on Chickamauga will only help all of us who write and study this battle, and I have no doubt Dr. Robertson's efforts will be top-shelf.

Keith Bohannon, Richard Manion, and Lee White have all become good friends over the course of this project. I know we share a comradeship in our own love of the park, and of the stories of the men who lived and died there. Rick led me on my first full tour of the battlefield, all those years ago. Keith and Lee have shared numerous pieces of information with me, as any perusal of my footnotes will quickly reveal. I thank them all for their help and support.

It is impossible to individually thank every archivist who helped me at every repository—they are legion. I appreciate every one of their efforts. Collectively, they keep safe the raw materials of history, and without them, no historian can succeed. For those of you who have family documents still in your possession—and I have met some of you—I thank you for showing them to me. I urge you to at least share fair use copies of those materials with an appropriate archival collection so your ancestor's experiences gain a wider audience.

John Reed, Zack Waltz, and a number of other war-gaming compadres have joined me on both research and battlefield excursions over the years. This project began as a humble war game, after all; and owes much of its existence and structure to that obscure hobby. Their help and encouragement has made the final product what it is today.

Eric Wittenberg is a friend and mentor who's own body of work is impressive and growing. He and I first met 21 years ago at Gettysburg and have been friends ever since. Eric has had his own interest in my work, and helped me make sure it found a home with such a quality publisher. Thank you Eric, for your efforts over the years. Now, finally, when you ask me "what are you working on," my answer will no longer be "Chickamauga."

This project would not exist at all if not for the willingness of Theodore P. Savas, managing director and owner of Savas Beatie, to take such a risk on a relatively untried and unknown author. And. . . he agreed to publish nothing less than a *full trilogy* on Chickamauga! I had casually commented more than once to Ted that I would love to tackle such a project, but always added, ruefully, that no one would want to publish it because it was so large. Who would want to buy it? Fortunately, I was wrong on both counts. Immense thanks are due to Ted and every member of the Savas Beatie team for their superb work in helping to craft *The Chickamauga Campaign* into the outstanding final product it has become. I have thoroughly enjoyed working with all of them. And, as I write this, the third printing of the hardcover of *A Mad Irregular Battle* (the first volume) has just reached the market, as has the paperback; I am sure the other volumes will follow in due time.

Some errors, of course, always creep through and those mistakes are all mine. Sometimes over the course of this project my understanding of a specific event has evolved; other times, I simply erred. We endeavor to correct all errors when we can. In the meantime, I take full responsibility. All I can say in my defense is that it usually made sense to me when I typed it. I also wish to thank those readers who found mistakes and pointed them out. Feel free to continue to do so. Your feedback only improves subsequent editions.

Finally, I want to thank everyone who has purchased and read my work. When I began, Chickamauga seemed to be the forgotten stepchild of American Civil War history, the subject of only two modern monographs in the past 50 years. Things are changing. I like to think I helped start a renaissance of interest in this great battle, the second bloodiest of the war. It may not be the single most important engagement, but it is at least equal in importance to any other of the Civil War's fierce combats.

In the last volume, I thanked my faithful research bloodhound, Killian. His efforts were no less invaluable in finishing this volume, as he labored (slumbered?) at my side through months of writing. Thank you Killian, for always being there.

I can't believe it is done. Huzzah!

David Powell
Chicago, IL
August, 2016

Who Won?

Chickamauga remains the only clear-cut battlefield victory ever won by the Army of Tennessee. Though these same Confederates achieved fleeting tactical success at Shiloh (Day 1), Perryville, and Stones River, each of those battles would be recorded as defeats, since the Rebels withdrew from the field each time. The smaller engagement at Richmond, Kentucky, was a triumph, but only a small part of the army was engaged there and so does not rise to the level of Chickamauga in terms of importance, ferocity, size, or sacrifice. Subsequent to September 1863, Chattanooga would go down as a Confederate disaster. The many fights on the road to Atlanta were mostly inconclusive (though the men in gray did administer a drubbing or two along the way, most notably at Kennesaw Mountain) and the final campaign in Tennessee was a catastrophe.

By all conventional measures, Chickamauga was a Confederate victory. The Union Army of the Cumberland fled the field, leaving its grisly spoils for the Rebels to harvest. The Army of Tennessee captured more guns, more flags, and took more prisoners than they lost. Roughly a third of the Federal army was routed so completely it could not reform until the next day. But those trophies all came at a dreadful cost.

Perhaps the most important facet was that when it ended, the Yankees held the city of Chattanooga—the strategic object of the campaign. Bragg's task was to defend it, and Rosecrans' task was to capture it. When the shooting stopped, Federal troops held it, dug in behind a series of entrenchments as daunting as any created during the war. The flag of the Confederacy would never fly over Chattanooga again. By the spring of 1864, the city had become a vast depot and supply hub, a secure base from which William T. Sherman would launch his campaign to capture Atlanta. Freed slaves would congregate there in the contraband camps, and regiments of United States Colored Troops would be formed there. A National Cemetery for Federals fallen in battle—with those who fell at Chickamauga among the first interments—would be created there.

For this reason, the men of the Army of the Cumberland would go to their graves insisting that Chickamauga was not a defeat. They are not wrong. So long as they held the critical objective of Chattanooga, a tactical setback a handful of miles away in North Georgia was inconsequential in the grand scheme of war. In the modern sense, Rosecrans suffered a tactical defeat, but he succeeded at the operational art of war because he captured and retained control of Chattanooga.

It is for this reason, despite all the hard-won tactical success achieved by the men of the Army of Tennessee in three days of immense bloodletting, Chickamauga must be acknowledged as a barren victory.

Chapter One

A Battle Won?

Morning, September 21st

By all appearances, as first light filtered through the trees on Monday morning, September 21, 1863, Braxton Bragg's Confederate Army of Tennessee had won a glorious victory. William Starke Rosecrans's Federal army had been driven from the field at all points. Thousands of prisoners had been captured, and the Army of the Cumberland's entire hospital complex was in Southern hands, as were large stores of armaments and many other sorely needed supplies. The Confederates had paid a bloody price for this stunning success, but the Northern enemy had been routed and had fled the field. Chattanooga, Tennessee—the important logistical and industrial river hub—seemed within the grasp of the Confederacy's outstretched fingers. Perhaps much of the state of Tennessee would soon be back in the Southern fold.

Unfortunately for the Confederates, Chickamauga was not a turning point in the war for Southern independence. The hard-fought and bloody three-day battle instead represented nothing more than a temporary check to the cause of restoring the Union. In time, this outcome would spark sharp accusations and sow bitter divisions within the Confederate army. Why was such a spectacular achievement not followed up immediately? Where was the vigorous pursuit needed to convert tactical success—one of the rarest events to unfold under a Southern banner in the Western Theater—into strategic victory?

Recriminations, virtually all of them leveled at Braxton Bragg, have muddied the historical waters. As darkness mantled the battlefield on

September 20, however, the state of affairs did not seem quite so clear-cut. The night brought with it a general Confederate halt. Fearing that a collision between the army's two wings somewhere between Horseshoe Ridge and Kelly Field would result in "serious consequences," Bragg ordered all of his generals to stop where they were and let the men sleep on their arms. Everyone expected the battle would renew with the dawn.

Bragg spent the night at his headquarters on the Brotherton Road near Jay's Mill. Even from that distance he could hear the enemy. "Desultory firing was heard until 8 p.m.," he noted, and "other noises, indicating movements and dispositions for the morrow, continued until a late hour." Bragg staffer Col. Taylor Beatty recorded the day's results in his diary: "About dark [the] enemy [was] routed. We expect him to rally though & the fight to be continued a few miles on tomorrow. Hope he will as I want daylight to follow him. Some though hope it is over as our loss is heavy."[1]

The Army of Tennessee's Left Wing commander, Lt. Gen. James Longstreet, sent two communiqués to Bragg that evening. The first, at 6:15 p.m., reported that things had "been entirely successful in my command today and [I] hope to be ready to renew the conflict at an early hour." Longstreet went on to note that Maj. Gen. Thomas C. Hindman's troops were badly scattered, and again asked Bragg for the loan of a division to replace Hindman in the line so that he "might collect his men." A second dispatch reported that Hindman believed the enemy even then were "fighting him hard," and reiterated the need for support from Lt. Gen. Leonidas Polk's Right Wing. As it stood that evening with darkness covering the field, Longstreet fully expected to reengage the Federals at dawn.[2]

Without waiting for Bragg to act, sometime after dark Longstreet turned to Brig. Gen. Evander Law's three brigades to bolster his battered front. After its sharp fight at midday on the 20th, Law's division spent the rest of the afternoon in the vicinity of Brotherton Field, recovering and awaiting a new mission.

---

1   U.S. War Department. *The War of the Rebellion: A Compilation of the Official Records of the Union and Confederate Armies*, 128 vols. (Washington, DC: U.S. Government Printing Office, 1880-1901) Series I, Volume 30, Part 2, 34. Hereafter cited as *OR*. All entries are to Series I unless otherwise noted. Entry for September 20, Taylor Beatty Diary, Southern Historical collection, University of North Carolina. Hereafter cited as Taylor Beatty Diary, UNC.

2   Longstreet to Bragg, September 20, 1863, Bragg Papers, Western Reserve Historical Society. Hereafter WRHS. On the afternoon of September 20, Longstreet asked Bragg for the loan of some of the men in Leonidas Polk's Right Wing to strengthen his ongoing efforts against Horseshoe Ridge. Bragg refused.

Longstreet directed the men back into the front line. It was fully dark by the time Col. William F. Perry led the way, marching his Alabamans north aligned with and just west of the La Fayette Road. They drew to a halt somewhere west of Kelly Field without contacting any Federals. Brigadier General Jerome Robertson, whose brigade followed Perry's, reported that "late in the evening, I was moved to the position of General Preston, where I relieved General [Joseph B.] Kershaw, and bivouacked for the night." During this exchange, at 10:00 p.m., Kershaw informed Robertson that the Federals were finally gone from their front. Kershaw "immediately communicated the fact to the Lieutenant General Commanding [Longstreet]." Presumably Brig. Gen. Henry L. Benning's Georgians filled out the remainder of this line, coming into place between Perry and Robertson, though the lack of filed reports makes any specific determination of these movements difficult[3]

Longstreet might have had a better understanding of his wing's relative positions had Brig. Gen. Bushrod Johnson been able to report in. By full dark, Johnson's three brigades were badly jumbled and short of ammunition, their ranks thinned due to exhaustion and heavy straggling. Colonel Cyrus A. Sugg was "thankful" to let Col. Robert Trigg's men (General Preston's division) take over his front. Colonel John S. Fulton ordered his Tennesseans to fall back south off the crest of Horseshoe Ridge to align his brigade with Brig. Gen. Arthur Manigault's men for the night, somewhere near the Vittetoe House. Colonel David Coleman, commanding McNair's brigade, made no mention of his actions after nightfall, but he likely emulated Fulton. With his men disengaged, about 8:00 p.m. Johnson sought new orders. Three hours of fruitless wandering ensued. "I . . . searched until about 11 o'clock for the headquarters of the army, or the wing, with a view to making a report of my position. Failing in this attempt I returned to my command, worn out with the toils of the day."[4]

On the army's right, Leonidas Polk found himself mired in similar difficulties. Around 8:00 p.m., while 1st Lt. William Gale, his aide-de-camp, was setting up Polk's camp amidst "the enemy's works at the state [La Fayette] road," Polk ordered Lt. Philip B. Spence to ride the length of the Right Wing's battle line to ascertain everyone's position. Once that laborious task was

---

3   OR 30, pt. 2, 505, 512. Perry continued to command the Alabama Brigade, since Law was the acting division commander and Col. James L. Sheffield was still incapacitated.

4   OR 30, pt. 2, 465, 476, 496.

accomplished, Spence had orders to locate General Bragg and report his findings to the army commander. Worn out by a very trying day, Polk went to bed.[5]

It took Spence a couple of hours to trace the lines and find Bragg, who was also asleep. The army leader shook himself awake to hear the news. "I . . . reported the situation of the Right Wing . . . as near as I could," recalled Spence, "drawing a diagram in the sand showing the position of each Corps Division and Brigade and as near as I could of each battery." Bragg received this report without comment, and sent the lieutenant off to summon Longstreet and Polk to a late-night meeting. Spence reached Polk first, informed him of Bragg's request, and then rode off in search of Longstreet. The rider met with no more success than had Bushrod Johnson and eventually gave up the hunt and spurred his horse back to Polk's fire.[6]

Leonidas Polk slept only fitfully, surrounded by the awful detritus of combat. "Within ten yards" of camp, recalled Lieutenant. Gale, "one poor devil . . . lay sobbing out his life all night long." Family concerns also troubled Polk's rest. Sometime around 11:00 p.m., Polk sent Gale off to check on his nephew, Brig. Gen. Lucius Polk, whose brigade was also camped within the confines of Kelly Field. "For two hours I rode around and among our men," Gale wrote, "most of the time in a dense forest. . . . The moon was shining . . . and gave a most unearthly appearance to this horrid scene. Wounded, dying and dead men and horses were strewn around me . . . for the field was yet hot and smoking from the last charge." Gale failed to locate the younger Polk (a common problem this night), and he, too, returned to headquarters. There, he found Lieutenant Spence back from his own horrific trip through the grotesque landscape.[7]

Their night was not yet done. Gale and Spence both recalled how they accompanied Lieutenant General Polk to meet with Bragg. By now the hour was very late, the ride trying, and Polk cross. At one point Bishop Polk complained "that he wished the commanding general would remain near the front." Spence recorded only that the party reached Bragg "some time after

---

5   William M. Polk, *Leonidas Polk, Bishop and General*, 2 vols. (Longmans, Green and Co., 1915), vol. 2, 266.

6   P. B. Spence to William M. Polk, August 5, 1874, Polk Papers, University of the South, Suwanee, TN.

7   Gale Letter, September 28, 1863, Polk Papers, University of the South.

midnight." Gale was equally vague. In one description he placed the meeting before midnight, but in another gave the time as 1:00 a.m. Discrepancies as to the timing of this meeting would prove much less important that its substance. Bragg did not mention in his report what passed between them. Polk never filed a regular report of the battle, mostly because he was about to become embroiled in a much larger controversy with the army commander, and also because he would be killed the next summer. In an 1882 letter to Polk's son William, Lieutenant Gale insisted it was Polk who first apprised Bragg that his army had won a great victory. General Polk, wrote Gale, told Bragg "that the enemy was routed and fleeing precipitously . . . and that then was the opportunity to finish the work . . . by prompt pursuit, before he had time to reorganize and throw up defenses at Chattanooga." As Gale subsequently discovered from Tennessee Governor Isham G. Harris, "the Commanding General would not believe the Federals had been beaten but insisted that we were to have a harder fight the next day."[8]

This story first appeared in 1893, long after Polk and Bragg were dead. By this time Bragg was being universally pilloried for his failure to pursue Rosecrans, a lapse that supposedly let the fruits of victory slip away. In reality it was not until well into the morning of September 21st that any senior Confederate, Polk included, understood the Army of the Cumberland had retired from the field.

The first bits of light on Monday morning were penetrating the smoke-shrouded woods covering Horseshoe Ridge when Lt. Clarence Malone roused the survivors of Company C, 10th Tennessee Infantry. When the combat closed the night before, Confederate troops all across the field dropped to the ground and spent the night wherever darkness found them. Malone and his men "encamped on the top [of the ridge] amid the grones of the dying and the prayers for assistance." None of these horrors overly bothered the exhausted Malone, who later recorded that he "slept soundly." As for the morrow, "all

---

8   P. B. Spence to William M. Polk, August 5, 1874, Polk Papers; Gale Letter, March 28, 1882, Polk Papers; Polk, *Leonidas Polk* vol. 2, 267. Harris accompanied General Bragg as a volunteer aide throughout the Chickamauga Campaign. For his part, Spence did not recall Gale's presence, noting only that General Polk, himself, and Lt. Col. H. C. Yeatman went to see Bragg. Spence also did not recall much of the conversation that transpired, writing only that he remembered Polk being "in favor of moving forward at once."

Brig. Gen. St. John Richardson Liddell was one of the more active Rebel commanders on the morning of September 21.

Library of Congress

thought [that September 21] would be another day of strife, but great was our surprise to awake and find the Yankees gone."[9]

But gone where? That was the question uppermost on every Confederate's mind from private to full general. A round of celebratory Rebel Yells had swept Bragg's army from one end to the other the night before, but most Confederates still expected the Federals to be waiting for them just over the next hill, having fallen back only as far the next piece of defensible ground. It seemed unlikely the battle could actually be over.

At 5:30 a.m., Longstreet sent a rider to Maj. Gen. Joseph Wheeler asking him to "send forward at once a strong cavalry force, and at once ascertain the position of the enemy." Just over an hour later, at 6:40 a.m., a courier from Bragg found Longstreet near the Dyer house and informed him that the army commander wished to confer. The big Georgian thought the invitation unwise and declined, explaining that he expected the fighting to resume at any minute, and he was even somewhat worried about a Federal counterattack.[10]

One of those who did suspect a wholesale enemy withdrawal was Brig. Gen. St. John Liddell. After his division was thrown out of McDonald Field by John Turchin's Federals, Liddell sent scouts cautiously forward later that night to investigate his front. They returned at 9:00 p.m. to report the Yankees had vanished. At first light, Liddell hunted up Polk, whom he "found in bed in his ambulance half asleep." After hearing Liddell's news, Polk ordered the

---

9 "Dear Miss Florence," September 28, 1863, Martha Clayton Harper Letters, Duke University. Hereafter DU.

10 *OR* 30, pt. 4, 682; Bragg Papers, WRHS.

Louisianan to press forward and discover where the Yankees might have gone. Before Liddell could depart, however, General Bragg rode up. "Near sunrise . . . [I] met the ever-vigilant Brigadier General Liddell," Bragg recalled, "who was awaiting to report . . . that the enemy had retreated during the night. . . . Instructions were promptly given to push our whole line of skirmishers to the front."[11]

Liddell recalled things a little differently. He remembered waiting for some time while Bragg and Polk conferred, expecting orders to pursue that never came. Finally, Liddell "left . . . in entire ignorance of the steps that had been determined upon." According to Liddell, he ordered out his skirmishers of his own volition and awaited additional instructions.[12]

Lieutenant General Daniel Harvey Hill's report recorded a similar series of events. At nightfall, Hill worried any new advance of his troops would stumble into Longstreet's men, who were understood to "be pressing northward" at right angles to Hill's own position. After halting his men once full night arrived, Hill rode forward far enough to determine that no Federals were in his front and that John B. Hood's men "were halted . . . but a short distance to our left." Later in the night Hill sent out scouts "with orders to proceed a mile in our front." When they returned having found nothing, Hill sent out more men, this time "to go 3 miles." Just before dawn additional scouts reported in bearing the same message: No Federals. Had Hill instructed his men to venture forward four miles instead of three, he might have found the enemy he sought, for the distance from Rossville to the McDonald farm was three and three-quarter miles.

In a rather curious observation, General Hill asserted that "never, perhaps, was there a battle in which the troops were so little mixed up and in which the organization was so little disturbed." However, he wrote that passage months after the fact, and well after he had been relieved from the army by Bragg. Other, more timely reports, including some of Hill's own communications,

---

11 Nathaniel Cheairs Hughes, Jr., ed., *Liddell's Record: St. John Richardson Liddell Brigadier General, CSA Staff Officer and Brigade Commander, Army of Tennessee* (Louisiana State University Press, 1985), 146; *OR* 30, pt. 2, 34-35. This might well be the meeting Gale and Spence remembered, but it happened at Polk's camp not Bragg's.

12 Hughes, *Liddell's Record*, 147. Writing in 1866, General Liddell's memory is also colored here by the universal condemnation heaped upon Bragg for not immediately launching a vigorous pursuit.

suggested this was far from the case, and that in fact the army was badly disrupted.[13]

While the generals were conferring, the troops were being fed. Assistant Quartermaster Samuel R. Simpson of the 30th Tennessee set out early to bring up "some ham & cold biscuit." While the men ate, Simpson wandered over Horseshoe Ridge, amazed at the carnage. "Such a sight I never want to see again," he wrote, with "dead men and horses, broken guns, & all kinds of accoutrements laying everywhere, some torn all to pieces."[14]

The primary responsibility for reconnaissance, of course, fell to Bragg's mounted arm. In addition to the infantry skirmishers pressing forward all across the front, Bragg also reported that "all the cavalry at hand, including my personal guard, were ordered to the front." With Maj. Gen. Joseph Wheeler's corps on the army's left and Brig. Gen. Nathan Bedford Forrest's troopers on the right, the cavalry should have been well situated for this mission and ready to exploit any lingering confusion within the Federal ranks. For differing reasons, however, neither Wheeler nor Forrest succeeded in doing so.[15]

At nightfall on September 20, Wheeler, with Brig. Gen. John Wharton's division in tow, withdrew to his old campsite near Doctor Anderson's house. These camps were on the wrong side of West Chickamauga Creek, southeast of Glass Mill, and seven miles from the battlefield. Wharton's 4,500 troopers would have to ride that distance and more back to the front before they could even start any reconnaissance. At least Brig. Gen. William T. Martin's division was closer, having spent the night at Crawfish Spring. Martin, however, lacked any orders concerning what to do on the morning after the battle.

Wheeler did exhibit some concern about a lingering Union presence to the south, down in McLemore's Cove, posting details to cover various crossings over Chickamauga Creek south of Lee and Gordon's Mills. Colonel Isaac Avery's 4th Georgia Cavalry camped east of the creek, along "the road running east from the old Glass home," with pickets left to guard the crossing at Glass Mill. Captain George W. Littlefield of Company I, 8th Texas Cavalry, was detailed to take a composite battalion (six companies drawn from the various

13 *OR* 30, pt. 2, 145.

14 Entry for September 21, Samuel Robert Simpson Diary, Tennessee State Library and Archives. Hereafter TSLA.

15 *OR* 30, pt. 2, 35. See also, generally, David Powell, *Failure in the Saddle: Nathan Bedford Forrest, Joseph Wheeler, and Confederate Cavalry Operations in the Chickamauga Campaign* (Savas Beatie, 2008).

regiments of Col. Thomas Harrison's brigade) and picket Owen's Ford, three miles upstream (south of) Avery's Georgia contingent.[16]

Though Captain Littlefield's assignment that night proved routine, it would have a profound effect on his psyche. Littlefield's route crossed over the southwest corner of the Chickamauga battlefield and through the Union hospital complex at Crawfish Spring—the scene of the morning cavalry fight at Glass Mill. Horrors abounded. He found it "a dreary ride at the head of the column, over the field of the dead and dying; the prayer of the conscious and the death rattle from the throats of the blue and the gray, could be heard as they lay mingled on that bloody field." Decades later, Littlefield admitted, "it was the most distressing ordeal of my career as a soldier to ride through that twelve miles of country, where the guns of both North and South had mowed the ground like a giant reaper."[17]

Though George Washington Littlefield was still a young man of 21, he was already a veteran. After two years of war, he was no stranger to battle or its aftermath. And yet these new scenes of carnage affected him deeply and in a way that earlier experiences had not. "In none of his letters prior to [this] ride," writes one longtime student of the man, "did he mention anything about the possibility of his death, though he had friends die all around him. Afterward, every letter said something about 'if I die' or 'promise to meet me in heaven.'" Littlefield's ride developed within him a keen awareness of his own fragile and potentially imminent mortality.[18]

Joe Wheeler failed to perform any important duty that morning. The new Federal positions on September 21 meant that Wheeler and Wharton faced not only a ten-mile ride to just encounter Federals on the far side of Missionary Ridge, but another crossing of the Chickamauga at Lee and Gordon's Mills. Once at the front Wheeler intended to "push forward through a perfectly desolate country in the direction of Lookout Mountain," recalled Robert Bunting of the 8th Texas Cavalry. More importantly, with Wheeler's camps so far from the front and with him now on the move, no one could easily find him.

---

16 A. F. Shaw, "My Experiences," *Walker County Messenger*, April 3, 1902; Lewis E. Daniell, *Types of Successful Men of Texas* (Eugene Von Boeckmann, Printer and Bookbinder, 1890), 348.

17 Daniell, *Successful Men of Texas*, 348; Mrs. Samuel Posey, *Confederate Veteran*, vol. 32, no. 4 (April 1924), 137-138.

18 Email exchange with David B. Gracie, II, archivist, University of Texas, November 12 to 14, 2014.

Neither Longstreet's request of 5:30 a.m. nor a similar order from Bragg's headquarters would reach Wheeler for hours.[19]

Lacking specific orders that morning, William T. Martin's Rebel troopers spent the early hours policing the battlefield or attending to personal matters. Private Nimrod Long of Company B, the 51st Alabama Partisan Rangers, managed a quick letter home for the first time in several days: "We have had several fights recently, two yesterday," wrote the private. "It is reported that we took 10,000 prisoners yesterday. I can't vouch for the truth of the report but I know that the enemy were driven several miles. It is about 8 o'clock and the fight has not yet opened this morning." Exhausted, many of Martin's men slept late. John Wyeth of the 4th Alabama Cavalry remembered that "when I awoke the sun was shining in my face." Wyeth had rounded up both forage for his horse and hardtack for his belly the night before, so upon arising he turned to other personal matters. "My trousers—the only pair I had—were soaked in wading the creek," he complained, "and had held the dust we raised as we marched over that much trodden field. They were now dry and as stiff as if they had been starched, and very uncomfortable." The trooper promptly headed toward the creek for a bath and a bit of laundry.[20]

Unlike Joe Wheeler, Nathan Bedford Forrest was on the scene commendably early. He was in the saddle at 4:00 a.m. on the 21st, well before first light, and since he had camped on the field did not have miles to cover before reporting in. The ever-aggressive Forrest set out along the La Fayette Road toward Rossville with Brig. Gen. Frank Armstrong's division, James T. Wheeler's brigade, in the van. George Dibrell's brigade followed. Brigadier General John Pegram's division, which reunited with John T. Scott's brigade overnight, would follow when ready and catch up on the move.[21]

After his early morning meeting with Polk, Bragg returned to his own camp to await developments. He was anxious, his demeanor grim and downbeat. That morning, as his column of troopers trotted past Bragg's headquarters along the Brotherton Road, General Pegram reined in his horse to converse with the army commander. The encounter proved alarming. Staff Captain

19 Robert F. Bunting Letter, *Rome Tri-Weekly Telegraph*, November 27, 1863.

20 "Dear Wife," September 21, 1863, W. E. Nimrod Papers, Emory University; John A. Wyeth, *With Sabre and Scalpel: The Autobiography of a Soldier and Surgeon* (Harper, 1914), 252.

21 Thomas Jordan and J. P. Pryor, *The Campaigns of General Nathan Bedford Forrest and of Forrest's Cavalry* (De Capo Press, 1996), 350.

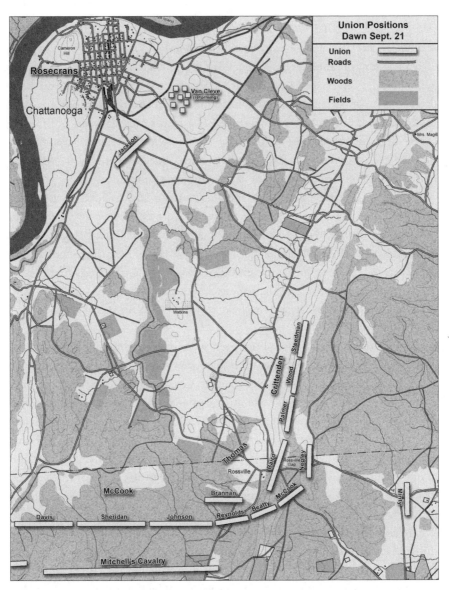

Shown here are the positions of the Union Army as of about dawn, September 21.

Henry B. Clay remembered Bragg "walking nervously and continually in front of the tents, wringing his hands. General Pegram, dismounting, approached him and said: 'I congratulate you, General, upon the brilliant victory you have won.' There was no stop in that walk, and the reply was: 'Yes, but it has been at a frightful sacrifice. The army is fearfully cut up, horribly demoralized.'" To Clay,

Bragg's pessimism felt "like a douche of ice water in the face." Suddenly subdued, both Clay and Pegram quickly mounted and rode on.[22]

Bragg sent off a similar assessment of the situation to Richmond, informing Secretary of War James Seddon that "after two days' hard fighting we have driven the enemy, after a desperate resistance, from several positions and now hold the field; but he still confronts us. The losses are heavy on both sides, especially, so in our officers." Closing on a more upbeat note, Bragg claimed the captures of "over twenty pieces of artillery and some 2,500 prisoners." Still, the battle seemed far from over, let alone a complete triumph.[23]

Moving towards Rossville, Forrest's troopers collided with their now-familiar adversaries: Col. Robert H. G. Minty's Federal cavalry. After dark on the 20th, Minty had pulled his brigade back from Red House Bridge to camp at McAfee Church, a mile and a half east of Rossville. There they spent a cold, fireless night, "bridles in hand," erecalled Joseph Vale, the brigade adjutant. "We were chilled and miserable, feeling that our army had been defeated, and that our only chance to regain the field was the timely arrival of Burnside . . . from Knoxville."[24]

Before dawn, the Yankee horsemen were disturbed by cheering coming from the west. Now fully aroused, some guessed Burnside had indeed arrived. The more cautious Minty sent riders back to Rossville to discover the meaning. They soon returned bearing heartening news: George Thomas was there, with the army reassembled and posted to defend the gap. The cheering some attributed to the arrival of Maj. Gen. Lovell Rousseau. Captain Richard Robbins of Company F, the 4th Michigan Cavalry, remembered the "intense disgust and disappointment we experienced when . . . informed of the cause of the row. . . . Rousseau was a good man, very popular with his troops . . . but we did not think he was worth all that fuss." Once Minty's scouts reported in from Red House Bridge and Mission Mills, bringing word that no Rebels posed any immediate threat at either place, Minty rode back to Rossville. "I found [Thomas] in the famous grove of large trees immediately back of the Gap," wrote Minty. "As soon as I reported to him he said: 'You should not be there, Colonel.' I replied, 'I know that, General; but there I am.'" Thomas, who better understood the

---

22 Henry B. Clay, "On the Right at Chickamauga," *Confederate Veteran*, vol. XIX (July 1911), 329-330.

23 *OR* 30, pt. 2, 23.

24 Joseph G. Vale, *Minty and the Cavalry* (Edwin K. Meyers, 1886), 235.

overall state of affairs and expected Bragg's vanguard to begin pressing forward soon, decided to use Minty to his advantage: "After a moment's thought, [Thomas] said, 'well, as you are there, delay the enemy all you can. Give me as much time as possible . . . to get ready for them.'"[25] Accordingly, Minty withdrew his force another quarter-mile west to the intersection of the Federal Road and a secondary road that intersected with the La Fayette Road. He deployed his men to cover both routes into Rossville and readied himself to receive Forrest's troopers.[26]

Instead of merely ordering out reconnaissance patrols and coordinating the movements of his two divisions, in a typically rash move, Forrest personally plunged ahead with division commander Frank Armstrong and 400 men, leaving the rest of his corps to catch up as best they could. Forrest's first encounter was with Surgeon Abraham Landis of the 35th Ohio, still manning John Brannan's divisional field hospital near Cloud Spring. Once again Landis and his comrades were prisoners, this time for good. "General Forrest told us to go ahead and attend to our wounded, and we should not be molested," explained Landis some months later. "He also told us that our wounded yet on the field should be removed to the hospitals and receive precisely the same treatment that their wounded received; also that parties had been detailed to bury the dead on both sides." The surgeon would have cause to remember that promise, as well as a similar guarantee offered up by Dr. E. A. Fluwellen, Bragg's Chief Surgeon, the following day. Moving on, Forrest set men to rounding up stragglers and collecting abandoned weapons. "The latter were . . . sent to the rear," reported Forrest, "using . . . several wagons and ambulances" found abandoned on the road.[27]

That detail attended to, Forrest rode on. Before long some of Minty's troopers came into sight. "Armstrong, let's give them a dare," shouted Forrest. The Rebel column thundered off at the charge. The Yankees belonged to one of Minty's picket posts and comprised just a handful of men. The surprised blue

25 Richard B. Robbins Memoir, Bentley Historical Library, University of Michigan. Hereafter Umich; Robert H. G. Minty, "Minty's Saber Brigade, the Part They Took in the Chattanooga Campaign, Part II," *National Tribune*, March 3, 1892. Thomas was referring to the exposed nature of Minty's camp, so far in front of the rest of the army.

26 Today this road is called Cross Street in Fort Oglethorpe, Georgia.

27 Thelma Hudson, *A History and Biographical Cyclopaedia of Butler County Ohio* (Western Biographical Publishing Company, 1882), 222; OR 30, pt. 2, 525.

troopers fell back quickly before the onrushing Rebels, but not before loosing a volley of carbine fire. Rebel battery commander John Morton, who was trying to get his guns unlimbered in order to support the attack, recalled that one of those bullets "passed through the neck of General Forrest's horse . . . and severed an artery." The quick-thinking Forrest stemmed the spurting stream of blood when he "stuck his finger into the opening and the horse carried him on." Within minutes, as the Federals thundered off, "General Forrest dismounted, and the faithful animal fell to the ground." This was the second mount shot out from under the cavalryman in three days.[28]

Once that skirmish ended, Forrest cast his eye westward. Remounted, he decided to take George Dibrell's brigade up Missionary Ridge, and then turn north to approach Rossville Gap from above. Armstrong was instructed to lead James Wheeler's brigade in a sweep "along the slopes, eastward," toward that same objective. Once Pegram's division arrived, he was to fall in on Armstrong's right, advancing straight up the La Fayette Road.[29]

Ascending the ridge proved difficult, for it was much steeper and narrower here than farther south, but it was also rewarding. Forrest reached the narrow crest of Missionary Ridge somewhere well to the south of where George Thomas had posted Union Brig. Gen. John Beatty's brigade of James S. Negley's division, before first light that morning. Beatty, who described his new position as "a high ridge, east of Rossville, and near it," had a joyful reunion with his troops the night before. Now, with a meal and a few hours of sleep, they began to feel as if the army were taking shape once again.[30]

Forrest halted his column about 7:30 a.m. and shimmied up a tree. Missionary Ridge rises to a knifed-edge crest here, and from that tree Forrest could see a great deal. All of Chattanooga Valley was spread out below him, with the city of Chattanooga off to the northwest, and with much of the terrain around Rossville also visible. Still clinging to his perch, Forrest dictated a hasty message to Capt. Charles W. Anderson, his aide-de-camp, who was sitting on his horse below. Using a saddle flap as a writing desk, Anderson scribbled:

28 John A. Wyeth, *That Devil Forrest: Life of General Nathan Bedford Forrest* (Louisiana State University Press, 1989), 235; John W. Morton, *The Artillery of Nathan Bedford Forrest's Cavalry* (R. Bemis Publishing, 1995), 126.

29 Jordan and Pryor, *Forrest's Cavalry*, 350.

30 John Beatty, *The Citizen-Soldier: The Memoirs of a Civil War Volunteer* (University of Nebraska Press, 1998), 345-346. Beatty, it will be recalled, became separated from his brigade about midday on September 20.

Genl,

We are in a mile of Rossville. Have been on the point of Missionary Ridge can see Chattanooga and every thing around. The enemy's trains are leaving going around the point of Lookout Mountain.

The prisoners captured report the pontoon thrown across for the purpose of retreating. I think they are evacuating as hard as they can go. They are cutting timber down to obstruct our passage.

I think we ought to press forward as rapidly as possible.

N.B Forrest
Brig Gen

Lt Gen L Polk
Please forward to Gen Bragg.[31]

This simple communiqué would become a key piece of evidence in building the historical prosecution's case that Bragg failed to launch a timely pursuit. One copy was saved by Captain Anderson, who grasped immediately its importance and kept it in his possession even after the war.

More important than what was included in Forrest's dispatch, however, is what he left out: The actual position of the Union army. At least eight Union divisions were deployed in and around Rossville Gap. The most visible enemy troops should have been Maj. Gen. Alexander McCook's XX Corps, facing south while stretched across Chattanooga Valley between Missionary Ridge and Chattanooga Creek, with Brig. Gen. Robert B. Mitchell's Federal cavalry out front as a screen. Beatty's brigade, as noted, was on the ridge just a short distance north, as Forrest would soon discover. Other Federal troops stood just west of Rossville in the flat, open ground beyond the gap, along with the ammunition trains for most of the Army of the Cumberland. The gap itself was defended by Thomas's XIV Corps and some of Granger's troops, while Maj. Gen. Thomas L. Crittenden's XXI Corps held the northward crest of the ridge

---

31 OR 30, pt. 4, 681. See also John Wyeth, *That Devil Forrest*, 236, for a more detailed description of the event. Anderson shared his copy of this document with Wyeth, who described it as "a pale blue sheet of paper, evidently torn out of a pocket memorandum book."

beyond Rossville. This was all vital information, unquestionably the most important news Forrest could have relayed to his superiors. Unfortunately, these details were completely absent from his dispatch.[32]

Unfortunately, what Forrest did include in his report, he misinterpreted. Wagons and large numbers of men were indeed fleeing Chattanooga, either by crossing the Tennessee River on Rosecrans's newly erected pontoon bridges or by swarming westward around the point of Lookout Mountain toward Wauhatchie. In the main, however, these were not combat troops. What Rosecrans was doing was akin to a man-o-war clearing the decks for action. If—as now looked increasingly likely—the Army of the Cumberland was about to be besieged in the city, the last thing Rosecrans needed were large numbers of non-combatant mouths to feed. Chattanooga had seethed with activity since falling into Union hands ten days earlier, for the Federals intended to use the city as its next major forward base for the army—the next stepping-stone on the long march to Atlanta. Hundreds, perhaps thousands, of laborers were already embarked on that endeavor, laying bridges, repairing existing facilities, and building new warehouses. The defeat at Chickamauga made these men a potential liability who would consume valuable stores without contributing to the army's combat strength. The city was also housing thousands of wounded men, both walking and non-ambulatory, who filled virtually every usable building in the city. They, too, had to be evacuated. In order to do so, every available wagon was pressed into service to move any injured soldier who could survive the trip.

Once that flood of army wagons offloaded their misery-laden cargos at the railheads, they had to rush back into Chattanooga as rapidly as possible. The stockpiled stores and ammunition crowding the depots at Bridgeport and Stevenson were now desperately needed in Chattanooga. Time was critical, for no Federal could tell how long it would be before Rebels moved to interdict the intervening roads and sever the Army of the Cumberland's lifeline.

One other factor contributed to the congestion pouring out of the city. Chaplain John Hight of the 58th Indiana, in town trying to sniff out news, found himself near the river. "The pontoon bridge was crowded with rebel prisoners, crossing over," he observed. "I confess I was surprised at their

32 Edward Betts and C. E. Park, *Atlas of the Battlefields of Chickamauga, Chattanooga, and Vicinity* (Chickamauga and Chattanooga National Park Commission, 1895), plate 8, shows the Federal deployments.

number." The Army of the Cumberland had been defeated, but at least 1,000 Confederates fell captive during the battle, and a sizeable number of Southern deserters were also still in Union hands. From a distance, all of this traffic pouring out of the city might look like a panic to an untrained eye, but that was far from the only—or even the most likely—interpretation of what was happening.[33]

After sending off his report, Forrest proceeded more slowly, moving northward along the spine of the ridge. If he had not noticed the Union infantry before, he found them now. At 10:00 a.m., reported Brig. Gen. John Beatty, the 15th Kentucky and 42nd Indiana were attacked by "a brigade of mounted infantry . . . under Colonel Dibble [Dibrell]." Ever aggressive, Forrest ordered the 8th Tennessee Cavalry and Shaw's Battalion to dismount and attack Beatty's line. "In a charge ordered by General Forrest in person," admitted Dibrell some years later, both commands "lost several good men killed." Members of the 42nd Indiana described the action as "nearly an hour's hard fighting. . . . [T]he enemy were repulsed, and withdrew from the field leaving their dead and wounded." According to Beatty, "One little boy, so badly wounded they could not carry him off, said, with tears and sobs, 'they have run off and left me in the woods to die.'" Taking pity on the young Rebel, Beatty ordered "the [Union] boys to carry him into our lines and care for him."[34]

While Dibrell's troopers were probing Beatty's line, John Pegram's cavalry arrived. He dismounted and deployed Brig. Gen. Henry B. Davidson's brigade directly in front of Rossville Gap and sent the men straight up the road. This advance soon collided with more Federals than either Pegram or Davidson expected. Still, the meeting engagement initially went well for the Rebels, as Davidson's troopers drove in Minty's picket line. Private John W. Minnich of the 6th Georgia Cavalry described the fight here as "a running skirmish" against the 7th Pennsylvania Cavalry. "[Our] brigade," Minnich noted, "moved steadily forward through the open fields . . . exchanging volley[s] and detached fire with the 7th, without any casualties on our side . . . and only one on theirs . . . a young fellow of less than twenty years." Minnich never forgot the sight of that dead

33 John J. Hight and Gilbert R. Stormont, *History of the Fifty-Eighth Regiment of Indiana Volunteer Infantry, Its Organization, Campaigns, and Battles from 1861 to 1865* (Press of the Clarion, 1895), 197.

34 John B. Lindsley, *The Military Annals of Tennessee*, 2 vols. (Broadfoot Publishing Company, 1995) vol. 2, 661; *Indiana at Chickamauga: Report of the Indiana Commissioners, Chickamauga National Military Park* (Sentinel Printing Co., 1900), 185; Beatty, *Citizen Soldier*, 346.

This modern view, taken from somewhere near Gen. Forrest's likely vantage point, shows how much Forrest should have been able to see of Rossville, the valley below, and the city of Chattanooga in the distance. *Author's Photograph*

Yank lying face down, shot through the forehead with a grisly exit wound "at the back near the crown." Farther on, Minnich scooped up a sergeant's daybook for the 7th's Company H, dropped during the fight.[35]

The advance came to an abrupt halt when the Confederates reached the foot of Missionary Ridge. The Rebel line stopped on a small hill just short of the gap. Taking the gap itself would require them to leave this smaller ridge, cross a shallow valley, and ascend Missionary Ridge at least as far as what Minnich called "the Ridge Road . . . which skirted the base of Missionary Ridge." Advancing in open order, they made it as far as the road, where they discovered they could go no farther. Minnich estimated Minty's main Federal line was "90 feet in front of us, and from sixty to eighty feet above us. Caught in a plunging fire, the Rebels sought shelter behind the lip of the road, where Federal lead pinned them down. "Lucky for us we did not try and push him further," Minnich concluded.[36]

35 John W. Minnich manuscript, 6th Georgia Cavalry file, Chickamauga-Chattanooga National Military Park. Hereafter, CCNMP.

36 Ibid.

Forrest now elected to send most of Dibrell's men back down the ridge to rejoin Frank Armstrong, and use Armstrong's entire division to reinforce Pegram. In one underreported incident, however, Forrest first ordered Col. William McLemore's 4th Tennessee Cavalry of Dibrell's brigade to venture down the west face of the ridge and into Chattanooga Valley. Postwar claims put McLemore within three miles of Chattanooga, riding "in the midst of large bodies of Federals . . . so panic-stricken as to not recognize his exposure." However, without additional evidence, determining exactly where McLemore went or how he got there is impossible. Worried that the 4th Tennessee might become cut off, Forrest soon recalled McLemore, who supposedly "came slowly back, full-handed with prisoners."[37]

Once Armstrong joined Pegram, Forrest's entire cavalry corps was concentrated in front of Rossville. John Morton unlimbered his guns, eager to try out the two new 3-inch Ordnance Rifles captured by Pat Cleburne on the night of the 19th and handed over to Morton's crews the next morning. "We shelled the city for several hours," recalled the artillerist, "but could not dislodge the batteries there." Forrest concurred. "My artillery . . . opened on and fought them for several hours, but could not move them."[38]

Though this cannonading accomplished little from the Rebel perspective, it did kill or wound several Federal infantrymen. Lieutenant John Otto of Company D, the 21st Wisconsin, suffered a most unusual injury when, as Otto himself related, a canister projectile "an inch and a quarter in diameter struck the ground in front of me." The round "ploughed through the ground nearly the length of my body, rubbing severely the inside of my right knee, then tearing off the sole of one shoe, not wounding but hurting the foot considerably." The round showered the lieutenant with dirt and resulted in "a three inch long blue mark" on his knee. Marveling at his narrow escape, Otto secured the offending missile and retained it as a souvenir. No skin was broken, but both knee and

---

37 Jordan and Pryor, *Forrest's Cavalry*, 352.

38 Lindsley, *Military Annals of Tennessee*, vol. 2, 849; Morton, *Forrest's Artillery*, 127; OR 30, pt. 2, 526. In his recollections, Morton thought the "city" he was shelling was Chattanooga, not Rossville. His memoir was published in 1909, when he was 67, which was 46 years after the events in question.

foot began to swell immediately, knocking Otto out of commission for the immediate future.[39]

At 11:30 a.m., Forrest, still on the ridge, indulged in a second bit of tree-climbing. While Armstrong and Pegram pressed the Federals at the gap, Forrest and his escort stumbled on a Union signal station atop the ridge. An amused Southern newspaper editor noted that they found "four Yankees concealed high up among the branches of a tree near them. Twenty guns were instantly leveled. 'Don't shoot,' screamed the blue birds, 'we'll come down.'" The tree, a "conspicuous" pine, had "holes [bored] in its sides" fitted with "a stairway of pegs along its trunk." Once the prisoners were secured, Forrest scurried up the pegs and enjoyed an even better view than before. His observations seemed to confirm his earlier impression of an enemy in full retreat.

Once back on terra firma, he sent General Polk another message:[40]

Missionary Ridge
On the Point opposite, south of Rossville
September 21, 1863 11:30 a.m.

Lieutenant General Polk:

General: I am on the point as designated, where I can observe the whole of the valley. They are evidently fortifying, as I can distinctly hear the sound of axes in great numbers.

The appearance is still as in last dispatch, that he is hurrying on toward Chattanooga. He is cutting timber on the point of this ridge. I have just captured a captain and 2 privates who were acting as a corps of observers. He (the captain) reports that a number of forces passed up the road toward Chattanooga, but does not know who, or what their numbers. They passed up about 5:00 p.m. yesterday.

---

39 John H. Otto Memoir, 268-269, Wisconsin Historical Society, Madison, WI. Hereafter WHS.

40 "Forrest Up a Tree," *Columbus Daily Sun*, November 13, 1863. Many of Forrest's biographers place this capture of the signal station and tree-climbing incident at 7:30 a.m., when he wrote his first dispatch. Forrest's specific mention of the signalers in the second dispatch, however, leads me to believe it happened as described above. Note that the newspaper story claims four prisoners, while in his own dispatch, Forrest mentions only "a captain and 2 privates."

N. B. FORREST
Brigadier General, Commanding[41]

Much like his earlier dispatch, this second message is most notable for what it did not say, as well as for its inherent contradiction. Were the Federals both fortifying *and* retreating in wholesale panic? Forrest must have concluded the force holding Rossville Gap was only a rearguard, with the rest of Rosecrans's army "hurrying on toward Chattanooga." But upon what evidence did he base this? Forrest makes no mention of the fact that Rossville was well defended, or that Federal troops had just stymied the advance of his corps, both atop the ridge and in trying to force their way through the gap. He made no mention of the enemy's current locations and dispositions. If he could indeed see the "whole of the valley," how could Forrest miss seeing the entire Union army spread out below him? Forrest's faulty observations would get widespread play, and create the widely held though false impression that the Army of the Cumberland had dissolved into blind panic. Largely because of these two dispatches, many of Bragg's chief subordinates within days would come to believe that one of the war's great opportunities had been missed.

In fact, the Federal army's circumstances were a lot less obvious at the time. Certainly James Longstreet did not initially believe that the Army of the Cumberland was fleeing in a panic on the morning of September 21. Longstreet spent the morning trying to determine what opposition his own front faced. Wheeler might be far to the rear, but Longstreet did have one regiment of cavalry on hand. Lieutenant Colonel Paul Anderson's 4th Tennessee Cavalry (not to be confused with McLemore's regiment—there were two 4th Tennessee Cavalry regiments in the Rebel army) was camped in Dyer field. Longstreet intended to put these men to work. "At an early hour [we] were ordered to report to him for orders," recalled regimental adjutant George B. Guild. "He sent us forward toward Chattanooga to report the whereabouts of the enemy." The Tennesseans passed the Dyer house, which Guild recalled being used as a field hospital complete with a huge mound of amputated limbs piled outside one window. Guild watched in horror as "a hog [ran] through the woods with a soldier's amputated leg in its mouth." Climbing the ridge north of the house, the troopers passed through the wreckage of Union Maj. John Mendenhall's gun line, overrun the previous afternoon. "Horses were piled

41 OR 30, pt. 4, 675.

thick one upon the other, mangled and torn in every conceivable shape. . . . A long line of Federals . . . had been killed where they lay," recalled Guild, their bodies blackened by fire. Moving farther west, the Tennesseans came upon another strange sight: "telegraph wires thrown over the top of bushes, connecting every part of the Federal line. These were incased in something resembling a cotton rope. Our men used them for bridle reins."[42]

While Longstreet's regimental patrols fanned out to look for Federals, Guild and his fellow Tennesseans spent a great deal of time picking through the wreckage of the Union retreat along the Dry Valley Road. None of the patrols ventured far enough to pass through McFarland's Gap. Had they done so, they would have found the Federals soon enough. Instead, they worked their way cautiously north along Missionary Ridge. As a result, it was several hours before any action worthy of the name broke out. Lieutenant William B. Corbitt of the 4th Tennessee Cavalry's Company K noted that at 8:00 a.m. they could hear infantry skirmishing, a fight that soon petered out within an hour. It wasn't until 9:30, he noted, that they "left camps this morning to ascertain the whereabouts of the enemy." Dismounted, Anderson's 4th Tennessee soon met Dibrell's men, and, about midday, took over for Dibrell's departing column as those men went to join Armstrong and Pegram.[43]

The morning's activity eased Longstreet's immediate worries. By 7:00 a.m. he was no longer concerned about either delivering or receiving an immediate attack. Even though it would be several hours before Forrest's reports made their way through the army, Longstreet's own efforts convinced him the Federals were no longer on his immediate front, and he could at last respond to Bragg's earlier summons. Before he could ride off to army headquarters, however, Bragg found him.

The exact time of their meeting passed unrecorded, but it must have been well after 7:00 a.m. Bragg reported that members of his own staff had already passed through Longstreet's lines that morning, and despite warnings that his officers "were entering neutral ground between us and the enemy," those same staffers had time enough to return, bringing back word that in fact, the enemy was gone from Longstreet's immediate front. Bragg also had enough information to know that Rossville Gap was held in some strength, though he

42 George B. Guild, *A Brief Narrative of the Fourth Tennessee Cavalry Regiment* (Cool Springs Press, 1996), 30-31.

43 Entry for September 21st, W. B. Corbitt Diary, Emory University.

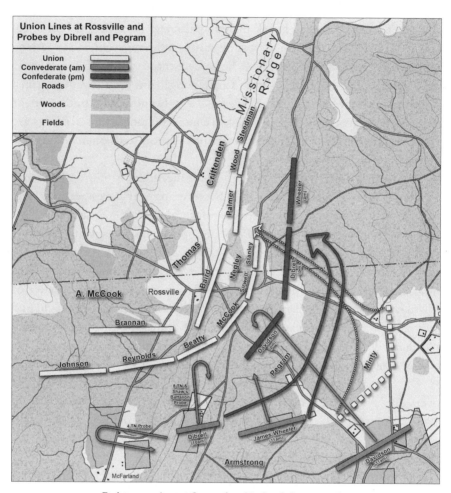

By late morning on September 21, Confederate cavalry
began to explore the Union defenses at Rossville.

probably was not yet fully aware of the extent of General Thomas's fortification efforts there. This knowledge suggests that Bragg probably rode up to Longstreet's camp some time after eight o'clock.[44]

Bragg left no record of their exact conversation. Longstreet described it variously, outlining the same basic course each time. It was clear to both men the Federals had disengaged successfully, and now held Rossville in sufficient

44 *OR* 30, pt. 2, 35.

strength to make a frontal attack there unpalatable. Accordingly, Longstreet advocated a solution that would have been right at home in Virginia: a turning movement. The Army of Tennessee, he argued, should move northeast, cross the Tennessee River upstream from Chattanooga, and operate either against Ambrose Burnside at Knoxville, Rosecrans's supply line back to Bridgeport, or more daringly, march back into Middle Tennessee. Longstreet's accounts are vague on details, offering up different versions of the discussion in his multiple descriptions of the encounter.

Longstreet wrote his first account of the meeting just four days later on September 25 in a confidential wire to Secretary of War James Seddon. In it, Longstreet "suggested at once to strike at Burnside, and if he made his escape, to march upon Rosecrans's communications upon rear of Nashville." The next version came in his official report, written sometime in October. Here Longstreet said he advocated "crossing the river above Chattanooga, so as to make ourselves sufficiently felt on the enemy's rear as to force his evacuation of Chattanooga, and indeed, force him back upon Nashville, and if we should find our transportation inadequate for a continuance of this movement, to follow up the railroad to Knoxville, destroy Burnside, and from there threaten the enemy's railroad communications in rear of Nashville." In an 1884 letter to D. H. Hill, Longstreet explained that he was "laying a plan by which we might overhaul the enemy at Chattanooga, or between that point and Nashville." In 1904 memoirs, the Georgian reiterated the version of the plan found in his official report: Cross the Tennessee, force Rosecrans out of Chattanooga, and then move on either Knoxville or Nashville[45]

Far from being fully formed, Longstreet's concept was really only a broad strategic outline. The variations in objective (the destruction of Burnside, flanking Rosecrans out of Chattanooga, or moving into Middle Tennessee) were simply the possibilities that suggested themselves to Longstreet as he contemplated what should come next, and should not be regarded as anything more definite. All three options were equally feasible and strategically sound, supposing the army could move with alacrity. His thinking foundered, however, on the shoals of logistical reality.

---

45 Polk, *Leonidas Polk*, vol. 2, 288; *OR* 30, pt. 2, 289-290; Daniel H. Hill, "Chickamauga: The Great Battle of the West," in Robert Underwood Johnson and Clarence Clough Buell, eds., *Battles and Leaders of the Civil War*, 4 vols. (Thomas Yoseloff, Inc., 1956), vol. 3, 659.

Longstreet had only recently arrived in North Georgia, and so had no way of knowing that the Army of Tennessee was crippled by a lack of transportation. Bragg's army may have recently doubled in size in terms of combat power, but all those reinforcements greatly complicated his army's logistical problems. None of Longstreet's nor William H. T. Walker's soldiers brought with them their own wagons from, respectively, Virginia or Mississippi. Leaving the wagons behind only exacerbated a problem Bragg already faced.

When he was operating in Tennessee, Bragg couldn't fully feed the men he had because, as historian Thomas Connelly observed, "Bragg's own transportation system had been on the verge of collapse since early 1863." Unless the army's supply trains could be vastly and rapidly augmented, the Confederates could not venture more than a handful of miles from a secure railhead. Longstreet's men were already feeling the effects of that limitation. Just that morning, Longstreet "complained to Bragg that many of his men needed provisions, and as his staff officers had not been provided with the means of supplying the troops, he [Longstreet] could do nothing" about the problem.[46]

Unfortunately for the Confederates, neither could Bragg. The Western & Atlantic Railroad, over which all of this logistical traffic must flow, was stressed to the breaking point. The rail line had spent the past week shuttling Longstreet's infantry to the front—a high priority for Bragg's army. The result was that the army was much stronger, and had won a decisive tactical victory, but the men were now short on rations. Catoosa Platform, where the rail line terminated, was 12 miles distant from the McDonald farmstead, which now marked the center of mass for Bragg's army. Ideally, Bragg wanted to advance the army's rail depot northward to Chickamauga Station, about 15 miles beyond Catoosa and just a couple of miles from McDonald's, but to do so the intervening line through Ringgold would have to be put back into service. Most significantly, four bridges destroyed by Forrest's men would have to be repaired before the railhead could be advanced. Bragg had already begun that job, ordering at least one company of the newly formed 3rd Confederate Engineers

---

46 Thomas L. Connelly, *Autumn of Glory: The Army of Tennessee, 1862-1865* (Louisiana State University Press, 1986), 230; Judith Lee Hallock, *Braxton Bragg and Confederate Defeat: Volume II* (University of Alabama Press, 1991), 83.

onto the task on September 17, but the work was nowhere close to complete by the morning of the 21st.[47]

Another huge obstacle to Longstreet's plans was the Tennessee River itself. The drought had made the Tennessee fordable in many places, at least by infantry and cavalry. Even some artillery might be rafted across. Crossing an entire army and keeping it supplied indefinitely, of course, required bridges. And bridging materials Bragg had in sufficient supply. In fact, he probably had more bridging assets than did Rosecrans. Back in July, during the retreat to Chattanooga, the Rebels had sufficient pontoons to span the Tennessee twice, once at Battle Creek and again at Kelly's Ferry. In August, these same pontoons were towed to Chattanooga, where later that month some of them formed the swinging bridge that occupied John T. Wilder's attention while Eli Lilly's guns shelled the city. A couple of weeks later, while he was preparing to abandon Chattanooga, Bragg ordered the bridges taken up and shipped south.[48]

On the 21st of September, Bragg's pontoon train was all the way back at Cartersville, Georgia, more than 60 miles to the south. Moving the boats back north would also require the use of the railroad—once again at the expense of other supplies like rations and ammunition. Once at Catoosa, more horses and mules would have to be assigned to pull those pontoons, a further drain on the army's already limited supply of livestock. However feasible that task might be in the long term, it certainly could not be accomplished quickly.[49]

The final problem with this solution, as Bragg saw it, was that Longstreet's proposed movement would mean exposing the Army of Tennessee's supply line to a direct thrust by Rosecrans. Despite all the new Confederate reinforcements, Bragg still harbored the misapprehension that the Union army was "now more than double our numbers." Who would defend Ringgold and Chickamauga Station once the army was on the far side of the Tennessee? To

---

47 Janet B. Hewitt, with Noah Andre Trudeau and Bryce A. Suderow, *Supplement to the Official Records of the Union and Confederate Armies*, 100 vols. (Broadfoot Publishing Co., 1995), vol. 85, 608. Hereafter cited as OR *Supplement*; Interview with Jim Ogden, CCNMP Park Historian, on July 20, 2012. Pegram's cavalry burned three bridges during its retreat from Ringgold on September 11, and at least one bridge at Graysville. The new railhead at Chickamauga Station would not be open until early October. The 3rd Confederate Engineer Regiment was organized out of existing pioneer detachments on August 1, 1863.

48 Interview with Jim Ogden, July 20, 2012.

49 OR *Supplement*, no. 85, 608. Company C of the 3rd Confederate Engineers comprised Bragg's pontonniers.

Bragg, the risks seemed too great. Moving the Army of Tennessee back into its namesake state exposed the Rebels to the very real danger of being isolated and destroyed in turn, more so than such a move threatened Rosecrans's Federals. It was far more likely that Union reinforcements could be quickly sent to defend Stevenson and Bridgeport than could more Rebels be stripped from other departments to defend Ringgold.[50]

For all of these reasons, Bragg understood that Longstreet's concept was simply impractical. However, Bragg failed to make that point clear to Old Pete. According to Longstreet, Bragg told him just the opposite. "He stated that he would follow that course," claimed the Georgian in his memoirs. Whether Bragg did a poor job of updating Longstreet, or whether Longstreet simply ignored the facts in order to further his own idea, this fundamental divide would produce no end of difficulties between these two men in the days to come.[51]

Meanwhile, Daniel Harvey Hill's mood had shifted dramatically overnight. After nearly a fortnight of constant pessimism and defensive-mindedness, Hill was suddenly advocating the *offensive a l'outrance*. Unlike Longstreet, Hill awoke certain the enemy had fled in wild abandon, and "that a 'pell-mell' straight into Chattanooga" would capture the place easily. Hill spent much of the early hours that morning awaiting orders to do just that. During that time he did not meet with Bragg, who was busy on the army's left. Instead, word came down only to "bury the dead and collect up arms and equipment." Four days later, in a September 25 letter to his wife, Isabella, Hill chafed at Bragg's focus on these trivialities.[52]

When his conference with Longstreet concluded, Bragg returned to the Right Wing, where at last things were coming into focus. Unlike D. H. Hill, and despite the postwar recollections of his aides, Leonidas Polk was not at all certain the battle was over. His first inkling came with Forrest's 7:30 a.m. dispatch that suggested the Union army's retreat went well beyond a mere tactical withdrawal. At 9:00 a.m., while awaiting Bragg's intentions, the bishop-general took time to compose a letter to his wife. In one telling passage

---

50 *OR* 30, pt. 2, 35.

51 James Longstreet, *From Manassas to Appomattox: Memoirs of the Civil War in America* (P. J. Lippincott, 1896), 461.

52 Hal Bridges, *Lee's Maverick General: Daniel Harvey Hill* (McGraw Hill, 1961), 225.

he noted, "we have just heard . . . that he [Rosecrans] has retreated to Chattanooga."[53]

News of the supposed Federal chaotic skedaddle traveled quickly through the army, coinciding with Bragg's arrival at Kelly Field. What followed there was an unprecedented scene for the men of the Army of Tennessee, and one described by Capt. John Ellis of the 16th Louisiana, Adams's Brigade, John C. Breckinridge's division:

> The brigade was bivouacked on the Chattanooga Road which was lined with officers and men, as Gen. Bragg with a portion of his staff rode along amidst the wildest cheering. The pale stern face of the chieftain beamed with animation; the dark eye . . . was softened with a milder light . . . the firm mouth and rigid lip had lost that sour sardonic grin so habitual to the face of Bragg. In the tightly wedged mass of shouting soldiers I saw Gen. Breckenridge, hat in hand and eager as a boy to do honor to the victorious general. There had been a feud between them, but Breckenridge seemed no longer to remember it.[54]

In a letter to his brother, Ellis further amplified this scene:

> After the battle . . . Bragg extended both hands and said 'General, let us be friends. Let the past be forgotten. Shall it not be so?' 'With all my heart,' answered the gallant Kentuckian. . . . As [Bragg] passed our brigade, I noticed Gen. Breckenridge down among the men with his hat off, whooping as lustily as any private. I am glad they have buried the hatchet.[55]

Surgeon Robert P. Myers of the 16th Georgia also witnessed such a scene. For Myers, fresh off the train from Virginia with the leading elements of Brig. Gen. William T. Wofford's Georgian brigade, this was his first introduction to Bragg's command. He noted some of those initial impressions in his diary: "Genl Bragg rode down the lines today, and was cheered long and hard, he had no uniform on simply a loose blouse. He rode a beautiful bay horse, his staff and escort very large—quite different from the Genls of the Army of Northern Va, Genl Lee and all of his Lieuts & Majors were accompanied with a small staff

---

53 Polk to Wife, September 21, 1863, as quoted in Polk, *Bishop and General*, vol. 2, 282.

54 Entry for September 21, E. John Ellis Diary, LSU.

55 "My Dear Brother," October 4, 1863, Ellis and Family Papers, LSU.

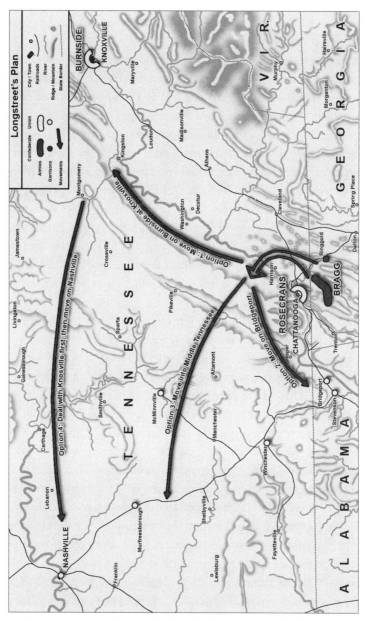

Longstreet's "plan" not really fully articulated, conceived only of first
outflanking Rosecrans to the north and then moving
into either Middle or East Tennessee.

and escort." Unfortunately for the Army of Tennessee, this rare heady moment of victory and comity would not last.[56]

By midday, Bragg was at last back at headquarters issuing new orders to stir the army into motion. The army would march—but not directly on Chattanooga. Instead, Bragg instructed Polk's wing "to move [north] . . . opposite Chickamauga Station" and form a line from there south to "Red House Ford" aligned on the west side of Chickamauga Creek. Longstreet was to follow as soon as the roads cleared, and deploy on Polk's left. Army headquarters and the army trains would relocate to Red House Ford, centered between the two wings. Both Wheeler and Forrest were to "press up close to the enemy," occupying Missionary Ridge. In addition, each corps was to detach two mounted regiments "to our rear to gather up the stragglers from this army and all arms left upon the field." If D. H. Hill was disappointed that the army was not marching 'pell-mell' on Rossville, Longstreet had reason to be pleased. This shift northward was the logical first step in a move across the Tennessee River upstream from Chattanooga.[57]

Bragg's instructions reached Joe Wheeler at Crawfish Spring near noon or shortly thereafter; not very long after Wheeler and Wharton arrived at that location from their overnight camps. Though Wharton's division was "early in the saddle" on Monday morning, they still had to travel six or seven miles just to reach the Spring. Once there, Wheeler pushed on to join Martin, deploying his cavalry across the valley between Missionary Ridge and the foot of Lookout Mountain, facing north against the similarly-arrayed Union cavalry under Robert Mitchell. Wheeler had the major portions of both Martin's and Wharton's divisions at hand, though sizeable detachments from each command were still picketing to the south or combing the field for prisoners and supplies. Bragg's instructions "to press up close" to the Union forces would likely have resulted in a substantial conflict that afternoon, had not other information come from those same southernmost pickets who reported that another Union cavalry column was working its way out of McLemore's Cove.[58]

Even as Wheeler's main body was deploying to face Mitchell, Captain Littlefield's Rebel picket post at Owen's Ford sent word that enemy cavalry was

---

56 Entry for September 21, 1863, Robert P. Myers Diary, Museum of the Confederacy, Richmond VA.

57 *OR* 30, pt. 4, 679.

58 Robert F. Bunting Letter, *Rome Tri-Weekly Telegraph*, November 27, 1863.

coming up from the south "in large force," apparently heading to Chattanooga and escorting "a large train of wagons." From his newly established headquarters at Crawfish Spring, Wheeler himself could see heavy dust clouds spiraling into the air marking the passage of that same Union column, moving (as Wheeler inaccurately described it) "toward McLemore Cove."[59]

This column was comprised of 600 Union cavalry under command of Col. Louis D. Watkins, encumbered with supply wagons and several hundred convalescents, which represented the very last of Rosecrans's army to leave Alpine. On the morning of September 20, Watkins was encamped at Steven's Gap. After leaving a detachment to hold that gap against any Rebel incursion, Watkins moved the rest of his men down into McLemore's Cove as far as the Shaw farmstead, about eight miles south of Crawfish Spring. Watkins's last instructions from Mitchell had been to join the main body at Crawfish Spring. Since then Watkins had heard nothing, and so knew he nothing of either the Union rout at Chickamauga or the Federals' wholesale retreat. As he moved northward on the morning of the 21st, however, Watkins encountered Captain Littlefield's six-company detachment at Owen's Ford. Uncertain that Crawfish Spring was even still in Union hands, Watkins halted and sent out scouts.[60]

Sensing an opportunity, Wheeler focused his attention on Watkins. Leaving only a picket to screen Mitchell's Yankees, Wheeler descended on Watkins's column with an overwhelming force, numbering between 3,000 and 5,000 men. Alerted to his peril by rising clouds of dust that all seemed to converge on his brigade, Colonel Watkins decided that his only hope of escape was to immediately ride west towards Cooper's Gap, from where he could ascend Lookout Mountain. Ordering one battalion of the Union 5th Kentucky under Lt. Col. William T. Hoblitzell to take the wagons on ahead, Watkins deployed his other two regiments (the 4th and 6th Kentucky cavalry regiments) to buy some time. With barely 400 Federals left to stem the gray tide, Watkins was hopelessly outmatched.[61]

The result was predictable. Watkins attempted a fighting withdrawal, but despite a couple of desperate stands, the battle devolved into a rout. Watkins officially described the ensuing retreat as a "running fight," but he was trying to

---

59 OR 30, pt. 2, 521.

60 Ibid., pt. 1, 917.

61 Ibid., 915.

put the best face on it. Charles H. Sowle of the 4th Kentucky Cavalry described the action more bluntly. The Rebels, he wrote, "routed us complete." Thomas Coleman of the 11th Texas Cavalry chortled that the affair was "a regular wolf chase."[62]

Watkins's Federals were driven back to the foot of Lookout at Cooper's Gap, jammed with Union wagons desperately seeking to escape. Watkins lost his entire 53-wagon train there, as well as 217 officers and men taken prisoner. Wheeler exaggerated the extent of this success, boasting that Watkins's command of "nearly 2,000" men was "badly scattered." He also claimed to have captured 400 prisoners, "18 stands of colors," and "their entire train, numbering about 90 wagons, loaded with valuable baggage."[63]

The action consumed most of the afternoon. Wheeler considered it a good day's work. Returning to Crawfish Spring, booty and prisoners in tow, he left only a picket line to face Mitchell and made no further effort to press the Yankees to the north or ascend Lookout Mountain. In truth, Wheeler's drubbing of Watkins was a sideshow. Bragg needed detailed information about the location of the Federal army, and secondarily, some effort should have been made to get into Lookout Valley. The massive flow of Union traffic between Chattanooga and Bridgeport should have been interrupted. Every hour the movement of goods continued improved Rosecrans's chances of holding the city.

Out on that picket line facing Mitchell, Robert Bunting of the 8th Texas Cavalry recalled a long, if mostly quiet, afternoon. "We had occasional skirmishing in front," he wrote, "and although the Yankee cavalry was in view, yet they did not press us." Eventually the Texans were recalled, returning to camp at "11 o'clock" that night. Once again the camp to which Wheeler and Wharton retired was their old one east of Glass Mill, six or seven miles from Crawfish Spring. This last decision compounded a day of poor judgments. By returning to that camp, Wheeler once again rode his invaluable horsemen out of position and far from where they would be needed the next morning.[64]

---

62 Ibid., 915; "Father and Mother," September 24, 1863, Charles H. Sowle Papers, DU; "Dear Parents and home folks," October 5, 1863, Tom Coleman Papers, University of Missouri, Rolla.

63 OR 30, pt. 1, 915-916; Ibid., pt. 2, 521. This fight is described in greater detail in Appendix I.

64 Robert F. Bunting Letter, *Rome Tri-Weekly Telegraph*, November 27, 1863.

By 4:00 p.m., Nathan Bedford Forrest's anger at the day's inactivity reached the boiling point. Despite the fact that his two divisions had made no headway that day against the Union position at Rossville, Forrest remained convinced the Federals were in full retreat. When Bragg's midday movement order reached him, Forrest decided his troopers could do no more. Leaving a picket line to watch the enemy, he moved his main body back to make camp along West Chickamauga Creek. According to Forrest's earliest biographers, Thomas Jordan and J. P. Pryor, the big cavalryman "was deeply chagrinned and depressed in view of the strange delay and inaction" that seemingly gripped the army. Agitated, he visited Bragg's new headquarters at Red House Bridge.[65]

The meeting that followed has been described in various ways. In 1868, writing while both men were still very much alive, Jordan and Pryor described the encounter with a great deal of circumspection. "At ten o'clock p.m., [Forrest] rode to General Bragg's headquarters. The Commander-in-Chief, receiving him graciously, had much to say in commendation of his action during the battle; after which, Forrest was directed to hold his command in readiness, next morning, for a general advance on Chattanooga."[66]

Others accounts differed considerably. The most dramatic was penned by biographer Andrew Lytle, an early 20th Century Southern novelist and poet, whose version was published in 1931. Lytle's account described an insolent Forrest facing down a cowed commanding general. Forrest "found him [Bragg] in his tent, sound asleep. . . . [G]oing in, he tried to impress upon Bragg what he considered the helpless condition of the enemy. . . . [I]f they pursued at once, capture was certain." In response, "Bragg asked him how he could move his army without supplies." According to Lytle, Forrest snapped back, "General Bragg, we can get all the supplies we want in Chattanooga." For a moment, the two men glared silently at each other until Forrest turned and "stalked out into the dark. . . . [T]here was more insolence and contempt in this silent departure than he could have put into a studied invective."[67]

---

65 Robert S. Henry, *First With The Most: Nathan Bedford Forrest* (Bobbs-Merrill, 1944), 193; Jordan and Pryor, *Forrest's Cavalry*, 352. D. H. Hill, in "Chickamauga," *Battles and Leaders*, vol. 3, 662, claims that in one angry dispatch, Forrest informed Bragg "that every hour was worth a thousand men," but there is no contemporary evidence of this communiqué.

66 Jordan and Pryor, *Forrest's Cavalry*, 353.

67 Lytle, *Bedford Forrest and His Critter Company*, 233. Wyeth, *That Devil Forrest*, 236-239, makes no mention of such an encounter. Henry, *First with The Most*, 193, says only that Forrest "interviewed" Bragg but does not record what passed between them. Andrew Lytle was a

Lytle's hyperbole was likely invented out of whole cloth, but there is no denying Forrest was bewildered by what he regarded as Bragg's peculiar paralysis. Back at his own headquarters, Forrest gave voice to his frustration and was overheard asking, "what does he fight battles for?" Despite his frustration with his commanding officer, Forrest would be ready early on September 22 to lead the army into Chattanooga, if Bragg ordered it done.[68]

Major General Lafayette McLaws of Longstreet's Corps reached the army on the 21st and witnessed the immediate aftermath of the battle. He would later defend Bragg. "It was generally believed that Gen. Bragg did not order the pursuit, but I bear witness that an immediate pursuit was ordered, and my division (three brigades of it) led, though no other force followed me." Unfortunately for Bragg's reputation, this movement accomplished very little.[69]

Joseph Kershaw's and Benjamin G. Humphreys's brigades arrived on September 19 as the battle was underway and played a prominent role in the breakthrough of the following day. The rest of McLaws's division, however (which consisted of Brig. Gens. William T. Wofford's and Goode Bryan's Georgia brigades) and the division commander did not begin detraining at Catoosa Platform until the night of the 19th. They were not fully assembled and ready to move until late the next afternoon, and did not start marching toward the sounds of battle until it was near dusk. "Marched . . . about 6 miles and camped," noted Lt. William R. Montgomery of the 3rd Georgia Sharpshooters. "Like to froze." Together, Wofford's and Bryan's men numbered about 3,700 troops. Additionally, Brig. Gen. Micah Jenkins's veteran 2,000-man brigade also detrained at Catoosa. Jenkins had been assigned to John B. Hood's division on September 11 as partial compensation for the loss of George Pickett's full division, who were deemed too shattered after their Pennsylvania experience to embark on a major new campaign across the country to North Georgia. True to form for the entire movement, Col. Asbury Coward of the 5th South Carolina recalled that Jenkins's troops reached "Ringgold in an exhausted state and found that our teams and baggage had not arrived." The South Carolinians

---

highly influential southern literary figure, a leader in the Agrarian Movement. Though he was a gifted writer and author of some note, he was not a trained historian.

68 Brian Steel Wills, *Battle from the Start: The Life of Nathan Bedford Forrest* (HarperCollins, 1992), 142; Henry, *First with the Most*, 193.

69 Lafayette McLaws, "Chickamauga," Cheeves Family Papers, South Carolina Historical Society, Charleston, SC.

followed McLaws's column, joining them in their bivouac along Chickamauga Creek somewhere near Reed's Bridge.[70]

Nearly 6,000 strong, all three brigades were up and moving early. During the march, Lieutenant Montgomery observed "Gens Bragg & Polk & Breckinridge," which helps place their route moving west to the battlefield along Reed's Bridge Road to the vicinity of the McDonald house. Once on the field, the new men had little to do but wait. They were not called upon until the day was almost over. According to McLaws, "I received an order about 5 o'clock to go in pursuit of the enemy, following General Breckinridge. At once I assembled three of my brigades, one of them [Kershaw] being sent to Ringgold to guard prisoners taken in the battle just ended."[71]

Here, of course, was more confusion, though whether McLaws was mistaken or Bragg's headquarters failed in some manner remains unclear. Breckinridge's division, part of D. H. Hill's Corps in Polk's Right Wing, was already marching toward Chickamauga Station. Breckinridge knew nothing about joining up with McLaws to move upon Chattanooga. Nor did anyone inform McLaws that the Federals were still staunchly defending Rossville, which would have abruptly cut short any pursuit. After spending some more time waiting for Breckinridge to appear, McLaws finally moved north along the La Fayette Road "until dark, and then bivouacked along the road side." Given the timing, he could not have gone far, and perhaps no more than a mile, before night fell. McLaws intended to resume the movement the next morning.[72]

For the Confederates, September 21 was characterized by uncertainty and caution. Time was slipping away. The Federals had been bloodied but not destroyed, and the sooner the Confederates could press their advantage, the better. Neither William Starke Rosecrans nor the rest of the Army of the Cumberland, however, would waste whatever gift of time they were granted. Crucial decisions needed to be made in Chattanooga as well. September 21 would be no less a critical day for the Federals than for the Confederates.

---

70 George F. Montgomery, ed., *Georgia Sharpshooter: The Civil War Diary and Letters of William Rhadamanthus Montgomery, 1839-1906* (Mercer University Press, 1997), 26; Natalie Jenkins Bond and Osmun Latrobe Coward, eds., *The South Carolinians: Colonel Asbury Coward's Memoirs* (Vantage Press, 1968), 84.

71 Montgomery, *Georgia Sharpshooter*, 26; Lafayette McLaws, "Chickamauga," Cheeves Family Papers.

72 Lafayette McLaws, "Chickamauga," Cheeves Family Papers.

Chapter Two

A Battle Lost?

September 21: Within Union Lines

Through the night and into the early morning hours of September 21, telegraph wires across the North hummed with activity. In Washington, President Abraham Lincoln, Secretary of War Edwin Stanton, and Union General-in-Chief Henry W. Halleck waited anxiously for news, pouncing on every morsel and firing off wire after wire in response. "Be of good cheer," Lincoln wired to General Rosecrans at 12:35 a.m. "We have unabated confidence in you and in your soldiers and officers. . . . I would say save your army by taking strong positions until [Maj. Gen. Ambrose] Burnside joins you, when I hope you can turn the tide. . . . We shall do our utmost to assist you." Burnside, whose forces in East Tennessee were the closest possible source of reinforcement for the Army of the Cumberland, now figured prominently in Lincoln's thoughts. At 2:00 a.m., the president wired a terse, unequivocal order to Burnside: "Go to Rosecrans with your force without a moment's delay."[1]

To those around him, the president clearly appeared downbeat. He had been so for several days, fearing the worst. Those doubts were now confirmed. In the small hours of Monday morning he visited his private secretary, John Hay, barging into Hay's bedroom while the latter was still abed. "Well, R[osecrans] has been whipped as I feared," blurted the frustrated commander-

---

1 OR 30, pt. 1, 146.

in-chief. "I have feared it for several days. I believe I feel trouble in the air before it comes." On the subject of Burnside, Lincoln vented his spleen. "Instead of obeying the orders . . . and going to R[osecrans]," he exploded in clear disgust, "[he] has gone up on a foolish affair to Jonesboro to capture a party of guerrillas."[2]

Especially vexing was the discovery that Robert E. Lee had sent most of James Longstreet's corps westward to reinforce Braxton Bragg's Army of Tennessee—a massive undertaking performed under the nose of a curiously passive Maj. Gen. George G. Meade. Meade and his Army of the Potomac had sat quietly around Culpeper, Virginia, while Lee coolly reduced his own forces by nearly one-third. "I asked what Meade was doing with his immense army," noted Secretary of the Navy Gideon Welles in his diary, given "Lee's skeleton and depleted show." Again Lincoln gave voice to his dismay: "It is . . . the same old story of this Army of the Potomac. Imbecility, inefficiency—don't want to do—is defending the capital. . . . Oh, it is terrible, terrible, this weakness, this indifference, of our Potomac generals." Welles felt Halleck should share equally in the blame. "General Halleck has earnestly and constantly smoked cigars and rubbed his elbows," sneered the derisive naval secretary, "while the rebels have been vigorously concentrating their forces to overwhelm Rosecrans."[3]

Gloom and despair might have gripped Washington, but at Rossville in Georgia, things improved steadily as the morning light brightened. Just west of the gap stood the John Ross house, named for the mixed-race Cherokee chief who had once lived there until the Indians were removed in the 1830s. Now the house was home to Thomas G. McFarland. Nearby was McFarland's Spring, which, similar to Crawfish Spring, acted as a magnet to all thirsty troops in this parched land. With such close access to good water, the house was soon

2   Martin Burlingame and John R. Turner Ettlinger, *Inside Lincoln's White House: The Complete Civil War Diary of John Hay* (Southern Illinois University Press, 1997), 85. Prior to the fight at Chickamauga, Burnside and Rosecrans had been in regular communication. With the capture of Chattanooga on September 9, it looked to both men as if Bragg were retreating, leaving Burnside nothing to fear from that quarter. Accordingly, Burnside took that part of his force not tied down occupying Knoxville towards Jonesboro, Tennessee, near the Virginia-Tennessee border, to secure his northern flank. A small force of Confederates under Maj. Gen. Samuel Jones still controlled southwest Virginia and, if reinforced, could pose a threat to Burnside's control of East Tennessee. At Jonesboro, Burnside was about 100 miles northwest of Knoxville and more than 200 miles from Chattanooga.

3   William E. Giennapp and Erica L. Gienapp, eds., *The Civil War Diary of Gideon Welles, Lincoln's Secretary of the Navy. The Original Manuscript Edition* (University of Illinois Press, 2014), 295.

This view shows the Ross house, with the Rossville Gap behind it. *Library of Congress*

commandeered as a hospital. General Thomas established his headquarters nearby.

As of 5:00 a.m., Colonel Minty reported that things were "all quiet on his front." At 6:45 a.m., Thomas reported his dispositions to Rosecrans. Major General James Negley was positioned "in the pass. . . . General McCook's corps on the right; General Crittenden's two divisions on the top of the ridge to the left . . . [and] the remainder of my corps and General Granger's massed in reserve."[4]

At 7:30 a.m., Negley passed his own update back to the army commander. Even though Thomas was present with him at the gap, Negley felt the need to inform Rosecrans "that everything is progressing most favorably. I have my division properly organized, armed, fed, and in position. Will have the other troops here in preliminary organization in less than an hour. Affairs present a

---

4   *OR* 30, pt. 1, 147. Maj. Gen. Thomas L. Crittenden's XXI Corps reported only two divisions ready for action that morning. Horatio Van Cleve's 3rd Division, the most badly scattered of all the Union commands on September 20, had not yet fully reconstituted.

very satisfactory appearance." Negley's wire directly to the army commander might well have been motivated by his growing unease over his decision to leave the field the day before, which was now looking increasingly premature. Other generals were beginning to talk, questioning that departure.[5]

The first dispatch of the morning penned by James Garfield, Rosecrans's chief of staff, was more equivocal than Negley's. Garfield was not "sure this line [w]as a good one for a general battle, and," he added gloomily, "I do not know how much reliance can be placed on the stampeded troops." Major General Thomas L. Crittenden, head of the XXI Corps, had informed Garfield that Rosecrans wanted Garfield back in Chattanooga, and, expecting to meet his boss there, Garfield suggested Rosecrans not come forward immediately. Wait "till we see the developments and organize the rear," advised the chief of staff.[6]

Major General Lovell H. Rousseau was also present and lending his considerable talents to restoring order. The hugely popular Rousseau normally commanded the First Division of Thomas's XIV Corps, but had been absent on army business for the past month or so, leaving his command in the hands of Absalom Baird. Rousseau arrived in Chattanooga on September 20 in time to learn of the army's stunning reverse. Departing for the front at 2:00 a.m., Rousseau arrived at Rossville that morning. He did not immediately replace Baird because Thomas put him to work rallying stragglers. His upbeat assessment, sent at 11:00 a.m., contradicted Garfield's pessimism: "I found the task comparatively easy," observed Rousseau, "the men separated from their regiments being in high spirits and not at all cowed." The men of his division certainly weren't cowed, and greeted their previous commander with wild enthusiasm. They raised "a tremendous shouting and cheering" which soon spread to other units, generating the tumult that Minty's cavalry mistook for the arrival of Burnside's long-awaited troops.[7]

By midday, the Federals were confident they could hold Rossville indefinitely. The chain of command had been largely reconstituted, and general order restored. The imposing ridge was a natural fortress, invulnerable to frontal attack if properly held. Moreover, the troops spent the day erecting sturdy defenses. When Chaplain John J. Hight located his regiment, the 58th

---

5 Ibid.

6 Ibid., 148.

7 Ibid., pt. 3, 762; Richard B. Robbins Memoir, Bentley Library, UMich.

Indiana, that morning, he found the men "in a very good position and seemingly able to hold it against the enemy." Hight could hear Forrest's cannons barking during the Rebel horseman's early afternoon effort to push through the gap, but for most Federals, this was of little concern. Instead, the day offered a chance to eat and rest. Private John Hollingsworth of the 101st Indiana, Maj. Gen. Joseph Reynolds's division, recorded that the men "laid in camp on the Chattanooga road and in line of battle half the day. Got 3 days rations, got supper, and laid down and slept" the rest of the afternoon.[8]

To Joe Reynolds's mingled amazement and joy, the men of the 105th Ohio, whom Reynolds was sure he had sent off to certain death or imprisonment when he ordered them to charge Brig. Gen. Henry Benning's Georgians in Poe Field on Sunday, reappeared. After marveling at the amazing tale of escape and evasion told by the Buckeyes, Reynolds stopped Thomas and had Capt. Charles Edwards of the 105th repeat the whole story. "Thomas turned to the regiment, then but a little company, and raising his hat, said: 'It was gallantly done!' No wonder the men cheered," observed Lt. Albion Tourgee.[9]

Captain William Boyd and Company B of the 84th Indiana awoke that Monday morning in the same spot they had camped on three days before, only in significantly fewer numbers. During Company B's morning roll call, the full impact of the prior day's fight hit them. "Of the thirty-six men I had taken into the three days' action," lamented Boyd, "five were too cowardly to fight and skulked away, six were left behind killed or mortally wounded and 18 others were more or less severely wounded." This left only Boyd and seven men fit for duty. Concerning the skulkers, apparently too disgusted by their failure of nerve, the captain never mentioned what became of them.[10]

The Federal position at Rossville might be all but impregnable to a direct assault, but Rosecrans and his key commanders understood that it was highly vulnerable to a flanking move. In large part this was because the army no longer had enough troops to defend all the possible avenues of approach. By 11:45 a.m., the Army of the Cumberland was shipshape enough to start assessing

---

8   John J. Hight, *History of the Fifty-Eighth Regiment of Indiana Volunteer Infantry, Its Organization, Campaigns, and Battles from 1861 to 1865* (Press of the Clarion, 1895), 197; Entry for September 21, Jonathan Hollingsworth Diary, Indiana Historical Society, Indianapolis. Hereafter INHS.

9   Tourgee, *The Story of a Thousand*, 226.

10   Entry for September 21, William Boyd Journal, University of California, Berkeley. Hereafter UCBerkeley.

Major General Lovell H. Rousseau arrived at Rossville on the morning of September 21.
Library of Congress

losses. The preliminary numbers were grim. Of the ten divisions in the XIV, XX, and XXI corps, six provided initial casualty counts, totaling 13,623 men killed, wounded, and missing. If the other four divisions reported in like proportion, Rosecrans's losses in infantry and artillery might top 22,000 men—more than half of the roughly 43,000 present for duty in those same formations on September 18. To make matters worse, this estimate did not include either the cavalry or Gordon Granger's three brigades of the Reserve Corps, who took a fearful pounding on Horseshoe Ridge during the final hours of the fighting.[11]

Fortunately for the Union, those numbers would improve dramatically within a short time as the lightly wounded returned to duty and the numerous stragglers came in. For most of the latter, Captain Boyd's harsh assessment of cowardice was probably too severe a charge. Many of these men, bewildered by the overwhelming confusion of a multi-day battle and the nighttime retreat, had simply become separated from their commands. When daylight arrived, they set out to find their regiments. As a result, the first loss estimates turned out to be too high by almost one-third. The combined final casualty count for those same six divisions eventually tallied 9,491 killed, wounded, and missing, or an improvement of more than 4,000 troops.[12]

Brigadier General James D. Spears's brigade, consisting of three Unionist East Tennessee regiments, played an important role in this resurgence of

11 OR 30, pt. 3, 761.

12 Ibid., pt. 1, 171-179. Note that this latter figure still included many lightly wounded men, some of whom would have returned to duty within a fortnight or so. A full discussion of losses for both sides can be found in Chapter 3.

numbers. Although its baggage was still toiling its way on the west side of Lookout Mountain, the brigade arrived in Chattanooga on the 20th and was ordered out to Rossville by Granger. Spears and his command never reached Rossville. Rosecrans found Spears and ordered him to take up a position on the Federal Road where it bridged Chattanooga Creek and halt "all officers and soldiers below the rank of Major General coming into Chattanooga." Spears expanded his role by spreading his three regiments—the 3rd, 5th, and 6th Tennessee—across all the most likely approaches. By first light on the 21st, he collected "between 8,000 and 12,000 officers and soldiers, who were . . . all thrown to the front again" with the coming of daylight.[13]

The improving numbers helped Rosecrans, but they still did not give him enough troops to fully defend the high ground surrounding Chattanooga. Though the looping nature of the Tennessee River meant that such a defensive line could run from bank to bank, giving any defender the advantage of secure flanks, a line that embraced both Missionary Ridge and Lookout Mountain would be too long for a force twice the size of Rosecrans's army. A defensive line that long would stretch as much as 15 miles. Rebels were already appearing in Chattanooga Valley, as evidenced by Brig. Gen. Mitchell's reports concerning the appearance of Joe Wheeler's troopers, but so far no enemy had appeared on the west side of Missionary Ridge north of the gap, or threatened Lookout Mountain. If they did, the Yankees could still be cut off from Chattanooga.

Chattanooga's unusual geography is defined by three features: The Tennessee River, Missionary Ridge, and Lookout Mountain. The town itself sits on the south bank of a shallow bend in the Tennessee, some 400 yards wide at that point, which then flows south for another mile and a half. There, the Tennessee makes an abrupt 180 degree turn, pushed aside by the rocky face of Lookout Mountain, called Moccasin Bend. Lookout Mountain marks the beginning of a 100-mile ridge that runs deep into northern Alabama, its steep sides pierced at infrequent intervals by gaps that allow traffic up and over the mountain. Its distinctive crest towers some 2,100 feet above the plain and the city. Two miles to the east, Missionary Ridge, another similar though much lower ridge, parallels Lookout. This ridge rises above the river basin at a place called Boyce's Station and runs roughly eight miles to Rossville Gap. It continues for a number of miles beyond that point all the way down into McLemore Cove. On September 21, Rosecrans's main concern was focused on

13 *OR* 30, pt. 1, 884.

that part of the ridge between Rossville and Boyce's. Lower ground lay between the northern end of Missionary Ridge and the river, which meant that swinging around the northern end of the ridge was the easiest way into Chattanooga, but also the longest route by several miles. Both of the rail lines entering Chattanooga from the south and east followed this course, with the Western and Atlantic (from Atlanta) skirting the ridge entirely, and the East Tennessee line piercing the ridge via a short tunnel near the northern end. Farther south the Federal Road, via Rossville Gap, was by far the most direct way between Ringgold and Chattanooga. However, between Boyce's Station and Rossville, Missionary Ridge is traversed by at least six other lesser roads, and while the ridge's western face was defined by a nearly sheer slope difficult to climb, the eastern aspect was more gradual and broken.

Between Missionary Ridge and Lookout Mountain lay a broad valley roughly two miles wide cut by Chattanooga Creek. Next came Lookout Mountain itself, with a significant shelf of plateau about one-third of the way up the mountain. The best roads around the northern nose of Lookout either followed the rail line, squeezed onto the floodplain between the river and the mountain's foot, or ran across this shelf. At the very top of the mountain sat a small village known as Summertown, with a prominent resort hotel. As its name suggested, it served mainly as a refuge from the valley's heat during the summer months.

If Rosecrans wanted to establish a line on this encircling high ground, he would need a large number of men to do so. Troops would have to man the entire length of Missionary Ridge at least as far as Rossville, more troops would be needed to hold the two miles of valley, and then additional forces at the foot, on the plateau, and on the top of Lookout. In all, this line would require about 100,000 men to properly man all the necessary defensive works. In the immediate aftermath of Chickamauga, however, Rosecrans had at most 30,000.

By the morning of the 21st, the Union army was deployed along a right-angled line, with the angle centered on Rossville. The northern shank of this line ran along the crest of Missionary Ridge, facing east. Brigadier General James Steedman's two-brigade division of the Reserve Corps anchored this northern flank, about a mile and a half north of the Rossville Gap. Next came Thomas Wood's and John M. Palmer's divisions of Crittenden's XXI Corps, also facing east and aligned atop the ridge. General Negley's division of the XIV Corps (minus John Beatty's brigade) defended Rossville Gap proper, its lines arcing east and a little in front of Crittenden's left astride the Federal Road. Colonel Dan McCook's brigade of the Reserve Corps was posted to Negley's left, facing southeast astride the La Fayette Road. McCook's command, still 2,000 strong and having suffered almost no loss in the earlier fighting, was now as large as some Federal divisions. It would not give ground easily.

Upslope from McCook, holding the knife edge of Missionary Ridge south of the Rossville Gap, were John Beatty's men. As described in the previous chapter, Beatty's command encountered Confederate cavalry. The first to find them were George Dibrell's troopers, and later, elements of Joe Wheeler's corps. Joe Reynolds's division of the XIV Corps, a much-reduced formation of only two brigades, deployed in the valley to Beatty's left, facing south to block the road from McFarland's Gap. Absalom Baird's and John Brannan's divisions formed George Thomas's main reserve, with Baird backstopping Negley in the gap and Brannan doing the same behind Reynolds.

Alexander McCook's XX Corps drew the duty of holding Chattanooga Valley. Richard Johnson's, Philip Sheridan's, and Jefferson C. "Jef." Davis's divisions were drawn up in a long single line running east to west between Reynolds's left flank and Chattanooga Creek. The stream, which flowed northward out of McLemore Cove into the Tennessee River, ran along the western foot of Lookout Mountain until it made a sharp bend eastward for more than a mile just south of the Tennessee state line, where it again turned northward toward the river. A road out of the cove ran northward between the creek and Lookout Mountain. Davis placed his strongest brigade, Col. Sidney Post's command, which had also escaped the bloodbath of the main battle, to defend it.

To the south, across McCook's front, Brig. Gen. Robert Mitchell's cavalry (with the exception of Col. Minty's brigade), and—for the time being, anyway—John T. Wilder's mounted infantry, jointly held a line stretching the length of the valley, covering both Thomas's right flank at Rossville and the direct approach to Chattanooga from the south. Wilder described this position as a line of about three miles running from "the base of Lookout Mountain" to the "low hills of Mission Ridge," about four and a half miles south of Rossville.[14]

A few other odds and ends were scattered about. The 1,200 troops of Brig. Gen. George P. Wagner's brigade, part of Tom Wood's division, still garrisoned Chattanooga. They were already beginning work to improve the preexisting Confederate defenses ringing the town. Bolstering these efforts were elements

---

14 Wilder Revised Report, John T. Wilder file, CCNMP.

of both the Pioneer Brigade and the 1st Michigan Engineers and Mechanics, perhaps another 1,000 men in all.

The only division not immediately reconstituted by Monday morning was Horatio Van Cleve's 3rd Division of Crittenden's XXI Corps. This command was among the most badly scattered of all of Rosecrans's combat formations, a situation exacerbated in part by Van Cleve himself. After falling back from Snodgrass Hill to Rossville, Col. George Dick located his division commander at 1:00 a.m. Van Cleve ordered Dick to continue into Chattanooga, where he arrived to join Wagner in the inner defenses by 4:00 a.m. Colonel Sidney Barnes's brigade, which had participated in the Kelly Field pullout, also reached the Rossville area around 1:00 a.m., spending the rest of the night there. At 2:00 a.m., Van Cleve stumbled on Brig. Gen. Samuel Beatty and two of his four regiments, the 79th Indiana and 13th Ohio. The 9th and 17th Kentucky, separated from Beatty since about midday on the 20th, had temporarily attached themselves to Wood's command. Unaware of Rosecrans's orders to Spears, Van Cleve instructed Beatty to take his rump of a brigade "to the crossroads at the foot of Lookout Mountain," and collect stragglers there. As a result, Van Cleve's division was scattered between Chattanooga, Lookout Mountain, and Rossville.

Thomas's deployment on the morning of September 21 encompassed less than one-third of the overall length needed to secure all of Chattanooga's approaches. A frontal attack aimed directly at the Rossville Gap could be handily repelled. Within a day, however, Bragg could maneuver all or part of his army—and after Sunday's disastrous outcome, Rosecrans and his generals believed Bragg's manpower advantage was enormous—to bypass Rossville Gap, either by going north along Missionary Ridge or by moving against Lookout Mountain itself. If either happened, the Army of the Cumberland was not in a position to meet those thrusts with anything like good odds.

Since his extant line held less than one-third of Missionary Ridge, George Thomas remained most concerned about his left. Additional forces for that mission, however, were lacking. A partial solution offered itself late that morning when Minty reported that the enemy was "advancing on him with a strong force of cavalry and infantry." With Negley and Dan McCook now holding Rossville in strength, Thomas could spare Minty, and directed the cavalryman "to retire through the gap and post his command on our left flank, and to throw out strong reconnoitering parties across the ridge to observe and report any movements on our left front." As he did so, Minty's latest news

Col. Robert H. G. Minty, whose brigade screened the Rossville Gap on the morning of September 21.
Joseph G. Vale, Minty and the Cavalry, 1886

played on Thomas's and Rosecrans's worst fears: "the enemy . . . are moving on both our flanks."[15]

Minty's few cavalrymen would hardly be sufficient force to hold the rest of the ridge if the Rebels showed in any strength to the north. Early that afternoon, after apprising both Alexander McCook and Tom Crittenden of Minty's news, Thomas must have appealed to Rosecrans for additional help, for Colonel Dick's brigade of Van Cleve's division made its way forward.[16]

By midday Dick's four regiments—the 44th and 86th Indiana, and the 13th and 59th Ohio—were ensconced in a Confederate redoubt called Fort Cheatham, originally named for the Rebel division commander whose men occupied that place when Bragg held the city. The fort, reported Dick, was about a mile east of Chattanooga proper and some distance west of Orchard Knob. The colonel's command was small. Dick entered the action at Chickamauga with fewer than 1,100 men and lost a quarter of his strength. On the morning of the 21st he fielded fewer than 800 muskets. Dick's new orders sent his command east another two miles to the crest of Missionary Ridge. This daunting assignment dispersed Dick's regiments across a wide front. "The Thirteenth Ohio," reported the colonel, was placed "on Missionary Ridge at the gap of the same name, the Forty-fourth Indiana at Shallowford Gap, one half-mile to the left of the Thirteenth . . . and the Fifty-Ninth Ohio at

15 *OR* 30, pt. 1, 254; ibid., pt. 3, 764.

16 Neither Van Cleve nor Dick specify who ordered Dick's men out of Chattanooga, but since Dick's brigade was manning the inner fortifications alongside Wagner, it is reasonable to assume it was acting under Rosecrans's authority.

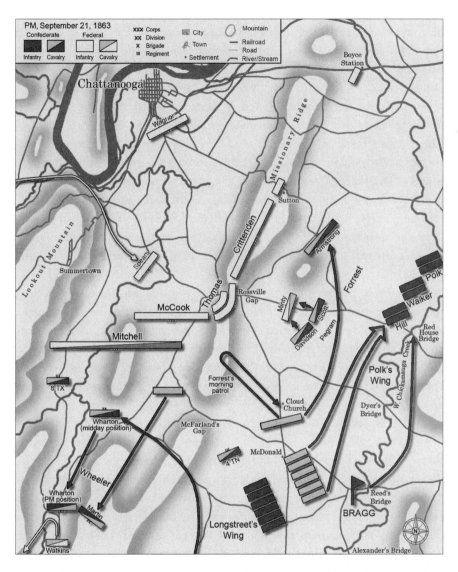

Chickamauga Bridge [near Boyce's Station] . . . 3 miles to the left of the Forty-fourth Indiana." The 86th Indiana deployed as skirmishers, sent down the ridge's east slope to help backstop Minty's picket line.[17]

Rosecrans also took steps to secure Lookout Mountain, which up to this point had been garrisoned only by a Union signal detachment. The only force

17 OR 30, pt. 1, 825. This site was later renamed Fort Wood.

he could spare for the important task, however, was Company L of the 15th Pennsylvania Cavalry. By noon the Keystoners were on the summit, thoroughly worn out after the arduous climb. After some rest, the troopers of the 15th Pennsylvania moved to Summertown, which, noted Pvt. John Williams, was "a noted resort of the chivalry." There Williams and his comrades found "an immense hotel," which was immediately appropriated as their living quarters. The men marveled at the furnishings. "Pianos, sofas, chairs, bedsteads and feather beds, statuettes, books, crockery-ware and cooking utensils—these we found in abundance," recalled one of the Pennsylvania troopers. They found every comfort but provisions, for as he noted, there was "not a scrap of anything eatable." The rest of the nearly deserted village was occupied by only "two women and some children." The Pennsylvanians established pickets along the road up to the crest, and at the south edge of Summertown across the plateau.[18]

Rosecrans, thinking like his old academy roommate James Longstreet, remained worried about a larger turning movement. After all, he had captured the important city of Chattanooga by eschewing direct assault in favor of a river crossing elsewhere. Why wouldn't Bragg try the same thing? Rosecrans needed an effective, independent, and reliable force to watch the river for just such an approach. Once again, he tapped Wilder's men, his Lightning Brigade, for the task.

Wilder's day began at 3:00 a.m., when he was awakened by a sergeant named Dawson bearing a message from George Thomas: Report in person at Rossville. Once there, Wilder and Thomas discussed the prior day's action, during which Wilder described in detail his assault against Brig. Gen. Arthur Manigault's brigade. Impressed, the Virginian informed the brash young colonel that the attack had bought Thomas two hours of valuable time to "rally the broken forces . . . on Snodgrass Hill." Thomas ordered Wilder to move his brigade back to Chattanooga. From there, one regiment would escort prisoners to Stevenson while the rest of the command crossed the Tennessee River and deployed upstream to guard against any Confederate trying to cross the waterway.[19]

18 John A. B. Williams, *Leaves from a Trooper's Diary* (Self published, 1869), 71.

19 Wilder Revised Report, CCNMP; *OR* 30, pt. 1, 143; Wilder, "Preliminary Movements of the Army," 271. In his revised report written in 1888, Wilder recalled being told, "I was reported

Once Wilder returned to his command, his brigade made a leisurely breakfast and moved off. The 98th Illinois drew the prisoner escort assignment. The Illini mounted infantry departed first and reached Chattanooga about noon, where Lt. Col. William Wiles of the provost marshal's office placed "1380 prisoners including 38 officers" into Lt. Col. Edward Kitchell's custody. "We moved out 6 miles and camped," reported Kitchell, who privately worried that his "effective force . . . to guard these prisoners is [only] 320 men."[20]

The rest of the Lightning Brigade broke camp about noon. "We arrived in town about 3:00 p.m. and found the streets blockaded with wagons," wrote Jerome Stubbins of the 123rd Illinois. "With some difficulty," Wilder's men crossed the Tennessee and moved upstream as far as Friar's Island—the same place they had crossed going in the opposite direction only eleven days before.[21]

This left only Mitchell's cavalry in place to screen Chattanooga Valley. Fortunately for Mitchell's frayed nerves, he and his Union troopers enjoyed an afternoon almost as quiet as their morning. The 1st Tennessee (Union) Cavalry, explained trooper Julius Thomas, "formed a line of battle on a hill . . . and throwed out skirmishers to the front and prepared to receive the rebs. . . . [We] waited two hours . . . and then fell back to our old camp . . . [again] formed line of battle and remained there all day."[22]

The tempo of the day's activities picked up slightly when Joe Wheeler arrived with Wharton's division and pushed both Wharton and Martin into Chattanooga Valley. This large-scale mounted effort rightfully alarmed Mitchell, who started receiving reports of Rebel contact shortly after 1:00 p.m. At 2:15 p.m., the Union commander sent word to Chief of Staff Garfield: "We have a hell of a front here," fretted Mitchell. "We will do the best we can. Their skirmishers are along my whole front. A soldier who left Crawfish Spring this morning and stole past them says two divisions of Longstreet's corps left there early this morning on this road."[23]

---

killed and my entire command captured at Widow Glenn's." This claim, however, conflicts with General Rosecrans's dispatch of the night before.

20 Entry for September 21, Edward Kitchell Diary, ALPL.

21 Entry for September 21, Jerome K. Stubbins Diary, Ohio Historical Society. Hereafter, OHS.

22 Entry for September 21, Julius Thomas Diary, TSLA.

23 OR 30, pt. 1, 154.

Brig. Gen. Robert B. Mitchell,
commanding the Union Cavalry Corps.
Library of Congress

Fortunately for Mitchell (if not for Colonel Watkins and his Kentuckians) Wheeler almost immediately turned his attention to the Union cavalry to the south. Watkins's small brigade was seeking a way out of McLemore's Cove that did not involve cutting through an entire Confederate cavalry corps. Wheeler sensed an opportunity and seized upon it with tremendous enthusiasm. The ensuing fight, begun at Lookout Church six or seven miles to the south, ended in Federal disaster at the foot of Cooper's Gap, but relieved pressure on Mitchell's line in Chattanooga Valley for the rest of the afternoon.[24]

Word of Longstreet's men pushing into that valley caught Rosecrans's attention. A strong force of enemy infantry in the Chattanooga valley would outflank Missionary Ridge and force Thomas to give up Rossville. Even worse, not only was the army commander concerned about a strong attack through the relatively open valley west of Missionary Ridge, but he also had to concern himself about the passes over Lookout Mountain. If Confederates crossed Lookout, they could do serious harm to the traffic in Lookout Valley bustling to and from Bridgeport. If Rosecrans hoped to withstand even a short-term siege, every wagonload of supplies that reached him might mean the difference between survival and surrender.

Rosecrans repeatedly inquired about Colonel Watkins, who he assumed was still in contact with Mitchell. "Is Watkins watching the gaps?" he asked. Rosecrans wanted Watkins's men deployed atop Lookout Mountain as far south as Cooper's Gap, and instructed Mitchell to "have him report often and fully all he sees." Watkins and his brigade, however, were missing. Mitchell had not heard from them in two days, despite numerous efforts to reestablish

24 For a full description of the fight between Watkins and Wheeler, see Appendix 1.

communication. Indeed, he feared them lost. And in fact, they came close to being annihilated in the running fight around Lookout Church and Cooper's Gap.[25]

Nor could Stevenson and Bridgeport be neglected. Stevenson was Rosecrans's main supply base, the entire town a veritable outdoor warehouse, its streets brimming with small mountains of supplies of every description. It and Bridgeport, five miles farther upstream, represented Rosecrans's current railhead, since the big bridge across the Tennessee River was still destroyed. From there, supplies had to be hauled across the Tennessee River by wagon, then via Running Water Creek Gap, Whiteside, Wauhatchie, and around the northern foot of Lookout Mountain before being delivered to Chattanooga. If Rebels slipped across the Tennessee quickly and struck at either town, the ensuing destruction could amount to a disaster equal to or greater than that which had already befallen the Army of the Cumberland in Brotherton Field.

Each town had a small garrison. On September 20, Bridgeport was defended by the 10th, 16th, and 60th Illinois infantry, augmented by the 10th Wisconsin battery. Stevenson held another five regiments and the headquarters of Brig. Gen. James S. Morgan, commanding the 2nd Division of the Union Reserve Corps. Having been alerted to the crisis the day before, the first thing on Monday morning Morgan dispatched two more regiments, the 34th Illinois and 10th Michigan, to Bridgeport. He also began calling additional Reserve Corps troops forward from back up the rail line toward Nashville.

For Pvt. Lyman S. Widney of the 34th Illinois, the day's orders were the first harbinger of the army's troubles. Widney was part of a detachment defending the pontoon bridge at Battle Creek a couple of miles from Bridgeport. On the 20th, while the battle was raging elsewhere, Widney and his comrades worked to finish their winter quarters, which they fully expected to occupy for the season. These quarters were substantial cabins complete with "fire places and chimneys." Then, remembered Widney, "during the night orders came that we must hold our bridge at all hazards so we were turned out at daybreak to build fortifications. This order is very disquieting."[26]

By the evening of September 21, Rosecrans concluded that the Army of the Cumberland's position at Rossville was too exposed to linger there any longer.

---

25 *OR* 30, pt. 1, 154.

26 Ibid., pt. 3, 752-753; Entries for September 20 and 21, 1863, Lyman S. Widney Diary, Kennesaw Mountain National Battlefield Park.

Granger and Garfield had both returned to Chattanooga during the day. Their descriptions of Thomas's deployments, coupled with Thomas's own opinion that his exposed flanks made Rossville untenable, decided the matter. Thomas would have to retreat once more, using the darkness as cover. By now, journalist William Shanks had also returned to Chattanooga. The observant Shanks left a characteristically colorful description of the moment: When Rosecrans sat down to draft the order, he began to compose a detailed missive delineating the order of march, measures needed to deceive the Rebels, and the like. "Oh, that's all nonsense, General," shot an impatient Granger. "Send Thomas an order to retire. He knows what he's about as well as you do." Whether or not Shanks's description was accurate, the sentiment surely was: George Thomas would get the army away safely.[27]

---

27 William F. G. Shanks, *Personal Recollections of Distinguished Generals* (Harper and Brothers, Publishers, 1866), 273.

Chapter Three

Into Chattanooga

Tuesday and Wednesday, September 22 and 23

George Thomas's careful, meticulous retreat from Rossville on September 22 was nothing like the barely controlled chaos two nights earlier. On the 20th, his men had been driven from a desperate position after an exhausting day's struggle, and in the case of the troops in Kelly Field, attacked midway through that movement. Now the men were rested, fed, and under no immediate pressure from pursuing Confederates.

The Union retreat from Rossville began the evening before. At 6:00 p.m. on September 21, noted Thomas, he received Rosecrans's order to fall back. The big Virginian immediately sent John Brannan's division half the distance back to the city to serve as a covering force and bulwark upon which to rally the rest of the army should such a thing be needed. The next to depart were the trains still massed in and around Rossville, mostly ammunition and ambulance wagons for the various divisions and corps. The remaining combat troops would slip away after full dark.[1]

To screen this movement, each division threw out a "strong skirmish line, under the direction of judicious officers," which remained in place until

---

1   OR 30, pt. 1, 255.

daylight. Behind that screen, each command had orders to evacuate its position in a carefully timed sequence of moves. Crittenden's XXI Corps, atop the ridge north of the gap, would pull out at 9:00 p.m. Steedman's men followed Crittenden. At 10:00 p.m., Negley's division would fall back, followed in turn by Reynolds's troops. After Reynolds, McCook's XX Corps would peel away one division at a time, following the general course of the movement from left to right. Each division, reported Thomas, would move "within supporting distance one after another" so no command could be caught on the march. Thomas turned once again to Rousseau, who had resumed command of his division from Absalom Baird, to oversee the rearguard. Colonel Minty's cavalry was tasked to support him.

Minty's troopers would be the last to leave, filtering south from their position on the eastern face of Missionary Ridge to hold the gap until dawn or thereafter—whatever was necessary to ensure the safe retreat of the last of the infantry skirmishers. The Federal horsemen could expect some difficulty, for the Rebels were all but certain to pursue once they discovered what was afoot.[2]

The entire operation was carried out smoothly, proving Granger's assertion of Thomas's competence. "The troops were withdrawn in a quiet, orderly manner, without the loss of a single man," reported Thomas with quiet pride, "and by 7 a.m. on the 22nd were in their positions in front of Chattanooga." The view from among the ranks was equally upbeat. "We were routed out about 3 o'clock and got out on the road towards Chattanooga. We stopped about 6 o'clock and got our breakfast and were then allowed to lay around," journaled Cpl. George Cooley of the 24th Wisconsin. The troops spent the rest of that Tuesday alternating between relaxation and bouts of working on the defenses beginning to ring the city.[3]

"This morning old Rosey came around, formed a line, and we began to fortify," wrote Pvt. Thomas Cantwell of Company D, the 26th Ohio. The new line ran about a mile and a half, forming an arc around Chattanooga to the south and west, anchored at each end on the banks of the Tennessee River. Crittenden's XXI Corps held the left, Thomas and his XIV Corps the center, and McCook's XX Corps the right. Eventually, the works would include both an inner and an outer line, each studded with forts, redoubts, and a series of additional fortified artillery positions on dominant terrain both around town

---

2   Ibid.

3   Ibid.; Entry for September 22, George Cooley Diary, WHS.

This was the view enjoyed by Private John Williams and his comrades
in the 15th Pennsylvania Cavalry, atop Lookout Mountain.
Library of Congress

and just across the river on Moccasin Bend. Rosecrans's defenses incorporated
the former Confederate works staked out by Rebel engineer Joseph Wampler
that July, but in a much-expanded and interconnected form. Some work had
begun on September 21, the labor provided by Wagner's troops and the army
pioneer battalions, but once the main army settled into position, dirt really
began to fly. Guided by Rosecrans, St. Clair Morton (active despite his arm
wound) and the army's other engineering officers, the troops began to dig in
earnest. Once finished, there would soon be no more strongly fortified place on
the continent.[4]

One Union observer had a birds-eye view of this industriousness. On
September 22, Pvt. John Williams of the 15th Pennsylvania Cavalry found
himself perched atop the crest of Lookout Mountain. The morning was crisp

---

4 Thomas Cantwell, "Day by Day with the Army of the Cumberland," *The Ohio Soldier*, vol.
XIII, no. 16, 241; George G. Kundahl, *Confederate Engineer: Training and Campaigning with John
Morris Wampler* (University of Tennessee Press, 2000), 221.

and clear, and Williams enjoyed a spectacular view. "Directly beneath our feet, it seemed, lay Chattanooga—an infinitesimal 'city'—encircled by yellow lines of earthworks, which extended unbrokenly from the mountains to the river," marveled Williams in a postwar memoir. "An inner circle of dark blue was still more apparent, from which the bayonets and the colors gleamed in the sunlight—as though visibly tipped with the glory of as gallant a fight as any in history."[5]

Rousseau's division brought up the rear of Thomas's retreat, retiring with caution. Despite the severe bruising to his leg the day before, Lieutenant Otto of the 21st Wisconsin was still with his regiment. "We were cautioned not to make any noise," he recalled, "were not even allowed to speak above a whisper. The battery wheels were muffled with blankets and carefully brought down. . . . We were the last ones to leave and consequently did not start until daylight. It was about four miles from the gap to the works at Chattanooga." This march presented Otto with a challenge, for his injured leg precluded him from keeping up, even after he fashioned a pair of crutches from sticks. Fortunately, "a pitying canonier helped me onto the limbers of a gun," he recalled, "[and] I rode proudly in the coveted fortifications of Chattanooga."[6]

Once Rousseau's men were clear, Minty's troopers settled into the gap. Their orders were to delay any Confederate advance as long as possible. Similarly, Colonel Dick's four small regiments and the 39th Indiana Mounted Infantry defended other gaps farther north in Missionary Ridge, while General Spears's Unionist Tennesseans still guarded the approaches to Lookout Mountain.

Missionary Ridge was an imposing natural wall, but it was not by any means impassible. Several roads traversed the ridge, which was also pierced by a railroad tunnel, and, as earlier noted, its northern end terminated short of the Tennessee River, leaving a broad flood plain of several hundred yards' width. While the Western & Atlantic tracks bypassed the ridge via the floodplain, the Chattanooga and Cleveland line leading to East Tennessee cut through the ridge, via the aforementioned tunnel. The two most important wagon roads surmounted the ridge about halfway between Boyce's Station and Rossville. Moore's Road branched off from the Rossville Road about three quarters of a

---

5   John A. B. Williams, *Memoir of John A. B. Williams, or Leaves from a Trooper's Diary* (Privately published, 1869), 72-73.

6   Otto memoir, 269, WHS.

mile south of Chattanooga before running almost due east for roughly two miles until it reached the western foot of Missionary Ridge at the Moore farmstead. From there, the road snaked its way up the side of the ridge, cresting at the Sutton farm, and then on to Chickamauga Station. A half-mile farther north, Shallow Ford Road traversed another gap in the ridge of the same name, joining Moore's Road some distance west of the Moore farm. Rosecrans lacked the troops to hold the entire ridge, but he knew he had to do what he could to delay the Confederates at these choke points.

Lieutenant Colonel Simeon Aldrich of the 44th Indiana commanded his regiment and the 13th Ohio of Dick's brigade at Moore's Road. Colonel Dick's entire command spent the morning of the 21st holding part of the Chattanooga defenses until midday, when Aldrich was ordered to "proceed to two gaps on Missionary Ridge." The Ohioans held the main road, while Aldrich's 44th Indiana moved a short distance north to Shallow Ford Gap "a half mile to the left." By nightfall, both regiments were in place behind hastily erected breastworks. Aldrich's combined force was small, barely 300 survivors in the two regiments, but the terrain was highly favorable for defense.[7]

Another of Dick's regiments, the 59th Ohio, was sent to defend Boyce's Station. Led by Lt. Col. Granville Frambes, the 59th mustered a little more than 200 bayonets. The Buckeyes were also in place by dark. Dick and his remaining regiment, the 86th Indiana, joined a reserve line about halfway between the ridge and the town. The reserve was commanded by Col. Peter Swaine of the 99th Ohio, of Col. Sidney Barnes's brigade, which in addition to Dick and the 86th was comprised, as Swaine described it, of his own command plus other "detachments from the First and Third Brigades." Supporting the entire force with firepower and roving patrols was Col. Thomas Harrison's 39th Indiana, which still had more than 500 men in the saddle. Harrison posted the bulk of his mounted infantry regiment near Aldrich's demi-brigade, but scattered additional pickets across the eastern slopes of Missionary Ridge to observe the numerous crossings over Chickamauga Creek.[8]

A smattering of Union cavalry also maintained watch in Chattanooga Valley between Missionary Ridge and Lookout Mountain, but no infantry remained there. The road from Chattanooga to Bridgeport along the south

7   OR 30, pt. 1, 825, 828.

8   Ibid., 849; Entry for September 22, 1863, Aurelius Willoughby Diary, InHS. Willoughby notes one such picket post was with the 59th Ohio.

bank of the Tennessee, however, squeezed between the river and the brow of that frowning summit. To protect that passage, Rosecrans posted General Spears's East Tennesseans. "In the event I was attacked by the enemy," Spears explained, "[my orders were] to contest the ground inch by inch and foot by foot, and to fall back across the mountain, and cross the river at Brown's Ferry, where a steamboat would be in waiting." Spears's force amounted to only "two pieces of regiments"—too few to effectively defend the passage against anything more than a token threat.[9]

By Tuesday morning the bulk of Mitchell's cavalry was gone, for Rosecrans had other missions for them. As with Colonel Wilder, Rosecrans wanted Mitchell's men on the north bank of the Tennessee River but not just to guard potential crossing sites. "You will please have the country . . . scoured for forage," Rosecrans ordered. "I want eight or ten days' [worth] collected, if possible." Fodder for the livestock would be depleted even more rapidly than rations for the men once everyone was penned up in the city, and Rosecrans needed his animals for both hauling supply wagons and for tactical mobility, especially for his artillery.[10]

*   *   *

Braxton Bragg awoke on the morning of September 22 with the intention of advancing directly toward Chattanooga, applying sufficient pressure to discover if the Yankees were going to abandon the city, as Forrest believed. Forrest's troopers would lead this advance, moving on a broad front to seize Missionary Ridge. Major General Benjamin F. Cheatham's infantry division was ordered to follow the cavalry and cross the ridge via Moore's Road. Simultaneously, General McLaws's column was to continue its march on the city but not via the heavily defended Rossville Gap. Instead, McLaws was ordered to turn west and move through McFarland's Gap into Chattanooga Valley, outflanking Rossville just as the Federals all feared. Bragg expected Joe Wheeler to contribute to this general movement by "push[ing] . . . closely and vigorously on our left," which should have put Wheeler's cavalry within

9   *OR* 30, pt. 1, 885; ibid., pt. 3, 783.

10 Ibid.

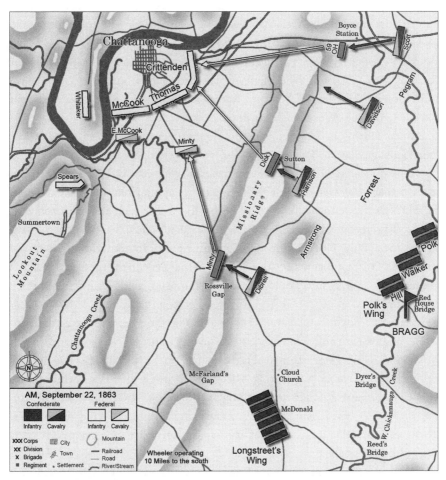

The final Union position was much more compact, with both flanks
anchored on the Tennessee River.

supporting distance of McLaws. Once more, Wheeler would be late to the
party.[11]

In fact, Wheeler had neglected his portion of the front almost entirely. That
morning, Union Capt. William E. Crane of the 4th Ohio Cavalry recorded his
surprise at the lack of Rebels to his front. "Last night . . . the enemy was known
to have a large force composed of infantry and cavalry at Crawfish Springs,"
wrote the Union officer. "We all expected them to advance upon us." At 3:00

11 Ibid., pt. 4, 694.

a.m., the 1st and 3rd Ohio regiments were sent forward on a patrol, riding a mile and a half south to look for those Confederates, noted Crane, all to no avail. The Buckeye captain got his own chance to see what was up when he was sent forward with a dispatch. By daylight he was also at the front, "but could see no indication of the enemy." With no Rebels in sight, the Union cavalry should have no trouble withdrawing as ordered.[12]

Bragg's army had difficulties completing even the simple movement to Chickamauga Station. The previous day, wagons snarled the few roads, slowing movement to a crawl. As a result, by nightfall, only part of Polk's wing of the army managed to take up Bragg's intended line along Chickamauga Creek. D. H. Hill's corps fell in behind, delayed by the traffic, and only reached Red House Bridge after midnight. James Longstreet's men (excepting McLaws) found their paths blocked and did not move at all. In addition to the traffic problems, Hill complained of "thousands of stragglers on the roadside." Clearly the army was not, as Hill would later disingenuously claim, "little disturbed" by the battle.[13]

At least Forrest was ready to move as ordered on September 22. By 8:00 a.m., his line was fully deployed, each division abreast, west of and facing Missionary Ridge. Armstrong's brigades held the left, with Dibrell directly opposite Rossville Gap (squaring off against Minty's bluecoats) while James Wheeler's brigade scaled the ridge along Moore's Road toward the Sutton farm. Pegram's two brigades fell in on Armstrong's right, moving against the northern end of the ridge, with Davidson to the left and Scott's troopers headed toward Boyce's Station.[14]

Minty's Federals gave ground slowly in the face of Dibrell's advance. Once again, Minty fell back in stages, regiment by regiment. The 4th U.S. made contact first. Much to Sgt. James Larson's disgust, he and his fellows were spread out and mounted in timber while Dibrell's troops approached them on foot. This, thought Larson, was bad tactics on the 4th's part. "They could take shelter behind trees so that we could seldom see any of them plainly. We had no shelter and sat high up among the leaves and limbs." Fortunately for Larson and his comrades, Minty had no intention of trying to slug it out with Dibrell amid

---

12 Entry for September 22, William E. Crane Journal, OHS.

13 *OR* 30, pt. 4, 693; ibid., pt. 2, 145.

14 David A. Powell, *The Maps of Chickamauga: An Atlas of the Chickamauga Campaign, Including the Tullahoma Operations, June 22 - September 23, 1863* (Savas Beatie, 2010), 255.

the trees. Pursuant to his orders, the Federal commander was only interested in delaying the Rebels as much as possible, buying time for Thomas to complete his retreat unmolested back toward Chattanooga. In this, Minty was successful. It would take several hours for Dibrell's Rebels to drive the Yankees back into the lines of Chattanooga, which Minty reached about 1:00 p.m. that afternoon. It was not only Minty's tactical acumen that held up Dibrell. The rest of Forrest's men faced tough resistance farther north, which combined to slow progress across Forrest's entire front.[15]

A sharp fight developed at the Sutton house, where Colonel Aldrich's detachment waited. The fight began as a picket skirmish, and soon took on a more personal aspect. Private Nicholas Ensley of the 44th Indiana began a duel with a Rebel, with each firing "four or five rounds" until Ensley hit his mark and wounded the man. When he moved forward and captured "his knapsack," the delighted Hoosier found it "full of fresh meat." Colonel Aldrich reported that the skirmishing began late that morning "about 10 a.m.," and involved both his skirmishers and those of the 39th Indiana.[16]

This initial Confederate probe revealed the presence of enough Yankees for Colonel Wheeler to call for infantry support. Frank Cheatham placed his arrival time at the foot of the ridge as 10:00 a.m., and soon determined "the enemy occupied the crest of the ridge in force." To counter this resistance, Cheatham shook out two brigades: Preston Smith's on the left (now under command of Col. Alfred J. Vaughan) and Brig. Gen. George Maney's on the right. Nearly 2,000 Rebel infantry were in line and ordered to assault the ridge.[17]

Maney's Tennesseans approached Aldrich's position directly. "I reserved my fire till they came in very short range," reported Aldrich, "my men being completely hid." This first engagement favored the Federals. "The enemy were taken completely by surprise and retreated in great disorder," Aldrich exulted. Facing this sudden fire, Pvt. Sam Watkins of the 1st Tennessee recalled that his regiment lost "about twenty men killed and wounded." Undeterred, the Confederates reformed and tried again, this time exercising more caution. Their steady approach, coupled with their numerical advantage, eventually outflanked the Union line. Still, both sides claimed a fair measure of success. Aldrich

15 James Larson, *Sergeant Larson, 4th Cavalry* (Southern Literary Institute, 1935), 195.

16 John H. Rerick, *The Forty-Fourth Indiana Volunteer Infantry: History of its Services in the War of the Rebellion and a Personal Record of its Members* (Lagrange, Indiana, 1880), 99.

17 *OR* 30, pt. 2, 80.

thought he repulsed three separate charges before "our mounted infantry giving way and the enemy appearing on our flanks, we were obliged to fall back." Maney admitted to "a spirited engagement of a few moments [until] the enemy was driven and the ridge top in our possession." Official Rebel losses were "18 in killed and wounded."[18]

Maney reported the crest and the road secure just before 2:00 p.m. Once atop the ridge, the Confederate brigadier was treated to a splendid view. "Chattanooga and river plainly in sight," he wrote. "Beef cattle being driven at ford above island; wagons crossing pontoon, going from Chattanooga." Less encouragingly, he noted that "no troops were crossing." Maney still faced a "light force of cavalry" in the valley below. His dispatch worked its way up the chain of command, and in a short while Bragg sent word back to "push the enemy vigorously," adding the encouraging news that General McLaws was moving into Chattanooga Valley via McFarland's Gap.[19]

While Cheatham's men were scrambling up Missionary Ridge, Pegram's Rebel troopers were working their way around the north end of that same feature to tackle the 59th Ohio at Boyce's Station. The Ohioans also erected a line of works astride the road, with three companies advanced as skirmishers. The 2nd Tennessee Cavalry of John Scott's brigade launched a mounted charge, surprising these Federals, captured several pickets, and sent the rest scrambling rearward. At the 59th's hastily constructed lunette, the Ohioans made a protracted fight of it. The commander of the 59th, Lieutenant Colonel Frambes, ordered the railroad bridge set ablaze while the regiment fought off repeated attacks. Scott's men advanced on foot, fighting with such determination that Frambes believed he was facing Rebel infantry. About noon, Frambes pleaded for reinforcements and warned that he would not be able to hold much longer without them. His plea passed unanswered. Unable to maintain his position, Frambes and his Buckeyes began a harrowing retreat toward the main Union line. Using the railroad embankment as an earthwork, and by leapfrogging detachments of his regiment in a splendid example of fire and maneuver, Frambes avoided repeated efforts by the Rebel cavalry to encircle his embattled command. Scott's men charged the Buckeyes several

---

18 OR 30, pt. 1, 828; Sam R. Watkins, with Ruth Hill Fulton McCallister, ed., *Co. Aytch: Maury Grays, First Tennessee Regiment, or A Side Show of the Big Show* (Providence House Publishers, 2007), 121; OR 30, pt. 2, 97.

19 Ibid., pt. 4, 691-692.

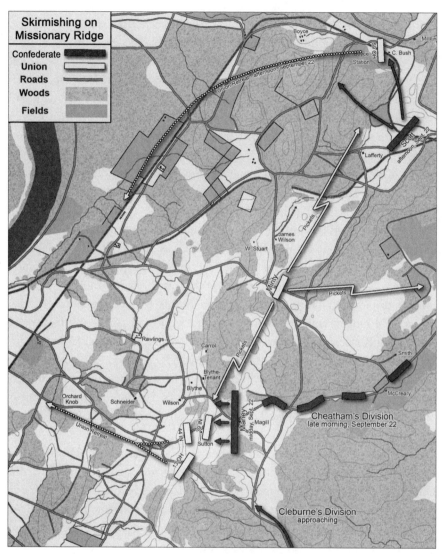

Small fights developed on Missionary Ridge and at Boyce's Station,
as Union rear guards confronted the advancing Confederates.

times while a Rebel battery shelled them, often at close range. Well versed in
skirmish drill, the Ohioans escaped with minimal loss considering the
circumstances.[20]

20 Ibid., pt. 1, 834-835.

The 59th's adroit escape frustrated their pursuers. According to Pegram, Scott would have captured the entire regiment if his men had not been fired upon at a critical moment by fellow Confederate cavalry. Pegram, however, failed to note whether this fratricidal fire came from some of Davidson's men or from another of Scott's own regiments. Frambes and his 59th regiment had been lucky and escaped only by the narrowest of margins, thought Lt. Edwin Perkins, the 59th's quartermaster. Perkins filled in the home folks on these doings: "The Regt was guarding a bridge some five miles from town and got cut off. . . . They came very near all being captured." When all was said and done, Frambes, reported a loss of 20 men and two officers, one killed and the rest made prisoners, which included all of the wounded.[21]

By early that afternoon, Forrest's men had control of the ridge and were moving into the plain beyond. Dibrell's brigade was through Rossville Gap, and his cavalry occupied most of the ground between the ridge and the burgeoning Union entrenchments ringing Chattanooga. In his shrewdest move of the day, Forrest dispatched Dibrell and a portion of his brigade westward toward Lookout Mountain with the intention of finally blocking the south bank road and sealing Rosecrans off from Bridgeport. Leaving Col. Daniel Holman with the 10th and Holman's own 11th Tennessee cavalry regiments on the Rossville Road to keep an eye on the main Union force in Chattanooga, Dibrell rode west with his remaining three regiments and Shaw's Battalion. The movement brought Dibrell's secessionist Tennesseans into direct conflict with Spears's Unionist Volunteer State men.[22]

In peacetime, James Gallant Spears and George Gibbs Dibrell were neighbors. Spears lived in Pikeville, Tennessee, fewer than 40 miles from Dibrell's farm in Sparta. Both men were noted lawyers before the war, active in regional and state politics. In 1861, both were also resistant to the idea of secession. Each man was elected as a Union delegate to Tennessee's secession convention. And there, the two parted ways. When the convention voted to take Tennessee out of the Union, Dibrell decided to follow his state while Spears remained loyal to the national government. In August 1861, Spears fled to Kentucky, where he organized like-minded men into the 1st Tennessee Infantry (Union) Regiment. He tasted combat at the small early-war battles of

21 *OR* 30, pt. 2, 529; "Dear Father and all at home," September 27, 1863, Edwin Perkins Papers, Western Reserve Historical Society, Cleveland, OH. Hereafter WRHS.

22 Jordan and Pryor, *Forrest's Cavalry*, 353.

Wild Cat Mountain and Mill Springs, helped the Federals capture Cumberland Gap in June 1862, and saw limited action in the final moments of Stones River. His middle name was an apt descriptor for his disposition in battle, but Spears was also quarrelsome and extremely opinionated. The Emancipation Proclamation, which he believed was illegal and designed to rob him of his property, had left him disillusioned with the war effort.[23]

The outspoken commander was also extremely unpopular with his men. Spears was assigned to commanded the 3rd Brigade, 3rd Division of Granger's Reserve Corps, assuming command at Alexandria Tennessee on August 31, 1863. The brigade, comprised of the 3rd, 5th, and 6th Tennessee Infantry, as well as the 1st Middle Tennessee Cavalry, was well acquainted with their new boss, and not happy with his arrival. Spears's new command was stationed at McMinnville, guarding supplies and patrolling the surrounding region. Their response to Spears's arrival was immediate. On September 3rd, 27 of the brigade's officers sent an unusual petition to General Rosecrans: "We . . . would most respectfully beg that you would relieve of Brigadier General Spears, who, we are informed, is to command us." Spears's "tyranny and ungentlemanly conduct," they charged, "will deplete the brigade by demoralization" within six weeks. They would prefer almost anyone else. Rosecrans ignored the petition.[24]

At first light on September 22, Spears, his three disgruntled infantry regiments, and the 1st Tennessee Artillery battery were all stationed at the eastern foot of Lookout Mountain. That morning Spears sent the Federal 3rd Tennessee atop the mountain to Summertown to reinforce the detachment of the 15th Pennsylvania Cavalry that had been sent up the previous day. Both units deployed to guard against any Rebel approach from the south. Spears next posted his 6th Tennessee and five companies of the 5th Tennessee to defend the road where it rose over the northern shoulder of the mountain and squeezed past the banks of the Tennessee River.

"At about noon," reported Spears, "the enemy, with one regiment of skirmishers . . . supported by three regiments of infantry or mounted infantry, and with artillery and cavalry, attacked my line." That enemy consisted of Dibrell's command, whose contact with Col. Joseph A. Cooper and his 6th

23 Ezra J. Warner, *Generals in Blue: Lives of the Union Commanders* (Louisiana State University Press, 1991), 466. In 1864, Spears would be dismissed from the army for his outspokenness on the subject.

24 *OR* 30, pt. 3, 330.

Tennessee sparked a fight that lasted about an hour and a half. "My forces fought well," insisted Spears, "and never yielded the ground until they were overpowered and compelled to fall back, which was done in good order." Spears retreated up the slope of Lookout to "the first bench," a plateau about one-third of the way up the mountain. Dibrell, having achieved his primary mission in blocking the road to Bridgeport, did not follow. His scattered units had to watch Spears's men as well as be on the alert for Federals who might come out of the works at Chattanooga to strike him in the rear. Also, Colonel Holman's two regiments were still back on the Rossville Road a mile or so to the east.[25]

Sometime after 1:00 p.m., with Dibrell still engaged at the foot of Lookout and Frank Cheatham's infantry clearing the slopes of Missionary Ridge, Colonel Holman tested the main Union defenses. Dibrell had left Holman with orders to proceed up the Rossville Road "as far as possible in the direction of Chattanooga." He pressed to within a half-mile of the place until he came upon Union entrenchments manned by elements of Thomas's XIV Corps. Holman dismounted both regiments and probed the forts. His first effort was rebuffed with loss. To support this thrust, Captain Morton unlimbered his four guns and opened fire. Holman's line pressed forward once more, but it soon came tumbling back. These Federals were more than just a mere rearguard.[26]

Holman was contemplating his next step when "Forrest came dashing up at full speed, followed by his escort, and asked impatiently (emphasizing the questions with an oath) 'What have you stopped here for? Why don't you go on into Chattanooga?'" The corps commander was in his usual lather, and still convinced Rosecrans was in full retreat. Momentarily stupefied by the sudden appearance of his superior and the series of rapid-fire queries, Holman hastily explained that "the enemy in considerable force was strongly entrenched not more than two hundred yards in front." Forrest scoffed, adding that "he believed he could take Chattanooga with [just] his escort." True to his nature, Forrest accepted nothing as fact until he had seen it demonstrated with his own eyes and so proceeded to test the theory personally. "Putting spurs to horse, he and a portion of his escort galloped in the direction of the enemy," leaving Holman to watch in dust-covered astonishment. Within minutes they were

---

25 Ibid., pt. 1, 885-886.

26 Lindsley, *Military Annals of Tennessee*, vol. II, 694.

back, having suffered a "hot fire" that cost Forrest yet another mount—this one also shot in the neck—and left several empty saddles among the escort.[27]

The significant skirmishes fought by Dibrell and Holman had collectively cost the brigade roughly 50 casualties.[28] The degree of resistance, personally confirmed by General Forrest and his escort on the Rossville Road, was a strong indication that Rosecrans was not conducting any panic-stricken retreat.

A short time later, General McLaws appeared up the Rossville Road, at the head of his division. McLaws's march had not passed without incident. After broaching McFarland's Gap, he reported, his column "became constantly engaged . . . sometimes with quite large organized bodies, but they gave way after some fighting."[29] The "organized bodies" consisted of Federals from Minty's rearguard, which skirmished with Brig. Gen. William T. Wofford's Georgians at the head of McLaws's column. Conspicuously, McLaws made no mention of seeing any Rebel cavalry until he encountered Forrest and his men somewhere on the Rossville Road. Wheeler's Corps, which should have been equally active in the Chattanooga Valley supporting his movement, had yet to put in any notable appearance. At the Watkins farmstead, where the Moore Road branched off from the La Fayette Road to turn toward Missionary Ridge, Forrest and McLaws conferred.

Descriptions of this meeting contradict one another. Forrest's biographers insist that Forrest was still full of fight, remaining convinced that every hour lost was a disaster for Confederate arms and that Rosecrans must be attacked before he escaped the trap of Chattanooga. Accordingly, "Forrest . . . proposed that they should venture an attack in the still demoralized condition of the enemy." According to these biographers, McLaws refused. His orders, he insisted, were to merely picket the roads into Chattanooga.[30]

McLaws recalled the encounter very differently. According to the Georgian, once Wofford "drove the enemy into the works about town, of course my further advance was checked, as my force was entirely too small to risk an assault." Instead, McLaws deployed his main line astride the intersection at the Watkins House, seized Watkins Hill as an artillery platform, and ordered

27 Ibid.

28 Jordan and Pryor, *Forrest's Cavalry*, 353.

29 Lafayette McLaws, "Chickamauga," Cheeves Family Papers.

30 Jordan and Pryor, *Forrest's Cavalry*, 353.

Union Brigadier General James G. Spears, charged with defending the approaches to Lookout Mountain.
Miller, Photographic History of the Civil War: Armies and Leaders

his men to throw up defensive works of their own. While in the process of doing so, continued McLaws, Forrest rode up. Not long before with Holman, the big cavalryman was all afire to pursue, heedless of caution, until he led his escort forward toward the enemy lines. Now—at least according to McLaws—Forrest was just the opposite. "Gen. Forrest joined me with a small body of cavalry," recalled McLaws, "and told me that I was risking the loss of my command, as the rest of the army was not within seven miles of me." (This was not entirely accurate, for Frank Cheatham's division was even then occupying Missionary Ridge at the Sutton house, but Cheatham's troops were at least two miles distant, and the bulk of the army was indeed much farther away.) As McLaws related the tale, Forrest now counseled immediate retreat. "I told him it was not my intention to retire unless driven back," insisted McLaws. Forrest next offered to scout McLaws's right flank, where there was a gap between his infantry and Cheatham's men. "He was gone perhaps half an hour, when he re-appeared riding a broken-down horse and with but two or three men. . . . [H]e had not gone over half a mile," recalled McLaws, "when he came upon a considerable body of infantry . . . who ordered them to surrender. The only reply he gave was for his men to charge, he leading it."[31]

The Confederate pursuit had been thoroughly blunted. It was clear to McLaws, if perhaps not to Forrest, that only a well-prepared large-scale assault could capture Chattanooga. Accordingly, McLaws determined to hold his ground and wait for reinforcements. Cheatham left his troops and made his way forward to visit McLaws about 10:00 p.m. that night. Cheatham "told me that

---

31 Lafayette McLaws, "Chickamauga," Cheeves Family Papers. McLaws may well have been relating a version of the same incident described by Holman.

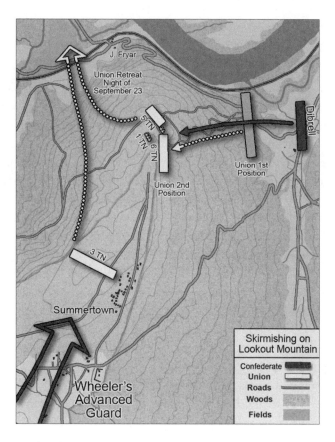

he had been ordered to report to me with his division," recalled McLaws, "but on crossing Missionary Ridge, had encountered such a large force of the enemy . . . that he deemed it wise to return to the ridge." McLaws ordered Cheatham to stay where he was and "to hold his command in readiness to come to my assistance" should the Yankees attack. No support was needed. The Federals were content to rest and strengthen their earthworks.[32]

Those Yankees high up on Lookout, meanwhile, observed all of this activity with intense interest. Trooper Williams and his Pennsylvania comrades had watched as Dibrell's Rebels swarmed around the eastern foot of the mountain and tested the Union lines. Then, "long, gray columns of infantry and strings of artillery appeared on the roads, barely distinguishable from the clouds of dust which they created. One gun was seen to move into an open field,

32 Ibid.

between the two main columns of the enemy." Williams wondered if the shelling and skirmishing foreshadowed "a still grander scene, an assault upon our works," but that turned out not to be the case.[33]

Aside from McLaws's and Cheatham's two divisions, no other Confederate infantry closed on Chattanooga that day. Instead, Bragg focused on administrative issues. An army-wide circular dictated a series of mundane but critical tasks that needed doing: ammunition wagons were ordered to Red House Ford for restocking, three days' rations, which had to be cooked before another forward movement was implemented, were to be issued; and losses and captures were to be tabulated. Bragg placed special emphasis on reporting captured standards, which would be sent via a personal messenger to Richmond. Each captured Federal flag was to "be labeled and properly prepared, giving as far as possible the names of the captors, with regiment and corps." Bragg also ordered the belated return of some of the troops loaned to him by Joe Johnston. John Gregg's and Matt Ector's brigades, the former still commanded by Col. Cyrus Sugg, marched to Catoosa, there to entrain for Atlanta and points west. Other brigades, reshuffled into new commands as a result of all the movement during the past two weeks, were returned to their proper places in the army's organization.[34]

Once rations were issued and cooked, the remainder of General Polk's wing prepared to follow Ben Cheatham's infantry division across Missionary Ridge the following morning. D. H. Hill's corps together with Thomas Hindman's division would move via Mission Mills, while W. H. T. Walker's Reserve Corps received ordered to advance along the Shallow Ford Road.[35] Longstreet's wing, which had barely moved on the 21st, would follow in Polk's wake. After concentrating around Red House Bridge, it would move toward Chattanooga via Rossville and McFarland's Gap, following and reinforcing McLaws's division.

In all likelihood, Bragg did not push an aggressive pursuit because he believed there was no need to do so. He had expected to renew the fight on the morning of the 21st. When that did not happen, Bragg now thought it likely Rosecrans would continue his retreat rather than risk another battle in an effort

33 Williams, *Leaves From a Trooper's Diary*, 74.

34 Entry for September 22, Brent Journal, Bragg Papers; *OR* 30, pt. 4, 689.

35 *OR* 30, pt. 4, 692.

Nathan Bedford Forrest and his escort company charging a Union position.
Tennessee State Historical Library and Archives

to hold Chattanooga. Forrest's initial reports might have been greeted with some skepticism at army headquarters, but the cavalryman continued to forward intelligence that suggested the Federals were poised to abandon the city. As late as 4:00 p.m. on the 22nd, a courier brought word to Brig. Gen. Marcus Wright, one of General Cheatham's commanders, that "the enemy [was] evacuating Chattanooga." Wright quickly passed the dispatch on up through the chain of command. It was a curious missive, coming so late in the day and well after Forrest and McLaws had their encounter on the La Fayette Road.

The news was apparently accepted as factual in General Bragg's command tent. General McLaws's observations seemed to match Wright's dispatch: From the Watkins house, McLaws informed Bragg that he could see Federals "crossing the river on their pontoons." A series of communiqués issued from Bragg's headquarters on the 22nd reflect this belief. Sometime that morning Brig. Gen. William Mackall, Bragg's chief of staff (a constant, if quiet, critic of his boss) dispatched a wire to his old friend Joseph E. Johnston in Mississippi, reporting "that the enemy was burning Chattanooga and crossing the Tennessee."[36]

Bragg's orders to Joe Wheeler reveal the fullest extent of the army commander's thinking on September 22. In the first such dispatch, Bragg informed Wheeler that "we are closely pressing the enemy on our right," and ordered the cavalryman to "push him closely and vigorously on our left." At 6:30 p.m., a second dispatch instructed Wheeler to "press the enemy hotly and vigorously as long as he remains this side of the river." A third message revealed Bragg's intentions most completely:

Headquarters, Army Of Tennessee
Red House, September 22, 1863

General Wheeler,
Commanding Cavalry Corps:

General: The general commanding directs that you will at once cross the Tennessee River and press the enemy, intercept and break up all his lines of communication and retreat.

I am, general, very respectfully, your obedient servant,

George WM. Brent
Assistant Adjutant-General

Major General McLaws has reported that the enemy are crossing the river on their pontoons. General Forrest has also been ordered to cross the Tennessee. General McLaws is now within two miles of Chattanooga.

G. W. B.

Forrest will cross on the right. You had better get into the mountains and cross on the left, if practicable. Press the enemy hotly.

Yours, &c.,

---

36 Ibid., 695-696. McLaws's original message is not found in the *Official Records*, but Bragg quotes it, see below.

George WM. Brent
Assistant Adjutant-General"[37]

By sending all his cavalry across the Tennessee River, Bragg hoped it would fall upon and savage the supposedly demoralized and retreating Union army as it made its way toward Bridgeport. If the Rebel troopers were to accomplish any of this before the Yankees got safely away, however, speed was of the essence.

Wheeler's corps, however, was once again tardy reaching the battlefield and Wharton's men especially so, having spent another night in their old campgrounds east of Glass Mill. "Reaching camp at 11 o'clock [on the 21st] all were tired," noted Robert Bunting of the 8th Texas Cavalry, freely admitting that "on Tuesday morning [we] did not move very early." Wheeler summarized his own description of the day's activity in one brief sentence: "[We] pressed on to within 1 1/4 miles of Chattanooga, driving the enemy's cavalry behind his infantry." Here, Wheeler concluded, "we remained in this position until night."[38]

Little of the private correspondence from men in Wheeler's corps adds much to the picture of their actions on Tuesday, September 22nd. Typical was that of Pvt. Julius Dowda of the 3rd Georgia Cavalry, part of Col. Charles Crews's brigade, who only recorded that the "regiment was ordered near Chattanooga" that afternoon "to support a battery," a task that resulted in at least one notable casualty. "Captain [Frank E.] Field of Co. G was killed by a canister shot."[39]

Wheeler was still short elements of his corps, notably Lt. Col. Paul Anderson's 4th Tennessee Cavalry, which was still helping to clear the debris of combat. The 4th Tennessee's Pvt. William Corbitt spent his day "with Captain Engles paroling prisoner[s] on the battle field. Returned to this command at sun down this evening, 2 miles from Chattanooga."[40]

That evening, when Wheeler received Bragg's orders to cross the river, he finally moved with some alacrity. During the night, he moved his command eight miles south toward Trenton, anticipating a crossing of the Tennessee

---

37 Ibid.

38 R. F. Bunting, *Rome Tri-weekly Telegraph*, November 27, 1863; OR 30, pt. 2, 522.

39 Typescript of Julius Lafayette Dowda Diary, Georgia Department of Archives and History, Morrow, GA. Hereafter GDAH.

40 Entry for September 22, W. E. Corbitt Diary, EU.

River somewhere between Battle Creek and Bridgeport.[41] Within hours, however, his orders would be changed again.

Sometime during that same night of September 22-23rd, Bragg finally grasped that, contrary to earlier reports, Rosecrans was not abandoning Chattanooga. That realization changed the army of Tennessee's plans, further souring Bragg's opinion of Forrest's ability to command a cavalry corps. It also engendered some anger amongst the headquarters staff. That night, with a nearly audible tone of disgust, Taylor Beatty recorded, "Forrest reports that the enemy have burned Chattanooga and fled—the truth turns out that he has never been within three miles of the place & the enemy are still there—having only burned a few houses which were in the way of the guns." If Bragg wanted Chattanooga back, he would have to fight for it.[42]

September 23 bore witness to a broad, if cautious, Confederate advance across Missionary Ridge that converted the outpost line established by Cheatham, McLaws, and Forrest into a full-fledged besieging circumvallation on the south bank of the Tennessee River. Once in place, the Rebels began their own digging, throwing up lines of works and artillery bastions with which to bombard the Yankees. Bragg, who considered himself outnumbered, believed at least part of Burnside's army was present and so approached the Federal lines as might a man facing a coiled rattlesnake. In one dispatch Bragg noted "the enemy are reported advancing," and urged General Polk to "move up your command promptly and form . . . [on] Longstreet's right" to ensure no Rebel flanks were exposed. This supposed Union advance was wholly illusory. Rosecrans, focused on his own defenses, gave no thought to attack.[43]

That same morning Bragg also decided to let Forrest's horsemen rest. Whatever other shortcomings Bragg thought Forrest might have possessed as a cavalry leader, sloth was not one of them. His men had been moving or fighting since September 18 without much let-up, and now desperately needed food, forage, and ammunition. Accordingly, Forrest's orders on the 23rd were welcome indeed. His corps was instructed to move to Tyner's Station, on the

---

41 *OR* 30, pt. 2, 522.

42 Entry for September 22, Taylor Beatty Diary, UNC.

43 *OR* 30, pt. 2, 23; *OR* 30, pt. 4, 696. Bragg mistakenly reported that one of the sets of colors captured on the field at Chickamauga belonged to a regiment of Burnside's IX Corps.

spur line of the East Tennessee and Georgia Railroad that connected Cleveland and Chattanooga, and refit.[44]

Within the Union lines, September 23's dawn was greeted with considerable optimism. The first line of Federal defenses was all but completed, and secondary lines were well under way. Sufficient supplies had poured into the city to avert any immediate prospect of starvation, though the long term situation was still precarious. At midday, Assistant Secretary of War Charles Dana wired a dispatch to Washington outlining these new circumstances: "The first great object of the campaign, the possession of Chattanooga and the Tennessee line, still remains in our hands, and can be held by this army for from fifteen to twenty days against all efforts of the enemy. . . . But to render our hold here perfectly safe," he continued, "no time should be lost in pushing 20,000 to 25,000 efficient troops to Bridgeport. If such reinforcements can be got there . . . this place—indispensable alike to the defense of Tennessee and the base of future operations in Georgia—will remain ours."[45]

There was still the matter of who would control Lookout Mountain. Dibrell's Confederate cavalry had not cleared the upper reaches of the mountain before being ordered to depart, leaving Spears's East Tennesseans still occupying the crest. As long as Spears did so, Bragg could not operate in Lookout Valley with any sizable force, and if Bragg couldn't control Lookout Valley, he couldn't interdict Rosecrans's supply route. Even though the Federals could no longer use the road skirting the foot of Lookout Mountain, pontoon bridges thrown across the river at Chattanooga and again at Brown's Ferry could easily bypass any Confederate interference there.

Rather than send infantry up the eastern face of Lookout to frontally assault Spears's infantry, Bragg decided to recall Wheeler, a decision that suspended indefinitely his earlier orders to cross the Tennessee River. Dispatched toward Trenton the day before, Wheeler's troopers were well to the south and preparing to cross the mountain during the coming day. Now, once atop Lookout's broad plateau, they could turn north and sweep the crest until they reached Summertown. Thus outflanked, the Federals would have to retreat or be trapped on Lookout's northern tip.[46]

44 Jordan and Pryor, *Forrest's Cavalry*, 354.

45 *OR* 30, pt. 1, 198.

46 Ibid., pt. 4, 699.

Major General Lafayette McLaws led the Confederate army toward Chattanooga on September 22. *Library of Congress*

Bragg's orders did not reach Wheeler until 2:00 p.m., during which time the cavalry gained additional distance southward. Bragg's courier found Wheeler's main body halted at the eastern foot of Cooper's Gap, roughly 20 miles from Chattanooga, cooking rations for the coming expedition. An advanced party of "550 picked men from the brigade" of Col. Thomas Harrison, noted Texas cavalryman Robert Bunting, was already atop Lookout and moving down the far side of the mountain toward Trenton, ordered to scout out an undefended crossing over the Tennessee River. Bragg's newest directive changed everything. Wheeler immediately sent a messenger to recall Harrison, and then personally set off for Cooper's Gap with an advanced guard of another 300 men. The rest of the corps was to finish their midday meal and follow as quickly as possible.[47]

Bragg might now want Wheeler's men at Summertown, but getting there would take some time. First Wheeler's Confederates had to ascend Lookout Mountain, then march another 20 miles back north, on top of their just completed 20-mile march south; a round trip of 40 miles within the space of 24 hours. The movement would be punishingly hard on both horses and men, leaving many animals knackered and the stragglers to catch up as best they could. However, Wheeler now seemed to fully grasp the urgency of Bragg's intentions and moved very rapidly. By 4:00 p.m., the leading elements of Wheeler's cavalry drove in the 15th Pennsylvania's pickets and then dismounted to attack the Union 3rd Tennessee Infantry. With considerably fewer than 300 men on hand and his main body still a long distance behind, Wheeler attempted to bluff his enemy with a surrender demand. Colonel Cross of the Federal 3rd Tennessee Infantry passed this request up to General Spears, who rejected it out of hand, telling Cross to "fight the enemy stubbornly." Wheeler then essayed an assault, easily repulsed, though the attack was promptly reported via signals to Rosecrans's departmental headquarters in Chattanooga. Lacking his full strength, Wheeler could not take Summerville by storm. He had no choice but to wait for the rest of his corps and try again in the morning.[48]

Alerted to this threat by the Union signalers' dispatch, William Rosecrans decided that he could spare no men to send to reinforce Spears; the Federal commander now saw no alternative but to abandon Lookout Mountain. At 2:00 a.m. on the 24th, Spears welcomed word to withdraw his command, leaving only the 6th Tennessee behind temporarily as rear guard. The movement was conducted nearly without incident. The 3rd and 5th regiments slipped down the mountain and across Chattanooga Creek to reach the safety of the Union lines near the rolling mill around first light. Wheeler must have gotten wind of the tail end of this movement. Just before dawn, reported the bantam Rebel, his force "charged their flanks, driving them for some distance," though the Rebel strength numbered only "105 dismounted men." For his part, Spears noted that the Union 6th Tennessee "was flanked and attacked by a superior force . . . early in the morning . . . but resisted the attack stubbornly until compelled to yield the ground." Their mission fulfilled, the 6th followed their comrades down the mountain, reaching Spears shortly after sunup, having lost only one man in the dustup.[49]

Joe Wheeler was fortunate Rosecrans decided not to make a fight of it, for some time after the 6th Tennessee Infantry disengaged, Wheeler received a surprising dispatch. The bulk of his corps was no longer moving up the spine of the mountain behind him to join in capturing Summertown. Instead, Bragg had changed his mind once again and diverted Wheeler's corps to Chickamauga Station, located east of Missionary Ridge, unwittingly leaving Wheeler and his small advanced guard to contend with an entire brigade of Yankees on their

---

48 *OR* 30, pt. 1, 885; ibid., pt. 3, 793.

49 *OR* 30, pt. 3, 797; ibid., pt. 2, 522; ibid., pt. 1, 886. Wheeler claimed he made this charge when he first arrived at dusk, but other reports show clearly the Federals did not leave the mountain until nearly dawn on the 24th.

own. Fortunately for the Rebels, Spears followed his orders promptly and efficiently, not realizing that Wheeler had so few men opposing him.

Due to this order, and unbeknownst to Wheeler, Wharton's and Martin's divisions reversed course again, marching back north out of McLemore Cove that afternoon and evening. In doing so they trekked "across the entire battle field [of Chickamauga] from the left through the centre," reaching Chickamauga Station by dark.[50]

Spears's retreat that night was conducted so stealthily that Company L of the 15th Pennsylvania and the Union signal station were left behind. According to Trooper Williams of the 15th, when these few remaining Yankees discovered their abandonment with the coming dawn on September 24, they were sure they were all about to be captured. The Confederates controlled the roads down off the mountain and blocked any avenue along the spine of Lookout. Early that morning, the Pennsylvanians searched for an escape path down the mountain's west face, but found nothing suitable for men afoot, let alone their horses. "We returned, slowly and despairingly, to Summertown," explained Williams. "Every mind was made up to submit with stolid grace to (apparently) inevitable capture." At the signal station, however, they found a man who appeared to be a Rebel, dressed in Confederate butternut. Far from being a secessionist, this new arrival proved to be "a noted Federal scout" who knew a secret path off the mountain—if they were willing to hazard it. They were. The new man asked for a coat of Union blue, lest he be captured in butternut "and swung for it to the first tree." Suitably re-equipped, he led the party away. Their escape took several hours, the guide picking out a path that at times seemed non-existent to his followers. There were some near-misses with Rebel pickets, but they made it down to safety and Union lines.[51]

This skirmish between Wheeler and Spears atop Lookout Mountain marked the last gasp of the Chickamauga Campaign, as well as what might be termed the end of the first phase of the campaign for Chattanooga. Confronted by an entrenched and determined enemy, Bragg quickly eschewed the idea of a frontal attack. He would need a new strategy in order to restore Chattanooga to the Confederacy. Bragg had won the battle, but not the city. Rosecrans had lost the battle, but retained the prize. Both sides would claim victory.

50 R. F. Bunting, *Rome Tri-weekly Telegraph*, November 27, 1863.

51 Williams, *Leaves from a Trooper's Diary*, 76-77.

Even as Bragg was sending troops back to join Johnston in Mississippi, the Federal government was turning all its power to reinforcing Rosecrans. At Vicksburg that September 22, Gen. Ulysses S. Grant received urgent word of the need for troops at Chattanooga. Grant's headquarters did not have a direct telegraph connection with Washington. Instead dispatches were wired to Memphis and then traveled via steamboat to Vicksburg. At the best of times this hand-off involved considerable delay. Now, with the drought and the rivers all very low, that delay could amount to several days' time-lag between messages sent and received. After digesting dispatches forwarded to him from September 15 through 17, Grant noted that he would send up to four divisions, plus an unnamed corps commander, as soon as he could manage. This reply would not be received in Washington until 12:40 a.m. on September 29—a full week after Grant responded. The troops themselves would take much longer to arrive.[52]

With Burnside fumbling around in East Tennessee and Grant apparently in limbo in Mississippi, Secretary of War Edwin Stanton decided that more immediate measures were required. If Lee could send troops to Bragg, then Meade could do the same for Rosecrans. Late on September 23, Stanton requested a cabinet meeting. John Hay, recalled that Lincoln was "considerably disturbed" by the demand, for never before had Stanton "ever sent for him." Was this a harbinger of some new crisis?[53]

Despite the president's gloomy expectations, when he reached the War Department offices, he found reason for reassurance. First, noted Hay, Stanton produced a "dispatch from Rosecrans [probably Dana's of that morning] stating that he could hold Chattanooga against double his number: [the city] could not be taken until after a great battle: his stampede evidently over." Secretary of the Treasury Salmon P. Chase was also present. "The summons really alarmed me," noted Chase. "I felt that disaster had befallen us. . . . Great was my relief when, reaching the War Department and asking 'more bad news?' Stanton replied 'No, what there is, is favorable.' He then handed me a telegram from Garfield . . . [stating] that Rosecrans could hold out ten days where he was, but earnestly urged reinforcements."[54]

52 OR 30, pt. 1, 162.

53 Hay, *Inside Lincoln's White House*, 86.

54 Ibid.; David Donald, ed. *Inside Lincoln's Cabinet: The Civil War Diaries of Salmon P. Chase* (Longmans, Green and Co., 1954), 201-202.

Fort Grose, defended by the 24th Ohio (left) and 36th Indiana (right)
of Crittenden's XXI Corps. *Battles and Leaders*

This brought up the second order of business: those reinforcements. Burnside, thought Halleck, could get 20,000 men to Chattanooga within ten days "if uninterrupted," and 12,000 in just over a week. Grant's forces might take ten days to arrive as well, estimated "Old Brains" Halleck—assuming the orders sent to Mississippi arrived in a timely fashion; they were still awaiting confirmation on that. As these reports were being digested, Stanton flummoxed everyone present by proposing a scheme to send 30,000 men (two corps) from Meade's Army of the Potomac in Virginia to reinforce Rosecrans immediately. Astoundingly, Stanton suggested that they could arrive at Bridgeport within five days.[55]

Stanton's bombshell was greeted skeptically, not the least by Lincoln. Halleck opined that it would take closer to 40 days than five. A rigorous discussion ensued, with most of the gathered men doubting the feat was possible within the needed time-frame, if at all. Stanton, however, had an ace in the hole: Col. Daniel C. McCallum, Superintendent of Military Railroads. Prior to the meeting, Stanton had asked McCallum and his staff to put together an

---

55 Roger Pickenpaugh, *Rescue by Rail: Troop Transfer and the Civil War in the West, 1863* (University of Nebraska Press, 1998), 4-5.

Col. Daniel C. McCallum (bearded, right) architect of the transfer of the Union XI and XII Corps; pictured here atop Lookout Mountain, as a brigadier general, sometime in 1864.
Library of Congress

estimate of how long such a project would take to complete. Now Stanton summoned McCallum into the room. "The transfer can be begun and fully completed within seven days," the Colonel confirmed. An ebullient Stanton beamed at his otherwise astonished audience. "'Good! I told you so,' shouted

Stanton. Then, scowling at Halleck, he added: 'Forty days! Forty days indeed, when the life of the nation is at stake!' The triumphant secretary turned to McCallum: "Go ahead, begin now."[56]

*   *   *

The war would inexorably move forward. The first round of contention for Chattanooga might be over, but the second round was about to begin.

56 Ibid., 6.

Chapter Four

The Cost

B y anyone's count, the combined toll for Chickamauga was staggering. William Rosecrans led 60,889 combatants on the field, while Braxton Bragg commanded 65,023 officers and men.. Each side lost roughly 27% of its engaged strength during three days of combat. Determining precise numbers, however, is a more complicated process.

Initially, Rosecrans's Army of the Cumberland reported 16,351 casualties at Chickamauga: 1,644 men killed, 9,262 wounded, and 4,945 captured or missing. Only Brig. Gen. Robert Mitchell's cavalry corps failed to break out losses in detail, providing instead an estimated figure of 500 total casualties. However, in a more detailed report, the army's chief surgeon subsequently recorded 16,170 casualties: 1,644 killed, 9,756 wounded, and 4,757 captured or missing. Here the cavalry losses are recorded in detail (468 killed, wounded and missing,) but this follow-on report adds an additional complication: It includes losses sustained up through September 22, 1863.[1]

My research establishes Union casualties of 1,657 killed, 9,747 wounded, and 4,811 captured or missing, for a total loss of 16,215. These Union numbers are relatively complete, and not much different from the official totals. The passage of time and broader research has allowed more men to be re-classified from "missing" to "killed" or "wounded." Note that these new figures are lower than those found in the army's preliminary report but higher than those

1   OR 30, pt. 1, 64, 171-179.

given the detailed breakdown, a factor further amplified by the fact that the second report includes those additional losses suffered on September 21 and 22. While detailed research at the regimental level might well turn up additional differences in these various totals, I believe any such changes would be minor in scope.

As is often the case, establishing Confederate losses is more problematic. Bragg's Army of Tennessee at Chickamauga included not only that army but troops from Northern Virginia, East Tennessee, and Mississippi. Unfortunately, unlike the Army of the Cumberland, Bragg's Army of Tennessee never filed a comprehensive tabulation. As a result, no definitive total of Confederate casualties is possible. In his official report, Bragg estimated his human loss at "two fifths," and about "one third" of his artillery horses. A partial accounting can be gleaned from the many regimental, battery, and battalion commanders who did file reports, as well as a host of unofficial sources including letters, diaries, and postwar memoirs. Period newspapers have been especially helpful in this regard. Estimates range from a low of 16,456 killed, wounded, and captured or missing (cited in an 1898 summary of the battle) to a high of 20,950, proffered by former Rosecrans staffer Henry Cist in his 1882 history of the Army of the Cumberland. Today, the most widely accepted number for Bragg's losses is 18,454: 2,312 killed, 14,674 wounded, and 1,468 captured or missing.[2]

The research here accounts for 2,141 killed, 13,328 wounded, and 1,339 captured or missing, for a total of 16,808 losses. However, these figures do not include most of the Rebel cavalry, for neither Wheeler nor Forrest filed casualty reports. Further, some of the reports for other formations (infantry and artillery) are obviously incomplete. In all likelihood, a methodical survey of the compiled service records of the men and units that fought at Chickamauga would produce substantially larger totals than those given above, pushing the numbers much closer to the official count of 18,454, and possibly higher.

The battlefield's trophies, as might be expected, were claimed almost exclusively by the Confederates. Rosecrans reported the loss of between 36 and

---

2   Henry M. Cist, *The Army of the Cumberland* (Charles Scribner's Sons, 1882), 228; Gustavus A. Fox, *Regimental Losses in the Civil War* (Morningside House, Inc., 1985), 544; Thomas Livermore, *Numbers and Losses in the Civil War, 1861-1865* (Riverside Press, 1901), 69; David J. Eicher, *The Longest Night: A Military History of the Civil War* (Simon & Schuster, 2001), 590. The number 18,454 is cited at the Chickamauga-Chattanooga National Military Park Visitor's Center. Bragg's initial loss estimate of 40%, if accurate, would amount to roughly 26,400 casualties.

39 cannon, along with attendant limbers and caissons; nearly 8,500 assorted infantry weapons, and much other needed equipment. In an early assessment on September 24, Bragg claimed "7,000 prisoners, of which 2,000 are wounded[;] . . . 25 stands of colors or guidons, 36 pieces of artillery, and . . . 15,000 small arms over and above those left on the field by our killed and wounded." In an undated but detailed report of ordnance and stores inventoried at Ringgold, Capt. Octavius T. Gibbes listed 51 cannon and 23,281 assorted small arms recovered from the field. In his final report, written in December 1863, Bragg embraced Gibbes's figures for the artillery, but stuck with the 15,000 number for small arms.[3]

And what of "engaged strength?" Those figures can be very amorphous. A few units (on both sides) simply failed to report their initial strengths, requiring a bit of mathematical guesswork to fill in the resultant gaps. Even for the units who did provide numbers, differing standards of counting gives rise to the question: Who should be included as "engaged" in the first place? Union regiments counted officers as well as enlisted men as a matter of course, but Confederate formations often omitted their officers in their own accounting—dichotomies which have to be adjusted for. Then there are troops involved around the periphery of the great battle who, for one reason or another, did not become engaged. How should they be tabulated? James Spears's Federal East Tennessee brigade and William Wofford's Georgia brigade were each involved in post-battle skirmishing between September 22 and 24. Neither brigade, however, is typically included as "engaged" at Chickamauga. In a similar vein, some units suffered additional loss after the battle—the 59th Ohio, for example, lost 78 men during the actions of September 19 and 20, and an additional 20 men on September 22. Should their losses be counted as 78 or 98? Including the September 22 casualties changes their loss percentage from 27% to 34%, a significant difference.

---

3   OR 30, pt. 1, 233-239; ibid., pt. 2, 23, 35, 40-43. Both sides made detailed inventories of material losses. Gibbes's list is very interesting, including such oddments as 3 copper bugles (damaged) 33 pounds of picket rope, and no less than 365 sets of assorted officers' shoulder straps. The Federals probably did lose only 36 guns to capture; the remaining 3 appear to have been damaged but extracted. Some of the 51 pieces eventually claimed by the Confederates were actually guns lost by their own batteries and recovered on the field. As for small arms, a combined total of nearly 35,000 men (or more) became casualties; how many of them bore their weapons off the field or had them recovered by their comrades is impossible to say. If anything, small arms captures are likely under counted. After refurbishment, these recovered infantry weapons went a long way toward completely re-arming the paroled Vicksburg garrison.

Early my research, I decided to count as "engaged" only those commands who were part of the fighting from September 18 to 21, 1863, and have further to confine loss figures to that same period of time. In some cases, however, determining a unit's strength still requires guesswork, and the losses inevitably include some who fell outside of this timeframe.[4]

As a result, these numbers (both engaged strengths and losses) must remain approximations. Thus, the Federal strengths and losses do not include Spears's men, or Brig. Gen. George Wagner's troops garrisoning in Chattanooga. On the Confederate side, the "engaged" numbers don't include more than half of James Longstreet's corps—five brigades and an oversized artillery battalion—which arrived too late to take part in the main battle. Those figures (or in some cases the best educated guess) are presented separately in Appendices III through VI.

As might be expected, Rebel cavalry numbers for both categories are especially uncertain. Forrest's and Wheeler's headquarters were often neglectful of such reports. The only reliable reports for Bragg's cavalry were made in August 1863, a full month before the battle. Worse, official loss returns are non-existent. Of the 34 regiments and battalions comprising the two Confederate cavalry corps, only 15 of those units provide any loss data at all, and most of those numbers are gleaned from contemporary newspapers.

Differing methodologies in each army further complicate statistical comparisons. The Union army tended to report as "killed" only those men who died outright on the field of battle, while the Confederates usually reported "killed and mortally wounded" as a single category, a figure that included both those who died immediately and those who were likely to die (or did perish) within a few days' time.

There is an additional complicating factor. On May 14, 1863, Gen. Robert E. Lee issued an order cautioning his officers to not include "those cases of slight injuries" in their reports. Such wounds, defined as "those . . . which do not incapacitate the recipients from duty," were also typically defined as those suffered by men who would return to the ranks within ten days. Lee took this action for reasons of morale. The previous practice, thought Lee, was "calculated to mislead our friends and encourage our enemies by giving false

---

4 Appendices III through VI.include a lengthy explanation of how I derived my figures, who got included or excluded, and why. I decided to include the actions on September 21, primarily to incorporate the fight between Col. Louis D. Watkins's brigade of the Union Cavalry (3/3/Cav) and Wheeler's Confederates, which occurred on that day.

impressions as to the extent of our losses." As a result, Confederate battle losses after mid-1863 in the Eastern Theater were often underreported, perhaps by as much as 10%, when compared to similar Union numbers. While Lee's order did not extend to other Confederate armies, we do not know whether Longstreet's officers used this recent methodology when they recorded their casualties at Chickamauga. Did Longstreet's staff instruct the non-Virginia portions of the left wing to follow this guideline when they made out their returns? Or did Longstreet's own report, which included losses for his wing, omit the lightly wounded category from the totals he reported? We do not know. It is possible that Rebel casualties for Chickamauga could approach Cist's estimate of 20,950 if some or all of the men in this last category were omitted from the official returns.[5]

We do know that almost 4,000 dead and a large number of those 25,000 injured men littered the 6,000+ acres of the Chickamauga battlefield. Losses among horses and mules, especially artillery animals, were also heavy. At a minimum, hundreds (and perhaps as many as 2,000) dead and crippled equines carpeted the field. It can only be described as a horrific scene, and one that would require an immense amount of labor to rectify. Given their possession of the field, this chore fell almost entirely upon the Army of Tennessee.[6]

Of course, even during the fighting both armies made tremendous efforts to get their wounded to safety as soon as possible. The walking wounded found their way to their respective field hospitals, which for both sides at this time of the war were organized at the division level. Every Federal hospital was captured on September 20, along with more than 1,000 of the non-ambulatory Union wounded. The Confederate field hospitals were mostly established along the banks of West Chickamauga Creek or lined the Reed's Bridge Road heading back toward Ringgold. None of these field hospitals were intended to be permanent, and each side did its best to evacuate those casualties who could be moved, as soon as possible, farther to the rear. For the Northerners, this meant an initial 10-mile trip to Chattanooga and, ultimately, another 30 difficult miles on to Bridgeport, either on foot or via horse-drawn ambulance. From there,

---

5   OR 25, pt. 2, 798.

6   This figure might seem low to many readers. At Gettysburg, there were reportedly 3,000 dead animals. However, most of the livestock losses came from artillery casualties, and both the Union and Confederate armies at Chickamauga contained substantially fewer cannon than their eastern counterparts. At Gettysburg the Union deployed 372 guns, the Confederates, 280, for a total of 652; at Chickamauga the Federals had 205, the Rebels, 166, for a total of 371.

things got a little easier. The injured could board rail cars destined for permanent hospitals in Nashville, Louisville, New Albany, Indiana, and other points north of the Ohio River. For some Yanks, however, Chattanooga would be as far as they could manage, and many of the city's structures would be put to use in the coming days.

The Confederate journey was shorter, just 10 miles back to Ringgold, where wounded could board their own trains southward. Ringgold was itself a destination for many. Two prewar resort hotels at Catoosa and Cherokee Springs had been converted into permanent hospitals in 1862. In August, just as the campaign opened, Braxton Bragg and his wife were recuperating from illness at Catoosa Springs. In early September, as the Federals approached Ringgold, both hospitals were evacuated. Now they were hastily reestablished in order to deal with the large influx of maimed men. Because there were far too few beds to deal with so many new casualties, additional buildings along the railroad from Dalton to Atlanta were commandeered for space.

Kate Cumming, the wife of Maj. Joseph Cumming (of Gen. W. H. T. Walker's staff) was one of the nurses staffing Catoosa Springs until she was evacuated to Atlanta in early September. She was in church on Sunday morning, September 20, and knew only that a great battle was raging 80 miles to the north. "[We] heard a very good sermon from the pastor," she recalled, "but [he] spoiled it by saying, with bitterness, that there would be no taking churches [in heaven] for hospitals. . . . All the churches here have been taken for hospital purposes, and this is the last Sunday service that will be held in that one." Though she understood the necessity, Mrs. Cumming sympathized with the pastor's anguish, "thinking of the ruin which would be wrought in making it ready for patients."[7]

No matter what color uniform a man wore, the trip from battlefield to hospital was almost always one of prolonged agony. Private Alfred D. French of the 89th Illinois was wounded in the left arm on September 19 during Brig. Gen. August Willich's charge near the Winfrey house. "Can you get back alone?" queried French's captain. "I said I thought I could," replied the injured private, and off he went. He made it only a few hundred yards when he began to feel faint. "Two men came and helped me back to where I would not be under fire, laid me on the ground and left me." French stayed there until about 10:00

---

7   Kate Cumming, with Richard Barksdale Harwell, ed., *Kate: The Journal of a Confederate Nurse* (Louisiana State University Press, 1987), 144.

a.m. the next morning, when he was taken by ambulance to Chattanooga and off-loaded in what he described as an "old Confederate barrack." On September 24, he was moved across the Tennessee River and laid out in the woods. Finally, at 9:00 p.m. that night, "for the first time I had a surgeon dress my wounds, received five days before."

French's ordeal was far from over. He remained in that grove for another forty-eight hours without any sort of shelter until tents could found and erected. In all, he spent the next month there, living on thin rations until he was finally hauled by wagon and then steamboat to Bridgeport. After another two days' wait there, French was among a group of 20 wounded loaded onto a "cattle car [with] some clean straw thrown in. Thirty-six hours later French reached Army Hospital Number 19 in Nashville, where, finally, "we got good care and plenty to eat." Thousands of wounded Federals faced a similar experience.[8]

Despite having better access to their rail line, the Confederates had their own difficulties. On September 28, responding to pleas for volunteers and supplies, Kate Cumming returned to Ringgold. About dark she reached Catoosa Springs, where she found the old resort crowded with injured men, "all shivering with cold," awaiting transportation. She spent the next two days here, dressing wounds, bringing food and water to the soldiers, and working without respite. On the 30th, she resolved to visit the battlefield itself, "not from any idle curiosity, but from a desire to know the worst." After much searching, she finally found a private citizen with a wagon who had been hauling wounded from the field hospitals to the rail platform, and who agreed to take her with him on his next return trip. They visited the Jeptha Hunt farmstead, now the site of Maj. Gen. Thomas Hindman's division hospital. "I found Mr. Hunt's home a very pretty cottage in the midst of a garden, which before the battle had been filled with fine shrubbery and flowers, but was now covered with tents, flies and sheds filled with wounded. . . . Every corner of the house was filled with wounded, many of them lying upon bunks made out of the branches of trees, a hard bed at any time, but much more so for these poor wounded veterans." As if to make things even more dreary, the long summer drought had broken, and in the week after the battle it started to rain. "We could see the men

---

8   Alfred D. French Memoirs, www.civilwar.ilgenweb.net/reg_html/089_reg.html, accessed September 2005. French's journey was delayed because he spent the month of October in Chattanooga awaiting the Federal effort to lift Bragg's siege of that place. He would have almost certainly died if he had to endure the jolting of a wagon journey over Walden Ridge to Bridgeport. With the reopening of the cracker line, he could travel via river steamer.

Confederate Nurse Kate Cumming, in her later years. *Cumming, Gleanings from Southland, 1985*

cooking out in the pouring rain; a perfect war between the two elements, fire and water. All had a most cheerless aspect. As we rode on the tents of the various field hospitals came in view," she added, "and the thoughts of the inmates and their sufferings added to the gloom."[9]

Many wounded did not get off the field for days. When General Forrest overran Brig. Gen. Absalom Baird's and Brig. Gen. John Brannan's hospitals at Cloud Church, the Rebel cavalryman promised Surgeon Abraham Landis of the 35th Ohio "that [the Union] wounded yet on the field should be removed . . . and receive precisely the same treatment that their wounded received." Dr. Landis was given a similar reassurance from Dr. Edward A. Flewellen, Bragg's medical director, the next day. Bragg also reiterated that same instruction in an army-wide order. Despite all these good intentions, the reality was that the Confederate medical and supply departments were completely overwhelmed, and many of the extra men detailed to bring in those wounded concentrated on their own side's casualties first.[10]

Certainly, the dead were prioritized. John Wyeth of the 4th Alabama Cavalry was one of those assigned to this gruesome task. "Most of the Confederate dead had been gathered in long trenches and buried," he recalled, "but the Union dead were still lying where they fell." Wyeth thought this was intentional, "for its effect on the survivors[.] It was the policy of the victor to

9 Cumming, *Kate: The Journal of a Confederate Nurse*, 144-145.

10 *Cyclopaedia of Butler County Ohio*, 222; OR 30, pt. 4, 690.

hide his own losses and let those of the other side be seen." Sadly, mixed in among those unburied "dead" were many men still clinging to life.[11]

One such was Merritt J. Simonds of the 42nd Illinois. Simonds was a 22-year-old resident of Dekalb, Illinois, who joined Company K in August, 1862. On September 20, he was wounded in the "right leg just above the knee, shatter[ing] the bone some." Unable to walk, he and several of his comrades in the 42nd watched as their regiment fell back, caught up Phil Sheridan's retreat off the field at midday. While he could not walk, Private Simonds remained clear-headed enough to write short entries in his diary over the course of the next week while he lay out on the battlefield where he fell, several hundred yards northeast of the Widow Glenn's ruined cabin. On the 21st, Simonds recorded that "the rebs carry off their wounded and bury their dead, but do not take us off." Two days later on the 23rd, he scribbled that "we have lain here now three nights and nearly four days and no signs of Relief Although the rebs continue to promise us." The next day produced an aid party, including a doctor, but though they shifted Simonds and those of his comrades who still lived a short distance away from the decomposing dead, they were still not removed to a hospital.[12]

Finally, on Saturday September 26, Simonds and his comrades were taken to a field hospital for treatment. The next Wednesday they were part of a prisoner exchange. Loaded into wagons and hauled to Chattanooga, nearly 1,000 Federals were finally back in friendly hands. It would be too late for Private Simonds, however. His leg became gangrenous, and the doctors told him he would die. He broke the news to his family in a letter home on October 27, 1863. "My leg is now mortifying above the knee and the Dr's say I cannot live more than two days at the longest. You must not take this to heart but look to a higher source for comfort, for it is God's will and I feel resigned to my fate. I hope to meet you all in a better world. I would like to have my body taken home and buried beside my mother." Sadly, even in death he never made it home, and was instead buried in Chattanooga.[13]

---

11 Wyeth, *With Sabre and Scalpel*, 254.

12 Entries for September 20 to 26, 1863, Merritt J. Simonds Diary, Northern Illinois University Dekalb, IL. Hereafter NIU.

13 "Dear Father," October 27, 1863, Merritt J. Simonds Papers, NIU. Simonds is buried in the Chattanooga National Cemetery, plot A, grave 234.

Simonds's fellow Illini, Pvt. Melville (Mell) C. Follett, also of the 42nd Illinois, was luckier—but only just. He also suffered a leg wound, struck in Viniard Field on Saturday, September 19. Unlike Simonds, Follett was moved to Sheridan's division field hospital that night. A doctor warned him that the injury might require amputation, but Follett avoided that fate when his leg began to improve. He was captured on September 20, and daily expected to be shipped south as a prisoner of war. The one benefit of his wound, however, was that he was too badly injured to stand the journey, and so was also paroled and exchanged along with Simonds and the others. On October 1, Follett recorded this agonizing journey:

> [We] were put in ambulances before daylight but did not start until 8 o'clock. Hauled about six miles when we halted for the rest of the train. I never knew what pain was before. It seemed at times as though I must die. We did not arrive until 10 o'clock at night. Got stuck in a pond hole and could not get out for two hours and then were helped out by the 10th South Carolina Regt. My wound is considered to be improving. I never shall have full use [of my leg] again. Such is a soldier's life. I shall be a cripple for the rest of my days.[14]

The Follett family got the news of Mell's wounding sometime in October, and his father A. H. Follett made the journey south to find his son. The elder Follett arrived in Chattanooga on November 8, 1863, and spent the next several months helping his son recover. "[I] found M[ell] alive but very weak & poor yet he seemed to be in good spirits. . . . The Surgeon in charge told me yesterday that Mell would have died if I had not come." Over the next few weeks, A. H. Follett helped his son journey home to recuperate, a process that would take almost a full year. Melville Cox Follett would finally be discharged in June 1864, due to the wounds received in at Chickamauga.[15]

Sergeant Ed Murray of the 96th Illinois also spent considerable time on the field, his distress compounded by the fact that he was paralyzed from the waist down due to a bullet lodged alongside his spine. Struck about 2:00 p.m. on the

---

14 Entry for October 1, 1863, Melville Cox Follett Diary, Ohio State University Digital History Collection, http://ehistory.osu.edu/osu/sources/letters/follett_melville/diary_index.cfm, accessed August 26, 2012.

15 "Dear Daughter," Chattanooga November 21, 1863, A. H. Follett Letter, Ohio State University Digital History Collection, http://ehistory.osu.edu/osu/sources/letters/follett_brothers/letters/AF631121.cfm, accessed August 26, 2012.

20th, Murray lay between the lines and under fire the rest of that desperate afternoon, during which he was hit twice more. Finally, after dark and as the temperature plunged, some compassionate Confederates moved Murray and several other wounded men to a campfire. Murray, who had seen other fallen men burned to death by fires ignited in the combustible ground litter, begged the soldiers to brush the leaves away from around him, for he could do little to protect himself given his paralysis. The Rebels did him a further kindness and covered him with a blanket. The next morning Murray watched as Bushrod Johnson's regiments formed up around him. Convinced he would be caught in the middle of another fight, Murray waited anxiously for the Confederates to move him to a field hospital. "It was a terrible suspense," he recalled later. "It seemed to me hours when it might have been but a few minutes, for I thought they would never come, but they did."[16]

Murray spent the next few days in a field hospital, still paralyzed, until he was also returned to Union lines in the exchange. Eventually, he was removed to a hospital in Nashville, enduring much of the same jolting agony described by Follett during the difficult journey from Chattanooga southwest to Stevenson, Alabama. As for his paralysis, each time Murray was examined the doctors decided the bullet was lodged too near the spine to be removed. Luckily, Murray's brother John arrived from the north and, with more personalized help, Ed began to regain some feeling and a little movement in his legs. Eventually, John escorted Sergeant Murray home where he continued to improve. By the spring of 1864, Murray could walk with crutches, but he was far from fit. He never returned to active duty, but he did survive, though he would carry the bullet in his back for the rest of his life, which left him with a permanent limp. Despite his wound, Ed Murray lived for another 37 years before passing away in 1900.[17]

---

16 Ed Murray, "A Soldier's Reminiscences," Lake County Discovery Museum, Wauconda, IL.

17 Ibid.; Email from Diane Dretske, Lake County Historian, Wauconda, IL, March 2, 2016. The U. S. Army had one final bit of irony to play out regarding Sergeant Murray when it ordered him to return to duty at the beginning of May 1864. The stunned soldier traveled to Chicago for an examination, where a doctor told him he was fit enough to rejoin his regiment—despite the fact that Murray could still only hobble around and had lung problems, to boot. Murray made it all the way to Nashville, reported in, and then he began coughing up blood. The surgeons wanted to send him back north immediately for the summer campaign of 1864 was underway and every bed was needed for men wounded in fighting for Atlanta. Murray begged to stay a few days, just long enough to recover some strength. Once he was stronger Murray traveled first to Louisville and then to a military hospital in Quincy, Illinois. He would not be officially

Merritt Simonds's, Melville Follett's, and Edward Murray's stories were repeated thousands of times across both the North and the South as maimed men fought to recover from their grievous injuries. In addition to those killed outright, roughly one-quarter of the injured would eventually die of their wounds. Another one-third could be considered as having been rendered permanently unfit to return to duty, meaning that only about six in ten, or about 40 percent, of those wounded in action would ever return to full service. Both armies paid heavily for the prize of Chattanooga.[18]

Prisoners of war had their own difficult tales to tell. Of the 6,400 unwounded men captured in the battle, the vast majority—4,800 of them—wore blue. Unlike Vicksburg, where General Grant paroled nearly the entire Confederate garrison (excepting officers), neither side paroled many prisoners after Chickamauga. Instead, captured men were shipped to distant prison camps. Confederate prisoners were moved north, first to Louisville and then to prison camps in Ohio, Indiana, and Illinois. Many of the officers were sent to Johnson's Island at Sandusky, Ohio, which was already heavily populated from previous battles. The enlisted men ended up at either Camp Morton in Indianapolis, or Camp Douglas in Chicago.

Few of these Confederates would ever return to duty. The exchange cartel between the North and the South was already foundering by July 1863, and would break down almost completely over the next few months due to what each side viewed as the other's improper handling of paroled men. The Federals were upset at the rapid return of many of the Vicksburg captures, as well as the Rebels' initial refusal to treat black soldiers as anything other than escaped slaves. The Confederates took umbrage over the North's refusal to honor paroles given to some Union troops during the Gettysburg campaign. These and other reasons were why many Rebels captured at Chickamauga would spend the rest of their war in prison.

One way out of that confinement was to "take the oath." If a Confederate prisoner of war took a loyalty oath and pledged not to raise arms against the government again, he could be released as long as he remained north of the Ohio River. As the war dragged on, this path out of the camps appealed to more

---

discharged until August 1864—eleven months after being wounded—when he was finally sent home with a full disability.

18 Given these statistics, it is reasonable to conclude that another roughly 6,000 men—2,300 Federals and 3,700 Rebels—might be considered "killed" as a result of Chickamauga.

Sergeant Edward Murray, of the 96th Illinois, was wounded and left on Horseshoe Ridge on September 20, 1863.

Partridge: History of the 96th Regiment, 1887

than a few. While only a small number of Confederates ever took the oath, some who did were Chickamauga men. One was Sgt. George W. Moody of the 24th Alabama, Manigault's brigade. Moody deserted to the Federals on September 20 and took the 24th's flag with him.[19]

Confederate Brig. Gen. Daniel Adams managed to avoid being shipped north after being wounded and captured. Instead, the one-eyed general was cared for in Chattanooga. On September 27, Adams informed his wife of his circumstances and noted optimistically that a Union surgeon "thinks I am doing very well." The courtesies of civilized war were much more in evidence for brigadier generals than for privates or sergeants. On the 28th, General Bragg inquired about Adams in the hope of having "Old Pelican" released back into Confederate lines on parole. Rosecrans agreed, though Adams's injuries precluded his actual return for another month. Thereafter Adams recuperated at Lagrange, Georgia, but would not return to duty any time soon. He would not be formally exchanged until the fall of 1864.[20]

Most Federal prisoners were destined for Virginia. Officers went to Richmond's Libby Prison, while enlisted men were initially housed on nearby Belle Isle in the James River. Like their Confederate counterparts, the trip was long and difficult, and captivity produced a spate of postwar prison reminiscences among the captured Yanks.[21]

19 David A. Powell, *The Chickamauga Campaign, Glory or the Grave: The Breakthrough, the Union Collapse, and the Defense of Horseshoe Ridge, September 20, 1863* (Savas Beatie, 2015), 307.

20 Adams to Wife, 27 September 1863, Adams Papers, Louisiana Historical Association Collection, Tulane University, New Orleans; Stuart Salling, *Louisianans in the Western Confederacy* (McFarland & Co. 2010), 135.

21 Later, many of these men would be transferred to Salisbury, North Carolina, and most infamously, Andersonville.

The prisoners were first marched in groups to Ringgold or Tunnel Hill, where they boarded trains for Atlanta. Captain Alonzo Keeler of the 22nd Michigan, one of those left behind on Horseshoe Ridge, recorded that his group reached Atlanta on the evening of September 23, hungry and cold. "After being gazed upon by an immense crowd," recalled Keeler, "we were marched officers and men to an open camp for the night." In Atlanta, the Federal captives were forced to surrender many personal items. Lieutenant Colonel William Robinson of the 77th Pennsylvania recalled the Rebels parading him and his fellows in a "triumphant march through Atlanta," which he described as "this miserable hole. The P.M. [Provost Marshall]," he continued, "refuses to let the people sell us anything— [and] took from us today our pocket knives, blankets, canteens cups, haversacks. [They] wanted pocket books, watches, etc."[22]

Several of these Federals were no strangers to the cheerlessness of an Atlanta imprisonment, for many served in the 2nd, 21st, and 33rd Ohio— participants in the Andrews Raid, also known as the Great Locomotive Chase. In 1862, more than a dozen of them had been captured in that affair and held in Atlanta for months while the Southern authorities debated whether or not to hang them as spies. In the end, only the mission's ringleaders met that fate, with the rest of the men exchanged in due time. They returned to their regiments, and some of them fought at Chickamauga. Now, five of these same men were back in Confederate hands, and fearful that the old charges of espionage would be revived. Two of them were too badly wounded to move and so never reached Atlanta. As invalids, they were instead exchanged at the end of September. The remaining three men survived the war but had very different experiences.

John Wollum of the 33rd Ohio was recognized as a raider, kept at Atlanta, and forced to wear a ball and chain. Despite this handicap, he somehow managed to escape in February 1864 and obtain his revenge by rejoining his unit in time to help William T. Sherman capture the Rebel city in early September 1864. Elihu Mason of the 21st Ohio, wounded in the arm at Chickamauga, spent a long time in Rebel prisons. He was not exchanged until December 1864. John Porter, also of the 21st, escaped from a train while being transported to the

22 Alonzo M. Keeler, with Robert D. and Cheryl J. Allen, eds., *A "Guest" of the Confederacy: The Civil War Letters and Diaries of Alonzo M. Keeler, Captain, Company B, Twenty-second Michigan Infantry* (Cold Tree Press, 2008), 65; Entry for September 23, William A. Robinson Diary, WRHS.

newly opened prison at Andersonville in May 1864. He was promptly recaptured but repeated the feat a month later and rejoined his regiment at the end of June—also in time to participate in Atlanta's fall.[23]

Despite their status, many prisoners managed to maintain good morale. Captain Keeler even described his fellow captives as "jubilant." On Friday, September 25, Keeler's group departed Atlanta for the trip east singing "The Star Spangled Banner," "The Red White and Blue," and other songs "until the rebel officer in charge of us forbids it." A young Georgia civilian named J. R. Kendrick watched one of these prison trains roll through the small town of Madison, just a few miles east of Atlanta, and took note of the defiance of the men jammed inside. "Great trains of cars came lumbering through our town, crowded with Union captives," recalled Kendrick. "The irrepressible prisoners shouted to me 'Old Rosey will be along here soon!' 'Old Rosey' never came, but 'Uncle Billy' came along in due time."[24] The train's route carried Keeler and his comrades through Augusta, Georgia, Colombia, South Carolina, and northward to Charlotte, North Carolina. The journey was not entirely without human comforts, noted Keeler: "After Midnight [on September 28th, some hours after leaving Charlotte] a female came into the cars and performed her peculiar evolutions." On the 30th, Keeler arrived at Libby.[25]

That same lax security that allowed prostitutes to sneak onto the train also allowed several captives to sneak off. One party of Federals gained their freedom this way at Danville, Virginia. The most famous Federal escape attempt by men captured at Chickamauga was hatched not inside a rail car but within the walls of Libby Prison itself. Colonel Thomas Rose of the 77th Pennsylvania, part of Col. Joseph Dodge's brigade, had fallen captive along with other comrades when they were overrun by Pat Cleburne's Rebels on the night of September 19. In February of 1864, Rose helped plan a mass breakout, leading 109 officers outside the walls. The method of escape was ingenious. First, the escapees had to pass "down the chimney through the fireplace by means of a rope ladder" to the cellar, where a tunnel was dug. The officers began slipping out on the night of February 9. The mass escape threw all of

---

23 Russell S. Bonds, *Stealing The General: The Great Locomotive Chase and the First Medal of Honor* (Westholme Publishing, 2007), 334-335.

24 J. R. Kendrick, "A Non-Combatant's War Reminiscences," *The Atlantic Monthly*, vol. 64 (October 1889), 458.

25 Keeler, *A "Guest" of the Confederacy*, 65-67.

Confederate Prisoners in Chattanooga. These men were captured in later battles,
probably at Missionary Ridge, but they endured much the same difficult
future as did those taken at Chickamauga.

Library of Congress

Richmond into an uproar. Of the 109 escapees, 59 eventually reached Union lines, 48 were recaptured, and two drowned in the James River.[26]

While some few of the Federals were exchanged in the spring of 1864 and returned to their units, most remained prisoners. The collapse of the cartel doomed many Federals, just as it did their Confederate counterparts imprisoned in the North, to linger in inadequate prison camps for the war's duration. Many Yankees would eventually end up at Andersonville, the most notorious camp of them all. A smaller handful of those who ended up there

---

26 Various entries, typescript of Frederick A. Bartleson Diary, 27-36, Rutgers University. Bartleson, a prewar attorney from Joliet, lost an arm at Shiloh. He was the colonel of the 100th Illinois at Chickamauga, where he was captured. He did not accompany the Libby Prison escapees, but he described the affair in detail. Bartleson was paroled in time to rejoin his command during the Atlanta campaign, and was killed on the skirmish line at Kennesaw Mountain on June 23, 1864.

would be so unfortunate as to die on the steamboat *Sultana* after finally being liberated.[27]

The impact on those civilians unfortunate enough to have their property turned into a battlefield was also devastating. Three of the humble homes that lent their names to immortalize parts of the field were left in ruins; Eliza Glenn's house, the Alexander farmstead, and the Poe cabin were all burned during the course of the battle. The McDonald house survived the combat only to catch fire and burn to the ground several weeks later. Those houses that did survive were crowded with wounded, leaving no home for their owners to return. On September 21, Larkin Poe relinquished his teamster duties and traveled to the battlefield, hoping to find his family. He reached the Brotherton house first, where, amid a host of wounded from the 100th Illinois and Rebels from John Fulton's brigade of Bushrod Johnson's division, Poe located his father-in-law, George Brotherton.

Together, the two men next traveled north to Poe's own home, which was now nothing but a smoldering ruin. "The piled up dead, the trampled and bloodstained ground, the torn and splintered timber, bore mute testimony to the terrible struggle that had taken place there." The fire that destroyed the cabin also savaged the dead. "Poe found one of the soldiers . . . with both legs burned off near the body." To his relief, Poe eventually located his family huddled with a number of other civilians in the woods behind the Snodgrass farm. His search, however, covered a large part of the field and filled him with memories that would haunt him until his death. In one place, recalled Poe, "I saw a piece of artillery . . . which had been knocked from the wheels by a direct hit from our guns and apparently most all of the horses and men belonging to the gun had perished there, for their bodies lay in grotesque heaps around their piece. The bodies I saw were apparently all Federals," he continued. "Their dead were yet unburied, and some of them lay on the field until after the battle of Missionary Ridge, ten weeks later."[28]

---

27 The *Sultana* sank in April 1865 as a result of a catastrophic boiler explosion, killing more than 1,600 of the 2,400 men crammed on board. The ship was contracted by the government to carry newly released prisoners up the Mississippi River, and was woefully overcrowded when the accident occurred.

28 James Alfred Sartain, *History of Walker County, Georgia*, 2 vols. (Thomasson Printing, 1972), vol. 1, 100; E. Raymond Evans, *Chickamauga: Civil War Impact on an Area: Tsikamagi, Crawfish Springs, Snow Hill, and Chickamauga* (City of Chickamauga, GA, 2002), 115. The original interview dates from a newspaper article printed in 1929.

Confederate brigade commander Daniel
Adams, wounded and captured on the
battlefield on the morning of September 20.
Library of Congress

For many, finding and burying the
dead was an intensely personal task.
Wherever possible, men on both sides
hurriedly buried friends and family,
marking their graves with hastily
scrawled identifiers in the hope the
deceased could be given a more fitting
interment at some later date. Private
Douglas Cater of Company E, 19th
Louisiana, Dan Adams's brigade, lost
his brother on the morning of
September 20 when Lt. Rufus Cater
was shot through the body while leading Company E that morning north of
Kelly Field. Douglas Cater found Rufus that evening amid distressing
circumstances. Rufus's body, remembered Douglas, had been looted by "devils
in human form [who] not yet satisfied, fired a rifle ball through his forehead."
Grief-stricken over his loss and enraged at this apparent murder of a wounded
man, Douglas spent an anguished night holding vigil over his brother's remains.
The next morning, he and a comrade, Pvt. Augustus Hendrick, buried both
Rufus and Hendrick's brother (killed in the same action) side by side. To mark
the graves, they "cut their names on the rough boards which marked 'the place
where they were laid.'"[29]

That same Monday, three Reed brothers found their friend John Ingraham,
who had been killed on the morning of September 19. The Reeds and Ingraham
were all members of the 2nd Battalion, 1st Confederate, and so local to the area.
Reed's Bridge, one of the battle's landmarks, was named for their family. The

---

29 Douglas John Cater, *As It Was: Reminiscences of a Soldier of the Third Texas Cavalry and the
Nineteenth Louisiana Infantry* (State House Press, TX, 1990), 163-164. Douglas Cater would
survive to the ripe old age of 90, passing away in San Antonio, Texas, in 1931. Augustus
Hendrick also survived to the end of the war. He was captured with the remnant of his regiment
at Spanish Fort in April 1865, but I was unable to find records concerning his postwar history.

brothers buried their boyhood friend near the intersection of the Alexander's Bridge Road and Brotherton Road, close to where they had experienced such hot fighting on Saturday. John's body had somehow remained untouched, missed by the human vultures who scoured battlefields to pillage from the dead. Charles Reed found and kept John's prized pocket watch as a memento. The Reeds also marked the spot of his burial with a board. For reasons that remain obscure, Ingraham's body was never removed from the battlefield. After the war, the Reed family marked his grave with a proper headstone and encircled it with an iron fence.[30]

Senior officers garnered more attention, even in death. Brigadier General Benjamin Helm died sometime during the night of September 20 in the Reed cabin, surrounded by members of his brigade. Fred Joyce of the 4th Kentucky lay alongside Helm and also near the slowly perishing artillery major, Rice Graves, who "was suffering the most intense agony." Helm "passed into an insensible condition and lingered until near midnight," recalled staff officer Capt. W. W. Herr, who attended his commander until the last, "when the spirit left the body" and only Helm's corpse "lay cold and pallid upon the floor." No battlefield grave with a hastily scrawled headboard awaited Helm. Instead, his remains were transported to Atlanta and given as elaborate a funeral as that wartime city could manage. His wife Emilie, who was residing in Selma when her husband was killed, arrived in time for the Atlanta ceremony. That December, a grief-stricken Emilie and their daughter Katherine traveled to Washington, D.C. to be with her half-sister Mary Todd Lincoln in the White House. They remained guests of the Lincolns for some time, and even returned several times between late 1863 and the end of the war, sometimes to the embarrassment of President Lincoln's political fortunes. It was not until 1884 that Helm's body found its final resting place in Elizabethtown, Kentucky, where a crowd of mourners estimated at 5,000 people were on hand to witness his interment.[31]

---

30 Evans, *Chickamauga*, 113. John Ingraham was an orphan who had lived with the Reeds and helped work their family farm. Today, Ingraham is the only casualty of the battle who is officially considered to be still on the field.

31 Fred Joyce, "The Mother and Two Sons," *Southern Bivouac* (September 1883 - August 1884), vol. 2, 314; W. W. Herr, "Death of Ben. Hardin Helm," undated clipping, Lewin Papers, Perkins Library, DU. Emilie Todd Helm tried to return to Kentucky after Helm's funeral, but in order to obtain a pass across Federal lines she would have to take an oath forsaking the Confederacy and swearing allegiance to the United States, which she refused to do. When

Similar pomp and ceremony attended William Haynes Lytle's remains. The Union brigadier general's corpse drew no small amount of attention from almost the minute he fell. Sometime on the 20th, Lytle was removed to Thomas Hindman's division hospital near Hunt's Ford, and interred there in a temporary grave. Dr. William Goodale of the 21st Michigan (of Lytle's brigade) was one of the captured Federal surgeons left behind to care for casualties. He met Rebel Brig. Gen. Patton Anderson on September 21, who informed him of Lytle's status and current whereabouts. Understanding that the family would want to recover the body, Goodale had Anderson carefully describe the site, the details of which the surgeon painstakingly recorded in his diary: "General Lytle was buried about one and a half miles below Lee & Gordon's Mills, about hundred yards below Hunt's Ferry [Ford] on west bank of West Chickamauga [Creek]." Captain Douglas West, an officer serving on Brig. Gen. Zachary C. Deas's staff, provided additional details: "[General Lytle was] buried at Hunt's Ford on the Chickamauga creek on the Chattanooga side of the river, left hand side of the road going from Chattanooga."[32]

Lieutenant Colonel William Ward of Lytle's former regiment, the 10th Ohio Infantry, appealed to General Rosecrans to ask for their former colonel's body back under a flag of truce. The Rebels readily acceded to Rosecrans's request, even providing an honor guard to escort the departed poet-general as far as their own picket lines. There, a similar detail of Buckeyes from the 10th Ohio took over, carrying their deceased commander to a funeral tent set up amidst the Ohioans' camp. Lytle was treated with all the ceremony the regiment could muster: "Major John Hudson . . . arranged for the coffin to be placed on a raised dais and draped with velvet and white linen. The American flag decorated

---

informed of the problem, Lincoln asked the Federal Provost Marshalls to bring her to Washington. The Lincolns tried to keep her presence a secret but to no avail. One evening, upon discovering that Mrs. Helm was living in the White House, an indignant Maj. Gen. Daniel E. Sickles chastised the President: "You should not have that rebel in your house," barked Sickles, who had lost a leg at Gettysburg only that summer. "My wife and I are in the habit of choosing our own guests," retorted Lincoln. "We do not need from our friends either advice or assistance in the matter." See David Herbert Donald, *Lincoln* (Simon & Schuster, 1995), 475. Emilie would later pester Lincoln for a permit to sell cotton.

32 Henry Goodale Recollections, Michigan State University, East Lansing, MI. Goodale did not give West's first name, and places him on Hood's staff. As far as I can tell, there was no Captain West serving with Hood at this time, but there was a Capt. Douglas West, an Assistant Adjutant General on Brigadier General Deas's staff, of Hindman's division. Deas's brigade engaged Lytle's command on September 20, and later occupied the ground; West would likely have been familiar with the Rebel efforts to secure Lytle's remains.

the opened outer coffin: Lytle's sword and scabbard lay over the flag in the form of a cross. Flowers, evergreens, drooping willow, and other greenery surrounded the coffin and filled the hall, while burning incense and candles perfumed it."[33]

After Lytle was suitably honored by the men of the regiment, his body was shipped home to Cincinnati, Ohio. There, on October 22, an elaborate cortege escorted him to his final resting place in Spring Grove Cemetery. The entire affair was the largest funeral procession in Cincinnati's memory, with some 5,000 mourners lining the route to witness the hours-long procession. In the best martial tradition, Lytle's riderless horse was led behind the coffin, with boots reversed. James Garfield— Rosecrans's chief of staff, a future president of the United States, and eventual victim of an assassin's bullet—was one of the pall-bearers.[34]

Of course, few casualties received such lavish attention. The vast majority of the fallen were, and indeed had to be, buried where they lay. Since the Confederates held the field, it was the Army of Tennessee's details that labored for several weeks to clear the former battleground. As a result, many of the Rebel dead were identified and interred by family or friends, such as Private Cater had done for his brother Rufus, and the Reed brothers for John Ingraham. The Federals, by way of contrast, were usually buried in mass graves that were nothing more than shallow trenches scraped out of the earth; this is one reason why the number of Federal "missing" is so much higher than for Bragg's army, and why the National Cemetery in Chattanooga has so many unknown graves.

In many cases corpses were covered by nothing more than a few shovels full of dirt, heaped atop them where they lay on the ground. It was common for slaves—either from the surrounding area or traveling with the army—to be impressed for this sort of work. One who wielded a spade at Chickamauga was Mark Thrash, a 40-year-old servant accompanying the Rebel army. "The orders was to bury the Rebs in one trench, the Yanks in another, and the horses in another," he wrote many years later. "They say Longstreet had ordered it that

---

33 Ruth C. Carter, ed., *For Honor Glory & Union*, 200.

34 Ibid. Rosecrans relieved Garfield of his duty as chief of staff on October 13, 1863, so that Garfield could take his place in Congress. Garfield was traveling to Washington with reports; he had stopped in Cincinnati to discuss affairs with Gen. Jacob D. Cox, commander of the department and an old friend and political ally.

Former Confederate cavalryman Larkin Poe, picture here many years later, at the site of his former house.

Sartain, History of Walker County, Georgia, 1932

way, 'cause he didn't want the Blues and Grays to rise up and fight the battle all over."[35]

The ultimate resting places for most of Chickamauga's Confederate dead are widely scattered. A fair number of the fallen were removed from the field and shipped home, at least where home could be reached. One was Lt. Col. Axalla J. Hoole of the 8th South Carolina. Hoole was killed early in the afternoon of September 20 during Brig. Gen. Joseph B. Kershaw's first assault against Horseshoe Ridge. On October 3, Hoole's widow sought permission from the army to retrieve his body. Three weeks later, on October 21, her husband's body was retrieved from his temporary resting place. Along with his sword, scabbard, a rifle, and other personal belongings, his remains were loaded onto the train at Ringgold, destined for his home town of Darlington, South Carolina. Across the South, others would follow, assuming their relatives had the means to do so.[36]

---

35 Roscoe E. Lewis, "The Life of Mark Thrash," *The Phylon Quarterly*, vol. 20, no. 4 (4th Qtr, 1959), 399. In the first half of the 20th Century, Mark Thrash was something of a Chickamauga institution. He claimed he was born on Christmas Day 1820, and he died December 18, 1943, one week short of what would have been (supposedly) his 123rd birthday. A former slave in Virginia and Georgia, Thrash worked for the park commission from the 1890s until his death. See also Stephen O. Addison, *Seen the Glory: Mark Thrash Buried the Dead at Chickamauga, The Story of the Oldest Person of our Country, 1820-1943* (Steven O. Addison, Publisher, 1991).

36 Elizabeth Hoole McArthur, *The Sword Returns to Chickamauga: A True Chronicle of the Sword of Lieutenant Colonel Axalla John Hoole, 8th South Carolina Infantry, C.S.A.* (Dog Ear Publishing, 2010), 85. The author is a great granddaughter of Colonel Hoole. She donated the sword and other artifacts to the Chickamauga-Chattanooga National Military Park in 2001.

A string of Confederate graveyards followed the railroad southward. Cemeteries were established at Dalton, Resaca, and Marietta; the latter was the largest. Initially populated by mortally wounded men who traveled that far and then no farther, each contains a mix of men who fought at Chickamauga, Chattanooga, and in the battles for Atlanta. Most of these reburials occurred after the war, starting as early as 1866, as a devastated South struggled to honor its fallen menfolk.

Similar efforts were made for the Federal dead, although most of the efforts to recover Union bodies for shipment home began months later. In December, after the Union victory at Missionary Ridge forced the Army of Tennessee back to its winter quarters around Dalton, Georgia, the Federals once again had access to the old battlefield. What they found horrified them. Unburied remains littered a grotesque landscape in what the Yankees angrily regarded as a deliberate barbarity on the part of the Confederates. How many dead had been left uncovered or otherwise improperly cared for will never be known.

In all fairness, however, Confederate burial details were simply overwhelmed by the task before them. The field was huge, the terrain varied, and the number of dead men and animals staggering. Many men had been hastily interred in shallow mass graves, not as a slight to the Federals but with a nod toward nature; corpses could only remain untended for a short time before they became so fetid that it was unhealthy and even dangerous to handle them. Many were unearthed by feral pigs and other wild animals. The incessant October rains also washed away loose soil, which helped create the appalling scene the Army of the Cumberland found when its men ventured back to the field. Once more labor details, this time dressed in blue, swarmed over the area to recover fallen comrades.

One such party was led by Lt. Col. Carter Van Vleck of the 78th Illinois Infantry. On January 4, 1864, Van Vleck set out with a 60-man detachment from his regiment, their objective the recovery of the body of his friend, Maj. William Broaddus, who had fallen on September 20. Van Vleck later described the melancholy expedition in a letter home to his wife, Patty. "No one can know how terrible the conflict was without visiting the ground," explained the Illinois officer. "Not a tree, not a bush, no not a twig was left without the marks of the missels of death. . . . In one little tree just in front of our position . . . not more than five inches in diameter, I counted 26 bullet holes. In another not more than 7 inches through, I counted 56." By this time, most of the corpses had been gathered and buried, and when the men of the 78th Illinois reached that familiar part of Horseshoe Ridge, they found one large fresh grave that contained all of the 78th's dead.[37]

Van Vleck set his men to work, and described their efforts in detail:

> I ordered the whole grave to be laid open, which being done it presented a most horrid sight. The remains . . . were here piled together in a common mass. Here a bunch of ribs, there a pile of heads, in another place a quantity of hair, feet or hands. The bodies had remained unburied until decomposition had so far taken place that the parts would not hold together. . . . I almost despaired of finding or identifying the remains of Major Broaddus, but I knew that none were buried here but our own regiment & that we lost no other officers but him.

Van Vleck assumed that Broaddus would be found near the center of the jumbled mess, given where he fell and that point's relative proximity to where the grave had been dug. The gruesome work continued. Finally, wrote Van Vleck,

> After looking through the whole horrid accumulation of human fragment[s], I thought I discovered a coat different from the others. . . .[T]he vest was also there and like his & there the fatal shot through the collar of each which pierced his neck & laid him low. The head was gone, it had decayed away & all but the breast was under another corpse, which being raise[d] we found that the boots the pants & the overcoat were gone, but there were the striped shirt, the blue socks & knit drawers which I at once recognized.

The men searched for the major's head, and Van Vleck despaired at ever being able to locate it. Two skulls were closely examined and rejected, for they had full sets of lower teeth, while Broaddus was missing most of his. Then, at last, they found what they were seeking. "I found another skull which had no doubt been buried with the body," explained Van Vleck. "There could be no mistaking it. There was still left a tuft of light brown hair, there were the few front teeth in the upper jaw & the lower jaw with none. . . . Not one that was present doubted for a moment that we had found the remains of our lamented Major."

---

37 Carter Van Vleck, with Theresa K. Lehr and Phillip K. Gerber, eds., *Emerging Leader: The Letters of Carter Van Vleck to His Wife, Patty, 1862-1864* (IUniverse, 2012), 188, 191-192. Van Vleck's original letters are at Duke University.

Obtaining final proof produced perhaps the most difficult moment of all. Major Broaddus's son Thomas was present through the whole ordeal. During the ghastly excavation, Van Vleck had deliberately kept Thomas away from the grave and out of sight of all the remains. Now, at last, the young man was called over to confirm that it was his father. "He at once recognized the clothing and all the other marks," recalled Van Vleck. Sadly, no other members of the 78th could be similarly identified. All of them were dressed too much alike, and few possessed singular characteristics such as the Major's dentition by which they could be singled out. That spring Major Broaddus's remains returned home to McComb, Illinois, where he was re-interred by his grieving widow.

Eleven months after that fateful September afternoon on Horseshoe Ridge, Carter Van Vleck would follow his friend in death, shot in the head outside Atlanta on August 11, 1864. He was more fortunate than most men who fell at Chickamauga, for his wife and daughter were able to reach him just before he died less than two weeks later.[38]

*   *   *

General Orders No. 296} Hdqrs. Dept. of the Cumberland
Chattanooga, Tenn., December 25, 1863

It is ordered that a national cemetery be founded at this place in commemoration of the battles of Chattanooga, fought November 23, 24, 25, 26, and 27, and to provide a proper resting-place for the remains of the brave men who fell upon the fields fought over on those days, and for the remains of such as may hereafter give up their lives in this region in defending their country against treason and rebellion.

The ground selected for the cemetery is the hill lying beyond the Western and Atlantic Railroad, in a southeasterly direction from the town.

It is proposed to elect a monument upon the summit of the hill, of such materials as are to be obtained in this vicinity, which, like all the work upon the cemetery, shall be exclusively done by the troops of the Army of the Cumberland.

Plans for the monument are invited to be sent in to these headquarters.

38 Ibid., 188-9, 198.

When the ground is prepared notice will be given, and all interments of soldiers will thereafter be made in the cemetery, and all now buried in and around the town removed to that place.

By command of Maj. Gen. George H. Thomas:

Wm. D. Whipple
Assistant Adjutant-General.[39]

Among those dead "removed to that place" would also be the fallen Federals of Chickamauga.

---

39 OR 31, pt. 3, 487.

Chapter Five

The Consequences

In an odd twist of irony, the victorious Army of Tennessee and the defeated Army of the Cumberland suffered similar fallout from the battle of Chickamauga: turmoil within the officer corps and a purging of each army's command structure. Braxton Bragg seized upon this moment of rare success to rid his army of unwanted troublemakers, and in doing so touched off a command crisis so serious that President Jefferson Davis traveled to Georgia to resolve it. In the Federal camp, William Rosecrans and several of his subordinates faced harsh criticism and, for some, courts of inquiry.

As the hours stretched into days, and the days into weeks of frustrating siege, many of Bragg's subordinates forgot the uncertainty of what they faced that Monday morning after the battle and became increasingly vocal about their commander's failure to pursue the "beaten foe." Could the Rebels have overwhelmed the Federals that morning and destroyed part, or even all, of the Union Army? Since Bragg did not order an immediate pursuit or attempt any significant attack on George Thomas's position at Rossville Gap, the question will remain forever unanswered.

The siege of Chattanooga that followed the tactical Southern victory at Chickamauga consumed October and most of November. It was lifted by the combination of large Union reinforcements and aggressive new leadership, coupled with a deteriorating and unfocused Confederate command situation, all of which culminated in a resounding Union victory in what has come to be called The Battles for Chattanooga (November 23-25, 1863). The Federal triumph there negated any Confederate success gained at Chickamauga.

Within days of Chickamauga, Bragg's attention became focused not on the Federals, but a pool of insubordinate officers within his own command. On September 25, less than a week after the battle ended, Bragg sent Lt. Col. William K. Beard, a member of his inspector general's department, to Richmond, Virginia. Beard carried with him 30 captured Union flags, but his real mission was to hand-carry an extraordinary confidential letter from Bragg to President Davis. The letter outlined Bragg's concerns, which Beard himself would be present to amplify in more detail.

Among other things, Bragg detailed the following:

> We failed to capture two divisions in McLemore's Cove on the 10th, first by General Hill deciding the movement . . . impracticable, and failing to execute, then by a direct failure of General Hindman to obey my order after a force under General Buckner had taken the place of Hill. When on the field of Chickamauga I ordered Gen'l Polk [to attack] at daylight. . . . I sent to Genl Polk and found him after seven o'clk two miles in rear . . . unable to account for the delay.

> Genl Polk, though gallant and patriotic, is luxurious in his habits, rises late, moves slowly, and always conceives his own plans the best. He has proved an injury to us on every field where I have been associated with him.

> Genl Hill is despondent, dull, slow, and tho gallant personally, is always in a state of apprehension, and upon the most flimsy pretext makes each report of the enemy about him as to keep up constant apprehension, and require constant reinforcements. His open and constant croaking would demoralize any command in the world. He does not hesitate at all times and in all places to declare our cause lost.
> With Buckner, Hood or Cleburne in place of these two officers our strength would be far greater.[1]

Bragg had begun his prelude to purging the army even before Beard left with his letter for President Davis. His first volley was aimed directed at Polk. On September 22, Bragg dictated a tersely worded formal note to the bishop:

---

1 "My Dear Sir," September 25, 1863, Charles C. Jones Papers, DU. Beard, the lieutenant colonel of the 1st Florida Infantry, had been detailed to General Bragg's staff as an inspector general since March of 1862. Bragg would come to regret his endorsement of Buckner, who proved to be one of Bragg's biggest detractors and would not hesitate to tell Jefferson Davis so when the Confederate president visited the army that October.

GENERAL: The General commanding desires that you will make as early as practicable a report explanatory of your failure to attack the enemy at daylight on Sunday last in obedience to orders.[2]

Polk knew what was coming. Instead of responding immediately, he began marshaling his own resources for a counterattack. The next day, Polk sought out the views of Generals Hill and Longstreet. Hill took little convincing for he had long been soured on Bragg and understood that he was also in the commanding general's crosshairs. Longstreet, also, was already growing disenchanted with the state of affairs within the Army of Tennessee and was willing to help. Polk decided to apply the same sort of political heat that had worked for him in the past. He intended to write to his old friend Jefferson Davis, and he urged Longstreet to do the same. Longstreet declined to address Davis directly, but he did agree to send missives to the Confederate Secretary of War and to General Lee. On September 26, Old Pete Longstreet penned a damning letter to James Seddon that Longstreet knew full well would come to Davis's attention as soon as the war secretary read it. After setting forth a litany of complaints, Longstreet closed with a sweeping indictment of Braxton Bragg. The head of the Army of Tennessee, Old Pete observed, "has done but one thing he ought to have done since I joined this army. That was to order the attack upon the 20th. All other things that he has done, he ought not to have done."[3]

Problems within his command structure were nothing new for Bragg. Six months earlier in the aftermath of the battles of Perryville and Murfreesboro, personality and control issues resulted in a full-blown command crisis that almost resulted in Bragg's being relieved of command at that time. In the end, nothing of substance was resolved and the matter remained to fester. Now, in the aftermath of his stunning North Georgia success, Bragg intended to see this fight through to victory. On September 27, writing to his wife Elise, the gaunt army commander summed up his intentions: "Again I have to complain of Genl Polk for not obeying my orders and I am resolved to bring the matter to an issue this time. One of us must stand or fall." That same day—five days after he had first requested it—Bragg reiterated his demand for Polk to explain Sunday's failure. When Polk finally answered on September 28, he put all of the blame at

2 OR 30, pt. 2, 54.

3 Longstreet, *Manassas to Appomattox*, 465; OR 30, pt. 4, 706.

D. H. Hill's feet, a stab in the back that could hardly have been calculated to please the acerbic North Carolinian.[4]

Bragg didn't put any stock in Polk's excuses. The very next day, on September 29, the army commander began cleaning house. Generals Polk and Hindman were suspended from command and ordered to Atlanta, there to await military trials. Hindman was already absent, invalided as a result of his September 20 neck wound. Polk departed immediately. For the time being, D. H. Hill remained with the army, but he and Bragg were now clearly at odds.[5]

These events triggered an acute leadership crisis within the army, one that everyone could see coming except, apparently, Braxton Bragg. Chief of Staff William Mackall tried to warn his boss of the looming trouble. That same day, in a private letter to Gen. Joseph Johnston, Mackall predicted that "if Bragg carries out his projects, there will be great dissatisfaction. I have told him so, but he is hard to persuade when in prosperity, and I do not think my warning will be heeded until too late." Mackall could not have been more correct: Bragg was feeling politically and militarily prosperous, and he had no intent of backing down.[6]

On the heels of Mackall's prediction came a petition during the first few days of October calling for Bragg's resignation. The document made the rounds surreptitiously, circulating amongst his chief subordinates. Most of the army's senior officers signed it, including Longstreet, Hill, and Buckner (who was most likely the author). This remarkable document—unprecedented in American military history—was sent to President Davis on October 4. Among other charges, it set in place the foundation for the longstanding accusation that Bragg had fumbled away a huge victory. In a remarkably short span of time, the signers' collective memory had undergone significant revision. "Two weeks ago this army," explained the document, "elated by a great victory which promised to be the most fruitful of the war, was in readiness to pursue its defeated enemy. That enemy, driven in confusion from the field, was fleeing in disorder and panic-stricken across the Tennessee River." Only Bragg's inexplicable hesitation, the conspirators charged, allowed the Federals to create "a new Sebastopol" at Chattanooga. Forgotten entirely was the formidable Union

---

4 "My Dear Wife," September 27, 1863, Bragg Papers, Missouri Historical Society, St. Louis MO; *OR* 30, pt. 2, 47; Steven E. Woodworth, *Jefferson Davis*, 239.

5 *OR* 30, pt. 2, 56.

6 "September 29, 1863," William W. Mackall Papers, UNC.

presence at Ringgold on September 21, the prostrated and provision-less condition of the Army of Tennessee immediately after the battle, and the uncertainty over where the Federals had gone.[7]

Wholesale mutiny now seemed in the offing. On October 5, Davis received a further alarming telegram from Brig. Gen. James Chesnut, previously dispatched to serve as Davis's eyes and ears in Georgia. "Your immediate presence in this army is urgently demanded," wired Chesnut.[8]

Alarmed by this turn of events Davis raced to Georgia. He met with Chesnut in Atlanta, "to receive some information in advance." While there, Davis also met with the embattled Polk, who handed him another lengthy letter filled with excuses and railing against Bragg. Among other things, Polk charged Bragg with "criminal incapacity." Despite their friendship Polk made little headway, for Davis was still not inclined to replace Bragg. Indeed, he seemed to believe that he could smooth over the difficulties between Bragg and his subordinates and restore harmony to the Army of Tennessee. As if to provide further evidence of the president's naiveté, he brought with him yet one more general in the person of John C. Pemberton. Despite the disaster at Vicksburg, Davis still had faith in Pemberton and was even then seeking a suitable position for him within Bragg's army, commensurate with his rank.[9]

If so, Davis was seriously out of touch. Pemberton was widely disparaged for his role in the surrender of Vicksburg, and no one in the Army of Tennessee would welcome him as a lieutenant, let alone a lieutenant general and corps commander. Muttering among the rank and file indicated that "they would desert before they would serve under the traitor Pemberton." Even Old Army friends like William Mackall found Pemberton overbearing and insufferable.[10]

Once with the army, the president made things decidedly worse by forcing a face-to-face confrontation between Bragg and his critics. Davis seemed to believe the dissention was overblown and could be dissipated with frank discussion. In the end, the only one who got something he wanted was Davis,

---

7   OR 30, pt. 2, 65. Sebastopol was Russia's heavily fortified and entrenched naval base on the Black Sea, and the primary Franco-British objective during the Crimean War. As a result of that war, the strength of Sebastopol's defenses became world renowned.

8   OR 52, pt. 2, 538.

9   OR 52, pt. 2, 540; Lynda Lasswell Crist, ed., *The Papers of Jefferson Davis*, 14 vols. (Louisiana State University Press, 1991-2015), vol. 10, 11.

10 Michael B. Ballard, *Pemberton: A Biography* (University Press of Mississippi, 1991), 184.

Confederate President Jefferson Davis
Library of Congress

when he sustained Bragg as commander of the Army of Tennessee. Polk would not be charged or tried for disobedience but neither could he return to the army while Bragg was at its head. Instead, Polk switched places with Lt. Gen. William J. Hardee, who was then in Mississippi. Hardee was no friend of Bragg's, but both Davis and Bragg naively believed that Hardee would at least help mend some of the disharmony ripping apart the army's command structure. "I hope General Hardee will be able to aid you effectively in checking such discontents as those indicated," was how Davis put it. The recuperating Tom Hindman was reinstated, but he would not return to the army until December after he was fully recovered and his wife had given birth to a son. Under protest, D. H. Hill was sent packing, back to North Carolina, now bereft of a command. John C. Breckinridge stepped up to command Hill's corps. Bragg also reorganized the army, discarding the wing structure; Longstreet reverted to command of his corps, while Buckner lost both his quasi-independent departmental status (East Tennessee, after all, was now in Union hands) and command of his corps, reverting to divisional command under the incoming Hardee.[11]

Although no one knew it at the time, Bragg would be gone before Hindman returned. The stinging Rebel defeat at Chattanooga that at the end of

11 Ibid., 555; Diane Neal and Thomas W. Kremm, *The Lion of the South: General Thomas C. Hindman* (Mercer University Press, 1993), 179-180. Bragg suggested the idea of a swap on October 2, once he was aware that President Davis favored returning Polk to command. Davis traveled to Mississippi after leaving the Army of Tennessee to confer with William Hardee. Davis's hopeful comment on Hardee's influence demonstrates the president was seriously out of touch with the command crisis ripping apart the Army of Tennessee.

November expunged the success of Chickamauga, and the Army of Tennessee's morale plunged to a new low. During the two months between Chickamauga and Missionary Ridge, the Federals were rushing troops into the region from all directions while Bragg's army was shedding troops at an alarming rate. Richmond ordered him to send troops back to Mississippi, and Bragg compounded the government's short-sightedness by sending Longstreet's command into East Tennessee on what amounted to a forlorn hope against Knoxville in order to rid himself of a troublesome subordinate.[12]

Bragg never understood the full import of Chickamauga. Perhaps his biggest blunder was in failing to grasp that, although his original plan had failed, Longstreet's stunning success on September 20 offered new and important opportunities. Polk's Right Wing did not achieve the success Bragg envisioned, but Longstreet's attack achieved everything he could have asked for. Once the Georgian's troops broke through the Union lines and enemy army was routed off the field, Bragg had two promising opportunities: reinforce that success with some of Polk's troops, or make sure by his personal presence that Polk launched a full-scale attack on the Kelly Field line earlier in the afternoon— while George Thomas's attention was centered on Horseshoe Ridge.

Bragg was a good strategist, a competent planner, a solid logistician, and demonstrably capable of turning civilians into first-rate soldiers through training and discipline. He was also a failure as a leader, incapable of inspiring loyalty among his subordinates or forging disparate personalities into a functioning combat command. He could be remarkably inflexible on a field of battle. These latter two qualities hamstrung any success he achieved, and ultimately rendered Bragg unfit for high command. Mackall, who had worked closely with Bragg as his chief of staff since April 1863, condemned him in the harshest of terms. Again writing to Johnston, Mackall lamented that Bragg "has not genius, and if our circumstances make *this call* [here Mackall was referring to the likely prospect of a second great battle before the fate of Chattanooga would be decided] upon him, he will fail in our hour of need. His mind is not fertile nor is his judgment good."[13]

---

12 Within days of the battle, both Brig. Gens. Mathew D. Ector's and Evander McNair's brigades were en route back to Meridian Mississippi.

13 Mackall to Johnston, "September 29, 1863," Mackall Papers, UNC. Mackall thought that Bragg was sincere in his patriotism and dedication to the cause of Southern independence, but that was about all the good Mackall could find to say about the man.

Confederate Brigadier General
William W. Mackall
Library of Congress

After the wholesale disaster of Missionary Ridge on November 25, 1863, which had been preceded one day earlier by the Union victory atop Lookout Mountain, even Bragg knew his days at the head of the Army of Tennessee were numbered. Four days later Bragg offered his resignation and President Davis accepted. The reins of the army were temporarily turned over to Hardee, and in December to Joe Johnston on a permanent basis. Davis, meanwhile, made Bragg an advisor in Richmond, which removed him from the day-to-day leadership of troops. He briefly held field command again during the final weeks of the war in North Carolina against William T. Sherman. After the surrender, Bragg tried his hand at several careers, and was working in Galveston, Texas, in 1876 as an inspector of railroads when he dropped dead on a street corner. His name has become something of a byword for failure in the popular culture of the American Civil War.[14]

Bragg's departure did not cure what ailed the Army of Tennessee. Joe Johnston's tenure at the head of the army would last but seven months before terminating at the gates of Atlanta the following July. Johnston never held Davis's confidence, the goodwill between the two men having been severed during the war's early months over a matter as petty as rank. As far as Davis was concerned, Johnston's performance outside Richmond in 1862 and during the Vicksburg campaign the following year as a department head had done little to justify the responsibility consummate with leading an army in the field, but the president did not believe he had another viable option. In addition to his

---

14 Davis first offered Hardee permanent command of the Army of Tennessee, but Hardee refused, necessitating Johnston's appointment.

troubled relationship with Richmond, Johnston's tenure at the head of the Army of Tennessee was wracked by a spirit of second-guessing and back-biting among his corps commanders, very similar to Bragg's experience. Mutiny, or something close to it, seemed to have become endemic to the Army of Tennessee by 1864, a wasting condition for which the rank and file paid in blood.

James Longstreet had a significant effect both on the outcome at Chickamauga and as part of the turmoil that followed. The gap created by Tom Wood's departure that September 20 was not the only misstep General Rosecrans made during the complex battle, or the only opportunity he dangled —however inadvertently—before the Confederates over the course of those three days. Breaks in the Union line had occurred several times on September 19 and again on the morning of the 20th. John Breckinridge penetrated all the way into Thomas's rear at Kelly Field before being thrown back. However, Bragg's Confederates were unable to convert these momentary lodgments into larger successes.

The difference Longstreet brought onto the field in North Georgia was profound. He had a consummate ability to handle large numbers of men, and unlike many commanders on both sides, managed to get more than a division or two into the fight simultaneously. Instead of piecemeal attacks, he launched his September 20 assault with nearly his entire wing of the army, with much of it arranged in-depth. That result proved overwhelming. While Longstreet's performance was not flawless, it was indeed remarkable—all the more so because he was completely new to the field, having arrived only late the night before, and unfamiliar with both the terrain and most of the men comprising his new command. The result was a victory more complete than any the Army of Tennessee had experienced before. His stunning success earned him a new nickname: "Bull of the Woods."

Unfortunately, the poisoned atmosphere clinging to Bragg's command was contagious and directly affected Longstreet's subsequent relations within that army. The politically charged mood, which Bragg's post-battle purge only made worse, dismayed Longstreet. When someone in the army wrote up the infamous petition and circulated it, Longstreet heartily endorsed the idea. Once he signed the petition seeking Bragg's removal, relations between the two men grew outwardly rancorous. Bragg became convinced that Longstreet was agitating to supersede him, while Longstreet's disdain for his unhappy and dyspeptic commander grew with each passing day. Longstreet did not create this dissension—it existed long before he arrived on the scene. However, he also did nothing to discourage it.[15]

Some writing about this chapter of the army's history ascribe a darker motive to Longstreet's involvement: overweening personal ambition. Bragg biographer Judith Hallock, among the most extreme of Longstreet's critics, accused the Georgian of scheming to supplant Bragg from the minute he left Virginia. According to Hallock, Longstreet endorsed the idea of coming west only to get out from under General Lee's shadow and to obtain an independent command of his own at Bragg's expense.[16]

This school of thought distorts the actual impact of Longstreet's presence in two ways. First, it minimizes Longstreet's clear and demonstrable contributions to the victory on September 20. Second, it recasts the conflict between Bragg and his subordinates as a struggle between Bragg and Longstreet for dominance of the army. This is understandable given Longstreet's popular reputation as one of the Confederacy's premier combat generals by the summer of 1863 and his willingness to openly criticize Bragg, but in truth, the deep troubles within the command ranks of the Army of Tennessee long pre-dated Longstreet's arrival and would continue well after Longstreet returned to Virginia. That is not to say that Longstreet was blameless. He did nothing to distance himself from the imbroglio, even to the point of failing to quell rumors that he would soon take command. William Mackall observed this deteriorating situation with growing dismay, and at one point thought that "Longstreet has done more injury to the general than all the others put together." Longstreet was clearly opposed to Bragg, but the animosity within the Army of Tennessee's high command is best understood as a conflict between Bragg and Polk, with everyone else choosing sides.[17]

---

15 The authorship of the petition has never been fully ascertained, but Buckner is the most likely candidate. See Arndt. M. Stickles, *Simon Bolivar Buckner: Borderland Knight* (University of North Carolina, 1940), 232-235, for a full discussion.

16 Judith Lee Hallock, *General James Longstreet in the West: A Monumental Failure* (Ryan Place Publishers, 1995), 16-24, presents a highly critical view of Longstreet's experience and motives.

17 "September 29, 1863," Mackall Papers, UNC. Numerous historians have weighed in on this issue. For a negative view of Longstreet, see Thomas L. Connelly, *Autumn of Glory: The Army of Tennessee, 1862-1865* (Louisiana State University Press, 1986), 238-239; Judith Lee Hallock, *Braxton Bragg and Confederate Defeat, Volume II* (University of Alabama Press, 1991), 98-99; and Peter Cozzens, *This Terrible Sound: The Battle of Chickamauga* (University of Illinois Press, 1992), 531-533. For a more positive view of Longstreet's role, see Donald Bridgman Sanger and Thomas Robson Hay, *James Longstreet: I. Soldier II. Politician, Office-holder, and Writer* (Louisiana

Longstreet had indeed lost faith in Bragg, but the idea that Longstreet wanted the command for himself is wholly speculative—and problematic on another front. Longstreet was an admirer of Joseph E. Johnston and had urged President Davis to bring Johnston in to command the Army of Tennessee. This is not the action of a man putting forth his own cap for the position. In his September 26 letter to James Seddon, Longstreet also pleaded for Robert E. Lee to come west and take the job—a request he reiterated to Lee himself in private letters dispatched to the Virginia general.

Lee had no desire to command the Army of Tennessee, and in any case Davis was highly unlikely to accede to any such request. Davis's long-standing feud with Johnston precluded that officer's chances at command, at least initially, and Lee, who was too valuable in Virginia protecting the Confederate capital at Richmond, strongly resisted the idea of coming west even on a temporary basis. Modern detractors have used these points as evidence of Machiavellian maneuvering on Longstreet's part by disingenuously putting forth candidates he knew that, for one reason or another, would be rejected. What can be asserted without supposition is that with Polk away from the army, Longstreet emerged (as Maj. Gen. Lafayette McLaws phrased it) "the nominal head of [the] cabal" against Bragg. In the end, all came to naught, for Davis sustained Bragg, with Longstreet reverting to corps command.[18]

In October, after a series of confused engagements at Brown's Ferry and Wauhatchie in Lookout Valley, Longstreet's troops failed to prevent the Union army from reopening a direct supply line to Bridgeport. Bragg sent him with his men into East Tennessee to operate against the Union forces holding Knoxville, a move designed as much to rid himself of Longstreet as to recapture East Tennessee. Short of both troops and especially transport, it was an effort unlikely to succeed. In what can only be described as a miserable winter campaign, Longstreet failed to retake Knoxville and fell to quarreling with

---

State University Press, 1952), 211-216. Despite the rather odd title, it is an interesting book that deserves more attention that it has heretofore garnered. See also William Garrett Piston, *Lee's Tarnished Lieutenant: James Longstreet and His Place in Southern History* (University of Georgia Press, 1987), 66-68, 73-76, which offers perhaps the most balanced view of the controversy. Jeffrey Wert, *General James Longstreet, The Confederacy's Most Controversial Soldier: A Biography* (Simon and Schuster, 1993), 324-325, concludes that Longstreet was, at the least, guilty of duplicity and self-promotion.

18 *OR* 30, pt. 4, 706; Wert, General James Longstreet, 325.

officers in his own command, a microcosm of the unfortunate miasma that permeated Bragg's army.

Longstreet's detachment also weakened Bragg's army outside Chattanooga just before the Federals struck back at the end of November. Bragg's retreat into North Georgia left Longstreet cut off, and had no choice but to retreat into southwest Virginia. In the spring of 1864, Longstreet and his men returned to Lee and the Army of Northern Virginia. In his first battle back, Longstreet was badly wounded in the Wilderness in early May and spent most of the rest of 1864 recuperating. He returned to limited field command later that year during the siege of Petersburg and Richmond, and was with Lee and the Virginia when the end arrived in early April 1865.

After the war, Longstreet urged rapid reconciliation, joined the Republican Party, and became a scapegoat for many of his fellow Confederates. Controversies erupted around his blunt criticisms of former commanders, especially Lee. He was blamed for a variety of mistakes, including his failure to make a supposed dawn attack at Gettysburg on July 2, which cost the South its chance at independence—at least according to his critics. These accusations have served to obscure his real record during the war.

The army's other wing commander, Leonidas Polk, had just a few months left to live. In May 1864, Polk and his Mississippi command rejoined the Army of Tennessee to help Johnston defend Atlanta against Maj. Gen. William T. Sherman. On June 14, at Pine Mountain north of Atlanta, Polk was killed instantly by a Union artillery shell that virtually disemboweled him. The affable Polk was popular with the rank and file, but his military talents were never equal to his high rank. More than any other general except Bragg, Polk's limitations cost the Army of Tennessee the fruits of a much more significant victory on September 20, 1863. While Maj. Pollack Lee's fanciful tale of finding Polk comfortably ensconced on a farmhouse porch taking a leisurely breakfast seems fabricated out of whole cloth, Polk's undeniable lack of attention in coordinating the dawn attack expected of him was still a shocking failure. Polk's inability to control D. H. Hill throughout the day highlights the Bishop-General's overall ineffectuality.

John Bell Hood earned a permanent corps command based on his performance at Chickamauga. While he exerted little influence in the confused fighting of the 19th, his role on the 20th was significant. After the breakthrough, he and Bushrod Johnson shifted the axis of attack from the west to the north, and Hood was in the process of orchestrating a larger effort against Horseshoe Ridge when he fell severely wounded. Had he died, it is quite possible he would be remembered today as another Stonewall Jackson, struck down at the pinnacle of success, a blow that cost the South ultimate victory. About the only thing Bragg and Longstreet could agree upon was that Hood should be promoted to lieutenant general, a course of action both men urged upon Secretary of War Seddon within days of Hood's wounding.

Hood lived to return to the Army of Tennessee, first at the head of a corps and then as the commander of that Army when Davis replaced Joe Johnston outside Atlanta in July 1864. Perhaps a bit of Polk's spirit inhabited Hood, for as a corps commander he repeatedly criticized his new chief in confidential, out-of-channels letters to President Davis and to Davis's new advisor, Bragg. Johnston was cautious by nature, and loathe to attack; Hood and Davis both embraced the spirit of the offensive. In Hood, Davis got all the offensive spirit he could ask for. Once he supplanted Johnston in July, Hood launched a series of attacks around Atlanta, all of which were bloody failures. That fall, with President Davis's blessing, Hood mounted a forlorn hope offensive into Middle Tennessee that brought about the disastrous battle of Franklin at the end of November and a final engagement outside Nashville that wrecked his army. Hood's tenure as army commander during the last half of 1864 had a tremendously negative effect on his postwar reputation. Today, he is largely seen as brilliant in brigade command, a competent division and corps leader, but promoted above his abilities, with disastrous results.[19]

Simon Bolivar Buckner was little more than a spectator during the battle of Chickamauga. When Bragg named Buckner as an able contrast to Polk or Hill in his letter to Davis, he woefully misjudged the Kentuckian. On September 19, one-half of his men were parceled out to other parts of the field. When called on to support Hood, however, instead of leading his remaining division into action, Buckner sent only a single brigade in response. On the 20th, Buckner's

---

19 Historians hold conflicting views about the propriety of these communiqués, which President Davis (and others) requested. There is less debate as to whether Hood's missives contributed to Davis's growing dissatisfaction with Joe Johnston. For a critical view of Hood's actions, see Connelly, *Autumn of Glory*, 322-324, 416-418. Brian Craig Miller, *John Bell Hood and the Fight for Civil War Memory* (University of Tennessee Press, 2010), 107-117, and Stephen M. Hood, *John Bell Hood: The Rise, Fall, and Resurrection of a Confederate General* (Savas Beatie, 2013), 19-29, offer more positive appraisals of Hood's conduct. The latter study is especially effective in its examination of what other authors have written or claimed about Hood's generalship and the sources, or lack thereof, upon which they relied. For more on this subject, see also Stephen M. Hood, ed., *The Lost Papers of General John Bell Hood* (Savas Beatie, 2015), a compilation with annotations of the general's wartime and postwar papers long thought lost or destroyed.

command responsibilities were effectively superseded by Longstreet exerting direct control over his divisions, leaving Buckner with little more to do than orchestrate artillery fire. The greatest missed opportunity for both Longstreet and Buckner came when Hood was struck down. Hood's loss removed the one man controlling the actions of the several divisions moving against Horseshoe Ridge, a situation that cried out for an immediate replacement. With Buckner at his side, Longstreet had an experienced senior officer who could step in and take charge. While it is impossible to know whether Buckner would have provided the continuity and coordination the Confederates so badly needed along Horseshoe Ridge, Longstreet's decision (or lack thereof) to not replace Hood as tactical commander of the First Corps was a serious error. Longstreet's failure to realize that the assault needed a directing hand resulted in a bloody series of piecemeal attacks against Horseshoe Ridge. Even George Thomas's sense of military pride was offended by the disjointed nature of the Confederate effort. At one point the Union general exclaimed, "The damned scoundrels are fighting without any system!"[20]

Simon Buckner's deep involvement in the various cabals against General Bragg damaged his credibility as a senior commander. Bragg must have been especially shocked when, in the face-to-face confrontation, Buckner spoke out against him. On October 13, two days after that extraordinary meeting, The Department of East Tennessee was disbanded; One part was merged into Bragg's sphere of authority, and the remainder was reassigned to Maj. Gen. Samuel Jones, who commanded in southwest Virginia. This decision effectively stripped Buckner of even the fiction of still holding an independent command. Nor did Buckner retain the command of a corps, reverting instead to lead but a division.

Subsequently, both Buckner and his troops were sent to join Longstreet in East Tennessee. Longstreet continued to hold him in high esteem, and General Lee concurred: Both men recommended that Buckner take permanent charge of Hood's old division that December. Instead, that position went to another, and in May 1864 Buckner was transferred to the Trans-Mississippi, where he ended the war as Gen. Kirby Smith's chief of staff. He met with more success once the shooting stopped when he was elected governor of Kentucky, in 1887, and, in 1896, when he ran for vice president alongside another governor,

---

20 Powell, *Glory or the Grave*, 570.

former Union general and fellow Chickamauga alumni John M. Palmer of Illinois.[21]

William H. T. Walker also lost his corps command after Chickamauga, not as retaliation for dissension, but through a lack of seniority. As Bragg shuffled troops and commanders in the wake of the attempted mutiny, Walker reverted to division command, which he retained through the next year. He was killed on July 22, 1864, during the battle of Atlanta leading his men into an attack. Given his limited sphere of authority, Walker performed well at Chickamauga. His aggressiveness was exactly the spirit the Confederate army needed on that field but which seemed lacking in so many other officers.

Daniel Harvey Hill was sure he would be scapegoated for the things that went wrong at Chickamauga. In fact, Hill deserves a significant share of blame in his own right. Hill's contrarian nature and gloomy, dyspeptic attitude cast a pall over Bragg's headquarters, just as had happened earlier with Lee's Virginia army. Hill's military judgments were often unsound. His advocacy of crossing the Tennessee River in early September to attack the Union XXI Corps was foolhardy and might have spelled disaster if Bragg had acted upon it. Hill's mulishness on Pigeon Mountain hampered Bragg's efforts to coordinate any attack against Negley in McLemore's Cove, and Hill's bad intelligence concerning the movements of the Union XX Corps on September 13 forced Bragg to turn away from his northern flank—at a critical moment—to deal with what proved to be a non-existent threat to La Fayette.

By the time Bragg received Hill's alarmist (and false) warnings of Federals crossing West Chickamauga Creek at Glass Mill on September 18, the commanding general was starting to routinely discount Hill's dispatches. Hill's attitude regarding the botched attack on September 20, however, did the most harm. His failure to find General Polk and receive his orders on the night of the 19th entirely disrupted Bragg's plans for the 20th. His deployment once the fighting finally commenced was poor. Hill's foolish quarrelling with Polk and Walker while Breckinridge's men desperately needed reinforcements was inexcusable. Hill compounded the errors of the morning by completely misreading the movement of the Union Reserve Corps that afternoon. He was chiefly responsible for the fact that Polk's wing played no role in the fighting for four critical hours while George Thomas's efforts were entirely focused on

21 David S. Heidler and Jeanne T. Heidler, eds. *Encyclopedia of the American Civil War*, 5 vols. (ABC-CLIO, 2000), vol. 1, 307-308.

Horseshoe Ridge. The right wing did not rejoin the fight until well after 4:00 p.m., largely due to Hill's unwillingness to attack. Hill's performance throughout all of September 20 was unrelievedly disappointing.

Given this poor track record, it is not surprising that Bragg shipped Hill off to Richmond as soon as he could, much to Hill's dismay. After visiting the Army of Tennessee, Davis concurred. On October 11, Bragg explained his reasons to the War Department: "With a view to the more efficient organization and command of this army I beg you will relieve Lieut. Gen. Hill from duty with it. Possessing some high qualifications as a commander he still fails to such an extent in others more essential that he weakens the moral and military tone of his command. A want of prompt conformity to orders of great importance is the immediate cause of this application." Believing that the stigma attached to being relieved would label him a coward, in an effort to clear his name Hill demanded, but never received, a court of inquiry. His temporary appointment to the rank of lieutenant general lapsed when Davis refused to send his name before the Confederate Senate for confirmation. Thereafter, D. H. Hill saw little service. In 1865 fate would bring Hill and Bragg together again for one last battle, at Bentonville.[22]

Both of Braxton Bragg's cavalry commanders failed him repeatedly throughout the campaign and battle, but Bragg held them to very different standards. From the middle of August, when the campaign began, until the end of September, Joseph Wheeler was repeatedly out of position, late, or insubordinate. His personal loyalty to Braxton Bragg, however, as exhibited by his refusal to have anything to do with the infamous petition, ensured that he would not only retain his command but see his responsibilities increase: In October, Bragg placed Forrest and his men under Wheeler's direct command.

Conversely, Forrest was sent away from the army, disgraced at least in Bragg's eyes. Though Forrest had his share of failures, he exhibited more energy than Wheeler and a growing degree of competence, a promise that might have served the Army of Tennessee well in time. But Forrest had little patience with what he perceived as incompetence, and he viewed Bragg as incapable. By the end of the campaign Bragg was equally disdainful of Forrest, dismissing the Tennessean as "nothing more than a good raider." Infuriated at being forced to

---

22 "October 11, 1863," Bragg to Davis, D. H. Hill Papers, North Carolina Division of Archives and History.

serve under Wheeler, Forrest applied for a transfer to Mississippi and Bragg was happy to let him leave.[23]

Eleven men commanded Confederate infantry divisions at Chickamauga. At least five (Liddell, Gist, Johnson, Kershaw, and Law) had been thrust into the new role at that level of command either because of Bragg's last-minute restructuring, or because of a temporary field promotion. Of the remaining six men (Breckinridge, Cleburne, Cheatham, Hindman, Preston, and Stewart), two (Preston and Hindman) were new to the Army of Tennessee, if not to senior command. This meant that only one-third of Bragg's division-level leadership had been previously tested at that rank prior to Chickamauga. Given the difficult terrain and the confused nature of the fighting, few of these men excelled there. In fact, there wasn't much chance to do so. Divisions were flung one after the other into the fight by Bragg or other senior officers with little or no support, and often with subordinate brigades peeled away at the last minute for divergent missions. Still, at least three men achieved impressive successes despite these obstacles, their commands tearing significant holes in the Union line. Bushrod Johnson's small provisional division fought well on all three days, and Johnson himself proved indefatigable in pressing the advantage wherever possible. Breckinridge and A. P. Stewart also did well. Had their earlier successes been properly supported, Rosecrans would have suffered a much more significant defeat at Chickamauga than the one history has recorded.

For Johnson, Chickamauga proved the apogee of his career track. Transferred to Virginia with Longstreet, he fought under Lee in 1864-5. Caught up in the final disasters leading to Appomattox, Johnson fell out of Lee's favor and was relieved of command and ordered home on April 8, 1865. He died in poverty in 1880. Breckinridge and Stewart both continued to rise in rank. Breckinridge commanded in the Shenandoah Valley in 1864, drubbing Union Maj. Gen. Franz Sigel's small army at the Battle of New Market. Breckinridge ended the war as the Confederacy's last secretary of war. A. P. Stewart rose to corps command in 1864 in the Army of Tennessee after Polk was killed outside Atlanta. Stewart finished the war in North Carolina as the last commander of the Army of Tennessee, by then only a division-sized remnant.[24]

23 Hughes, *Liddell's Record*, 150. See also Powell, *Failure in the Saddle*, 205-213, for a more detailed analysis of both cavalry commanders.

24 Charles M. Cummings, *Yankee Quaker, Confederate General: The Curious Career of Bushrod Johnson* (The Generals Books, 1993), 328.

Patrick Cleburne, who would become one of the most famous of all Confederate generals, simply had no chance to shine at Chickamauga. While he made no egregious blunders there, his star had yet to fully ascend. He would do better in later battles, most notably in saving the army at Ringgold Gap after its devastating defeat at Missionary Ridge. Cleburne was cut down at the battle of Franklin in November 1864, achieving Confederate martyrdom akin to Stonewall Jackson and Jeb Stuart.

*   *   *

The turmoil within Union ranks was even more turbulent. The scope of the Federal defeat, coupled with the ignominy of a virtual rout that included about one-third of the Federal army, came with severe repercussions.

On October 9, the War Department issued an order that radically restructured the Army of the Cumberland. The first to go were Thomas Crittenden, Alexander McCook, and James Negley. This directive merged the XX and XXI corps, renamed the IV Corps, with Gordon Granger in command. Granger's Reserve Corps was similarly folded into George Thomas's existing XIV Corps. The merger left Crittenden and McCook without official duties; both officers were ordered to retire to Indianapolis and await courts of inquiry into their conduct during the battle. Negley, who commanded a division in Thomas's corps, was also relieved pending investigation, and the regiments in his division were reassigned, reducing the XIV Corps from four divisions to three.[25]

William Starke Rosecrans was relieved of command on October 17, 1863, though the order did not reach him until the 19th. In the immediate aftermath of the Chickamauga disaster, Ulysses S. Grant was given authority over the entire Western Theater and ordered to go to Chattanooga to take personal charge of operations there. En route from Mississippi, Grant met with Secretary of War Edwin Stanton, who gave the general the choice of keeping Rosecrans or replacing him. Grant decided to sack Rosecrans and elevate George Thomas in his stead. Soon thereafter, Rosecrans and Grant met briefly

---

25 *OR* 30, pt. 4, 126, 253-4. Ultimately, a large number of regiments were reshuffled, even between the two remaining Union corps during this reorganization, changing corps and commanders.

at Stevenson, Alabama, where the former army commander summarized the current situation in the department for the new man.[26]

Rosecrans took his leave of the army on the morning of October 20 as quietly as he could manage. That quiet would not last long. Rosecrans's removal was a major story, and the news of his removal filled papers across the country with accusation, speculation, and refutation. Rosecrans's arrival in Cincinnati was met by an enormous reception, an overwhelming outpouring of public support for him, and a harsh repudiation of his replacement. Rumors, each more wild than the last, flew from the pens of editors and reporters alike. Democratic papers saw Machiavellian machinations in the news and waxed vitriolic: "They slew him with poison whom they feared to meet with steel. Already the maggots are active on the carcass of the fallen lion."[27] Pro-administration papers charged Rosecrans with incompetence, cowardice, and even drug use. In Richmond, the *Daily Dispatch* gleefully repeated these tidings for its own readers. "[Rosecrans] exceeded his instructions and was unsuccessful," repeated the *Dispatch* editor, quoting the *Philadelphia Inquirer*. "[H]e aimed to take Atlanta, when he should have been content with Chattanooga." Alternatively, word from Washington suggested there was "the mortifying [reason] of cowardice in the presence of the enemy," supposedly bolstered by "charges . . . preferred against him by Generals McCook and Crittenden of unofficer-like conduct on the battlefield." The rumor "that he had an attack of epilepsy during the battle, and that he was subject to that disease, is untrue," noted the *Daily Dispatch*. More credible was this idea: That Rosecrans "was constitutionally and by education subject to fits of religious depression of the profoundest character . . . is well known. In connection with this it may not be unsuitable to add that it is understood that the fourth specification of the preferred charge is an excessive use of opium."[28]

The men of the Army of the Cumberland would remember Rosecrans's relief with great sadness. Over time, they came to see Chickamauga as a victory, not a defeat. "Although Rosy was removed from us by red tape," complained Illinois Pvt. W. H. Austin, "Chattanooga was taken and held to a certainty. . . . The day Rosecrans was removed [t]here were more long faces that day than I

26 Lamers, *The Edge of Glory*, 398. [NC?]

27 Ibid., 401.

28 "Latest from the North," *Richmond Daily Dispatch*, October 26, 1863. Rosecrans laughed off these charges in his speech to the crowd at Cincinnati.

ever saw in the army[,] for when we started for a place we always expected to take it. We never knew what defeat was, and I think that every soldier that belonged to that army felt as I did."[29]

Of course, neither Crittenden nor McCook tried to bring charges against Rosecrans, and he had not suffered an attack of epilepsy or consumed opium—but he did leave the field before the battle was over, and that act doomed him. Rosecrans was denied a formal inquiry and, in January 1864, given command of the Department of Missouri. In effect, an assignment that sidelined him for the duration of the fighting.

George Thomas was given command of the Army of the Cumberland, a position he would hold until the close of the war. Thomas, sometimes thought a little slow to move, had always been respected by his peers. Now his public reputation soared. One afternoon of fighting had turned him into "The Rock of Chickamauga"—a moniker bestowed on him by Garfield—the man who saved the army when all seemed lost. It was a reputation fully earned, and his steadiness in the face of crisis was essential to the successful defense of Horseshoe Ridge. The Virginia native served well throughout the upcoming Chattanooga and Atlanta campaigns. His last battlefield success, at Nashville in December of 1864, smashed what was left of the Rebel Army of Tennessee. Sent west after the war, Thomas died in 1870, in California. Thomas was throughout his life a reserved and intensely private man. In an act lamented by historians ever since, upon his death, his grieving wife burned all of George Thomas's personal papers.

John Brannan and Thomas Wood also emerged with enhanced reputations. These two men and their commands, more than any others, made the defensive stand possible. Despite having his division flanked and shattered, Brannan orchestrated the initial defense of Hills One and Two. His various brigades never fully regained their cohesion that afternoon, but that fact did not seem to affect the tenacity of their defense. Brannan refused to give up, rallied his enough of his own and parts of several other divisions—perhaps as many as 2,500 men—to hold the position long enough for reinforcements to arrive. His efforts earned Brannan a Regular Army brevet promotion, and Thomas ultimately made him chief of the army's artillery.

Despite his central role in the army's most controversial order, Tom Wood's subsequent actions earned him promotion and continued success. Had

29 W. H. Austin, "How the Boys Remember Rosy," *National Tribune*, June 14, 1883.

he simply sought a defensive line for Harker's men or, even worse, followed Negley off the field, the first Rebel push against Horseshoe Ridge could have gone much differently. Instead, Wood launched a counterattack that bought Brannan the critical time he needed to forge a new line atop Horseshoe Ridge. Charles Harker's advance back down the Glenn Kelly Road and then through Dyer Field repulsed Jerome Robertson's Texans at an important juncture. When the Texans fell back, their retreat triggered similar withdrawals by fellow Confederates David Coleman and William F. Perry, crippling Bushrod Johnson's advance and effectively removing Evander Law's division from the battle. Perhaps most the most critical loss during this time was Hood himself, which disrupted Confederate command and control at a pivotal moment in the action. In the event, Joe Kershaw made the first attack against the ridge with only part of his brigade, barely supported by some of Ben Humphreys's Mississippians. If Hood had still been in effective control, it is very possible he would have attacked Brannan's line with as many as four or five Rebel brigades. All of those factors changed with Wood's decision.

Though Rosecrans would later attack Wood for not questioning the infamous order directing him "to close up and support Reynolds," at the time Rosecrans seems to have borne no grudge against the division commander. In fact, Wood was one of those Rosecrans singled out for promotion and praise. On October 15, Rosecrans made special mention of Wood and Brannan. Of Wood, he wrote, "On the battle on the 19th he did his duty in the fight well. In that of the 20th, after the right was shattered, he, with two brigades of his division and one of Van Cleve's, maintained himself against attacks of the rebels with firmness, skill, and determination."[30]

Subsequently, Wood's division played an integral role in the successful attack on Missionary Ridge that November and performed well in the Atlanta Campaign the following year. Badly wounded in September 1864, he refused to leave the field and again played a central role in inspiring his command. He ultimately rose to lead a corps at the battle of Nashville under Thomas. Wood retired from the army in 1868, was granted a full pension for his wounds, and vigorously defended his reputation concerning the order of September 20 during the last three decades of his life.

Two other men rode away from Snodgrass Hill with public plaudits: Gordon Granger and James B. Steedman. Some of the hyperbole concerning

30 OR 30, pt. 4, 387.

their march to join Thomas is overwrought, for Rosecrans's orders for September 20 authorized Granger to support Thomas, and Granger was not exceeding those orders when he marched south. Of course, he was also expected to protect the Rossville Gap. The conflict inherent in those two missions posed something of a dilemma, and Granger did take a risk: had a significant Rebel thrust materialized to seize the gap while he led Steedman's brigades south, any subsequent blame would certainly have fallen upon his shoulders.

Nonetheless, Granger's decision to take two of his three brigades as well as his ammunition train to Thomas was no less important in sustaining the defense of Horseshoe Ridge than the earlier efforts by Brannan and Wood. Once there, however, his impact on the rest of the battle was minimal. He did not play a prominent role in leading his infantry regiments during the struggle. In fact, he seems not to have left Thomas's side for most of the afternoon except to sight and fire cannon, a task normally reserved for sergeants and corporals. When Thomas left for Kelly Field, as senior officer Granger's leadership was needed to orchestrate the final retreat. In those last minutes, however, Granger was nowhere to be found – instead he returned to Rossville.

Granger's uneven performance on September 20 foreshadowed later problems. When the army was reorganized, Granger received command of the newly created IV Corps. His troops played a prominent role at Missionary Ridge, but he failed to inflict much damage against James Longstreet's forces in East Tennessee later that winter. A sarcastic telegram sent from Knoxville in December (perhaps imprudently composed while intoxicated) earned the displeasure of Granger's superiors, and he was banished to peripheral operations on the Gulf coast for the rest of the war. Gordon Granger served in the postwar U. S. Army until his death in 1876. Chickamauga was the high point of his career.[31]

James Steedman's role in the fight was dramatic. While Granger busied himself playing with artillery near Thomas's headquarters, Steedman led his division into the very teeth of the action. His personal presence kept more than one regiment on the line at a critical moment, and his penchant for seizing flags ensured that all eyes were drawn to him throughout the battle. He proved to be exactly the kind of leader most needed that afternoon, and played a significant role in holding Thomas's right flank.

---

31 Heidler and Heidler, *Encyclopedia of the Civil War*, vol. 2, 862.

Despite the accolades won at Chickamauga, promotion did not come quickly. Steedman was, after all, a Democrat, and his Ohio newspaper had questioned the wisdom of immediate emancipation. In the radical-controlled Republican Senate, where all promotions were vetted, both of these were black marks against him. Still, he rose to major general in April 1864.[32]

Ironically, black troops would play a prominent role in the rest of Steedman's military career. He commanded rear area forces during the Atlanta campaign and, in August 1864, defended Sherman's supply line at Dalton while leading a relief column composed in part of black soldiers. His aggressive tactics drove off Joe Wheeler's Rebel troopers.[33] That December at Nashville, Steedman led two brigades of U.S. Colored Troops in another dramatic attack. By the end of the war, he was a stout defender of the qualities of blacks as soldiers and citizens. He left the Army in 1866 for a variety of government jobs and also ran his newspaper in Toledo, Ohio.

The dark side of Steedman's quest for fame manifested itself in his postwar quarrels with Granger. Steedman claimed it was he, not Granger, who had made the decision to march to Thomas, and falsely asserted that he was not under Granger's command at the time. Partisans of the two men squared off in print and public oration, beginning a feud that would last many years. Steedman performed heroics enough at Chickamauga. He had no need to attempt to steal Granger's thunder as well, but his personality would not let the matter rest.

*   *

Thousands of men on both sides, from brigade commanders to young drummer boys, fought in the terrible battle in North Georgia, and many played more important roles than the handful of senior officers discussed above. The nature of the terrain meant that senior officers often had little sense of the moment-to-moment fight and little or no control or influence over specific actions. As a result, the burdens of command fell heavily upon junior and non-commissioned officers—the tough men who rallied their broken units when they were flanked, or seized the moment when fleeting tactical opportunity beckoned.

32 Warner, *Generals in Blue*, 473.

33 Shanks, *Personal Recollections*, 287.

On September 18, this burden fell most heavily upon John T. Wilder and Robert H. G. Minty, who with a mere handful of men badly disrupted General Bragg's planned offensive, forcing the Confederates to fight for the creek crossings and costing them an entire day—time that Rosecrans put to good use to gather his own scattered army. The following day, September 19, saw some of the most confused fighting of the war. Time and again, division and brigade commanders on both sides were thrust into action with only the sketchiest of ideas of where their own units or the enemy were to be found. Bragg's parting injunction to Maj. Gen. Alexander P. Stewart that he must be "governed by circumstances" applied equally to any number of other officers that day on either side of the line.

September 19 bears the hallmarks of a large-scale meeting engagement, albeit one seemingly conducted with most of the participants blindfolded. On multiple occasions men found themselves fighting on radically changed axes, oriented east-west one minute, and north-south the next. Units were repeatedly outflanked. Even the steadiest of veterans willing to sustain gruesome losses in a frontal fight will collapse into rout when their flanks are threatened and being surrounded seems a real possibility.

It is a tribute to the veteran nature of both armies that despite these repeated episodes of flanking and routing, time and again units reformed and returned to action. It is worth noting that in most of the great battles of the Civil War, the pace and nature of combat was quite different from that seen at Chickamauga. In many other battles, units engaged, endured terrific fighting for a period of time, and then passed to the flanks or rear to let fresh troops join the combat. Alternatively, the focus of action might shift from sector to sector, again letting new commands bear the brunt of the next encounter. This was not typical of Chickamauga. There, regiment after regiment found itself in the midst of the firestorm not once, but twice or even three times over the course of a single day, and double that over the span of the entire three days' engagement. The men of John Croxton's Federal brigade, for example, faced two major engagements on the morning of the 19th, and two more major combats on the 20th, the last concluding with the prolonged firefight atop Horseshoe Ridge. John Fulton's Confederate brigade spearheaded major efforts on all three days of the battle, and it was engaged from the opening shots on the 18th until the very last hour on the 20th. By the time Arthur Manigault's combined Alabama-South Carolina brigade was struggling up those same steep slopes alongside Fulton's Tennesseans on the afternoon of September 20, Manigault's men were making their third assault of the day, all within three hours.

Any one of the engagements just related might have been enough to shatter a given regiment and render it at least temporarily combat ineffective. But that didn't happen at Chickamauga. Even after the large-scale disaster of September 20, the Federals who rallied atop Horseshoe Ridge did so of their own volition, and the initial gathering there had as much to do with individual tenacity and a stubborn unwillingness to admit defeat as it did with the presence of any general. Men rallied individually or in small groups, knitting together a hasty line that had little to do with unit integrity. A number of regiments later justified the placement of their monuments on Horseshoe Ridge because of the fragmentary knots of men who had collected themselves—at times haphazardly so—to become that first defensive line. Modern visitors often leave with the mistaken impression that those knots were preexisting, well organized tactical formations. Except in rare instances, such as when Harker's brigade exhibited such splendid fire discipline out in the Snodgrass cornfield, the men who rallied and initially held Horseshoe Ridge did so with little regard to tactical manuals. They simply refused to quit.

Storming the hill from below, the Confederates displayed no less tenacity, despite their own increasing disorganization. Repeated charges by the same formations, time and again, proved that they bore the same determination as exhibited among the blue ranks. Kershaw's South Carolinians entered the fight about 1:00 p.m. with their first rush toward the crest. The survivors were still in the fight at dusk, supporting Archibald Gracie's brigade. A nucleus of Bushrod Johnson's men was even more obdurate: they eventually drove Steedman's Federals off the crest after hours of exhausting fighting. By the close of fighting on September 20, tactical organization was largely gone; men advanced or retreated in small bands, fighting as they went, without regard to dressing ranks.

All of this explains why, in the collective memories of North and South, Chickamauga became the quintessential soldiers' battle. Sergeants, lieutenants, captains, and natural leaders from the ranks directed the action far more than brigade or even regimental commanders. Panoramic vistas were luxuries mostly found on other fields. At Chickamauga, visibility might extend as far as a couple of hundred yards, dropping to a fraction of that distance once the fighting began and the thick powder smoke filled the woods.

The survivors of the battle who returned in later years fully understood the importance of the man in the ranks, so much so that they regarded the creation of the National Park as a tribute to them. Unlike Gettysburg, Chickamauga does not contain imposing statues of Thomas, Longstreet, or any other general officer. A few individuals are represented on bas-reliefs or statues adorning individual monuments, but those representations are the exception and not the rule. Chickamauga, more than any other military park, pays tribute to the private in the ranks as much as any officer.[34]

34 There is one qualified exception to this rule: Bushrod Johnson's division marker along the Brotherton Road includes an unusual half-profile of the general. However, it was erected in the 1970s, long after the veterans themselves had passed on.

Last Clash at Chickamauga

By Dave Powell and Steven L. Wright

One *other notable action took place on September 21, 1863, that would have a bearing on the outcome of the Chickamauga Campaign. As noted in the main text, Col. Louis D. Watkins's brigade of three Kentucky cavalry regiments was the last Federal force to extricate itself from North Georgia and safely reach Chattanooga, though these Federals did not do so without suffering considerable loss. It was a near run thing. Their sacrifice was not in vain, however, for in turning his attention to Watkins's force, Confederate cavalryman Joe Wheeler probably allowed Rosecrans an extra half-day, at least, to gather supplies and make Chattanooga a bit stronger. Since Watkins's adventure is separate from the main battle story, it is presented here as a separate narrative.*

This chapter was originally written as a stand-alone piece in a collaboration between myself and Steven Wright. It arose out of a discussion we had concerning Watkins's engagement on September 21. Over the years, we have never found a home for it, until this volume. My thanks to Steve Wright and the publisher for allowing its inclusion here.

* * *

In the early afternoon of June 27, 1863, the 6th Kentucky Cavalry held a dress parade outside of Franklin, Tennessee. The occasion was a sword presentation to the regiment's commanding officer, Col. Louis Douglas Watkins. Also present were the officers and men of the 5th Kentucky Cavalry. In about ten days Watkins would relinquish command of his regiment and take charge of the newly formed Third Brigade, First Division, Cavalry Corps and tasked with screening the right flank of the Union Army of the Cumberland. The magnificent ivory-handled sword, ornate silver scabbard, and belt cost $500, and rivaled any similar blade given to general officers. It was a rare occasion that Colonel Watkins could be taken unawares, but he "manifested his genuine gratitude by a moment's profound silence." Regaining his composure he remarked "that the surprise at being the recipient of so handsome a gift was the predominant emotion of his nature and all he was able to do was to accept their appreciated donation with as warm a heart as was ever borne by officer to soldiers."[1]

Only the men of the 6th Kentucky Cavalry could appreciate the full meaning of their splendid gift and their commander's response. When Watkins was given command of the 6th that February, it probably had the lowest morale of any regiment in the army. The unit had been cobbled together from three disparate groups of men. Companies A through E had answered the governor's first call for troops in September 1861 and, under the command of Lt. Col. Reuben Munday, operated through the spring and summer of 1862 in the Cumberland Gap campaign. Munday and a detachment from his battalion were unluckily caught up in the maelstrom of the 1862 Confederate invasion and were unfairly tarred with the defeats of the Union forces at Big Hill and Richmond, Kentucky. As a result, the 53-year-old Munday resigned the following spring, leaving his officers and men embittered by their experience.[2]

Over the summer of 1862, Dr. Dennis J. Halisy of Washington County, Kentucky, recruited what would become Companies F through K in the area around Lebanon. Simultaneously, two companies recruited by Col. William E. Woodruff, in Louisville (ostensibly for the 29th Kentucky Infantry, which was never formed) were added to Halisy's roster and became Companies L and M of the 6th. There was great dissatisfaction among many of these men who, having volunteering for the infantry, were unceremoniously dumped into a cavalry unit full of strangers. Halisy's raw recruits were forced to hit the ground running and were in the saddle and under fire almost from the start. Confederate cavalry raids led by Cols. John Hunt Morgan and John S. Scott of the 1st Louisiana Cavalry kept the area in constant turmoil. Later in the year General Bragg invasion culminated in the battle of Perryville.[3]

During Morgan's Christmas Raid in December 1862, Halisy's cavalrymen were employed in attacking the Rebel rearguard as Morgan attempted to escape back into Tennessee. Colonel Halisy was killed near the foot of Muldraugh Hill on the last day of the year. The surviving field grade officers of the now-consolidated regiment were distrustful of each other as they aspired to fill the shoes of their dead commander. They

1 *Louisville* Journal, July 2, 1863. Watkins's presentation sword is in the holdings of The Frazier Historical Arms Museum, Louisville, Kentucky.

2 Compiled Service Records of Union Soldiers, Lieutenant Colonel Reuben Munday M397-roll 70, National Archives and Records Administration. Hereafter cited as NARA; Daniel W. Lindsey, *Report of the Adjutant General of the State of Kentucky, 1861-1866*, 2 vols. (Kentucky yeoman office, 1866-1867), vol. 1, 179; William H. Perrin, Ed., *History of Fayette County, Kentucky* (O.L. Baskin, 1882), 459; *Louisville Journal*, September 2, 1862; OR 16, 910-916.

3 Compiled Service Records 6th Kentucky Veteran/Volunteer Cavalry microfilm M397-rolls 60-75, NARA; *Louisville Journal* July 7, July 12, July 14, July 15, July 30, July 31, and September 8, 1862; "History of Lebanon, Ky.", *Lebanon Standard & Times*, January 19, 1887.

Union Col. Louis D. Watkins
Library of Congress

were all to be disappointed. Upon the recommendation of Maj. Gen. Gordon Granger, Capt. Louis D. Watkins of the 5th U.S. Cavalry was given the command.[4]

Watkins was not a Kentuckian, though he had some familial ties with the state. He was born in Tallahassee, the pioneer capital of the Florida Territory, in about 1828, where his father was one of the first physicians. He spent his youth in Waynesboro, Georgia, and other rural communities before his family settled in Savannah. He was educated in the best schools of that city. When it was announced that gold was found in California, Watkins headed for the west coast. According to one source, "He dug gold, hunted wild game and fought Indians alternately. Whenever the miners proposed an expedition in search of grizzly bears or Digger Indians, Watkins was among the first to join the chase."[5]

After a few years Watkins rejoined his mother, who was now a widow, in Washington, DC. Not more than a month after John Brown's raid on Harpers Ferry in October 1859, Watkins helped form a militia company, the National Rifles, in the nation's capital and was elected first lieutenant. Although he was a Southern man, Watkins remained loyal to the old flag and espoused the cause of the Union. "Faithful among the faithless," Watkins assisted Col. Charles P. Stone in thwarting the attempts of his company commander, Capt. Francis B. "Frank" Schaeffer, to offer an insult to President Lincoln at his inauguration. Almost immediately afterward Schaeffer led about 70 of his men across the Long Bridge and joined the Confederacy.[6]

4 *Louisville Journal,* January 3, January 6, 1863; Francis B. Heitman, *Historical Register and Dictionary of the United States Army,* 2 vols. (Government Printing Office, 1903), vol. 1, 1008.

5 C. J. Wood, *Reminiscences of the War, Biography and Personal Sketches of All the Commanding Officers of the Union Army* (n.p., 1880), 178.

6 Francis E. Spinner, Treasurer of the United States to Secretary of War Edwin M. Stanton, May 27, 1863; Personnel Records of General Officers, microfilm M1064-roll 311, NARA;

Watkins was rewarded for his loyalty with a first lieutenant's commission in Stone's newly formed 14th U.S. Infantry. He turned it down, opting instead for a commission that had just become vacant when an officer in the 2nd U.S. Cavalry resigned to join the Confederacy. Lieutenant Watkins commanded the company until the battle of Gaines's Mills on June 27, 1862. Near the end of that day the regiment was ordered to make a brave but ill-conceived charge against Confederate infantry. Watkins was shot and fell from his horse. Trampled underfoot, he sustained severe head injuries. Upon his recovery he was promoted to captain and sent to Kentucky. He was temporarily assigned as aide-de-camp to Brig. Gen. Samuel P. Carter and breveted major in the U.S. Army for his services during a successful raid into East Tennessee. Subsequently, Watkins was briefly assigned as chief of cavalry for the Army of Kentucky before accepting a commission in the volunteers to become colonel of the 6th Kentucky Cavalry.

Colonel Watkins wasted no time instilling discipline and good order in his regiment and requisitioneing much-needed arms and equipment. Two weeks after taking command, the 6th was on its way to Nashville to join Maj. Gen. William S. Rosecrans's Army of the Cumberland. From there, the unit was ordered to Franklin, Tennessee. It was not long before the 6th was skirmishing with enemy cavalry. As he had in Virginia, Watkins led from the front, which prompted an admonishment from his commanding officer. "The orderly who brought the last message from you reports you as constantly in the front exposing yourself unnecessarily. This display of reckless bravery might cost you your life . . . should a necessity exist for you to head the column no one doubts but you would be equal to the emergency. But some care of your person is requisite."

On the March 25, while under the command of Brig. Gen. Green Clay Smith, Watkins and the 6th Kentucky, along with the 4th Kentucky and 2nd Michigan Cavalry, repulsed an enemy attack along the banks of the Little Harpeth River. During that skirmish Watkins "knocked a rebel from his horse with the butt of his pistol while the rebel was aiming at one of our men." General Smith reported "I cannot speak too earnestly of the coolness and courage and daring gallantry of Col. L. D. Watkins." He went on to commend Maj. William H. Fidler, and lieutenants George Williams, Daniel Cheatham, and Warren H. Mead, also of the 6th, who "with twelve men were cut off in one of the charges made by Col. Watkins [and] gallantly fought their way out, killing seven rebels, wounding several and capturing six prisoners."[7]

Charles P. Stone "Without them Lincoln would never have been Inaugurated," in *Battles and Leaders of the Civil War*, 4 vols. (Thomas Yoseloff, Inc., 1956), vol. 1, 11-23.

7   Personnel Records of General Officers, Hq Army of Kentucky to Col. L.D. Watkins, March 23, 1863, NARA; Report of Green Clay Smith, in Personnel Record of Louis D. Watkins,

Watkins continued to improve the performance of his regiment through the spring of 1863 while skirmishing against forces under Generals Van Dorn, Wheeler, and Forrest. Early on the morning of April 27, Watkins, with his own regiment and a detachment from the 4th Kentucky, made a daring surprise attack on the camp of the Texas Legion within sight of General Van Dorn's main camp near the Carter's Creek Pike. The Texans who escaped did so mostly without their pants, boots, saddles, and arms. A large number of prisoners, horses, mules, wagons and other equipage were captured. "Watkins made a feint of attacking [the other] camp about a mile off, and by thus diverting the attention of the enemy, he was enabled to withdraw all the stores which he had taken without loss," explained one newspaper account. Understandably, the men of the 6th Kentucky now held Colonel Watkins in high esteem and followed his lead through their many skirmishes that summer.[8]

On the 8th of June Watkins was credited with capturing two Confederate spies at Franklin after they had already received passes from the post commander and gone on their way. Watkins, however, sensed something false about the two men and captured them. Closer examination revealed that these men—Col. William Orton Williams and Lt. Walter G. Peter—were Confederates. Watkins gave them a drumhead trial and executed them. Ironically, it was Colonel Williams who had resigned his commission in the 2nd U.S. Cavalry, which in turn left the vacancy filled by Louis D. Watkins.[9]

At the end of June 1863, Rosecrans initiated the Tullahoma Campaign, an elaborate scheme to maneuver the Rebels out of Middle Tennessee. Watkins's men were in the thick of it. After more than a week of campaigning, Colonel Watkins led a combined force (some 1,200 men) of the 5th and 6th Kentucky Cavalry on the 4th of July 1863 against General Bragg's rearguard at University Depot, skirmishing with the Rebels as they retreated over the mountains toward Chattanooga. The Federals captured 15 men of the 3rd and 4th Georgia and a set of brass instruments, which the musically inclined members of the 6th Kentucky used to form an impromptu band. Four days later, Watkins took command of the Third Cavalry Brigade, which consisted of his own regiment and the 4th and 5th Kentucky Cavalry.[10]

July and August were relatively quiet months for the Kentuckians. With Rosecrans on one side of the Tennessee River and Bragg on the other, the two armies had very

---

March 27, 1863, NARA; Undated clipping from the Cincinnati Commercial referring to the Little Harpeth fight.

8 *Louisville Journal,* April 28, April 29, and December 5,1863; *The Federal Knapsack,* May 2, 1863.

9 *Louisville Journal,* June 10, 1863; *Nashville Daily Union,* June 11, 1863; *Nashville Daily Press,* June 10, 1863.

10 Frederick H. Dyer, *A Compendium of the War of the Rebellion* (Morningside Press, 1994), 860, 1192; Michael R. Bradley, *Tullahoma: The 1863 Campaign for the Control of Middle Tennessee* (Burd Street Press 2000), 89; Personnel Records of General Officers, NARA.

little contact, though Watkins' men were kept busy chasing reports of Rebels in Northern Alabama. The end of August, however, brought new challenges. With a surprise crossing of the Tennessee, Rosecrans initiated a new campaign aimed at turning Bragg out of the mountains, capturing Chattanooga, and possibly driving deep into North Georgia. On September 2, Watkins's Kentuckians crossed the river along with the rest of their division to open the campaign. Alongside the Federal XX Corps, they marched towards Valley Head, Alabama, and Winston's Spring, the site of the best source of water in the region.[11]

Despite difficult crossings over the mountains, contact with the enemy remained limited. Rosecrans's surprise worked well, and by September 8 the Rebels were abandoning Chattanooga and in full retreat. Bragg was falling back towards Rome and Dalton in an effort to protect the Western and Atlantic Railroad. Once Chattanooga was so easily captured, Rosecrans urged the Federal cavalry eastward to try and cut Bragg off.

For the Kentuckians, this meant more action. After a few days at Valley Head, Watkins's brigade headed toward Alpine. En route, Watkins reported a successful skirmish with two companies of the Confederate 3rd Georgia Cavalry at Summerville, Georgia. On September 10, the Federals captured a dozen Georgians and killed or wounded several more at the cost of one Kentuckian dead and a couple others wounded. The Rebels fell back towards Lafayette.[12]

The next week saw the Federals press on toward Lafayette, where they discovered that Bragg had stopped retreating and occupied the town in strength. This was alarming news for Rosecrans, for his forces were scattered in difficult terrain. By September 14 the Union commander was no longer chasing Bragg; the Rebel army commander had turned the tables and was now seeking out Rosecrans. The XX Corps and the cavalry at Alpine, some 40 miles from the rest of the army, had no choice but to turn north and move back to Chattanooga.

After nearly three weeks of active campaigning, the Third Brigade returned to Valley Head and their old camps on September 18, 1863. The first time around Winston's Spring's had hosted nearly 30,000 men of the Union XX Corps and the bulk of the Cavalry Corps. Now, as the rear guard of this massive force, Colonel Watkins and his 1,175 men had the springs to themselves except for 400 sick Yankees and four captured Rebel officers Watkins was charged with protecting.[13]

September 19 was a welcomed day of rest. Awaiting orders, the Kentuckians spent the day quietly, unaware that the battle of Chickamauga was raging just 20 miles to the

11 OR 30, pt.1, 890-891.

12 Ibid., 913.

13 Ibid., 915.

north. Late that afternoon, however, Watkins received orders to come north as far as Stevens' Gap in Lookout Mountain, about 10 miles south of Crawfish Springs, and bring any stray Federals along with him. Early on the 20th, with baggage, the sick, and the captured Confederates in tow, Watkins moved out.[14]

The column marched about 15 miles that day. Once he reached Stevens' Gap, Watkins received a second order to join the rest of the army at Crawfish Springs, leaving Maj. Christopher T. Cheek and one battalion of the 5th Kentucky Cavalry to guard the gap. The Federals could now hear the muffled thunder of heavy cannon, their first intimation of the great battle raging to their north. The sounds bred caution, since Watkins did not have a firm idea of the location of any of the combatants. Brigadier General Robert B. Mitchell's orders telling Watkins to join the main force concluded with the ominous and vague admonition to "look out for the enemy. We have been fighting all along the line." That evening Watkins halted several miles south of Crawfish Springs at a local farmhouse to avoid stumbling into the middle of a battle after dark.[15]

That farm belonged to William Shaw, who was unprepared to receive the roughly 1,500 Union "guests" that descended upon him that late afternoon. The 42-year-old Shaw had at least one son in the Rebel army. Arba (or Arby) F. Shaw was serving in the 4th Georgia Cavalry, Col. C. C. Crews' brigade, Maj. Gen. Wheeler's Cavalry Corps. The younger Shaw was not at home on the 20th, but he had visited recently while on a 60-day convalescent leave at nearby Cherokee Springs. He was now with his unit but on light duty, and managed to get home again the day after Watkins's visit. "When I was last home," he wrote, "the farms [were] all under good fences, the fields laden with corn and . . . good wheat, and an abundance of fine stock of all kinds. . . .When I came back after the battle, what did I see? The whole valley was one sea of deep dust and not a sign of a fence to be seen and the corn and all the stock was gone and not a chicken was left to crow for day. They poured the wheat in their dust for their horses to eat."[16]

The stop at the Shaw farm provided food, fodder, and fuel for the campfires, but not, apparently, any solid intelligence. The next morning the Kentuckians saddled up and resumed their march, with farmer Shaw pressed into service as a guide. The cannon had fallen silent, which suggested the fighting was over—though who had triumphed remained in doubt. The first contact with the enemy came quickly. Near Owens's Ford, the leading Federals collided with a Rebel picket who fired at the Yankees and fell back. Watkins continued on until he estimated he was about three miles south of Crawfish Spring, when he encountered a second Rebel patrol. These Confederates were also

14 "From Watkins' Cavalry Brigade" *Louisville Daily Journal*, October 9, 1863.

15 *OR* 30, pt.1, 917.

16 Arba F. Shaw, "My Experiences" *Walker County Messenger*, April 3 and 10, 1902.

driven back, but they provided enough of an alarm that Watkins decided to halt the column, send scouts out to reconnoiter, and question some more locals.[17]

The scouts returned an hour later, the bearers of bad news. An anonymous member of the brigade, writing home on September 28h, described their "great astonishment" at running into Rebels, and that the "reconnaissance discovered the enemy to be in force at the springs." The civilians did not know much more. They thought Rosecrans had moved, but apparently did not know of the extent of the Union disaster on the 20th. They also offered that Union Maj. Gen. Alexander McDowell McCook's XX Corps still held the Chattanooga Valley Road, five miles to the west. This last detail was soon confirmed by two Yankee stragglers.[18]

Watkins' options were limited. Heading back south would only carry him farther away from Chattanooga and friendly lines. Moving west, toward McCook's supposed position, was also dangerous as it would expose his flank to the enemy holding Crawfish Springs. The wagons and the sick men limited his mobility; if attacked, he would not be able to escape quickly. According to reports from the locals, however, McCook's Federals were only five miles away. Watkins decided to make for McCook, and pressed another local in to service as a guide.[19]

The initial portion of the movement was successful. The Kentucky Unionists reached Lookout Valley without further incident. They had just turned north again, toward Chattanooga, when according to the *Daily Journal* correspondent, "an immense dust was seen rising to our front." Sergeant Charles H. Sowle of Company F in the 4th Kentucky angrily concluded that the guide had deliberately "led us into two divisions of Rebel Cavalry." Watkins knew immediately that his command was heavily outnumbered.[20]

Watkins was right. The approaching force included the bulk of Wheeler's cavalry corps—two divisions under William H. Martin and John A. Wharton, each composed of two brigades. Wheeler's men began the morning widely scattered, with Martin's brigades dispersed on picket and escort duties, and Wharton's men camped a couple of miles southeast of Crawfish Springs. When word reached Wheeler of Watkins's approach, he gathered those forces he had to hand and set off after the Yankees.[21]

The sketchy nature of Wheeler's reports make it difficult to determine exactly how many men he deployed against Watkins. From Wharton's division, the 8th Texas

17 Shaw, "My Experiences"; *OR* 30, pt.1, 917.

18 *OR* 30, pt.1, 917; "From Watkins's Cavalry Brigade" *Louisville Daily Journal*, October 9, 1863.

19 *OR* 30, pt.1, 915.

20 *Louisville Daily Journal*, October 9, 1863; "Father and Mother," September 26, 1863 Letter, Charles H. Sowle Papers, Perkins Library, Duke University, Durham, NC. Hereafter DU.

21 *OR* 30, pt. 2, 19.

Cavalry was left behind to watch McCook's XX Corps near Chattanooga, and Anderson's 4th Tennessee Cavalry had been assigned to Lt. Gen. James Longstreet's infantry command the day before to gather up supplies and Yankee stragglers. Wheeler used the 'balance of [his] command'" to attack Watkins. That "balance" included the rest of Col. Thomas Harrison's brigade, three regiments strong, and the four regiments of Colonel Crews's mixed Alabama and Georgia brigade, who made first contact with Watkins's column. Wharton's full division contained about 4,400 troopers, and after subtracting the two detached regiments, could theoretically muster 3,600 men against Watkins.[22]

Additionally, Wheeler could call on all or part of Martin's command. Martin's division was much smaller and numbered only 2,400 men. Once again, official reports are lacking specific details. However, a letter from a member of the 3rd Alabama Cavalry, part of Col. John T. Morgan's brigade, indicates that the Alabama outfit also participated in the day's action; John Wyeth's memoir from his days in the 4th Alabama Cavalry, part of Col. A. A. Russell's brigade, also described engaging Watkins.[23]

With accounts from regiments in each of Wheeler's four brigades describing their role against Watkins, and after making allowances for the various detachments and pickets not explicitly detailed by the surviving records, Wheeler clearly deployed a much stronger force against Watkins's lone Federal brigade. Depending upon how large his detachments were, Wheeler's strength numbered somewhere between 2,000 and 5,000 men. In either case, the Federals were outnumbered, and Watkins's situation was now desperate.

Any hope the Federals making their way north along the Chattanooga Road could now reach McCook had vanished. Their only viable escape route lay four miles south at Cooper's Gap, where the column could then ascend Lookout Mountain. Watkins ordered the wagons to turn around, and sent the remaining battalion of the 5th Kentucky under Lt. Col. William T. Hoblitzell ahead to hold the gap. The 4th and 6th Kentucky would have to fight it out to buy time for the wagons to get away. With Cheek's battalion detached the day before, and now Hoblitzell riding hard for Cooper's Gap, Watkins had barely 500 left to slow down Wheeler. He advanced with this small force to meet the oncoming Rebels.[24]

---

22 R. F. Bunting letter, *Rome Tri-Weekly Telegraph*, November 27, 1863; George B. Guild, *A Brief Narrative Of The Fourth Tennessee Cavalry Regiment* (Cool Springs Press, 1996), 30; *OR* 30, pt.2, 521.

23 William Robert Stevenson, "Robert Alexander Smith: A Southern Son," *Alabama Historical Quarterly* (Vol. XX, 1958), 45-46; Wyeth, *With Sabre and Scalpel*, 253.

24 *OR* 30, pt. 1, 915; "From Watkins' Cavalry Brigade," *Louisville Daily Journal*, October 9, 1863. Watkins's report claims only 400 effectives, but this number seems low when based upon the reported brigade strength, and it might not include officers.

The Federals collided with the Confederates just more than a mile farther north. Both Union regiments dismounted and went into line, Maj. Lewis A. Gratz's 6th Kentucky on the left and Col. Wickliffe Cooper and the 4th Kentucky on the right. The Union line was centered on the Chattanooga Road. Rebels swarmed their front and flanks, and almost immediately the Federals began falling back. Watkins retired the 4th first to a position near Lookout Church, where it halted to cover the 6th's retreat. In describing this movement, a member of the 6th wrote, "Unaccustomed to retreat, the 6th fell back slowly and sullenly. . . . Knowing that they outnumbered us ten to one the cowardly traitors advanced with a yell. The well directed volleys of the 4th brought them to a halt." The 4th managed to hold the Rebels in check at the church while the 6th fell back to take up the next defensive position.[25]

This stand, too, was only temporary. Cooper's 4th, assailed on both front and flank was, in Watkins' words, "compelled to fall back slowly, fighting with desperation, and rallied on the Sixth Kentucky." From here, both Federal units fought side-by-side in an action that lasted about 20 minutes. The Rebels once again swarmed in front and on both flanks, and the situation deteriorated for Watkins and his men. Tom Coleman, one of the attackers in the 11th Texas Cavalry, described the fight: "[They] made a short stand of five or six rounds [and then] they fled precipitously, every one of them taking care of himself the best way he could." Watkins described the ensuing retreat as a "running fight," but he was trying to put the best face on things. Sergeant Sowle called the action more bluntly, noting the Rebels "routed us complete." To Rebel Coleman, the fight was "a regular wolf chase." Coleman sarcastically admired the fine riding of the Kentuckians, noting that on "this occasion a stake and ridered fence was not in the way at all" as the Federals scattered across fields to escape.[26]

Major Gratz, writing to an uncle in Poland, described a similarly chaotic scene this way: "[W]e were attacked by 3,000 enemy cavalrymen. We fought as long as we could, but when I saw that nothing was left to me but to become a prisoner . . . I rallied my men and we broke through the line of the enemy. . . . The Chaplain . . . was shot down at my side; my orderly, a young German, dropped from his horse dead no more than three steps behind me. My adjutant was made prisoner no more than ten paces away from me." Leonidas B. Butner, the 6th Kentucky's imposing, six-foot, three-inch color bearer, was captured as well, but somehow managed to hide the regimental flag under his shirt. He successfully concealed the banner on his person up to the time of his death

25 *OR* 30, pt. 1, 915; "From Watkins' Cavalry Brigade," *Louisville Daily Journal*, October 9, 1863.

26 *OR* 30, pt. 1, 915; "Dear Parents and home folks" October 5th, 1863, Tom Coleman Papers, University of Missouri, Rolla; *OR* 30, pt. 1, 915; "Father and Mother" September 24th, 1863, Charles H. Sowle Papers, DU.

at Andersonville where, at the very last, he entrusted it to a comrade who bore it back to a postwar reunion in 1866 and presented it there to Colonel Watkins.[27]

The two Federal battalions, retreated in considerable confusion back to where the wagons were jammed up at the foot of Lookout Mountain, where they were still being hauled up Cooper's Gap to safety. Here, Watkins made another disheartening discovery. Hoblitzell's battalion, which he had sent back to protect the gap, had already climbed the mountain well ahead of the trains, which now left Watkins with no reserve. The furious colonel later claimed that if Hoblitzell had not ascended the mountain "at a very rapid rate," his force would have been enough to "check the enemy [and] save the whole brigade." Whether or not this was true, the damage had been done. The entire train, 53 wagons in all, fell into Rebel hands, including all the personal and regimental baggage for the three battalions. Watkins also reported 217 officers and men as missing or captured, most of whom were taken amidst the confusion of the traffic-jam. At the crest of the mountain, Watkins rallied the fragments of his command and placed the troopers along a rocky ledge overlooking the roadway—a stand that finally ended the Rebel pursuit. From there, the remnant of the brigade limped into Chattanooga, reaching the city about 10:00 p.m. that night. They brought with them another small train of wagons from the Union XIV Corps discovered en route.[28]

For the rest of 1863 Watkins's now-depleted brigade performed relatively light duty by scouting and guarding fords. The Third Brigade went on furlough in January, as the 4th, 5th and 6th Kentucky cavalry regiments became "veteranized." All three regiments successfully recruited replacements for those lost the previous year.[29]

During the 1864 Atlanta Campaign, the Third Brigade, which now included the 7th Kentucky Cavalry, operated in the rear of General Sherman's army guarding the railroad lines and communications stretching south in North Georgia. At LaFayette on June 24, Brig. Gen. Gideon J. Pillow made an unsuccessful surprise attack on Watkins and detachments of the 6th and 7th Kentucky. Pillow got the worst of it, and Watkins received his brigadier general's star, by brevet, the following November. Once he received this honorary promotion, Watkins was separated from his brigade and appointed post commander at Louisville, Kentucky. His Kentucky cavalrymen were split up among various brigades and participated in Wilson's Great Cavalry Raid through Alabama and Georgia.[30]

27 Jacob R. Marcus, *Memoirs of American Jews, 1774-1865* (Jewish Publication Society of America, 1955), 233-234; *Louisville Daily Journal*, April 7, 1866.

28 *OR* 30, pt. 1, 915-916.

29 Dyer, *Compendium*, 1192-1193.

30 *Louisville Daily Journal*, June 28, 1864; "The Late Exploit of Jack the Giant Killer," *Nashville Daily Union*, June 29, 1864.

Watkins was promoted to brigadier general of volunteers on March 13, 1865, and while serving as post commander of Louisville, the remnants of two of his former regiments (the 6th and 7th Kentucky Cavalry) were consolidated and served as his Provost Guard until their muster-out in September, 1865.[31]

On the 28th of July 1866 Watkins was appointed lieutenant colonel in the 20th U.S. Infantry and assigned to Baton Rouge. Sadly, less than two years later, on March 29, 1868, he succumbed to injuries he suffered nearly six years earlier on the battlefield at Gaines Mills. The men of the 6th Kentucky never forgot their old commander. In 1883, the Hays-Watkins Post No. 21, of the Grand Army of the Republic was organized at Lebanon, Kentucky. Watkins was honored jointly in the title with Col. William H. Hays, of the 10th Kentucky Infantry.[32]

Veterans of the 6th Kentucky Cavalry met for their only reunion during the G.A.R. encampment at Louisville in 1895. "Notwithstanding the thirty years that have elapsed since the war," editorialized the *Lebanon Enterprise*, "there was a goodly number of this fine regiment at the late encampment at Louisville. . . . No mounted regiment underwent more trying experiences, whether on the march through hostile country, in the prison camp, [or] in deadly battle. . . . May the true reward of honesty, patriotic, and gallant men be theirs."[33]

31 Heitman, *Historical Register*, 1008; *Report of the Adjutant General of the State of Kentucky*, vol. I, 179, 208.

32 Ibid.; *Lebanon Standard and Times*, December 12, 1883.

33 *Lebanon Enterprise*, October 4, 1895.

Rosecrans, Garfield, and Dana

William Starke Rosecrans departed the Army of the Cumberland early on the fall morning of October 20, his once-ascendant star having waned. He would spend months waiting for another command before being ordered to the Department of Missouri, where he finished the war chasing guerrillas and raiders while riding a desk in St. Louis. His presidential ambitions, if indeed he ever harbored any, had also come to an end.

Generals Tom Crittenden, Alexander McCook, and James Negley would at least receive a chance to clear their names via official inquiries. Not so Rosecrans. No charges were ever brought against him for his action at Chickamauga, so there was no need for such a court. The court of public opinion, however, conducted its own informal hearing that continued for many decades. It proved a harsh venue, indeed.

Neither Ulysses S. Grant nor Edwin Stanton was a Rosecrans partisan, and the general's ultimate relief from command was their doing. Rosecrans came to believe that two other men took a hand in his downfall: James A. Garfield and Charles A. Dana. In 1863 Rosecrans considered Garfield a friend, and Dana an enemy. He was certainly right about Dana. But over time his view of Garfield changed and he concluded Garfield wielded one of the knives plunged deeply into his back in 1863.

Despite his time as a civilian engineer and inventor, Rosecrans was at heart a soldier, with all of the professional's disdain for meddling politicians and amateur generals. Garfield, by contrast, should have represented everything Rosecrans most distrusted. He was a political general and a Radical Republican. Garfield viewed West Pointers with suspicion, and his service on the court that tried and convicted Maj. Gen. Fitz-John Porter of disloyalty after Second Bull Run unsettled—and even enraged—many Regular Army officers. Garfield was also a friend and protégé of

Secretary of the Treasury Salmon P. Chase, a fellow Ohioan, vehement abolitionist, and perhaps the most radical of all of Lincoln's cabinet members. Despite these stark differences, when Rosecrans and Garfield met during the winter of 1863, the two men quickly became friends.

Garfield was a congressman-elect, having easily won the race for Ohio's 19th district after being put forward by Chase. Since the new Congress wouldn't convene until December 1863, Garfield continued to hope for a field command in the interim. When Rosecrans offered him the job of the army's new chief of staff he accepted, somewhat to his own surprise. While not a field command, it was a prominent and important post, and one that would put Garfield closer to the heart of critical military decision-making than he had initially expected to be.

The first real differences of military opinion between the two arose over Tullahoma, which Garfield thought had been unnecessarily delayed. Even though April brought good campaigning weather in Tennessee, Rosecrans refused to advance until everything was in place. Active operations in Virginia and Mississippi, however, commenced immediately. May passed into June without significant action, and Garfield (along with the Washington authorities) chafed at the inaction. In his private correspondence he first anticipated action, and then bemoaned the lack of it. "I hope this army will move in a day or two," wrote Garfield on May 26 in a letter to his friend Burke Hinsdale. Four days later, however, Garfield informed another friend, "I hope you will soon hear that this army is in motion. It is in admirable condition and ought to give a good account of itself." On June 2, he informed his wife that "after long delays we have at last reached the verge of a movement. Indeed, the movement has begun and I confidently expect to be in the saddle by Saturday. . . . Bragg's army has been reduced . . . [and] it is our purpose to go out and offer battle, and if he declines we shall drive him away from the line of the Duck River."[1]

On June 6 Garfield was hedging his bets when he wrote, "we do not want to begin a general movement on Sunday and so I think we shall have no more fighting before Monday next. It is quite impossible to tell in so large an army as this precisely when any general movement will be made." Five days later he expressed his growing frustration to another civilian friend, Harrison Rhodes: "A sense of disappointment akin to mortification . . . has kept me from answering any letters for some time . . . in hopes of having something decisive to say. I had drafted a plan of campaign, drawn the first rough draft of the order for movement," he continued, "and submitted the document to General Rosecrans, who had approved it, and all things seemed ready. But . . . just on the eve of our movement there seemed to fall down upon the leading officers of this

---

1   Garfield, *Wild Life*, 272-274.

army . . . a most determined and decided opinion that there ought to be no immediate or early advance."[2]

Garfield's frustration with the army's cautious spirit stemmed from a June 8 questionnaire Rosecrans sent to his corps and divisional commanders concerning the desirability of an immediate advance. The results were disheartening. On the question of whether or not the army could advance "with strong, reasonable chances of fighting a great and successful battle, only two generals answered yes and 11 no. More specifically, when asked "Do you think an *immediate* advance of this army advisable, the results were unanimous, 15 generals replied no. On the question of making an "early advance," most demurred. No one answered yes, but only two firmly replied in the negative. On June 12, it fell to Garfield to summarize the results. In this communique, he also included an intelligence estimate of Bragg's strength, noting recent Rebel detachments to Mississippi. Garfield concluded the Army of the Cumberland had the advantage over Bragg by some 20,000 troops. Garfield ended this lengthy document with his own opinion, which placed him at odds with the majority of the army's generalship: "I believe an immediate advance of all our forces is advisable, and under the providence of God will be successful."[3]

It would be more than two weeks before Rosecrans finally ordered the army to move on June 24. The result was the Tullahoma Campaign, a wildly successful movement that cleared Middle Tennessee, though Bragg's army escaped to fight another day.

It is fair to say that this season of delays tempered Garfield's previously high opinion of Rosecrans. On July 27, the army chief of staff wrote a heartfelt letter to his mentor and political benefactor, Salmon P. Chase. In it, Garfield outlined the degree to which he and Rosecrans differed on military affairs and his concern over Rosecrans's command style:

> I have for a long time wanted to write to you . . . to say some things confidentially on the movements in this department; but I have refrained hitherto, lest I do injustice to a good man and say to you things which were better left unsaid. We have now, however, reached a point upon which I feel it proper . . . to acquaint you with the condition of affairs here. I cannot conceal from you the fact that I have been greatly tried and dissatisfied with the slow progress that we have made . . . since the Battle to Stone River.

---

2   Ibid., 275-276.

3   OR 23, pt. 2, 420-424. The number of responding officers varied. Of the first four questions, 17 replied to the first, 13 to the second, 14 to the third, and 15 to the fourth.

. . . it would be in the highest degree unjust to say that the 162 days which elapsed between . . . Stone River and the next advance of this army were spent in idleness or trifling. During that period was performed the enormous and highly important labor which made the Army of the Cumberland what it is—in many respects by far the best the country has ever known.

But for many weeks prior to our late movement [June 24] I could not but feel that there was not that live and earnest determination to fling the great weight of this army into the scale and make its power felt in crushing the shell of the rebellion. . . . I could not justly say we were in any proper condition to advance till the early days of May. At that time . . . I plead[ed] for an advance, but not till June . . . did General Rosecrans begin seriously to meditate an immediate movement.

In the first week the month a council of war was called, and out of eighteen generals whose opinion was asked seventeen were opposed to an advance. I was the only one who urged upon the General the imperative necessity of striking a blow at once."

In closing, Garfield summarized:

Thus far the General has been singularly disinclined to grasp the situation with a strong hand and make the advantage his own. I write this with more sorrow than I can tell you, for I love every bone in his body, and next to my desire to see the rebellion blasted is my anxiety to see him blessed. But even the breadth of my love is not sufficient to cover this almost fatal delay.[4]

Despite these policy differences, Garfield's personal and professional relations with Rosecrans remained warm. Rosecrans continued to rely on his chief of staff, taking Garfield into his every confidence. Nor was Rosecrans in the dark regarding Garfield's concerns, as evidenced by Garfield's June 12 report. But as subsequent events would demonstrate, Rosecrans was almost certainly unaware of how much of that concern Garfield conveyed to Chase via his private correspondence.

On September 10, 1863, a new player appeared on the scene when Assistant Secretary of War Charles A. Dana reached Bridgeport. Dana's report to Washington at 5:00 p.m. that evening foreshadowed the detailed, speculative reports he would provide Edwin Stanton. For example, Dana outlined the army's logistical problems, supply shortfalls due to depleted depots and insufficient rail capacity, and the Union fears of Rebel cavalry attacks on that tenuous rail link stretching its way back to Nashville. "The

---

4   Garfield, *Wild Life*, 289-290.

reserve ammunition train of 800 wagons," Dana observed, was then only at Stevenson. "No further advance of the army can take place until this gets up to Trenton or Chattanooga. . . . [I]t will be ten days before any new step is taken," he predicted, and possibly longer, for "it will require a month at least to replace the railroad bridge."[5]

The next day, however, Dana reached Rosecrans's headquarters in Chattanooga. Despite suspicions about his motives, Rosecrans accepted Dana's role at face value and took the man fully into his confidence. For his part, Dana's reports up through the battle of Chickamauga trended to the positive. On September 11, for example, Dana wired welcome news indeed: "my report . . . that the advance would be stopped . . . was incorrect."[6]

Though they were destined to become bitter personal and political enemies, there is little contemporary evidence to reveal how Garfield viewed Dana at this time. They were probably at least moderately friendly. Garfield's political leanings made him more compatible with Dana's perceived role than most of the Army of the Cumberland's leadership. For his part, Dana's communiqués praised Garfield often, especially for his conduct during and immediately after the battle of Chickamauga.

On September 20, not only was the Union right flank overwhelmed and driven from the field, but Rosecrans himself left the scene. Had Rosecrans returned to join General Thomas on Snodgrass Hill, or even halted his flight at Rossville to take charge of the troops forming there, the course of future events might have been much different. Instead, Rosecrans rode to Chattanooga, a further five miles to the rear. That decision had a dramatic impact on the lives of all three men.

For Charles Dana, that day marked the moment where he lost faith in Rosecrans and began agitating for his replacement (ideally, Grant.) Dana's subsequent career was enhanced by his relationships with both Stanton and Grant. For Rosecrans, it probably made replacement inevitable; Stanton's already low opinion of the army commander was confirmed. General Henry Halleck's limited support turned to outright antipathy, and it crystallized President Lincoln's thinking that Rosecrans needed to go. The impact on the relationship between Rosecrans and Garfield, while less dramatic, was no less impactful and eventually, extremely deleterious.

Mindful of the existing animosity between himself and Washington (which emanated primarily from Secretary Stanton and General Henry Halleck) Rosecrans adopted one narrative in describing what happened at Chickamauga. That narrative relied on official channels, and via dispatches and army reports Rosecrans could choose his words with great care. Dana adopted a different narrative.

---

5   OR 30, pt. 1, 184.

6   Ibid.

Rosecrans had no choice but to inform his superiors in Washington of the scope of the battlefield disaster. He simply could not hide plain facts. Union soldiers had been routed and driven from the field, he and two of his corps commanders had left that same field before the fighting had completely ended, and the last hours of the battle were conducted by Thomas, who likely saved the army. He did try and minimize the bad news, especially when it came to any hint of questionable actions on his or his subordinates' part. His 5:00 p.m. September 20th message from Chattanooga, for example, admitted that "we have met with a serious disaster," and that "the enemy overwhelmed us, drove our right, pierced our center, and scattered troops there." Rosecrans insisted, however, that "Thomas, who had seven divisions, remained intact at last news." He then added what would become the second thread of a long-running defense: Rebels "from Charleston, Florida, Virginia, and all along the seaboard are found among the prisoners. It seems every available man was thrown against us."[7]

Through the end of September Rosecrans's daily communications with Washington tended to be brief, hitting on the twin themes of reinforcements, which were badly needed in light of the Confederates' overwhelming odds, and supplies, which were limited. Starting on September 27, Rosecrans's direct communications with the War Department dwindled, mainly because of the arrival of Union Brig. Gen. Montgomery C. Meigs, the Quartermaster General of the United States Army. Meigs had come to examine the Army of the Cumberland's circumstances for himself. Once in Chattanooga, he conferred with Rosecrans daily and sent his own detailed reports back to Stanton.

In Meigs Rosecrans found a sympathetic ear. The quartermaster general's reports struck a positive note, while at the same time supporting Rosecrans's own narrative about the immense difficulties his army faced due to the terrain and the enemy hordes confronting him. On the 27th, Meigs reported, "I have with General Rosecrans visited the lines of defense of this place. I have seen the men vigorous, hearty, cheerful, and confident." On the subject of Chickamauga, he noted, "It is difficult for the leaders to abstain from claiming a complete victory. They believe they could have remained on the battlefield and that in that case the enemy would have retired . . . As I now see this field . . . the great effort of the rebels by which, concentrating in Georgia, they hoped to crush this army . . . has failed. If so, the fruits of victory are with Rosecrans . . . though the trophies" were not. Meigs also reported on Rosecrans's plans to reopen the river, which was the only viable means of supplying the army for the long-term, and which even a week after the battle seemed well advanced. Finally, added Meigs, "things look much better here than I expected to find them when I left Nashville; still success demands efforts from the army and the country." In closing, Meigs noted, "of the

---

7   OR 30, pt. 1, 142-143.

rugged nature of this region, I had no conception when I left Washington. I never traveled on such roads before."[8]

Similarly, on October 1 Meigs described the "road from Bridgeport over the mountains [as] execrable, and wearing out teams. All our supplies, except forage . . . come that way at present." He also marveled at the Army of the Cumberland's myriad talents: "This army is most ready, and laborious as well as courageous. It builds its own bridges, makes pontoons, and lives within itself. It is in many respects most remarkable." Rosecrans could hardly ask for a better representative to speak on behalf of himself and his men.[9]

Rosecrans was smart to let Meigs take point in his communications with the government. Ever a font of ideas, when Rosecrans chose to wire Washington directly, he sometimes overstepped. He did exactly that on October 3 when he advised the president on war policy. "If we can maintain [our] position in such strength that the enemy are obliged to abandon their position . . . would it not be well to offer a general amnesty to all officers and soldiers in the rebellion?" he asked. "It would give us moral strength and weaken them very much." This suggestion exceeded his authority—and it could not have come at a worse time for him. Lincoln replied that he intended "doing something like you suggest whenever the case shall appear ripe," but right now, such an offer would be seen as "a confession of weakness and fear." Stanton, irascible at the best of times, was offended both by the suggestion and by the fact that Rosecrans bypassed the secretary of war to communicate directly with Lincoln on the matter. That particular telegram would have an outsized effect on Rosecrans's future.[10]

Despite Meigs's welcome presence, Rosecrans could not afford to ignore Charles Dana. His dealings with Dana remained unchanged, holding daily discussions with the man and letting him convey those impressions back to Stanton. Here, however, Rosecrans underestimated the amount of damage Dana's new-found malice could do him.

Rosecrans had already warned Washington repeatedly that the Army of the Cumberland would be forced to retreat unless help was quickly forthcoming, warnings bolstered by Meigs's own detailed reports. Rosecrans was correct in pointing out that unless a better supply line was opened there would be no choice in the matter: Chattanooga would have to be abandoned, for the army could not be sustained through the winter via Walden Ridge. Rosecrans's intent was to impress the government with the urgency of his circumstances, and to make sure the help he needed would come as quickly as possible. He was not hinting that it was his own desire to fall back, or even

8   Ibid., pt. 3, 890-891.

9   Ibid., pt. 4, 9.

10 Ibid., 57, 79.

laying groundwork to prepare Stanton for the worst. Rosecrans had no intention of retreating unless he absolutely had no other choice. Dana's disingenuous spin on the subject created the impression that Rosecrans favored a retreat, and soon. Rosecrans probably thought he was using Dana. In reality, Dana was playing him.

Another important arrival in Chattanooga during this time documented the Rosecrans-Dana relationship. Journalist Henry Villard reached the city on October 5. "Northern papers, "noted Villard, "had been full of all sorts of accounts of the two days' battles, the causes of our defeat, and the behavior of Generals Rosecrans, McCook, Crittenden, Negley, Davis, Sheridan, Wood, and Van Cleve. . . . There was so much contradiction and partisanship . . . that I resolved to ascertain the truth and to write a review of the battle." Villard found Rosecrans and his chief-of-staff Garfield more than willing to talk. "Generals Rosecrans and Garfield expressed their readiness to place at my disposal all the information they had, including the official reports . . . as fast as they came." This was a huge help to Villard's intended article, and a splendid chance for Rosecrans to get his own version of events in the public forum via a sympathetic scribe.[11]

Rosecrans, noted Villard, extended the same access to Dana. "Dana had intimate intercourse, day and night, with General Rosecrans, and he enjoyed his personal hospitality, sitting at the same table, and sleeping in the same building." Looking back many years later, Villard found this to be a dire miscalculation. "[Dana's] reports . . . prove that he deliberately drew the General into confidential communications, the substance of which he used against him, and that he held talks with general officers regarding Rosecrans which were nothing less than insubordination."[12]

Dana's post-battle stream of criticism began, of course, with the fateful telegram of 4:00 p.m., September 20, which likened Chickamauga to another Bull Run. In subsequent dispatches, Dana described Rosecrans as alternating between desiring to make a determined stand at Chattanooga and contemplating an abrupt retreat. In outlining the extent of the disaster on the 20th, Dana first blamed "the dangerous blunderhead McCook, who always imperils everything." He also strongly criticized Rosecrans for two serious tactical errors: "too much extending his line originally, . . . and a more pregnant error in the mode of contracting it which he adopted." However, Rosecrans's most glaring fault, argued Dana, was "his temporizing nature." It was obvious Dana found both McCook and Crittenden wanting, and that sentiment within the army was running strongly against both men; clearly they should be relieved.

11 Henry Villard, *Memoirs of Henry Villard, Journalist and Financier 1835-1900*, 2 vols. (Boston, 1904), vol. 2, 184-185.

12 Ibid.

Rosecrans, however, refused to relieve the generals. He could not do so, thought Dana, for two reasons. First, Rosecrans was "greatly lacking in firmness and steadiness of will . . . [and] hates to break with McCook and Crittenden." Second, while "McCook and Crittenden . . . fled to Chattanooga . . . from that glorious field where Thomas and Granger were saving their army and their country's honor . . . [Rosecrans] fled also."[13]

Throughout the first half of October, Dana's daily dispatches continually undermined Rosecrans, criticizing the Union commander at every opportunity. Dana analyzed the defeat of the 20th at length, passing on every bit of discontented gossip that caught his ear and in doing so, painted an increasingly bleak picture of the army's circumstances. On October 12, for example, he described Rosecrans as being "sometimes as obstinate and inaccessible to reason as at others he is irresolute, vacillating and inconclusive. . . . He has inventive fertility and knowledge, but he has no strength of will and no concentration of purpose. His mind scatters. . . . He is a feeble commander."[14]

Dana played on Stanton's worst fears by stressing the theme of retreat. At midday on October 16, reported Dana, "nothing can prevent the retreat of the army from this place within a fortnight . . . except the opening of the river." That same day, in a wire sent at 4:00 p.m., Dana summarized a "full conversation" with the army commander, which sounded even more alarming. The river must be reopened, claimed Rosecrans, but only Maj. Gen. Joseph Hooker (with the reinforcements from the Potomac army) could do that, and Hooker had to wait for his trains to get up. Worse, "as soon as the weather would allow the enemy will cross . . . in force . . . and then it will be necessary to fight a battle . . . or retreat from here." Given the parlous state of the army's logistics, fighting a battle seemed unlikely, leaving withdrawal as the only option. Worst of all, Dana charged that Rosecrans seemed oblivious to his peril, "insensible to the impending danger, and dawdl[ing] with trifles."[15]

Dana was sending pure, if vitriolic, nonsense. Rosecrans was neither inactive nor feeble. Meigs's reports show Rosecrans in firm control, working day and night to address his various logistical, organizational, and morale problems. By mid-October Rosecrans had already worked out a complete plan for opening the river and returning the troops to full rations. Implementation only waited on the completion of several riverboats, then under construction at Bridgeport, and the production of at least 50 pontoon boats in Chattanooga, which would do double-duty as assault boats.[16]

---

13 OR 30, pt. 1, 202.

14 Ibid., 215.

15 Ibid., 218-219.

16 Ulysses S. Grant, *Personal Memoirs of U. S. Grant*, 2 vols. (New York, 1886), vol. 2, 28. In his memoirs, Grant described meeting Rosecrans and hearing his "excellent suggestions" for

All the while Dana secretly urged that Rosecrans be immediately replaced by George Thomas—even though Thomas had already quietly refused the notion, not wanting to be seen as undermining a commander he still greatly respected—and pitched Grant as the only man who could come and save a deteriorating situation. With that last, Stanton heartily agreed.

On the morning of October 16, while at Cairo, Illinois, Grant was summoned to Louisville. En route at Indianapolis, he met with the man who summoned him—Edwin Stanton. While riding on to Kentucky, Stanton presented Grant with two nearly identical orders. Each created the Military Division of the Mississippi, which embraced the entire Western Theater with Grant in charge. The only difference was that one order left Rosecrans in command of the Army of the Cumberland, while the other replaced him with Thomas. Grant immediately chose Thomas. On October 17 the secretary and the general pulled into Louisville. From there, Grant continued on to Stevenson, Alabama, while Stanton remained in Kentucky.[17]

Meanwhile, on October 10, Rosecrans published the order relieving Garfield of his chief of staff duties so Garfield could take up his congressional seat, replaced by Maj. Gen. Joseph J. Reynolds. It would take Garfield several more days to hand over army affairs, but on October 15 Rosecrans authorized Garfield to "proceed to Washington with all convenient dispatch, and deliver . . . the report of the operations of this army to the close of the battle of Chickamauga." Additionally, Garfield was "to see the Secretary of War and the General-in-Chief, and explain to them in detail our condition here." Garfield was further authorized to also "give them as full information as may be desired as to the condition of the troops and the administrative branches of the service." Many years later, author and Garfield political biographer James Gilmore asserted that George Thomas put things much more succinctly, telling Garfield, "You know the injustice of all these attacks on Rosecrans. Make it your first business to set these matters right."[18]

Garfield spent the next several days making his way to Nashville, reporting back to Rosecrans along the way. He reached reached Anderson's Crossroads on October 16, where he painstakingly forded the "booming" Sequatchie River, swollen by recent rains. The next morning found him at Battle Creek on the north bank of the Tennessee River, and that night reached Bridgeport. From there, travel became easier for Garfield could at last ride the rails. He arrived in Nashville on the evening of October 18 and

---

relieving the siege. "My only wonder was that he had not carried them out." The reason was simple enough; Rosecrans had been relieved before everything was ready, and going off half-cocked would have only tipped his hand.

17 See OR 30, pt. 4, 404, for the orders that followed. Note they are dated October 16, 1863.

18 OR 30, pt. 4, 249-250, 389-390; James R. Gilmore, "The Relief of Rosecrans," in *Burial of General Rosecrans, Arlington National Cemetery, May 17, 1902* (Cincinnati, 1903), 85.

wired Rosecrans that he would depart for Louisville on the 20th. It was there that Garfield caught wind of a disturbing rumor: "General Grant and the Secretary of War are at Louisville and start for [Nashville] by special train tomorrow morning. What does it mean?"[19]

Rosecrans already knew what it meant. By the time Garfield's latest was in hand, the army commander had also already received Grant's order relieving him of command. Grant's missive arrived in Chattanooga about midday on the 19th, while Rosecrans was out on an inspection tour. Gordon Granger, standing duty at headquarters at the time, examined the order and set it on Rosecrans's desk. When Rosecrans returned and read it, he quietly gathered his officers and informed them of the change and of his intention to depart the army without fuss or fanfare at 5:00 a.m. the next morning.[20]

It is possible Grant would not have relieved Rosecrans via telegram (with the added snub that method implied) had not Charles A. Dana struck one last egregious blow. On the morning of October 18, Dana telegraphed his direst warning to date. The river was still not open to transports, he observed, the rains had made the mountain roads impassable, the artillery horses were starving, and the men not far behind. "If the effort which Rosecrans intends to make to open the river should be futile, the immediate retreat of this army will follow." Even worse, "amid all this, the practical incapacity of the general commanding is astonishing, and it often seems difficult to believe him of sound mind. His imbecility appears to be contagious, and it is difficult for anyone to get anything done." With that last bit of slander transmitted, Dana departed Chattanooga almost immediately thereafter for Louisville to meet with Stanton in person.[21]

According to Grant, that evening, when Stanton received this latest wire, he immediately went looking for Grant at the Galt House. Grant was out, so Stanton waited impatiently for the general to return. Both men agreed there was no time to observe military courtesies. Of course, as per Gen. Meigs's dispatches, Rosecrans was not acting like an imbecile, he was not contemplating a retreat, and the situation was not nearly as desperate as Dana claimed. No matter. Dana's reports suited Stanton's needs perfectly, while Meigs's did not. It was time to show Rosecrans the door. Grant was agreeable and, late on the evening of October 18 signed the order formally assuming his

19 *OR* 30, pt. 4, 415-416, 435-436, 479.

20 Lamers, *Edge of Glory*, 391-392.

21 *OR* 30, pt. 4, 221; Charles A. Dana, "Reminiscences of the Civil War," *New York Sun*, November 26, 1879. Grant might have waited to relieve Rosecrans in person.

new command, along with the new department's first directive, Special Orders No. 1, which appointed Thomas in Rosecrans's stead.[22]

Rosecrans acknowledged each of these orders on the evening of the 19th, tersely informing both Washington and Grant of his compliance. Grant next wired Thomas, instructing the Virginian to "hold Chattanooga at all hazards." Thomas shot back, in his classic gruff fashion, "I will hold the town till we starve." Rosecrans, who was still present when this insulting communiqué arrived, would remember that both he and Thomas "regarded it as an aspersion on the Army of the Cumberland and its commander, founded either in ignorance or malice." Rosecrans insisted that "we had as little idea of abandoning Chattanooga as anybody in the world."[23]

Garfield received the answer to his question ("What does it mean?") on the same day Rosecrans departed Chattanooga. The former chief of staff left Nashville on the morning of the 20th and arrived in Louisville that evening, where he and Brig. Gen. James B. Steedman (who was also heading north) were "summoned into conference by Secretary Stanton."[24]

This meeting continues to be controversial because of what Garfield supposedly told Stanton about Rosecrans, and the effect it had on Rosecrans's career. Rosecrans's supporters have generally held it to be Garfield's moment of betrayal. Historian Frank Varney, for example, charged that Garfield, in "a secret meeting," informed Stanton that "Rosecrans had lost his nerve" on September 20. "His reason for denouncing Rosecrans was simple," Varney insisted. "He wanted the reputation as one of the men who had saved the Army of the Cumberland, in order to advance his political career." Garfield partisans insist otherwise. Theodore Clarke Smith, Garfield's most extensive biographer, maintained that Garfield's own claim (made in a letter to Rosecrans in 1880) that "he defended [Rosecrans] stoutly against Stanton's criticism," should be taken at face value.[25]

Certainly there was nothing "secret" about the meeting itself. After all, Rosecrans expressly authorized Garfield to meet with Stanton and Halleck and "explain in detail" the army's circumstances. Moreover, whatever transpired had nothing to do with Rosecrans's relief, for that event had already transpired nearly 48 hours earlier. Stanton

---

22 *OR* 30, pt. 4, 450, 455.

23 *OR* 30, pt. 4, 478-479; see also Grant, *Personal Memoirs*, 2, 26; William S. Rosecrans, "The mistakes of Grant," *The North American Review*, vol. 141, issue 349 (December 1885), 595-596. Grant combined these events in his memoirs, placing both the order relieving Rosecrans and his instructions to Thomas on the night of October 19. In fact, they happened a day apart.

24 Smith, *Garfield Life and Letters*, vol. 2, 354.

25 Frank P. Varney, *General Grant and the Rewriting of History: How the Destruction of General William S. Rosecrans Influenced Our Understanding of the Civil War* (El Dorado Hills, CA, 2013), 215; Smith, *Garfield Life and Letters*, vol. 2, 354.

was certain of the need to give Rosecrans the boot as early as the end of September. The orders for doing so (nominally left to Grant's discretion, to satisfy Lincoln's remaining concerns) were inked before Stanton even ventured west.

As proof of the fact that the secretary of War's mind was already made up, Stanton conferred with the governor of Indiana, Oliver P. Morton, prior to meeting Grant's train at Indianapolis on October 17. The governor was also a Radical Republican and the head of an important Midwestern state and thus a close ally of the administration. Stanton informed the astounded Morton that "relieving General Rosecrans . . . [was] the object of his trip." He was removed, continued Stanton, because of "a telegram which the General had sent to President Lincoln after the battle, recommending an armistice with a view of agreeing on terms of peace." Stanton's statement could only refer to Rosecrans's October 3 wire suggesting an amnesty for Confederate deserters. The suggestion of course had been rejected by Lincoln, and its contents now grossly distorted by Stanton. This alarming statement filled Morton with "apprehension . . . [and] with grief at the discovery that Rosecrans should have proved so weak and faltering."[26]

The Stanton-Morton incident is important for two reasons: It clearly demonstrates that Rosecrans's fate was already a fait accompli, and it stands as a fine example of Stanton's mendacity and his willingness to twist facts to suit his needs of the moment. Rosecrans's telegram might have been out of channels, but it said nothing about an armistice or a negotiated peace. Stanton lied to Morton to justify the general's relief.

At least five people were present at the meeting in Louisville between Garfield and Stanton. In addition to the two principals, Brig. Gen. James Steedman, Col. Anton Stager, head of the Union Military Telegraph Bureau who accompanied Stanton to Louisville, and Andrew Johnson, the Military Governor of Tennessee, were also witnesses to what transpired. Garfield never publicly spoke or wrote his version of what happened in that train car, but he did privately describe the meeting to Brig. Gen. Jacob D. Cox, a close friend and fellow Ohio Republican, when the pair met in Cincinnati on October 23. According to Cox, Garfield said that Stanton "not only had dispatches full of information from General Meigs, who now also met with him at Louisville, [but also] . . . Dana's . . . series of cipher dispatches giving a vivid interior view of affairs and of men." Stanton thus demonstrated "such knowledge of the battle . . . that it would be impossible for Garfield to avoid mention of [those] incidents which bore unfavorably upon Rosecrans." Conducting what amounted to a cross-examination, former prosecutor Stanton, "one of the great courtroom lawyers of his generation," extracted the information he needed. Steedman apparently corroborated what Garfield told Cox. "Generals Garfield and Steedman are here," Stanton wired Washington once the

---

26 "Rosecrans' Removal," *Indianapolis Times*, March 13, 1882.

meeting was over. "Their representations of the incidents of the Battle of Chickamauga more than confirm the worst that has reached us as to the conduct of the commanding general." Garfield, of course, disputed this version of affairs. In an 1880 letter to his former commander, Garfield insisted that far from condemning Rosecrans, when Stanton "denounced you . . . I rebuked him and earnestly defended you against his assaults."[27]

Rosecrans came to doubt Garfield's trustworthiness because he believed that at least one other witness, Colonel Stager, recalled the army chief of staff siding with Stanton. In 1881, former Colonel Francis A. Darr, the former quartermaster of Thomas's XIV Corps, claimed to have met Stager the previous year at West Point's annual military exercises. According to Darr, Stager told him that "Garfield in my presence denounced Rosecrans as incompetent, unworthy of his position, as having lost the confidence of his army, and should be removed." This strong and unequivocal statement seemed to conclusively settle the matter of Garfield's duplicity.[28]

Or did it? By the summer of 1882 the Garfield-Rosecrans drama was drawing a good deal of press coverage, in large part because Garfield had been elected president in 1880 and martyred by an assassin's bullet in September of 1881. By this time Rosecrans's efforts to vindicate his reputation were in full swing, and he had repeatedly publicized Stager's condemnatory comments about Garfield in interviews and speeches.

Naturally, the press asked Stager for comment on Rosecrans's claims. Stager, a postwar industrialist and financier, was living in Chicago. According to the June 15, 1882, edition of the Chicago Daily Tribune, Stager denied that "he told Gen. Rosecrans or anyone else that what occurred at the Louisville meeting with Stanton was the reverse of what was stated by Gen. Garfield." When a reporter later clarified that Rosecrans was not claiming to have met Stager personally, but that Colonel Darr was the source of the quote, Stager offered an even more emphatic denial, which appeared two days later in the same paper. "I never made any such statement . . . to Gen. Darr or anybody else. It wasn't a fact—Gen. Garfield did not denounce his superior officer—and I couldn't therefore have said he did. I met Gen. Darr at West Point; but if

---

27 Jacob D. Cox, *Military Reminiscences of the Civil War*, 2 vols, (New York, 1900), vol. 2, 7-8; Allan Preskin, *Garfield: A Biography* (Kent OH, 1978) 217; Lamers, *Edge of Glory*, 411. Contrary to some reports, Stanton did not meet personally with Dana at this time. When Dana reached Nashville he encountered Grant, who informed Dana that he would be returning to Chattanooga on Grant's own train. Dana, *Recollections*, 127. Garfield to Rosecrans, January 19, 1880, Rosecrans Papers, University of California, Los Angeles. Hereafter UCLA.

28 Francis Darr to Rosecrans, July 16, 1881, Rosecrans Papers, UCLA.

he says I made such a statement he misapprehended me." Stager's comments were picked up and carried by other newspapers and the store spread.[29]

So what did Garfield have to say about Rosecrans's conduct on September 20? Short of simply lying, Garfield could not avoid conveying at least some distressing details to Stanton, who (as would Garfield describe this interview to Cox) clearly was already armed with most of those same details via Dana.

Garfield left Louisville for Cincinnati, where he met with Cox, who was of course deeply interested in everything Garfield had to say. As Cox later related, Garfield told him that after Rosecrans tried to rally his broken troops, and after Phil Sheridan's counterattack failed, "with the conviction that nothing more could be done, mental and physical weakness seemed to overcome the general. He rode silently along, abstracted, as if he neither saw nor heard." Most damning of all, thought Cox, was Garfield's description of "the collapse of nerve and of will that had befallen his chief. The words," Cox added, "burned themselves into my memory."[30]

How accurate was Cox's memory? Corroborating evidence seems to come from Rosecrans own hand less than three weeks after the battle. In a letter to his brother, the general admitted that "it was possibly one of the most trying and anxious periods of my life." More specifically, Rosecrans turned to prayer: "I prostrated myself in spirit at the feet of our Crucified Lord and implored his most Sacred Heart to pity us." If Rosecrans spent that ride in contemplation and internal prayer, he would indeed appear to be riding "silently along, abstracted." Similarly, even Capt. Henry Cist (a former staff officer and loyal Rosecrans man) admitted that once Rosecrans reached Chattanooga, the general was so enervated that he could not dismount under his own power. He had to be helped from his horse and into the house serving as his headquarters. A third bit of evidence comes from journalist Henry Villard. Based upon interviews made with those who rode with him, Villard stated that Rosecrans completed the ride in "gloomiest despondency."[31]

Years later Rosecrans offered a considerably different version of that ride. He insisted he was in full possession of his mental and physical faculties, so much so that his mind was racing—as evidenced by the sudden barking of orders (the ones Garfield couldn't follow) as the command party reached the junction of the Rossville-Chattanooga road. It is worth noting that Rosecrans described this incident

29 "Stager Denies," *Chicago Daily Tribune*, June 15, 1882; "Garfield-Rosecrans," *Chicago Daily Tribune*, June 17, 1882; see also "Rosecrans receives another facer from General Stager," *Sacremento Daily Record-Union*, June 16, 1882; and "Stager's Statements," *Rock Island Argus*, June 15, 1882.

30 Cox, *Military Reminiscences*, vol. 2, 10. See David A. Powell, *The Chickamauga Campaign: Glory or the Grave* (El Dorado Hills, CA, 2015), 315-319, for a full description of this ride.

31 Powell, *The Chickamauga Campaign: Glory or the Grave*, 315-319.

repeatedly in various publications, but none of these versions were published before Garfield's death in September 1881.

Garfield fully understood the dangerous political waters in which he now found himself, and took time to write Rosecrans on October 23. He reiterated his support and that he hoped to meet with Rosecrans in Cincinnati, since Rosecrans was now also headed north. Unfortunately, that was not to be. "[B]ut I must go tonight, or I cannot reach home before Monday [October 26.] I therefore must go away without seeing you. The action of the War Dep't fell upon me like the sound of a fire bell. I am sure that it will be the verdict of the people that the War Dep't has made a great mistake and have done you a great wrong."[32]

After a very short trip home, Garfield reached Washington by the 28th. He reported to General Halleck and formally delivered the reports entrusted to him and "had several interviews with the President and General Halleck [concerning] the military situation at Chattanooga." On December 16, 1863, Garfield wrote another letter to Rosecrans in which he described the substance of at least one of those meetings. Garfield, along with Ohio Senator Benjamin F. Wade—"a staunch and ardent friend" of Rosecrans—met with Lincoln to plead the general's case. They had a "full, direct, and very satisfactory talk," explained Garfield, and Lincoln was apparently agreeable to the idea of returning Rosecrans to active service in some capacity. What gave the president pause, continued Garfield, "was the tone of your [Rosecrans's] dispatches from Chickamauga several days after the battle that led him to fear that you did not feel confident that you could hold the place; and hence the consolidation of the three armies to make Chattanooga sure. It was still at that time [Lincoln's] intention to keep you at the head of the Army of the Cumberland . . . with Grant the ranking officer in command of the whole, BUT GRANT MADE IT A CONDITION OF ACCEPTING THE COMMAND THAT YOU SHOULD BE REMOVED [emphasis in the original]." Here, then, was the smoking gun as Garfield saw it, likely relayed to Lincoln by Stanton, perhaps in order to shift the responsibility away from the secretary's own shoulders. Dana's malign influence was evident.[33]

Were these meetings as Garfield described them? Lincoln died in 1865, of course, long before Rosecrans went public. Garfield's version would be disputed, but often second- or even third-hand. One of Rosecrans's informants was Postmaster General Montgomery Blair. Writing in 1880, Blair penned Rosecrans that he had heard Lincoln state that the rumors of Rosecrans's "misconduct" were "substantiated" by Garfield, presumably in one of these personal encounters. Blair himself was not present for any

32 Garfield to Rosecrans, October 23, 1865, Rosecrans Papers, UCLA.

33 Smith, *Garfield Life and Letters*, vol. 2, 355. Lamers, *Edge of Glory*, 413; and Garfield to Rosecrans, December 16, 1863, Rosecrans Papers, UCLA.

of those meetings, nor did Blair claim that Lincoln elaborated beyond that point. Did Garfield's corroboration came face-to-face or, more likely (given the similarities in wording), was Lincoln repeating his own recollection of Stanton's condemnatory telegram?

Of one thing we can be sure: Blair's claim that Garfield's evidence was the reason Lincoln agreed to let Rosecrans go is clearly wrong; Garfield's interviews with both Stanton and Lincoln came after that decision was already made. Blair's contribution to the entire affair amounts to self-contradictory hearsay and his evidence sheds no light on what actually occurred.[34]

In December 1863 Garfield took up his Congressional duties, resigning his commission despite the added inducement of a promotion to major general, which had been back-dated to September 19. According to autobiographical notes Garfield penned in 1873, the added incentive stemmed from George Thomas's desire to have Garfield return to the field. "Thomas . . . was exceedingly anxious to have me come back into the army and tendered me, in a private letter, the command of a corps if I would go," Garfield wrote. "I very much wanted to go back." Instead, he stayed in Congress, where Lincoln needed every vote he could get, and where Garfield could bring his martial expertise to use as a member of the Committee on Military Affairs. He entertained vague hopes of returning to uniform in the summer of 1864, for "Secretary Stanton assures me that he will hold my place in the army open for me at any time I choose to return." It was not to be. Garfield would remain in Congress until his surprising election to the presidency in 1880.[35]

One of the first things Garfield did in the House of Representatives was to try and win justice for his former commander. In February 1864, a joint resolution was offered thanking General Thomas and the Army of the Cumberland "for their conduct in the battle of Chickamauga." Rosecrans's name was deliberately omitted from the resolution. Outraged at the snub, Garfield swayed enough members to amend the resolution and get it passed with Rosecrans's name included, but the bill died in the Senate.[36]

That was not Garfield's last effort on behalf of Rosecrans. It was now a presidential election year and Lincoln grip on the officer was uneasy, at best. Many Republicans were disillusioned with him and had formed an offshoot party, nominating John C. Fremont that in May. The bulk of the party met that June in Baltimore, changed the name to the National Union Party, re-nominated Lincoln, and looked to form a coalition with War Democrats. Doing so required the dumping of the current vice

34 Lamers, *Edge of Glory*, 412; Preskin, Garfield, 215.

35 Smith, *Garfield Life and Letters*, vol. 1, 355-356.

36 Jacob D. Cox, "The Chickamauga Crisis," *Scribner's Magazine*, vol. 28, no. 1, (July 1900), 331.

Secretary of War Edwin M. Stanton
Library of Congress

president, Maine Radical Republican Hannibal Hamlin, in favor of a more acceptable man for the second slot. Garfield thought Rosecrans would be perfect for the job. "Will you allow your named to be used for vice-president on the ticket with Mr. Lincoln?" Rosecrans's reply was verbose and not a little opaque. The nomination went instead to Andrew Johnston of Tennessee.[37]

*   *   *

In a postwar military dominated by Grant and Sherman, Rosecrans saw little chance for advancement and resigned his commission shortly after the war ended. He spent the next several years in various business ventures, with but limited success. In 1868, he was appointed Ambassador to Mexico by President Andrew Johnson, only to be replaced five months later by Ulysses S. Grant when his old nemesis moved into the White House.[38]

Rosecrans received multiple offers to run for public office, but declined them all until 1880, when he ran for Congress as a Democratic representative from California. That election year was important in other ways for James Garfield emerged as the dark-horse candidate for president after a deadlocked Republican convention in Chicago. Garfield went on to win the White House, but the ensuing hoopla reignited Chickamauga's lingering controversies.

Despite their political differences, staunchly Republican Garfield and Democrat Rosecrans remained friendly over the years, with Garfield very careful not to discuss that fateful day of September 20, 1863—at least in public. The two men saw each other rarely, but communicated often. In 1874, Charles A. Dana was the editor of the New

---

37 Lamers, *Edge of Glory*, 424-425; Preskin, *Garfield*, 239-240. Per Lamers, Rosecrans apparently believed that Stanton intercepted his reply, leaving Garfield in the dark and thus acquiescing to Johnston. Preskin, however, notes that there is a copy in the Garfield papers dated June 7, 1864, which suggests Garfield did receive the response.

38 Lamers, *Edge of Glory*, 441.

York Sun, which published an accusation that Rosecrans was relieved because of a confidential wartime letter Garfield penned to Salmon P. Chase suggesting the general was not fit to retain his command. A more serious strain on the relationship five years later when Dana repeated that same charge, asserting that "he [Dana] never had any quarrel with Gen. Rosecrans. . . Neither is it true . . . that Rosecrans was removed on account of facts alleged in [my] reports . . . sent to Washington. . . .[I]t was not until the situation exhibited in [my] reports was emphatically illustrated by a private communication which Gen. J. A. Garfield . . . addressed to Secretary Chase that the administration resolved to act decisively." Garfield reiterated his denial. "Any charge that I was in any sense untrue to you," " he assured Rosecrans, "has no particle of truth in it." With both men now running for office—Garfield for the highest office—the case of "The Letter" would become a cause célèbre. Garfield, Rosecrans, and Chickamauga were all fodder for the media gristmill.[39]

Garfield's political biographers made much of Garfield's courageous ride to join Thomas in his determined end-of-day stand on Snodgrass Hill, portraying him as the savior of the army while Rosecrans fled to Chattanooga. This, coupled with Dana's recent charge that Garfield had penned a secret letter of betrayal that was used to supplant his commander while Garfield returned to Washington in triumph, made the whole contretemps downright Shakespearean. Cumulatively, these accusations drove a rift between Rosecrans and his former chief of staff, one that never had time to heal before Garfield's untimely death the next year.

Dana remained undeterred despite Garfield's martyrdom. In 1882, he published Garfield's July 27, 1863, letter to Chase. It was not the smoking gun Dana had earlier claimed that had precipitated Rosecrans's removal (that, Dana asserted, was a different letter entirely), but its publication enraged Rosecrans. Chase's former private secretary, Mr. J. W. Shuckers, explained how the July 27 letter was used. Though Chase considered it private correspondence, after Chickamauga he decided to show it to President Lincoln. This act, asserted Schuckers, "determined [the President] to remove Rosecrans from command of the Army of the Cumberland. Perhaps it was so, but Dana's version of what happened was very different and became the version widely embraced by Rosecrans partisans. Dana continued to insist that the second, far more damning letter existed, and it, not the July 27 missive, decided Rosecrans's fate.[40]

Writing in 1895, aforementioned novelist James R. Gilmore added more detail to the story. Gilmore recounted a meeting between himself and Salmon Chase on

39   Smith, *Garfield Life and Letters*, 863-864. Charles A. Dana "Recollections of the Civil War," *New York Sun*, November 26, 1879; Garfield to Rosecrans, January 19. 1880, Rosecrans Papers.

40   "Garfield and Rosecrans: Mr. J. W. Schuckers's contribution to the history of the controversy," *New York Times*, June 12, 1882.

Christmas Day 1863. Gilmore claimed he met with Garfield the day before, December 24, where Gilmore "questioned him particularly as to the bearing of [Rosecrans] during the battle. . . .You know there never was a commander so cool in battle as old Rosecrans," responded Garfield, adding that Rosecrans "expressed a little surprise, nothing more, when he saw McCook was broken; but at once prepared to meet the emergency by sending [Garfield] with orders, on to Thomas, and going himself to Chattanooga to rally there our men and hold the place, for that was the objective of the campaign." According to Gilmore, when he asked why Rosecrans had been removed Garfield replied that "he did not know; that the deed was done sometime before his arrival in Washington, and he found it would be a waste of words to attempt to stem the opposition against the General."[41]

Gilmore related this conversation to Chase the next day at Christmas dinner. "Mr. Chase seemed to hesitate for a moment," recollected Gilmore, "then said, 'General Garfield has not been entirely frank with you.'" The secretary went on to relate how he had received a letter from Garfield "soon after Chickamauga," describing Rosecrans as "demoralized, panic-stricken and totally unfitted to command." Troubled, Chase carried the letter for several days before showing it to Lincoln, who insisted he read it before the entire cabinet. "At once Mr. Stanton suggested the removal of Rosecrans and the substitution of General Thomas." Gilmore's tale was widely circulated in a number of newspapers and eventually published as part of the memorial tribute to General Rosecrans at his funeral.[42]

Did this letter ever exist? Dana was later forced to admit that, "all I know of Garfield's letter is what Mr. Stanton told me; I never saw it—do not know where it is, and suppose it to be destroyed. . . . Of its contents I have never known anything, except as I have stated."[43]

Other inconsistencies abound. The reading of the letter to the cabinet is one example, for neither Chase's personal diary nor that of Secretary of the Navy Gideon Welles mentions such an incident. In addition, why would Chase have Schuckers destroy this supposedly embarrassing post-Chickamauga letter, but save the almost equally embarrassing July 27 letter? During the winter of 1868-1869, when Schuckers and Chase went through all of Chase's correspondence with an eye toward saving material that held either sentimental value or historical import, all of Garfield's military correspondence was preserved. Since Dana never saw the letter, Gilmore's story merely

41 James R. Gilmore, "Rosecrans' Removal," *Norfolk Virginian*, December 22, 1895. See also James R. Gilmore, "Why Rosecrans was removed," *Atlanta Constitution*, December 22, 1895, and James R. Gilmore, "The Relief of Rosecrans," *Burial of General Rosecrans, Arlington National Cemetery, May 17, 1902* (Cincinnati, The Robert Clarke Company), 98-99.

42 Gilmore, "Rosecrans' Removal," Norfolk Virginian, December 22, 1895.

43 Smith, Garfield Life and Letters, vol. 2, 870.

echoes Dana's hearsay, embellished with a verbal confirmation purportedly from Chase—but only described long after Chase was dead. Nor is there any contemporary eyewitness account (such as Chase's or Welles's diaries) to corroborate the letter's existence. It is unlikely that this letter ever existed.

All of the evidence purporting to describe Garfield's "betrayal" of Rosecrans is similarly suspect, presented second- or third-hand, and worthy of closer scrutiny. Here is a summary of all participants and the circumstances surrounding their statements:

Edwin M. Stanton: He was unquestionably the driving force behind Rosecrans's dismissal. His purpose was fixed on that outcome before he even left Washington, and well before the fateful meeting with Garfield. His telegram stating that Garfield and Steedman confirmed "everything" remains the primary evidence of Garfield's duplicity, and seeming irrefutable, but the telegram offers no specifics about what Garfield actually said. Stanton's interpretation is highly suspect, as exemplified his gross distortion of Rosecrans's "amnesty" telegram to Governor Morton. Stanton presents direct evidence, buy it is not unbiased and, without corroboration, untrustworthy. At best, we are left with too many questions about what Garfield actually said, and at worst, we can assume Stanton merely confirmed his own pre-conceived notions;

Col. Anson Stager: Most historians rely on Stager's corroboration of Stanton's claim. Stager's supposed condemnation of Garfield, via Colonel Darr in 1881, appears to be the clinching argument for Garfield's duplicity. However, in no discussion of that meeting is there any mention of Stager's adamant denial of Darr's allegations, or of Stager's public statements asserting just the opposite: that Garfield in fact vehemently defended his chief, exactly as Garfield claimed. Stager's own public statements should be given more weight than Darr's second-hand assertion;

Charles A. Dana: Dana of course was Rosecrans's principle slanderer, and that might be motive enough for him to want to shift the blame to Garfield. But it is also worth noting that Dana's animosity toward Garfield surfaced in the mid-1870s when Dana was the editor and co-owner of the New York Sun and in the midst of a particularly nasty political fight. It is interesting to note that United States Senator Roscoe Conkling's brother was also a stockholder in that newspaper. Conkling, a New York powerbroker, led the faction of the Republican Party known as the "Stalwarts," who fully endorsed political patronage (the spoils system) and bitterly opposed merit-based civil service reform—the opposite of what Garfield championed. Conkling rightly regarded Garfield, a progressive, as a major threat to his patronage power, much of which was centered on who controlled appointments to the highly lucrative job of running the New York Customs House. The two men locked horns throughout the decade. Naturally enough, Dana's paper was a Stalwart mouthpiece, which explains much of the animosity shown toward Garfield—especially after Garfield's surprise nomination as the Republican candidate for president (at the expense of a Stalwart favorite, U. S. Grant) in 1880. Moreover, Dana's own dispatches from Chattanooga in 1863 are full of distortions and outright lies. It is no stretch to presume that his accusations against Garfield are any more truthful than Stanton's;

Montgomery P. Blair. Blair's evidence dates from 1880 and is detailed in a letter to Rosecrans. Blair's account is confusing. He stated that Lincoln removed Rosecrans only after Garfield confirmed rumors of Rosecrans panicking and leaving the field. Blair heard this secondhand from the president, and was not sure if this was in the form of a letter read before the cabinet, or from a direct interview between Garfield and Lincoln. The latter is impossible, since Stanton's and Lincoln's face-to-face meetings with Garfield only occurred well after the decision to replace Rosecrans had been made. The former, however, is highly improbable. According to Mr. Schucker, Chase's confidential secretary, the only letter Chase presented to Lincoln was Garfield's July 27th missive. That letter could not possibly have included anything about Rosecrans's conduct at Chickamauga since it was written nearly two months before the battle. This means that Blair could only be referring to the mythical "second letter," which Dana claimed to have heard about but had never seen, and Gilmore claimed that Chase referenced during the Christmas dinner. However, Schucker made it clear the letter in question was in fact the July communiqué—and that no other letter existed. The contradictions in Blair's version of events simply cannot be reconciled, which leave us with a very unsatisfactory set of unanswered questions. Blair's motives, too, are suspect.

Montgomery Blair, the son of Francis P. Blair, was Lincoln's postmaster general and by nature a quarrelsome man. In the words of Lincoln's secretary John Hay, the Blairs were a "close corporation. . . . They have a way of going with a rush for anything they undertake." They also feuded with the radicals, especially Chase, whom they charged with corruption. As a congressman, Garfield led the investigation stemming from those charges. They cleared Chase, much to the Blairs' long-lived disgust. Montgomery Blair's accusation against Garfield came just after Garfield's surprise nomination in 1880, and, according to Blair, after Garfield's betrayal of yet another ally, Senator John Sherman of Ohio—who was supposed to be the party's nominee. Blair had plenty of ulterior motive in writing to Rosecrans when he did;[44]

---

44 Doris Kearns Goodwin, *Team of Rival, The Political Genius of Abraham Lincoln* (New York, Simon and Schuster, 2005), 314.

James R. Gilmore: Gilmore was a young Bostonian who made his fortune in cotton before the war. Business trips down south inspired him to write. Under the pseudonym Edmund Kirke, Gilmore penned several novels describing the South and Southerners. His tracts were ardently abolitionist, aimed at showing the evils of slavery. During the war he became a journalist and lecturer. Though never a soldier, he was fond of inserting himself into moments of action. He acted as Horace Greeley's emissary to Rosecrans in the summer of 1863 in order to sound out Rosecrans on the idea of a presidential run against Lincoln, assuming Rosecrans could be shown to be "sound on the goose"—i.e. a firm opponent of slavery and supporter of immediate abolition. According to his memoirs, Gilmore also undertook a peculiar informal peace mission to Richmond in 1864, to no avail.[45]

In 1880 Gilmore published a laudatory campaign biography of Garfield, hastily written and full of fanciful details, especially concerning Garfield's return to Thomas. Gilmore had Garfield barely escaping capture and repeatedly cheating death. In 1895, Gilmore expanded this episode into a widely circulated article that included even more embellishments. This time Gilmore had Garfield dodging a hot fire of "shot and shell and canister [which] plowed up the ground all about [him.]" Very little of this article had any basis in fact. Gilmore also erroneously placed Garfield with Thomas in time to witness Gordon Granger's arrival on Snodgrass Hill, crafting suitably melodramatic (and wholly fictitious) dialogue to fit the moment.[46]

Neither of these efforts contained any hint of a Garfield betrayal. Nor did Gilmore include any details of his previously described Christmas dinner at Chase's Washington residence in Gilmore's own *Personal Recollections of Abraham Lincoln and the Civil War* (1898). The flaws in Gilmore's account of that dinner have already been examined, but it is worth noting the overall lack of consistency in Gilmore's various iterations of the history, as well as the amount of manufactured detail generally included in his historical writings. Gilmore never really stopped being a novelist, whether he was writing fiction or nonfiction;

Jacob D. Cox: Although Cox's Military Reminiscences were not published until 1900, they were drawn in part from his own diaries. Cox—a friend and political ally—had Garfield's confidence and was in a position to record Garfield's observations. Garfield's recounting of both the ride back to Rossville and later, of the meeting with

45 James R. Gilmore, *Personal Recollections of Abraham Lincoln and the Civil War* (Boston, L. C. Page and Company, 1898), 101.

46 James R. Gilmore, "Garfield's Perilous Ride at Chickamauga," *Chicago Tribune*, May 26, 1895.

Stanton, were relayed to Cox barely a month after they occurred. They remain the most detailed descriptions of each event ever to see print. Cox's account is notable for conveying not just factual details, but also Garfield's impressions of each moment, including Rosecrans's demeanor.

The salient features of Cox's account are: (1) Garfield felt Rosecrans had suffered "a collapse of nerve and will" during the ride to Rossville, and (2) Garfield's conclusion that, despite his good qualities, Rosecrans "lacked poise . . . and the steadiness of will necessary to handle great affairs successfully." Cox himself thought that Rosecrans had a "fatal defect . . . the liability to be swept away by excitement and to lose all efficient control of himself and others in the very crisis when complete self-possession is the essential quality of a great general."[47]

Did Garfield agree wholeheartedly with these sentiments, as Cox related them? If so, did he also tell the same to Stanton in Louisville? We can't know for certain, but nothing in Garfield's own writings indicates this to be true. Of course, Garfield subsequently said very little about what happened on September 20. He also left no details about his Louisville meeting. We do know that he worked to get Rosecrans either a field command or, potentially, the vice-presidential nomination. Would Garfield put forth Rosecrans's name for important new positions if he thought Cox's assessment was true?

Henry Villard: Villard, like Gilmore, was another wealthy businessman turned journalist. His memoir echoes Cox's: Villard thought the chief of staff lost confidence in his commander after Chickamauga. Writing in 1900, Villiard wrote that "Garfield, knowing he was safe with me, took me freely into his confidence. He told me how fully convinced he was that his chief was making a mortal mistake in going to Chattanooga, how he tried to dissuade him from it, and how relieved [Garfield] himself was to be permitted to rejoin Thomas. . . . While he did not say so directly, it could be inferred from his remarks that his faith in Rosecrans' military qualifications were shaken, if not lost."[48]

It is impossible to state definitively that Garfield never said anything detrimental about William Starke Rosecrans. As evidenced by his letters in the summer of 1863, he did criticize his commander. In Louisville, he almost certainly related facts that cast Rosecrans in a bad light when he was interrogated closely by Stanton and could not

47 Cox, *Military Reminiscences*, vol. 2, 8-10.

48 Villard, *Memoirs*, vol. 2, 185-186.

avoid describing the difficult details of that afternoon. Rosecrans made bad decisions that day, and it would require outright lies on Garfield's part to paper over those mistakes—and perjury was simply not part of Garfield's character. But did he argue for Rosecrans's removal? On this issue Stanton's telegram is of no help. According to Stanton, Garfield "confirmed the worst . . . [about] the conduct of the commanding general," but made no reference as to whether or not Garfield thought Rosecrans should go. For his part, Garfield claimed he "rebuked" Stanton and "earnestly defended" Rosecrans. Secondhand, Colonel Darr claimed Stager told him that Garfield thought Rosecrans "should be removed." Contrast this with Stager's own emphatic denials of ever having said anything of the sort. Stager's own testimony instead corroborated Garfield's account. On the whole, the balance tilts in Garfield's favor.

One other consideration should not be overlooked. Where did Garfield's duty lie? Both Jacob Cox and Theodore Clarke Smith were quick to point out that Garfield had an obligation to Stanton and Lincoln the truth as he saw it. To do anything else would amount to dereliction of duty. Moreover, as Cox described, Stanton already had considerable information on the event in question, which would have made it difficult for Garfield to obfuscate certain actions even if he had been inclined to do so.

It is apparent that the most critical accusation lodged against Garfield—the mysterious letter Dana accused Garfield of penning right after Chickamauga, which Chase supposedly read aloud to Lincoln, and which was supposedly the tipping point in convincing Lincoln of Rosecrans's need to go—is a fabrication. At best this is a garbled tale concerning the July 27, 1863, letter, and at worst it is a deliberate lie invented by Dana, repeated by Gilmore, and embraced by Rosecrans.

It is also inarguable that Garfield had nothing to do with Rosecrans's removal. That decision was made well before Garfield ever met with Stanton or Lincoln. The root cause rested with Rosecrans's already adversarial relationship with Stanton, a relationship Rosecrans sometimes seemed to deliberately aggravate. Rosecrans's decision to ride to Chattanooga instead of returning to Thomas sealed his fate with the war secretary. Dana's grossly distorted dispatches describing the Army of the Cumberland's circumstances after Chickamauga, and of the army commander's purported feebleness, cemented his removal.

Rosecrans was brought down by Dana's deceptive backstabbing in 1863. The ultimate irony is that in seeking to justify his own actions, Rosecrans was more than ready to believe Dana's new falsehoods when it came to James Garfield.

Union Order of Battle

The research presented here is the cornerstone of my entire Chickamauga project, which commenced in 1997 as research for a war game. My goal was to determine an accurate and comparable initial strength (as well as combat loss) for each regiment, battalion, or battery engaged at Chickamauga. Equally important, since the two armies used several different categories of numbers when counting men, and each side counted people a little differently, the final "engaged" numbers needed to equalized in order to make valid comparisons between the combatants.

"Aggregate Present" (AP) included all officers and men currently with the unit, including sick, excused duty, and detailed men. This number is useful in understanding a force's logistical needs, but not for determining combat strength.

"Present for Duty" (PFD) excluded the sick and excused duty men, but usually included detailed men. This was the general strength of a unit.

"Present for Duty, equipped" (PFDE) excluded sick, excused duty and detailed men, giving only the unit's current combat strength. Usually used by Federal units.

"Effectives" was more often than not used by the Rebels. At first glance it might seem comparable to PFDE, but it was not. For the Confederates, "effectives" meant only men in the ranks carrying rifles and ready to fight. Not only did this number omit musicians, ambulance corps members, etc., it also excluded all officers—who would be included in PFDE numbers. Since officers amounted to between 9% and 15% of a unit's total strength (at Chickamauga they averaged 9.8%) a straight comparison between "engaged" and PFDE would undercount Confederate strengths significantly.

Finally, a word on data. In the historian's perfect world, bureaucracy reigns triumphant. Every form is filled out correctly and filed on time. Every battle report is clear, detailed, accurate, and includes all pertinent numbers. Once filed, these records are stored safely, never lost, misfiled, or (gasp) destroyed. We do not live in that world.

In reality, there are many gaps in the records, especially Confederate records. I have used a broad range of sources for the information presented below, but the numbers for some units remain incomplete. Where necessary, I resorted to estimates and averages, extrapolated from the numbers I do have. (All such approximations are clearly noted.) Even that methodology, however, is often insufficient.

One final note concerns artillery. By 1863, both armies were supposed to have centralized their divisional artillery into battalions instead of assigning a battery to each brigade. In practice, not every division fought this way. As a result, if no artillery battalion commander is shown (for either army), that battalion did not operate tactically as a unit.

Union Sources and Methodology

The primary source for most Union numbers is the *Official Records*. About two-thirds of the Army of the Cumberland's engaged units report their strength somewhere in the *OR*. Not all those numbers are equally accurate. Some regiments reported their strength at the moment of combat, and in rare instances, separately for each day. Some brigade and divisional reports use figures drawn from earlier in the month, or even (in some cases) from the last monthly returns in August. The final Union numbers provided here are culled from and cross-checked against several different sources.

Sources, in Order of Precedence

1) Monuments: Some monuments provide detailed numbers of men taken into action. Veterans put a lot of effort into making the information on their monuments accurate, so I believe it is safe to rely on these. In some cases, the monument numbers match the regimental report numbers (see below), but in a surprising number of cases they do not.

There is one additional bias to consider. Veterans had a vested interest in the size of the unit as it went into battle, and the smaller the better. Given the currency of the time, the percentage of loss was often seen as a measure of valor and sacrifice. Further, a small unit defeating a larger enemy is obviously more dramatic than a large unit defeating a smaller foe; conversely, there was no shame in giving way to overwhelming numbers.

As a result, while the numbers presented on the monuments are not fabrications, they are pared to the bone: Men detailed to guard packs, sent to get water, the unarmed (infirmary corps) or otherwise not directly engaged on the firing line are usually not counted—even though they likely should be for the sake of direct comparison.

2) Regimental and Battery Reports. Each regimental and battery commander was supposed to file a report detailing his unit's actions and losses. For the Federals, most of these appear in the *OR.* About half of those provide engaged strengths, usually broken out as officers and men, and then a total. Nearly all these reports come from the morning roll calls made on September 18, 19, and 20. In general, such numbers are from the PFDE category.

3) Brigade Reports. Just as with regimental reports, brigade commanders were supposed to file their own reports. Brigadiers sometimes reported their strengths as of the last semi-weekly return. In most cases at Chickamauga, that return was dated September 14 or 15. These returns use the less restrictive PFD category in most cases, making precise accounting more difficult. However, I have used the brigade reports as-is because it is not always clear if the report was a PFD or PFDE number, and any attempt to modify those numbers would introduce as many errors as it corrects.

4) Higher Echelon Reports. Sometimes, the division or even corps commanders provided detailed regimental strengths in their reports. These come from a variety of sources, and have to be evaluated separately. One very accurate report, for example, is the Chief Surgeon's addendum to the XXI Corps report: this report details the casualties of each unit in the corps, and also details the strength taken into action for every regiment and battery actually engaged at Chickamauga. In only a few cases do the regimental reports differ from this corps report, and then usually by only a handful of men. The record-keeping in XXI Corps has clearly survived much better than in the rest of the army, and I came to trust these numbers a great deal. The First Division of the Reserve Corps provided a similar summary. Finally, the army consolidated returns were useful in determining the strength of the provost guard and escorts, where listed. Since these organizations reported directly to corps or division, they are not buried in various brigade totals but broken out separately. (See *OR* 30, pt. 1, 169-170.)

5) Morning Reports. Each company was required to take roll and turn in a report every morning. These rolls were recorded and consolidated at regimental headquarters. Most of the numbers found in the regimental battle reports, above, are derived from these morning roll calls. They represent perhaps the most accurate view of a unit's available combat power on any given day. Unfortunately, these reports didn't always survive the rigors of campaigning. For the Union, these reports are found in the national archives, bound in into regimental volumes.

6) Brigade and Division Returns. These are the Army of Cumberland returns (Record Group 94, National Archives). Returns were usually filed every ten days. I've used the September returns, which should have been taken on the 10th, 20th, and 30th

of the month. For obvious reasons, the September 20 returns are spotty. Most of the surviving returns date from September 30—ten days after the battle. Each return itemizes the regiments, battalions, or batteries as a line item, in each case indicating the number of officers and men present "for duty" at the end of the month. Since they do not specifically include "Present for duty, equipped" as a separate category, I relied upon these numbers only as a last resort, with the Chickamauga battle losses added to them. These are likely mildly inflated, as some of the lightly wounded had already returned to duty, and detailed men returned to the ranks. Again, I have not attempted to modify those figures in any effort to reconcile such discrepancies; estimates based on previous estimates merely compound mistakes and reduce the process to a guessing game. Instead I have chosen to use the September 30 numbers plus losses as-is, which provides the likely maximum strength a given unit would have taken into action.

6) The Quarterly Ordnance Reports. These National Archive records list the government property on hand in each regiment once a quarter. As such, they can sometimes provide a good cross check for the rough size of a unit, but cannot be relied upon for precise head counts. These reports itemize weapons on hand, not the men to use them, and the dates of each return vary greatly. Ordnance returns were filed once a quarter. I used the September 30, 1863 numbers where possible.

Union artillery armament comes from *OR* 30, pt. 1, 233-236. This report details the equipment of all engaged batteries. For those batteries detached or otherwise not engaged, see *OR* 23, pt. 2, 967-969, which details artillery weaponry for June 30, 1863.

Nomenclature Notes

1/XIV means 1st Division, XIV Corps.

1/1/XIV means 1st Brigade, 1st Division, XIV Corps.

1/15 US means 1st Battalion, 15th US Infantry Regiment.

SS = Sharpshooters.

Lt. = Light if artillery, or Lieutenant if a rank.

Bn. = Battalion.

(k) = killed in action

(w) = wounded, (mw) = mortally wounded.

(c) = captured

(Units in *Italics* were not engaged.)

Union Order of Battle

Maj. Gen. William S. Rosecrans
Commanding, Army of the Cumberland

Formation	Companies	Strength	Sources
Force engaged	1,589	60,889	
Escort, Army	**25**	**988**	
1 Bn Ohio SS Capt. Gershom M. Barber	3	154	OR 30, pt. 3,914
10 Ohio Lt. Col. William M. Ward	10	396	OR 30, pt. 3, 914
15 Penn. Cav Col. William J. Palmer	12	438	OR 30, pt. 1, 170
XIV Corps (guns)	**458** (64)	**18,138**	
XX Corps (guns)	**367** (54)	**13,048**	
XXI Corps (guns)	**333** (52)	**12,111**	
Reserve Corps (guns)	**150** (18)	**5,894**	
Cavalry Corps (guns)	**194** (7)	**7,751**	
Wilder's Brigade (guns)	**49** (10)	**2,378**	
39th Indiana	10	581	

Formation	Companies	Strength	Sources
Troops nearby, but not engaged, September 18-20			
3/3/Res	*26*	*1,000 (estimate)*	
(guns)	*(6)*		
38 Ohio	*10*	*513*	
2/1/21	*41*	*1,570*	
(guns)	*(6)*		
110 Illinois Bn	*4*	*255*	
Pioneers	*23*	*883*	
3 Indiana Cav	*4*	*159*	
Total	**108**	**4,380**	
(guns)	*(12)*		

Maj. Gen. George H. Thomas
XIV Army Corps

Formation	Companies	Strength	Sources
XIV Corps	**458**	**18,138**[1]	
(guns)	(64)		
Escort	**10**	**441**	
9 Michigan Col. John G. Parkhurst	*9*	*384*	OR 30, pt. 3, 914[2]
L, 1 Ohio Cav Capt. John D. Barker	1	57	OR 30, pt. 3, 914
1/XIV Col. Benjamin F. Scribner (guns)	**131** (18)	**4,964**	
1/1/XIV Col. Benjamin F. Scribner	**50**	**1,730**[3]	
38 Indiana Lt. Col. Daniel F. Griffin	10	354	OR 30, pt. 1, 292[4]
2 Ohio Lt. Col. Obadiah C. Maxwell (w), Maj. William T. Beatty (w&c), Capt. James Warnock	10	412	OR 30, pt. 1, 294, and Monument[5]

Formation	Companies	Strength	Sources
33 Ohio Col. Oscar F. Moore	10	415	*OR* 30, pt. 1, 289
94 Ohio Maj. Rue P. Hutchins	10	309	*OR* 30, pt. 1, 289
10 Wisconsin Lt. Col. John H. Ely (c), Capt. Jacob W. Roby	10	240	Monument[6]
2/1/XIV Brig. Gen. John C. Starkweather	**40**	**1,512**	
24 Illinois Col. Geza Mihalotzy (w), Capt. Augustus Mauff	10	362	*OR* 30, pt. 1, 308[7]
79 Penn. Lt. Col. Harry A. Hambright	10	390	Monument[8]
1 Wisconsin Lt. Col. George B. Bingham	10	391	*OR* 30, pt. 1, 308[9]
21 Wisconsin Lt. Col. Harrison Hobart (w), Capt. Charles H. Walker	10	369	*OR* 30, pt. 1, 308[10]
3/1/XIV Brig Gen. John H. King	**38**	**1,375**	
1/15 US Capt. Albert B. Dod	7	276	*OR* 30, pt. 1, 312 and Monument
1/16 US Maj. Phillip Sidney Coolidge (k), Capt. R. E. A. Crofton	8	308	*OR* 30, pt. 1, 312
1/18 US Capt. George W. Smith	8	300	*OR* 30, pt. 1, 312 and Monument
2/18 US Capt. Henry Haymond	7	287	*OR* 30, pt. 1, 312 and Monument
1/19 US Maj. Samuel K. Dawson (w), Capt. Edmund L. Smith	8	204	*OR* 30, pt. 1, 322 and Monument[11]

Formation	Companies	Strength	Sources
Artillery/1/XIV	**3**	**347**	
4th Indiana Lt. Lt. Henry Flansburg (w), Lt Henry J. Willits	1	99	OR 30, pt. 3, 796[12]
	(6) 2xNapoleon, 2xJames Rifle, 2x 12# Howitzer		
A, 1 Michigan Lt Lt. George W. Van Pelt (k), Lt. Almerick W. Wilbur	1	118	OR 30, pt. 1, 289
	(6) 6x10# Parrott		
H 5 US Lt Lt. Howard M. Burnham (k), Lt. Joshua A. Fessenden	1	130	OR 30, pt. 1, 312
	(6) 4xNapoleon, 2x10# Parrott		
2/XIV Maj. Gen. James S. Negley (Guns)	**112** (18)	**4,282**	
1/2/XIV Brig. Gen. John Beatty	**40**	**1,191**	*OR* **30, pt. 1, 371**
104 Illinois Lt. Col. Douglas Hapeman	10	299	OR 30, pt. 1, 371
42 Indiana Lt. Col. William T. B. McIntire	10	328	OR 30, pt. 1, 371[13]
88 Indiana Col. George Humphrey	10	259	*OR* 30, pt. 1, 371
15 Kentucky Col. Marion C. Taylor	10	305	OR 30, pt. 1, 371
2/2/14 Col. Timothy R. Stanley (w), Col. William L. Stoughton	**29**	**1,018**	
19 Illinois Lt. Col. Alexander W. Raffen	9	333	Brigade Return, NARA[14]

Formation	Companies	Strength	Sources
11 Michigan Col. William L. Stoughton, Lt. Col. Melvin Mudge	10	341	Morning Report, NARA[15]
18 Ohio Lt. Col. Charles H. Grosvenor	10	344	Brigade Return, NARA[16]
3/2/XIV Col. William Sirwell	**40**	**1,729**	
37 Indiana Lt. Col. William D. Ward	10	361	Brigade Return, NARA[17]
21 Ohio Lt. Col. Dwella M. Stoughton (w), Maj. Arnold McMahan (c), Capt. Charles H. Vantine	10	561	Monument[18]
74 Ohio Capt. Joseph Fisher	10	300	Brigade Return, NARA[19]
78 Penn. Lt. Col. Archibald Blakeley	10	507	Brigade Return, NARA[20]
Arty/2/XIV	**3**	**344**	
Bridges Illinois Capt. Lyman Bridges	1	126	OR 30, pt. 1, 371
	(6) 2x Napoleon, 4x 3 Inch Rifle		
G 1 Ohio Lt Capt. Alexander Marshall	1	100	Divisional Return, NARA[21]
	(6) 4x Napoleon, 2x 3 Inch Rifle		
M 1 Ohio Lt Capt. Frederick Schultz	1	118	Artillery Return, NARA[22]
	(6) 4x James Rifle, 2x 3 Inch Rifle		
3/XIV Brig. Gen. John M. Brannan (guns)	**122** (16)	**5,163**	
1/3/XIV Col. John M. Connell	**29**	**1,220**[23]	

Formation	Companies	Strength	Sources
82 Indiana Col Morton C. Hunter	10	285	OR 30, pt. 1, 412
17 Ohio Lt. Col. Durbin Ward	10	454	OR 30, pt. 1, 412
31 Ohio Lt. Col. Frederick W. Lister	10	465	OR 30, pt. 1, 412
38 Ohio	det.	16	OR Supplement, 64, 258[24]
38 Ohio *Col. Edward H. Phelps*	*10*	*513*	*train guard*[25]
2/3/XIV Col. John T. Croxton (w), Col. William H. Hays	**50**	**1,998**	
10 Indiana Col. William B. Carroll (k), Lt. Col. Marsh B. Taylor	9	366	Monument[26]
74 Indiana Col. Charles W. Chapman (w), Lt. Col. Myron Baker	10	400	OR 30, pt. 1, 419[27]
4 Kentucky Lt. Col. P. Burgess Hunt, Maj. Robert M. Kelly	10	351	Brigade Return, NARA[28]
10 Kentucky Col. William H. Hays, Lt. Col. Gabriel C. Wharton	10	421	OR 30, pt. 1, 423
14 Ohio Lt. Col. Henry D. Kingsbury	10	460	OR 30, pt. 1, 424[29]
3/3/XIV Col. Ferdinand Van Derveer	**40**	**1,643**	
87 Indiana Col. Newell Gleason	10	366	Monument[30]
2 Minnesota Col. James George	10	384	Monument
9 Ohio Col. Gustave Kammerling	10	502	Troutman, *We Were the Ninth*, 147[31]
35 Ohio Lt. Col. Henry Van Ness Boynton	10	391	Monument[32]

Formation	Companies	Strength	Sources
Arty/3/XIV	**3**	**302**	
D, 1 Michigan Lt Capt. Josiah W. Church	1	106	Brigade Return, NARA[33]
	(6) 2x 10# Parrott, 2x James Rifle, 2x 12# Howitzer		
C, 1 Ohio Lt Lt. Marco B. Gary	1	122	Brigade Return, NARA[34]
	(6) 4x James Rifle, 2x Napoleon		
I, 4 US Lt. Frank G. Smith	1	74	Brigade Return, NARA[35]
	(4) 4x Napoleon		
4/XIV Maj. Gen. Joseph J. Reynolds (guns)	**83** (12)	**3,288**[36]	
1/4/XIV Col. John T. Wilder	**48**	**2,283** (detached, reporting to Army Headquarters)	
92 Illinois Col. Smith D. Atkins	8	383	BaumGartner, 152[37]
98 Illinois Col. John J. Funkhouser (w), Lt. Col. Edward Kitchell	10	485	Brigade Return, NARA[38]
123 Illinois Col. James Monroe	10	422	Brigade Return, NARA[39]
17 Indiana Maj. William T. Jones	10	513	Brigade Return, NARA[40]
72 Indiana Col. Abram O. Miller	10	480	Morning Reports, NARA[41]
2/4/XIV Col. Edward King (k), Col. Milton S. Robinson	**40**	**1,476**	
80 Illinois *Capt. James Cunningham*	*10*	*400*	*Morning Reports and* *Q.O.R.*[43]

Formation	Companies	Strength	Sources
68 Indiana Capt. Harvey J. Espy	10	356	Monument
75 Indiana Col. Milton S. Robinson, Lt. Col. William O'Brien	10	360	Monument[44]
101 Indiana Lt. Col. Thomas Doan	10	400	Brigade Return, NARA[45]
105 Ohio Maj. George T. Perkins (w)	10	382	Brigade Return, NARA[46]
3/4/XIV	**40**	**1,612**	
Brigade Provost A, 18 Kentucky Capt. John W. Robbins	1	29	Calculation[47]
18 Kentucky Lt. Col. Hubbard K. Milward (w), Capt. John B. Heltemes	9	266	OR 30, pt. 1, 478[48]
11 Ohio Col. Philander P. Lane	10	433	Monument, *OR* 30, pt. 1, 479.
36 Ohio Col. William G. Jones (k), Lt. Col. Hiram F. Devol	10	484	Brigade Return, NARA[49]
92 Ohio Col. Benjamin D. Fearing (w), Lt. Col. Douglas Putnam, Jr.	10	400	OR 30, pt. 1, 482[50]
Arty/4/XIV	**3**	**295**	
18 Indiana Lt Capt. Eli Lilly	1	95	Brigade Return, NARA[51]
(10) 6x 3 Inch Rifle, 4x Mountain Howitzer			
19 Indiana Lt Capt. Samuel J. Harris (w), Lt. Robert S. Lackey	1	100	Division Return, NARA[52]
(6) 4x Napoleon, 2x 3 Inch Rifle			

Formation	Companies	Strength	Sources
21 Indiana Lt Capt. William W. Andrew	1	100	Division Return, NARA[53]
(6) 6x Napoleon			

Maj. Gen. Alexander McDowell McCook
XX Army Corps

Formation	Companies	Strength	Sources
Escort I, 2 Kentucky Cav Lt. George W. L. Batman	1	39	Brigade Return, NARA[54]
Corps Provost H, 81st Indiana Capt. William J. Richards	1	25	OR 30, pt. 1, 523[55]
D, 1st Ohio Capt. Alexander Varian	1	41	Brigade Return, NARA[56]
1/XX Brig. Gen. Jefferson C. Davis	**121**	**3,926**	
(guns)	(18)		
1/1/XX Col. P. Sidney Post	**40**	**1,239**[57]	
59 Illinois Lt. Col. Joshua C. Winters	10	285	Morning Reports, NARA[58]
74 Illinois Col. Jason Marsh	10	354	Morning Reports, NARA[59]
75 Illinois Col. John E. Bennett	10	200	OR 30, pt. 1, 512[60]
22 Indiana Col. Michael Gooding	10	400	Morning Reports, NARA[61]
2/1/XX Brig. Gen. William P. Carlin	**40**	**1,190**	
21 Illinois Col. John W. S. Alexander (k), Capt. Chester K. Knight	10	416	OR 30, pt. 1, 518[62]
38 Illinois Lt. Col. Daniel H. Gilmer (k), Capt. Willis G. Whitehurst	10	301	OR 30, pt. 1, 522

Formation	Companies	Strength	Sources
81 Indiana Capt. Nevil B. Boone (relieved), Maj. James E. Calloway	9	230	OR 30, pt. 1, 523[63]
101 Ohio Lt. Col. John Messer (w), Maj. Beden B. McDonald (w), Capt. Leonard D. Smith	10	243	OR 30, pt. 1, 528[64]
3/1/XX Col. Hans Heg (k), Col. John A. Martin	**38**	**1,218**	
25 Illinois Maj. Samuel D. Wall (w), Capt. Wesford Taggart	10	337	OR 30, pt. 1, 531
35 Illinois Lt. Col. William P. Chandler	10	299	OR 30, pt. 1, 531
8 Kansas Col. John A. Martin, Lt. Col. James L. Abernathy	10	406	OR 30, pt. 1, 531
15 Wisconsin Lt. Col. Ole C. Johnson (c), Capt. Mons Grinager	8	176	OR 30, pt. 1, 531[65]
Arty/1/XX	**3**	**279**	
2 Minnesota Lt Lt. Albert Woodbury (mw), Lt. Richard L. Dawley	1	76	Division Return, NARA[66]
(6)	2x 10# Parrott, 4x Napoleon		
5 Wisconsin Lt Capt. George Q. Gardner	1	115	Division Return, NARA[67]
(6)	2x Napoleon, 2x 10# Parrott, 2x Mountain Howitzer		
8 Wisconsin Lt Lt. John D. McLean	1	88	Division Return, NARA[68]
(6)	2x Napoleon, 4x 3 Inch Rifles		

Formation	Companies	Strength	Sources
2/20 Brig. Gen. Richard W. Johnson	**122**	**4,658**	
1/2/XX Brig. Gen. August Willich (guns)	**40** (18)	**1,499**	
89 Illinois Lt. Col. Duncan J. Hall (k), Maj. William D. Williams	10	391	Morning Reports, NARA[70]
32 Indiana Lt. Col. Frank Erdelmeyer	10	378	Brigade Return, NARA[71]
39 Indiana Col. Thomas J. Harrison (Detached, reporting to Corps Headquarters)	10	581	Morning Reports, NARA[72]
15 Ohio Lt. Col. Frank Askew	10	325	OR 30, pt. 1, 550
49 Ohio Maj. Samuel F. Gray (w), Capt. Luther M. Strong, Maj. Samuel F. Gray	10	405	Brigade Return, NARA[73]
2/2/XX Col. Joseph B. Dodge	**40**	**1,130**	*OR* **30, pt. 1, 536**[74]
79 Illinois Col. Allen Buckner	10	263	Morning Reports, NARA[75]
29 Indiana Lt. Col. David M. Dunn	10	315	*Stueben Republican*, 10/31/63[76]
30 Indiana Lt. Col. Orrin D. Hurd	10	299	Calculation[77]
77 Penn. Col. Thomas E. Rose (c), Capt. Joseph J. Lawson	10	253	Calculation[78]
3/2/XX Col. Philemon P. Baldwin (k), Col. William W. Berry	**39**	**1,627**	
6 Indiana Lt. Col. Hagerman Tripp (w), Maj. Calvin D. Campbell	10	467	Brigade Return, NARA[79]

Formation	Companies	Strength	Sources
5 Kentucky Col. William W. Berry, Capt. John M. Huston	10	334	Brigade Return, NARA[80]
1 Ohio Lt. Col. Bassett Langdon	9	367	Brigade Return, NARA[81]
93 Ohio Col. Hiram Strong (w), Lt. Col. William H. Martin	10	459	Brigade Return, NARA[82]
Arty/2/XX	**3**	**402**	
5 Indiana Lt Capt. Peter Simonson	1	124	Brigade Report, NARA[83]
(6) 4x James Rifle, 2x Napoleon			
A, 1 Ohio Lt Capt. Wilbur F. Goodspeed	1	152	Divisional Return, NARA[84]
(6) 4x James Rifle, 2x Napoleon			
20 Ohio Lt Capt. Edward Grosskopff	1	126	Divisional Return, NARA[85]
(6) 4x 3 Inch Rifle, 2x Napoleon			
3/XX Maj. Gen. Philip H. Sheridan	**122**	**4,359**	
1/3/XX Brig. Gen. William H. Lytle (k), Col. Silas Miller	40	1,556	
36 Illinois Col. Silas Miller, Lt. Col. Porter C. Olson	10	358	Morning Report, NARA[86]
88 Illinois Lt. Col. Alexander S. Chadbourne	10	449	Brigade Return, NARA[87]
21 Michigan Col. William B. McCreery (w & c), Maj. Seymour Chase	10	262	A. B. Morse Letter, NARA[88]
24 Wisconsin Lt. Col. Theodore S. West (c), Maj. Carl Von Baumbach	10	487	Brigade Return, NARA[89]

Formation	Companies	Strength	Sources
2/3/XX Col. Bernard Laiboldt	**39**	**1,100**	
44 Illinois Col. Wallace W. Barrett	10	269	Brigade Return, NARA[90]
73 Illinois Col. James F. Jacques	10	300	Morning Report, NARA[91]
2 Missouri Maj. Arnold Beck	10	281	Brigade Report, NARA[92]
15 Missouri Col. Joseph Conrad	10	250	Morning Report, NARA[93]
3/3/XX Col. Luther P. Bradley (w), Col. Nathan W. Walworth	**40**	**1,391**	
22 Illinois Lt. Col. Francis Swanwick	10	314	Brigade Return, NARA[94]
27 Illinois Col. Jonathan R. Miles	10	463	Brigade Return, NARA[95]
42 Illinois Col. Nathan H. Walworth, Lt. Col. John A. Hottenstein	10	305	Morning Report, NARA[96]
51 Illinois Lt. Col. Samuel B. Raymond	9	309	Brigade Return, NARA[97]
Arty/3/XX	**3**	**312**	
C, 1 Illinois Lt Capt. Mark H. Prescott	1	114	Divisional Return, NARA[98]
	(6) 4x 3 Inch Rifle, 2x 12# Howitzers		
11 Indiana Lt Capt. Arnold Suitermeister	1	117	Divisional Return, NARA[99]
	(6) 4x Napoleon, 2x 3 Inch Rifle		
G, 1 Missouri Lt Lt. Gustavus Scheuler	1	81	Divisional Return, NARA[100]
	(6) 4x Napoleon, 2x 10# Parrott		

Formation	Companies	Strength	Sources

Maj. Gen. Thomas L. Crittenden

XXI Army Corps

Formation	Companies	Strength	Sources
XXI Corps (guns)	**333** (52)	**12,111**[101]	
K, 15 Illinois Cav. Capt. Samuel B. Sherer	1	83	OR 30, pt. 3, 918[102]
1/XXI Brig. Gen. Thomas J. Wood (w) (guns)	**80** (12)	**2,932**[103]	
1/1/XXI Col. George P. Buell	**40**	**1,333**	
100 Illinois Col. Frederick A. Bartleson (c), Maj. Charles M. Hammond	10	339	OR 30, pt. 1, 615
58 Indiana Lt. Col. James T. Embree	10	397	OR 30, pt. 1, 661[104]
13 Michigan Col. Joshua B. Culver (w), Maj. Willard G. Eaton	10	220	OR 30, pt. 1, 615
26 Ohio Lt. Col. William H. Young	10	377	OR 30, pt. 1, 675[105]
2/1/21 *Brig. Gen. George D. Wagner*	*40*	*1,438*[106]	
15 Indiana *Col. Gustavus A. Wood*	*10*	*351*	*OR 30, pt. 1, 680*
40 Indiana *Col. John W. Blake*	*10*	*375*	*OR 30, pt. 1, 680*
51 Indiana *Captain D. W. Hamilton*	*8*[107]		
57 Indiana *Lt. Col. George W. Leonard*	*10*	*278*	*OR 30, pt. 1, 680*[108]
97 Ohio *Lt. Col. Milton Barnes*	*10*	*434*	*OR 30, pt. 1, 680*

Formation	Companies	Strength	Sources
3/1/XXI Col. Charles G. Harker	**38**	**1,346**	
73 Indiana Capt. D. W. Hamilton	10[109]		
3 Kentucky Col. Henry C. Dunlap	10	401	*OR* 30, pt. 1, 615
64 Ohio Col. Alexander McIlvain	10	325	*OR* 30, pt. 1, 615
65 Ohio Lt. Col. Horatio N. Whitbeck (w), Maj. Samuel C. Brown(w), Capt. Thomas Powell	10	306	*OR* 30, pt. 1, 615
125 Ohio Col. Emerson Opdycke	8	314	*OR* 30, pt. 1, 709[110]
Arty/1/XXI	**2**	**253**	
8 Indiana Lt. Capt. George Estep	1	134	*OR* 30, pt. 1, 615
	(6) 4x 10# Parrott, 2x Napoleon		
10 Indiana Lt Lt. William A. Naylor	1	122	*OR* 30, pt. 1, 680[111]
	(6) 4x 10# Parrott, 2x 12# Howitzer		
6 Ohio Lt Capt. Cullen Bradley	1	119	*OR* 30, pt. 1, 615
	(6) 4x 10# Parrott, 2x Napoleon		
2/XXI Maj. Gen. John M. Palmer	**129**	**5,043**[112]	
(guns)	*(22)*		
Escort			
C, 7 Illinois Cav. Capt. Prescott Bartlett	1	36	*OR* 30, pt. 1, 719

Formation	Companies	Strength	Sources
Provost			
110 Illinois *Capt. E. Hibbard Topping*	*4*	*255*	*OR 30, pt. 1, 680*[113]
Train Guards			
Bn., 1 Kentucky Maj. James W. Mitchell	5	178	OR 30, pt. 1, 745[114]
G, 23 Kentucky	1	29	OR Supplement 34, 575-576[115]
1/2/XXI Brig. Gen. Charles Cruft	**34**	**1,280**	
31 Indiana Col. John T. Smith	10	380	OR 30, pt. 1, 615
1 Kentucky Lt. Col. Alva R. Hadlock	4	118	OR 30, pt. 1, 615[116]
2 Kentucky Col. Thomas D. Sedgewick	10	367	OR 30, pt. 1, 615
90 Ohio Col. Charles H. Rippey	10	415	OR 30, pt. 1, 615
2/2/XXI Brig. Gen. William B. Hazen	**40**	**1,443**	
9 Indiana Col. Isaac Suman	10	328	OR 30, pt. 1, 616[117]
6 Kentucky Col. George T. Shackelford (w), Lt. Col. Richard Rockingham (k), Maj. Richard T. Whitaker	10	302	OR 30, pt. 1, 616
41 Ohio Col. Aquila Wiley	10	360	OR 30, pt. 1, 616[118]
124 Ohio Col. Oliver H. Payne (w), Maj. James B. Hampson	10	453	OR 30, pt. 1, 616
3/2/XXI Col. William Grose	**49**	**1,631**	
84 Illinois Col. Louis H. Waters	10	382	OR 30, pt. 1, 616

Formation	Companies	Strength	Sources
36 Indiana Lt. Col. Oliver P. Carey (w), Maj. Gilbert Trusler	10	347	*OR* 30, pt. 1, 616
23 Kentucky Lt. Col. James C. Foy	9	263	*OR* 30, pt. 1, 792[119]
6 Ohio Col. Nicholas L. Anderson(w), Maj. Samuel C. Irwin	10	362	*OR* 30, pt. 1, 616[120]
24 Ohio Col. David J. Higgins	10	277	*OR* 30, pt. 1, 616
Arty/2/XXI	**4**	**446**	
B, 1 Ohio Lt Lt. Norman A. Baldwin	1	132	*OR* 30, pt. 1, 616
	(6) 4x James Rifle, 2x 6# Gun		
F, 1 Ohio Lt Lt. Giles J. Cockerill	1	110	*OR* 30, pt. 1, 616
	(6) 4x James Rifle, 2x 12# Howitzer		
H, 4 US Lt. Harry C. Cushing	1	87	*OR* 30, pt. 1, 616
	(4) 4x 12# Howitzer		
M, 4 US Lt. Francis L. D. Russell	1	117	*OR* 30, pt. 1, 616
	(6) 4x Napoleon, 2x 24# Howitzer		
3/XXI Brig. Gen. Horatio P. Van Cleve	**123**	**4,053**	
(guns)	*(18)*		
Provost			
A, 9th Kentucky	1	30	*OR* 30, pt. 1, 814[121]
1/3/XXI	**39**	**1,384**	
79 Indiana Col. Frederick Knefler	10	300	*OR* 30, pt. 1, 616

Formation	Companies	Strength	Sources
9 Kentucky Col. George H. Cram	9	213	OR 30, pt. 1, 616[122]
17 Kentucky Col. Alexander M. Stout	10	487	OR 30, pt. 1, 616
19 Ohio Lt. Col. Henry G. Stratton	10	384	OR 30, pt. 1, 616
2/3/XXI Col. George F. Dick	**40**	**1,084**	
44 Indiana Lt. Col. Simeon C. Aldrich	10	229	OR 30, pt. 1, 616[123]
86 Indiana Maj. Jacob C. Dick	10	261	OR 30, pt. 1, 616
13 Ohio Lt. Col. Elhannon M. Mast (k), Capt. Horatio G. Cosgrove	10	304	OR 30, pt. 1, 616
59 Ohio Lt. Col. Granville A. Frambes	10	290	OR 30, pt. 1, 616[124]
3/3/XXI Col. Sidney M. Barnes	**40**	**1,202**	
35 Indiana Maj. John P. Dufficy	10	229	OR 30, pt. 1, 616
8 Kentucky Lt. Col. James D. Mayhew (w & c), Maj. John S. Clark	10	297	OR 30, pt. 1, 845[125]
21 Kentucky *Col. S. Woodson Price*	*10*[126]		
51 Ohio Col. Richard W. McLain(c), Lt. Col. Charles H. Wood	10	319	OR 30, pt. 1, 616
99 Ohio Col. Peter T. Swaine	10	357	OR 30, pt. 1, 616
Arty/3/XXI	**3**	**353**	
7 Indiana Lt Capt. George R. Swallow	1	122	OR 30, pt. 1, 806

(6)   4x 10# Parrott,
2x Napoleon

Formation	Companies	Strength	Sources
26 Penn Capt. Alanson J. Stevens (k), Lt. Samuel M. McDowell	1	112	*OR* 30, pt. 1, 806
	(6) 4x 6# Gun, 2x James Rifle		
3 Wisconsin Lt Lt. Courtland Livingston	1	119	*OR* 30, pt. 1, 806
	(6)4x 10# Parrott, 2x 12# Howitzer		

Maj. Gen. Gordon Granger

Reserve Corps[127]

Formation	Companies	Strength	Sources
Reserve Corps	**150**	**5,894**	
(guns)	*(18)*		
1/Res Brig. Gen. James B. Steedman	**99**	**3,819**	
(guns)	*(12)*		
1/1/Res Brig. Gen. Walter C. Whitaker	**58**	**2,695**[128]	
96 Illinois Col. Thomas E. Champion	10	419	Partridge, *History Of The Ninety-Sixth*[129]
115 Illinois Col. Jesse H. Moore	10	426	*OR* 30, pt. 1, 858[130]
84 Indiana Col. Nelson Trusler	10	374	*OR* 30, pt. 1, 858[131]
22 Michigan Col. Heber Le Favour (c), Lt. Col. William Sanborn (w), Capt. Alonzo M. Keeler	10	455	*OR* 30, pt. 1, 858[132]
40 Ohio Lt. Col. William Jones	10	537	*OR* 30, pt. 1, 858[133]
89 Ohio Col. Caleb H. Carlton (c), Capt. Isaac C. Nelson	10	389	*OR* 30, pt. 1, 858[134]

Formation	Companies	Strength	Sources
18 Ohio Lt Capt. Charles C. Aleshire	1	95	*OR* 30, pt. 1, 858
	(6) 6x 3 Inch Rifle		
2/1/Res Col. John G. Mitchell (guns)	**38** (6)	**1,124**	
78 Illinois Lt. Col. Carter Van Vleck (k), Lt. George Green	10	353	*OR* 30, pt. 1, 858
98 Ohio Capt. Moses J. Urquhart (w), Capt. Armstrong J. Thomas	7	181	*OR* 30, pt. 1, 858[135]
113 Ohio Lt. Col. Darius B. Warner	10	355	*OR* 30, pt. 1, 858
121 Ohio Lt. Col. Henry B. Banning	10	235	*OR* 30, pt. 1, 858
M, 1 Illinois Lt Lt. Thomas Burton	1	112	*OR* 30, pt. 1, 858
	(6) 4x Napoleon, 2x 3 Inch Rifle		
2/2/Res Col. Daniel McCook (guns)	**51** (6)	**2,075**	
85 Illinois Col. Caleb J. Dilworth	10	371	Morning Reports, NARA[136]
86 Illinois Lt. Col. David W. Magee	10	420	Morning Reports, NARA[137]
125 Illinois Col. Oscar F. Harmon	10	439	Morning Reports, NARA[138]
52 Ohio Maj. James T. Holmes	10	417	Morning Reports, NARA[139]
69 Ohio Lt. Col. Joseph B. Brigham	10	350	Morning Reports, NARA[140]

Formation	Companies	Strength	Sources
I, 2 Illinois Lt Capt. Charles M. Bennett	1	78	Morning Reports, NARA[141]
(6) 2x Napoleon, 2x James Rifle, 2x 10# Parrott			
3/3/Res *Brig. Gen. James G. Spears*	**26**	**1,000**	**estimate[142]**
(guns)	*(6)*		
3 Tenn. *Col. William Cross*	*10*	*300*	*estimate*
5 Tenn. *Col. James T. Shelley*	*8*	*300*	*estimate[143]*
6 Tenn. *Col. Joseph A. Cooper*	*7*	*300*	*estimate[144]*
A, 1 Tenn. Lt. *Capt. Ephraim P. Abbott*	*1*	*100*	*estimate[145]*
(6) 4x James Rifle, *2x 6# gun*			

Brig. Gen. Robert B. Mitchell

Cavalry Corps

Formation	Companies	Strength	Sources
Cavalry Corps	**195**	**7,751**	
1/Cav Col. Edward M. McCook	**114**	**4,087**	
Escort			
L, 4th Indiana Cav	1	32	Estimate[146]
1/1/Cav Col. Archibald P. Campbell	**35**	**1,348**	
2 Michigan Cav Maj. Leonidas S. Scranton	12	273	Brigade Return NARA[147]
9 Pennsylvania Cav Lt. Col. Roswell M. Russell	11	397	Brigade Return NARA[148]
1 Tennessee Cav Lt. Col. James P. Brownlow	12	678	Brigade Return NARA[149]

Formation	Companies	Strength	Sources
2/1/Cav Col. Daniel M. Ray	**48**	**1,532**[150]	
2 Indiana Cav Maj. Joseph B. Presdee	12	388	OR 30, pt. 3, 833[151]
4 Indiana Cav Lt. Col. John D. Deweese	10	284	OR 30, pt. 3, 833[152]
2 Tennessee Cav Lt. Col. William R. Cook	12	476	Brigade Return, NARA[153]
1 Wisconsin Cav Col. Oscar H. Lagrange	12	384	OR 30, pt.3, 833[154]
3/1/Cav Col. Louis D. Watkins	**32**	**1,175**	
4 Kentucky Cav Col. Wickliffe Cooper	10	288	Brigade Return, NARA[155]
5 Kentucky Cav Lt. Col. William T. Hoblitzell	10	363	Brigade Return, NARA[156]
6 Kentucky Cav Maj. Louis A. Gratz	12	524	Brigade Return, NARA[157]
2/Cav Brig. Gen. George Crook	**79**	**3,542**	
1/2/Cav Col. Robert H. G. Minty	**36**	**1,696**[158]	
3 Indiana Cav Bn *Lt. Col. Robert Klein*	*4*	*159*	*OR 30, pt. 1, 680*[159]
4 Michigan Cav Maj. Horace Gray	12	489	Brigade Return, NARA[160]
7 Penn. Cav Lt. Col. James G. Seibert	12	496	Brigade Return, NARA[161]
4 U.S. Cav Capt. James B. McIntyre	12	711	Brigade Return, NARA[162]
2/2/Cav Col. Eli Long	**43**	**1,846**	

Formation	Companies	Strength	Sources
2 Kentucky Cav Col. Thomas P. Nicholas	9	347	Brigade Return, NARA[163]
1 Ohio Cav Lt. Col. Valentine Cupp (k), Maj. Thomas J. Patten	10	404	Brigade Return, NARA[164]
3 Ohio Cav Lt. Col. Charles B. Seidel	12	550	Brigade Return, NARA[165]
4 Ohio Cav Lt. Col. Oliver P. Robie	12	545	Brigade Return, NARA[166]
Arty/Cav	**1**	**122**	
CBOT Battery Capt. James H. Stokes	1	122	Divisional Return, NARA[167]
(7) 4x 6# Gun, 3x James Rifle			
Pioneer Brigade *Capt. Patrick O'Connell*	*23*	*883*[168]	*OR 30, pt. 3, 769*
1st Bn *Capt. Charles J. Stewart*	*10*	*388*	*September 20 Report,* *NARA*[169]
2nd Bn *Capt. Correll Smith*	*2*	*65*	*September 20 Report,* *NARA*[170]
3rd Bn *Capt. Robert Clements*	*10*	*334*	*September 20 Report,* *NARA*[171]
1st Squadron *Lt. Wyman Murphy*	*1*	*61*	*OR 30, pt 3, 769*[172]

Endnotes

1. Wilder's brigade (1/4/14), is not included in this total.

2. On September 17, 1863, one company of the 9th Michigan was sent to Stevenson, where it remained. On September 19, the other nine companies escorted the 14th Corps baggage train to Chattanooga. On the 20th, eight of those companies returned to the battlefield, escorting a medical train, but saw no fighting.

3. The brigade OR report (OR 30, pt. 1, 289) provides the effective strength of all units as of September 15, 1863. Two regiments of the brigade, 38th Indiana and 10th Wisconsin, reported much lower strengths actually engaged, while one, the 2nd Ohio, reported 412 instead of the 414 found in the September 15th return.

4. On September 15, 1863, the regiment reported 410. OR 30, pt. 1, 289.

5. On September 15, 1863, the regiment reported 414. OR 30, pt. 1, 289.

6. On September 15, 1863, the regiment reported 323. OR 30, pt. 1, 289.

7. The 24th Illinois numbered 379, based on the September 23, 1863 return plus losses suffered. *OR* 30, pt. 3, 796.

8. The 79th Pennsylvania reported 445 on September 14, 1863. *OR* 30, pt.1, 308. Alternatively, the regiment reported 485, based on the September 23rd return plus losses.

9 The 1st Wisconsin numbered 398, based on the September 23, 1863 return plus losses. *OR* 30, pt. 3, 796.

10. The 21st Wisconsin numbered 342, based on the September 23, 1863 return and losses suffered. *OR* 30, pt. 3, 796. James M. Randall Diary of September 23, 1863 states that the "regiment went into the fight with 250 men."

11. Strength given as 199 in brigade report, *OR* 30, pt. 1, 312.

12. The 4th Indiana battery reported 2 officers and 77 men present on September 23. This figure, added to the 20 casualties reported in the battle, gives a pre-battle strength of 99 officers and men.

13. Lt. Col. McIntyre reported 19 officers and 200 enlisted men present, 30 enlisted men on extra duty, and 30 men sick; for a total 219 for duty and 60 detached and sick: 279 aggregate present on September 21, 1863. He also lists 104 officers and men as casualties. 104 losses added to the 219 for duty gives a total of 321 present for duty on the 18th, but we do not know the extra duty and sick totals for that date, which is likely where the discrepancy lies. Indiana State Archives, 42nd Indiana file. A letter to the *Evansville Daily Journal*, October 7, 1863, claims that 323 men entered action.

14. RG 94, Entry 65, Box 28. The September return shows 262, plus 71 losses. The August Return shows 336 PFD. Only nine companies listed as present on return, Company G was detached.

15. Includes field and staff.

16. RG 94, Entry 65, Box 28. The return shows 270, plus 74 losses.

17. RG 94, Entry 65, Box 28. The return shows 352, plus 9 losses.

18. 539 in *OR* 30, pt. 1, 390.

19. RG 94, Entry 65, Box 28. The return shows 291, plus 9 losses.

20. RG 94, Entry 65, Box 28. The return shows 502, plus 5 losses.

21. RG 94, Entry 65, Box 28. The return shows 100, no losses reported.

22. RG 94, Entry 65, Box 28. The return shows 114, plus 4 losses.

23. Strengths were determined by subtracting 10% of the strengths found in *OR* 30, pt. 1, 412 for each regiment, as per the brigade report, since the Brigade commander indicated that at least 10% of these figures were not engaged. In this case, the OR strength totals were clearly PFD, not PDFE figures. The 38th Ohio is also not included.

24. 1 officer and 15 men, serving with the brigade pickets, who were engaged.

25. Brigade Return, NARA, RG 94, Entry 65, Box 28. The strength is given for the September Return. No losses reported. The 38th Ohio was detached and escorted the trains of 14th and 20th Corps to Chattanooga on the 18th, and remained there throughout the battle, except for those men with the brigade pickets.

26. *Indianapolis Daily Journal*, October 6, 1863, shows that company E, 10th Indiana was not engaged, and shows no losses. No reason for the detachment is given.

27. *Stueben Republican*, October 10, 1863 reports 376 engaged, but this figure only counts the enlisted men.

28. RG 94, Entry 65, Box 28. The August return shows 390. Comparing the August strengths for the other four regiments to the known engaged strengths produces figures that range from 79% to 94% of the August reporting strength. This estimate represents 90% of the reported August strength.

29. 449 men in 14th Ohio, Fox, *Regimental Losses*, 32.

30. 380 men in 87 Indiana, Fox, *Regimental Losses*, 29. *Indianapolis Daily Journal*, October 3, 1863 shows 350 engaged.

31. Constantine Grebner, with Frederick Trautman, Trans.. *We were the Ninth* (Kent, OH: Kent State University Press, 1987), 147.

32. *OR* 30, pt. 1, 435, gives the strength as 464 present, but notes that 73 men did not enter action for various reasons.

33. RG 94, Entry 65, Box 28. The September return lists 95, plus 11 losses.

34. RG 94, Entry 65, Box 28. The August Return lists 122. The same number is found in the *OR*.

35. RG 94, Entry 65, Box 28. The August return lists 74. The September return lists 58, plus 22 losses, for a total of 80. It is assumed that some of the losses had returned to duty by the end of September, 10 days after the battle.

36. 1/4/14 is not included.

37. Richard A. Baumgartner, *Blue Lightning* (Blue Acorn Press, 1997), 152. Two companies, C and K, of the 92nd were on Lookout Mountain guarding trains and thus not present. Their strength would add another 95 men, based on averages in the other companies, for a total PFD of 478. Of the eight companies present, three carried Spencer Rifles, while five carried Enfield rifled muskets. NARA, RG 94, Entry 65, Box 28, lists 472, plus 26 losses, for 498.

38. RG 94, Entry 65, Box 28. The September return lists 450, plus 35 losses.

39. RG 94, Entry 65, Box 28. The September return lists 398, plus 24 losses.

40. RG 94, Entry 6, Box 28. The September return lists 497, plus 16 losses.

41. 380 present for duty in 8 companies on September 17, 1863, in Morning Reports, NARA. Records for companies C and F not available. 95 men assumed for these two companies, based on the average strength of the other eight, and 5 added for field and staff, also not reported. The September brigade return shows 508 officers and men, plus losses of 21, for a total of 529.

42. exclusive of the 80th Illinois, not present.

43. 156 men in three companies, morning reports, NARA. 363 rifles on hand, as shown in the December 31, 1863 Quarterly Ordnance Returns. I have estimated the PFD strength at approximately 400. This unit was originally stationed at Nashville. It was transferred to Bridgeport on September 7th, and was not present at the battle.

44. Peter Cozzens, *This Terrible Sound* (Urbana IL, 1992), gives the strength as over 700. The monument, however, lists only 360, and the Morning Reports in NARA show 365 on 8/31/63. On 9/10/63, the morning report in the Indiana Adjutant Generals Records shows 32+494, for 526 officers and men, so the regiment's strength did fluctuate considerably during this period.

45. RG 94, Entry 65, Box 28. The September Return shows 281 officers and men, plus 119 losses. The Morning Reports give 330 men in 8 companies. Adding 82 men for the remaining two companies, based on the average company strength, and 5 for estimated field and staff, not reported, gives 417.

46. RG 94, Entry 65, Box 28. The September return lists 312 officers and men, plus 70 losses. The Morning Reports give 174 men in 5 companies. Another 174 men added for the other 5 companies based on the average company strength., and 5 for field and staff, not reported, would give 353. The *OR* report for this unit suggests that the strength was 900 men, a figure that is clearly much too high. Companies C and H were detached, serving as train guard, and engaged elsewhere; they numbered approximately 70 men.

47. Company A serving as provost guard for the brigade. Strength based on average company strength, see below.

48. Company A detached for guard duty. 250 enlisted men plus 6.5% added for officers (average of known officer to enlisted ratios for the Army of Cumberland.) in the remaining nine companies.

49. RG 94, Entry 65, Box 28. The September return lists 393 officers and men, plus 91 losses.

50. *OR* report gives a total of "about 400 men" as the effective total. This is assumed to be for both officers and men.

51. RG 94 Entry 65, Box 28. The September return lists 92 officers and men, plus 3 losses. This battery served with Wilder's Brigade.

52. The September return lists 80 officers and men, plus 20 losses.

53. The September return lists 88 officers and men, plus 12 losses.

54. See note for 2nd Kentucky Cavalry. This figure is 10% of the "for duty" total of 386 found in the September 30th Report, plus losses. RG 94, Entry 65, Box 64.

55. 10 % of regimental strength.

56. RG 94, Entry 65, Box 44. This figure represents 10% of the September 30th strength plus losses.

57. This brigade was detached and escorting trains. It reached Crawfish Spring on September 20.

58. 168 men present in the six companies that show reports for the 19th, plus 112 men added as estimated strength of the remaining four companies (based on average company strength) and 5 added for field and staff, not reported.

59. All ten companies reporting as of September 19, 1863, with 5 added for field and staff, not reported. On October 5, a letter from the regiment noted that the aggregate present was 380. *Rockford Register*, October 24, 1863.

60. As of September 14, 1863.

61. 277 men present in the seven companies reporting as of September 17, 1863. Additionally, 118 men added for missing three companies, based on average company strength, and 5 added for field and staff, not reported.

62. The regimental strength was derived by subtracting the other regiments' strengths from the brigade total.

63. A letter in the *New Albany Daily Ledger*, September 26, 1863, shows 249 engaged.

64. 97 officers and men present on September 22, plus 146 casualties. Alternatively, "232 guns," according to Lt. I.B. Reed, *Norwalk Reflector*, October 5, 1863.

65. Companies G and I detached and serving at Island No. 10. They rejoined the regiment on September 22.

66. RG 94, Entry 65, Box 44. The September 30th return shows 3 officers and 72 men, with 1 loss reported.

67. RG 94, Entry 65, Box 44. The September 30th return shows 4 officers and 111 men, no losses reported.

68. RG 94, Entry 65, Box 44. The September 30th return shows 4 officers and 84 men, no losses reported.

69. The 39th Indiana, detached, is not included here. It is considered serving with corps headquarters.

70. The last report made by the 89th Illinois before the battle is September 10, except for company I, which was on August 31, 1863. The report for September 20 totals 308 officers and men, plus battle losses of 132, for a total of 440 present on the 18th. Additionally, on September 20 another 44 recruits were reported present as a separate category, suggesting a total of 484 total present on the 19th. This latter number seems too high. It remains unclear where the recruits came from, if they were in the fight, or if they were somehow double-counted. I have elected to go with the figures from September 10, plus 10 field and staff reported present for duty. The September 30 return found in RG 94, Entry 65, Box 44, shows 267 present, plus 132 losses, which gives 399 engaged.

71. RG 94, Entry 65, Box 44. The September 30 strength is 256 present, plus 122 losses.

72. The 39th Indiana was detached and serving as mounted infantry. It moved about the field independently, and on the 20th fought with Wilder's Brigade. The number given here is from the last recorded morning report before the battle, September 10, 1863. 5 added for field and staff, not reported. The September 30 divisional return found in RG 94, Entry 65, Box 44, shows 550 present, plus 40 losses, for a strength of 590 on the field.

73. RG 94, Entry 65, Box 44. The September return shows 306 present, plus 99 losses.

74. The Brigade report in *OR* 30, pt. 1, 556, gives 1130 'aggregate." The brigade report also lists a post-battle strength as 598, which, if added to the losses of 523, gives the initial strength as 1121. The Brigade return is not on file, but the Divisional return for September 30 shows 44 officers and 628 men PFD, total of 672. Adding that figure to the reported losses gives us 1195 PFD as of September 19, but certainly double-counts some of the lightly wounded.

75. The report dated September 15 includes 9 for field and staff, reported separately.

76. A letter from Capt. J. H. M. Jenkins of the 29th, dated Sept 23, 1863, appears in the *Stueben Republican*, October 24, 1863, reports 305 men engaged. A second letter from Capt. Jenkins, however, dated October 6th, shows 297 "guns" and 18 commissioned officers.

77. There were no reports for either the 30th Indiana or 77th Pennsylvania. The known strengths of the two regiments above were subtracted from the brigade total, and then the remainder was divided among the 30th and 77th, based on the proportion of losses each regiment suffered.

78. See footnote for 30th Indiana, above.

79. RG 94, Entry 65, Box 44. The September return shows 317 present, plus 160 losses.

80. RG 94, Entry 65, Box 44. The September return shows 209 present, plus 125 losses.

81. RG 94, Entry 65, Box 44. The September 30th strength was 266, plus 142 losses, giving a total of 408, all ten companies reporting. Company D was detached and serving as provost at XX Corps Headquarters (see note 56, above) so 10% was deducted from the total to derive the "engaged" figure.

82. RG 94, Entry 65, Box 44. The September return shows 329 present, plus 130 losses.

83. RG 94, Entry 65, Box 44. The September return shows 115 present, plus 9 losses.

84. RG 94, Entry 65, Box 44. The September return shows 3 officers and 129 men present, plus 20 losses. This number is a bit high for a single battery, but I have found no better information.

85. RG 94, Entry 65, Box 44. The September return shows 1 officer and 121 men present, plus 4 losses.

86. Reports for nine companies, dated September 19, number 318 PFD. Company K was not reported, so 35 men were added, based on the average strength of the other nine companies. 5 added for field and staff, also not reported. Alternatively, the September return (RG 94, Entry 65, Box 44) shows 223 present, plus 141 losses, for 364. *The American Tribune*, March 17, 1892, reported 370 men engaged, with 141 losses.

87. RG 94, Entry 65, Box 44. The September return shows 361 present, plus 88 losses.

88. RG 94, Entry 65, Box 44. The September return shows 193 present, plus 106 losses, for 299. Allen Benton Morse Letter, September 26, 1863, Burton Historical Library, Detroit Public Library. reports 22 officers and 240 men taken into action.

89. RG 94, Entry 65, Box 44. The September return shows 382 present, plus 105 losses.

90. RG 94, Entry 65, Box 44. The September return shows 169 present, plus 100 losses.

91. All companies reported with field and staff estimated at 5. Of the company reports, five date from September 19, three are from September 10, and two from September 1. Col. Jacquess would later apply for a disability pension, claiming to have suffered a double inguinal hernia when he had two horses shot out from under him on September 20, but he did not make this claim until many years later.

92. RG 94, Entry 65, Box 44. The September return shows 189 present, plus 92 losses.

93. Seven companies reported a strength of 173. I have estimated the strength of the remaining three companies at 24 men each, or 72 total, with field and staff estimated at 5. The September return (RG 94, Entry 65, Box 44) shows 169 present, plus 100 losses, for 269 total.

94. RG 94, Entry 65, Box 44. The September return shows 184, plus 130 losses.

95. RG 94, Entry 65, Box 44. The September return shows 372, plus 91 losses.

96. All ten companies reporting, with field & staff estimated at 5. On September 19 the regiment reported 305 PFD; on September 20, 308 PFD.

97. RG 94, Entry 65, Box 44. The September return shows 160 present, plus 149 losses. The 51st had only nine companies until February 1865.

98. RG 94, Entry 65, Box 44. September 30th return shows 110 present, plus 4 losses.

99. RG 94, Entry 65, Box 44. September 30th return shows 98 present, plus 9 losses.

100. RG 94, Entry 65, Box 44. The September return shows 81 present, plus 5 losses.

101. The 21st Corps OR report included a summary of the strength of all regiments and batteries taken into action. This summary appears to be based on the September 19, 1863 semi-weekly returns for the Corps, as the numbers in both documents, where found, match very closely. In some instances, regimental reports gave slightly different numbers, and in those cases I deferred to the regimental figures, rather than the summaries.

102. Originally, this unit was Cavalry Company B of the 36th Illinois Infantry, also known as Sherer's Independent Cavalry. When first raised, the 36th had ten infantry companies and two of cavalry.

103. Wood had a horse shot out from him on September 19, suffering an inguinal hernia. He remained on the field, but the injury would force his retirement from active service in 1865.

104. Strength given as 400 in OR 30, pt. 1, 615.

105. The 26th Ohio's reports give some idea of how strength fluctuated from day to day, or even mission to mission. In the corps return of casualties found in OR 30, pt. 1, 615; the listed strength is 362 men "taken into action." The regimental report gives two figures. OR 30, pt. 1, 671, records 24 officers and 335 men, for a total of 359 engaged, but on page 675, the table of strength and losses closing out that same report shows 23 officers and 354 men "in action," for a total of 377. Finally, in a letter to the *Madison County Union* dated September 24, 1863, J. A. Trahern reports the September 20 strength as 335 men, which clearly omits officers.

106. This entire brigade was not engaged. With the exception of the 51st Indiana, Wagner's command was stationed at Chattanooga.

107. The 51st Indiana participated in Streight's raid, with most of the regiment being captured in May, 1863. They were taken to Richmond, where the enlisted men were exchanged. The officers remained in Libby Prison. At Indianapolis the 51st and 73nd Indiana (captured in similar circumstances, and also without officers) were consolidated and placed Capt. D. W. Hamilton of the 7th Indiana. A small detachment (size unknown, comprised of those men who were never captured) of the 51st was with Wagner in Chattanooga. Eight companies of the consolidated 51st & 73rd were at Nashville. Two companies were still en route from Indiana.

108. reported 25 officers and 261 men on October 8, 1863, for 286 total; Indiana Adjutant General records.

109. See note 107 for the 51st Indiana, above.

110. Only companies A-H present. Companies I and K were stationed at Camp Denison, Ohio.

111. Not engaged, stationed at Chattanooga.

112. This total does not include the 110th Illinois Battalion, see below.

113. Detached and serving at Chattanooga. The Battalion consisted of companies A-D.

114. Comprised of companies A, C, F, H, and I, this battalion was guarding the 2nd Division baggage trains. It was in Chattanooga on September 18, marched to Crawfish Spring on the 19th, and to Rossville on the 20th. It returned to regular duties on September 23. The strength is as reported by the regiment on September 23, plus the losses suffered at Chickamauga; and less the 118 reported engaged strength of the other four companies. See OR 30, pt. 3, 800.

115. Co. G was guarding the divisional ammunition train. Strength estimated by taking the average of the other nine companies.

116. Only four companies—B, D, G, and K—were in action.

117. *Logansport Journal*, October 3rd, 1863, shows a 275 men engaged. *Marshall County Republican*, Oct. 8th, 1863, reports 316 engaged.

118. Jacob Cressinger, in a letter home on September 24, 1863, gives the regiment's strength as 430 officers and men.

119. Strength given as 274 in *OR* 30, pt. 1, 616. Company G was guarding the Second Division ammunition train.

120. Regimental report cites 23 officers and 324 men, for 347 present on September 18th. *OR* 30, pt.1, 796.

121. The strength of Company A can only be guessed at. The regimental report says it was the largest company in the command, and the average company strength for the rest of the command was about 24 men per company. It seems unlikely that there were more than 30 men in Company A.

122. A Company was serving as escort and provost to 3rd Division, 21 Corps. Additionally, another detachment of 30 men was guarding trains.

123. *Fort Wayne Weekly Sentinel*, October 17, 1863, shows 215 men engaged.

124. Edwin Perkins noted that the 59th had "300 plus officers" on September 27, 1863. Edward Perkins Papers, Western Reserve Historical Society.

125. Regimental strength given as 318 in both corps and brigade reports. See *OR* 30, pt. 1, 616.

126. The 21st Kentucky was stationed in Chattanooga.

127. Until August 1863, The Reserve Corps's headquarters escort was Company F, 1 Missouri Cavalry. At the beginning of September, that company was ordered to St. Louis, where it rejoined its regiment. *OR Supplement*, 34, 447.

128. The ratio of September 30th strength to engaged strength for each of the five regiments who reported both is 86%. This figure includes some of the lightly wounded that had already returned to duty.

129. Charles Partridge, *History of the Ninety-Sixth Regiment Illinois Volunteer Infantry* (Chicago: 1887), 192. See also the George Pepoon Letters, Northern Illinois University, Dekalb IL. *OR* 30, pt. 1, 858 shows 21 officers and 380 men, for 401 engaged. George Pepoon was on the brigade staff during the battle. Additionally, several other manuscript sources cite the 419 figure.

130. 490 on September Return plus losses, NARA RG 94 Entry 65 Box 64.

131. 422 on September return plus losses, NARA RG 94, Entry 65, Box 64.

132. 561 on September return plus losses, NARA RG 94, Entry 65, Box 64. Company B was serving as headquarters guard for Granger.

133. 577 on September return plus losses, NARA RG 94, Entry 65, Box 64.

134. The 89th Ohio was technically part of 3/4/14, but had been detached earlier and was now serving with the Reserve Corps.

135. Companies A, D, and G on detached duty, not engaged; per the *Cadiz Republican*, October 7, 1863. Anonymous, "98th Ohio," *National Tribune*, June 30, 1887; gives 11 officers and 190 men, for 201 total.

136. This is the total strength given for September 18, 1863, including field and staff. 414 reported in September Brigade Return, NARA, RG 94 Entry 65, Box 64.

137. Only five companies reported for either September 18 or 19, giving 206 PFD. doubling that number for the other five companies would give a total of 412. The Field and Staff reported 8, for a total of 420. On July 23, 1863, the last full report of the whole regiment, there were 470 PFD, which makes the 420 estimate a reasonable one. 447 were reported in September Brigade Return, RG 94, Entry 65, Box 64, NARA.

138. Reports for all ten companies plus the field and staff, dated September 19. The September Brigade Return shows 440 PFD, RG 94 Entry 65 Box 64 NARA.

139. The 52nd Ohio reported this figure at the end of September, RG 94 Entry 65 Box 64, NARA. For other regiments, the ratio between the Morning Report figures and the September Brigade Return plus battle losses is 92%.

140. RG 94, Entry 65, Box 28, NARA. As above, the losses for the 69th are not specified. The 69th Ohio was technically part of 2/2/14, but had been detached and was serving with the Reserve Corps.

141. RG 94, Entry 65 Box 64. NARA, from the September Brigade Return. This figure seems low for a six-gun battery.

142. The strength shown here is a guess. These regiments were shuffled around a great deal in 1863, and changed higher organizations several times. Their OR records are sketchy at best.

143. 2 companies left at Carthage Tennessee, September 13, 1863. *Tennesseans in the Civil War*, vol. 1, 386.

144. This regiment was organized with 7 companies. *Tennesseans in the Civil War*, vol. 1, 388.

145. Also known as the 1st Middle Tennessee Battery.

146. The Regiment reported 316 men in ten companies. This figure represents 10% of that total.

147. RG 94, Entry 65, Box 64. The return is for the end of September. The 2nd lost 11 men at Chickamauga, which I added to the 262 officers and men reported on the return.

148. RG 94, Entry 65, Box 64. End of September return of 394 officers and men, plus 3 losses at Chickamauga.

149. RG 94, Entry 65, Box 64. End of September return shows 677 officers and men, plus 1 loss at Chickamauga.

150. This brigade provides some of the basis for contrasting the known strengths of all the cavalry at the end of September with engaged strengths. The OR report is from September 24, 1863. The three regiments reported there, plus losses, total 1088. The brigade returns for these same units, a week later, show 1181. Thus, the engaged strengths of these units at Chickamauga total 92% of the present for duty numbers given at the end of September. The three regiments also detail 58 dismounted men not counted "for duty" on September 24th. It is unlikely that these men would have recovered mounts and be counted in the "for duty" column on the brigade return at the end of the month. Nor is it clear when these men were dismounted, leaving it an open question as to whether some or all of them were at Chickamauga. They are not counted in the final strength because it is assumed that there is always a small portion of a cavalry command that is dismounted due to attrition of the animals (horses tended to be much more fragile than men) and these men or others in similar numbers would not be available for service.

151. Return dated September 24 shows 383, plus 5 losses at Chickamauga. 9 dismounted men not included above. Brigade Return for September 30 shows 411 PFD.

152. Return dated September 24 shows 307, plus 9 losses at Chickamauga. The 284 figure subtracts 10% of this strength for the detached company serving as escort. Also, 21 dismounted men were not included. The Brigade Return of September 30 shows 359 PFD. Company C was detached, serving in General N.P. Banks' command; Company L was acting as escort to 1st Division. Richard Reid, *Fourth Indiana Cavalry Regiment: A History* (Fordsville, KY: 1994), 94.

153. RG 94, Entry 65, Box 64, shows 517 officers and men "for duty." 92% of this figure is 476, the final figure used here.

154. Return for September 24, 1863 shows 378, plus 6 losses at Chickamauga. 28 dismounted men are not included. The Brigade Return for September 30 shows 411 present for duty.

155. The 4th Kentucky reported 193 "for duty" plus 95 losses at Chickamauga. They also reported only 10 troops present. RG 94 Entry 65, Box 64.

156. The 5th Kentucky reported 343 "for duty" plus 20 losses at Chickamauga. RG 94, Entry 65, Box 64.

157. The 6th Kentucky reported 393 "for duty" plus 131 losses at Chickamauga. RG 94, Entry 65, Box 64.

158 Minty's Brigade was the most difficult of the Cavalry numbers to reconcile. The September 30 Brigade returns show this strength. However, in his official report Minty stated that he only had 973 men opposing the Rebel advance on the 18th; see OR 30, pt. 1, 923. On September 2, Minty reported that he had 1100 men in the 4th US, 4th Michigan, and 7th Pennsylvania, OR 30, pt. 3, 316; excluding the 3rd Indiana Cavalry, stationed at Chattanooga. Minty's report counts only the men he had contesting the Rebel advance on the 18th, and makes

mention of large detachments watching area roads that did not become engaged. How large or numerous these detachments were is not reported. However, see note for the 4th Michigan, below, which suggests that they were substantial–at least one battalion of the 4th Michigan, strength 260, was not present at Reed's Bridge. Also, Crittenden reported that the 4th US, "650 strong" reported to him for duty on September 13, see OR 30, pt. 1, 604.

159. Detached, at Chattanooga. This figure for September 14. The September 30 Brigade return reports 175 "for duty," RG 94, Entry 65, Box 64.

160. The 4th Michigan reported 470 "for duty" plus 19 losses at Chickamauga. RG 94, Entry 65, Box 64. Capt. Henry Potter recorded that on the 19th, the day after the 4th's engagement at Reed's Bridge, Major Mix and a battalion of 260 men joined the regiment, "which makes our regiment about 400 strong." Henry Potter Journal, Bentley Historical Library, University of Michigan.

161. The 7th Pennsylvania reported 477 "for duty" plus 19 losses at Chickamauga. RG 94, Entry 65, Box 64.

162. The 4th US reported 704 "for duty" plus 7 losses at Chickamauga. RG 94, Entry 65, Box 64. In his report, Crittenden noted that the 4th US numbered "650 strong" on September 13. OR 30, pt. 1, 604.

163. The 2nd Kentucky reported 323 "for duty" plus 63 losses at Chickamauga. One troop was detached and serving as escort for XX Corps. RG 94, Entry 65, Box 64. The figure given here is 90% of the regimental total, accounting for the detached company.

164. The 1st Ohio reported 382 "for duty" plus 22 losses at Chickamauga. RG 94, Entry 65, Box 64.

165. The 3rd Ohio reported 533 "for duty" plus 17 losses at Chickamauga. RG 94, Entry 65, Box 64.

166. The 4th Ohio reported 511 "for duty" plus 34 losses at Chickamauga, RG 94, Entry 65, Box 64.

167. RG 94, Entry 65, Box 64. The Chicago Board of Trade Battery reported no losses at Chickamauga. In OR 30, pt. 1, 170, the battery reported 166 PFD, but this figure seems high. I chose to rely on the Divisional report instead.

168. None of the Pioneer troops were actually on the field at Chickamauga. The September 20 report, however, lists their location as Chattanooga. In fact, the command was still widely dispersed, with elements at Chattanooga, Bridgeport, and various other locations.

169. Tri-monthly report for Sept 20th, RG 94, Entry 65, Box 64. OR 30, pt. 3, 769 shows 396.

170. Tri-monthly report for Sept 20th. RG 94, Entry 65, Box 64. The return lists 10 companies present, but only 7 officers and 58 men. Almost 600 officers and men are on detached duty. It is likely that only 2 companies were actually present in Chattanooga, the rest scattered across Tennessee on various duties.

171. Tri-monthly report for Sept 20th. RG 94 Entry 65, Box 64. OR 30, pt. 3, 769 shows 338.

172. Mounted.

Union Losses

Determining accurate losses poses a problem in its own right: Which figures to use? While loss data is more abundant for both sides, there are also numerous small conflicts to resolve.

The official Union return of casualties for Chickamauga includes smaller skirmishes along Missionary Ridge and Lookout Mountain on September 21 and 22, although these fights do not add more than a handful of losses to the total. Where specified, I have tried to edit out losses not suffered September 18-20, an admittedly arbitrary time frame. Official losses do not include the preliminary skirmishing during the week leading up to the battle, which could easily be included. Shifting boundaries of what should and should not count as the "Battle of Chickamauga" creates additional confusion. I decided to follow the more tightly defined path.

Further, figures in the regimental and brigade reports are sometimes higher than the figures found in the official army return. Lower echelon returns tend to include lightly wounded, some of whom had returned to duty, and also because the number of missing declined as more men were accounted for in other categories or rejoined their regiments. I chose to use the regimental or brigade figures as far as the wounded go, but not for the missing.

I consulted hundreds of newspapers for losses and descriptions of the battle. They are a treasure trove of information. The reported loss figures from this source, while generally in overall agreement with the official figures, also varied by small margins and often had different proportions of killed/missing/wounded. A couple of factors account for these discrepancies.

Once again, the slightly wounded may or may not have been counted. Additionally, newspaper reports stem from news sent home within a day or two of the battle, and—as with the higher echelon reports—many of the missing turn out to actually be killed or wounded. For both these reasons I have included the newspaper losses as footnotes, but continued to use the official return for my final count. The overall numbers would not change much, if at all, by relying on these accounts, for as many regiments under-reported as over-reported.

All losses are listed as follows—"killed / wounded / missing = total." Percentages are calculated based on the engaged for the Federal unit strengths as listed in the first chapter of this volume. Staff losses, where broken out separately, are noted with their own line for division, corps, and brigade. Staff losses are counted where staff strengths are not, which will change the percentage losses by a minuscule amount, but I simply have no good figures for brigade staff sizes, or how many staff members were under fire, as opposed to serving in the rear, so I have omitted to count them as engaged. Ignoring their battle losses, however, seemed wrong: Men who were killed or wounded on the field of battle should not be ignored.

All told, just as I discovered with the engaged strengths, battle losses proved to be a slippery concept, more so than a fixed, immutable figure. Lightly injured men who did not leave the ranks, for example, might be counted as wounded in one regiment's report and not in another's. In the end, where conflicting information presented itself, I relied primarily on the Union losses found in *OR* 30, pt, 1, 171-179 as the final arbiter.

Formation	Strength	Losses K/W/M=T	Percent
Army	**60,889**	**1,657/9,747/4,811=16,215**	**27%**
Escort	988	0/2/4=6	1%
1 Bn Ohio SS	154	0/0/0=0	0%
10 Ohio	396	0/0/1 = 1	.3%
15 Penn. Cav	438	0/2/3 = 5	1%
Independent	581	5/35/0=40	7%
39 Indiana	581	5/35/0=40	7%
XIV Army Corps			
XIV Corps	**20,516**	**666/3,552/1,920=6,138**	**30%**
Staff		0/0/1=1	--
9 Michigan	384	0	0%
L, 1 Ohio Cav	57	0	0%
1/XIV	**4,964**	**181/785/1,202=2,168**	**44%**
1/1/XIV	**1,730**	**49/247/411=707**	**41%**
38 Indiana	354	13/57/39=109	31%[1]
2 Ohio	412	9/50/122=181	44%

Formation	Strength	Losses K/W/M=T	Percent
33 Ohio	415	14/63/83=160	39%
94 Ohio	309	2/22/22=46	15%
10 Wisconsin	240	11/55/145=211	88%
2/1/XIV	**1,512**	**64/262/251=577**	**38%**
24 Illinois	362	19/68/56=143	40%
79 Penn.	390	16/67/42=125	32%
1 Wisconsin	391	27/84/77=188	48%
21 Wisconsin	369	2/43/76=121	33%[2]
3/1/XIV	**1,375**	**48/237/510=795**	**58%**
1/15 US	276	9/49/102=160	58%
1/16 US	308	3/19/174=196	64%[3]
1/18 US	300	19/71/68=158	53%
2/18 US	287	14/81/50=145	51%
1/19 US	204	3/17/116=136	67%
Artillery/1/XIV	**347**	**20/39/30=89**	**26%**
4th Indiana Lt	99	1/14/5=20	20%
A, 1 Michigan Lt	118	6/7/12=25	21%
H 5 US	130	13/18/13=44	34%
2/XIV	**4,282**	**67/431/295=793**	**19%**
1/2/XIV	**1,191**	**11/173/100=284**	**24%**
104 Illinois	299	2/46/16=64	21%[4]
42 Indiana	328	1/52/53=106	32%[5]
88 Indiana	259	3/33/16=52	20%
15 Kentucky	305	5/42/15=62	20%
2/2/XIV	**1,018**	**20/142/49=211**	**21%**
19 Illinois	333	10/45/16=71	21%[6]
11 Michigan	341	5/42/19=66	19%
18 Ohio	344	5/55/14=74	22%[7]
3/2/XIV	**1,729**	**30/96/142=268**	**16%**
37 Indiana	361	1/8/2=11	03%[8]
21 Ohio	561	28/84/131=243	43%
74 Ohio	300	1/2/6=9	03%
78 Pennsylvania	507	0/2/3=5	01%

Formation	Strength	Losses K/W/M=T	Percent
Arty/2/XIV	**344**	**6/20/4=30**	**09%**
Bridges Illinois	126	6/16/4=26	21%
G 1 Ohio Lt	100	0/0/0=0	0%
M 1 Ohio Lt	118	0/4/0=4	03%
3/XIV	**5,163**	**325/1,652/214=2,191**	**42%**
Staff		0/1/0	--
1/3/XIV	1,220	49/316/66=431	35%
82 Indiana	285	20/68/23=111	40%
17 Ohio	454	16/114/21=151	33%
31 Ohio	465	13/134/22=169	36%
38 Ohio	16	0/0/0=0	0%
2/3/XIV	**1,998**	**127/719/79=925**	**46%**
10 Indiana	366	24/136/6=166	45%
74 Indiana	400	22/125/10=157	39%[9]
4 Kentucky	351	25/157/9=191	54%
10 Kentucky	421	21/134/11=166	39%
14 Ohio	460	35/167/43=245	53%
3/3/XIV	**1,643**	**144/579/65=788**	**48%**
87 Indiana	366	40/142/8=190	52%
2 Minnesota	384	35/113/14=162	42%[10]
9 Ohio	502	48/185/16=249	50%
35 Ohio	391	21/139/27=187	48%
Arty/3/XIV	**302**	**5/37/4=46**	**15%**
D, 1 Michigan Lt	106	0/7/4=11	10%
C, 1 Ohio Lt	122	4/9/0=13	11%
I, 4 US	74	1/21/0=22	30%
4/XIV	**5,666**	**93/684/175=952**	**17%[11]**
1/4/XIV	**2,283**	**12/92/18=122**	**05%**
92 Illinois	383	2/22/2=26	07%[12]
98 Illinois	485	2/31/2=35	07%[13]
123 Illinois	422	1/13/10=24	06%
17 Indiana	513	4/10/2=16	03%
72 Indiana	480	3/16/2=21	04%

Formation	Strength	Losses K/W/M=T	Percent
2/4/XIV	**1,476**	**48/347/69=464**	**31%**
68 Indiana	356	17/108/12=137	38%
75 Indiana	360	17/108/13=138	38%
101 Indiana	400	11/90/18=119	30%
105 Ohio	382	3/41/26=70	18%[14]
3/4/XIV	**1,612**	**30/215/86=331**	**21%**
A, 18 Kentucky	29	0/0/0=0	0%
18 Kentucky	266	7/46/33=86	32%
11 Ohio	433	5/36/22=63	15%
36 Ohio	484	12/65/14=91	19%
92 Ohio	400	6/68/17=91	23%
Arty/4/XIV	**295**	**3/30/2=35**	**12%**
18 Indiana Lt	95	1/2/0=3	03%
19 Indiana Lt	100	2/16/2=20	20%
21 Indiana Lt	100	0/12/0=12	12%

XX Army Corps

Formation	Strength	Losses K/W/M=T	Percent
XX Corps	**13,048**	**417/2,669/1,253=4,339**	**33%**
I, 2 Kentucky Cav	**39**	**0/0/0=0**	**0%**
D, 1 Ohio Infantry	41	0/0/0=0	0%
1/XX	**3,951**	**125/824/424=1,373**	**35%[15]**
1/1/XX	**1,239**	**1/4/19=24**	**02%[16]**
59 Illinois	285	0/1/1=2	01%
74 Illinois	354	0/1/4=5	01%
75 Illinois	200	0/0/10=10	05%
22 Indiana	400	1/2/4=7	02%
2/1/XX	**1,215**	**54/299/298=651**	**54%**
21 Illinois	416	22/70/146=238	57%
38 Illinois	301	15/87/78=180	60%
81 Indiana	255	4/60/23=87	34%[17]
101 Ohio	243	13/82/51=146	60%
3/1/XX	**1,218**	**70/519/107=696**	**57%**
25 Illinois	337	10/171/24=205	61%
35 Illinois	299	17/130/13=160	54%
8 Kansas	406	30/165/25=220	54%
15 Wisconsin	176	13/53/45=111	63%

Formation	Strength	Losses K/W/M=T	Percent
Arty/1/XX	**279**	**0/2/0=2**	**01%**
2 Minnesota Lt	76	0/2/0=2	03%
5 Wisconsin Lt	115	0/0/0=0	00%
8 Wisconsin Lt	88	0/0/0=0	00%
2/XX	**4,658**	**141/905/553=1,599**	**34%**
1/2/XX	**1,499**	**55/306/114=475**	**32%**
Staff		0/1/1=2	--
89 Illinois	391	14/88/30=132	38%[18]
32 Indiana	378	21/81/20=122	32%[19]
15 Ohio	325	10/77/33=120	37%
49 Ohio	405	10/59/30=99	24%
2/2/XX	**1,130**	**27/198/307=532**	**47%**
Staff		0/2/7=9	--
79 Illinois	263	3/21/97=121	46%
29 Indiana	315	11/92/69=172	55%
30 Indiana	299	10/55/61=126	42%
77 Pennsylvania	253	3/28/73=104	42%
3/2/XX	**1,627**	**56/378/125=559**	**34%**
Staff		1/1/0=2	--
6 Indiana	467	13/116/31=160	34%[20]
5 Kentucky	334	14/79/32=125	37%
1 Ohio	367	13/96/33=142	39%
93 Ohio	459	15/86/29=130	28%[21]
Arty/2/XX	**402**	**3/23/7=33**	**08%**
5 Indiana Lt.	124	1/7/1=9	07%
A, 1 Ohio Lt.	152	2/14/4=20	13%
20 Ohio Lt.	126	0/2/2=4	03%
3/XX	**4,359**	**151/940/276=1,367**	**31%**
1/3/XX	**1,556**	**52/309/80=441**	**28%**
Staff		1/0/0=1	--
36 Illinois	358	20/101/20=141	39%
88 Illinois	449	12/62/14=88	20%
21 Michigan	262	16/73/17=106	40%
24 Wisconsin	487	3/73/29=105	22%

Formation	Strength	Losses K/W/M=T	Percent
2/3/XX	**1,100**	**37/240/107=384**	**35%**
44 Illinois	269	6/60/34=100	37%
73 Illinois	300	13/57/22=92	31%
2 Missouri	281	7/56/29=92	33%
15 Missouri	250	11/67/22=100	40%
3/3/XX	**1,391**	**58/372/84=514**	**37%**
Staff		0/1/0=1	
22 Illinois	314	23/76/31=130	41%
27 Illinois	463	2/79/10=91	20%
42 Illinois	305	15/123/5=143	47%
51 Illinois	309	18/93/38=149	48%[22]
Arty/3/XX	**312**	**4/19/5=28**	**09%**
C, 1 Illinois Lt.	114	0/4/0=4	04%
11 Indiana Lt.	117	3/12/4=19	16%
G, 1 Missouri Lt.	81	1/3/1=5	06%

XXI Army Corps

Formation	Strength	Losses K/W/M=T	Percent
XXI Corps	**12,111**	**322/2,382/699=3,403**	**28%**
K, 15 Illinois Cav	83	0/3/0=3	04%
1/XXI	**2,932**	**132/743/194=1,069**	**36%**
1/1/XXI	**1,333**	**79/443/129=651**	**49%**
100 Illinois	339	23/117/24=164	48%[23]
58 Indiana	397	16/119/34=169	43%[24]
13 Michigan	220	13/67/26=106	48%
26 Ohio	377	27/140/45=212	56%
3/1/XXI	**1,346**	**51/283/58=392**	**29%**
3 Kentucky	401	13/78/22=113	28%
64 Ohio	325	8/50/13=71	22%
65 Ohio	306	14/71/18=103	34%[25]
125 Ohio	314	16/84/5=105	33%[26]
Arty/1/XXI	**253**	**2/17/7=26**	**10%**
8 Indiana Lt	134	1/9/7=17	13%
6 Ohio Lt	119	1/8/0=9	08%
2/XXI	**5,043**	**134/1,031/203=1,368**	**27%**
Staff	--	1/2/3=6	--
C, 7 Illinois Cav	36	0/0/0=0	0%

Formation	Strength	Losses K/W/M=T	Percent
1 Kentucky	178	0/0/0=0	0%
G, 23 Kentucky	29	0/0/0=0	0%
1/2/XXI	**1,280**	**24/213/53=290**	**23%**
31 Indiana	380	5/61/17=83	22%
1 Kentucky	118	2/26/3=31	26%
2 Kentucky	367	10/64/18=92	25%
90 Ohio	415	7/62/15=84	20%
2/2/XXI	**1,443**	**46/378/76=500**	**35%**
9 Indiana	328	13/91/22=126	38%
6 Kentucky	302	12/95/11=118	39%
41 Ohio	360	6/100/9=115	32%[27]
124 Ohio	453	15/92/34=141	31%[28]
3/2/XXI	**1,631**	**53/399/65=517**	**32%**
Staff	-	0/3/0=3	--
84 Illinois	382	13/83/9=105	27%
36 Indiana	347	13/99/17=129	37%
23 Kentucky	263	11/52/6=69	26%
6 Ohio	362	13/102/17=132	36%
24 Ohio	277	3/60/16=79	29%
Arty/2/XXI	**446**	**10/39/6=55**	**12%**
B, 1 Ohio Lt	132	1/8/4=13	10%
F, 1 Ohio Lt	110	2/8/2=12	11%
H, 4 US	87	5/17/0=22	25%
M, 4 US	117	2/6/0=8	7%
3/XXI	**4,053**	**56/604/302=962**	**24%**
Staff	--	0/0/1=1	--
A, 9th Kentucky	30	0/0/0=0	0%
1/3/XXI	**1,384**	**16/254/61=331**	**24%**
79 Indiana	300	1/44/10=55	18%
9 Kentucky	213	2/45/13=60	28%
17 Kentucky	487	6/105/15=126	26%
19 Ohio	384	7/60/23=90	23%
2/3/XXI	**1,084**	**16/180/83=279**	**26%**
44 Indiana	229	3/61/10=74	32%
86 Indiana	261	1/31/21=53	20%

Formation	Strength	Losses K/W/M=T	Percent
13 Ohio	304	5/47/22=74	24%
59 Ohio	290	7/41/30=78	27%
3/3/XXI	**1,202**	**20/135/144=299**	**25%**
35 Indiana	229	5/23/37=65	28%
8 Kentucky	297	4/47/28=79	27%
51 Ohio	319	8/35/55=98	31%
99 Ohio	357	3/30/24=57	16%
Arty/3/XXI	**353**	**4/35/13=52**	**15%**
7 Indiana Lt	122	0/8/1=9	7%
26 Pennsylvania	112	2/14/1=17	15%
3 Wisconsin Lt	119	2/13/11=26	22%

Reserve Corps

Formation	Strength	Losses K/W/M=T	Percent
Reserve Corps	**5,894**	**215/972/635=1,822**	**31%**
Staff		1/0/0=1	--
1/Res	**3,819**	**212/962/613=1,787**	**47%**
1/1/Res	**2,695**	**154/654/518=1,326**	**49%**
Staff		0/1/0=1	--
96 Illinois	419	39/134/52=225	54%
115 Illinois	426	22/151/10=183	43%
84 Indiana	374	23/97/13=133	36%
22 Michigan	455	32/96/261=389	85%
40 Ohio	537	19/102/11=132	25%
89 Ohio	389	19/63/171=253	65%
18 Ohio Lt Arty	95	0/10/0=10	11%
2/1/Res	**1,124**	**58/308/95=461**	**41%**
78 Illinois	353	17/77/62=156	44%
98 Ohio	181	9/41/13=63	35%[29]
113 Ohio	355	21/98/12=131	37%
121 Ohio	235	9/83/7=99	42%
M, 1 Illinois Lt	112	2/9/1=12	11%
2/2/Res	**2,075**	**2/10/22=34**	**2%**
85 Illinois	371	0/2/0=2	1%
86 Illinois	420	1/1/5=7	2%
125 Illinois	439	1/2/4=7	2%
52 Ohio	417	0/5/0=5	1%

Formation	Strength	Losses K/W/M=T	Percent
69 Ohio	350	0/0/13=13	4%[30]
I, 2 Illinois Lt	78	0/0/0=0	0%

Cavalry Corps

Formation	Strength	Losses K/W/M=T	Percent
Cavalry Corps	**7,751**	**32/136/300=468**	**6%**
1/Cav	**4,087**	**6/24/254=284**	**7%**
1/1/Cav	**1,348**	**2/6/7=15**	**1%**
2 Michigan Cav	273	2/6/3=11	4%
9 Pennsylvania Cav	397	0/0/3=3	1%
1 Tennessee Cav	678	0/0/1=1	0.1%
2/1/Cav	**1,564**	**2/10/11=23**	**1%**
2 Indiana Cav	388	1/4/0=5	1%
4 Indiana Cav	316	0/2/7=9	3%
2 Tennessee Cav	476	1/2/0=3	1%
1 Wisconsin Cav	384	0/2/4=6	2%
3/1/Cav	**1,175**	**2/8/236=246**	**21%**
4 Kentucky Cav	288	0/1/94=95	33%
5 Kentucky Cav	363	0/0/20=20	6%
6 Kentucky Cav	524	2/7/122=131	25%
2/Cav	**3,542**	**26/111/46=183**	**5%**
1/2/Cav	**1,696**	**7/32/8=47**	**3%**
Staff	--	0/2/0=2	--
4 Michigan Cav	489	1/12/6=19	4%
7 Pennsylvania Cav	496	5/13/1=19	4%
4 US Cav	711	1/5/1=7	1%
2/2/Cav	**1,846**	**19/79/38=136**	**7%**
2 Kentucky Cav	347	11/50/2=63	18%
1 Ohio Cav	404	2/13/7=22	5%
3 Ohio Cav	550	2/7/8=17	3%
4 Ohio Cav	545	4/9/21=34	6%
Arty/Cav	**122**	**0/0/0=0**	**0%**
CBOT Battery	122	0/0/0=0	0%

Endnotes

1. *Evansville Daily Journal*, October 5, 1863, has a letter from Col. Scribner that shows how severe straggling can be in combat: On the morning of the 21st, Col. Scribner reported that the 38th Indiana had only 160 men present for duty, even though, after subtracting the reported loss of 109 from the engaged strength of 354, it should have had 245 men PFD that morning. The 85 extra missing likely include both lightly wounded men and stragglers. They reflect an "unofficial" extra loss of nearly 80% above the reported casualties.

2. James M. Randall Letter, Tennessee Sourcebook, Sept 23, 1863, states that out of 250 engaged, there were 131 present, making a loss of 119.

3. In his report, Captain Robert E. A. Crofton initially reported his losses as 10/16/215=241, or 78%.

4. *Chicago Evening Journal*, October 5, 1863, reports 2/44/16=62.

5. *Evansville Daily Journal*, October 7, 1863, shows 6/36/55=97.

6. In the *Chicago Evening Journal*, October 5, 1863, the regiment reported 11/44/19 = 74, but at least one man was killed on September 11th, one on the 29th, and one wounded on the 25th. All of the remaining 71 losses except one wounded occurred on September 20th.

7. *Athens Messenger*, October 8, 1863, shows 10/67/11=88.

8. The official losses reported were 0/7/2=9. The *Aurora Commercial*, Aurora Indiana, October 15, 1863, reported 1 mortally wounded, 8 wounded, (including 2 lightly wounded) and 2 missing=11.

9. *Stueben Republican*, Angola Indiana, Saturday, October 10, 1863 reports 17/124/24=165.

10. George Lamphear, in a letter home, reported the loss as 153 total. October 11, 1863, Lamphear papers, University of Tennessee, Knoxville.

11. Without Wilder's Brigade and the 18th Indiana Light Artillery, 1/4/14, the division lost 80/590/157=827 out of 3288 engaged, for 25% losses.

12. *Chicago Evening Journal*, October 3, 1863, shows 2/24/5 = 31, including an additional 2 wounded and 3 missing. However, the brigade was involved in skirmishing both before and after the battle proper, and the newspaper reports do not specify when the losses were incurred.

13. *Robinson Argus*, Crawford County, IL, September 20, 1882, shows 5/36/1 = 42, found in a historical sketch of the regiment.

14. *Jeffersonian Democrat*, October 23, 1863, shows 3/39/25=67.

15. Without Post's Brigade and 5th Wisconsin Light Artillery, this division lost 124/820/405=1349 out of 2597 engaged, for 52% losses.

16. This brigade was not engaged in the main battle, but sustained losses skirmishing and protecting the army trains between September 18-20.

17. *Indianapolis Daily Journal*, October 6, 1863, reports 8/59/22 = 89.

18. *Chicago Evening Journal*, October 5, 1863 shows 15/88/31 = 134.

19. *Indianapolis Daily Journal*, October 6, 1863 shows 21/78/17 = 116.

20. Same figure reported in the *Indianapolis Daily Journal*, October 6, 1863.

21. *Dayton Weekly Journal*, September 29, 1863, shows 5/56/0=61. The early date and the fact that the letter writer was wounded himself, and thus not with the regiment following the battle, explains the fact that the official losses are more than double those given here. It is possible, though not stated, that this figure represents only losses suffered on September 19.

22. *Chicago Evening Journal*, October 3, 1863, gives losses of 17/95/25 = 137.

23. *Chicago Evening Journal*, October 5, 1863, gives 21/112/26= 159.

24. *Evansville Daily Journal*, October 3, 1863, lists 17/113/25 (17 missing and 8 captured) = 155.

25. *Cleveland Morning Leader*, October 3, 1863, shows 16/68/20=104.

26. *Cleveland Plain Dealer*, October 8, 1863, shows 17/82/0=99.

27. Jacob Cressinger, in a letter home on September 24th, 1863 gives the losses as "150 killed wounded and missing." UT Austin.

28. Cleveland Morning Leader, October 3, 1863, reports 29/84/22=135.

29. *Cadiz Republican*, October 7, 1863, gives 7/38/4=49.

30. A water detail, consisting of 2 men from each company, was captured on the morning of Sept. 19. Gam Pease, "Chickamauga. The Part Taken by the Sixty-ninth Ohio and McCook's Brigade." *The National Tribune*, July 3, 1890.

Confederate Strength

Sources and Methodology

As might be expected, Confederate numbers are less well documented. Many fewer units filed battle reports, or reports that were filed have been lost. There are also fewer surviving monthly returns and morning reports. There is not even a full casualty return for the entire Confederate army. As a result, I was forced to rely much more on unofficial sources (like newspapers) to reach realistic numbers.

In general, the Confederates used the same reporting categories, (PFD, PFDE, etc.) as the Federals, since their regulations were essentially rewrites of the Old Army regulations. The glaring exception is "effectives," which reported only enlisted men ready for combat, excluding officers. Where "effectives" were reported—and battle reports recorded "effectives" more often than not—I had to add in 9.8% for officers. Fortunately, enough regiments reported both officers and men that I could determine fairly accurately a reasonable army-wide average for the ratio of officers to men. However, even this category can be deceiving. Some reports include figures for "aggregate effective," which includes officers. Care must be taken in distinguishing between these categories.

A Word on Confederate Cavalry Strengths

Of all the Rebel numbers, cavalry strengths remain the most speculative. Virtually no reports were filed for the mounted arm, and those few that were are silent on numbers. A few fragmentary scraps can be found here and there, but nothing substantial. Confederate numbers found in the few brigade or regimental reports are usually little more than brief mentions of detachments, and so give few if any clues as to real strength at the time. Additionally, picket duty, courier work, and HQ escorts drained a large number of mounted men out of the line units. Where possible, I have accounted for the escorts separately. Finally, the command and organizational structure of the Confederate cavalry was undergoing significant changes during the month immediately before the battle. For these reasons, Rebel cavalry strengths at Chickamauga are largely estimates.

Fortunately, however, there are some solid numbers to work from at the corps and divisional level. Firm returns on July 31, August 10, and August 20 give consistent numbers for the overall strength of Forrest and Wheeler's commands.

Forrest's command is misleading, however, because the above returns report only the strength of his division of two brigades and two batteries—and not the additional division that was added to his command from the Department of East Tennessee in August, which expanded his command to corps size. Despite the fact that these men were assigned to Forrest, they continued to report separately, which led to confusion among early historians. One of the earliest histories of Forrest and his command estimates that both divisions numbered only "3500 rank and file" during the battle.[1]

The following table shows a solid consistency in the strengths of the cavalry over the month leading up to the battle. The August numbers actually show a slight increase in strength over the July totals, of about 5% across the board.

Date	Cavalry Officers	Cavalry Men	Artillery Officers	Artillery Men	Total
Wheeler 7/31	527	5,961	9	214	6,711
Forrest 7/31	286	3,287	6	129	3,708
Wheeler 8/10	539	6,356	10	238	7,143
Forrest 8/10	292	3,410	8	132	3,842
Wheeler 8/20	495	6,377	10	260	7,142
Forrest 8/20	290	3,450	9	127	3,876[2]

East Tennessee Strengths

	Offiers	Men	
7/1/63	425	5,331	5,756
8/10/63	425	5,332	5,757[3]
8/31/63	405	4,825	5,205[4]

Not all of the cavalry in East Tennessee actually joined Forrest. On July 31, the total mounted force in the Department of East Tennessee included nine regiments, six battalions, two squadrons, and two independent cavalry companies. Of those formations, a total of eight regiments and two battalions (which were merged to form a new regiment, the 6th North Carolina) joined the Army of Tennessee. Of a total of approximately 137 cavalry companies stationed in East Tennessee, by the beginning of September only 96 of those companies were included in John Pegram's newly organized cavalry division, or about 70% of the whole.[5]

Extrapolating from above, 70% of the reported strength for the department on August 10 is 4,029 officers and men. Note that this strength does not include Morgan's detachment—the two battalions of stragglers and returned men organized from the remnants of John Hunt Morgan's cavalry division lost during his raid into Ohio that July. This detachment was not organized until August 1, 1863, and was not included in either the August 10 or August 31 returns.

All told, General Bragg's cavalry numbered 15,287 officers and men by early September (just before the battle of Chickamauga). About 7,000 served with Wheeler and another 8,000 under Forrest. These figures offer a departure point in providing a baseline accuracy check for those numbers we do have, and for estimating the remaining regimental and battalion strengths.

Admittedly, calculating this figure required some assumptions, but in the absence of more detailed information I think my assumptions are reasonably accurate. The Federals thought so too, based on their intelligence. On September 12, a "Lt. Thomas" of the 3rd Kentucky Cavalry (CSA) was captured. He informed his captors that "they [the Confederates] have their cavalry all concentrated, and about 15,000 of them."[6]

This was not a bad guess on Thomas's part. The overall strength return for August 31 1863, shows 16,248 officers and men present for duty. In a letter to Emerson Opdycke after the war, William Rosecrans provided a more conservative estimate of 13,000—a combined total in Wheeler and Forrest's Corps.[7]

General Polk's Corps: The October 22 1863 Strength Return from the Bragg Papers

One month after Chickamauga, four divisions of the Army of Tennessee reported their regimental strengths on October 22 1863. From this data it was possible to extrapolate September 18 strengths for about a dozen regiments where no other sources were available. Since this report was made a full month after Chickamauga, however, simply adding each regiment's combat losses to the October 22 numbers would potentially double count a number of the wounded who had already returned to duty. Instead, I compared the ratio of known engaged strengths to these October 22 strengths and used that ratio to extrapolate numbers for the remaining unknown units.

Surprisingly, by October 22 many units had already returned to pre-battle strengths. Based on the numbers found in these four divisions, Bragg effectively replaced roughly 80% of his losses within one month of the fight, which suggests that most of his combat losses did not pose the permanent drain on manpower logic suggests they should be.

A Special Case: Govan's Brigade

Brig. Gen. Daniel C. Govan's Arkansas Brigade presents its own interesting numbers problem. Govan's brigade was part of Brig. Gen. St. John Liddell's division. Liddell reported that his division numbered 1,498 men PFD on September 21, and suffered 1,646 casualties in three days of fighting, for a total of 3,144 officers and men engaged. Brig. Gen. Edward C. Walthall's brigade report gives his September 18 engaged strength as 1,827. This leaves 1,317 officers and men available for Govan.

That calculation seems simple enough. However, two out of Govan's five regiments reported their own engaged strengths, a total of 837 men PFD. This leaves only 480 in the other three regiments, or 160 men per unit. This is very low. Even worse, we have a September 25 report from the brigade adjutant reporting the three regiments in question with 594 "effectives" not including officers. Once those officers were added back in, those same three regiments totaled 650—a force nearly one-third larger than the 480 calculated above—and we still haven't accounted for casualties.

Approaching things from another angle, Govan estimated his brigade losses at nearly 50%, and reported his casualties as 858 officers and men. If Govan's engaged strength was really 1,317, then his estimate of his loss percentage would be way off (he would have suffered 65% losses, not 50%). However, the percentage of loss of the two known regiments is 45% and 44%, which is more in keeping with Govan's brigade estimate.

All of this arithmetic suggests that the 1,317 figure is too low. For the losses and statistics to bear out, Govan had to have substantially more men. Working backward from the September 25 strengths, I used those figures as a base and added in an apportioned share of the 485 losses found in the brigade report, but not already accounted for in regimental reports. This produced a brigade engaged strength of 1,975 men PFD, about 650 more men than shown in Liddell's report. While it is possible that significant numbers of stragglers rejoined Govan between September 21 and 25, I have found no evidence of this (unlike, for example, some of the Georgians in Claudius C. Wilson's brigade). In the end, I decided the larger figure for Govan's strength had to be more accurate.

Nomenclature Notes

SS = Sharpshooters.
Bn. = Battalion.
(k) = killed in action, (w) = wounded, (mw) = mortally wounded.
(c) = captured

(Units in *Italics* were not engaged.)

Gen. Braxton Bragg
Commanding, Army of Tennessee

Formation	Companies (Guns)	Strength	Principle Sources
Escort Capt. Guy Dreux	6	344	
Dreux La. Co. Cav Lt. O. Dubuis	1	68	*OR* 30, pt. 4, 518[8]
K, 3rd Ala Cav Capt. E. M. Holloway	1	68	*OR* 30, pt. 4, 518[9]
Miners and Sappers	3	160	*OR* 23, pt. 2, 957, 962[10]
C, 1 Louisiana Reg	1	48	*OR* Supplement, 35, 669[11]
Polk's Corps	372	13,225	
Hill's Corps	265	9,216	
Reserve Corps	225	8,005	
Buckner's Corps	252	9,537	
1st Corps - Hood	398	11,056	
Forrest's Cav Corps	189	6,553	
Wheeler's Cav Corps	153	6,870	

Formation	Companies	Strength	Principle Sources
	Troops nearby or arriving too late, all unengaged		
Total	**165**	**6,689**	
16 South Carolina	10	398	
Ferguson Battery (guns)	1 (4)	87	
Jenkins' Brigade	62	2,000	
Bryan's Brigade	40	1,500	
Wofford's Brigade	52	2,200	
Alexander's Artillery (guns)	6 (24)	504	

Lt. Gen. Leonidas Polk
Polk's Corps

Formation	Companies	Strength	Principle Sources
Polk's Corps	**372**	**13,225**	
Escort	**1**	**33**	
Greenleaf La. Cav Capt. Leeds Greenleaf	1	33	OR 23, pt. 2, 957[12]
Cheatham's Division Maj. Gen. Benjamin F. Cheatham	**218**	**7,046**	
Escort	**1**	**32**	
G, 2 Ga. Cav Capt. Thomas M. Merritt	1	32	OR 23, pt. 2, 957[13]
Jackson's Brigade Brig. Gen. John K. Jackson	39	1,311	
2 Bn. 1 Conf. Maj. James Clarke Gordon	5	194	OR 30, pt. 2, 86[14]
2 Georgia Bn. SS Maj. Richard H. Whiteley	4	108	OR 30, pt. 2, 86[15]
5 Georgia Col. Charles P. Daniel	10	353	OR 30, pt. 2, 86[16]

Formation	Companies	Strength	Principle Sources
5 Mississippi Lt. Col. Walter L. Sykes (k), Maj. John B. Herring	10	252	OR 30, pt. 2, 86[17]
8 Mississippi Col. John C. Wilkinson	10	404	OR 30, pt. 2, 86[18]
Maney's Brigade Brig. Gen. George Maney	**33**	**1,293**	
1+27 Tennessee Col. Hume R. Field	10	703	OR 30, pt. 2, 82[19]
4 Tennessee (PA) Col. James A. McMurray (mw), Lt. Col. Robert N. Lewis (w), Maj. Oliver A. Bradshaw (w), Capt. Joseph Bostick	10	179	OR 30, pt. 2, 100[20]
6+9 Tennessee Col. George C. Porter	10	368	OR 30, pt. 2, 103[21]
24 Tennessee Bn SS Major Frank Maney	3	43	OR 30, pt. 2, 104[22]
Smith's Brigade Brig. Gen. Preston Smith (k), Col Alfred J. Vaughan, Jr.	**40**	**1,642**	
11 Tennessee Col. George W. Gordon	8	383	Bragg Papers[23]
12+47 Tennessee Col. William M. Watkins	8	351	Bragg Papers[24]
13+154 Tennessee Col. Alfred J. Vaughan, Jr., Lt. Col. Robert W. Pitman	9	222	Company Rolls, NARA[25]
29 Tennessee Col. Horace Rice	10	413	Company Rolls, NARA[26]
Dawson's Bn SS Maj. John W. Dawson (w), Maj. William Green (w), Maj. James Purl	5	273	OR 30, pt. 2, 115[27]

Formation	Companies	Strength	Principle Sources
Strahl's Brigade Brig. Gen. Otho F. Strahl	**50**	**1,181**[28]	
4+5 Tennessee Col. Jonathan J. Lamb	10	380	Bragg Papers[29]
19 Tennessee Col. Francis M. Walker	10	266	OR 30, pt. 2, 134[30]
24 Tennessee Col. John A. Wilson	10	245	Bragg Papers[31]
31 Tennessee Col. Egbert E. Tansil	10	168	Bragg Papers[32]
33 Tennessee Col. Warner P. Jones	10	122	Bragg Papers[33]
Wright's Brigade Brig. Gen. Marcus J. Wright	**50**	**1,113**	
8 Tennessee Col. John H. Anderson	10	285	OR 30, pt. 2, 121[34]
16 Tennessee Col. David M. Donnell (w)	10	266	OR 30, pt. 2, 121[35]
28 Tennessee Col. Sidney S. Stanton	10	279	OR 30, pt. 2, 121[36]
38 Tennessee + Murray's Tennessee Bn Col. John C. Carter	10	278	OR 30, pt. 2, 121[37]
51+52 Tennessee Lt. Col. John G. Hall	10	255	OR 30, pt. 2, 121[38]
Artillery/Cheatham	**5**	**474**	
Carnes's Tennessee Capt. William W. Carnes	1	87	Calculation[39]
	(4) 2x 6# Gun, 2x 12# Howitzer		
Scogin's Georgia Capt. John Scogin	1	89	OR 30, pt. 2, 86
	(4) 2x 6# Gun, 2x 12# Howitzer		

Formation	Companies	Strength	Principle Sources
Scott's Tennessee Lt. John H. Marsh(w), Lt. A. T. Watson, Capt. William L. Scott	1	114	Bragg Papers[40]
	(4) 2x 6# Gun, 2x 12# Howitzer		
Smith's Mississippi Lt. William B. Turner	1	87	Bragg Papers[41]
	(4) 4x Napoleon		
Stanford's Mississippi Capt. Thomas J. Stanford	1	97	Bragg Papers[42]
	(4) 4x 3 Inch Rifles		
Hindman's Division Maj. Gen. Thomas C. Hindman (w), Brig. Gen. Patton Anderson	**153**	**6,146**[43]	
Escort	**1**	**75**	
I, 3 Alabama Cav Capt. Thomas M. Lenoir	1	65	Company Rolls, NARA[44]
Sharpshooters Lt. William L. Mead	Det.	10	Bragg Papers[45]
Anderson's Brigade Brig. Gen. Patton Anderson, Col. Jacob H. Sharp	**53**	**1,865**[46]	
7 Mississippi Col. William H. Bishop	10	291	Company Rolls, NARA[47]
9 Mississippi Maj. Thomas H. Lyman	10	355	OR 30, pt. 2, 324[48]
10 Mississippi Lt. Col. James Barr	10	311	OR Sup., 45, 184[49]
41 Mississippi Col. William F. Tucker	10	502	OR 30, pt. 2, 327[50]
44 Mississippi Col. Jacob H. Sharp, Lt. Col. Robert G. Kelsey	10	272	OR 30, pt. 2, 328[51]
9 Mississippi Bn Maj. William C. Richards	3	134	Company rolls, NARA[52]

Formation	Companies	Strength	Principle Sources
Deas' Brigade Brig. Gen. Zachariah C. Deas	**52**	**1,932**	**OR 30, pt. 2, 331**
19 Alabama Col. Samuel K. McSpadden	10	515	OR 30, pt. 2, 335[53]
22 Alabama Lt. Col. John Weedon (k), Capt. Henry T. Toulmin	10	371	OR 30, pt. 2, 337[54]
25 Alabama Col. George D. Johnston	10	330	OR 30, pt. 2, 338[55]
39 Alabama Col. Whitfield Clark	10	340	OR 30, pt. 2, 338[56]
50 Alabama Col. John G. Coltart	10	313	Calculation[57]
17 Alabama SS Capt. James F. Nabers	2	63	Calculation[58]
Manigault's Brigade Brig. Gen. Arthur M. Manigault	**43**	**2,025**	**Manigault, 102[59]**
24 Alabama Col. Newton N. Davis	10	381	OR 30, pt. 2, 347[60]
28 Alabama Col. John C. Reid	11	629	Calculation[61]
34 Alabama Maj. John N. Slaughter	10	329	Manigault, 96[62]
10+19 S. Carolina Col. James F. Pressley	12	686	Calculation[63]
Artillery/Hindman guns	**3** (14)	**249**	
Dent's Alabama Capt. Samuel H. Dent	1	87	OR 30, pt. 2, 332
	(6) 6x Napoleon		
Garrity's Alabama Capt. James Garrity	1	89	Bragg Papers[64]
	(4) 2x 6 # Gun, 2x Napoleon		

Formation	Companies	Strength	Principle Sources
Waters's Alabama Lt. Charles W. Watkins	1	73	OR 30, pt. 2, 345[65]
(4) 2x 6# Gun, 2x 12# Howitzer			

Lt. Gen. Daniel H. Hill
Hill's Corps

Formation	Companies	Strength	Principle Sources
Hill's Corps	**265**	**9,216**	
Escort	**1**	**51**	
Raum's Cav Capt. W. C. Raum	1	51	OR 23, pt. 2, 940, 945[66]
Breckinridge's Div Maj. Gen. John C. Breckinridge	**135**	**3,785**	
Adam's Brigade Brig. Gen. Daniel W. Adams (w&c), Col. Randall L. Gibson	**42**	**1,221**	
32 Alabama Maj. John C. Kimbell	10	145	OR 30, pt. 2, 219
13+20 Louisiana Col. Randall L. Gibson, Capt. E. M. Dubroca, Col. Leon Von Zinken	10	309	OR 30, pt. 2, 222[67]
16+25 Louisiana Col. Daniel Gober	10	319	OR 30, pt. 2, 219[68]
19 Louisiana Lt. Col. Richard W. Turner (w), Maj. Loudon Butler (k), Capt. Hyder A. Kennedy	10	349	OR 30, pt. 2, 224[69]
14 Louisiana Bn Maj. John E. Austin	2	99	OR 30, pt. 2, 219[70]
Helm's Brigade Brig. Gen. Benjamin H. Helm (k), Col. Joseph H. Lewis	**50**	**1,384**	
41 Alabama Col. Martin L. Stansel	10	357	OR 30, pt. 2, 208[71]

Formation	Companies	Strength	Principle Sources
2 Kentucky Lt. Col. James W. Hewitt (k), Lt. Col. James W. Moss	10	302	OR 30, pt. 2, 209[72]
4 Kentucky Col. Joseph P. Nuckols (w), Maj. Thomas W. Thompson	10	275	OR 30, pt. 2, 206[73]
6 Kentucky Col. Joseph H. Lewis, Lt. Col. Martin H. Cofer	8	220	OR 30, pt. 2, 206[74]
9 Kentucky Col. John W. Caldwell (w), Lt. Col. John C. Wickliffe	10	230	OR 30, pt. 2, 206[75]
Stovall's Brigade Brig. Gen. Marcellus A. Stovall	**40**	**897**	
1+3 Florida Col. William S. Dilworth	10	298	OR 30, pt. 2, 232[76]
4 Florida Col. Wylde L. L. Bowen	10	238	OR 30, pt. 2, 232
47 Georgia Capt. William S. Phillips (w), Capt. Joseph S. Cone	10	193	OR 30, pt. 2, 232
60 N. Carolina Lt. Col. James M. Ray (w), Capt. James Thomas Weaver	10	168	OR 30, pt. 2, 232[77]
Artillery/Breckinridge Maj. Rice E. Graves (k)	**3**	**283**	
guns	(15)		
Cobb's Kentucky Capt. Robert Cobb	1	84	OR 30, pt. 2, 202
	(5) 4x Napoleon, 1x 12# Howitzer		
Mebane's Tennessee Capt. John W. Mebane	1	73	OR 30, pt. 2, 202

Formation	Companies	Strength	Principle Sources
(4) 12# Howitzer			
Slocomb's Louisiana Capt. Cuthbert H. Slocomb	1	126	OR 30.2.202
(6) 4x Napoleon, 2x James Rifle			
Cleburne's Division Maj. Gen. Patrick R. Cleburne	**129**	**5,380**[78]	
Escort	**1**	**51**	
Sanders' Cavalry Capt. C. F. Sanders	1	51	OR 30, pt. 2, 940[79]
Deshler's Brigade Brig. Gen. James Deshler (k), Col. Roger Q. Mills	**30**	**1,693**	
19+24 Arkansas Lt. Col. Augustus S. Hutchison	10	226	OR 30, pt. 2, 192
6+10+15 Texas Col. Roger Q. Mills, Lt. Col. T. Scott Anderson	10	700	OR 30, pt. 2, 193[80]
17+18+24+25 Texas Col. Franklin C. Wilkes (w), Lt. Col. John T. Coit, Maj. William A. Taylor	10	767	OR 30, pt. 2, 194
Polk's Brigade Brig. Gen. Lucius E. Polk	**50**	**1,390**	
1 Arkansas Col. John W. Colquitt	10	430	OR 30, pt. 2, 179
3+5 Confederate Col. James A. Smith	10	290	Calculation[81]
2 Tennessee Col. William D. Robison	10	264	OR 30, pt. 2, 181[82]
35 Tennessee Col. Benjamin J. Hill	10	236	OR 30, pt. 2, 184[83]
48 Tennessee Col. George H. Nixon	10	170	OR 30, pt. 2, 185-186[84]

Formation	Companies	Strength	Principle Sources
Wood's Brigade Brig. Gen. Sterling A. M. Wood	**45**	**1,982**	
16 Alabama Maj. John H. McGaughy (w), Capt. Frederick A. Ashford	10	414	OR 30, pt. 2, 162[85]
33 Alabama Col. Samuel Adams	10	459	Morning reports, NARA[86]
45 Alabama Col. Ephraim B. Breedlove	10	423	CCNMP[87]
18 Alabama Bn Maj. John H. Gibson, Col. Samuel Adams	3	87	Calculation[88]
32+45 Mississippi Col. Mark P. Lowrey	10	541	Morning Reports, NARA[89]
15 Mississippi Bn SS Maj. A. T. Hawkins (mw), Capt. Daniel Coleman	2	58	Calculation[90]
Artillery/Cleburne Maj. Thomas R. Hotchkiss (w), Capt. Henry C. Semple	**3**	**264**	
Calvert's Arkansas Lt. Thomas J. Key	1	87	Calculation[91]
	(4) 2x 6# Gun, 2x 12# Howitzer		
Douglas's Texas Capt. James P. Douglas	1	90	OR 30, pt. 2, 191[92]
	(4) 2x 6# Gun, 2x 12# Howitzer		
Semple's Alabama Capt. Henry C. Semple, Lt. R. W. Goldthwaite	1	87	Calculation[93]
	(4) 4x Napoleon		

Maj. Gen. William H. T. Walker
Reserve Corps

Reserve Corps	**225**	**8,005**	

Formation	Companies	Strength	Principle Sources
Escort	*1*	*51*	
Nelson's Cavalry Co. *Capt. Thomas M. Nelson*	*1*	*51*	OR 24, pt. 3, 1040[94]
Gist's Division Brig. Gen. Matthew D. Ector, Brig. Gen. States Rights Gist	**123**	**3,974**[95]	
Gist's/Colquitt's Bde Brig. Gen. States Rights Gist, Col. Peyton H. Colquitt (k), Lt. Col. Leroy Napier	**27**	**1,400**	OR 30, pt. 2, 246[96]
46 Georgia Col. Peyton H. Colquitt (k), Maj. Alexander M. Speer	10	591	Calculation[97]
8 Georgia Bn Lt. Col. Leroy Napier, Major Z L. Watters	7	399	Calculation[98]
16 South Carolina *Col. James McCullough*	*10*	*398*	*Company rolls, NARA*[99]
24 South Carolina Col. Clement H. Stevens (w), Lt. Col. Ellison Capers	10	410	Jones, p. 123[100]
Ector's Brigade Brig. Gen. Matthew D. Ector	**55**	**1,199**	
Stone's Bn Ala. SS Maj. Thomas O. Stone	3	111	*Mobile Daily Advertiser*[101]
Pound's Bn Miss. SS Capt. Merryman Pound	2	42	*Mobile Daily Advertiser*[102]
29 North Carolina Col. William B. Creasman	10	215	*Mobile Daily Advertiser*[103]
9 Texas Col William H. Young	10	145	*Mobile Daily Advertiser*[104]
10 Texas DC Lt. Col. Cullen R. Earp	10	272	*Mobile Daily Advertiser*[105]
14 Texas DC Col. John L. Camp	10	197	*Mobile Daily Advertiser*[106]
32 Texas DC Col. Julius A. Andrews	10	217	*Mobile Daily Advertiser*[107]

Formation	Companies	Strength	Principle Sources
Wilson's Brigade Col. Claudius C. Wilson	40	1,317	OR **30**, pt. 2, 249[108]
25 Georgia Lt. Col. A. J. Williams	11	383	Company Rolls, NARA[109]
29 Georgia Lt. Col. George R. McRae	10	220	CCNMP[110]
30 Georgia Lt. Col. James S. Boynton	9	334	CCNMP[111]
1 Georgia SS Bn Maj. Arthur Schaaff	4	104	*Savannah Republican*[112]
4 Louisiana Bn Lt. Col. John McEnery	6	276	Calculation[113]
Artillery/Gist	1	58[114]	
Ferguson's SC Lt. R. T. Beauregard	1	87	Calculation[115]
	(4) 2x 6# Gun, 2x Napoleon		
Howell's Georgia Capt. Evan P. Howell	1	58	Company Returns, NARA[116]
	(6) 2x 6# Gun, 4x 12# Howitzer		
Liddell's Division Brig. Gen. St. John R. Liddell	102	4,031	
Govan's Brigade Col. Daniel C. Govan	49	1,975	**Calculation[117]**
2+15 Arkansas Lt. Col. Reuben F. Harvey (mw), Capt. A. T. Meek	10	349	CCNMP[118]
5+13 Arkansas Col. Lucius Featherston (k), Lt. Col. John E. Murray	10	450	OR 30, pt. 2, 266[119]
6+7 Arkansas Col. David A. Gillespie (mw), Lt. Col. Peter Snyder	10	388	CCNMP[120]

Formation	Companies	Strength	Principle Sources
8 Arkansas Lt. Col. George F. Baucum (w), Maj. A. Watkins	10	387	OR 30, pt. 2, 269
1 Louisiana Reg. Lt. Col. George F. Baucum (w), Maj. A. Watkins	9	401	CCNMP[121]
Walthall's Brigade Brig. Gen. Edward C. Walthall	**51**	**1,827**	**OR 30, pt. 2, 276**[122]
24 Mississippi Lt. Col. Robert P. McKelvaine (w), Maj. William C. Staples (w), Capt. John D. Smith (w), Capt. Benjamin F. Toomer	10	428	*Memphis Daily Appeal*[123]
27 Mississippi Col. James A. Campbell	11	362	Calculation[124]
29 Mississippi Col. William F. Brantley	10	368	OR 30, pt. 2, 282
30 Mississippi Col. Junius I. Scales (w&c), Lt. Col. Hugh A. Reynolds (detached), Maj. James M. Johnson	10	362	Calculation[125]
34 Mississippi Maj. William G. Pegram (w), Capt. Henry J. Bowen, Lt. Col. Hugh A. Reynolds (mw)	10	307	OR 30, pt. 2, 285
Artillery/Liddell Capt. William H. Fowler	**2**	**229**	
Fowler's Alabama Capt. William H. Fowler	1	142	Company Returns, NARA[126]
(4) 4x Napoleon			
Warren Lt. Artillery (Swett's Mississippi) Lt. Harvey Shannon	1	87	Calculation[127]
2x Napoleon, 2x James Rifle			

Formation	Companies	Strength	Principle Sources

Maj. Gen. Simon B. Buckner
Buckner's Corps

Formation	Companies	Strength	Principle Sources
Buckner's Corps	252	**9,537**	
Escort	4	100	
Clark's Cav Capt. J. W. Clark	1	**20**	OR **31, pt. 1, 531**[128]
Train Guard	3	80	Calculation[129]
Preston's Division Brig. Gen. William Preston	122	**4,862**	
Gracie's Brigade Brig. Gen. Archibald Gracie Jr.	43	**1,927**[130]	
43 Alabama Col. Young M. Moody	10	364	Tabular Statement[131]
1 Alabama Bn Lt. Col. John H. Holt (w), Capt. George W. Huguley	7	281	Tabular Statement[132]
2 Alabama Bn Lt. Col. Bolling Hall Jr. (w), Capt. W. D. Walden (mw), Lt. Crenshaw Hall	6	282	Tabular Statement[133]
3 Alabama Bn Lt. Col. John W. A. Sanford	6	331	Tabular Statement[134]
4 Alabama Bn Maj. John D. McLennan	4	243	Tabular Statement[135]
63 Tennessee Lt. Col. Abraham Fulkerson (w), Maj. John A. Aiken	10	426	Tabular Statement[136]
Kelly's Brigade Col. John H. Kelly	36	**1,146**[137]	
65 Georgia Col. Robert H. Moore	8	272	Tabular Statement[138]
5 Kentucky Col. Hiram Hawkins	10	252	Tabular Statement[139]
58 North Carolina Col. John B. Palmer	10	359	Tabular Statement[140]

Formation	Companies	Strength	Principle Sources
63 Virginia Maj. James M. French	8	263	Tabular Statement[141]
Trigg's Brigade Col. Robert C. Trigg	**40**	**1,536**[142]	
1 Florida Cav Col. G. Troup Maxwell	10	271	Tabular Statement[143]
6 Florida Col. Jesse J. Finley	10	402	Tabular Statement[144]
7 Florida Col. Robert Bullock	10	391	Tabular Statement[145]
54 Virginia Lt. Col. John J. Wade	10	472	Tabular Statement[146]
Artillery/Preston Maj. A. Leyden	**3**	**253**	
Jeffress' Virginia Capt. William C. Jeffress	1	79	Bragg Papers[147]
	(5) 4x 10# Parrott, 1x 12# Blakely Rifle		
Peeples's Georgia Capt. Tyler M. Peeples	1	87	Calculation[148]
	(4) 2x Napoleon, 2x 24# Howitzer		
Wolihin's Georgia Capt. Andrew M. Wolihin	1	87	Calculation[149]
	(4) 2x 6# Guns, 2x 12# Howitzer		
Stewart's Division Maj. Gen. Alexander P. Stewart	**122**	**4,298**	
Escort	1	35	
Foules's Co. MS Cav. Capt. Henry L. Foules	1	35	OR 30, pt. 2, 365[150]
Bate's Brigade Brig. Gen. William B. Bate	**43**	**1,217**	
58 Alabama Col. Bushrod Jones	10	287	OR 30, pt. 2, 390[151]

Formation	Companies	Strength	Principle Sources
37 Georgia Col. Anthony F. Rudler (w), Lt. Col. Joseph T. Smith	10	425	OR 30, pt. 2, 388[152]
4 Georgia Bn SS Maj. Thomas D. Caswell (w), Capt. Benjamin M. Turner, Lt. Joel Towers	3	92	OR 30, pt. 2, 388[153]
15+37 Tennessee Col. Robert C. Tyler (w), Lt. Col. R. Dudley Frayser(w), Capt. R. M. Tankesley	10	230	OR 30, pt. 2, 388[154]
20 Tennessee Col. Thomas B. Smith (w), Maj. William M. Shy	10	183	OR 30, pt. 2, 388[155]
Brown's Brigade Brig. Gen. John C. Brown (w), Col. Edmund C. Cook	**45**	**1,340**[156]	
18 Tennessee Col. Joseph B. Palmer (w), Lt. Col. William R. Butler (w), Capt. Gideon H. Lowe	10	362	OR 30, pt. 2, 373[157]
26 Tennessee Col. John M. Lillard (mw), Maj. Richard M. Saffell	10	239	OR 30, pt. 2, 373[158]
32 Tennessee Col. Edmund C. Cook, Capt. Calaway C. Tucker	10	341	OR 30, pt. 2, 373[159]
45 Tennessee Col. Anderson Searcy	10	254	OR 30, pt. 2, 373[160]
23 Tennessee Bn Maj. Tazewell W. Newman (w), Capt. W. P. Simpson	5	144	OR 30, pt. 2, 373[161]
Clayton's Brigade Brig. Gen. Henry D. Clayton	**30**	**1,446**	
18 Alabama Col. James T. Holtzclaw (w), Lt. Col. Richard F. Inge (mw), Maj. Peter F. Hunley	10	527	OR 30, pt. 2, 404[162]

Formation	Companies	Strength	Principle Sources
36 Alabama Col. Lewis T. Woodruff	10	429	OR 30, pt. 2, 404
38 Alabama Lt. Col. Augustus R. Lankford	10	490	OR 30, pt. 2, 404
Artillery/Stewart Maj. J. Wesley Eldridge (guns)	**3** (12)	**260**	
Humphreys's Ark. Capt. John T. Humphreys	1	89	OR 30, pt. 2, 365
Dawson's Georgia Lt. R. W. Anderson	1	65	OR 30, pt. 2, 365
	(4) 2x Napoleon, 2x 12 # Howitzer		
Eufala Alabama Capt. McDonald Oliver	1	106	OR 30, pt. 2, 365
	(4) 4x 3 Inch Rifles		
Reserve Artillery Maj. Samuel C. Williams (guns)	**4** (14)	**277**	
Baxter's Tennessee Capt. Edmund D. Baxter	1	53	Bragg Papers[163]
	(2) 2x 3 Inch Rifle		
Darden's Mississippi Capt. Putnam Darden	1	60	Company returns, NARA[164]
	(4) 4x Napoleon		
Kolb'sAlabama Capt. Reuben F. Kolb	1	86	Bragg Papers[165]
	(4) 2x 12# Howitzer, 2x 6# Gun		
Mecants's Florida Capt. Robert P. MeCants	1	78	Bragg Papers[166]
	(4) 1x 10# Parrott, 3x 6# Gun		

Formation	Companies	Strength	Principle Sources

Maj. Gen. John Bell Hood (w)
1st Corps, Army of Northern Virginia

Formation	Companies	Strength	Principle Sources
1st Corps - Hood	398	11,056[167]	
Escort	2	60	
A, 1 La. Cav	1	30	Calculation[168]
E/C, 1 La. Cav	1	30	Calculation[169]
Johnson's Division Brig. Gen. Bushrod R. Johnson	158	3,755[170]	
Fulton's Brigade Col. John S. Fulton	40	874	
17 Tennessee Lt. Col. Watt W. Floyd	10	249	*OR* 30, pt. 2, 479[171]
23 Tennessee Col. Richard H. Keeble	10	186	*OR* 30, pt. 2, 484[172]
25 Tennessee Lt. Col. R. B. Snowden	10	145	*OR* 30, pt. 2, 477[173]
44 Tennessee Lt. Col. John L. McEwen, Jr. (w), Maj. George M. Crawford	10	294	*OR* 30, pt. 2, 477[174]
Gregg's Brigade Brig. Gen. John Gregg (w), Col. Cyrus A. Sugg	65	1,419	
3 Tennessee Col. Calvin H. Walker (w), Lt. Col. Calvin J. Clack	10	274	*OR* 30, pt. 2, 497[175]
10 Tennessee Col. William Grace	10	190	*OR* 30, pt. 2, 497[176]
30 Tennessee Lt. Col. James J. Turner (w), Capt. Charles S. Douglas	10	185	*OR* 30, pt. 2, 497[177]
41 Tennessee Lt. Col. James D. Tillman (w), Maj. Thomas G. Miller	10	325	*OR* 30, pt. 2, 497[178]

Formation	Companies	Strength	Principle Sources
50 Tennessee Col. Cyrus A. Sugg, Lt. Col. Thomas W. Beaumont (k), Maj. Christopher W. Robertson, Col. Calvin H. Walker	10	186	*Confederate Veteran,* March, 1898[179]
1 Tennessee Bn. Maj. Stephen H. Colms (w), Maj. Christopher W. Robertson	5	82	OR 30, pt. 2, 497[180]
7 Texas Col. Hiram B. Granbury (w), Maj. Kleber M. Van Zandt	10	177	OR 30, pt. 2, 497[181]
McNair's Brigade Brig. Gen. Evander McNair (w), Col. David Coleman	**50**	**1,207**	
1 Ark Mtd. Rifles Col. Robert W. Harper (mw), Lt. Col. Daniel H. Reynolds	10	273	OR 30, pt. 2, 501[182]
2 Ark Mtd. Rifles Col. James A. Williamson	10	139	OR 30, pt. 2, 501[183]
25 Arkansas Lt. Col. Eli Hufstedler	10	133	OR 30, pt. 2, 501[184]
4+31+4 Bn Ark Maj. J. A. Ross	10	415	OR 30, pt. 2, 501[185]
39 North Carolina Col. David Coleman, Lt. Col. Frank A. Reynolds	10	247	OR 30, pt. 2, 501[186]
Artillery/Johnson	**3**	**255**	
Bledsoe's Missouri Lt. R. L. Wood	1	84	OR 30, pt. 2, 497
(4) 2x 3 Inch Rifle, 2x 12# Howitzer			
Culpepper's SC Capt. James F. Culpepper	1	84	OR 30, pt. 2, 501[187]
(4) 2x 6# Gun, 2x 12# Howitzer			

Formation	Companies	Strength	Principle Sources
Everett's Georgia Lt. William S. Everett	1	87	OR 30, pt. 2, 467[188]
	(4) 4x Napoleon		
Law's Division Brig. Gen. Evander M. Law	**132**	**3,957**[189]	
Benning's Brigade Brig. Gen. Henry L. Benning	10	1,200[190]	
2 Georgia Lt. Col. William S. Shephard (w), Maj. William W. Charlton	10	427	Calculation[191]
15 Georgia Col. Dudley M. DuBose (w), Maj. Peter J. Shannon	10	285	Company rolls, NARA[192]
17 Georgia Lt. Col. Charles W. Matthews	10	250	*Columbus Weekly Enquirer*[193]
20 Georgia Col. James D. Waddell	10	238	CCNMP[194]
Robertson's Brigade Brig. Gen. Jerome B. Robertson, Col. Van H. Manning	**42**	**1,300**	**OR 30, pt. 4, 652**[195]
3 Arkansas Col. Van H. Manning	10	380	Alexander Papers[196]
1 Texas Capt. Richard J. Harding	12	409	Company Rolls, NARA[197]
4 Texas Lt. Col. John P. Bane (w), Capt. Robert H. Bassett (w), Capt. James T. Hunter	10	264	Calculation[198]
5 Texas Maj. Jefferson C. Rogers (w), Capt. John S. Cleveland (w), Capt. Tacitus T. Clay	10	247	*Memphis Daily Appeal*[199]
Sheffield's Brigade Col. James L. Sheffield (w), Col. William F. Perry	**50**	**1,457**	**Laine and Penny, 370**[200]

Formation	Companies	Strength	Principle Sources
4 Alabama Col. Pinckney D. Bowles	10	249	Laine and Penny, 370[201]
15 Alabama Col. William C. Oates	10	373	Laine and Penny, 370[202]
44 Alabama Col. William F. Perry, Lt. Col. John A. Jones	10	276	Laine and Penny, 370
47 Alabama Maj. James M. Campbell	10	283	Laine and Penny, 370
48 Alabama Lt. Col. William M. Hardwick	10	276	Laine and Penny, 370
Anderson's Brigade *Brig. Gen. George T. Anderson*	*50*	*1,728*[203]	
7 Georgia *Col. William W. White*	*10*	*344*	*Company Rolls, NARA*[204]
8 Georgia *Col. John R. Towers*	*10*	*338*	*Company Rolls, NARA*[205]
9 Georgia *Col. Benjamin Beck*	*10*	*318*	*Company Rolls, NARA*[206]
11 Georgia *Col. Francis H. Little*	*10*	*317*	*Company Rolls, NARA*[207]
59 Georgia *Lt. Col. Bolivar H. Gee*	*10*	*411*	*Company Rolls, NARA*[208]
Jenkins' Brigade *Brig. Gen. Micah Jenkins*	*62*	*2,000*[209]	
1 South Carolina *Col. Franklin W. Kilpatrick*	*10*	*312*	*Calculation*[210]
2 SC Rifles *Col. Thomas Thomson*	*10*	*316*	*Company Rolls, NARA*[211]
5 South Carolina *Col. Asbury Coward*	*10*	*368*	*Company Rolls, NARA*[212]
6 South Carolina *Col. John Bratton*	*10*	*313*	*Calculation*[213]
Hampton Legion *Col. Martin W. Gary*	*10*	*316*	*Charleston Mercury*[214]
Palmetto SS *Col. Joseph Walker*	*12*	*375*	*Calculation*[215]

Formation	Companies	Strength	Principle Sources
Kershaw's Division Brig. Gen. Joseph B. Kershaw	**102**	**2,822**[216]	
Humphreys' Brigade Brig. Gen. Benjamin G. Humphreys	**41**	**1,226**	
13 Mississippi Lt. Col. Kennan McElroy	10	300	Company Rolls, NARA[217]
17 Mississippi Lt. Col. John C. Fiser	10	338	Company Rolls, NARA[218]
18 Mississippi Capt. William F. Hubbard	10	260	Company Rolls, NARA[219]
21 Mississippi Lt. Col. Daniel N. Moody	11	328	Company Rolls, NARA[220]
Kershaw's Brigade Brig. Gen. Joseph B. Kershaw	**61**	**1,596**[221]	
2 South Carolina Lt. Col. Franklin Gaillard	10	230	Egleston Letter, Screvin diary[222]
3 South Carolina Col. James D. Nance	10	343	Company Rolls, NARA[223]
7 South Carolina Lt. Col. Elbert Bland (k), Maj. John S. Hard (k), Capt. E. Jerry Goggins	12	283	Company Rolls, NARA[224]
8 South Carolina Col. John W. Henagan	12	215	Company Rolls, NARA[225]
15 South Carolina Col. Joseph F. Gist	10	343	Company Rolls, NARA[226]
3 South Carolina Bn. Capt. Joshua M. Townsend (k), Capt. Benjamin M. Whitener	7	182	Calculation[227]
Bryan's Brigade *Brig. Gen. Goode Bryan*	*40*	*1,500*	*Calculation[228]*
10 Georgia *Col. John B. Weems*	*10*	*330*	*Calculation*
50 Georgia *Col. W. R. Manning*	*10*	*330*	*Calculation*

Formation	Companies	Strength	Principle Sources
51 Georgia *Col. Edward Ball*	*10*	*330*	*Calculation*
53 Georgia *Col. James P. Simms*	*10*	*510*	*Calculation*
Wofford's Brigade *Brig. Gen. William T.* *Wofford*	*52*	*2,200*	*CCNMP*[229]
16 Georgia *Col. Henry P. Thomas*	*10*	*356*	*Calculation*
18 Georgia Col. *Solon Z. Ruff*	*10*	*475*	*Calculation*
24 Georgia *Col. Robert McMillan*	*10*	*396*	*Calculation*
3 Georgia SS *Maj. P. E. Devant*	*6*	*220*	*Calculation*
Cobb's Legion *Lt. Col. Luther J. Glenn*	*7*	*327*	*Calculation*
Phillips Legion *Lt. Col. E. S. Barclay*	*9*	*426*	*Calculation*[230]
Reserve Artillery Maj. Felix H. Robertson	**5**	**462**	
(guns)	(18)		
Barret's Missouri Capt. Overton W. Barret	1	94	OR 31, pt. 3, 828[231]
	(4) 2x 6# Gun, 2x 12# Howitzer		
Le Gardeur's La. Capt. G. Le Gardeur, Jr.	1	87	Calculation[232]
	(4) 2x 6# Gun, 2x 12# Howitzer		
Havis's Georgia Capt. M. W. Havis	1	100	OR 31, pt. 3, 828[233]
	(3) 2xNapoleon, 1x James Rifle		

Formation	Companies	Strength	Principle Sources
Lumsden's Alabama Capt. Charles L. Lumsden	1	90	OR 31, pt. 3, 828[234]
	(5) 3xNapoleon, 1x10# Parrott, 1x12# Howitzer		
Massenberg's Georgia Capt. T. L. Massenberg	1	91	OR 31, pt. 3, 828[235]
	(2) 2x 10# Parrott		
Alexander's Battalion *Col. E. Porter Alexander* (guns)	*6* (24)	*504*	*Calculation*[236]
Fickling's SC Capt. William W. Fickling	*1*	*84*	*Calculation*[237]
	(4) 4x12# Howitzer		
Jordan's Virginia Capt. Tyler C. Jordan	*1*	*84*	*Calculation*[238]
	(4) 4x3 inch Rifles		
Moody's Louisiana Capt. George V. Moody	*1*	*84*	*Calculation*[239]
	(4) 4x24# Howitzer		
Parker's Virginia Capt. William W. Parker	*1*	*84*	*Calculation*[240]
	(4) 3x3 inch Rifle, 1x 10# Parrott		
Taylor's Virginia Capt. Osmond B. Taylor	*1*	*84*	*Calculation*[241]
	(4) 4xNapoleon		
Woolfolk's Virginia Capt. Pichegru Woolfolk, Jr.	*1*	*84*	*Calculation*[242]
	(4) 2xNapoleon, 2x 20# Parrott		

Brig. Gen. Nathan Bedford Forrest
Forrest's Cavalry Corps

Forrest's Cav Corps	**189**	**6,553**	

Formation	Companies	Strength	Principle Sources
Escort	1	67	
Jackson's Company Capt. J. C. Jackson	1	67	OR 31, pt. 2, 646[243]
Armstrong's Division	**95**	**3,486**	
Escort			
Bradley's Company Capt. John Bradley	1	47	Weinert, 38[244]
Wheeler's Brigade Col. James T. Wheeler	35	1,221	
Brigade Escort			
E, 6th Tennesee Cav Capt. James H. Polk	1	30	Calculation[245]
3 Arkansas Cav Col. Anson W. Hobson		300	OR 30, pt. 2, 73[246]
2 Kentucky Cav Lt. Col. Thomas G. Woodward	9	427	Calculation[247]
6 Tennessee Cav Lt. Col. James H. Lewis	9	300	OR 30, pt. 2, 73[248]
18 Tennessee Bn Maj. Charles McDonald	6	164	OR 31, pt. 2, 646[249]
Dibrell's Brigade Col. George G. Dibrell	**59**	**2,218**[250]	
4 Tennessee Cav Col. William S. McLemore	10	200	OR 30, pt. 2, 527[251]
8 Tennessee Cav Capt. Hamilton McGinnis	11	300	OR 30, pt. 2, 527[252]
9 Tennessee Cav Col. Jacob B. Biffle	10	350	OR 31, pt.1, 550[253]
10 Tennessee Cav Col. Nicholas Nickleby Cox	10	474	Calculation[254]
11 Tennessee Cav Col. Daniel W. Holman	10	474	Calculation
Shaw's Battalion Col. Daniel W. Holman	6	284	Calculation

Formation	Companies	Strength	Principle Sources
Huggins's Tennessee Capt. A. L. Huggins	1	65	OR 30, pt. 4, 518[257]
	(4)　2x 6 # Guns, 2x 12# Howitzers		
Morton's Tennessee Capt. John W. Morton, Jr.	1	71	OR 31, pt. 2, 646[258]
	(4)　2x3 Inch Rifles, 2x 12# Howitzers		
Pegram's Division Brig. Gen. John Pegram	**93**	**3,000**	**Estimate[259]**
Davidson's Brigade Brig. Gen. John Pegram, Brig. Gen. Henry B. Davidson	**55**	**1,900**	**Minnich[260]**
1 Georgia Cav. Col. James J. Morrison	10	295	Calculation[261]
6 Georgia Cav Col. John R. Hart	11	400	Calculation[262]
6 North Carolina Cav Col. George N. Folk	10	520	Website[263]
10 Confederate Cav Col. Charles T. Goode	10	250	CCNMP[264]
Rucker's Legion Col. Edmund W. Rucker	13	385	Calculation[265]
Huwald's Battery Capt. Gustave A. Huwald	1	50	Estimate[266]
	(4)　2x 12# Mtn Howitzer, 2x Mtn Rifle		
Scott's Brigade Col. John S. Scott	**38**	**1,100**	**Estimate[267]**
Morgan's Detachment Lt. Col. R. M. Marton	10	240	OR 30, pt. 2, 524[268]
1 Louisiana Cav Lt. Col. James O. Nixon	7	210	Estimate[269]

Formation	Companies	Strength	Principle Sources
2 Tennessee Cav Col. Henry M. Ashby	10	300	Estimate[270]
5 Tennessee Cav Col. George W. Mckenzie	10	300	Estimate[271]
Robinson's Louisiana Lt. Winslow Robinson	1	50	Estimate[272]

(3) 2x Mtn Howitzer,
2 x 3 Inch rifle[273]

Maj. Gen. Joseph Wheeler
Wheeler's Cavalry Corps

Formation	Companies	Strength	Principle Sources
Wheeler's Corps	**153**	**6,870**	
Wharton's Division Brig. Gen. John A. Wharton	**94**	**4,439**	
Escort			
B, 8 Texas Cav.	1	41	Calculation[274]
Crew's Brigade Col. Charles C. Crews	**42**	**2,125[275]**	
Malone's Ala Regt. Col. James C. Malone, Jr.	12	502	Calculation[276]
2 Georgia Cav Lt. Col. F. M. Ison	9	600	Ives, 42[277]
3 Georgia Cav Col. Robert Thompson	10	418	Calculation[278]
4 Georgia Cav Col. Isaac W. Avery	10	605	Company Rolls, NARA[279]
Harrison's Brigade Col. Thomas Harrison	**51**	**2,273[280]**	
3 Confederate Cav Col. William N. Estes	10	550	OR 30, pt. 1, 928[281]
3 Kentucky Cav Lt. Col. J. W. Griffith	10	418	Calculation[282]
4 Tennessee Cav Lt. Col. Paul F. Anderson	10	418	Calculation[283]

Formation	Companies	Strength	Principle Sources
8 Texas Cav Lt. Col. Gustave Cook	10	412	Bush, *Terry's Texas Rangers*[284]
11 Texas Cav Col. George R. Reeves	10	398	Calculation[285]
White's Tennessee Capt. B. F. White	1	77	OR 32, pt. 2, 641[286]
(4) 4x 6# guns			
Martin's Division Brig. Gen. William T. Martin	**59**	**2,431**[287]	
Escort			
A 3 Alabama Cav	1	34	Company Rolls, NARA[288]
Morgan's Brigade Col. John T. Morgan	**37**	**1,533**	
1 Alabama Cav Lt. Col. David T. Blakey	10	418	Calculation[289]
3 Alabama Cav Lt. Col. T. H. Mauldin	7	279	Company Rolls, NARA[290]
51 Alabama Cav Lt. Col. Milton L. Kirkpatrick	10	418	Calculation[291]
8 Confederate Cav Lt. Col. John S. Prather	10	418	Calculation[292]
Russell's Brigade Col. Alfred A. Russell	**21**	**864**[293]	
4 Alabama Cav Lt. Col. J. M. Hambrick	10	418	Calculation[294]
1 Confederate Cav Capt. C. H. Conner	10	418	Calculation[295]
Wiggins's Arkansas Lt. J. P. Bryant	1	28	OR 32, pt. 2, 641[296]
(2) 2x 12# Howitzer			

Endnotes

1. Thomas Jordan and J.P. Pryor, *The Campaigns of General Nathan Bedford Forrest and of Forrest's Cavalry* (De Capo Press, 1996), 310.

2. *OR* 23, pt. 2, 941 details the strengths of the various units on July 31st. *OR* 23, pt. 2, 957 for August 10th, and *OR* 30, pt. 4, 518 for August 20th.

3. *OR* 23, pt. 2, 945, 962.

4. Emerson Opdycke Papers, strength return for Pegram's Division, Ohio Historical Society. This date of this return and the classification of the cavalry as Pegram's Division suggest that this figure represents only the cavalry that did move with Buckner to join Bragg, but if so, the numbers seem high. Since the return does not provide a detailed listing of the composition of Pegram's division at this time, we cannot know exactly who is and who is not counted in this return.

5. See organizational chart for Dept of East Tennessee, July 31st, 1863, in *OR* 23, pt. 2, 945-946, and compare to organization of Pegram's division, *OR* 30, pt. 2, 20. Also the 5th and 7th North Carolina Battalions, listed separately with 6 companies each in East Tennessee, were merged to form the new 6th North Carolina Cavalry Regiment, with only 10 companies, creating a seeming discrepancy among the numbers of companies.

6. See *OR* 30, pt. 3, 604.

7. See August 31 "summary of strength," Opdycke Papers, Ohio Historical Society.

8. Strength of the escorts is listed as 136, August 20, 1863. The strength given for each individual company is simply assumed to be half. These escorts show a consistent pattern of attrition during the month of August: on July 31st, they numbered 152 (*OR* 23, pt. 2, 941,) but by August 10, they numbered 141 (*OR* 23, pt. 2, 957.)

9. Listed as Holloway's Company Alabama Cavalry in the *OR*. The Website for the 3rd Alabama identifies company K as the escort. See note above for strength.

10. Strength reported as of August 10. Two companies were with the Army of Tennessee and one company was from Buckner's Department of East Tennessee. On September 16 Buckner's company was with his corps at La Fayette, Georgia. *OR* 30, pt. 4, 658.

11. This company was detached on August 18, 1863 as train guard, serving in that capacity until October. Strength was taken from Company rolls for August 31, 1863, RG 109, NARA.

12. On August 10th, the three cavalry escorts total 130 officers and men, with the staff broken out separately, at 17. On August 20th, the return lumps all staff and escorts together, for an aggregate of 157. If the staff numbers remained unchanged, the three escort companies would now number 140, a gain of ten men between August 10 and 20. Given the active operations between August 20th and the time of the battle, I assumed that the gain would be offset by later attrition. From that 130 total, I subtracted the reported strength of the Lenoir Company, which was 65 on June 30. That left 65 to divide between the other two escort companies, or 32.5 men per company.

13. The August 10 return lists only the total for all three escorts in Polk's Corps, or 130 total. From that I have subtracted the strength of Hindman's Escort, the Lenoir Cavalry, which reported 65 on June 30. The remainder was divided in half to account for the other two escorts reported. See noted for Lenoir's and Greenleaf's Cavalry companies.

14. This figure is the "Aggregate effective" taken into action, which includes officers. Companies C, D, G, I and K were present. The remaining companies were still stationed at Fort Gaines, Alabama during the battle. See *OR Supplement*, 85, 436-455.

15. As above, the figure is "Aggregate effective" taken into action. Companies A-D present at Chickamauga. *OR Supplement*, 18, 112-116.

16. As above, the figure is "Aggregate effective" taken into action.

17. "Aggregate effective," includes officers.

18. "Aggregate Effective" includes officers.

19. The Brigade Ordnance report shows 1,177 "men" taken into action. This figure does not include officers. The other units in the brigade reported a total of 537, leaving 640 in the 1+27 Tennessee. 9.8% added for officers.

20. PA= Provisional Army. This regiment was also known as 34th Tennessee. 163 "men" reported, plus 9.8% added for officers.

21. The regimental report says "about 335 men." 9.8% added for officers.

22. The battalion report lists "39 men under arms" 9.8% added for officers. Companies A-C present.

23. Bragg Papers, folder 10, Palmer Collection, Western Reserve Historical Society. Regimental returns of Polk's Corps for October 22nd. The figure given is for "total effective" and from the context of the report, includes officers. Comparing known strengths of other regiments in Smith's Brigade going into action on the 19th with those same units for this October 22nd Return suggests that strengths were roughly equal, as returning wounded, stragglers, and extra duty men had largely rebuilt the ranks. 8 companies present, two companies detached to form part of Dawson's Sharpshooter Battalion.

24. Bragg Papers, Folder 10, Palmer Collection, WRHS. On September 11, a deserter gave the strength of Company A at 53 men, with the regiment as a whole numbering "between 400 and 500." See NARA, RG 94, Army of the Cumberland, Summaries of intelligence received. 8 companies present, two companies detached to form part of Dawson's Sharpshooter Battalion.

25. Nine companies reported 217 officers and men present as of August 1, 1863. 5 added for field and staff. One company was detached on September 9 to form part of Dawson's Sharpshooters.

26. Nine companies reported 367 officers and men present on August 31, 1863. 41 men added for Company I, not reported, the average of the strength of the other companies, and 5 added for field and staff.

27. The battalion was formed on September 9. Two companies from the 11 Tennessee, two companies from the 12+47 Tennessee, and one company from the 13+154 Tennessee comprised the battalion. The battalion reported 252 "rifles" on September 19th. 8.4% added for officers.

28. The brigade ordnance report says 1,149 "men" were taken into action, see *OR* 30, pt. 2, 82. Note, however, if the standard 9.8% for officers were added, the brigade strength would be 1,262, or 81 men higher than reflected using the October 22 return. I suspect that the brigade strength given here is actually somewhat low.

29. October 22 return, Bragg Papers, folder 10, Palmer Collection, WRHS.

30. 242 "rank and file" plus 9.8% added for officers.

31. October 22 return, Bragg Papers, folder 10, Palmer Collection, WRHS.

32. October 22 return, Bragg Papers, folder 10, Palmer Collection, WRHS.

33. October 22 return, Bragg Papers, folder 10, Palmer Collection, WRHS.

34. Brigade ordnance report gives the 8th Tennessee 260 "guns" engaged. 9.8% added for officers.

35. Brigade ordnance report lists 242 "guns" engaged. 9.8% added for officers. Col. Donnell was reported as "injured" but did not relinquish command.

36. Brigade ordnance report lists 254 "guns" engaged. 9.8% added for officers. Regimental reports the total as 308 aggregate, but including Infirmary Corps. OR 30, pt. 2,.126.

37. Brigade Ordnance report lists 254 "guns" engaged. 9.8% added for officers. This regiment may not have had a company C, but a company L instead. Casualty reports in the *Memphis Daily Appeal*, October 6, 1863, do not show C Company, but do report two wounded men in L company. This regiment had been re-organized several times, with the companies changing designations, in some cases as many as three times.

38. Brigade ordnance report lists 232 "guns" engaged. 9.8% added for officers.

39. The strengths for a number of batteries proved impossible to find. Carnes's battery was all but destroyed at Chickamauga, and does not appear on the October 22nd report, nor were any

company rolls found. The number here is simply an average of the strengths of the 24 known batteries in the army.

40. Capt. Scott was absent, sick, at the start of the battle. He returned to command on September 20. The strength is from the October 22 return, Bragg Papers, folder 10, Palmer Collection, WRHS.

41 October 22 return, Bragg Papers, folder 10, Palmer Collection, WRHS.

42. October 22 return, Bragg Papers, folder 10, Palmer Collection, WRHS.

43. On August 31, 1863, this division numbered 7,697 officers and men, per Army of Tennessee field returns, RG 109, NARA; copy at Combat Studies Institute, Ft. Leavenworth. Hindman was sick during the battle, resumed command only on the 19th, and was subsequently lightly wounded in the neck on September 20. Anderson commanded the division during when Hindman was incapacitated.

44. Company rolls for June 30, 1863, show 65 officers and men. This unit was more commonly called Lenoir's Company. On August 19, 1863, the company had 61 men.

45. Report of William L. Mead, October 14, 1863, Braxton Bragg Papers, Western Reserve Historical Society. Mead commanded a sharpshooter detachment of nine men armed with Whitworth Rifles.

46. Anderson reported that his command numbered 1865 officers and men on the 20th, OR 30, pt. 2, 319. Four of the six units in the brigade report engaged strengths, leaving just two formations as unknown. Subtracting the known strengths from the reported brigade total yields a total of 425 officers and men in the 7th Mississippi and the 9th Sharpshooters. Starting with the August 19 strengths, which are available for both of these commands, each has been reduced proportionally in order to match the 425 men calculated from the brigade report.

47. Strength as of August 19, last reported date for regiment, gives 368 officers and men. This figure has been reduced by 77 men to bring it in line with the brigade total. See brigade note, above.

48. Strength given is "effective aggregate." Maj. Lyman's name is misspelled in the OR.

49. 29 officers, 282 men.

50. Strength given is "aggregate."

51. Report specifies "officers and men."

52. Strength as of August 19, 1863, the last reported date for the battalion, was 170 officers and men. This figure has been reduced by 36 men to bring it in line with the brigade total, see brigade note, above.

53. Strength given as "about 469 guns." 9.8% added for officers.

54. 31 officers, 340 men. A letter from Thaddeus Marion Brindley in the CCNMP 22nd Alabama file states that the regiment "carried 384" into action but does not indicate categories. Likely Brindley's figure includes ambulance corps or other non-combatants.

55. Strength given as "about 330 officers and men."

56. Strength given as "310 muskets." 9.8% added for officers.

57. In *Confederate Military History*, the regiment's strength is given as "500 aggregate." However, Deas reports his exact strength as 157 officers and 1,785 enlisted men, for a total of 1,932. (OR 30, pt. 2, 331.) The other regiments in the brigade also provide exact totals. Dividing the remainder of 376 by the 12 companies of the 50th and the sharpshooters, gives an average of 31.5 men per company.

58. See the note for the 50th Alabama, above. The 17th Battalion, formed in June 1862, was comprised of two companies. Company A was formed from men of the 19th Alabama; Company B, from the 39 Alabama. On October 22, 1863 the battalion reported 54 present. They suffered 12 losses during the battle.

59. Arthur M. Manigault, *A Carolinian goes to War* (Columbia, SC: 1983), 102. Manigault's numbers are precise enough to suggest that he had access to his brigade returns, and so I take them as accurate. Unfortunately, he did not provide exact numbers for each regiment. Working backwards from the brigade numbers, I determined that the two unreported regiments were

roughly twice the size of the reported units. Checking loss figures seemed to confirm this ratio: losses in the 10+19 South Carolina were just about twice as many (236 versus 116) for the 24th Alabama.

60. Strength given as "aggregate," officers included.

61. Strength derived by subtracting other known regimental strengths from the brigade total, and then divided by the number of companies remaining to determine an average company strength, in this case 57 men. Finally, the company average was multiplied by the number of companies in each regiment.

62. Manigault gives the figure as "300 rifles." 9.8% added for officers.

63. See note above for the 28th Alabama.

64. October 22 return, Bragg Papers, folder 10, Palmer Collection, WRHS.

65. "Effective" strength given as 70, 3 officers added.

66. On July 31st, the three companies comprising the escorts numbered 137 officers and men. Subtracting Foules's strength (given as 35 in Stewart's *OR* report) leaves 102 officers and men in the two remaining companies, or 51 men per unit. While almost two months shy of the actual battle, this is the closest hard number yet found for these units. Raum's company was formerly Company G, Adams's 1st Mississippi Cavalry. There is some evidence that Raum's men were ordered to follow their former commander, Lt. Gen. William J. Hardee, to Mississippi, but I cannot confirm that movement. I have included them here because I believe that even if Raum and his men were in Mississippi, some unit would have been detailed to serve as Hill's escort.

67. Col. Gibson, in the regimental report, says he "carried into action 275 muskets." to which has been added the 34 officers found in *OR* 30, pt. 2, 219. Lt. John McGrath noted that the regiment fired "buck and ball," meaning they carried smoothbore muskets. See McGrath letters, Louisiana State University, Baton Rouge. Col. Von Zincken, serving on the divisional staff, took command on the afternoon of September 20.

68. E. John Ellis letter, Oct 4th, 1863, Louisiana State University, Baton Rouge; says the regiment lost 110 out of 293, but likely he refers only to the "effective" strength.

69. The brigade report says 33 officers and 317 men. *OR* 30, pt. 2, 219

70. Companies A and B. The battalion was formed out of the disbanded 11th Louisiana Regiment in August, 1862.

71. The Brigade report shows 401 officers and men, see *OR* 30, pt. 2, 206; but the regimental commander reports 325 "men." 9.8% added for officers.

72. The brigade report shows only 28 officers and 254 men, for a total of 282.

73. No strength given in the regimental report.

74. No strength given in the regimental report. The 6th Kentucky had no company F or K, each of whom were consolidated with other companies in 1862 and never re-formed.

75. The regimental report, *OR* 30, pt. 2, 214, gives the same figure.

76. The brigade report lists 273 "total" and 298 "aggregate." The regimental report (*OR* 30, pt. 2, 234) says "273 carried into the fight." The lower figure includes enlisted men only.

77. On September 10th, the morning report showed 234 officers and men present for duty. Morning reports for the 60th North Carolina, RG 109, NARA.

78. In *OR* 30, pt. 2, 158, Cleburne reported a divisional strength of 5,115 officers and men, with 4,875 "bayonets." This figure appears to only count the infantry and their officers, omitting the artillery and escort. Adding in those missing units gives a new total of 5,380.

79. See footnote 233, for Raum's Escort, above.

80. The "effective" total on September 19 was 667, with 5% added for officers. Due to the converged nature of the command and its size, I added in only half the normal average of 9.8% for officers. Otherwise, the unit would have had nearly 70 officers, about double the normal complement.

81. On August 31, 1863, 181 men were present in the 3rd Confederate, 7 out of 10 companies reporting. The 5th Confederate reports were not found. The 3rd Confederate was formed largely out of the 19th Arkansas, while the 5th derived mostly from the 40th Tennessee.

Since both formations had companies from other states, they were re-designated "Confederate" units in 1862. They were combined later, and finished out the war together. It is assumed that they operated tactically as a ten company formation, though it is clear from the few surviving records that they maintained separate administrative routines. The strength was determined by subtracting all known strengths from the reported infantry total in Cleburne's Report, *OR* 30, pt. 2, 158. The balance, 435, was then divided by the remaining 15 companies of unreported units, determining an average company strength.

82. *Memphis Daily Appeal*, Oct. 9, 1863; a letter from Col. Robison shows 275 officers and men.

83. 215 "men" reported, plus 9.8% officers.

84. 150 "men" reported on September 20. 5 losses from 9/19 and 9.8% officers added.

85. 412 engaged, *Hunstville Daily Confederate*, October 3, 1863.

86. 9 companies reported 409 PFD on August 31, 1863 The rolls for Company H were incomplete, reporting 2 officers, 9 non-commissioned officers, and an unknown number of privates. Adding in 5 for field and staff, not reported, and the average company strength of 45 for company H gives a total of 459.

87. CCNMP Regimental file; *Montgomery Weekly Advertiser*, October 4, 1863, reported "385 engaged" 9.8% added for officers.

88. Companies A-C. For strength, see note for 3+5 Confederate, above. The 18th battalion was attached to Col. Adams's 33rd Alabama for much of the battle.

89. This number dates from August 31, 1863. Like most combined units, the 32nd and 45th still reported their strengths separately. The 32nd has reports on file for all 10 companies, while only 7 company reports were found for the 45th. Tactically, the two regiments formed into 10 companies for battle.

90. See note for 3+5 Confederate, above.

91. Average strength of known artillery battery strengths in the army.

92. The battery strength was determined by subtracting the regimental strengths from the brigade total, given here.

93. Average strength of known artillery battery strengths in the army.

94. This company numbered 78 officers and men in December, 1863, and was serving as Maj. Gen. S.D. Lee's escort, in Mississippi. It served as Walker's divisional escort in August 1863, but was ordered to remain behind on August 13, when Walker was transferred to Bragg's army. Nelson was supposed to be replaced by another company to accompany Walker. Nelson remained in Mississippi, but it is unclear if Walker was ever assigned a new escort. The strength given here is for July 31, 1863.

95. The 16th South Carolina and Ferguson's Battery are omitted, as they were not engaged. Ector commanded the division until the morning of September 20, when Gist reached the field.

96. Gist was the brigade commander, but stepped up to divisional command by reason of seniority when he reached the field on the 20th. Initially, he reported the brigade strength at 980 "aggregate," but this number included only the 24th South Carolina, the 8th Georgia Battalion, and three companies of the 46th Georgia who had reached the field that morning. On the afternoon of the 20th, the remaining seven companies of the 46th Georgia arrived, adding another 420 men to the ranks, and Gist then reported his strength as 1,400 men and officers. see *OR* 30, pt. 2, 244-246. These figures give us some idea of the effective strengths of the regiments, which averaged about 60 men per company.

97. Only three companies of the 46th were engaged on the morning of September 20. The remaining seven companies arrived that afternoon. The strength was determined by various calculations. For the first three companies, the strength was calculated by subtracting 410 (strength of the 24th South Carolina, below) from 980, the brigade aggregate. This calculation yielded a company average of 57 men, or 171 men total. Next, the remaining seven companies brought with them 420 men, or 60 men per company, (see *OR* 30, pt. 2, 246) which added to the first number gives 591men total for the regiment. This number is in line with the other known

strengths of the regiment. At the end of June, 1863, the regiment reported 754 officers and men PFD. In December, it reported 595 PFD. All numbers were derived from the company muster rolls, RG 109, NARA.

98. Companies A-G present. Strength determined by subtracting 410 (Strength of the 24th South Carolina, see note below) from 980, the aggregate reported for the brigade. The remainder, 570, was divided by the number of companies present (the seven of the 8th Georgia Battalion plus three of the 46th Georgia regiment then present to produce a company average of 57 men per company, multiplied by seven, for 399. Working with the known muster rolls gives some strange findings. In June, Companies A and B each had 79 officers and men present for duty, total 158, plus the staff, 7 more, giving a total of 165. On August 31st, the entire battalion of seven companies reported 125 men total, with an average company strength of 18. By October, the next reporting period, with only A and B providing numbers, A had 45, B and 67, with 9 field and staff present. Extrapolating from the known numbers, in June, the battalion would have numbered over 500 men, while in October it would have more than 400 men PFD. Clearly, the battalion suffered from significant absenteeism in August, but based on the numbers provided in Gist's Report, had recovered a large portion of its strength by the time of the battle.

99. Six companies reported for September. Two companies reported for August, and two companies only had strengths from December, well after the battle. Alternatively, taking only the 6 reported companies and averaging in the other four yields 432 officers and men. Finally, given the overall low losses in the brigade once the 24th South Carolina losses are factored out, the probable losses added back to the two companies reporting post-battle strength would only change the numbers by a man or two.

100. Eugene W. Jones, *Enlisted for the War* (Longstreet House: 1997), 123. Jones cites no source for this number.

101. *Mobile Daily Advertiser*, October 10, 1863.Stone's battalion was formed from three companies of the 40th Alabama: A, D, and I. The remainder of the regiment had been captured at Vicksburg. On October 5th the battalion reported 105 present, not including losses, which amounted to 23.

102. *Mobile Daily Advertiser*, October 10, 1863. The battalion operated as a two-company command. On October 5, 1863, the battalion reported a strength of 40officers and men, with 10 casualties. This battalion also formed from men whose regiments were captured at Vicksburg: elements of companies A, H, and I, 43rd Mississippi; and company A, 38th Mississippi.

103. *Mobile Daily Advertiser*, October 10, 1863.

104. *Mobile Daily Advertiser*, October 10, 1863. Company Rolls, NARA, show 170 present on 10/5/63.

105. *Mobile Daily Advertiser*, October 10, 1863. On October 5, the company muster rolls, NARA, show 224 PFD. Zachariah Bailey Letter, October 11, 1863, reports 196 men engaged. Zachariah Bailey Letter, Navarro College, Corsicana, Texas.

106. *Mobile Daily Advertiser*, October 10, 1863. On October 5, the company muster rolls, NARA, show 206 PFD.

107. *Mobile Daily Advertiser*, October 10, 1863. N. B. Littlejohn, "Memories of Many Conflicts," *Confederate Veteran*, vol. XVIII, no. 12 (December, 1910), 559; shows 320 engaged.

108. In the brigade report Wilson states that his brigade entered the fight with an effective strength of 1200 men. Adding 9.8% for officers gives Wilson's brigade a strength of 1317.

109. This regiment underwent multiple reorganizations between 1862 and 1863. It was comprised of eleven companies in mid-1862. I have assumed that it still contained eleven companies at Chickamauga, but it is possible that the 25th had been consolidated into a ten company organization by the fall of 1863. There were 172 men present in five companies on August 31, 1863. Taking an average of 34 men per company, and adding in 5 more for field and staff, produces an estimate of 383 officers and men.

110. A letter in the 29th Georgia Regimental file, CCNMP, says "200 men." 9.8% added for officers. Robert G. Mitchell Letter, University of Georgia Archives, dated Sept. 21, 1863, also states "200 men."

111. Unpublished regimental report, 30th Georgia files, CCNMP. Companies A-I present, Company K on detached duty at Savannah.

112. *Savannah Republican*, October 26, 1863. This casualty listing gives company figures for 101 men carried into action, but omit the field and staff.

113. The battalion's strength was derived by subtracting the known strengths of the other units from the brigade total of 1317. Available company rolls were limited. Of the 6 companies, A and B only had numbers for February, 1864, while C through F only had rolls for February 1863. Combined numbers from these sources shows 252 officers and men, while just using the 1863 rolls shows 187 men in four companies, or an average of 47 men per company.

114. Ferguson's strength omitted, as it was not engaged. See below.

115. Ferguson's Battery was at Rome Georgia, awaiting transport. No strength numbers have been found. The strength given here is the average battery strength of the known reported batteries in the army. The armament shown is as equipped in 1864.

116. On October 5, 1863, the battery reported 51 officers and men, plus 7 losses at Chickamauga. This number seems low for a six-gun battery. The command was also known as Martin's Battery.

117. Two regiments in the brigade reported both engaged strength and losses. Each suffered about 45% casualties. Govan's Brigade report suggests that losses were about 50%. For the unknown commands, I have adopted the following formula: Starting with the known strength on September 25, I added in 9.8% for officers, and then also added a percentage of the unaccounted-for brigade losses (derived by subtracting the known losses of the two regiments who did report, from the known losses of the brigade overall, as found in *OR* 30, pt. 2, 243) and then apportioning those losses to the unreported regiments based on unit size after the battle. Each regiment is assumed to have suffered about 43% loss.

118. 181 "effectives" on September 25, 1863, plus 9.8% added for officers. 150 losses added in. Williams report, CCNMP regimental file.

119. The regimental report says about 450 "carried into action." The Williams report shows 215 "effectives" on September 25. Losses were 202, for a total of 417, plus 9.8% added for officers, which gives a final tally of 458 officers and men.

120. The regiment had 535 officers and men on June 17, 1863, based on the closest company muster rolls. The William report shows 203 "effectives" on September 25, plus 9.8% added for officers, and 165 casualties, produces 388.

121. The Williams report lists the 1st Louisiana as being combined with the 8th Arkansas, with a combined total of 210 "effectives" on September 25. This figure differs radically from other sources. The 8th Arkansas's official report states that the 8th numbered 216 officers and men PFD on September 21, 1863 - higher than the combined total for both regiments four days later. I have assumed that the "210" number found in the Williams report is for only the 1st Louisiana. As a further check, we have reports from two 1st Louisiana companies on August 31, showing strength of 48 and 50, respectively. If those strengths are indicative of the whole command, the August 31st strength would be about 500, or 450 after subtracting the one company on detached duty. Accordingly, following the brigade formula, I have taken 210 men, plus 9.8 for officers, for a total of 231; adding in the 170 losses produces an engaged total of 401. The 1st Regiment's numbers declined after Chickamauga. By December 1863 they only had 4 officers and 64 men PFD.

122. The brigade strength was reported at 1,827, see *OR* 30, pt. 2, 276. Two regiments report their engaged strengths in the *OR*, and another comes via the *Memphis Daily Appeal*, September 26, 1863. The total for the remaining two units were derived by subtracting the known strengths from the brigade total, and dividing by two.

123. *Memphis Daily Appeal*, September 26, 1863. In a list of losses, the writer reported that the 24th took 428 men into the fight. Additionally, the 24th reported 432 "effectives" on August 24, 1863; see Company Returns, NARA. Nominally, the regiment included 11 companies, A-L; but Companies B and G were merged into one for tactical reasons. Captain Smith was the senior captain, and Captain Toomer held command only briefly, after Smith was slightly wounded on September 20. Smith returned to command on September 21.

124. The 27th reported 446 "effectives" on August 24, 1863. On September 3, the morning report showed "total enlisted present - 476." see 27th Mississippi morning reports, RG 109, NARA.

125. The 30th reported 370 "effectives" on August 23, 1863; company returns, RG 109, NARA. Lieutenant Colonel Reynolds was assigned to command the 34th Mississippi after Major Pegram was wounded, and in turn, mortally wounded on September 20.

126. 142 officers and men present, August 19, 1863; company returns, RG 109, NARA. While this number is almost certainly a little too high, it is the last firm number that could be found.

127. Average strength of the known reported battery strengths in the army.

128. On November 22, 1863, the escort moved with parts of Buckner's command into East Tennessee. Clark's effective strength was listed as 20 at this time.

129. Companies C and I, 63rd Virginia, and one unspecified company of the 65th Georgia. The two companies of the 63rd Virginia numbered approximately 49 men, while the one company of the 65th Georgia numbered 31 men, for a total of 80.

130. The core of Gracie's Brigade was Hilliard's Legion, consisting of three battalions of infantry and one artillery battalion, serving as infantry. The Legion made up more than half of the brigade. (A cavalry battalion had been detached earlier and was now part of the 10th Confederate Cavalry.) The four battalions all served as independent commands, After Chickamauga, the four battalions were merged to form the 59th and 60th Alabama infantry. For more detail, see *OR Supplement*, 13, 855-876. See also Joseph H. Crute, Jr., *Units of the Confederate States Army* (Derwint Books, 1987), 19 (23 Bn Sharpshooters), 34 (59th and 60th Regiments), 37 (Hilliard's Legion.) See also website: http://www.tarleton.edu/~kjones/hilliard.html. In the *Abingdon Virginian*, Oct 9, 1863, a letter from a quartermaster in the division gives the brigade strength as "1,800 men."

131. Return of strength "actually under arms and carried into action," October 7, 1863, Wickliffe-Preston Papers, University of Kentucky, shows 27 officers and 337 men. A note in the regimental file at CCNMP says "400 aggregate."

132. Wickliffe-Preston Papers, University of Kentucky. Hilliard's Legion, Companies A-G. *OR* 30, pt. 2, 245 shows 260 engaged, but this number is exactly equal to the enlisted only figure on the tabular statement.

133. Wickliffe-Preston Papers. Hilliard's Legion. Companies A-F. *OR* 30, pt. 2, 426, shows 230 engaged, but the Tabular statement shows 17 officers and 265 enlisted.

134. Wickliffe-Preston Papers. Hilliard's Legion. Companies A-F. The *OR* 30, pt. 2, 426, says 229 were carried into action, of those, 56 officers and men were detailed for fatigue duty on the 19th, and served with Kelly's Brigade.

135. Wickliffe-Preston Papers. Hilliard's Legion. Companies A-D. Originally the artillery contingent of the Legion, this command once had five companies, but at Chickamauga, one (Company C) was detached and serving as artillery - Kolb's Battery. The remaining companies fought as infantry. *OR* 30, pt. 2, 428, shows 205 engaged.

136. Wickliffe-Preston Papers. *OR* 30, pt. 2, 429 shows 402 engaged. *Confederate Veteran*, Vol. XXII (January 1914), 37 shows 404 engaged. Both of those figures are probably enlisted men only.

137. William M. Owen provides a strength report for Preston's Division, which shows the regiments of this brigade as having 1,805 men PFD on August 26th. Desertion badly crippled this command as it moved out of East Tennessee to join Bragg. William M. Owen, *In Camp and Battle*

with the Washington Artillery of New Orleans (Gretna, LA: 1998), 268. The *Abingdon Virginian*, Oct 9, 1863, gives the brigade total, exclusive of the 65th Georgia, as "850 Effectives."

138. Wickliffe Preston Papers, University of Kentucky. 25 officers and 247 enlisted men. The regimental report says eight companies were engaged (two serving elsewhere) with 229 "effectives," *OR* 30, pt. 2, 442. Company H was detached and acting as engineering troops in East Tennessee, see *OR Supplement*, 19, 197-198. The other absent company is not specified, but the report of 63rd Virginia indicates that two companies Virginians and two from the 65th Georgia were escorting ordnance trains. See note, below, for 63rd Virginia.

139. Wickliffe-Preston Papers, University of Kentucky. On August 31, 1863, eight companies reported their strength, for a total of 294. 8 field and staff were present as well. The average strength for the two companies not reporting added another 75 men, for a total strength of 377 officers and men; see Company Reports, RG 109, NARA. In Kellar Anderson, "The Rebel Yell," *Confederate Veteran*, vol. I, no. 4, (April, 1893), 107; the strength was given at 700 men, which is much too high, though it might well have been closer to the 5th Kentucky's strength before leaving East Tennessee.

140. Wickliffe-Preston Papers, University of Kentucky. This statement actually gives two strengths for the regiment: 359, the number "held in readiness on 19th," and 361, given as strength in action on the 20th. The Website: http://members.aol.com/jweaver301/nc/58ncinf.htm indicates that losses for the regiment were 161, or "50%" of the initial strength, with no source listed for that figure.

141. Wickliffe-Preston Papers, University of Kentucky. Companies C and I were escorting the corps ordnance train; see *OR Supplement*, 84, 812-830. As with the 5th Kentucky, there is fragmentary evidence of significant desertion: Company D reported that 22 men deserted in August, substantially more than the "15 guns" they reported taking into action. Company A reported "heavy desertion," and only had 20 men in the fight.

142. "1,750 men" *Abingdon Virginian*, Oct 9, 1863.

143. Tabular Statement, Trigg's Brigade, September 24, 1863, Wickliffe-Preston Papers, University of Kentucky. The last company rolls prior to the battle were for July 9, 1863, which shows 300 PFD. After the battle, the first rolls available were for October 31, and show 137 officers and men PFD; see company rolls, RG 109, NARA. The October 22, 1863 return in the Bragg Papers, folder 10, Palmer Collection, WRHS; shows 231 total present, with an effective present of 201. Battle losses for the 1st Florida amounted to 27 men.

144. Wickliffe-Preston Papers. In July 1863, the company rolls show 470 PFD, and for October, 217; see company rolls, RG 109, NARA. The October 22, 1863 return in the Bragg Papers, folder 10, Palmer Collection, WRHS; shows 293 total present.

145. Wickliffe Preston Papers. Company rolls for July, 1863 show 431 PFD, see company rolls, RG 109, NARA. The October 22 1863 return in the Bragg Papers shows 398. Losses were not specified, but described as "few."

146. Wickliffe-Preston Papers. The October 22 1863 return in the Bragg Papers shows 477. Battle losses were 47. The company rolls for December 1863, RG 109, NARA, show 458 officers and men.

147. October 22, 1863 return, Bragg Papers.

148. Average strength of known batteries in the army.

149. Average strength of known batteries in the army. Wolihin's armament is not known, but given here as the most common equipment for a Confederate battery at Chickamauga. The battery was sent to East Tennessee in 1862, when 6 pounders and 12 pound Howitzers were both extremely common in the Confederate inventory, and would not likely have received newer cannon in the interim.

150. Foules's Company of Mississippi Cavalry is listed as Breckenridge's Escort in the OR chart on *OR* 30, pt. 2, 13, but in his report, A. P. Stewart compliments Foules and his men, and details the strength of the company as part of the strength of his division. Foules was a graduate of Yale University.

151. September 18th strength. The brigade report indicates 284 went into action.

152. September 18th strength. The regimental report only reports "400 men" omitting officers.

153. Companies A-C. September 18th strength.

154. September 18th and 19th strength. The regimental report lists 202 "taken into action, which clearly refers to enlisted only. *Daily Huntsville Confederate*, Sept 22, also lists 220 "in action."

155. September 18th strength. W. J. McMurray, "The Gap of Death at Chickamauga," *Confederate Veteran.* vol. II, no. 11 (November, 1894), 329-330, says "140 strong."

156. The brigade also took 67 men of the infirmary corps into action, as noted below.

157. 12 infirmary corps not counted. On September 11th, one deserter from this unit reported the strength at 'about 450" while another gave a strength of 330. See summaries of intelligence received, Army of the Cumberland, RG 94, NARA.

158. The 26th Tennessee Infantry has proven surprisingly hard to pin down. This figure is taken from the official reports of Stewart's Division. However, in a letter home the regimental commander, Major Saffell, reported that he had 332 engaged, and lost 117, see Mike Miner, "A Brave Officer: The letters of Richard Saffell, 26th Tennessee, C.S.A" *Military Images*, vol. XII, no. 2 (September-October, 1990), 16-18. 11 infirmary corps men are not counted. I have elected to go with the OR report, for consistency's sake.

159. 19 infirmary corps men not counted.

160. 10 infirmary corps men not counted.

161. 11 infirmary corps men not counted. William F. Fox, *Regimental Losses in the Civil War* (Dayton, OH: 1985), 557, gives a strength of 181.

162. Col. Holtzclaw was thrown from his horse during the battle and had to relinquish command.

163. October 22 Return, Bragg Papers, folder 10, Palmer Collection, WRHS.

164. This strength report dates from July 17, 1863, two months before the battle.

165. October 22 Return, Bragg Papers, folder 10, Palmer Collection, WRHS.

166. October 22 Return, Bragg Papers, folder 10, Palmer Collection, WRHS.

167. From the Army of Northern Virginia. Longstreet commanded the corps. However, on the 18th and 19th, Longstreet had not yet arrived, so Hood assumed command in his absence. On the 20th, Longstreet was placed in charge of the Left Wing, with Hood continuing in command of First Corps. Law commanded Hood's Division.

168. Average size of other companies in the regiment. A company was serving as James Longstreet's escort.

169. Average size of other companies in the regiment. C and E companies were consolidated, and serving as Hood's escort.

170. Johnson's Provisional Division was created by detaching Johnson's Brigade (and Everett's Battery) from A. P. Stewart's Division to defend Ringgold, and then joining McNair's and Gregg's brigades, newly arrived from Mississippi, with Johnson. As the senior brigadier, Johnson took command of all three brigades. Col. John S. Fulton stepped up to command Johnson's brigade. On September 18, Johnson's force was further augmented by Robertson's brigade from Hood's (Longstreet's) Corps. On September 19 Robertson reverted to Hood's division, now commanded by Evander Law.

171. 122 officers and men sent to the rear, barefoot.

172. 26 men sent to the rear, barefoot.

173. 23 men sent to the rear, barefoot.

174. 56 men sent to the rear, barefoot.

175. "Officers and men taken into action on September 19."

176. "Officers and men taken into action on September 19." On September 28, Lawrence C. Malone wrote that there were 168 engaged, which probably omits the officers.

177. "Officers and men taken into action on September 19."

178. "Officers and men taken into action on September 19."

179. *OR* 30, pt. 2, 497, lists only 104 "officers and men taken into action on September 19." However, C. W. Tyler, "Patriotism in a Tennessee County," *Confederate Veteran*, vol. VI, no. 3 (March, 1898), 125-126, quotes a letter from Colonel Sugg, commanding the 50th Tennessee and later the brigade, as saying the regiment carried 186 into action, with only 54 men unwounded at the end. The record of events for the regiment in the *OR Supplement*, 67, 450, says 190 men entered, "about 50" came out. Col. Sugg's letter, coupled with the estimate in the *OR Supplement*, make 186 the most likely engaged figure. Part of the confusion may stem from the fact that the 50th was involved in a train collision during the move from Mississippi to North Georgia, incurring nearly 100 casualties on September 14, 1863. After the battle, the 50th was temporarily merged with the 3rd Tennessee.

180. "Officers and men taken into action on September 19." Companies A-E present. Major Robertson was assigned to command the battalion after Colms was wounded.

181. "Officers and men taken into action on September 19."

182. "Aggregate engaged."

183. "Aggregate engaged."

184. "Aggregate engaged." Col. A. C. Avery of the 39th North Carolina indicated that the 25th was "not over 150 strong." Avery Letter, 39th NC File, CCNMP.

185. "Aggregate engaged." Originally, these three units comprised 25 companies.

186. The number includes officers and enlisted men. The *Atlanta Register*, Oct 4 1863, reported 238 men, but does not include officers. Lt. John M. Davidson, wrote on September 24 1863, that the regiment went into the fight with "240 men" and lost 102. See Jane Bonner Peacock, ed. "A Wartime Story: The Davidson Letters," *The Atlanta Historical Bulletin*, vol. XIX, no. 1, (Spring, 1975), 9-75.

187. This is the equipment of the battery as of December 1862. In May 1863, Culpepper was transferred from Charleston to Mississippi. In September it joined Bragg in Georgia. See *OR* 14, 702.

188. Also known as Company E, 9th Georgia Artillery, and York's Battery. Everett only had three guns with him during the battle. One gun broke down on the 17th, was repaired, and joined Lumsden's Alabama Battery for the duration of the fight. Since all four guns and crews saw action, their strength is given as shown.

189. Technically Hood's division, temporarily commanded by Law.

190. Wright's dispatch from Atlanta gives Benning 1,200 men in *OR* 30, pt. 4, 652. The *Columbus Georgia Sun*, Sept. 26, 1863, reported that the brigade had "about 900 engaged." Even if, as is probable, the 900 figure is for enlisted men only and we add in the average of 9.8% for officers; this only increases the brigade strength to 988, leaving a discrepancy of more than 200 men between the engaged estimate and the 1,200 reported as leaving Atlanta. Lacking better information, I have decided to use the 1,200 figure as the baseline strength, with the understanding that the actual engaged number is likely much lower. Absenteeism was a problem in Benning's command at this time, as these men had not seen their homes in two years. Benning reported that 50 such men joined his command on the night of the 19th.

191. The *Columbus Georgia Sun*, Sept. 26, 1863, reported 117 losses in the 2nd Georgia. Based on the brigade engaged figure of 900, if we subtract the known or estimated strengths of the other regiments, that leaves only 127 men present in the 2nd. Losing 117 men out of 127 engaged would be near- annihilation, and a far higher percentage loss than suffered in the rest of the brigade. Assuming 988 to be more accurate, re-doing the math now gives the 2nd Georgia 215 engaged, a more reasonable figure, but still lower than the 427 given above. Again, the degree of temporary absenteeism cannot be known.

192. Existing company rolls for companies E-K, August 31, 1863. Additionally, the *OR Supplement* lists the strength of company D for the same period. All told, these seven companies add up to 196 officers and men, or an average of 28 per company. This average was then added for companies A-C giving a total of 280 officers and men. 5 more were added for field and staff. In David Dameron, *Benning's Brigade: A History and Roster of the 15th Georgia* (Spartanburg, South

Carolina, 1997), 61-65; Dameron only notes that in October, the 15th had "approximately" 200 men, and suffered 31 casualties at Chickamauga, for a total engaged strength of 231. However, Dameron's losses are much too low. *Memphis Daily Appeal*, September 25 1863, shows 82 casualties, which would give a strength of 282.

193. "About 250 engaged." *Columbus Weekly Enquirer*, September 29, 1863. Alexander papers, Museum of the Confederacy, shows 166 present, and also shows 250 present at Knoxville, two months later.

194. Per CCNMP Park Ranger Lee White. A letter from Captain Mims of Co. I, dated September 21, 1863, reports 6 officers and "about 100 men" present after the battle. Adding in the 142 reported losses gives a total of 248 engaged. *Columbus Daily Sun*, Sept. 26, 1863. In the Alexander Papers, the Museum of the Confederacy, the regimental questionnaire says 236 "engaged."

195. In the OR 30, pt. 2, 18, Manning is shown as succeeding Robertson in command. Neither Robertson nor Manning report Robertson being injured, or Manning replacing him. Robertson was transferred to Texas in December 1863, after disciplinary run-ins with James Longstreet and Micah Jenkins during the Wauhatchie and East Tennessee Campaigns.

196. Regimental Questionnaire, Alexander Papers, Museum of the Confederacy.

197. Company rolls for August 31, 1863. RG 109, NARA.

198. Subtracting the strengths of the other three regiments from the brigade total leaves 264 men. Capt. R. H. Bassett, Co. G, gives the strength as "about 260" in a letter dated September 26th, 1863. R. H. Bassett Letter, Letters received by the C.S. Adjutant and Inspector General's Office, RG 109, NARA.

199. *Memphis Daily Appeal*, Sept 28, 1863, says 225 "men" 9.8% added for officers.

200. Law's Brigade, temporarily commanded by Sheffield. Wright's dispatch from Atlanta gives a strength of 2,000 men, OR 30, pt. 4, 652.

201. J. Gary Laine and Morris M. Penny, *Law's Alabama Brigade in the War between the Union and the Confederacy*, (White Mane Publishing, 1996), 370. "300 present" in Alexander Papers, Regimental Questionnaire. Oates was slightly wounded on the 20th, but did not relinquish command.

202. "425 present," in Regimental Questionnaire, Alexander Papers, Museum of the Confederacy.

203. Not engaged. A copy of a telegram in the CCNMP files indicates that Anderson's Brigade numbered 1,900 men on September 14. Anderson's brigade was diverted to Charleston on September 16th, and did not arrive at Chattanooga until October 9. Anderson is included here for completeness, but his command is not included in the unengaged total listed at the beginning of this section. See also Warren Wilkinson and Steven Woodworth, *A Scythe of Fire* (Harper Collins, 2002), 269. All regimental commanders are as of August 31, 1863, unless otherwise noted.

204. Strength as of August 31, 1863.

205. Strength as of December 31, 1863.

206. Nine companies reported, December 31, 1863. Company A added 31 as average strength for the other companies, plus 5 added for field and staff.

207. Eight companies reported 250 in April, 1864, the only date given. 62 added in for the average for the other two companies, plus 5 for Field and staff. The late date of this report makes this figure speculative, at best.

208. Field and staff, and nine companies reported for October 31, 1863. Company C not reported, estimated at 42, the average of the other nine companies. On August 31, 483 were reported present. In OR 29, pt. 2, 683 and OR 31, pt. 1, 452 (for August 31 and November 30, 1863) the regimental commander is listed as "Col. Jack Brown." However, Col. William Andrew Jackson Brown was wounded and captured at Gettysburg, and not exchanged until March, 1864. In his absence, Lieutenant Colonel Gee commanded the regiment.

209. Not engaged. Jenkins's Brigade numbered approximately 2,000 men, per *OR* 30, pt. 4, 675. Jenkins's brigade reached the battlefield on September 22. All regimental commanders are as of October 31, 1863.

210. Subtracting the known strengths of the brigade leaves 1,000 men unaccounted for in three regiments, or 32 companies. That figure was then divided by 32 to produce an average of 31.25 men per company, or 312.5 men each for the 1st and 6th South Carolina, and 375 for the Palmetto Sharpshooters.

211. All ten companies reported, August 31, 1863, Field and staff estimated at 5.

212. All ten companies reported, August 31, 1863, except for Company G, reported for December 31st. Field and staff estimated at 5.

213. See note for 1st South Carolina, above.

214. Engaged strength at the battle of Wauhatchie, October 28, 1863. *The Charleston Mercury*, November 11, 1863.

215. See note for 1st South Carolina, above.

216. McLaws's Division, temporarily commanded by Kershaw.

217. Regimental questionnaire, Alexander Papers, Museum of the Confederacy. Company rolls for August 31, 1863, show 177 officers and men present in six companies. 118 officers and men estimated in the four unreported companies, giving 295 total, and 5 estimated for field and staff.

218. Five companies reported 162 officers and men present on August 31, 1863. Company B reported 24 aggregate for October, the only roll available, and also lost 14 men at Chickamauga, (*OR Supplement*, 45, 443) giving a total of 38. Total strength of 6 reported companies: 200. The estimated strength of the 4 unreported companies was 133, with field and staff estimated at 5. The regimental questionnaire, Alexander Papers, Museum of the Confederacy; says "300 engaged" a figure which probably includes only the enlisted men.

219. All ten companies reported 255 officers and men as of August 31, 1863. 5 additional were added for estimated field and staff.

220. Companies A-L. Eight of eleven companies and the field and staff reported their strength as of August 31, 1863, and one reported as of September 30, 1863. This totals 270, including 11 field and staff. The average for the two unreported companies was 29 each, for another 58 officers and men, estimated. Final total, 328.

221. A telegram in the CCNMP files shows Kershaw with 1,850 men on September 14. The regimental questionnaire, Alexander Papers, Museum of the Confederacy; shows 1,344 engaged. Kershaw retained command of both his brigade and the division.

222. Dubose Egleston Letter, September 27, 1863, Southern Historical Collection, UNC, and Reginald Screvin diary, South Carolina Historical Society; both record a strength of 230, with 101 losses. Mac Wyckoff, *A History of the 2nd South Carolina Infantry: 1861-65* (Sgt Kirkland's Press, 1994), 96, says that only 225 went into action, but gives no specifics on officers and men.

223. All ten companies reporting, for August 31, 1863, show 338 officers and men. Field and staff was estimated at 5.

224. Companies A-M. Eleven of twelve companies reported for August 31, 1863, showing 255 officers and men. Company B, for whom no reports were found, was estimated at 23, the average of the other eleven companies. Field and Staff estimated at 5.

225. Companies A-M. All twelve companies reported a total of 210 officers and men on August 31, 1863. Field and staff estimated at 5.

226. All ten companies reported for August 31, 1863, showing 338 officers and men. Field and staff estimated at 5.

227. The last numbers found for this unit date from Gettysburg. There, the battalion took 203 men into action and lost 46, leaving 157 present after the fight. None of the other units in the brigade were stronger at Chickamauga than their engaged strengths at Gettysburg, though some had recovered to nearly that strength. This suggests that the Battalion should number somewhere between 160 and 200 officers and men. The average company strength for the rest of the brigade

ran from a low of 18 men per company to a high of 34, with an overall brigade average of about 26. I finally decided to simply multiply the brigade average company strength - 26 - by the 7 companies in the battalion to produce this total, essentially splitting the difference between the high and the low estimates. Lt. Col. William G. Rice commanded the battalion after Gettysburg, but he was granted sick leave on September 14, 1863; as senior Captain, Townsend took over. Who replaced Captain Townsend remains unclear. The regimental history suggests Whitener assumed command, though it could also have been Capt. Edward S. Percival. Rice would be back with the battalion in October. See Sam B. Davis, *A History of the 3rd South Carolina Volunteer Infantry Battalion (James Battalion):1861-1865* (Broadfoot Publishing Co. 2009), 174-175; OR 31, pt. 2, 657; and *Compiled Service Records of Confederate Soldiers who served in Organizations from the State of South Carolina*, 3rd South Carolina Battalion, microcopy 267, roll 181.

228. Not engaged. The strength of this unit was determined by subtracting the known strength of the other brigades in the division from the divisional return, dated October 1, 1863. These numbers reflect the aggregate present rather than effectives. Had they reached the field in time to see action, the actual engaged figures would likely have been 10-15% lower, based on similar comparisons with other regiments. The regimental estimates come from the relative sizes of the units after Gettysburg, and then simply applying those same percentages to the brigade total. All regimental commanders are as of August 31, 1863, unless otherwise noted.

229. Not engaged. The brigade strength was 2,200 per a telegram dated September 14, tracking their movement through Wilmington North Carolina; found in the CCNMP files. Wofford's Brigade arrived on the 21st, and lost at least one man killed in skirmishing outside Chattanooga on the 22nd. Actual combat strengths would have likely been 10-15% lower. The regimental estimates are derived from the relative sizes of the units after Gettysburg, complicated by the fact that though the Sharpshooters were organized in the spring of 1863, and fought at Gettysburg, their status was not given official recognition until after Gettysburg. The Sharpshooters were formed from the other units in the brigade, so here I have assumed that each of the other units gave up 10% strength to form the battalion. All regimental commanders are as of August 31, 1863, unless otherwise noted.

230. The company structure of Phillips Legion was very complicated. Originally, it had companies lettered A to P. The infantry battalion was comprised of companies A, B, C, D, E, F, L, M, and O. The cavalry battalion accounted for the remaining 6 companies, G, H, I, K, N, and P. See *OR Supplement*, 7, 256-270.

231. Strength and equipment as of December 14, 1863. The guns were the same as at Stone's River in January, 1863, indicating that this was also the battery's armament at Chickamauga. OR 31, pt. 3, 828.

232. Average battery strength of known units in the army. Le Gardeur's battery and men were transferred, without guns, to Charleston to reinforce the Dept. of South Carolina in November, 1863. On October 31, 1863, they were reported as being having "no pieces," see OR 28, pt. 2, 465. I speculate that their equipment was merged or re-organized, leaving them without weapons and available to be sent to Charleston. Battery equipment shown here is guess work, representing the most common pieces in the Confederate army.

233. Gun types from Park Tablet. Strength is from December 14, 1863, OR 31, pt. 3, 828.

234. Gun types from Park Tablet. Strength is from December 14, 1863, OR 31, pt. 3, 828. In December this battery was re-armed with 4 Napoleons.

235. Gun types from Park Tablet. Strength from December 14, 1863, OR 31, pt. 3, 828. This strength is very high for having only two guns in the battery.

236. Alexander's battalion was the only artillery sent to Georgia. Longstreet's other corps artillery battalion, plus each of the battalions normally assigned to Hood's and McLaws's infantry divisions, were left behind in Virginia. Alexander's guns reached Ringgold at 2:00 a.m. on Friday, September 25, 1863. E. Porter Alexander, *Military Memoirs of a Confederate: A Critical Narrative*, (New York: 1907), 449. The strength is the average battery strength for First Corps Artillery on October 31, 1863, OR 31, pt. 2, 656. Alexander's Battalion numbered 576 engaged at Gettysburg,

and suffered 139 losses, John W. Busey and David G. Martin, *Regimental Strengths and Losses at Gettysburg* (Longstreet House, 1986), 284.

237. This battery numbered 71 at Gettysburg, and lost 36.

238. This battery numbered 78 at Gettysburg, and lost 9.

239. This battery numbered 135 at Gettysburg, and lost 33.

240. This battery numbered 90 at Gettysburg, and lost 18.

241. This battery numbered 90 at Gettysburg, and lost 13.

242. This battery numbered 103 at Gettysburg and lost 28.

243. Strength as of November 7, 1863, at time of their transfer to West Tennessee.

244. Richard P. Weinert, Jr., *The Confederate Regular Army* (White Mane Publishing Company, 1991), 38. Officially, Bradley's men were Company A of the 1st Confederate Regular Cavalry Regiment. Weinert cites the company muster roll for June 30th, 1863, that shows 1 officer and 46 men present for duty. In early November, the company totaled only 28 officers and men.

245. Ten percent of the regimental strength.

246. On September 11, 1863, Armstrong reported that he was moving to Reed's Bridge with two regiments, numbering 600 men. In the same message, he detailed Col. Woodward of the 2nd Kentucky cavalry to make a scout elsewhere. By process of elimination, the two regiments he took to Reed's Bridge should be the 3rd Arkansas and the 6th Tennessee; and each is assumed to have about 300 men.

247. Companies A-I. Strength determined by subtracting the known strengths from the 3740 officers and men reported for this division on August 20, 1863, then dividing that remainder by the number of companies left unaccounted for, producing an average of 47.4 men per company. Multiplying by the 9 companies in the 2nd Kentucky, we get 427 men.

248. See the note for 3rd Arkansas Cavalry, above. Company E detached as escort for the brigade commander. *Tennesseans in the Civil War in Two Parts* (Civil War Centennial Commission, 1964), vol. 1, 66.

249. Companies A-F. Strength at time of transfer to West Tennessee, November 7, 1863.

250. Dibrell reported 94 officers and 944 men present PFD in January 1864 (not including Shaw's Battalion or the two artillery batteries) for a total of 1,038. OR 32, pt. 2, 641.

251. In his report Dibrell mentions being reinforced by Col. McLemore and 200 men on August 17th. It is not known if this is the full regiment or just a portion.

252. The Company rolls, NARA, show Companies A-L. L Company assigned on August 1st, 1863. Nine companies report 505 officers and men present, mostly June 30th rolls, one from August 31st. Company average was 56 men, giving 112 men added back in for the two missing companies, plus 5 for field and staff., or a total of 622. Admittedly, this strength is speculative, but the overall strength of the Forrest's Cavalry Division on August 10 shows a slight increase from June, before the Tullahoma retreat; which indicates fairly consistent strengths for this period. Dibrell reported that he had "not over 300 men present" On August 9, 1863, in a skirmish near Sparta Tennessee. However, Dibrell also mentions sending out many scouts over a wide area, and it is unclear how much of the regiment was detached. See OR 23, pt. 1, 848. In his dispatch from August 18th, Dibrell reported that over half the regiment was absent gathering supplies, which would reconcile with the 622 shown on the rolls. Finally, several Union reports give the impression that several hundred Confederates where wandering all over White County Tennessee at this time, foraging. I have decided that while the 622 figure is likely accurate for how many were with the regiment in August, no more than half were available for combat duties.

253. Dibrell, brigade commander, estimates Biffle's regiment at 350 strong on November 5, 1863.

254. See note for 2nd Kentucky, above. 47.4 men per company, times 10 companies.

255. Companies B-L. Company A transferred to McDonald's Battalion May 1, 1863. For strength, see the note for 2nd Kentucky, above.

256. The Brigade return in OR 30, pt. 2, 20, shows this unit as being comprised of Shaw's and Hamilton's Battalions, and Allison's Squadron; all consolidated. The OR *Supplement*, 78,

292-295 shows Allison's Squadron with 3 companies, A-C. Pages 315-9 indicate that Shaw's and Hamilton's command were the same unit, commanded in secession by Hamilton and then Shaw, and likely also had 3 companies (only the muster roll for company C is shown.) Also see the note for 2nd Kentucky, above.

257. In August, the total strength of the two batteries in Forrest's division was 136 officers and men. When Morton was transferred in November, his strength was listed as 71 officers and men. Subtracting that strength from the 136 gives 65 left for Huggins' Battery. Admittedly, Morton's strength is from well after the battle. Alternatively, Huggins reports 91 total (5 officers and 86 men) present for duty in January, 1864; see OR 32, pt. 2, 641. Equipment is as of November 1862, found in OR 20, pt. 2, 399.

258. The battery strength is as of time of transfer to West Tennessee, November 7, 1863. Equipment is as described in Morton's memoir, John Watson Morton, *The Artillery of Nathan Bedford Forrest's Cavalry* (Bemis Publishing, 1995), 176-177. A report from May 1864 in OR 31, pt. 2, 624, says that Morton had four 3 inch rifles, but Morton himself says that the battery did not have four rifles until two more were captured at Bryce's Crossroads in June 1864, and exchanged on the spot for the two brass 12 pound howitzers in his command.

259. A report for August 31, 1863, in the Emerson Opdycke Papers, Ohio Historical Society shows 405 officers and 4825 men PFD in Pegram's Division, for a total of 5230. Desertion, attrition, and the exact composition of Pegram's command at this time make it difficult to tell if that figure reflects only the troops who accompanied Buckner to join Bragg.

260. J. W. Minnich, of the 6th Georgia Cavalry, estimates the brigade as 1600 or 1650 strong on the morning of the 19th. It is unclear if he includes the 10th Confederate, which was nominally a part of Scott's Brigade. Since the 10th was not a regular part of the brigade, I believe Minnich did not include it. I have also estimated Huwald's battery - somewhat arbitrarily - at 50 men, assuming that Minnich's '1650' estimate included the battery. Overall, I think this number is more likely a minimum than a maximum, and using other estimates described below, Davidson's Brigade could have numbered much closer to 2500 men than 1600. Pegram personally commanded both the division and the brigade until Davidson arrived sometime during the morning of September 19.

261. Strength derived by subtracting the known strengths of the other regiments in the brigade, and calculating a company average strength for this regiment and for Rucker's command. On October 19, Col. Morrison reported that this regiment, plus the 6th Georgia and 3rd Confederate, together numbered 1800 men, or 600 men per unit. Hence, this figure might well be low, or not reflect detachments. See note for Third Confederate, below.

262. This is at best, an educated guess. Davidson's brigade reportedly lost about one quarter of its strength in the battle. J. W. Minnich, a member of the 6th, reported the regimental losses at 84 killed and wounded, with no missing specified. A crude estimate of overall losses might be 100. Applying the brigade loss ratio of 25% gives a ballpark strength for the regiment of around 400 men. On October 19 Col. Morrison reported this regiment, plus the 1st Georgia and 3rd Confederate, at 1800 men, or 600 men per unit. See note for 3rd Confederate, below. On April 30, 1863, this regiment reported 25 officers and 482 men present for duty in nine out of the ten companies, for 507, or 56 men per company average. Adding back in 56 men for company E, not reported, would give the regiment a strength of 563. See box 198, RG 109, NARA.

263. Originally the 5th and 7th Battalions, North Carolina Cavalry, which numbered 27 officers and 493 men following their consolidation into the 6th North Carolina Cavalry Regiment on August 3, 1863. This figure is drawn from the memoirs of Capt. Martin V. Moore. See website: http://members.aol.com/jweaver301/nc/6nccavhi.htm.

264. Strength given as of June 9, in *Macon Daily Telegraph*, June 23, 1863.

265. Rucker's 1st East Tennessee Legion was a field organization created by consolidating the 12th and 16th Tennessee Cavalry Battalions. The 12th had seven companies, A-G, the 16th had six companies, A-F. Strength derived by subtracting the known strengths of the other regiments from the brigade total, and then finding a company average. In January, 1864, Rucker's

Legion reported 19 officers and 171 men present for duty, total 190, but this was after much hard service and the loss of many horses during the East Tennessee campaign, so a figure about double that seems fairly reasonable for Chickamauga. See *OR* 32, pt. 2, 641. In a post war account from 1867, Leroy Moncure Nutt estimates the strength at "about 300" in each battalion, which would give Rucker a strength of close to 600. Note how this number compares to the estimates of the 1st Georgia, 6th Georgia, and 3rd Confederate Regiments, above - all also estimated at 600 strong on October 19th, 1863. Leroy Moncure Nutt Letters, Southern Historical Collection, University of North Carolina.

266. Huwald's battery was armed with two mountain howitzers and two mountain rifles. The latter was a 2.56 inch rifle scaled down from the 3" model and mounted on a carriage similar to that of a mountain howitzer.

267. In Scott's report of the battle, he gives his strength as 500 men for the entire brigade, including Morgan's remnants. However, within the text of the report, Scott mentions that that heavy detachments for patrols and pickets were not counted in this total. Moreover, the strength reported at the beginning of the month was far higher. An article in the *Charleston Mercury* from Saturday, October 10, 1863 gives the total for just the 1st Louisiana, 2nd and 6th Tennessee as 590 men, without indicating if this figure included officers. Using the newspaper figure gives a total of 900 men, or 990 if officers are added back in. I have settled on the 1,100 figure as the likely one to reflect scouts, detachments, and officers not reported, assuming the figures we do have are all "effectives." Jordan and Pryor, in *Forrest's Cavalry*, 307; give Scott's strength on September 11 as "900 men."

268. In July, Morgan's Division of Kentucky Cavalry was sent on a raid deep into Federal territory. Morgan crossed the Ohio River and most of his men were captured. On August 1st, 1863, two battalions were formed from the survivors of that raid, and of detached men left behind. The 1st Battalion had six companies, the 2nd Battalion had four; See *OR Supplement*, 35, 24-25, 52-53. One battalion was mounted, the other lacked horses. However, the army organization lists only Morgan's "detachment" as serving in Scott's Brigade. Forrest, in his report, says only that they had "about" 240 men.

269. Company A detached and escorting Longstreet. Companies E/C detached and escorting Hood, 1st Corps, ANV. Scott reported the brigade has having 900 men on August 7, 1863. for an average of 300 men per regiment. He had lost heavily to straggling on his Kentucky Raid in July/early August. *OR* 23, pt. 1, 841.

270. See note above, for 1st Louisiana.

271. See note above, for 1st Louisiana.

272. This strength is based on the relative size of other horse batteries equipped with mountain howitzers. Robinson's battery was merged with Wiggins' in October, and disappeared from the rolls.

273. *OR* 30, pt. 2, 531.

274 10% of the regimental strength given below. Bennett is assumed to be in command due to the absence of the other ranking officers.

275. Crews reported 63 officers and 730 men present for duty, total of 793, January 1864. *OR* 32, pt. 2, 641. However, this figure includes the 1st and 6th Ga. Cavalry, attached after the battle.

276. Also known as the 7th/9th Alabama Cavalry. Their strength is derived by subtracting the strengths of the known regiments from the August 20, 1863 strength report of the Corps, and then dividing by the number of companies left in the unknown regiments. This calculation produced an average of 48.8 men per company.

277. Jim R. Cabaniss, Ed. *The Civil War Journal and Letters of Washington Ives* (Tallahassee Florida, 1987), 42. Company G was detached and serving as Escort to Cheatham's Division, Polk's Corps.

278. See note for Malone's Regiment, above.

279. Strength given as of August 31, 1863. On September 10, a deserter from the 4th told the Federals that this regiment numbered 300 men. See Summary of Intelligence Received, Army of the Cumberland, RG 94; and also Box 197, Confederate Records, RG 109, NARA.

280. Harrison reported 73 officers and 642 men present for duty, total 715, in January 1864. *OR* 32, pt. 2, 641 However, this number includes only the 3rd Confederate, 8th and 11th Texas, as the other units were not in the brigade at this time. The same force here numbers 1,360.

281. This strength is given in a Union report, local intelligence gathered by a civilian. Certainly not the most reliable of accounts, but the numbers are close to reasonable. Further, on October 19, 1863, Col. J.J. Morrison reported taking three regiments on a mission across the Hiwassee River: the 1st and 6th Georgia, and 3rd Confederate; with a reported strength as 1,800 men, roughly 600 men per regiment. See *OR* 31, pt. 1, 14. Finally, on November 20, 1863, Col. H.B. Lyon reported the 3rd Confederate as having 260 "effective men" (286 with officers) see *OR* 31, pt. 3, 722. All Confederate reports, however, including Morrison's, report dramatic straggling and desertion in the fall of 1863 For example, while Morrison reported 1,800 men at the start of his week-long expedition he ended it with only 1,000; but recorded actual combat losses of just 14 killed and 82 wounded. Something like 700 men were unaccounted for, more than 1/3 of the command.

282. See note for Malone's regiment, above.

283. See note for Malone's regiment, above. In *Military Annals*, vol. 2, 631, George Guild claimed that "the regiment went into the fight eight hundred strong." This seems high.

284. Bryan S Bush, *Terry's Texas Rangers: The Eighth Texas Cavalry* (Turner Publishing, 2002), 100. Bush's source cites the strength for the "closing days of August." Company A, companies C-L. Company B was detached and serving on escort duty. At the end of the year, the Company Rolls, RG 109, NARA; show six companies reported their strength, at 168 men, as of December 31, 1863. The average company strength was 28 men, with 112 more men added in for the four non-reporting companies. Additionally, 5 added for field and staff, for a total of 285.

285. This strength derived by comparing the strength for the 8th Texas at the end of August, (412) to the known strength on December 31st (285.) That ratio was then applied to the known strength of the 11th Texas, ten companies plus field and staff reporting on December 31, 1863; for a total of 277. Company Rolls, Confederate Records, RG 109, NARA. Assuming a similar ratio of strength gain and loss in the 11th, the 277 figure was multiplied by 1.44 to produce an estimated strength for the end of August.

286. 3 officers and 74 men present for duty on January 30, 1864. While this date is pretty far removed from the battle, it remains the closest firm number found. The Union Provost's report on Bragg's order of battle, assembled from prisoner interrogations, lists White's Battery as present with 6 guns, see *OR* 30, pt. 1, 232. The January report shows only 4 guns present. Bush, *Terry's Texas Rangers*, 104 lists the armament.

287. In Wheeler's report, he gives Martin's strength as "about 1,200 men" but makes reference to at least two regiments detached, who are apparently not counted in that number. Further, later in the same report, Wheeler notes specifically that he did not count men who were screening or guarding flanks as part of his effective total. Hence, his report is useless for determining actual strength available at the time of the battle. See *OR* 30, pt. 2, 519-522.

288. Entry 18, part 101, Alabama Box 3, RG 109, NARA. Company A reported the same number present on both June and December, 1863.

289. See note for Malone's regiment, above.

290. Entry 18, part 101, Alabama Box 3, RG 109, NARA. Six companies reported 235 men present on June 30, 1863, 39 men added in as average strength for company C, not reported, and 5 added for field and staff. Companies B-H present. Company A was serving as escort to General Martin, company I (Lenoir) serving as escort to General Hindman, and Company K (Halloway) escorted General Bragg. *OR* 30, pt. 4, 585, indicates that a "detachment" of this command numbered 250 men.

291. See note for Malone's regiment, above.

292. See note for Malone's regiment, above.

293. Russell reported 65 officers and 724 men present for duty in January 1864, a total of 789; but this figure includes the 1st, 3rd, 4th, 51st and Malone's regiments, all of Alabama cavalry, as well as the 1st Confederate.

294. See note for Malone's regiment, above.

295. See note for Malone's regiment, above.

296. This figure is from January 30, 1864. In June, Capt. Wiggins and one section numbering 30 men were captured at Shelbyville. A year later, in 1864, after a number of cavalry transfers, the strength of the battery was 45, 30 in one section and 15 in the other, see *OR Supplement*, 14, 266. The equipment is an either-or situation. Sometime in April or May, the battery received two 12# howitzers in exchange for two guns from its current complement of four 6 Pound guns. Hence, by June, one section had 6-Pounders and one section had the howitzers. When Wiggins and his section were captured, nothing indicates which pieces were lost. However, Wheeler in his report of his October raid, says that two guns of Wiggins' battery had to be abandoned, and that they were howitzers. I have assumed that these were the pieces present at Chickamauga. See *OR* 30, pt. 2, 725.

Confederate Losses

Determining total Confederate losses is an uncertain (and difficult) business. No consolidated army-wide return of losses appears in the *Official Records* akin to the Union loss figures provided there. Confederate troops from several different departments moved to reinforce Bragg's Army of Tennessee, and in a process that began shortly after the battle, many of those same troops eventually returned to other theaters. Many reports are thus missing—if they were ever filed at all—and in the case of Bragg's cavalry, completely non-existent.

Fortunately, there are enough reports in the OR to gain a solid basis of casualties for most units. Additionally, I relied heavily on newspapers, especially the *Memphis Daily Appeal*. Despite its name, the *Appeal* had long ago fled Memphis, and at the time of the battle was being published in Atlanta. It is a prime source of news and information for the Army of Tennessee and published dozens of casualty reports and other important correspondence from the army during that critical fall of 1863.

The data presented below is admittedly incomplete, and remains very much a work-in-progress. Historically, losses have been estimated as low as 14,000 and as high as almost 21,000, a dramatic variance indeed.

Unless otherwise noted, the losses presented in the tables that follow are taken from OR 30, pt. 2.

Formation	Strength	Losses K/W/M=T	Percent
		Army of Tennessee	
Army of Tennessee		**2,141/13,328/1,339=16,808**	
Escort	344	0/0/0=0	0%
Dreux La. Co	68	0/0/0=0	0%
K, 3rd Ala Cav.	68	0/0/0=0	0%
Miners and Sappers	160	0/0/0=0	0%
C, 1 Louisiana Reg.	48	0/0/0=0	0%
		Polk's Corps	
Polk's Corps	**13,205**	**450/3,334/127=3,911**	**30%**
Greenleaf La. Cav	33	0/0/0	0%
Cheatham's Division	7,046	194+/1,670(?)/75+=1,939	28%[1]
G, 2 Ga. Cav	32	0/0/0	0%
Jackson's Brigade	**1,311**	**54/419/4=477**	**36%**
Staff		0/0/1=1	
2 Bn, 1 Conf. Regt	194	10/73/0=83	43%
2 Georgia Bn SS	108	3/27/0=30	28%
5 Georgia	353	27/165/2=194	55%
5 Mississippi	252	4/70/1=75	30%
8 Mississippi	404	10/84/0=94	23%
Maney's Brigade	**1,293**	**50/305/32=387**	**30%**
1+27 Tennessee	703	14/75/0=89	13%
4 Tennessee (PA)	179	10/43/12=65	36%[2]
6+9 Tennessee	368	26/168/17=211	57
24 Tennessee Bn SS	43	0/19/3=22	51%
Smith's Brigade	**1,642**	**38/302/7=347**	**21%**
11 Tennessee	383	8/44/0=52	14%[3]
12+47 Tennessee	351	11/76/0=87	23%
13+154 Tennessee	222	8/67/0=75	34%[4]
29 Tennessee	413	4/66/1=71	17%
Dawson's Bn SS	273	7/49/6=62	23%
Strahl's Brigade	**1,181**	**250 total**	**21%[5]**
4+5 Tennessee	380	3/30/0=33	9%
19 Tennessee	266	8/66/20=94	35%
24 Tennessee	245	43 total	18%
31 Tennessee	168	1/26/0=27	16%[6]

Formation	Strength	Losses K/W/M=T	Percent
33 Tennessee	122	53 total	43%[7]
Wright's Brigade	**1,113**	**30/379/6=415**	**37%**
8 Tennessee	285	3/78/1=82	29%[8]
16 Tennessee	266	1/67/0=68	26%
28 Tennessee	279	9/76/0=85	30%
38 Tennessee	278	4/56/5=65	23%[9]
51+52 Tennessee	255	13/102/0=115	45%
Artillery/Cheatham	**474**	**10/47/6=63**	**13%**
Carnes	87	7/16/0=23	26%
Scogin	89	1/11/1=13	15%
Scott	114	2/14/0=16	14%
Smith	87	0/2/5=7	8%
Stanford	97	0/4/0=4	4%
Hindman's Division	**6,146**	**256+/1,664/52=1,972**	**32%[10]**
I, 3 Alabama Cav	65	0	-
Sharpshooter Det.	10	0/1/0	10%
Anderson's Brigade	**1,865**	**80/454/24=558**	**30%**
7 Mississippi	291	10/64/1=75	26%
9 Mississippi	355	9/75/9=93	26%
10 Mississippi	311	17/59/0=76	24%
41 Mississippi	502	24/164/9=197	39%
44 Mississippi	272	81 total	30%
9 Mississippi Bn	134	36 total	27%[11]
Deas' Brigade	**1,932**	**125/586/24=735**	**38%**
19 Alabama	515	34/158/12=204	40%
22 Alabama	371	44/161/0=205	55%
25 Alabama	330	15/95/2=112	34%
39 Alabama	340	14/82/0=96	28%
50 Alabama	313	17/81/8=106	34%[12]
17 Alabama SS	63	1/9/2=12	19%
Manigault's Brigade	**2,025**	**656 Total**	**32%[13]**
24 Alabama	381	22/91/3=116	30%
28 Alabama	629	266 total	42%[14]
34 Alabama	329	38 total	12%
10+19 S. Carolina	686	26/210/0=236	34%

Formation	Strength	Losses K/W/M=T	Percent
Artillery/Hindman	**249**	**3/18/1=22**	**9%**
Dent	87	3/13/0=16	18%
Garrity	89	0/5/0=5	6%
Waters	73	0/0/1=1	1%

Hill's Corps

Formation	Strength	Losses K/W/M=T	Percent
Hill's Corps	**9,216**	**384/2,508/211=3,103**	**34%**
Staff		0/1/0=1	
Raum's Cav	51	0/0/0=0	0%
Breckinridge's Div	**3,785**	**177/899/176=1,252**	**33%**
Adams's Brigade	1,221	66/238/91=395	32%
Staff		1/0/0=1	
32 Alabama	145	0/4/0=4	3%
13+20 Louisiana	309	16/64/44=124	40%
16+25 Louisiana	319	21/49/36=106	33%[15]
19 Louisiana	349	28/114/11=153	44%
14 Louisiana Bn	99	0/7/0=7	7%
Helm's Brigade	**1,384**	**60/399/39=498**	**36%**
41 Alabama	357	27/120/11=158	44%
2 Kentucky	302	13/107/26=146	48%[16]
4 Kentucky	275	7/51/0=58	21%
6 Kentucky	220	2/32/0=34	15%[17]
9 Kentucky	230	11/89/2=102	44%
Stovall's Brigade	**897**	**37/232/46=315**	**35%**
1+3 Florida	298	9/70/13=92	31%
4 Florida	238	9/67/11=87	37%
47 Georgia	193	11/59/6=76	39%
60 N. Carolina	168	8/36/16=60	36%
Artillery/Breckinridge	**283**	**14/30/0=44**	**16%**
Cobb	84	3/7/0=10	12%
Mebane	73	0/1/0=1	1%
Slocumb	126	11/22/0=33	26%
Cleburne's Division	**5,380**	**207/1,608/35=/1,850**	**34%[18]**
Sanders' Cavalry	51	0/1/0=1	2%[19]
Deshler's Brigade	**1,693**	**52/366/29=447**	**26%**
19+24 Arkansas	226	8/97/1=106	47%

Formation	Strength	Losses K/W/M=T	Percent
6+10+15 Texas	700	20/95/28=143	20%
17+18+24+25 Texas	767	24/174/0=198	26%
Polk's Brigade	**1,390**	**56/548/6=610**	**44%**[20]
1 Arkansas	430	13/180/1=194	45%
3+5 Confederate	290	13/104/1=118	41%[21]
2 Tennessee	264	13/145/1=159	60%
35 Tennessee	236	7/54/0=61	26%
48 Tennessee	170	10/65/3=78	46%[22]
Wood's Brigade	**1,982**	**99/677/0=776**	**39%**
16 Alabama	414	25/218/0=243	59%[23]
33 Alabama	459	19/166/0=185	40%
45 Alabama	423	22/95/0=117	28%
18 Alabama Bn	87	5/34/0=39	45%
32+45 Mississippi	541	25/141/0=166	31%
15 Mississippi Bn	58	3/23/0=26	45%
Artillery/Cleburne	**264**	**0/16/0=16**	**6%**
Calvert	87	0/6/0=6	7%
Douglas	90	0/0/0=0	0%
Semple	87	0/10/0=10	11%

Reserve Corps

Formation	Strength	Losses K/W/M=T	Percent
Reserve Corps	**8,108**	**346/2,036/672=3,054**	**38%**
Gist's Division	**3,974**	**208/1,013/254=1,475**	**37%**
Colquitt's Brigade	**1,400**	**49/251/36=336**	**24%**
46 Georgia	591	5/48/19=72	12%[24]
8 Georgia Bn	399	14/59/0=73	18%[25]
24 South Carolina	410	30/144/17=191	47%[26]
Ector's Brigade	**1,199**	**60/329/138=527**	**44%**[27]
Stone's Ala. Miss. SS	111	5/17/1=23	21%[28]
Pound's Bn Miss. SS	42	1/8/1=10	24%[29]
29 North Carolina	215	14/72/25=111	52%[30]
9 Texas	145	6/36/18=60	41%[31]
10 Texas DC	272	11/84/24=119	44%[32]
14 Texas DC	197	10/47/29=86	44%[33]
32 Texas DC	217	13/65/40=118	54%[34]

Formation	Strength	Losses K/W/M=T	Percent
Wilson's Brigade	**1,317**	**99/426/80=605**	**46%**
25 Georgia	383	29/123/0=152	40%[35]
29 Georgia	220	24/97/8=129	59%[36]
30 Georgia	334	20/106/0=126	38%[37]
1 Georgia SS	152	5/52/4=61	40%[38]
4 Louisiana Bn.	228	21/48/68=137	60%[39]
Artillery/Gist	**58**	**0/7/0=7**	**12%**
Howell	58	0/7/0=7	12%[40]
Liddell's Division	**4,031**	**138/1,023/418=1,579**	**39%**
Govan's Brigade	**1,975**	**73/502/283=858**	**43%**
2+15 Arkansas	349	150 total	43%[41]
5+13 Arkansas	450	38/131/33=202	45%
6+7 Arkansas	388	165 total	43%
8 Arkansas	387	14/92/65=171	44%
1 Louisiana Reg.	401	170 total	42%[43]
Walthall's Brigade	**1,827**	**57/497/133=687**	**38%**
24 Mississippi	428	10/103/19=132	31%
27 Mississippi	362	10/88/19=117	32%
29 Mississippi	368	17/139/38=194	53%
30 Mississippi	362	5/76/38=119	33%
34 Mississippi	307	15/91/19=125	41%
Artillery/ Liddell	**229**	**8/24/2=34**	**15%**
Fowler	142	6/18/2=26	18%[44]
Warren	87	2/6/0=8	9%[45]

Buckner's Corps

Formation	Strength	Losses K/W/M=T	Percent
Buckner's Corps	**9,537**	**418/2,574/92=3,086**	**32%**
Clark's Cav	20	-	0%
Ordnance Escort	80	-	0%
Preston's Division	**4,862**	**199/1,086/60=1,345**	**28%[46]**
Gracie's Brigade	**1,927**	**90/606/27=725**	**38%[47]**
43 Alabama	364	16/78/4=98	27%[48]
1 Alabama Bn.	281	24/135/8=167	59%[49]
2 Alabama Bn.	282	16/82/8=106	38%[50]
3 Alabama Bn.	331	5/44/0=49	15%[51]

Formation	Strength	Losses K/W/M=T	Percent
4 Alabama Bn.	243	13/84/1=98	40%[52]
63 Tennessee	426	16/183/6=205	48%[53]
Kelly's Brigade	**1,146**	**62/247/28=337**	**29%[54]**
65 Georgia	272	0/4/0=4	1%
5 Kentucky	252	14/75/2=91	36%
58 North Carolina	359	36/123/13=172	48%[55]
63 Virginia	263	12/45/13=70	27%[56]
Trigg's Brigade	**1,536**	**46/231/5=282**	**18%[57]**
1 Florida Cav	271	3/24/1=28	10%
6 Florida	402	38/147/1=186	46%
7 Florida	391	1/16/1=18	5%
54 Virginia	472	4/44/2=50	11%
Artillery/Preston	**253**	**1/2/0=3**	**1%**
Jeffress	79	0/0/0	-
Peeples	87	1/2/0=3	3%
Wolihin	87	0/0/0=0	-
Stewart's Division	**4,298**	**216/1,484/32=1,732**	**40%**
Foules Company	35	1/0/1=2	6%
Bate's Brigade	**1,211**	**65/515/11=591**	**49%**
Staff		0/1/0=1	
58 Alabama	287	21/128/0=149	52%
37 Georgia	425	19/168/7=194	46%[58]
4 Georgia Bn. SS	92	2/36/0=38	41%
15+37 Tennessee	230	15/102/4=121	53%
20 Tennessee	183	8/80/0=88	48%[59]
Brown's Brigade	**1,340**	**57/419/4=480**	**36%**
18 Tennessee	362	20/114/1=135	37%
26 Tennessee	239	12/79/1=92	38%[60]
32 Tennessee	341	9/112/2=123	36%[61]
45 Tennessee	254	13/85/0=98	39%
23 Tennessee Bn.	144	3/29/0=32	22%
Clayton's Brigade	**1,446**	**90/528/16=634**	**44%**
Staff		0/2/0=2	
18 Alabama	527	37/250/8=295	56%
36 Alabama	429	16/133/3=152	35%
38 Alabama	490	37/143/5=185	38%

Formation	Strength	Losses K/W/M=T	Percent
Artillery/Stewart	**260**	**3/22/0=25**	**10%**
Humphreys	89	1/3/0=4	4%
Dawson	65	1/6/0=7	11%
Eufala	106	1/13/0=14	13%
Reserve Artillery	**277**	**3/4/0=7**	**3%**
Baxter	53	0/0/0=0	0%
Darden	60	1/2/0=3	5%
Kolb	86	2/1/0=3	3%
Mecants	78	0/1/0=1	1%

Longstreet's Corps
1st Corps, Army of Northern Virginia

Formation	Strength	Losses K/W/M=T	Percent
1st Corps, ANV	**11,056**	**535/2,853/231=3,619**	**33%**
A, 1 La Cav	30	0/0/0=0	0%[62]
E/C, 1 La Cav	30	0/0/0=0	0%[63]
Johnson's Division	**3,755**	**190/1,076/167=1,433**	**38%**
Fulton's Brigade	**874**	**28/271/98=397**	**45%**
17 Tennessee	249	0/61/69=130	52%
23 Tennessee	186	8/77/13=98	53%
25 Tennessee	145	10/45/1=56	39%
44 Tennessee	294	10/88/15=113	38%
Gregg's Brigade	**1,419**	**110/465/15=590**	**42%**
3 Tennessee	274	22/87/6=115	42%[64]
10 Tennessee	190	24/86/4=114	60%[65]
30 Tennessee	185	21/73/3=97	52%[66]
41 Tennessee	325	11/67/1=79	24%[67]
50 Tennessee	186	9/46/0=55	30%[68]
1 Tennessee Bn.	82	13/24/1=38	46%[69]
7 Texas	177	10/82/0=92	52%[70]
McNair's Brigade	**1,207**	**51/322/54=427**	**35%**
Staff		0/2/0=2	
1 Ark MR	273	14/76/16=106	39%
2 Ark MR	139	6/43/3=52	37%
25 Arkansas	133	7/51/3=61	46%
4+31+4 Bn. Ark	415	14/60/29=103	25%
39 North Carolina	247	10/90/3=103	42%

Formation	Strength	Losses K/W/M=T	Percent
Artillery/Johnson	**255**	**1/18/0=19**	**7%**
Bledsoe	84	1/1/0=2	2%
Culpepper	84	0/14/0=14	17%
Everett	87	0/3/0=3	3%
Law's Division	**3,957**	**209/1247/63=1,519**	**38%**
Benning's Brigade	**1,200**	**60/424/8=492**	**41%**[71]
Staff		0/2/0=2	--[72]
2 Georgia	427	16/101/0=117	27%[73]
15 Georgia	285	7/75/0=82	29%[74]
17 Georgia	250	9/132/8=149	60%[75]
20 Georgia	238	28/114/0=142	60%[76]
Robertson's Brigade	**1,300**	**90/463/38=591**	**45%**[77]
3 Arkansas	380	32/150/9=191	50%[78]
1 Texas	409	19/124/12=155	38%[79]
4 Texas	264	26/102/5=133	50%[80]
5 Texas	247	13/87/12=112	45%[81]
Sheffield's Brigade	**1,457**	**59/360/17=436**	**30%**[82]
4 Alabama	249	12/45/1=58	23%[83]
15 Alabama	373	11/121/0=132	35%[84]
44 Alabama	276	10/71/8=89	32%
47 Alabama	283	7/56/7=70	25%
48 Alabama	276	19/67/1=87	32%
Kershaw's Division	**2,817**	**134/524/1=659**	**23%**
Humphreys' Brigade	**1,226**	**21/134/0=155**	**13%**
13 Mississippi	300	1/7/0=8	3%[85]
17 Mississippi	338	12/76/0=88	26%[86]
18 Mississippi	260	1/8/0=9	3%[87]
21 Mississippi	328	7/43/0=50	15%[88]
Kershaw's Brigade	**1,596**	**113/390/1=504**	**32%**[89]
2 South Carolina	230	26/75/0=101	44%[90]
3 South Carolina	343	51/115/0=166	48%[91]
7 South Carolina	283	10/76/1=87	31%[92]
8 South Carolina	215	5/23/0=28	13%[93]
15 South Carolina	343	14/57/0=71	21%[94]
3 South Carolina Bn.	182	7/44/0=51	28%[95]

Formation	Strength	Losses K/W/M=T	Percent
Reserve Artillery	**462**	**2/6/0=8**	**2%**
Barret's Battery	94	0/0/0=0	0%
Le Gardeur's Battery	87	0/0/0=0	0%
Havis' Battery	100	1/1/0=2	2%
Lumsden's Battery	90	1/1/0=2	2%
Massenberg's Battery	91	0/4/0=4	4%
Forrest's Cavalry Corps			
Forrest's Cav Corps	**6,553**	**59/234/24/37=354**	**?%[96]**
Jackson's Company	67		
Armstrong's Division	**3,486**		
Bradley's Company	47		
Wheeler's Brigade	**1,221**		
E, 6th Tennessee Cav	30		
3 Arkansas Cav	300	2/2/0=4[97]	
2 Kentucky Cav	427[98]		
6 Tennessee Cav	300		
18 Tennessee Cav Bn.	164		
Dibrell's Brigade	**2,218**	**18/63/6=87**	**4%[99]**
4 Tennessee Cav	200	3/22/3=28	14%[100]
8 Tennessee Cav	300	4/11/0=15	5%[101]
9 Tennessee Cav	350	1/7/0=8	2%[102]
10 Tennessee Cav	474	3/6/2=11	2%[103]
11 Tennessee Cav	474	3/3/1=7	1%[104]
Shaw's Battalion	284	4/3/0=7	2%[105]
Huggins Battery	65	0/11/0=11	17%[106]
Morton's Battery	71		
Pegram's Division	**3,000**		**263 in units reported**
Davidson's Brigade	**1,900**		**163 in units reported**
1 Georgia Cav	295		
6 Georgia Cav	400	12/72/0=84[107]	21%
6 North Carolina Cav	520	5/6/18=29[108]	6%
10 Confederate Cav	250	2/11/0=13[109]	5%
Rucker's Legion	385	37 total[110]	10%
Huwald's Battery	50		

Formation	Strength	Losses K/W/M=T	Percent
Scott's Brigade	**1,100**	**20/80/0=100**	**9%**
Morgan's Det.	240	3/7/0=10[111]	4%
1 Louisiana Cav	210	10/42/0=52[112]	25%
2 Tennessee Cav	300	5/14/0=19	6%
5 Tennessee Cav	300	2/14/0=16	5%
Robinson's Battery	50	0/3/0=3	6%

Wheeler's Cavalry Corps

Formation	Strength	Losses K/W/M=T	Percent
Wheeler's Corps	**6,870**		**76 total in units reported[113]**
Wharton's Division	**4,439**		
B, 8 Texas Cav	41		
Crew's Brigade	**2,125**		
Malone's Regiment	502		
2 Georgia Cav	600		
3 Georgia Cav	418	2/16/16=34[114]	
4 Georgia Cav	605		
Harrison's Brigade	**2,273**		
3 Confederate Cav	550		
3 Kentucky Cav	418		
4 Tennessee Cav	418	40 total[115]	
8 Texas Cav	412		
11 Texas Cav	398		
White's Battery	77		
Martin's Division	**2,431**		
A 3 Alabama Cav	34		
Morgan's Brigade	**1,533**		
1 Alabama Cav	418		
3 Alabama Cav	279		
51 Alabama Cav	418		
8 Confederate Cav	418		
Russell's Brigade	**864**		
4 Alabama Cav	418		
1 Confederate Cav	418		
Wiggins Battery	28		

Endnotes

1. All losses from the 24th and 33rd Tennessee were counted as wounded, though these certainly included killed and perhaps missing as well, which is why the divisional totals for those categories are off. The number of killed is certainly higher.

2. An additional 2/8/0=10 were suffered on September 22, 1863.

3. 6/32/0=38, *Memphis Daily Appeal*, Sept 28, 1863, 8/32/0=40, Unit file, Tennessee State Library and Archives.

4. *Memphis Daily Appeal*, Sept 28, 1863.

5. *Tennesseans in the Civil War*, vol. 1, 241.

6. *Memphis Daily Appeal*, Oct 8, 1863.

7. Calculation, subtracting known losses from other units.

8. *Memphis Daily Appeal*, Oct. 6, 1863.

9. *Memphis Daily Appeal*, Oct. 6, 1863.

10. Some losses from Manigault's Brigade, not broken down by category, were included in the wounded total. There should be more killed and less wounded.

11. Calculation, subtracting all known losses from brigade total given in the *OR*.

12. *Huntsville Daily Confederate*, October 3, 1863.

13. Manigault, 102. Manigault does not give a standard breakdown of losses in his memoir, but instead listed the killed and seriously wounded together, at 540; the slightly wounded as 69, and the captured, 47. Jerome P. Wilson Papers, Emory University, lists a much lower overall figure, of 66/426/47=539.

14 Calculation, subtracting known losses from brigade total, above.

15. E. John Ellis Letters, LSU, says losses were "110 out of 293."

16. *Memphis Daily Appeal*, Oct. 6, 1863, lists 13 killed and 107 wounded, no missing; but the regimental report indicates that total losses were 146. *OR* 30, pt. 2, 209.

17. The *Memphis Daily Appeal*, October 6, 1863, shows 1/32/0=33.

18. In his report, Cleburne recorded 204/1539/6 = 1749, or 101 less casualties than recorded here. I have chosen to use the brigade and regimental reports wherever possible, which often produce higher numbers. Cleburne does not explain the discrepancy, nor are the consolidated brigade loss returns shown in the *OR*. It is clear from the context that Cleburne was not counting the artillery or escort in his totals for either engaged strengths or losses, but these formations only account for 17 casualties. There are detailed regimental losses for all but one regiment and two small battalions of Cleburne's command. There are also firm numbers for two of the three brigades, and a solid estimate for the remaining brigade. I feel reasonably certain that the number given here is closer to accurate for the losses in the division that that which Cleburne provided.

19. In Cleburne's report, he notes that one private from the escort was wounded in the hand.

20. Polk's report does not provide a detailed breakdown, but instead gives loss estimates for three discrete actions: the night of the 19th, where he estimated the loss at "not over 60 men killed and wounded"; the morning of the 20th, where he reported "350 killed and wounded"; and the afternoon of the 20th, where he reported a loss of "nearly 200 men." *OR* 30, pt. 2, 176-178. Since there are reported losses of all but one regiment in the brigade, these figures provide a handy cross-check for Polk's estimates. Since a total of each category is impossible, known subtotals are given where it is possible, with the remaining 118 losses added on at the end. Proportionally, those 118 would break down to 10/106/2.

21. The regimental report does not give a total loss, only reporting 25 men killed and wounded in the night engagement of the 19th. Losses were clearly much heavier on September 20. As noted above, in Polk's report the total estimated brigade loss is 610 men. Subtracting the known losses of the other regiments leaves 118 casualties unrecorded for the 3rd+5th Confederate. This percentage of loss is consistent with most of the other regiments in the brigade. Finally, killed and missing were extrapolated by comparing the reported killed and missing from the divisional report to the other known units in the brigade. Since there are still some discrepancies between the divisional and the brigade totals, these figures can only be an estimate.

22. *Memphis Daily Appeal*, Oct. 9, 1863.

23. 261 killed and wounded, 'with a few missing' *Huntsville Daily Confederate*, October 3, 1863.

24. *Columbus Daily Sun*, Sept. 29, 1863, documents 10 killed and mortally wounded, 40 wounded, and 6 missing - a total of 56 casualties. Several companies show few or no losses, however, and are likely incomplete. Subtracting the other unit losses from the reported brigade losses produces this figure instead.

25. *Memphis Daily Appeal*, Oct. 9, 1863.

26. *Charleston Mercury*, October 2, 1863.

27. Ector's brigade reported a total of 536 losses in the *OR* 30, pt. 2, 243. However, the numbers only add up to 436, and no detailed reports from the regiments survive. Given the detail in the newspaper accounts, including names, I have elected to rely on those figures, since they were reported to the paper by the Brigade Adjutant.

28. *Mobile Daily Advertiser*, October 10, 1863.

29. *Mobile Daily Advertiser*, October 10, 1863.

30. *Mobile Daily Advertiser*, October 10, 1863.

31. *Mobile Daily Advertiser*, October 10, 1863.

32. *Mobile Daily Advertiser*, October 10, 1863.

33. *Mobile Daily Advertiser*, October 10, 1863. Zachariah Bailey Letter, Navarro College, October 11th, 1863, reports that of 196 engaged, only 76 were present on Sunday night, but "many have since returned." Bailey reports a final casualty total of 86. This suggests that another 34 men were lightly wounded and not reported, or stragglers.

34. *Mobile Daily Advertiser*, October 10, 1863.

35. *Savannah Daily Morning News*, September 29, 1863.

36. Numbers provided by Ranger Lee White, CCNMP.

37. Regimental file, CCNMP.

38. Numbers provided by Ranger Lee White, CCNMP.

39. No regimental report survives, and I have found no newspaper account. These figures were derived by subtracting all other losses from the brigade total found in *OR* 30, pt. 2, 243. Two oddities become obvious when doing so - the high ratio of killed to wounded, and the very high number of missing. Clearly a large number of the missing were also wounded, likely captured when Wilson's Brigade was flanked on the 19th. On October 8, the survivors of the battalion numbered "about one hundred." See unidentified soldier's diary, Hill Library, LSU.

40. Lee White, CCNMP.

41. Casualties were determined by subtracting the known regimental losses from the brigade total given in Liddell's report, and then apportioned on a percentage basis to the three unreported regiments.

42. Casualties were determined by subtracting the known regimental losses from the brigade total given in Liddell's report, and then apportioned on a percentage basis to the three unreported regiments.

43. Casualties were determined by subtracting the known regimental losses from the brigade total given in Liddell's report, and then apportioned on a percentage basis to the three unreported regiments.

44. Losses shown as 6/16/1=23 in Fowler battery file, CCNMP. See also Jerome Wilson Papers, Emory University, Atlanta. In the *OR*, Fowler reports 6/17/1=24, *OR* 30, pt. 2, 287.

45. Lee White, CCNMP.

46. *Abingdon Virginian*, October 9, 1863, gives the figure as 202/1,080/96 = 1,367 (note, the article is in error, the correct total is 1,378.) The discrepancy is not explained, but of the 96 missing, the correspondent goes on to report that 6 have returned to the regiment and 14 were killed or wounded, making in all, 1,347 total losses.

47. The loss figures shown here for all units in the brigade are taken from the Wickliffe-Preston Papers, University of Kentucky. Most losses in the statement are very close to the losses given in the OR regimental reports, except as noted below. The Brigade losses are given as 90 killed, 576 wounded, and 2 missing, 668 total. *OR* 30, pt. 2, 291. The individual losses, however, add up to considerably higher, which is reflected in the numbers shown above. *The Mobile Daily Register*, October 10, 1863, shows a total brigade loss of 735, but the casualty lists for three battalions of Hilliard's Legion also shown in that newspaper instead confirm the totals in the regimental reports.

48. The *OR* shows 16/83/0=99.

49. The *OR* shows 24/144/0=168.

50. The *OR* shows 16/75/0=91.

51. The *OR* shows 5/45/0=50.

52. The *OR* shows 15/87/0=102.

53. The *OR* shows 16/184/0=200. *Confederate Veteran*, vol. XXII, no. 1 (January, 1914), 37; shows 47 killed and 155 wounded, total 202.

54. The *OR* report shows only 66/241/3=310. I have chosen to use the report found in the Wickliffe-Preston Papers, because it shows more detail on individual regimental losses.

55. Report of Casualties, Wickliffe-Preston Papers, University of Kentucky. Ranger Lee White of the CCNMP, and regimental website each show 161 casualties. The G. D. Gouge Letter of September 29, 1863, in the 48th North Carolina file, CCNMP, shows 37/132/0=169.

56. Report of Casualties, Wickliffe-Preston Papers, University of Kentucky.

57. All losses taken from Report of Casualties, Trigg's Brigade, Wickliffe-Preston Papers.

58. 142 of these were suffered on September 19. *Huntsville Daily Confederate*, Sept 22, 1863.

59. 140 engaged, 98 killed and wounded, according to Dr. W. J. McMurray, "The Gap of Death at Chickamauga," *Confederate Veteran*, vol. II, no. 11 (November 1894), 329-330.

60. In a letter home, reprinted in Military Images Magazine, Maj. Saffell gives his numbers as 332 engaged and 117 lost, for a 35% loss rate.

61. The *Chattanooga Daily Rebel*, October 8, 1863, reports 5/156/0=161, or 47%. Many of the wounded listed there, however, are noted as only slightly wounded.

62. The 1st Louisiana Cavalry lost 10/42/0= 52 for the battle. It is not clear if these losses include casualties suffered by the escorts serving with Hood and Longstreet.

63. See note above.

64. Lee White, CCNMP.

65. Lee White, CCNMP.

66. Lee White, CCNMP.

67. *Memphis Daily Appeal*, October 1, 1863.

68. *Memphis Daily Appeal*, October 1, 1863.

69. Lee White, CCNMP.

70. Lee White, CCNMP.

71. *OR* 30, pt. 2, 291, shows 488 losses.

72. *Memphis Daily Appeal*, September 25, 1863.

73. *Columbus Daily Sun*, September 29, 1863.

74. *Memphis Daily Appeal*, Sept 25, 1863. Dameron, *Fifteenth Georgia*, 61, shows only 12 killed and 19 wounded for 31 losses total. No source is cited for these figures.

75. *Columbus Daily Sun*, Sept 26, 1863. Alexander Papers shows 24/100/0=124.

76. Lee White, CCNMP. Alexander Papers show 28/114/2=144.

77. *OR* 30, pt. 2, 291, shows 570 losses.

78. CCNMP files show a loss of 25/120/12=157.

79. *Memphis Daily Appeal*, Sept 28, 1863.

80. *Memphis Daily Appeal*, Sept 28, 1863.

81. *Memphis Daily Appeal*, Sept 28, 1863.

82. All losses taken from Laine and Penny, *Law's Alabama Brigade*, 370. *OR* 30, pt. 2, 291, shows 390 losses. Note different figures for the 4th and 15th Alabama, below.

83. Alexander Papers, Museum of the Confederacy, shows 14/54/6=74.

84. Alexander Papers, Museum of the Confederacy, shows 19/173/2=194.

85. *Memphis Daily Appeal*, September 28, 1863.

86. *Memphis Daily Appeal*, September 28, 1863. Alexander papers shows 12/88/0=100.

87. *Memphis Daily Appeal*, September 28, 1863. Alexander Papers shows 3/10/0=13.

88. *Memphis Daily Appeal*, September 28, 1863. Alexander Papers shows only 8/22/3=33.

89. Alexander papers show 65/424/0=489.

90. The Reginald Screvin Diary, South Carolina Historical Society, also gives 101 losses.

91. Wycoff, *Third South Carolina*, 142.

92. *Charleston Mercury*, October 2, 1863.

93. *Charleston Mercury*, October 2, 1863.

94. Losses were derived by subtracting the other regimental casualties from the brigade totals, to arive at the regiment's total losses. Within the brigade, the ratio of killed to wounded is 1 in 5, which matches the known losses in company A; 2 killed and 8 wounded.

95. *Charleston Mercury*, October 2, 1863.

96. Alexander, *Military Memoirs of a Confederate*, 464, gives the Confederate cavalry a total of 250 casualties, provides no details. His figure includes both Forrest and Wheeler, and is much too low. The known casualties given here, from only 17 of 34 regiments reported, amount to 430. Total Confederate cavalry losses are probably between somewhere 800 and 1000 men.

97. Calvin L Collier, *The War Child's Children* (Pioneer Press, 1965), 67.

98. One company commander reported that he lost 1/3 of his command. Given Campbell Papers, UNC.

99. Lindsley, *Military Annals of Tennessee*, vol. 2, 660. Alternatively, the *Memphis Daily Appeal*, October 9, 1863, reports 10/40/0=50, from the Brigade Adjutant's report, but with no figures reported for Shaw' Battalion or the artillery. Michael Cotten, *The Williamson County Cavalry: A History of Company F, Fourth Tennessee Cavalry Regiment, CS*, (n.p., 1994), 134; repeats the figures found in *Military Annals*, of 18/63/6=87.

100. Lindsley, *Military Annals of Tennessee*, vol. 2, 660. *Memphis Daily Appeal*, October 9, 1863, shows 2/16/0=18. Cotten, *Williamson County Cavalry*, 134, also shows 3/22/3 = 28.

101. Lindsley, *Military Annals of Tennessee*, vol. 2, 660. *Memphis Daily Appeal*, October 9, 1863 shows 3/11/0=14.

102. Lindsley, *Military Annals of Tennessee*, vol. 2, 660. *Memphis Daily Appeal*, October 9, 1863 shows 0/18/0=8.

103. Lindsley, *Military Annals of Tennessee*, vol. 2, 660. *Memphis Daily Appeal*, October 9, 1863 shows 3/3/0=6.

104. Lindsley, *Military Annals of Tennessee*, vol. 2, 660. *Memphis Daily Appeal*, October 9, 1863 shows 2/2/0=4.

105. Lindsley, *Military Annals of Tennessee*, vol. 2, 660.

106. Lindsley, *Military Annals of Tennessee*, vol. 2, 660.

107. Minnich manuscript, 6th Georgia Cavalry file, CCNMP. Minnich details 9 killed and 71 wounded on September 19th, and also includes some losses - unspecified - from the action on September 21st.

108. Jeffrey C Weaver, *The 5th and 7th Battalions North Carolina Cavalry*, 133. I feel that this list is incomplete.

109. *Columbus Daily Sun*, Sept ember 29, 1863.

110. Leroy Moncure Nutt Papers, Southern Historical Collection, University of North Carolina, Chapel Hill, NC. Nutt says only that the Legion had "37 killed and wounded." No further details are given, nor are any missing noted.

111. The 1st Kentucky Cavalry shows 1 man killed at Chickamauga. Since the only portion of the 1st that was present at that battle was in Morgan's detachment, that loss is incorporated here. Some of the sources for Morgan's cavalry present wildly inflated figures. Thomas F. Berry, *Four Years with Morgan and Forrest* (Harlow, Ratliff and Company, 1914), 235, 244; claims that the detachment lost 4/11/0=15 on September 18, and a staggering "362 killed or wounded" out of a claimed "570" engaged, or "about two thirds of the whole number." These figures are not supported by any other source.

112. Howell Carter, *A Cavalryman's Reminiscences of the Civil War*, 92.

113. See note for Forrest's Cavalry, above. There are almost no loss reports from Wheeler's Corps.

114. Clipping from the *Columbus Daily Enquirer*, 3rd Georgia cavalry file, CCNMP, and from Dr. Keith Bohannon.

115. "About 40," George B. Guild Scrapbook, 4th Tennessee Report, TSLA.

Polk's Corps
October 22, 1863 Return

In October, General Bragg reorganized the Army of Tennessee. Leonidas Polk's Corps was comprised of Cheatham's, Hindman's, and Buckner's (formerly Preston's) divisions, as well as Walthall's brigade from the Reserve Corps. All of these commands reported their strength for every regiment, battalion, and battery on October 22, 1863. Coming one month after the battle of Chickamauga, but before the next major action (battles for Chattanooga), these returns allow a comparison between the known engaged Chickamauga strengths for 43 separate regiments and battalions, and their subsequent PFD numbers one month after the battle.

Some explanation is in order. Wherever possible, the September 18 strengths are the "aggregate effective," counting officers and men. Units where such numbers were not available were omitted from this sample.

Next, the loss column shows two figures: killed or mortally wounded (and hence permanent losses) / and the total loss suffered.

The October 22 return specifies three numbers for each command: "effective present," "aggregate present," and "total present," The "effective present" are most likely those men who are ready for combat, including officers. The "total present" probably includes all men with their commands, including some sick and (perhaps) some of the lightly wounded. I have presented both the "effectives" and the "total present" here for comparison's sake; those numbers can and do vary significantly.

In theory, the "aggregate present" figures should make for a better comparison than the "effectives present" figures, but in going through these returns, I noted some additional discrepancies, including a number of units that reported the same number for each category, which led me to believe the "effectives" number already included both officers and men.

Finally, for each unit I have expressed the October 22 "effectives present" and "total present" numbers as a percentage of the September 18 engaged strength in order to give some idea of how much Confederate combat strength had recovered (or not) after Chickamauga.

Unit	Sept 18 Engaged Strength	Sept 18-20 Losses Killed/Total	October 22 Eff/Total Present	Oct 22 % of Sept 18 Strength
Overall				72%/94%
Cheatham's Division				
Jackson's Brigade				67%/100%
2 Bn., 1 Conf.	194	10/83	100/181	52%/93%
2 GA SS Bn.	108	3/30	75/102	69%/94%
5 GA	353	27/194	166/276	47%/78%
5 Miss	252	4/75	187/310	74%/123%
8 Miss	404	10/94	355/451	88%/112%
Maney's Brigade				61%/80%
1+27 Tenn	703	14/89	402/476	57%/68%
4 Tenn	179	12/75	116/168	65%/94%
6+9 Tenn	368	unknown	235/340	64%/92%
24 Tenn SS	43	0/22	30/50	70%/116%
Strahl's Brigade				85%/103%
19 Tenn	266	8/94	227/273	85%/103%
Wright's Brigade				78%/98%
8 Tenn	285	unknown	258/286	91%/100%
16 Tenn	266	1/68	226/270	85%/102%
28 Tenn	279	15/85	250/316	90%/113%
38 Tenn	278	unknown	157/233	56/84
51+52 Tenn	255	17/115	178/235	70%/92%

Unit	Sept 18 Engaged Strength	Sept 18-20 Losses Killed/Total	October 22 Eff/Total Present	Oct 22 % of Sept 18 Strength
Hindman's Division				
Anderson's Brigade				**78%/95%**
7 Miss	291	13/75	255/293	88%/101%
9 Miss	355	9/93	281/328	79%/92%
10 Miss	311	unknown	208/301	67%/97%
41 Miss	502	24/197	416/480	83%/96%
44 Miss	272	?/81	187/250	69%/92%
9 Miss Bn	134	unknown	101/120	75%/90%
Deas' Brigade				**68%/81%**
19 Alabama	515	34/204	384/435	75%/84%
22 Alabama	371	15/205	235/280	63%/75%
25 Alabama	330	15/112	281/321	85%/97%
39 Alabama	340	14/96	276/334	81%/98%
50 Alabama	500	16/105	228/287	46%/57%
17 Alabama SS	76	1/12	54/60	71%/79%
Manigault				**96%/121%**
24 Alabama	381	22/116	272/355	71%/93%
34 Alabama	329	unknown	408/506	124%/154%
Buckner's Division				
Gracie's Brigade				**69%/94%**
43 Alabama	400	16/99	245/330	61%/82%
1 Bn	260	24/168	116/143	45%/55%
2 Bn	230	16/91	184/240	80%/104%
3 Bn	229	4/46	197/316	86%/139%
4 Bn	205	23/102	133/180	65%/88%
63 Tenn	402	16/200	323/421	80%/104%
Kelly				**77%/95%**
65 GA	251	0/4	218/272	87%/108%
5 Kentucky	377	15/91	183/218	49%/58%
58 NC	322	half	281/326	87%/101%
63 VA	196	one third	198/272	101%/138%

Unit	Sept 18 Engaged Strength	Sept 18-20 Losses Killed/Total	October 22 Eff/Total Present	Oct 22 % of Sept 18 Strength
Trigg				
No units reported for engaged strengths.				
Walthall's Brigade				79%/101%
24 Miss	428	10/132	328/416	77%/97%
27 Miss	362	10/117	337/408	93%/113%
29+30 Miss	730	313	502/648	69%/92%
34 Miss	307	15/125	284/381	93%/124%

Bibliography

The goal of this bibliography is to support the three volumes of *The Chickamauga Campaign* and establish a broad bibliographic resource so interested parties can utilize it. I hope this is similar to Dr. Richard A. Sauers's masterful *The Gettysburg Campaign, June 3-August 1, 1863: A Comprehensive, Selectively Annotated Bibliography* (Butternut & Blue, 2004). The major difference is that I have not annotated each entry because of space limitations.

This bibliography is intended to be as far-reaching as possible, organized (hopefully) for ease of use. Some explanation is required. There is some duplication of sources, where items can be found in multiple archives, or where archival material has also been published. Additionally, I have included the regimental affiliation of the material, wherever possible, if the title of citation does not already make that connection obvious. Many readers have a particular regimental or brigade interest, and this feature should help them isolate materials specific to their subject matter.

The large number of articles found in the *National Tribune, Confederate Veteran, Military Order of the Loyal Legion of the United States (MOLLUS Papers)* and similar collections of veteran reminiscences demand separate sections, for clarity's sake.

Newspapers, other than those listed above, are handled in one of two ways. For reasons of space, period newspapers (1863-1864) are listed only by title and location. Individual articles are not itemized, except in the footnotes. Postwar articles are listed in the "Articles" section, alphabetically by author.

Despite the very large number of archival holdings and publications listed here, I am under no illusion that this is a complete list. As of this writing I am still discovering related material, a trend which I expect will continue even after publication.

Sources marked with an * include transcriptions prepared by Dr. William Glenn Robertson while he worked at the Combat Studies Institute, Fort Leavenworth, Kansas.

Internet Sources

Sadly, internet links come and go. My research spans fifteen years, and now many of these links are no longer active. Early on, I did not record the date when I accessed each site, which explains why some citations give only the year. In each case, I printed off copies of the material in question, all of which remain in my collection.

First Battalion Georgia Sharpshooters—Regimental History. http://members.tripod.com /k_thurman/1st_battalion_georgia_sharpshoot.htm, accessed 11/13/2015.

Civil War Career of Henry Harrison Adney, (36th Ohio Infantry) http://worldconnect.rootsweb.ancestry.com/cgi-in/igm.cgi?op=GET&db=thezubers&id=I12495, accessed 5/24/12..

Augustus Cabot Abernathy Letters (19th/24th Arkansas Infantry) http://freepages.Genealogy.rootsweb.ancestry.com/~bandy/kestletters.html, accessed 11/13/2015.

The Civil War Letters of Gershom M. and Huldah L. Barber (Ohio Sharpshooters) http:// 285bc.com/285bc/tillotsons/GM_1.htm, accessed 1/04/2016.

George D. Barnett Letters, (25th Illinois Infantry) http://www.douglascountyil.com/_images/1_CW_MORE_LETTERS.pdf Accessed 9/04/2011.

John Beals Letter (101st Indiana Infantry) http://101stindiana.tripod.com/id4.html, accessed 2/15/2010.

Daniel A. Bellware, "Colonel Leon Von Zinken," online essay, 2006, http://cvacwrt.tripod.Com/zinken.html, accessed 10/2/2011.

John F. Beasley Autobiography, 3rd Georgia Cavalry website, accessed 2008.

Pelatiah Bond Letters (4th Indiana Cavalry) http://www.genealogy105.com/letterindex.html accessed 11/13/2015.

C. C. Bowen Letter, (6th Ohio Infantry) from Ironton *Register*, March 17, 1887 http:// soldierstudies.org, accessed 03/13/2011.

Edward Ebenezer Brewer Diary (30th Georgia Infantry) http://www.authentic-campaigner.com/forum/showthread.php?7248-Diary-of-Edward-Brewer-30th-Ga-Inf, accessed 11/13/2015.

James I. Brewer Letters (34th Mississippi Infantry) http://www.rootsweb.ancestry.com/ ~mscivilw/brewerletters.htm, accessed 8/16/2013.

Samuel Broughton Memoir and Journal (21st Illinois Infantry) http://www.rootsweb. Com/~ilcivilw/scrapbk/broughtjourn.html, accessed 9/4/2011.

C. E. Brown Letter (Company H, 2nd Ohio Infantry) transcript from Ebay Auction, accessed 11/16/2012. Copy in author's collection.

Life History of W. C. Brown (23rd Tennessee Infantry Battalion) http://home.flash.net/ ~coley/WCBrown.html, accessed 2009.

James Edward Caldwell, *Recollections Of Events Of The Civil War, 3rd South Carolina Infantry,* http://gen.1starnet.com/civilwar/caldwelj.htm. Accessed 11/03/2013.

Francis M. Carlisle Autobiography, 42nd Indiana Infantry, http://freepages.history.rootsweb.ancestry.com/~indiana42nd/fcarlisleauto.htm, accessed 8/14/2013.

Dean R. Chester letter extracts, Abraham Lincoln Papers at the Library of Congress, digital collections (88th Illinois) http://memory.loc.gov/ammem/alhtml/alhome.html, accessed 11/13/2015.

Chickamauga campaign roadside markers, "The Xzanders G. McFarland House and McFarland Gap," http://chickamaugacampaign.org/pdfs/TheXzanders.pdf, accessed 2/18/12.

Civil War Generals from West Point, http://sunsite.utk.edu/civil-war/wpclasses.html, accessed 8/14/2013.

Charles T. Clark letter to Ezra Carmen, "Dear Sir," February 12, 1909 (125th Ohio Infantry) http://home.earthlink.net/~nhaldane/ctc-letter.html, accessed 10/22/2012.

William M. Cockrum Reminiscences, *Oakland City Indiana Journal*, Sept. 10, 1894, http://freepages.history.rootsweb.ancestry.com/~indiana42nd/Chickamauga_Cockrum_Article.htm, accessed 9/7/2011.

Thomas Cobb Letters (10th Indiana Infantry) www.indianainthecivilwar.com/ letters/10th/cobb.htm, accessed 2009.

Charles D. Cruft Biography, Civil War Indiana Website, http://civilwarindiana.com /biographies/cruft_charles_d.html, accessed 11/3/2012.

William Crutchfield Biography, Hamilton County Genealogical Society Website, http://www.hctgs.org/Biographies/crutchfield_william.htm, accessed 10/29/2012.

"Details of Col. Davis's resignation," Indiana Civil War Message Board, http:// www.history-sites.net/cgi-bin/bbs62x/incwmb/webbbs_config.pl?md=read;id=796, accessed 12/11/2011.

Seaborn Dominey Letters, M 1st Texas, Texas in the Civil War Message board. http://history-sites.com/cgi-bin/boards/txcwmb/index.cgi?read=1480, accessed 2009.

Henry Figures to "Dear Mother," September 26th, 1863, (4th Alabama Infantry) http://www.mqamericana.com/4th_AL_Hds_Brig_Chick_btieh.html, accessed 9/19/2011.

Civil War consolidated service records, Fold3 Website, https://www.fold3.com/.

Melville Cox Follett Diary, E-History online. (Illinois regiment, unknown) https://ehistory. Osu.edu/exhibitions/letters/follett_melville/default, accessed 11/15/2015.

History of Freedom's Champion, newspaper, http://www.kshs.org/p/kansas-territorial- newspapers/13875, accessed 10/13/2013.

Alfred D. French Memoirs, (89th Illinois Infantry) http://www.rootsweb.com/ ~ilcivilw/scrapbk/frenchmemoirs.html, accessed 2008.

John Harris Letter, Tennessee Civil War Sourcebook, http://tennessee.civilwarsourcebook.com/collection.pdf/1863-09/1863-09-Article-323-Page412.pdf, accessed 5/28/2011.

Robert Box Helm Diary, (79th Illinois Infantry) http://www.douglascountyil.com/images/ 1_CW_DIARIES_AND_LETTERS.pdf.

Michael Hileman Memoir, (96th Illinois Infantry) http://www.rootsweb.com/~usgenweb /sd/buffalo/hileman.html, accessed 3/11/2010.

William Henry Huntzinger diary, (79th Indiana Infantry) http://www.lafavre.us/ huntzinger/huntzinger.htm, accessed 11/15/2015, (see also CCNMP files).

William G. Kendrick letter, (Croxton Staff) http://www.bivouacbooks.com/bbv7i2s2.htm, accessed 03/13/2011.

Civil War Diary of Private Jesse Leeper, (Co. I, 4th Indiana Cavalry) http://www.nps.gov/stri/historyculture/upload/Leeper_Jesse_Diary.pdf, accessed 11/15/2015.

Jim R. Martin Letter, (22nd Alabama Regiment) http://geocities.com/~bobjones/ 22nd_docs.htm, accessed 9/4/2011.

Sergeant Jesse McClave diary, (89th Ohio Infantry) http://www.89thohio.com/Mcclave/ mcclave02.htm, accessed 5/19/2012.

Duncan C. Milner recollections, (98th Ohio Infantry) http://www.drwilliams.org/iDoc/ index.htm?url=http://www.drwilliams.org/iDoc/Web-50.htm—accessed 3/15/2010.

Isaac V. Moore diary, (37th Georgia Infantry) http://www.knoxscv.org/csa.htm—accessed 2/15/2010.

Charles Morfoot letter, (101st Ohio Infantry) http://www.mqamericana.com/ 101st_OH_Vol_Chickamauga.html, accessed 4/18/2010.

John G. Munsell letters, (110th Illinois Infantry) http://www.griffincunningham.net/ ldmunselle/LDMpg7aJohnG.htm, accessed 11/15/2015.

William H. Nichols memoir, (Morgan's Cavalry) from the *Honolulu Advertiser*, September 22, 1930. http://rootsweb.com/~kypendle/nichols.html, accessed 2009.

John L. McBride letters, (51st Illinois Infantry) http://51stillinois.org/mcbrideletters.html, accessed 11/15/2015.

Online transcript of letter describing the battle of Chickamauga, September 23, 1863, Samuel Patton letters, (M, 1st Illinois Light Artillery) Cowan's Historical auctions, Lot 259, November 20, 2012, http://cowanauctions.com/auctions/item.aspx?Itemid=3852; accessed 12/06/2013. Copy in author's possession. Also spelled "Patten."

Quiner Scrapbooks, (various regments) Wisconsin History Digital Civil War Collection, 102-103, http://content.wisconsinhistory.org/cdm4/document.php?CISOROOT=/quiner&CISOPTR=18427&CISOSHOW=18135&REC=4, accessed 6/20/2012.

James M. Randall diary, ehistory online, (21st Wisconsin Infantry) http://ehistory.osu.edu/osu/sources/letters/randall/index.cfm, accessed 3/4/2012.

Letter: Chaplain Lewis Raymond to Clarissa McBride, (51st Illinois Infantry) http://www.51illinois.org/mcbride_raymond.html, accessed 2/22/2010.

Lucias C. Runion diary, (92nd Illinois Infantry) http://www.rootsweb.com/~ilcivilw/scrapbk/runiondiary2.html, accessed 2009.

John Rutherford letter, (24th Ohio Infantry) http://www.geocities.com/CapitolHill/Senate/1861/higgins.html, accessed 8/16/2013.

Winfrey Scott to Mrs. E. C. Scott, Oct 3rd, 1863, (19th Louisiana Infantry) http://www.louisianacivilwar.com/2010/02/19th-louisiana-at-kelly-field.html, accessed 2/15/2010.

George A. Smith Letter, Overton County, TN Website www.tngenweb.org/tnletters/over1.htm, accessed 11/15/2015.

Oliver Smith letter (98th Ohio Infantry) http://www.mojaveweblog.com/98thOVI/index.html, accessed 3/20/2010.

Cyrus W. Spade Letter, (5th Co, Ohio Sharpshooters) http://www.geocities.com/srhackettbr/spadeoct2_1863.htm, accessed in 2009.

Strieby Family Letters, (30th Indiana Infantry) http://home.att.net/~cwletters/Pages/Wm631017P1.htm, accessed in 2009.

Marcellus Stovall description, http://www.aug.edu/~liblsc/Grant/Stovall/Stovall_description.html, accessed 9/1/2011.

Charles Swett, "A Brief Narrative of the Warren Light Artillery," http://www.Perryvillebattlefield.org/html/ms-swett-charles-cs.html, accessed 5/28/2012.

Edward Leroy Tabler diary, (51st Illinois Infantry) http://www.51illinois.org/TablerJul_Dec1863.html, accessed 2/22/2010.

Henry Clay Taylor Papers, (21st Wisconsin Infantry) http://digital.library.wisc.edu/1711.dl/WI.TaylorH03, accessed 11/15/2015.

John W. Turner letters, (84th Indiana Infantry) Indiana in the Civil War, Henry County letters. http://www.rootsweb.ancestry.com/~inhenry/letters1863.htm, accessed 11/15/2015.

James M. Walker biography, (Battery A, 1st Ohio Light Artillery) http://ohiocivilwar.com/stori/walker.html, accessed 11/15/2015.

John Weatherred Diary, (9th Tennessee Cavalry & Morgan Detachment) http://www.jackmasters.net/9tncav.html, accessed 11/15/2015.

Jeffrey Weaver, "58th North Carolina Infantry, Confederate States Army" http://nc58thinf.tripod.com/id1.html, accessed 1/31/2015.

William E. Whittsett Letter, (9th Texas Infantry) http://9thtexas.tripod.com, accessed 7/16/2008.

"Lieutenant John Wilson on Snodgrass Hill" (6th Florida Infantry) http://www.rootsweb.com/~fljackso/SnodgrassHill/SnodgrassHill.html, accessed 11/15/2015.

Wisconsin Battle Flags. http://www.wisconsinbattleflags.com/units-flags/1st-wisconsin.php, accessed 6/17/2012.

Ebay electronic collections: (transcriptions and copies of original material taken from Ebay auctions, which are no longer available online.) Copies in author's possession.

Joseph J. Baker Letter, (54th Virginia Infantry)
Frank M. Phelps Letter, (10th Wisconsin Infantry)
Unknown author, Letter of March 23, 1863, (73rd Illinois Infantry)

Manuscript Sources

Abraham Lincoln Presidential Library, Springfield (Formerly Illinois Historical Society)
William Montgomery Austin Diary (22nd Illinois Infantry)*
John Batchelor Diary (78th Illinois Infantry)
William H. Brown Diary (92nd Illinois Mounted Infantry)
Allen Buckner Papers (79th Illinois Infantry)*
Martin Van Buren Coder Letters (15th Kentucky Infantry)
Benjamin F. Campbell Diary, 36th Illinois file.
James M. Cole Letters (49th Ohio Infantry, serving with 101st Ohio?)
James T. Colehour Reminiscences (92nd Illinois Mounted Infantry)
George A. Cummins Diary (36th Illinois Infantry)*
Henry G. Davidson Letters (10th Kentucky Infantry)
George W. Dodd Papers (21st Illinois Infantry)*
Robert Everett Letters (84th Illinois Infantry)
Allan L. Fahnestock Diary (86th Illinois Infantry)
James Fenton Diary (19th Illinois Infantry)
James Frazee Letters (73rd Illinois Infantry)
John Glenn Papers (27th Illinois Infantry)*
Douglas Hapeman Diary (104th Illinois Infantry)
Jacob Harding Papers (79th Illinois Infantry)*
James C. Hogue Papers (36th Illinois Infantry)
Samuel Bateman Hood Papers (22nd Illinois Infantry)*
Theodore H. Jansen Diary (27th Illinois Infantry)
Riley M. Hoskinson Journal (73rd Illinois Infantry)*
Edward Kitchell Diary (98th Illinois Infantry)*
A. W. Lester Diary (Chicago Board of Trade Battery)*
Francis Marion Letters (31st Ohio Infantry)*
George Marsh "War Reminiscences," (104th Illinois Infantry)*
Elgin H. Martin Letters, Parkhurst T. Martin Papers (115th Illinois Infantry)
Lyman H. Needham Papers (42nd Illinois Infantry)*
David Woodman Norton Papers (General Palmer's Staff)*
Henry M. Nurse Letter (86th Illinois Infantry)
William H. Onstot Letters (27th Illinois Infantry)
John M. Palmer Papers*
William Elwood Patterson Diary (38th Illinois Infantry)*
George O. Pratt Memoir, Journal, and Letters (51st Illinois Infantry)
Samuel B. Raymond Report (51st Illinois Infantry)
Gifford S. Robinson Memoir and Diary (115th Illinois)
Levi A. Ross Diary (86th Illinois Infantry)
Benjamin T. Smith Letters and Diary (51st Illinois Infantry)
James P. Suiter Diary (84th Illinois Infantry)

Nadine Turchin Diary
Thomas Winston Letters and Papers (92nd Illinois Mounted Infantry)

Alabama Department of Archives and History
  "Army Correspondence, Letter from Tennessee," 2nd/4th Alabama Infantry Battalion File*
  George W. Athey Letters
  Thomas T. Bigbie Letters (33rd Alabama Infantry) (See also Auburn)
  Robert Lewis Bliss Letters (S. A. M. Wood Staff)*
  Brown Letters (45th Alabama Infantry)
  Robert T. Coles. "History of the 4th Regiment Alabama Volunteer Infantry, CSA" 4th Alabama file
  John F. Davenport Letter (Hilliard's Legion)
  Davis Letter (Hilliard's Legion)
  Newton N. Davis Letters, 24th Alabama File
  A. Doss Letters, 19th Alabama File.
  Benjamin R. Glover Letters (6th Florida Infantry)
  Archibald Gracie Letter (Trigg's Brigade)*
  Alexander K. Hall Letter (Holloway's Escorts, K, 3rd Ala. Cav.)
  Andrew Malone Hill Recollections, 16th Alabama File.
  Wilson P. Howell manuscript, 25th Alabama File*
  Robert Dandridge Jackson Reminiscences (51st Alabama Cavalry)
  Harvey Jones Papers
    Archibald Gracie IV Letter
  Charles L. Lumsden Diary (Lumsden's Battery)
  I. W. McAdory memorandum, 25th Alabama File.*
  Solomon Palmer Diary (19th Alabama Infantry)
  William E. Preston Memoir, 33rd Alabama Infantry File.
  Hezekiah Rabb Letters (33rd Alabama Infantry)
  James T. Searcy Letters (Reserve Artillery Battalion)*
  Semple's Battery File
  Smith Letter (3rd Alabama Cavalry)
  Isaac Burton Ulmer Reminiscences, 3rd Alabama Cavalry File*
  "Most Lovely Lizzie," Samuel King Vann Letters (19th Alabama Infantry)
  Joseph Wheeler Papers
    S.A.M. Wood Papers*
    S.A.M. Wood Letters*
  M. P. Lowrey Report*
  Belser L. Wyman Letters (Semple's Battery)*

Allara Library, Pikeville College, Pikeville KY
  Henry Scalf Papers (5th Kentucky Infantry CSA)

Arkansas History Commission, Little Rock, Arkansas
  Nat G. Pierce Papers (14th Ohio Infantry)*
  W. C. Guest Letter (2nd Arkansas Infantry)
  J. C. Sharp Letters (51st/52nd Tennessee)

Ashland University, Ashland Ohio
  George Nicholson Diary (6th Ohio Infantry)

Atlanta History Center, Atlanta GA
    Charles F. McCay letters (Wheeler staff and escort)

Auburn University
    William H. Ball Letters (5th Wisconsin Battery)
    Thomas Bigby Letters (33rd Alabama Infantry)
    I. J. Rogers Letter, Boldwig Papers (27th Alabama Infantry)
    J. Q. Burton, "Sketch of Co. H, 47th Alabama"
    John Crittenden Letters and Collection (34th Alabama)
    Benjamin Mason Papers (Hilliard's Legion)
    Richard C. McCalla Letters, Speake- McCalla Correspondence (Pioneers)
    William E. Preston Memoir (33rd Alabama Infantry)
    Steiner Family Papers (16th Alabama Infantry)
    William T. Stockton Papers (1st Florida Dismounted Cavalry)
    Williams Papers (33rd Alabama Infantry)

Author's Collection
    John T. Wilder Tactical Notes

Birmingham Public Library, Birmingham AL
    John W. Sparkman Diary (48th Tennessee Infantry)
    R.S. Reed Letters (19th Alabama Infantry)

Ball State University, Muncie, IN
    Cassady-Nelson Family Collection (37th Indiana Infantry)
    G.W.H. Kemper Letter (17th Indiana Mounted Infantry)

Personal collection of Ken Bandy, Beloit OH
    Ken Bandy notes on 65th Ohio casualties
    Henry Elliott Letters (65th Ohio Infantry)
    Thomas M. Taylor Letter (65th Ohio Infantry)

Personal collection of David Bash
    Letters and inspector Log of Capt. William G. Kendricks (Stanley's Brigade)

Baylor University, The Texas Collection, Waco, TX
    Edward Rotan reminiscences (16th Tennessee Infantry)

Boston Public Library
    Lewis Hanback Letters (27th Illinois Infantry)

Bowling Green State University, Bowling Green OH
    Brigham Family Papers
        L. E. Chenoweth Letter (69th Ohio Infantry)
    Silas Canfield Reminiscences (21st Ohio Infantry)
    Isaac Cusac Letters (21st Ohio Infantry)
    Robert S. Dilworth Journal (21st Ohio Infantry)
    Thomas J. Doughman Recollections (89th Ohio Infantry)
    Dumont Family Papers (69th Ohio Infantry)

Richard H. Foord Diary (35th Ohio Infantry)
B. B. Jackson Letter (14th Ohio Infantry)
Leonard Kleckner Letters (21st Ohio Infantry)
George Kryder Papers (3rd Ohio Cavalry)
John C. Leonard Letter (21st Ohio Infantry)
Linus Anthony Patrick Papers and Letters (121st Ohio Infantry)
William Shanks Diary (21st Ohio Infantry)
Stanton/Searles Family Papers (21st Ohio Infantry)
William Strahl Diary and Papers (49th Ohio Infantry)
William J. Sullivan Collection (21st Ohio Infantry)
   H. H. Alban Letter, June 12, 1889
   H. M. Bayliss Letter, July 1, 1889
   J. W. Bishop Letter, August 10, 1889
   S. S. Canfield Letter, June 7 and July 18, 1889
   C. H. Carlton Letter, August 8, 1889
   Isaac Cusac Letter, March 13, 1909
   George Dolton Letters, Feb. 3 and April 14, 1890
   John Mahony Letter, July 23, 1889
   Arnold McMahan Papers
Liberty Warner Papers (21st Ohio Infantry)
James Inman Letter, Waddell Family Papers (21st Ohio Infantry)
John K. Welk Diary (15th Ohio Infantry)
Loyal Barber Wert Letters (21st Ohio Infantry)

Brigham Young University, Provo UT
Eugene Banks Diary (39th Alabama)

Buffalo and Erie County Historical Society, Buffalo NY
"The Battle of Chickamauga" by William R. Johnston.

Carroll College Civil War Institute, Waukesha WI
Orson and Hastings Clinton Letters (1st Wisconsin Cavalry)
Robert S. Merrill Diaries (1st Wisconsin Cavalry)

Chicago History Museum, Chicago IL
John J. Ballard Diary (2nd Georgia Infantry)
Lucien B. Case Letters (18th US Infantry)
Day Elmore Letters (36th Illinois Infantry)
Joseph S. Johnston Diary and Letters (19th Illinois)*
Cyrus Watson Pomeroy Memoir (96th Illinois Infantry)
Levi H. Sipes Memoir (29th Indiana Infantry)
Silas Curtis Stevens Memoir (Chicago Board of Trade Battery)
Henry T. Wulff Letter (24th Alabama Infantry)

Chattanooga-Hamilton County Library, Chattanooga TN
Thomas W. Davis Diary (6th Tennessee Cavalry, Confederate)
Alfred Tyler Fielder Diary (12th Tennessee Infantry)
Reminiscences of Chickamauga, by Capt. S.J.A. Frazier (19th Tennessee) 1909*
Reminiscences of a Soldier Who Fought At Chickamauga, by Capt. S. J. A. Frazier (19th Tennessee) 1921*
James Perry Fyffe Papers (59th Ohio)*

Lieutenant Thomas L. Steward Diary, newspaper clipping, *Chattanooga New Free Press*, September 21, 1938. (11th Ohio Infantry)*

"A Union Soldier's Diary" newspaper clipping from *Chattanooga Times*, April 25, 1937. (36th Illinois Infantry)*

Chickamauga-Chattanooga National Military Park, Fort Oglethorpe GA

Anonymous, By CHARLIE, "Camp in the field near Chattanooga," September 24, 1863, 2nd Georgia Sharpshooters file

William K. Armstrong Diary, 52nd Ohio file.

A. C. Avery Letters, 39th North Carolina file*

C. O. Bailey Letter, 7th Florida Infantry file

Henry Banta Diary, 17th Indiana file

James S Boynton Report, 30th Georgia file

Sergeant Marvin Boget Letter, 22nd Michigan file

Charles R. Brand Letter, 9th Michigan file

John M Brannan Letter, 31st Ohio file.

August Bratnober Diary, 10th Wisconsin Infantry file

Joseph Brenling Letter, 3rd Wisconsin Battery file

Thaddeus Marion Brindley Letter, 22nd Alabama file

John W. Bryson Memoir, 3rd South Carolina file

George Butler Reminiscences, 96th Illinois file

Ellison Capers notebooks, 24th South Carolina file

Francis Carlisle Reminiscences, 42nd Indiana file*

William W. Carnes Letter and Memoir, Carnes' Battery file

William P. Chandler Letter, 35th Illinois file

Orville T. Chamberlain Letters, 74th Indiana file.

Thomas Claiborn Letter, Eyewitness accounts file (Buckner Staff)*

E.H. Clark Letter, 51st Alabama Partisan Ranger file

Thomas A. Cobb Letters, 10th Indiana Infantry file

Sam Houston and Alexander Smith Collins Letters 63rd Virginia file*

Albert Cone Letter, 19th Illinois Infantry file*

John Conover Letters, 8th Kansas file*.

James F. Culpepper, Culpepper's SC Battery file

John H. Davenport Letter, 1st Battalion Hilliard's Legion file.

Lt. Col. Davis Letter, 82nd Indiana file*.

Francis Warrington Dawson Report, Longstreet's Corps.

George E. Dolton, *Capsule History Battery M, 1st Illinois Light Artillery* file

John Ely Diary, 88th Illinois file.

Horace N. Fisher Letters, Alexander M. McCook file*

Nathan B. Forrest Letter to Joseph Wheeler, Wheeler file.

James H. Fraser Diary extracts, 50th Alabama Infantry file.

Henry Gale Letter, 96th Illinois file.

Milton Garrigus Letters, 39th Indiana Mounted Infantry file*.

W. W. Gifford Letter, 36th Illinois file.

J. S. Gilbert Letter, 7th South Carolina file*

William Ross Glisan Diary, 6th Ohio Infantry file*

Harlow B. Godard Letter, 100th Illinois Infantry file.

G. E. Goudelock Letter, 2nd Arkansas Mounted Rifles file.

G. D. Gouge Letters, 58th North Carolina file.

Archibald Gracie-L.W. Harper correspondence, 58th North Carolina file.

George A. Grammer Diary, Warren Light Artillery file.

George Green Letter, 78th Illinois file.

Joseph Haddock recollections, 4th Indiana Battery file.

Charles D. Hammer Reminiscences, 124th Ohio file

Charles G. Harker Letter, Harker file

"History of the 18th Alabama Infantry,"Gleeson 18th Alabama Infantry file.

W. G. Houghton Memoir, 2nd Georgia file

Col. Morton C. Hunter Report, 82nd Indiana Infantry file

William H. Huntzinger Diary, 79th Indiana Infantry file

J. L. Irwin Letters, 84th Illinois Infantry file*

F. M. Ison Letter, 2nd Georgia Cavalry file

Fred Knefler Correspondence, 79th Indiana Infantry file*

John Levering Diary Extracts, Reynolds Division file*

Ramy L. Lafitte Letters, 19th Louisiana Infantry file

Longstreet Troop Movement Telegrams, Longstreet file

William Edgar McAnally Journal, 37th Tennessee file.

Dyer B. McConnell, "Address given at the 1891 Reunion of the 9th Indiana," 9th Indiana file

Jim B. Martin Letter, 22nd Alabama Infantry file

William T. Martin Letter, Martin file

Samuel Mason Diary, 31st Indiana Infantry file

James T. Mills Letter, 10th Kentucky file*

J. W. Minnich account, 6th Georgia Cavalry file

S. B. Moe Correspondence, 96th Illinois Infantry file*

Monument Correspondence, 121st Ohio Infantry file*

William R. Montgomery Letters, 3rd Georgia Sharpshooters file

Sgt. I. V. Moore Diary, 37th Georgia file

Ed Murray Reminiscences, 96th Illinois file.

Samuel Pasco Diary, 1st/3rd Florida Infantry file

R. J. Redding Letter, 46th Georgia file

J. J. Reynolds Statements, 19 and 20 September, Reynolds file

D. N. Sharp Letter, 15th Kentucky file*

Frank G. Smith Letter, Battery I, 4th US Artillery file*

Joseph Henry Smith Diary, 33rd Alabama file

Thomas Smyrl Letter, 34th Alabama file

John Snow Letter, Lumsden's Alabama Battery file

A. N. Speer Letter, 46th Georgia file

George W. Steele Letters, 101st Indiana file*

S. H. Stevens account, Crook's Division* Crook file

Sylvanus H. Stevens Letter, Chicago Board of Trade Battery file*

James Thompson Diary, 4th Ohio Cavalry file

William M. Thompson Letter, 3rd Georgia Cavalry file

J. J. Turner Report, 1891 30th Tennessee Infantry file*

Undated clipping, 4th Tennessee Cavalry CS file

Unknown Letter, 3rd Kentucky US file

Durbin Ward Letter, 31st Ohio file.

Darius B. Warner Letter, 113th Ohio file

William G Webber letters, 6th Ohio file

James E. White Reminiscences, 46th Georgia file.

John T. Wilder Revised Report,* Wilder file

Claudius C. Wilson Correspondence, 30th Georgia file

J. Russell Wright Reminiscences, 7th South Carolina file

In addition to the park's manuscript files, Both the War Department interpretive tablets and the monuments themselves were heavily consulted.

Cincinnati Historical Society, Cincinnati OH
    Isaac Anderson Papers, James Anderson Letter (93rd Ohio Infantry)
    Cist Family Papers*
        Frank Bond Diary (Rosecrans staff)
    William E. Crane Journal (4th Ohio Cavalry)*
    Frank Johnston Jones Papers (20th Corps staff)*
    Lytle Family Papers
        Howard Greene Letter (24th Wisconsin & Lytle Staff)
        Alfred Pirtle Memoir "Leaves of my Journal," (Lytle Staff)

Citadel, The Military College of South Carolina, Charleston SC
    James D. Nance Letter (3rd South Carolina Infantry)*

Clark County Historical Society and Museum, Springfield OH
    A. W. Black Letters (90th Ohio Infantry)

Combat Studies Institute, Command and General Staff College, Ft. Leavenworth, KA
    Allen Barksdale Letter, 7th South Carolina file
    Thesis on John Belue Diary, 15th South Carolina file
    David S. Blackburn papers, 21st Illinois file*
    A. S. Bloomfield Letters, Battery A, 1st Ohio Light Artillery file
    William Alexander Brown Diary, 63rd Tennessee Infantry file
    William Brown Notebook, Stanford's Mississippi Battery file
    William Watts Carnes Memoir, Carnes's Battery file
    David M. Cleggett, 17th Kentucky Infantry US file
    S. A. Cunningham Reminiscences, 41st Tennessee file
    James H. Frasier Letter, 50th Alabama file
    Thomas E. Green Letter, 85th Illinois Infantry file*
    Jason Hurd Diary, 19th Ohio file, (from collection of William Acree*)
    James Madison Jones Recollections, 2nd Indiana Cavalry file*
    William Kennedy Ketes Diary, 48th Tennessee file
    W. E. Miller Letter, 16th South Carolina file
    Wesley Nichols newspaper clipping, 15th South Carolina file*
    Melvin R. Norman Letters, 63rd Virginia Infantry file*
    J. A. Reep Memoir, 19th Ohio Infantry file, (collection of William Acree*)
    E. H. Rennolds Diary, 4th/5th Tennessee Infantry file
    John Sanders Letter, 84th Indiana Infantry file
    William Ralston Talley Autobiography, Havis' Georgia Battery file
    Charles Frederick Terrill, 2nd Georgia Infantry file*
    Henry M Weiss Letter Excerpts, 27th Illinois Infantry file
    Edgar N Wilcox Diary and court martial records, 18th US Infantry file* (Wiley Sword Coll.)
    Thomas J. Wood Correspondence (Collection of Stephen Wood)*
    XIV Corps Headquarters Locations, XIV Corps file

Creighton University, Reinert Library, Omaha NE
    Jasper Newton Hall Diary (113th Ohio)

Danville Public Library, Danville IL
  George Dillon Letters (125th Illinois)

Dayton Public Library, Dayton OH
  Samuel B. Smith Autobiography (93rd Ohio Infantry)
  Hiram B. Strong Papers (93rd Ohio Infantry)

Dekalb History Center, Decatur GA
  Papers of Col. J. J. Morrison, (1st Georgia Cavalry)

Depauw University, Greencastle IN
  William D. Ward Journal and Unpublished Recollections (37th Indiana Infantry)

Detroit Public Library, Burton Historical Collection, Detroit MI
  August Henry Bachman Letters (Battery A, 1st Michigan Artillery)
  William Brownall Diary (4th Michigan Cavalry)
  Robert Burns Letters (4th Michigan Cavalry)
  Oscar Chamberlain Letters, Chamberlain Family Papers (9th Michigan Infantry)
  Anson T. Gilbert Letters (11th Michigan Infantry)
  Allen Benton Morse Letters, Marion Morse Davis Papers, (21st Ohio Infantry)
  James Stephenson Letter, (2nd Michigan Cavalry)
  James Vernor Letters, Vernor Family Papers (4th Michigan Cavalry)

Duke University, Perkins Library, Durham NC
  George Brent Papers (Bragg Staff)*
  William Broaddus Papers (78th Illinois Infantry)
  John C. Brown Letter, Longstreet Papers
  Lt. Witt Clement Letters (Post's Brigade)
  William DeLong Letter (11th Ohio Infantry)
  Hemphill Family Papers (7th South Carolina)
  Braxton Bragg letter, Charles Colcock Jones Papers *
  "Death of Gen. Ben Hardin Helm," William C. Leman Papers
  Malone Letter, Martha Harper Clayton Papers (10th Tennessee Infantry)
  John Euclid MaGee Diary (Stanford's Mississippi Battery)*
  Benjamin Nourse Diary (Chicago Board of Trade Battery)
  Benjamin Williams Papers (47th Georgia Infantry)
  James H. Wiswell Papers (4th US Cavalry)*
  Elisha Peterson Papers (Union Cavalry Corps)*
  John Snow Papers (Lumsden's Battery)*
  Charles H. Sowle Papers (4th Kentucky Cavalry US)
  Daniel Augustus Tompkins Papers
  Anonymous, "Lieut. Col. Elbert Bland Late Commander of the 7th Regiment S.C.V." (7th South Carolina
      Infantry)
  Joseph T. Woods Papers (99th Ohio Infantry)*
  Confederate Veteran Papers
      W. H. Cunningham Letter (Hindman's Staff)*
      J. T. Gaines Recollections (5th Kentucky Infantry CS)*
      R. M Henderson Reminiscences (9th Texas Infantry) *
      Austin Peay Reminiscences (Dibrell's Brigade)
      W. F. Shropshire Reminiscences (1st Georgia Cavalry)

Emory University, Robert W. Woodruff Library, Atlanta GA
  Alexander Miller Ayers Letters (125th Illinois Infantry)
  William E. Corbitt Diary, Confederate Miscellany File (4th Tennessee Cavalry)*
  James Preston Crowder Letters (47th Alabama Infantry)
  William M. Crumley Reminiscences (Kershaw Aide)
  William H. Davis Letters and Diary (9th Tennessee Infantry)
  William Cary Dodson Memoir, Confederate Miscellany II (51st Alabama Cav.)
  Theodore Fogle Letters (2nd Georgia Infantry)
  Ephraim Hampton Letters (54th Virginia Infantry)
  Hannoll Family Collection, W. B. Hannoll letter (24th Mississippi Infantry)
  Nimrod W. E. Long (51st Alabama Cavalry)*
  James A. McMurtrey Letters (York's Georgia Battery)
  J. B. Mason Letters (58th Alabama Infantry)
  Thomas Henry Pitts Letters (3rd South Carolina Infantry)*
  Isaac Rosenberry Diary (1st Michigan Engineers)
  Stout Family Letters (Surgeon, Army of Tennessee)
  Benjamin S. Williams Reminiscences (47th Georgia Infantry)
  Jerome P. Wilson Papers (Hindman's Division)*

Filson Historical Society, Louisville KY
  John C. Breckinridge Papers
  Alfred Pirtle Papers (Lytle Staff)
  James Shera Diary (68th Indiana Infantry)
  John H. Tilford Diary (79th Indiana Infantry)
  John L. Williams Letter (4th Kentucky Infantry)
  Thomas J. Wood Collection

Florida State Archives, Tallahassie FL
  Roderick Gospero Shaw Letter (4th Florida)
  William T. Stockton Papers (1st Florida Dismounted Cavalry)
  Robert Watson Diary (7th Florida)

Florida State University, Tallahassee FL
  James Patton Anderson Letter
  Henry T. Wright Letters, (1st Florida Infantry)

Galveston and Texas History Center, Rosenberg Library, Galveston TX
  Bunting, R. F. "True Merit Brings It's Own Reward." (8th Texas Cavalry)

Geneva History Center, Geneva IL
  Daniel Terry Letter (36th Illinois Infantry)

Georgia Department of Archives and History, Morrow GA
  Ben F. Abbott Letters, (2nd Georgia Infantry)
  David Richard Childers Letter, Sallie B. Veal Collection (34th Mississippi)
  Joseph B. Cumming Letters (Jackson staff, 2nd Bn, 5th Georgia Infantry)
  William Sylvester Dillon Diary (4th Tennessee Infantry)
  Julius Lafayette Dowda Diary (3rd Georgia Cavalry)
  Sketch of Lt. Col. A. R. Harper (1st Georgia Cavalry)

James Longstreet Papers
J. H. Martin Reminiscences, UDC Collection, vol. XI (17th Georgia Infantry)*
W. H. Reynolds Letter, Dickey Family Papers (29th Georgia Infantry)
Frank T. Ryan Reminiscences (1st Arkansas Mounted Rifles)*

Hill College, Hillsboro TX
  Jesse P. Bates Letters, (G, 9th Texas Infantry)
  Solomon S. Boss Letters (6th Georgia Cavalry)
  Louis T. Botto Papers (154th Tennessee Infantry)
  C. H. Clark memoir, copied from newspaper (16th Tennessee Infantry)
  John M. Claypool Reminiscences (47th Tennessee Infantry)
  Jeremiah Ellis Letters (38th Alabama Infantry)
  Andrew J. Fogle Letters (Co. C, 9th Texas Infantry)
  Abram M. Glazener Letters (18th Alabama Infantry)
  Isaiah Harlan Letters (G, 10th Texas Infantry)
  George Lea Letters (7th Mississippi Infantry)
  J. W. Minnich Letters (6th Georgia Cavalry)
  Lycurgus A. Sallee Letter (Polk's Brigade)
  George Simmons Memoir (23rd Tennessee Infantry Battalion)
  J. B. Smyth Letter (32nd Texas Dismounted Cavalry)
  John Templeton Letters (10th Texas Dismounted Cavalry)
  William B. Tunnell Recollections (B, 14th Texas Dismounted Cavalry)
  Henry Watson Letters (F, 10th Texas Dismounted Cavalry)
  William P. White Letters (36th Alabama Infantry)
  William G. Young Letters (A, 15th Texas dismounted Cavalry)
  32nd Tennessee Infantry casualty list, from Chattanooga Daily Rebel, Oct 8 1863.

Historical Society of Pennsylvania, Philadelphia PA
  Captain Charles Malone Betts Letters, (15th Pennsylvania Cavalry)
  Captain Thomas S. McCahan Diary (9th Pennsylvania Cavalry)

Huntington Library, San Marino CA
  W. W. Carnes Letter, James William Eldridge Papers (Carnes's Battery)
  James Monro Forbes Letters (92nd Illinois Infantry)
  James M. Goff Letters, Goff-Williams Collection (10th Wisconsin Infantry)
  Nelson G. Huson Letters (96th Illinois Infantry)
  William Devereux Kendall Letters (5th Tennessee Infantry)
  Duncan McKercher Diaries (10th Wisconsin Infantry)
  Lovell Newton Parker Memoir (105th Ohio Infantry)
  George S. Phillips Diary and Letters (49th Ohio Infantry)

Indiana Historical Society, Smith Memorial Library, Indianapolis IN
  Chesley D. Bailey Letters (31st Indiana Infantry)
  Jacob W. Bartmess Letters (39th Indiana Infantry)
  John M. Barnard Letters (72nd Indiana Infantry)
  George W. Baum Papers (2nd Indiana Cavalry)
  John Beals Letters (68th Indiana Infantry)
  William Blair Report and Letter (Surgeon, XXI Corps)
  Benjamin F. Brown Letter (87th Indiana Infantry)

Bergun H. Brown Papers (29th Indiana Infantry)*

Orville Chamberlain Letters, Camberlain Family Papers (74th Indiana)

Jesse B. Connelly Diary (31st Indiana Infantry)*

W. O Crouse Manuscript, History of the 18th Indiana Battery

John Day Diary (31st Indiana Infantry)

Helim C. Dunn Letters (74th Indiana Infantry)

William H. Dunn Letters (4th Indiana Cavalry)

James William Ellis Letters (72nd Indiana Infantry)

James G. Essington Diary (75th Indiana Infantry)

William D. Evritt Letter (81st Indiana Infantry)

James Frank Fee Letters, (31st Indiana Infantry)

William Forder Letters (10th Indiana Battery)*

Frederick G. Fried Memoir (74th Indiana Infantry)

Arthur J. Gates Diary (68th Indiana Infantry)

William B. Graham Reminiscences (101st Indiana Infantry)

Joseph C. Haddock Papers, Historical sketch of the 4th Indiana Battery

James Henry Harris Diary (4th Indiana Cavalry)

Thomas J. Harrison Letters (39th Indiana Mounted Infantry)*

Daniel Wait Howe Papers

   Daniel Waite Howe Diary (79th Indiana Infantry)*

   Samuel Olyer Letters (79th Indiana Infantry)

Horace Hobart Letter (17th Indiana Mounted Infantry)

Jonathan Hollingsworth Diary (101st Indiana Infantry)

Elijah W. Israel Letters (87th Indiana Infantry)

Sylvester M. Jessup Letter, Jessup Family Papers, (79th Indiana Infantry)

Luman Jones Letter (79th Indiana Infantry)

Jeptha King Letter (6th Indiana Infantry)

John Klingman Diary (88th Indiana Infantry)

Garrett Lerew Diary (86th Indiana Infantry)

Horace C. Long Letter (87th Indiana Infantry)

Benjamin B. Mabrey Letters (82nd Indiana Infantry)

Benjamin Magee Recollections (72nd Indiana Infantry)

John Mendenhall Diary (2nd Indiana Cavalry)*

Jacob S. McCullough Diary (Pioneer Brigade)*

Josiah F. McNair Diary (74th Indiana Infantry)

William S. Mead Diary (6th Indiana Infantry)

William Bluffton Miller Journal (75th Indiana Infantry)

John Otto Papers, History of the 11th Indiana Battery

Robert J. Price Letters (68th Indiana Infantry)*

Thomas Prickett Letters (9th Indiana Infantry)

William Jasper Ralph Diary (39th Indiana Infantry)

Regimental Clipping File

   Albert Cripe Prospectus, (84th Indiana Infantry)

Jackson Risley Letter (42nd Indiana Infantry)

Elisha J. Robinson Letter (82nd Indiana Infantry)

A. R. Ryman Letters (68th Indiana Infantry)

Joseph A. Scott Reminiscences (18th Indiana Battery)

Benjamin F. Scribner Letters and Papers*

Robert P. Shanklin Letters (3rd Indiana Cavalry)

Oliver Shelly Letters (88th Indiana Infantry)

Thomas M. Small Diary (10th Indiana Infantry)
Joseph Taylor Smith Letters (75th Indiana Infantry)
Thomas J. Stephenson Letter, Joseph Gullion Collection, (10th Indiana Infantry)
W. R. Stuckey Letters (42nd Indiana Infantry)
James S. Thomas Letters (10th Indiana Infantry)*
John Q. Thomas Collection
    W.L. Hilligos Letter, October 2nd,1863 (75th Indiana Infantry)
    D.L. Thomas Letters, Sept. 28th & Oct. 4th, 1863 (68th Indiana Infantry)
Peter S. Troutman Letter (87th Indiana Infantry)
Unknown Diary, 72nd Indiana Mounted Infantry
William D. Ward Diary (37th Indiana Infantry)
Williamson D. Ward Diary and Letter (39th Indiana Mounted Infantry)
William Weidner Recollections (37th Indiana Infantry)
John C. Wysong Diary (30th Indiana Infantry)

Indiana State Archives, Indianapolis IN
    Adjutant General's Records
        10th Indiana report, 10th Indiana Regimental Correspondence file
        75th Indiana Infantry Regimental Correspondence file
        81st Indiana Infantry Regimental Correspondence file
        Nelson Trusler Report, 84th Indiana Regimental Correspondence file
        Thomas Doan Report, 101st Indiana Regimental Correspondence file

Indiana State Library, Indianapolis IN
    Bevington Papers
        George Johnson Letter, (65th Ohio Infantry)
    Henry V. Brown Papers
        Shaw narrative, (3rd Indiana Cavalry)
    Chauncy Brooks Letters (unknown unit)
    Daniel E. Bruce Memoir (Teamster, 87th Indiana Infantry)
    John Combs Letter (6th Indiana Infantry)
    Jesse B. Connelly Diary (31st Indiana Infantry)
    William H. Doll Reminiscences, (6th Indiana Infantry)
    James W. Ellis Letters (72nd Indiana Mounted Infantry)
    James Embree Report (58th Indiana Infantry)
    William B. Galway Journal (125th Illinois Infantry)
    Solomon Glick Letters, (4th Indiana Cavalry)
    Alva C. Griest Journal (72nd Indiana Mounted Infantry)
    Porter Griffin Letter (38th Indiana Infantry)
    Hiram Hines Diary (supply trains)
    John M. Hook Letters (6th Indiana Infantry)*
    William D. Hynes Letters (22nd Illinois Infantry)*
    Peter Keegan Diary (87th Indiana Infantry)
    W. E. Ludow letter concerning Oliver S. Rankin (Union spy)
    George H. Martling Diary (87th Indiana Infantry)
    Samuel F. Mason Diary (31st Indiana Infantry)
    McCullough Diary (37th Indiana Infantry)
    John S. McGraw Letters (57th Indiana Infantry)
    William H. Records Diary, (72nd Indiana Mounted Infantry)
    Isaac H.C. Royce Diary (115th Illinois Infantry)

Shepardson Letters (30th Indiana Infantry)
William H. Springer memoir, Springer-Brayton Papers (38th Indiana Infantry)
John T. Wilder Papers (17th Indiana)
    H. Jordan Letter*
    Robert H.G. Minty Dispatch
Aurelius M. Willoughby Diary (39th Indiana Mounted Infantry)
Joshua Wilson Letters (58th Indiana Infantry)

Indiana State University, Terre Haute IN
    John H. Rippetoe Letters, (18th Indiana Battery)
    Indiana University, Lilly Library, Bloomington IN
    Milton C. Crist Letters, (17th Ohio Infantry)
    Samuel Day Diary, (8th Indiana Light Artillery)
    Henry F. Dillman Diary (31st Indiana Infantry)*
    William G. Jacques memoir, "Account of my experiences in, and capture in the Battle of Chickamauga,"
        (73rd Illinois Infantry)
    Ambrose Remley Letters, (72nd Indiana Mounted Infantry)

Iowa Historical Society, Des Moines IA
    Stephen A. McCollum Letter (64th Ohio Infantry)
    James Norman Letters, Vance Family Papers (74th Indiana Infantry)
    O. H. Payne Papers (124th Ohio Infantry)

Iowa Historical Society, Iowa City IA
    John C. McLain Diary (4th Michigan Cavalry)
    Job D. Wilkinson Papers (19th Illinois Infantry)

Jackson County Historical Society, Independence MO
    Aaron Flint Sawyer Letters (8th Kansas Infantry)

Kalamazoo Valley Museum, Kalamazoo MI
    Orville Harrison Dewaters Letters (13th Michigan Infantry)

Kennesaw Mountain National Military Park, Kennesaw GA
    John J. Cloud Letters (113th Ohio Infantry)
    Daniel O'Leary Letters (15th Kentucky Infantry US)*
    J. Ben Settle Letter (32nd/45th Mississippi Infantry)
    Lyman S. Widney Diary and Letters (34th Illinois Infantry)

Kentucky Historical Society, Frankfort, KY
    Hiram Hawkins Papers (5th Kentucky Infantry, CS)
    George R Mattingly, "Reminiscences Of The Nelson Grays" (9th Kentucky CS)
    John W. Tuttle Diary (3rd Kentucky Infantry US)

Lake County Museum, Regional History Archives, Wauconda IL
    Edward Murray, "A Soldier's Reminiscences" (Sgt, C, 96th Illinois Infantry)
    George Smith Letters, David Minto Collection (96th Illinois Infantry)
    Orson Van Ness Young Letters, (96th Illinois Infantry)

Lake County Historical Society, Kirtland Hills, OH
  George H. Sharp Diary (105th Ohio Infantry)

Lane Public Library, Smith Library of Regional History, Oxford OH
  Sterrett Graham Smith Memoir (93rd Ohio Infantry)
  Van Derveer Family History
  Ferdinand Van Derveer letters

Library of Congress. Washington DC
  Braxton Bragg Papers*
  Caleb Henry Carlton Papers (89th Ohio Infantry)
  Ezra Carman papers
    William Perry Letter (44th Alabama)
  Josiah Dexter Cotton Letter (92nd Ohio Infantry)
  David Douglass Letters (79th Indiana Infantry)
  Charles C. Hood Collection (31st Ohio Infantry)
  John Wesley Marshall Journal (97th Ohio Infantry)
  McCook Family Papers (Alexander McDowell McCook materials)
  John Patton Memoirs (98th Ohio Infantry)
  Leonidas Polk Papers
  Horace Porter Papers (Rosecrans Staff)
  Alfred Roman Papers (Wheeler inspection report)
  Philip H. Sheridan Papers*
  John Powers Smith Papers (Braxton Bragg Letter)
  John H. Tower Papers, Naval Historical Foundation
    Rueben S. Morton Diary (Civilian, Rome Georgia)
  Samuel S. Yoder Papers (51st Ohio Infantry)

Louisiana State University, Noel Memorial Library, Shreveport LA
  John Harris Letter (19th Louisiana Infantry)

Louisiana State University, Hill Memorial Library, Baton Rouge LA
  Lemuel Conner Family Papers (Slocomb's Battery)
  E. John Ellis Letters and Diary (16th Louisiana Infantry)*
  John Foster Letters (10th Mississippi Infantry)
  Marshall Furman Family Papers (8th Mississippi Infantry)
  Charles E. Leverich Diary (Robinson's Battery)*
  John McGrath Papers (8th Texas Cavalry, 13th Louisiana Infantry)
  Leonidas Polk Letters
  Unidentified soldier's diary (4th Louisiana Battalion)

Mahoning Valley Historical Society, Youngstown OH
  Samuel Platt Diary (26th Ohio Infantry)

Mankato State University, Mankato MN
  Edgar Van Buren Dickey Letters (2nd Minnesota Infantry)

Marietta Museum of History, Marietta GA
  "Testimony of a Union Spy That Lived in Marietta"

Marietta College, Marietta OH
  Samuel Hildreth Putnam Letters (Co. L, 1st Ohio Cavalry & Thomas Escort)
  Joseph P. Snyder Letters, William Rufus Putnam Papers (92nd Ohio)

Marshall University, Huntington WV
  Charles Aleshire Letters, Aleshire Family Papers (18th Ohio Battery)

Maryland Historical Society, Baltimore MD
  Osmun Latrobe Diary* (Longstreet Staff)

Massachusetts Historical Society, Boston MA
  Horace Newton Fisher Papers (XX Corps Staff)
  Henry W. Hall Letters (51st Illinois Infantry)

McLean County Historical Museum, Bloomington IL
  Virgil E. Reed Letters (34th Illinois Infantry)

Miami University, Havighurst Special Collections, Oxford OH
  Henry Richards Letters, Richards-Gilbert Papers (93rd Ohio)

Michigan State Archives, Lansing MI
  Henry Albert Potter Letters and Diary (4th Michigan Cavalry)

Michigan State University, East Lansing MI
  George Farr Autobiography (Battery H/M, 4th US Artillery)
  Harry Goodale Recollections (21st Michigan Infantry)
  Othniel Gooding Letters (4th Michigan Cavalry)
  John McClain Diary (4th Michigan Cavalry)
  Jan Nies Letters, Katherine Rickey Papers (2nd Michigan Cavalry, written in Dutch)
  John G. Parkhurst Diaries (9th Michigan Infantry)
  Henry Dean Warden Letters (22nd Michigan Infantry)

Midway Village and Museum, Rockford IL
  Horace B. Utter Diary (74th Illinois Infantry)

Milwaukee County Historical Society, Milwaukee WI
  Byron Abert Letters, Abert Family Papers. (21st Wisconsin Infantry)

Milwaukee Public Library, Milwaukee WI
  Ole Steensland Reminiscences (15th Wisconsin Infantry)

Minnesota Historical Society, Minneapolis MN
  Robert Burns Letters (4th Michigan Cavalry)*
  Jeremiah Chester Dunahower Papers (2nd Minnesota Infantry)
  Horatio P. Van Cleve Papers*

Mississippi Department of Archives and History, Jackson MS
  T. Otis Baker Papers (10th Mississippi Infantry)

James G. Bullard Letter (10th Mississippi Infantry)
Robert Dacus memoir, "History of Company H, 1st Arkansas Mounted Rifles"
George Dodson Letters, David Colin Humphreys collection (10th Mississippi)
William Hill Diary (13th Mississippi Infantry)
Robert A. Jarman, "The History of Company K, 27th Mississippi Infantry"
George Lea Letters (7th Mississippi Infantry)
James S. Oliver Papers (9th Mississippi Infantry)
Sil J. Quinn Manuscript (13th Mississippi Infantry)
James Miller Rand Diary (41st Mississippi Infantry)
John C. Rietti Diary and Letters (10th Mississippi Infantry)
Oscar J. E. Stuart Family Papers (D. H. Hill Staff)*

Mississippi State University, Starkville, MS
    Tacitus Clay Letters (5th Texas Infantry)
    Captain Thomas H. Dickson Diary (9th Mississippi Infantry)
    Charles Hill Letters (115th Illinois Infantry)
    George Sledge Diary (Stanford's Mississippi Battery)
    Isham W. Thomas Letters (Stanford's Mississippi Battery)

Missouri Historical Society, St. Louis MO
    Patrick Ahern Reminiscences, Jesse P. Henry Papers (13th Arkansas Infantry)
    Braxton Bragg Letters, Sept. 22 and 27, 1863
    Angus Waddle Letters, Eleanor W. McCoy Papers (33rd Ohio Infantry)
    Civil War Miscellaneous collection
        Trumbull Griffin Reminiscences (Chicago Board of Trade Battery)
        James E. Love Autobiography and Letters (8th Kansas Infantry)
        John F. Norton Letter (113th Ohio Infantry)

Morrison-Reeves Library, Richmond IN
    John A. Mendenhall Diary (2nd Indiana Cavalry)

Museum of the Confederacy, Richmond VA
    E. P. Alexander Papers (Papers related to Longstreet's Corps)
    Records of the Military Court, Longstreet's Corps*
    W. T. Holt, Army of Tennessee Scout Book
    Robert P. Myers Diary (16th Georgia Infantry)

Nashville Public Library, Nashville TN
    Peter J. Williamson letters (1st Wisconsin Cavalry)

National Archives and Records Administration, Washington DC.
    Compiled Service Records of Confederate Soldiers
    Compiled Service Records of Union Soldiers
    RG 94, Records of the U.S. Adjutant General's Office
        Strength returns for the Army of the Cumberland, September 1863
            General Thomas's Papers*
            William E. Crane Diary (4th Ohio Cavalry)*
            Edward Grosskopf to Edward Ruger, June 23, 1867*
            Moses B. Walker Report (31st Ohio Infantry)*

Union Battle Reports, Box 56*
  E. S. Watts Report (2nd Kentucky Cavalry US)*
Letters, 1875-1877. Transcripts of Reynolds court of Inquiry.
  RG 109 Confederate Records
    Letters received by the C.S. Adjutant and Inspector General's Office,
      R. H. Bassett letter, (4th Texas Infantry)
    Returns of Hindman's Division
    Returns of Patton Anderson's Brigade*
    Returns of J. K. Jackson's Brigade*
    Bushrod R. Johnson Diary
    Letters Sent by General Polk's Command*
    Orders and Circulars, Army of Tennessee*
  RG 393
    Part 1, Entry 986, Summaries of news reaching Rosecrans*
    Entry 925, Dept. of the Cumberland, letters received.*

Navarro College, Pearce Civil War Collection, Corsicana TX
  Zachariah Bailey Letters (14th Texas Dismounted Cavalry)
  Wallace W. Darrah Papers (10th Wisconsin Infantry)
  Benjamin I. Franklin Letters (5th Texas Infantry)
  Henry Haymond Letter (2/18th US Infantry)
  Willis Jones Letters (84th Illinois Infantry)
  Samuel Kessler Letter, Thomas J. Kessler Papers (15th Ohio Infantry)
  George Lutze Letter (22nd Michigan Infantry)
  William M D. Martin Letter, Martin Family Papers
  Unknown letter, Union Soldier's Letters 1861-65.
  Elijah S. Watts Diary (2nd Kentucky Cavalry Union)
  Thomas White Papers (Union, unit unknown)
  Albert Woodcock Papers (92nd Illinois Mounted Infantry)

Nebraska State Historical Society, Lincoln NE
  John Holden McBride Correspondence (51st Illinois Infantry)*

New York Historical Society, Gilder-Lehrman Collection, New York NY
  Gustave Cook Letters (8th Texas Cavalry)
  J. William Flinn Letters (17th Mississippi Infantry)
  Joseph Jones Letters (79th Illinois Infantry)
  John J. McCook Letter (XXI Corps Staff)
  William McRae Letters (101st Indiana)
  Hillary Shifflet Letters (1st Ohio Infantry)

New York Public Library, New York NY
  Ezra Carman Papers
    Charles T. Clark Letter, February 12, 1909 (125th Ohio)
    J. H. Jennings Letter, November 28, 1893 (17th Kentucky)*
    John T. Wilder Letter, November 19, 1908
  Lucius Brown Letters (18th US Infantry)
  Theater Manuscripts Division
    Reminiscences of Nate Salsbury (89th Illinois Infantry)

New York State Library, Albany NY
    William LeRoy Watson Papers (21st Wisconsin Infantry)

Newberry Library, Chicago IL
    Daniel E. Bernard Letters, Howe-Bernard Family Papers (88th Illinois Infantry)
    Edward W. Curtis Letters (88th Illinois Infantry)
    John C. Fleming Letters (Chicago Board of Trade Battery)
    William T. Foster Letters (84th Illinois Infantry)

North Carolina Department of Archives and History, Raleigh NC
    D. H. Hill Papers*

North Dakota State Historical Society, Bismarck ND
    Hustus R. Kerr Papers and Diary (36th Ohio Infantry)
    North Dakota State University, Fargo ND
    Oscar B. Barrett Diary (1st Wisconsin Cavalry)

Northern Illinois University, Regional History Center, Founder's Library, DeKalb IL
    George Pepoon Letters (96th Illinois Infantry)
    Merritt Simonds Diary and Letters (42nd Illinois Infantry)

Northern Kentucky University, Highland Heights KY
    B. F. James Diary (51/52nd Tennessee Infantry)

Norwich University, Northfield VT
    James Evans Reminiscences (41st Ohio Infantry)

Ohio Genealogical Society, Mansfield OH
    Military History of Harrison Emmons (15th Ohio Infantry)

Ohio Historical Society, Columbus OH
    James Anderson Letter (93rd Ohio Infantry)
    Anonymous, "First Ohio Cavalry Reunion Pamphlet"
    George W. Botkin Letters, Sidney Baker Collection, (1st Kentucky Infantry US)
    John William Baldwin Letters (74th Ohio Infantry)
    A. S. Bloomfield Letters (A, 1st Ohio Light Artillery)
    John H. Bolton Letters and Diary (21st Ohio Infantry)
    John T. Booth papers (36th Ohio Infantry)
    Clark-Williams Family Letters (13th Ohio Infantry)
    William L. Curry Papers (1st Ohio Cavalry)
    Dilworth Journal (15th Ohio Infantry)
    Robert Newell Elder Letters (94th Ohio Infantry)
    Richard T. Foster Reminiscences (17th Ohio Infantry)
    Thomas Corwin Honnell Letters (99th Ohio Infantry)
    A. L. Gierhart Recollections (17th Ohio Infantry)
    John D. Innskeep Diary (17th Ohio Infantry)
    William H Kemper Diary (17th Indiana Infantry)
    Capt. R. Lyle Letter, Hoff Family Papers (86th Ohio Infantry)
    Silas S. Mallory recollections (64th Ohio Infantry)

John Wesley Marshall Diary (97th Ohio Infantry)
Joseph K Marshall Diary (90th Ohio Infantry)
William McKean Letters (35th Ohio Infantry)
Robert Thomas McKee Diary (31st Indiana Infantry)
James P. Mitchell Reminiscences (94th Ohio Infantry)
William B. Mitchell Letter (1st Ohio Infantry)
Emerson Opdyke Papers (125th Ohio Infantry)
Lewis Oglivie Letter, William Oglevie collection (14th Ohio Infantry)
William M. Parkinson Letters (31st Ohio Infantry & US Engineers)
George M. Patton Diary (98th Ohio Infantry)
Styles W. Porter Diary (52nd Ohio Infantry)*
Nelson Purdum Diary (33rd Ohio Infantry)
John P. Sanderson Letters (Rosecrans's Staff)*
Harry E. Sark, Recollections of Grandfather (John Burton, 90th Ohio Infantry)
Isaac N. Schnorf (94th Ohio Infantry)
Jerome K. Stubbins Diary (123rd Illinois Infantry)
Eben P. Sturges Letters (M, 1st Ohio Light Artillery)
John Thompson Papers (24th Ohio Infantry)
George Butler Turner Letters (92nd Ohio Infantry)
Oscar N Wheeler Diary (31st Ohio Infantry)
Jonathan Wood Recollections (14th Ohio Infantry)

Ohio University, Athens OH
William Parker Johnson Letters (18th Ohio Infantry)
Joseph Alpin Martin Letters (97th Ohio Infantry)

Oregon Historical Society, Portland OR
James W. Nesmith Papers (Civilian, Union)

Private collection of John Krotec, Sarasota Florida
Captain Peter Marchant letter (47th Tennessee Infantry)
Robert Nails letter (47th Alabama Infantry)

Rutgers University, New Brunswick NJ
John T. Brown Letter, Ellen M. Stuart Brown Collection (86th Illinois Infantry)
Frederick A. Bartleson Diary (100th Illinois Infantry)

Rutherford B. Hayes Presidential Center, Fremont OH
Charles Barney Dennis Memoir (101st Ohio Infantry)

Shorter College, Livingston Library, Rome GA.
G.W. Bradley Letters (4th Georgia Infantry)

South Carolina Historical Society, Charleston SC
Lafayette McLaws Letter, Cheves Family Papers*
Reginald Screvin Diary (2nd South Carolina Infantry)*

Stones River National Battlefield Park, Murfreesboro TN
William H. Buskey Diary (1st Kentucky Infantry US)*

David H. Chandler, "History of the Fifth Indiana Battery"*
E. John Ellis Recollections (16th Louisiana) (original at LSU Baton Rouge)
Risenar Etter Diary (16th Tennessee)* (Roryson Robertson Etter, see TSLA)
Lewis Hanback Letters, (51st Illinois Infantry)
James S. McCarty Letters (27th Illinois Infantry)
L. Jackson Sanders Diary (30th Tennessee Infantry)*

Sullivan Munce Cultural Center, Zionsville IN
James M. Hickerson Diary transcripts (10th Indiana Infantry)

Swarthmore College, Swarthmore PA
Joseph Turner Papers (10th Ohio Infantry)

Tennessee State Library and Archives, Nashville TN
William Gibbs Allen Memoirs (5th Tennessee Cavalry)
David Shires Myers Bodenhamer Memoirs (32nd Tennessee Infantry)
Robert F. Bunting Letters (8th Texas Cavalry)
Terry Cahal Letter (A. P. Stewart's Staff)
Newton Cannon Memoirs (11th Tennessee Cavalry)
Carroll Henderson Clark Memoirs (16th Tennessee Infantry)
Samuel A. Cooke Memoirs (17th/18th/24th/25th Texas Cavalry)
Col. James L. Cooper Memoir (20th Tennessee Infantry)
Edwin Cook Report (32nd Tennessee Infantry)
William Wirt Courtney Diary (32nd Tennessee Infantry)
Thomas W. Davis Diary (5th Tennessee Cavalry)*
W. R. Dyer Diary (Forrest Escort)
George Washington Dillon Diary (18th Tennessee Infantry)
Roryson Robertson Etter Diary (16th Tennessee Infantry)
John H. Freeman Diary (34th Mississippi Infantry)*
D. G. Godwin Letters (51st Tennessee Infantry)
George B. Guild Scrapbook (4th Tennessee Cavalry)
William Henry Harder Reminiscences (23rd Tennessee Infantry)*
John Harris Letter (Preston Smith's Staff)
Milton P. Jarnigan Memoirs (Buckner's Staff)
Isaac Madden Letters (Cleburne's Division, unit unknown)*
Philip M. Matlock Memoirs (20th Tennessee Infantry)
William Mebane Pollard Diary (1st Tennessee Infantry)
Bradford Nichol Diary and Memoir (Bragg's Staff)
Nimrod Potter Diary (3rd Tennessee Cavalry)
G. A. Rutledge Letters, Rutledge Family Papers (63rd Tennessee Infantry)
Samuel Robert Simpson Papers (30th Tennessee Infantry)*
William E. Sloan Diary (5th Tennessee Cavalry)*
Theodore Gillard Trimmier Letters (41st Alabama Infantry)
J. F. Wheless Memoirs (Polk's Staff)
James Franklin Witherspoon Papers (Morgan's Detachment)*
W. E. Yeatman Memoirs (2nd Tennessee Infantry)
Unknown Memoir, 5th Tennessee Infantry, Confederate Collection
Unknown Memoir, 50th Tennessee Infantry, Confederate Collection
Tennessee Veterans Questionnaires:
    John Ephriam Gold (24th Tennessee Infantry)*

Texas Tech University, Lubbock TX
    Kleber Miller Van Zandt Papers (7th Texas Infantry)

Tippecanoe County Historical Association Library, Lafayette IN
    W. O. Crouse Journal & Letters (18th Indiana Battery)
    William E. Ogburn Letters (17th Indiana Infantry)
    Winfield S. Street Letters (15th Indiana Infantry)

Toledo Public Library, Toledo OH
    Isaac M. Keller Reminscence, in "Sketches of War History" GAR Ford Post
    Frank Kemp Letter (35th Ohio Infantry)
    Joseph C. Skiles Diary and Letters (44th Illinois Infantry)

Tulane University, New Orleans LA
    Sister Edie Letter - author unknown. (Deshler's Brigade)
    Braxton Bragg Papers
    George Brent Papers (Bragg's Staff)
    Simon B. Buckner Report, Bragg Papers
    J. A. Charlaron Papers (Slocomb's Battery)*

Transylvania University, Lexington KY
    Samuel Woodson Price Letters (21st Kentucky Infantry)
    U.S. Army Heritage and Education Center, Carlisle PA
    John Arrick Letter (75th Indiana Infantry)
    Jacob H. Bender Letters (24th Wisconsin Infantry)*
    Luther P. Bradley Papers
    Almon Brower Letters (96th Illinois Infantry)
    William H. Brown Reminiscences (92nd Illinois Infantry)
    William D. Cole Letter (38th Alabama Infantry)
    George W. Cheney Recollections (105th Ohio Infantry)
    Rufus W. Daniel Diary (6th Arkansas Infantry)
    James E. Edmonds Diary (94th Ohio Infantry)
    John Eicker Papers, Harrisburg CWRT Collection (79th Pennsylvania Infantry)
    Jesse and Stroder W. Evans Letters, 125th Illinois Infantry)
    Horace Cecil Fisher Papers (Rosecrans's Staff)
    Cecil Fogg Letter, Wiley Sword Collection (36th Ohio Infantry)
    S. B. Franklin Reminiscences (77th Pennsylvania Infantry)
    Fulton Lenz Correspondence, Longenecker letters (Pioneer Corps)*
    Abram M. Glazener Letters, (18th Alabama Infantry)
    Thomas Green Letters (85th Illinois Infantry)
    Albert M. Haskett Papers (57th Indiana Infantry)
    Stephen H. Helmer Diary (93rd Ohio Infantry)
    William Kerns Diary (89th Ohio Infantry)
    Eli Long Papers
    George Lea Papers (7th Mississippi Infantry)
    Samuel Mays Reminiscences (50th Tennessee Infantry)
    Jacob Miller recollections (9th Indiana Infantry)
    K. A. Moore Letters (77th Pennsylvania Infantry)
    Thomas E. Morrow Recollections (11th Ohio Infantry)

Mungo F. Murray Letters (31st Ohio)*
James A. Price Diary (10th Indiana Infantry)
Hezekiah Rabb Letter (33rd Alabama Infantry)
John Russell Letters (21st Illinois Infantry)*
Asa B. Smith Memoir (97th Ohio Infantry)
David S. Stanley Papers
William Strahl Diary (49th Ohio Infantry)
Eben P. Sturges Papers, (M, 1st Ohio Light Artillery)* (see also Ohio Historical Society)
Spenser Brown Talley Memoirs (28th Tennessee Infantry)
Lester Dewitt Taylor Diary (105th Ohio Infantry)
Lewis Tripp Letters (18th Ohio Infantry)
Levi Wagner Recollections (1st Ohio Infantry)*
John J. Warbinton Letters (59th Ohio Infantry)
C. F. Weller Letters & Journal (17th Indiana)
E. G. Whiteside Diary (125th Ohio Infantry)
David M. Wynn Letters (49th Ohio Infantry)

University of Akron, Akron OH
    William Henry Greenwood Diary and Letters (Union Cavalry Corps Staff)

University of Arkansas, Fayetteville AR
    Samuel Wesley Fordyce, Fordyce Family Papers (Crook's Staff)
    Joseph Hubbard Jones Memoir, (1st Arkansas Infantry)
    Daniel Harris Reynolds Diary, (1st Arkansas Mounted Rifles)

University of California, Bancroft Library, Berkeley CA
    Samuel S. Boyd Letters, Boyd Family Papers (84th Indiana Infantry)
    Frederick Christian Hess Letters, (104th Illinois Infantry)

University of California, Los Angeles CA
    William S. Rosecrans Collection
        James P. Drouillard diary*
        William E. Margedant Letter*
        William S. Rosecrans Letters

University of Florida, P.K. Yonge Library of Florida History, Gainesville, FL
    J. Patton Anderson Papers
    Casermo O. Bailey Papers (7th Florida Infantry)

University of Georgia, Hargrett Rare Book and Manuscript Library, Athens GA
    Edgeworth Bird Letters (Benning Brigade Quartermaster)
    Telamon Cuyler Collection
        Henry C. Wayne Letter, Governor's Correspondence (GA State Line)
    Alfred Long Dearing Diary (Walker's staff)
    Robert G. Mitchell Letters (29th Georgia Infantry)
    Munday Letters (Buckner's Staff)
    William J. Short Letters (Co. G, 2nd Georgia Cavalry)
    Henry Smith memoirs (Preston Smith's Staff)
    Robert G. Stone Letters (15th Georgia Infantry)

University of Illinois, Illinois Historical Survey, Champaign-Urbana IL
  John Hoch Diary (96th Illinois Infantry)
  Jones and Heath Letter, William E. Lodge Collection (73rd Illinois Infantry)
  Duncan C. Milner Letters and Memoirs (98th Ohio Infantry)
  Benjamin Franklin Reed Letters (21st Illinois Infantry)
  Montraville Reeves Letters (79th Illinois Infantry)
  James E. Withrow Diary (M, 1st Illinois Artillery)

University of Iowa, Iowa City IA
  Harrison Allspaugh Diaries (31st Ohio Infantry)

University of Kansas, Spencer Research Library, Lawrence KS
  Douglas O. Lilley Diary (8th Kansas Infantry)
  Joseph Murray Raymond Papers (101st Ohio Infantry)

University of Kentucky, Lexington KY
  John T. Gunn Letter, Gunn Family Papers (Barnes's Staff)
  William Johnson Stone Biography (Morgan's Detachment)
  John W. Tuttle Journal (1st Kentucky Infantry US)
  Henry M. West Letters (17th Kentucky Infantry US)
  Wyckliffe-Preston Papers (Buckner's Staff)*

University of Michigan, Bentley Historical Library, Ann Arbor MI
  Harold J. Bartlett Letter (D, 1st Michigan Light Artillery)
  William J. Carroll Letter (13th Michigan Infantry)
  George W. Chase Letters (4th Michigan Cavalry)
  Thomas Conely Letters (9th Michigan Infantry)
  James L Curry Letters (21st Ohio Infantry)
  D. H. Haines Recollections (4th Michigan Cavalry)*
  Henry Hempstead Diary (2nd Michigan Cavalry)
  Alonzo M. Keeler Diary and Papers (22nd Michigan Infantry)
  John C. Love Letters and Journal (9th Michigan Infantry)
  James Martin Letter (11th Michigan Infantry)
  Seymour Chase Letter, McCreery Family Papers (21st Michigan Infantry)
  John Parkhurst Letters (9th Michigan Infantry)
  Henry Albert Potter, "Account of the battle of Chickamauga and Wheeler's Raid," (4th Michigan Cavalry)
  Richard B. Robbins Reminiscences (4th Michigan Cavalry)
  Andrew Tousley Letter, Nina Ness Collection (64th Ohio Infantry)

University of Michigan, Clements Historical Library, Ann Arbor MI
  Charles Barnett Journal (Battery I, 2nd Illinois Artillery)
  William L. Curry Journal and Letters (1st Ohio Cavalry)
  Lewis Carlisle Mead Letters (22nd Michigan Infantry)
  Henry H. Seys Letters (15th Ohio Infantry)
  Washington Irving Snyder Diary (11th Michigan Infantry)
  Heinrich Spaeth Letters (9th Ohio Infantry)
  William D. Travis (22nd Illinois Infantry)
  James Verity Journal (18th Ohio Infantry)
  Henry H. Willard Letter (4th Indiana Cavalry)

University of Mississippi, J.D. Williams Library, University MS
    J.H. Buford Letter, Juanita Brown Collection (32nd Mississippi Infantry)
    Given Campbell Letter, Juanita Brown Collection (Polk's Staff)
    John C. Campbell Collection (29th Mississippi Infantry)
    William Sylvester Dillon Diary (4th Tennessee Infantry)
    B. F. Gentry Letters (29th Mississippi Infantry)
    Robert A. Jarman, "History of Company K, 27th Mississippi Infantry"
    Robert Augustus Moore Diary (17th Mississippi Infantry)
    Charles Roberts Collection (Strahl's Brigade Staff)
    T. B. Setttle Letters, Settle Collection (32nd Mississippi Infantry)
    Edward Cary Walthall Papers

University of Missouri, Western Historical Manuscript Collection, Rolla, MO
    Bergun H. Brown Letter (29th Indiana Infantry)
    Tom Coleman Letters (11th Texas Cavalry)
    William Elwood Patterson Memoir (38th Illinois Infantry) (See also ALPL)
    Lot Dudley Young Memoir (4th Kentucky Infantry)

University of Memphis, Memphis TN
    William B. Gilliland Letters (22nd Alabama Infantry)
    J. Edward James Letters (96th Illinois Infantry)
    Joseph G. Rhea (Confederate Commissary)
    E. M Strahl Diary (84th Illinois Infantry)

University of North Carolina, Southern Historical Collection, Chapel Hill
    J. Patton Anderson Memoir
    Taylor Beatty Diary (Bragg's Staff)
    Henry L. Benning Papers*
    John Bratton Papers (6th South Carolina Infantry)
    Gavin Campbell Papers (2nd Kentucky Cavalry)
    Clinton A. Cilley Papers (2nd Minnesota Infantry)
    D. Coleman Diary (Hawkins Sharpshooter Battalion)
    Confederate Veteran Papers
        J. T. Gaines, "Recollections of Chickamauga" (5th Kentucky Infantry CS)
    Joseph B. Cummings Recollections (Walker's Staff)
    Espey Family Papers (65th Georgia Infantry)*
    Gale-Polk Papers
        William T. Gale Letters
        Leonidas Polk Letters
        Lycurgus A. Sallie Letter
    Franklin Gaillard Papers (2nd South Carolina Infantry)*
    Daniel C. Govan Papers
    R. M. Gray Reminiscences (37th Georgia Infantry)
    James Iredell Hall Memoir (9th Tennessee Infantry)
    G. W. F. Harper Papers (58th North Carolina Infantry)
    John F. Leonard Letters (125th Illinois Infantry)
    W. W. Mackall Papers (Bragg's Staff)
    James A. McLean Letter, Jeannette Bonebrake Correspondence (125th Illinois)
    George Knox Miller Papers (8th Confederate Cavalry)*
    Willis J. Milner Diary (33rd Alabama Infantry)

Martin Van Buren Moore Papers (6th North Carolina Cavalry)
Leroy Moncure Nutt Letters (Rucker's Legion)
James W. Patton Letters (60th North Carolina Infantry)
Ruffin, Roulhac & Hamilton Papers
    DeBose Egleston Letter (2nd South Carolina Infantry)*
Henry Semple Papers
    Samuel Hall Letter (7th Alabama Cavalry)
    T. C. Randolph Letter, (Semple's Battery)
Thomas Bog Slade Papers (58th North Carolina Infantry)
James K. Street Letters (9th Texas Infantry)
John and Sallie Thurman Papers (3rd Tennessee Cavalry)
William H. Tillson Diary (84th Illinois Infantry)
Richard A. Torrence autobiographical sketch (8th Texas Cavalry)
Isaac Barton Ulmer Papers (3rd Alabama Cavalry)*
Paul Turner Vaughn Papers (4th Alabama Infantry)
James H. Whiswell Letters (4th US Cavalry)
Thomas B. Wilson Reminiscences (11th Tennessee Cavalry)
Marcus J. Wright Collection
    Braxton Bragg Letter
Henry Duplessis Wells Papers (18th Tennessee Cavalry Battalion)*

University of Notre Dame, South Bend IN
    Caley Family Correspondence (105th Ohio)

University of South Carolina, South Caroliniana Library, Columbia SC
    Jasper Brobham Letter (1st South Carolina Infantry)
    Ellison Capers Papers (24th South Carolina Infantry)*
    Childs Family Papers, J.B. Palmer Letter (58th North Carolina Infantry)
    David Crawford Letter, (Longstreet Staff & 15th South Carolina)*
    A. H. Dalton Letters (Hampton Legion)
    Charles Manning Furman Letters (16th South Carolina Infantry)
    Jesse S. McGee Letter, McGee-Foster Papers (7th South Carolina Infantry)
    James Drayton Nance Letters (3rd South Carolina Infantry)
    John Henry Steinmeyer Diary (24th South Carolina Infantry)
    James C. Tinkler Letter (6th South Carolina Infantry)

University of Southern Mississippi, McCain Library, Hattiesburg MS
    Mark P. Lowery Autobiography (S.A.M. Wood's Brigade)

University of the South. Suwannee TN
    Leonidas Polk Papers

University of Tennessee, Martin TN
    Martin Van Buren Oldham Diaries (9th Tennessee Infantry)

University of Tennessee, Knoxville TN
    Joseph E. Boyd Letters (115th Illinois Infantry)
    Harry C. Cushing Letters (Battery H, 4th US Artillery)
    Orlando L. French Letters (75th Illinois Infantry)

B. F. James Memoir (51st/52nd Tennessee Infantry)
George Lamphear Letters (2nd Minnesota Infantry)
Edward Summers Letter (6th Kentucky Cavalry US)
Julius E. Thomas Diary (1st Tennessee Cavalry US)
T. J. Walker Reminiscences (9th Tennessee Infantry)
Milton Weaver Letters (74th Ohio Infantry)
Unknown Letter, from "Willie" (1st Alabama Cavalry)

University of Texas, Briscoe Center for American History, Austin TX
John Crittenden Letters (34th Alabama Infantry)*
Jacob Cressinger Letters (41st Ohio Infantry)
George A. Gordon Letters (Georgia State Troops)*
Thomas B. Hampton Letters (63rd Virginia)*
John W. Hill Papers (8th Texas Cavalry)*
James H. Manahan Letters (4th Texas Infantry)
William T. Martin Papers
Roger Q. Mills Letters (6th/10th/15th Texas)*
James and William Nicholson Letters (8th Texas Cavalry)
Unidentified Soldier's diary (4th Louisiana Battalion)*
J. W. Ward Letters (24th Mississippi Infantry)*

University of Virginia, Charlottesville VA
John Levering Collection (Reynolds's Staff)
Walter Gibson Peter Letters (Martin's Cavalry division)
Jeremiah Crook Letters (13th Tennessee Infantry)

University of Washington, Seattle WA
James Forsyth Papers (King's (Regulars) staff)
Riley M. Hoskinson Letter and Journal (73rd Illinois Infantry)

University of West Florida, Pensacola FL
Timothy W. Bludworth Letters, William H. Watson Papers (6th Florida Infantry)

University of Wisconsin, Golda Meir Library, Milwaukee WI
William S. Mitchell Letters (1st Wisconsin Infantry)
James Pillar Letters (21st Wisconsin)

Urbana Free Library, Champaign County Archives, Urbana IL
Oliver Perry Hunt Letters (125th Illinois)

Vanderbilt University, Heard Library, Nashville TN
William R. McMahan Diary, (Union Pioneers)

Vigo County Public Library, Terre Haute, IN
Daniel S. Schenk Diary (79th Illinois Infantry)
Harrison Nay Letter (79th Illinois Infantry)

Virginia Historical Society, Richmond VA
James Madison Brannock Papers (5th Tennessee Infantry)*

George Binford Letters (18th Tennessee Infantry)
John Walter Fairfax Papers (Longstreet's Staff)*
James Miller Wysor Letters (54th Virginia Infantry)*

Virginia Military Institute, Preston Library, Lexington VA
Septimus Knight Diary, in John F. Hanna Papers (15th Pennsylvania Cavalry)
J. R. Hurley Papers (39th Alabama Infantry)

Virginia Polytechnic Institute and State University, Blacksburg VA
Thomas Morris Burns Letters (52nd Ohio Infantry)
William Wallace Hensley Autobiography (21st Illinois Infantry)

Virginia State Library, Richmond VA
D. H. Hill Papers*
L. F. Moody Letter, J. B. Snyder Collection (7th Texas Infantry)*

Wabash College, Robert T. Ramsey Archival Center, Crawfordsville IN
Henry Campbell, "Three Years In The Saddle," (18th Indiana Battery)

Washington State History Research Center, Tacoma WA
Harlow M. B. Wittum Papers (10th Wisconsin)

Waukegan Historical Society, Waukegan IL
96th Illinois File
    John Baker Letter
    John Corson Smith Letter
GAR Memorial Book, Waukegan Post #374 Personal War Sketches
    John W. Swansbrough sketch (96th Illinois)
    Edward Murray sketch (96th Illinois)

West Virginia University Library, Morgantown WV
Allen D. Frankenberry Diary (15th Pennsylvania Cavalry)*

Western Illinois University. McComb IL
Robert Everett Letters (84th Illinois Infantry)
Christopher Wetsel (84th Illinois Infantry)

Western Kentucky University, Bowling Green, KY
Cincinattus D. Bell Diary (2nd Kentucky Cavalry CS)
David McKee Claggett Diary (17th Kentucky Infantry US)
Dewitt Clinton Downing Letters (9th Kentucky Infantry US)
Robert Alan Dearman Diary (2nd Minnesota Infantry)
E. John Ellis Letters, Ellis Family Papers (16th Louisiana Infantry)
John Frost Letter, George W. Simons Papers (17th Kentucky Infantry US)
George W. Hughes Letters (18th Ohio Infantry)
Charles E. Leverich Diary (Buckner's Staff)
A. W. Randolph Letter (1st Kentucky Infantry, CS)
Richard C. Thomas Letter (Morgan's Cavalry)

Western Michigan University, Regional History Collection, Kalamazoo MI
  "A Civil War Diary and Letters By A Union Officer Jeremiah Doran Likens
     Compiled by Cheryl Eastwood Suazo (30th Indiana Infantry)
  James Brady Collection, Col. R. P. Rowley Papers (C.S.A. Engineers)
  Boyce Collection, Eli Russell Letters (4th Michigan Cavalry)
  Don DeYoung Collection
     Charles R. Pomeroy Letters (33rd Ohio Infantry)
     John Wesson Letters, (2nd Michigan Cavalry)
  James W. King Letters (11th Michigan Infantry)
  Joseph Lawhead Collection, Eugene Bronson Letters (4th Michigan Cavalry)
  Lester Mange Collection, John J. Snook Diary (22nd Michigan Infantry)
  Lola J. Warrick Collection, William G. Eaton Letters (13th Michigan Infantry)
  Betty Yenner Collection, Augustus L Yenner Diary (121st Ohio)

Western Reserve Historical Society, Cleveland, OH
  Charles K. Bailer Letters (18th US Infantry)*
  James Barnett Papers (1st Ohio Artillery, various batteries)
  Alden F. Brooks Memoir (105th Ohio Infantry)
  Charles Ransley Green Letter, (101st Ohio Infantry)
  Albert G. Hart Papers (41st Ohio Infantry)*
  George Hodges Letters (41st Ohio Infantry) *
  Wilbur F. Hinman Papers (65th Ohio Infantry)
  George Landrum Letters (Signal Corps, 14th Corps)
  Stanley B. Lockwood Letters (105th Ohio Infantry)
  Benjamin H. Lossing Papers
     William B. Hazen Letter*
  Silas Mallory Recollections (64th Ohio Infantry)
  James M Nash Diary (19th Ohio Infantry)
  Nesbitt-Raub Collection
     J. W. Nesbitt Letters (105th Ohio Infantry)
     Isaac P. C. Raub Letters (105th Ohio Infantry)
  William Palmer Collection
     Braxton Bragg Papers
  Edward Perkins Papers (59th Ohio Infantry)*
  Elbert Squires Letters (101st Ohio Infantry)
  William A. Robinson Diary (77th Pennsylvania Infantry)*
  Alexander Varian Letters (1st Ohio Infantry)
  Aquila Wiley Papers (41st Ohio Infantry and various regiments)

Wichita State University, Wichita, KS
  Robert Stevenson Letters, Mark Bassett Collection. (73rd Illinois)

Williams Research Library, Historic New Orleans Collection, New Orleans LA
  Vaught, William C.D. Letter, October 4th, 1863. (Washington Artillery)

Winthrop College, Rock Hill SC
  John Belue Diary (15th South Carolina Infantry)

Wisconsin Historical Society, Madison WI
  Kelsey M. Adams Letters (1st Wisconsin Infantry)

Robert J. Bates Letters (10th Wisconsin Infantry)
William Boyd Letter, Charles L. Ballard Letters (1st Wisconsin Infantry)
Willis Chase Letters (1st Wisconsin Cavalry)
Eugene C. Comstock Letters, (24th Wisconsin Infantry)
George F. Cooley Diary (24th Wisconsin Infantry)
Gasharie Decker Letters (3rd Wisconsin Battery)
Alfred Galpin Diary and Letters (1st Wisconsin Infantry & 4th Indiana Battery) Lucius Dwight Hinkley
    Papers (10th Wisconsin Infantry)
Ole C. Johnson Letter, Barton Papers (15th Wisconsin Infantry)
Newton Jones Letters (1st Wisconsin Cavalry)
Theodore Kellogg Papers (1st Wisconsin Cavalry)
Abraham V. Knapp Diary (10th Wisconsin Infantry)
Hugh A. McLaurin Letters (7th Mississippi Infantry)
John Henry Otto Memoirs (21st Wisconsin Infantry)
Paine Family Papers, "history of Co. G, 1st Wisconsin Cavalry"
Horace T. Persons Letters and Diary (1st Wisconsin Cavalry)
Milo K. Swanton Papers, "Historical Narrative of the Lt. Rollin Olson family heritage" (15th Wisconsin
    Infantry)
Jerry Swart Letters (1st Wisconsin Cavalry)
Henry Clay Taylor Letters (1st Wisconsin Infantry)
Michael Thompson Diary (15th Wisconsin Infantry)
Samuel F. Thompson Diary (10th Indiana Infantry)
Ole Thostenson Reminiscences (15th Wisconsin Infantry)

Wisconsin Veterans Museum, Madison WI
James M. Chatfield Letters (2nd Michigan Cavalry)
Horatio Kirkland Foote Letters (1st Wisconsin Cavalry)
William C. Pitt Memoir and Diary (24th Wisconsin Infantry)
James W. Skeels Letters (1st Wisconsin Cavalry)

Wyoming Historical Society, Cheyenne WY
Henry B Freeman Papers (US Regulars)

Wright State University, Dayton OH
Oliver Protsman Diary (1st Ohio Infantry)
William L. Patterson Letters (1st Ohio Infantry)

Yale University, New Haven CT
Augustus B. Carpenter Letters (19th US Infantry)*

Unpublished Theses

Blackford, Robert W. *The Civil War Service of General Gordon Granger U.S.A.* MA Thesis, Southern Illinois University, Edwardsville IL, 1990.
Blackwell, Sam M. Jr. *The History of the 123rd Illinois Infantry In The Civil War.* MA thesis, Northern Illinois University, 1976.
Brewer, Richard J. *The Tullahoma Campaign: Operational Insights.* US Army Command And General Staff College, Ft. Leavenworth, 1991.

Broome, Doyle D. *Intelligence Operations of the Army of the Cumberland During the Tullahoma and Chickamauga Campaigns.* US Army Command and General Staff College, Ft. Leavenworth, 1989.

Corns, Evan Robert. *Daniel Harvey Hill and the Peninsular, Maryland, and Chickamauga Campaigns.* MA Thesis, University of North Carolina, Chapel Hill, 1961.

Coryell, Keith R. *Three Volunteers: Personal Realities of the Civil War.* MA Thesis, Northern Illinois University, 1987.

Edwards, Lawyn C. *Confederate Cavalry at Chickamauga: What Went Wrong?* US Army Command And General Staff College, Ft. Leavenworth, 1990.

Eiserman, Frederick A. *Longstreet's Corps at Chickamauga: Lessons in Inter-Theater Deployment.* U.S. Army Command and General Staff College, Ft. Leavenworth, 1985.

Eresman, Raymond Scott. *Union and Confederate Infantry Doctrine in the Battle of Chickamauga.* U.S. Army Command and General Staff College, Ft. Leavenworth, 1991.

Griffin, Kevin. *History of the 35th Indiana Regiment.* MA Thesis, Notre Dame University, 1992.

Johnson, Robert Louis. *Confederate Staff Work at Chickamauga: An Analysis of the Staff of the Army Of Tennessee.* US Army Command and General Staff College, Ft. Leavenworth, 1992.

Kapaun, David M. Jr. *Major General Joseph J. Reynolds and his Division at Chickamauga: A Historical Analysis.* US Army Command and General Staff College, Ft. Leavenworth, 1999.

King, Michael R. *Brigadier General ST. John Liddell's Division at Chickamauga: The Study of a Division's Performance in Battle.* US Army Command and General Staff College, Ft. Leavenworth, 1997.

Londa, John J. *The Role Of Union Cavalry During The Chickamauga Campaign.* US Army Command and General Staff College, Ft. Leavenworth, 1991.

Lott, Robert P. Jr. *Van Cleve At Chickamauga: The Study of a Division's Performance in Battle.* US Army Command and General Staff College, Ft. Leavenworth, 1996.

Mammay, Michael J. *Union Artillery at the Battle of Chickamauga.* US Army Command and General Staff College, Ft. Leavenworth, 2001.

Manville, Craig J. *The Limits of Obedience: Brigadier General Thomas J. Wood's Performance During the Battle of Chickamauga.* U. S. Army Command and General Staff College, Ft. leavenworth, 2005.

Mendoza, Alexander. *Struggle For Command: General James Longstreet and the First Corps in the West, 1863-1864.* Phd. Dissertation, Texas Tech University, 2002.

Moore, James Orville. *Men of the Bayou City Guards.* University of Houston at Clear Lake, 1988. (5th Texas Infantry)

Newsom, James Lynn. *Intrepid Gray Warriors: the 7th Texas Infantry, 1861-1865.* Phd. Dissertation, Texas Christian University, 1995.

Richardson, Robert D. *Rosecrans' Staff at Chickamauga.* US Army Command and General Staff College, Ft. Leavenworth, 1989.

Rubenstein, David A. *A Study of the Medical Support to the Union and Confederate Armies During the Battle For Chickamauga.* U.S. Army Command And General Staff College, Fort Leavenworth, 1990.

Taylor, James Carlisle. *The 60th North Carolina Regiment: A Case Study of Enlistment and Desertion in Western North Carolina During the Civil War.* MA Thesis, Western Carolina University, 1996.

Thornton, Leland W. *When Gallantry was Commonplace: A History of the Michigan Eleventh Volunteer Infantry, January 1863 to September 1864.* MA Thesis, Western Michigan University, 1986.

Government Publications

Adjutant General's Office, *Official Military History of Kansas Regiments during the War for the Suppression of the Great Rebellion.* Leavenworth, KS: W. S. Burke, 1870.

Adjutant General of the State of Kansas. *Military History of the Kansas Regiments.* Topeka: Kansas State Printing Co. 1896.

Barnes, Joseph K. *The Medical and Surgical History of the War of the Rebellion: Appendix to Part I.* Washington, DC: Government Printing Office, 1870.

Belknap, Charles E. *History of the Michigan Organizations at Chickamauga, Chattanooga, and Missionary Ridge, 1863*. Lansing, MI: Robert Smith Printing Company, 1897.

Benham, Calhoun. *A System for Conducting Musketry Instruction*. Ashland, VA: J.W. Henry Publishing, Inc. 1998. Reprint of 1863 C.S.A. pamphlet.

Boynton, Henry V. *Dedication of the Chickamauga and Chattanooga National Military Park, September 18-20, 1895*. Washington, DC: Government Printing Office, 1896.

Boynton, Henry V. *The National Military Park, Chickamauga-Chattanooga. An Historical Guide, with Maps and Illustrations*. Cincinnati: The Robert Clarke Co., 1895.

Commissioners. *Indiana at Chickamauga: 1863-1900, Report of Indiana Commissioners, Chickamauga National Military Park*. Indianapolis: Sentinel Printing Co., Printers and Binders, 1900.

Heitman, Francis B. *Historical Register and Dictionary of the United States Army, From Its Organization, September 29, 1789, to March 2, 1903*. 2 vols. Washington: Government Printing Office, 1903.

Hewitt, Janet B., Noah Andre Trudeau, and Bryce Suderow, eds. *Supplement to the Official Records of the Union and Confederate Armies*,100 vols. Wilmington, NC: Broadfoot Publishing Co., 1995.

Fry, James B. *Official Register of the Officers and Cadets of the U.S. Military Academy, West Point, New York*. New York: James F. Baldwin, Printer, 1858.

Lindsey, Daniel W. *Report of the Adjutant General of the State of Kentucky, 1861-1866*, 2 vols. Frankfort: Kentucky Yeoman Office, 1866-1867.

McElroy, Joseph C. *Chickamauga: Record of the Ohio Chickamauga and Chattanooga National Park Commission*. Cincinnati: Earhart and Richardson, Printers, 1896.

Memorial Addresses on the Life and Character of Robert M. A. Hawk (A Representative from Illinois) Delivered in the House of Representatives and in the Senate, Forty-Seventh Congress. Washington, DC: Government Printing Office,1883. (92nd Illinois Mounted Infantry).

Robertson, John, Compiler. *Michigan in the War*. Lansing, MI: W. S. George & Co, State Printers, 1882.

Skinner, George W., Ed. *Pennsylvania at Chickamauga and Chattanooga: Ceremonies at the Dedication of the Monuments Erected by the Commonwealth of Pennsylvania to mark the positions of the Pennsylvania Commands engaged in the Battle*. Harrisburg, PA: William Stanley Ray, State Printer of Pennsylvania, 1897.

South Carolina Chickamauga Commission. *Ceremonies At The Unveiling Of The South Carolina Monument On The Chickamauga Battlefield, May 27th, 1901*. Columbia, SC: n.p., 1901.

Terrill, W. H. *Report of the Adjutant General of the State of Indiana*. Indianapolis: Indiana Adjutant General's Office, 1866.

United States War Department. *War of the Rebellion, A Compilation of the Official Records of the Union and Confederate Armies*. 70 volumes in 128 parts. Washington, DC: Government Printing Office, 1880-1901.

Contemporary Newspapers

The months following the battle of Chickamauga saw an explosion of stories appearing in newspapers around the country. While the larger papers had their own correspondents (whose articles were widely reprinted) many hometown papers had informal soldier-correspondents serving with the army, who filled their pages with personal accounts and provided casualty lists. If cited individually, that material would run to dozens of extra pages. Articles from postwar papers are not listed here.

Abbeville Press, 1863 (South Carolina)
Abingdon Virginian, 1863 (Virginia)
Akron-Summit County Beacon, 1863 (Ohio)
Aledo Record, 1863 (Illinois)
Allegan Journal, 1863 (Michigan)
Amboy Times, 1863 (Illinois)

Army And Navy Journal, 1863 (Washington DC)
Ashtabula Weekly Telegraph, 1863 (Ohio)
Athens Messenger, 1863(Ohio)
Atlanta Constitution, 1863 (Georgia)
Augusta Chronicle, 1863 (Georgia)
Augusta Newspaper Digest, 1863 (Georgia)
Aurora Beacon, 1863 (Illinois)
Aurora Commercial, 1863 (Indiana)
Beaufort Free South, 1863 (South Carolina)
Belvedere Standard, 1863 (Illinois)
Burlington Standard, 1863 (Wisconsin)
Cadiz Republican, 1863 (Ohio)
Canton American Citizen, 1863 (Mississippi)
Canton-Stark County Republican, 1863 (Ohio)
Carroll County Weekly Mirror, 1863 (Illinois)
Centralia Sentinel, 1863 (Illinois)
Chardon Jeffersonian Democrat, 1863 (Ohio)
Charleston Daily Courier, 1863 (South Carolina)
Charleston Mercury, 1863 (South Carolina)
Chicago Evening Journal, 1863 (Illinois)
Chicago Tribune, 1863 (Illinois)
Chillicothe-Scioto Gazette, 1863 (Ohio)
Cincinnati Commercial, 1863 (Ohio)*
Cincinnati Daily Enquirer, 1863 (Ohio)
Cincinnati Gazette, 1863 (Ohio)
Clarksville Standard, 1863 (Texas)
Cleveland Herald, 1863 (Ohio)
Cleveland Morning Leader, 1863 (Ohio)
Cleveland Plain Dealer, 1863 (Ohio)
Clinton County Republican, 1863 (Ohio)
Columbus Daily Express, 1863 (Ohio)
Columbus Daily Ohio State Journal, 1863 (Ohio)
Columbus Sun, 1863 (Georgia)
Columbus Weekly Enquirer, 1863 (Georgia)
Covington People's Friend, 1863 (Indiana)
Daily Wisconsin, 1863 (Wisconsin)
Dayton Weekly Journal, 1863 (Ohio)
Delaware Gazette, 1863 (Ohio)
Delphi Journal, 1863 (Indiana)
Detroit Free Press, 1863 (Michigan)
DeWitt County Weekly Transcript, 1863 (Illinois)
Elgin Gazette, 1863 (Illinois)
Evansville Daily Journal, 1863 (Indiana)
Fort Wayne Weekly Sentinel, (Indiana)
Frankfort Daily Commonwealth, 1863 (Kentucky)
Frankfort Tri-Weekly Commonwealth, 1863 (Kentucky)
Franklin Repository, 1863 (Pennsylvania)
Freedom's Champion, 1863 (Kansas)
Fremont Journal, 1863 (Ohio)
Galena Northwestern Gazette, 1863 (Illinois)

Gallipolis Journal, 1863 (Ohio)

Goshen Democrat, 1863 (Indiana)

Grant County Witness, 1863 (Wisconsin)

Hancock County Courier, 1863 (Ohio)

Harrisburg Patriot Union, 1863 (Pennsylvania)

Hendersonville Times, 1863 (North Carolina)

Houston Tri-Weekly Telegraph, 1863 (Texas)

Huntsville Confederate, 1863 (Alabama)

Illinois State Journal, 1863 (Illinois)

Indiana State Sentinel, 1863 (Indiana)

Indianapolis Daily Journal, 1863 (Indiana)

Island City Times, 1863 (Wisconsin)

Jackson Standard, 1863 (Ohio)

Joliet Signal, 1863 (Illinois)

Keithsburg Observer, 1863 (Illinois)

Lafayette Daily Courier, 1863 (Indiana)

LaGrange Standard, 1863 (Indiana)

Lancaster Daily Evening Express, 1863 (Pennsylvania)

Lancaster Gazette, 1863 (Ohio)

Lancaster Ledger, 1863 (South Carolina)

Lima Weekly Gazette, 1863 (Ohio)

Logansport Democratic Pharos, 1863 (Indiana)

Logansport Journal, 1863 (Indiana)

Louisville Daily Democrat, 1863 (Kentucky)

Louisville Daily Journal, 1862-1863 (Kentucky)

Macomb Weekly Journal, 1863 (Illinois)

Macon Daily Telegraph, 1863 (Georgia)

Macon Journal and Messenger, 1863 (Georgia)

Madison County Democrat, 1863 (Ohio)

Madison County Union, 1863, (Ohio)

Marshall County Republican, 1863 (Indiana)

Marysville Tribune, 1863 (Ohio)

Mattoon Gazette, 1863 (Illinois)

McArthur Register, 1863 (Ohio)

Marietta Register, 1863 (Ohio)

Memphis Daily Appeal, 1863 (Originally Tennessee, published in Atlanta at the time)

Milledgeville Southern Recorder, 1863 (Georgia)

Milwaukee Daily News, 1863 (Wisconsin)

Milwaukee Sentinel, 1863 (Wisconsin)

Mobile Daily Advertiser, 1863 (Alabama)

Mobile Daily Register, 1863 (Alabama)

Mobile Register and Advertiser, 1863 (Alabama)

Montgomery Daily Advertiser, 1863 (Alabama)

New Albany Daily Ledger, 1863 (Indiana)

New Castle Courier, 1863 (Indiana)

New Philadelphia Democrat, 1863 (Ohio)

New York Herald, 1863 (New York)

New York Tribune, 1863 (New York)

Norwalk Reflector, 1863 (Ohio)

Oregon Statesman, 1863 (Oregon)

Oshkosh Courier, 1863 (Wisconsin)
Paris Western Citizen, 1863 (Kentucky)
Paulding Independent, 1863 (Ohio)
Perrysburg Weekly Journal, 1863 (Ohio)
Polk County Press, 1863 (Wisconsin)
Quincy Daily Whig and Republican, 1863 (Illinois)
Raleigh Daily Progress, 1863 (North Carolina)
Rensselaer Weekly Gazette, 1863 (Indiana)
Richmond Times, 1863 (Virginia)
Richmond Palladium, 1863 (Indiana)
Rochester Chronicle, 1863-64 (Indiana)
Rock Island Evening Argus, 1863, (Illinois)
Rock River Democrat, 1863 (Illinois)
Rockford Register, 1863 (Illinois)
Rome Tribune, 1863 (Georgia)
Rome Tri-weekly Courier, 1863 (Georgia)
Rushville-Schuyler County Citizen, 1863 (Illinois)
Sandusky Ohio Commercial Register, 1863 (Ohio)
Savannah Morning News, 1863 (Georgia)
Savannah Republican, 1863 (Georgia)
Shelby Union Banner, 1863 (Indiana)
St. Clairsville Gazette, 1863 (Ohio)
St. Clairsville Belmont Chronicle, 1863 (Ohio)
St. Louis Daily Missouri Republican, 1863-64 (Missouri)
St. Louis Missouri Daily Democrat, 1863 (Missouri)
St. Louis Missouri Daily Union, 1863 (Missouri)
Steuben Republican, 1863 (Indiana)
Steubenville Weekly Herald, 1863 (Ohio)
Talladega Democratic Watchtower, 1863 (Alabama)
Tiffin Weekly Tribune, 1863 (Ohio)
Toledo Blade, 1863 (Ohio)
Toledo Commercial, 1863 (Ohio)
Troy Times, 1863 (Ohio)
Wabash Plain Dealer, (Indiana)
Wabash Weekly Intelligencer, 1863 (Indiana)
Warren Independent, 1863 (Illinois)
Washington Telegraph, 1863 (Arkansas)
Waukegan Weekly Gazette, 1863 (Illinois)
Waupun Times, 1863 (Wisconsin)
Western Reserve Chronicle, 1863, (Ohio)
Winchester Journal, 1863 (Indiana)
Wisconsin State Journal, 1863 (Wisconsin)*
Woodstock Sentinel, 1863 (Illinois)
Youngstown Mahoning Register, 1863 (Ohio)
Zanesville Courier, 1863 (Ohio)

Articles published in *The American Tribune* (Indiana)

Anonymous, "At Chickamauga." January 14, 1892.
Anonymous. "Told by a Johnny Reb," October 19, 1893. (Maney's Brigade).

Anonymous, "Told by the Veterans of Chickamauga," February 22, 1894.

Brewer, Lewis. "A Reminiscence of the Battle of Chickamauga," November 28, 1890. (29th Indiana).

Correspondent of the St. Louis Globe-Democrat, "Stubborn Fighting at Chickamauga," September 12, 1890.

Correspondent of the St. Louis Globe-Democrat, "Chickamauga: One of the Remarkable Battles of the War," September 12, 1890.

Correspondent of the St. Louis Globe-Democrat, "Bloody Pond-Chickamauga," September 12, 1890.

Dolton, George E. "Chickamauga," October 26, 1893. (M, 1st Illinois Light Artillery).

Dolton, George E. "Chickamauga continued," December 28, 1893. (M, 1st Illinois Light Artillery).

Dolton, George E. "Chickamauga, part three," January 4, 1894. (M, 1st Illinois Light Artillery).

Dolton, George E. "Chickamauga, part four," January 25, 1894. (M, 1st Illinois Light Artillery).

Doyle, W. E. "Wilder's Brigade, part 2," October 21, 1897.

Doyle, W. E. "Wilder's Brigade, part 3," November 4, 1897.

Emmington, J. G. "Scenes At Chickamauga," February 27, 1891.

E.E.L, "14 Months in Hades," January 14, 1892. (36th Illinois Infantry).

Kilmer, George L. "Sheridan's Pets," March 17, 1892. (36th Illinois Infantry).

Kilmer, George L. "Ohioans in Battle," January 4, 1894. (49th Ohio Infantry).

Ohlwine, J. N. "Chickamauga," October 5, 1893. (30th Indiana Infantry).

Articles published in *Confederate Veteran* Magazine

Allen, J. W. "Bullet in a Testament," vol. VI, no. 4 (April, 1898), 154. (19th Louisiana Infantry).

Allen, W. G. "Reminiscences of Chickamauga," vol. XIX, no. 11 (November, 1911), 511. (2nd Tennessee Cavalry).

Allen, W. G. "Severe Cavalry Fighting at Chickamauga," vol. XX, no. 2 (February, 1912), 87. (2nd Tennessee Cavalry).

Anderson, Chas. A. "Gracey - Chickamauga-Whitaker," vol. III, no. 8 (August, 1895), 251-252. (Forrest's Staff).

Anderson, Kellar. "The Rebel Yell," vol. I, no. 4 (April, 1893), 106-107. (5th Kentucky Infantry CSA).

Anderson, Keller. "The Rebel Yell," vol. XXXIII, no. 8 (August, 1925), 295-296. (5th Kentucky Infantry CSA, reprint of above, first name spelled differently.)

Anonymous. "Henry Fugate," vol. XXII, no. 1 (January 1914), 37. (63rd Tennessee Infantry).

Anonymous, "Col. Robert C. Trigg of Virginia," vol. XVII, no 2 (February, 1909), 65. (54th Virginia Infantry).

Anonymous. "Capt. W. T. Hardison," vol. XXVII, no. 11 (November, 1919), 430-432. (1st Tennessee Cavalry).

Atkins, Smith D. "Crushing McCook's Corps at Chickamauga," vol. XII, no. 10 (October, 1904), 483. (92nd Illinois Mounted Infantry).

Bell, C. W. R. "Reminiscences of Chickamauga," vol. XII, no 2 (February, 1904), 71. (6th Georgia Cavalry).

Boothe, J. B. "The Tallahatchie Rifles-'Cap' Houston." vol. XXXII, no. 12 (December, 1924), 458-460. (21st Mississippi Infantry).

Carnes, W. W. "An Unusual Identification," vol. XXXVII, no. 5 (May, 1929), 188. (Carnes's Battery).

Chandler, A. M. "Reminiscences of Chickamauga," vol. II, no. 3 (March, 1894), 79. (44th Mississippi).

Charlaron, J. A. "Vivid Experiences of Chickamauga," vol. III, no. 9 (September, 1895), 278-279. (Slocomb's Battery).

Clay, H. B. "Concerning the Battle of Chickamauga," vol. XIII no. 2 (February, 1905), 72. (Pegram's Staff).

Clay, H. B. "The Right at Chickamauga," vol. XIX, no. 7 (July, 1911), 329-330. (Pegram's Staff).

Clay, H. B. "On the Right at Chickamauga," vol. XXI, no. 9 (September, 1913), 439-440. (Pegram's Staff).

Corn, T. I. "Brown's Brigade at Chickamauga," vol. XXI, no. 3 (March, 1913), 124-125. (32nd Tennessee Infantry).

Coxe, John. "Chickamauga," vol. XXX, no. 8 (August, 1922), 291-294. (2nd South Carolina Infantry).

Goodrich, John T. "Gregg's Brigade in the Battle of Chickamauga," vol. XXII, no. 6 (June, 1914), 263-264.

Green, Curtis, "Sixth Georgia Cavalry at Chickamauga," vol. VIII, no. 7 (July, 1900), 324.

Hawkins, Judge W. M. "Mississippians at Chickamauga," vol. XVII, no. 7 (July, 1909), 334. (18th Mississippi Infantry).

Herr, W. W. "Kentuckians at Chickamauga," vol. III, no. 10 (October, 1895), 294-295. (Helm's Kentucky Brigade).

Hunter, J. T. "Hard Fighting of Fourth Texas," vol. XIV, no. 1 (January, 1906), 22.

Johnston, J. Stoddard."Gen. J. B. Hood and Chickamauga," vol. XIII, no. 12 (December, 1905), 552. (Buckner's Staff).

Lee, W. H. "Major John C. Thompson of Mississippi," vol. XVI, no. 11 (November, 1908), 588. (44th Mississippi Infantry).

LeMonnier, Y. R. "Gen. Leonidas Polk at Chickamauga," vol. XXIV, no. 1 (January 1916), 17-19. (Orleans Guard, Polk's Escort).

Littlejohn, N. B. "Memories of Many Conflicts," vol. XVIII, no. 12 (December, 1910), 559. (32nd Texas Dismounted Cavalry).

McCown, J. G. "Ábout Ector's and McNair's Brigades," vol. IX, no. 3 (March, 1901), 113.

McMurray, Dr. W. J. "The Gap of Death at Chickamauga," Confederate Veteran. vol. II, no. 11 (November, 1894), 329-330. (20th Tennessee Infantry).

Martin, Rev. P. T. "Recollections of a Confederate," vol. XV, no. 5 (May, 1907), 231. (23rd Tennessee Infantry).

Massenburg, T. L. "Capt. W. W. Carnes' Battery at Chickamauga," vol. VI, no. 11 (November, 1898), 517-518.

Minnich, J.W. "Liddell's Division at Chickamauga," vol. XIII, no. 1 (January, 1905), 22-24. (6th Georgia Cavalry).

Minnich, J. W. "Tunnels to Release Prisoners" vol. XVII, no. 11 (November, 1909), 554. (6th Georgia Cavalry).

Minnich, J. W. "Unique Experiences in the Chickamauga Campaign," vol. XXXV, no. 6 (June, 1927), 222-225. (6th Georgia Cavalry).

Minnich, J. W. "Unique Experiences in the Chickamauga Campaign," vol. XXXV, no. 10 (October, 1927), 381-384. (6th Georgia Cavalry).

Moore, J. C. "McNair's Arkansas Brigade," vol. XIV, no. 3 (March, 1906), 124.

Otey, W. N. Mercer, "Operations of the Signal Corps," vol. VIII, no. 3 (March, 1900), 129-130. (Leonidas Polk's Staff).

Otey, W. N. Mercer, "Story of Our Great War," vol. VIII, no. 8 (August, 1900), 342. (Leonidas Polk's Staff).

Phillips, N. W. "The Greatest Victory of the War," vol. XVI, no. 9 (September, 1908), 467. (43rd Alabama Infantry).

Phillips, N. W. "Gracie's Scouts at Chickamauga," vol. XIX, no. 1 (January, 1911), 37. (43rd Alabama Infantry).

Pilsbury, W. K. "The Fifth Georgia at Chickamauga," vol. III, no. 11 (November 1895), 330.

Parrott, S. F. "The Gray and The Blue" vol. I, no. 3 (March, 1893), 75-76. (15th Texas).

Posey, Mrs. Samuel. "A Story of Terry's Texas Rangers," vol. XXXII, no. 4 (April, 1924), 137-138. (8th Texas Cavalry).

Ratchford, George. "Gen. D. H. Hill at Chickamauga," vol. XXIV, no. 3 (March, 1916), 120-121. (D. H. Hill's Staff).

Red. B. F. "McLaw's Division at Chickamauga," vol. XXI no. 12 (December, 1913), 585. (Phillips Legion).

Ridley, B. L. "Daring Deeds of Staff and Escort," vol. IV, no. 10 (October, 1896), 258. (A. P. Stewart's Staff.).

Ridley, B. L. "Southern Side at Chickamauga, Article I," vol. VI, no. 9 (September, 1898), 407-409. (A.P. Stewart's Staff).

Ridley, B. L. "Southern Side at Chickamauga, Part II," vol. VI, no. 11, (November, 1898), 514-517. (A.P. Stewart's Staff).

Robinson, G. S. "A Mutual Mistake," vol. XXII, no. 9 (September, 1914), 414-415. (115th Illinois Infantry).

Rone, John T. "First Arkansas Brigade at Chickamauga," vol. XIII, no. 4 (April, 1905), 166-167. (5th Arkansas Infantry).

Semmes, B. J. "Chickamauga Reminiscences," vol. III, no. 10 (October, 1895), 293-294. (154th Tennessee Infantry).

Smith, J. D. "Walthall's Brigade at Chickamauga," vol. XII, no. 10 (October, 1904), 483-484. (24th Mississippi Infantry).

Smith, W. H. "Melanchthon Smith's Battery," vol. XII, no. 11 (November, 1904), 532. (Turner's Battery).

Stradley, J. H. "Ector's Brigade at Chickamauga," vol. XIII, no. 7 (July, 1905), 308. (29th North Carolina Infantry).

Templeton, J. A. "A Chickamauga Prisoner," vol. XXXI, no. 6 (June, 1923), 238. (10th Texas Dismounted Cavalry).

Trantham, William D. "Wonderful Story of Richard R. Kirkland," vol. XVI, no. 3 (March, 1908), 105.

Tutweiler, Mrs. J. B. "Lieut. John Wilson on Snodgrass Hill." vol. XXI, no. 2 (February, 1913), 62. (6th Florida Infantry).

Tyler, C. W. "Patriotism in a Tennessee County," vol. VI, no. 3 (March, 1898), 125-126.

Weiser, J. M. "Trigg's Brigade at Chickamauga," vol. XXXIV, no. 12 (December, 1926), 452-453. (54th Virginia Infantry).

Williams, Mrs. S. F. "Out of the Past," vol. XXXII, no. 8 (August 1924), 295. (9th Tennessee Infantry).

Wiseman, Elijah. "Tennesseans at Chickamauga," vol. II, no. 7 (July, 1894), 205. (17th Tennessee Infantry).

Womack, J. K. "Chickamauga as I Saw It," vol. XXV, no. 2 (February, 1917), 74. (4th Tennessee Cavalry).

Articles published in *The Milwaukee Sunday Telegraph*

Anonymous. "The Twenty-First Wisconsin, Chapter III," May 22, 1881.

Anonymous. "Old Chicamauga," January 27, 1884. (Maj. Gen. John B. Steedman Obituary).

Anonymous. "The Rock of Chickamauga," August 5, 1888. (George H. Thomas).

Anonymous. "Forward March Rosecrans' Summer Campaign, 1863," August 5, 1888.

Anonymous. "Gen. W. H. Lytle-How He Died At Chickamauga," August 19, 1888.

Anonymous. "Chickamauga," September 16, 1888.

Cist, Henry M. Interview, "Rosecrans At Chickamauga," June 25, 1882.

Correspondent of the Chattanooga Times, "About Chickamauga," January 22, 1882.

Correspondent of the Chattanooga Times, "About Chickamauga, continued," January 29, 1882.

Correspondent of the Chattanooga Times, "About Chickamauga, concluded," February 2, 1882.

Laine, J. R. "The First Wisconsin Infantry," June 19, 1881.

Sherman, W. B. "Old Army Letter," March 9, 1884. (letter of September 29 1863, 24th Wisconsin Infantry.).

Woods, T. J. "About Chickamauga," January 8, 1882. (Steedman's Division).

Articles Published in the *Military Order of the Loyal Legion of the United States* (MOLLUS Papers) 70 vols. Broadfoot Publishing, 1991 and 1993

Atkinson, William F. "The Rock Of Chickamauga," vol. 51, 5-11. (22nd Michigan Infantry).

Anderson, Edward L. "Colonel Archibald Gracie's The Truth about Chickamauga," vol. 7, 447-475. (52nd Ohio Infantry).

Carnahan, James R. "Personal Recollections of Chickamauga," vol. 1, 401-422. (86th Indiana Infantry).

Carnahan, James R . "Indiana At Chickamauga," vol. 24, 86-116. (86th Indiana Infantry).

Castle, Henry A. "Sheridan with the Army of the Cumberland," vol. 43, 159-184.

Curry, William L. "Raid Of The Confederate Cavalry Through Central Tennessee In October, 1863, Commanded By General Joseph Wheeler," vol. 7, 227-245. (1st Ohio Cavalry).

Ford, Augustus C. "Midnight On Missionary Ridge," vol. 24, 239-246. (31st Indiana Infantry).

Hascall, Milo S. "Personal Recollections and Experiences Concerning the Battle of Stones River," vol. 13, 152-154.

Hicks, Borden M. "Personal Recollections of the War of the Rebellion," vol. 31, 519-540.

Hosea, Lewis M., "Regular Brigade Of The Army Of The Cumberland," vol. 5, pp. 328-360. (16th U.S. Infantry).

Johnson, R. W. "War Memories," vol. 26, 4-28.

Jones, Frank J. "Personal Recollections and Experience of a Solder During the War of the Rebellion," vol. 6, 111-131. (Alexander McD. McCook's Staff).

Kemper, Dr. and C. "William Haines Lytle," vol. 1, 19-35.

Kniffen, Gilbert C. "The Cavalry of the Army of the Cumberland in 1863," vol. 42, 417-432.

Ostrander, James S. "Two September Days," vol. 24, 322-150. (2nd Ohio Infantry and 18th U. S. Infantry).

Patton, J. T. "Personal Recollections of Four Years in Dixie," vol. 50, 409-440.

Richards, William J. "Rosecrans and the Chickamauga Campaign," vol. 24, 465-475.

Snider, S. P. "Reminiscences of the War," vol. 27, 234-44. (65th Ohio Infantry).

Waterman, Arba A. "The Battle of Chickamauga," vol.10, 231-245.

West, Granville C. "Personal Recollections of the Chickamauga Campaign," vol. 45, 419-432.

Wilder, John T. "Preliminary Movements of the Army of the Cumberland Before the Battle of Chickamauga." vol. 7, 261-272.

Wilson, George S. "Wilder's Brigade of Mounted Infantry in Tullahoma-Chickamauga Campaigns," vol. 15, 45-76.

Yaryan, John Lee. "Stone River," vol. 24, 157-177.

Articles published in *The National Tribune*

This list could not have been nearly as complete without the invaluable help of Dr. Richard A. Sauers, who generously shared his detailed subject index for this paper long before The National Tribune became available on the internet.

Abbott, J. N. "Opening of Chickamauga Fight," April 9, 1914. (98th Illinois Infantry).

Addington, Thomas. "The Story of Chickamauga," March 29, 1900 (84th Indiana Infantry).

Allspaugh, H. "Chickamauga," October 7, 1886. (31st Ohio Infantry).

Anonymous, "Johnny Clem—Drummer Boy of Chickamauga," October 1, 1879. (22nd Michigan Infantry).

Anonymous, "Garfield-Rosecrans," March 18, 1882.

Anonymous "Harker's Brigade at Chickamauga," April 26, 1882.

Anonymous, "Chickamauga, an Incident of the Great Battle in Georgia," January 4, 1883.

Anonymous, "the 21st Ohio at Chickamauga," September 11, 1884.

Anonymous. "98th Ohio," June 30, 1887.

Avery, Oscar F. "The Chickamauga Campaign A Success," May 31, 1883.

Ball, John C. "John C. Ball," June 15, 1933 (113th Ohio Infantry).

Banks, N.P " Steedman's Division," March 1, 1900. (Miller's Illinois Battery).

Banks, N. P. "Chickamauga Again," December 15, 1887. (M, 1st Illinois Artillery).

Banta, Fred. "The Twenty-First Corps at Chickamauga," May 24, 1883. (44th Indiana Infantry).

Barbour, James M. "the 21st Ohio at Chickamauga," October 27, 1921.

Barnes, W. M. "What became of the 89th Ohio's Colors?" June 14, 1883.

Barnes, W. M. "A Touching Meeting," August 23, 1883. (89th Ohio Infantry).

Barton, C. C. "Bravest of Them All," July 16, 1903. (18th Ohio Battery).

Beach, John N. "Chickamauga," May 1, 1890. (40th Ohio Infantry).

Bishop, J. W. "Van der Veer's Brigade. A Splendid Organization of Crack Regiments which was Magnificently Handled on the Field of Chickamauga and Won Decisive Results, part one," June 9, 1904. (2nd Minnesota Intantry).

Bishop, J. W. "Van der Veer's Brigade. A Splendid Organization of Crack Regiments which was Magnificently Handled on the Field of Chickamauga and Won Decisive Results, part two," June 16, 1904. (2nd Minnesota Infantry).

Bonn, John H. "Taking of Chattanooga," December 31, 1885. (92nd Illinois Infantry).

Bonn, John H. "Wilder's Brigade at Chickamauga," October 14, 1886. (92nd Illinois Infantry).

Bonner, J. W. "Burning Reed's Bridge," March 26, 1896 (69th Ohio Infantry).

Boon, W. J. "Reed's Bridge," May 14, 1914. (125th Illinois Infantry).

Booth, John T. "Turchin's Charge," July 19, 1888 (36th Ohio Infantry).

Booth, John T. "Turchin's Brigade Cut Their Way Through the Rebels," October 16, 1890. (36th Ohio Infantry).

Booth, John T. "Chickamauga: A Campaign unrivaled in the Annals of War. Part I," October 2, 1890. (36th Ohio Infantry).

Booth, John T. Chickamauga: A Campaign unrivaled in the Annals of War. Part II," October 9, 1890. (36th Ohio Infantry).

Booth, John T. Chickamauga: A Campaign unrivaled in the Annals of War. Part III," October 16, 1890. (36th Ohio Infantry).

Booth, John T. Chickamauga: A Campaign unrivaled in the Annals of War. Part IV," October 23, 1890. (36th Ohio Infantry).

Booth, John T. "Chickamauga: Comrade Booth Replies to his Critics," November 13, 1890. (36th Ohio Infantry).

Boyle, Robert E. "Chickamauga," January 10, 1907. (10th Kentucky Infantry US).

Boynton, H.V. "Chickamauga," March 12, 1885. (35th Ohio Infantry).

Boynton, H. V. "Chickamauga." May 3, 1888. (35th Ohio Infantry).

Bradley, Cullen. "Chickamauga: The True Story of the Break in the Line of Battle on Sunday, September 20th, 1863," September 20, 1906. (6th Ohio Light Artillery and Thomas J. Wood's Staff).

Bradner, J. W. "Reed's Bridge," November 15, 1914. (4th U.S. Cavalry).

Braley, A. A. "Reed's Bridge," September 30, 1909. (4th Michigan Cavalry).

Brandley, A. "A Kentucky Regiment at Chickamauga," February 15, 1894. (23rd Kentucky Infantry US).

Brasher, C. A. "Chickamauga," May 9, 1889. (17th Kentucky Infantry US).

Brown, C. A. "Chickamauga: The Memorable Night March," November 20, 1890. (92nd Ohio Infantry).

Brown, William G. "At Chickamauga," August 31, 1911. (93rd Ohio Infantry).

Burlingame, E. P. "Reed's Bridge," August 27, 1914. (1st Ohio Cavalry).

Burnes, John. "Fourth Corps at Chickamauga," March 24, 1910. (23rd Kentucky Infantry US).

Burns, J. "Chickamauga," May 19, 1887. (39th Indiana Mounted Infantry).

Burns, J. E. "Indiana at Chickamauga," August 5, 1915. (39th Indiana Mounted Infantry).

Camp. G.L. "Turchin's Brigade at Chickamauga," October 22, 1908.

Camp, G. L. "To Booth's Rescue," November 13. 1890. (92nd Ohio).

Camp, W. M. "Cruft's Brigade," March 16, 1922. (Battery B, 1st Ohio).

Campbell, Henry. "The 18th Ind. Battery," November 1, 1906.

Canfield, George S. "Chickamauga and Stones River Fields After Twenty Years," August 16, 1883.

Carlin, William P. "Military Memoirs," April 2, 1885.

Carlin, William P. "Military Memoirs," April 16, 1885.

Carlin, William P. "Military Memoirs," April 23, 1885.

Carleton "Saving the Nation, the Story of the War Retold for our Boys and Girls, part 69," August 27, 1885.

Carleton "Saving the Nation, the Story of the War Retold for our Boys and Girls, part 70," September 3, 1885.

Carson, W. J. "A Bugler Replies to Gen. Wiley," June 23, 1887. (15th U. S. Infantry).

Cates, Isaac. "When and Where. It Was on Monday Night, Sept., 22d, 1863, Near Midnight, that Those Guns Were Wrapped," April 12, 1894. (52nd Ohio Infantry).

Chamberlain, R. S. "The Break at Chickamauga," September 15, 1921. (64th Ohio Infantry).

Chamberlain, R. S. "Gen. Wood's Order," December 11, 1924. (64th Ohio Infantry).

Cincinnati Commercial Gazette correspondent. "Chickamauga: The Historic Root on which Gen. Thomas sat during the Battle," October 12, 1886.

Clark, O. A. "21st Ohio at Chickamauga," November 21, 1907.

Clayton, B. M. "Turchin's Great Charge," August 18, 1921. (36th Ohio Infantry).

Columbus Herald Correspondent. "Chickamauga," November 22, 1883.

Conner, J. A. "Praises The Fourteenth Corps," May 19, 1910. (18th Kentucky Infantry US).

Cooper, R. J. "The 96th Illinois at Chickamauga," November 29, 1883.

Coulter, S. L. "Taking of Chattanooga," November 12, 1885. (64th Ohio Infantry).

Curtis, A. F. "The Reserve Corps at Chickamauga," January 13, 1916. (125th Illinois Infantry).

Cusac, Isaac. "The 21st Ohio at Chickamauga," September 5, 1907.

De Wolf, W. P. "Stands Up for the Fourteenth," May 19, 1910. (105th Ohio Infantry).

Dace, E. W. "An Incident of Chickamauga," June 6, 1901. (115th Illinois Infantry).

Dahuff, Amos. "That Awful Sunday," November 1, 1917. (9th Indiana Infantry).

Dickennan, Albert. "The 9th Ohio at Chickamauga," October 18, 1906.

Dilley, John W. "Thomas at Chickamauga," September 26, 1901. (84th Illinois Infantry).

Dimm, B. A. "The Close of Chickamauga," May 2, 1907. (9th Indiana Infantry).

Dixon, Henry C. "Sheridan's Division at Chickamauga," December 19, 1918. (27th Illinois Infantry).

Dolton, George E. "Chickamauga," October 17, 1887. (M, 1st Illinois Artillery).

Dolton, George E. "Chickamauga," February 13, 1890. (M, 1st Illinois Artillery).

Dolton, George E. "Snodgrass Ridge, Chickamauga," February 27, 1890. (M, 1st Illinois Artillery).

Dolton, George E. "Another Blast from Battery M's Bugle," May 1, 1890. (M, 1st Illinois Artillery).

Dolton, George E. "Dolton Once More," May 1, 1890. (M, 1st Illinois Artillery).

Dolton, George E. "Another Blast from Dolton's Bugle," November 13, 1890. (M, 1st Illinois Artillery).

Dolton, George E. "Chickamauga," June 25, 1891. (M, 1st Illinois Artillery).

Dolton, George E. "Chickamauga," December 3, 1891. (M, 1st Illinois Artillery).

Dolton, George E. "Where was General Lytle Killed?" August 27, 1896. (M, 1st Illinois Artillery).

Dove, J. W. "Chickamauga," March 13, 1884. (115th Illinois Infantry).

Doyle, Robert. "Chickamauga," April 7, 1887.

Doyle, William E. "Chickamauga," June 6, 1901. (Wilder's Brigade).

Doyle, William E. "Wilder's Brigade," August 29, 1901.

Dreifus, Arthur. "Their 'Dutch' Was Up," August 31, 1899 (9th Ohio Infantry).

Dunn, B.A. "That Mysterious Volley," September 17, 1908. (9th Indiana Infantry).

Durand, O. H. "Steedman at Chickamauga," February 10, 1916. (115th Illinois Infantry).

E.N.N. "Gen. Steedman," August 4, 1887. (18th Ohio Battery).

E.N.N. "Steedman at Chickamauga," September 1, 1887. (18th Ohio Battery).

Ehrisman, Christian. "An Incident at the Battle of Chickamauga," January 1, 1891. (5th Kentucky Infantry US).

Erwin, J. L. "Steedman at Snodgrass Hill," December 30, 1915. (98th Ohio Infantry).

Erwin, J. L. "The Battle of Chickamauga," November 29, 1925. (98th Ohio Infantry).

Fahnestock, Allan H. "Opened the Battle of Chickamauga," September 29, 1904 (86th Illinois Infantry).

Fahnestock, Allan H. "The Fight of McCook's Brigade On Friday and Saturday," November 25, 1909 (86th Illinois Infantry).

Fallis, Leroz S. "Chickamauga," March 29, 1900. (39th Indiana Mounted Infantry).

Fisher, James "Wilder's Brigade at Chickamauga," May 13, 1886. (17th Indiana Infantry).

Fleming, James S. "At Chickamauga," August 3, 1898. (24th Wisconsin Infantry).

Floyd, D. B. "Turchin's Brigade Cut Their Way Through the Rebels," November 13, 1890. (75th Indiana Infantry).

Fox, A. B. "Dan McCook's Brigade," October 30, 1924. (86th Illinois Infantry).

Fry, John W. "James A. Garfield," January 21, 1886.

Gates, F. W. "Chickamauga," April 7, 1887. (115th Illinois Infantry).

Gleason, A. J. "Heard His Bullet Coming," July 15, 1909. (15th Ohio Infantry).

Glenn, D. L. "the 82nd Ind. at Chickamauga," December 9, 1915.

Halsey, M. W. "That Terrible Chickamauga Week End," December 8, 1927. (18th Ohio Infantry).

Hanes, J. T. "Captured at Chickamauga," August 8,1908. (92nd Ohio Infantry).

Haigh, G. W. "Chickamauga: Skirmishers from Croxton's Brigade Open the Battle," January 14, 1915. (10th Indiana Infantry).

Hartzell, J. C. "The Pole Bridge Across the Tennessee," January 6, 1910 (105th Ohio Infantry).

Hawk, Philip A. "How Philip A. Hawk of Co. G, 104th Ill. Spiked a Brass Cannon at Chickamauga," October 18, 1906.

Hendrick, Rev. S. "Chickamauga," November 5, 1891. (C, 1st Ohio Light Artillery).

Hill, John F. "Good-bye to Dixie," March 29, 1883. (89th Ohio Infantry).

Hill, W. A. "The 121st Ohio at Chickamauga," May 1, 1884.

Hills, Frank E. "Chickamauga," November 26, 1891. (100th Illinois Infantry).

Hills, H.H. "Charging Without Orders" January 4th, 1900. (2nd Minnesota Infantry).

Hinson, J. "Kicked with Artillery," March 26, 1896 (33rd Ohio Infantry).

Holmes, G. W. "Reserves at Chickamauga," October 14, 1926. (Union Reserve Corps).

Holmes, I. W. "Demand Granted," April 4, 1912. (69th Ohio Infantry).

Homer, J. W. "Saved the Whole Army," May 19, 1904 (69th Ohio Infantry).

Hoskinson, R.S. "A Father and Son Escape from the Rebels," September 25, 1884. (73rd Illinois Infantry).

Hubbard, P. L. "The Capture of the 8th Ind. Battery," June 6, 1907.

Hunter, Morton C. "Where Bones Crashed. What General Hunter had to Say About the Battle of Chickamauga," June 28, 1883. (82nd Indiana Infantry).

Hunter, Morton C. "At Chickamauga," November 24, 1887. (82nd Indiana Infantry).

Hunter, Morton C. "Chickamauga," May 31, 1888. (82nd Indiana Infantry).

Huntley, J. "Bragg Knew Thomas," December 3, 1908. (D.H. Hill's Staff).

Irwine, J.A. "At Chickamauga," December 12, 1912. (4th U.S. Cavalry).

J. "The 21st Ohio at Chickamauga," September 11, 1884.

Jennes, George B. "General A. McD. McCook: A Soldier's Pen in Defense of a Gallant Officer," March 18, 1886.

Johnson, Amasa. "Chickamauga," June 16, 1887. (9th Indiana Infantry).

Jones, J. N. "Chickamauga," July 4, 1901. (39th Indiana Mounted Infantry).

Jones, J.N. "The Widow Glenn's," October 31, 1901. (39th Indiana Mounted Infantry).

Keeran, Samuel. "Chickamauga," September 10, 1891. (124th Ohio Infantry).

Kelley, Walden. "Losses of the 26th Ohio at Chickamauga," June 26, 1890.

Kemper, A. C. "General W. H. Lytle," July 5, 1883.

Kingdon, Cassell C. "17th Ohio at Chickamauga," December 8, 1928.

Larson, James. "Outwitting a Picket Guard," September 12, 1912 (4th U.S. Cavalry.

Magee, B. F. "Chickamauga: Comrade Magee wants Facts, not Fancies," July 22, 1886. (72nd Indiana Infantry).

Magee, George C. " A Reminiscence of Chickamauga-Gen. Steadman's Division," September 1, 1879. (98th Ohio Infantry).

Martin, E.H. "Steedman at Chickamauga," November 22, 1883. (115th Illinois Infantry).

Martin, W. H. "Death of Col. Richmond," October 1, 1891. (93rd Ohio Infantry).

Mason, LeRoy. "The Gap at Chickamauga," June 23, 1887. (121st Ohio Infantry).

McElroy, John. "The Army of the Cumberland and The Great Central Campaign. Chapter XXIX," September 20, 1906.

McElroy, John. "The Army of the Cumberland and The Great Central Campaign. Chapter XXX," September 27, 1906.

McElroy, John. "The Army of the Cumberland and The Great Central Campaign. Chapter XXXI," October 4, 1906.

McElroy, John. "The Army of the Cumberland and The Great Central Campaign. Chapter XXXIII," October 18, 1906.

McClellan, W. G. "Chickamauga," February 14, 1884. (78th Illinois Infantry).

McCollum, D. C. "Chickamauga," April 2, 1885. (87th Indiana Infantry).

McCollum, D. C. "Gen. H. V. Boynton," April 23, 1885. (87th Indiana Infantry).

McConnell, Dyer P. "The Ninth Indiana," November 11, 1886.

McFarland, H. M. "Where the 78th Illinois Held On," October 1, 1925.

McMahan, Arnold "Chickamauga Again," June 7, 1888 (21st Ohio Infantry).

McNeil, S. A. "At Chickamauga," April 14, 1887. (31st Ohio Infantry).

McNeil, S. A. "Chickamauga, A Comrade Replies to Gen. Wiley's Criticisms of Gen. Thomas," August 18, 1887. (31st Ohio Infantry).

McNeil, S. A. "The 31st Ohio at Chickamauga," February 9, 1888.

McNeil, S. A. "Were They Demoralized," November 5, 1891. (31st Ohio Infantry).

McTeer, Will. A. "Shot a Disturber," November 24, 1910 (4th U.S. Cavalry).

Miller, G. W. "On Chickamauga's Bloody Field," November 3, 1904. (31st Ohio Infantry).

Miller, G. W. "The 31st Ohio at Chickamauga," February 21, 1907.

Minty, Robert G. "Minty's Saber Brigade: The Part They Took in the Chattanooga Campaign. Part I," February 25, 1892.

Minty, Robert G. "Minty's Saber Brigade: The Part They Took in the Chattanooga Campaign. Part II," March 3, 1892.

Minty, Robert G. "Fighting Them Over: The Saber Brigade," September 22, 1892.

Minty, Robert G. "Minty Speaks, Apropos the Story of Being Left on a Skirmish Line," November 9, 1893.

Minty, Robert G. "Cast No Discredit. Gen. Minty Raises but One Question with Comrade Larson," January 18, 1894.

Minty, Robert G. "Rossville Gap. Gen. Minty Has a Word to Say About Who Left It Last," March 8, 1894.

Mitch, John L. "Croxton at Chickamauga," November 5, 1925.

Mosgrove, George Dallas. "Longstreet at Chickamauga," August 14, 1902.

Neff, A. Y. "Bloody Times at Chickamauga," March 22, 1906. (13th Ohio Infantry).

Newman, George S. "Chickamauga: Reminiscences of the 38th Indiana," October 16, 1884.

Nye, Jas. S. "Chickamauga," November 11, 1884. (17th Ohio Infantry).

Pair, A. L. "First Shot at Chickamauga," February 26, 1914 (18th Indiana Battery).

Patton, M. "Turchin's Charge at Chickamauga," August 30, 1888. (92nd Ohio Infantry).

Pearson, Samuel W. "Met Again at Salt Lake," May 19, 1910.

Pease, Gam. "Chickamauga. The Part Taken by the Sixty-ninth Ohio and McCook's Brigade." July 3, 1890. (69th Ohio Infantry).

Pepoon, G. W. "An Incident of Chickamauga," October 7, 1886. (96th Illinois, Whitaker Staff).

Perry, F. W. "Chickamauga," June 28, 1883. (10th Wisconsin Infantry).

Porter, John R. "One of the 'Engine Thieves' Recaptured at Chickamauga," February 13, 1908. (21st Ohio Infantry)

Pressler, George. "Johnson's Division at Chickamauga," March 6, 1884. (93rd Ohio Infantry).

Putney, W. G. "Chickamauga," September 24, 1885. (B, 2nd Illinois Light Artillery).

Putney, W. G. "Chickamauga," January 15, 1891. (B, 2nd Illinois Artillery).

Quiggle, Horatio R. "Chickamauga. A Comrade Corrects Capt. Webster in Some Minor Particulars," October 15, 1891 (14th Ohio Infantry).

Radcliffe, Charles K. "Battle of Chickamauga," September 1, 1921 (105th Ohio Infantry).

Radcliffe, Charles K. "Reynolds at Chickamauga," November 20, 1924. (105th Ohio Infantry).

Radcliffe, Charles K. "As to Rosecrans," September 10, 1925. (105th Ohio Infantry).

Rapp, Edward. "At Chickamauga," November 20, 1913. (9th Ohio Infantry).

Rea, William P. "Roasted Bacon at Bridge," October 15, 1914. (69th Ohio Infantry).

Rea, William P. "Burning Reed's Bridge," December 10, 1914. (69th Ohio Infantry).

Records, W. H. "Wilder at Chickamauga," August 30, 1883.

Reed, A. H. "Vandervere's Brigade," February 23, 1888. (2nd Minnesota Infantry).

Reed, A. H. "At Chattanooga," January 28, 1915 (2nd Minnesota Infantry).

Reed, A. H. "Reed's Bridge," September 16, 1915. (2nd Minnesota Infantry).

Reed, A. H. "It Was the Last to Leave Snodgrass Ridge at Chickamauga," December 16, 1915. (2nd Minnesota Infantry).

Reed, A. H. "Chickamauga," September 21, 1916. (2nd Minnesota Infantry).

Reed, A. H. "Thomas Shook His Leg," September 14, 1922. (2nd Minnesota Infantry).

Reed, A. H. "Van Derveer's Brigade at Chickamauga," October 16, 1924. (2nd Minnesota Infantry).

Reed, Henry M. "Letter," April 23, 1885. (4th Kentucky Infantry US).

Reese, G. J. "Why Negley Retreated," April 5, 1906. (78th Pennsylvania Infantry).

Reppert, W. E. "Rosecrans - A Great General," May 19, 1910. (15th Pennsylvania Cavalry).

Rilea, S. W. "The Action of his Brigade at Chickamauga," October 18, 1906. (86th Illinois Infantry).

Rilea, S. W. "Reed's Bridge," August 13, 1914. (86th Illinois Infantry).

Robbins, R. B. "At Reed's Bridge," November 14, 1895. (4th Michigan Cavalry).

Robinson, G. S. "Chickamauga," August 7, 1884. (115th Illinois Infantry).

Robinson, G. S. "Steedman's Charge at Chickamauga," December 20, 1906. (115th Illinois Infantry).

Rose, L. A. "From Chickamauga to Andersonville," August 7, 1884. (42nd Illinois Infantry).

Rosecrans, William S. "General Sherman's Letter," October 8, 1881.

Rosecrans, William Starke. "Tullahoma Campaign," March 11, 1882.

Rosecrans, William Starke, "Chattanooga Campaign," March 25, 1882.

Rosecrans, William S. "What Old Rosey Says: 'Carlton' criticized," September 24, 1885.

Royce, Isaac H.C. "The Iron Brigade at Chickamauga," December 31, 1908. (115th Illinois Infantry).

S. W. L. "Chickamauga," March 27, 1890. (possibly 21st Michigan Infantry).

Salt, William C. "Among the First," November 29, 1917. (59th Ohio Infantry).

Scott, A. "Just Tribute to the Valor of the Twentieth Corps," May 24, 1883. (78th Illinois Infantry).

Scott, Launcelot L. "On Snodgrass Ridge," July 14, 1910. (18th Ohio Infantry).

Scott, Launcelot, L. "With Negley's Division," June 8, 1911. (18th Ohio Infantry).

Scott, R. S. "At Chickamauga," December 18, 1913. (3rd Kentucky Infantry US).

Seaman, W. E. "Death of Col. Hall at Chickamauga," July 8, 1886. (89th Illinois Infantry).

Seiler, Christian. "Premonitions That Came True," February 24, 1910. (29th Indiana Infantry).

Shafer, A. C. "An Exploit of Turchin's Brigade," July 11, 1898. (92nd Ohio Infantry).

Shafer, A. C. "An Incident of Chickamauga," May 21, 1914. (92nd Ohio Infantry).

Shafer, A. C. "Longstreet at Chickamauga," July 8, 1915. (92nd Ohio Infantry).

Shafer, A. C. "Chickamauga," October 21, 1915. (92nd Ohio Infantry).

Shafer, A. C. "Losses at Chickamauga," November 4, 1915. (92nd Ohio Infantry).

Shafer, A. C. "Chickamauga," October 12, 1916. (92nd Ohio Infantry).

Shafer, A. C. "Army of the Cumberland," July 4, 1918. (92nd Ohio Infantry).

Shafer, A. C. "Second Day at Chickamauga," October 17, 1918. (92nd Ohio Infantry).

Shafer, A. C. "The Gen. Thomas Myth," September 10, 1925. (92nd Ohio Infantry).

Shafer, A. C. "Chickamauga No Disaster." October 8, 1925. (92nd Ohio Infantry).

Shafer, A. C. "Stands Up for Rosecrans," October 8, 1925. (92nd Ohio Infantry).

Shafer, A. C. "Incident at Chickamauga," October 16, 1930. (92nd Ohio Infantry).

Shafer, A. C. "Veterans Writes of Second Day of Bitter Struggle at Chickamauga," January 28, 1932. (92nd Ohio Infantry).

Shafer, A. C. "Bullet that Killed His Colonel Passed Over Head of Vet," November 22, 1934. (92nd Ohio Infantry).

Shaughnessy, D. "The Fires that Comrade Booth Saw," December 11, 1890. (124th Ohio Infantry).

Shellenberger, John K. "Garfield at Chickamauga," March 18, 1886. (64th Ohio Infantry).

Shellenberger, John K. "The Yelling at Chickamauga," May 5, 1887. (64th Ohio Infantry).

Shively, Joseph H. "10th Ky. at Chickamauga," May 23, 1907.

Shuster, James H. "Holding Reed's Bridge," August 11, 1910.

Smart, Isaac. "Snodgrass Hill Again," November 7, 1907. (9th Indiana Infantry).

Smith, J.C. "As Gen. Smith Saw It. The True Story of General Steedman's Gallantry at Chickamauga," January 10, 1884. (Steedman Staff).

Smyth, W. H. "Holding Snodgrass Hill," September 14, 1922. (98th Ohio Infantry).

Snodgrass, Robert M. "Steedman's Division," November 2, 1899. (84th Indiana Infantry).

Stanford, I. N. "Canteen Carriers," December 27, 1906. (18th U.S. Infantry).

Stanford, I. N. "The Regular Brigade," July 21, 1887. (18th U.S. Infantry).

Stanford, I.N. "The 9th Ohio to the Rescue," October 5, 1899. (18th U.S. Infantry).

Starkey, C. H. "No Fourth Corps There," May 19, 1910. (42nd Indiana Infantry).

Stebbins, A. E. "A Daring Movement," October 19, 1899. (88th Illinois Infantry).

Stevens, J. W. "Chickamauga," May 28, 1908. (87th Indiana Infantry).

Stevens, John W. "Chickamauga," February 3, 1910. (87th Indiana Infantry).

Stone, Israel W. "Fifer-boy Criticized," April 2, 1896. (M, 2nd Illinois Artillery).

Swan, Joseph. "At Chickamauga," November 30, 1893. (52nd Ohio Infantry).

Sweetland, A. F. "Reed's Bridge at Chickamauga," June 17, 1915. (55th Ohio, not present at Chickamauga.).

Swick, Henry F. "Fourteenth Corps and Regulars," May 19, 1910. (18th U.S. Infantry).

Taylor, J. C. "Left for Dead on the Field," November 19, 1914. (21st Michigan Infantry).

Thompson, D. B. "Reed's Bridge," December 10, 1914. (69th Ohio Infantry).

Turchin, John B. "Bayonet and Saber," February 11, 1886.

Turchin, John B. "The 89th Ohio: Gen. Turchin Tells How it was Captured at Chickamauga," November 11, 1886.

Turnbull, John M. "Chickamauga," April 14, 1896. (36th Illinois Infantry).

Van Camp, H. H. "Chickamauga," September 4, 1884. (21st Ohio Infantry).

Van Doren, John A. "Chickamauga: Who Did the Best Fighting in that Battle?" October 30, 1884. (21st Indiana Battery).

W. H. G. "A Chickamauga Incident," August 14, 1884. (78th Illinois Infantry).

Webster, I. B. "Chickamauga," July 2, 1891. (10th Kentucky Infantry US).

Wetmore, E. G. "The 21st Ohio at Chickamauga," October 2, 1884.

Whallon, James M. "Chickamauga," August 25, 1887. (11th Michigan Infantry).

Whallon, James M. "Chickamauga," May 17, 1888. (11th Michigan Infantry).

Whallon, James M. "Chickamauga," April 17, 1890. (11th Michigan Infantry).

White, Elias. "In Close Quarters," September 16. 1909 (18th U.S. Infantry).

Wilson, F. E. "Who Burned Reed's Bridge?" February 19, 1914. (69th Ohio Infantry).

Widney, Lyman S. "From Louisville to the Sea. A Soldier's Diary of the Civil War. Part I," October 24, 1901. (34th Illinois Infantry).

Widney, Lyman S. "From Louisville to the Sea. A Soldier's Diary of the Civil War. Part II," October 31, 1901. (34th Illinois Infantry).

Widney, Lyman S. "From Louisville to the Sea. A Soldier's Diary of the Civil War. Part III," November 7, 1901. (34th Illinois Infantry).

Widney, Lyman S. "Maj. Gen. W. S. Rosecrans," September 1, 1921.

Wildman, John E. "The 105th Ohio at Chickamauga," May 10, 1888.

Wiley, Aquila. "Gen. Hill Answered," May 19, 1887. (41st Ohio Infantry).

Wiley, Aquila. "Battle Statistics," October 29, 1891. (41st Ohio Infantry).

Wilkins, A. "Soldiering with a Vengeance," February 15, 1900. (49th Ohio Infantry).

Williams, J.E. "No Insubordination," August 20, 1896. (Col. Daniel McCook's Brigade).

Wilson, F. E. "At The Burnt Bridge," April 8, 1915. (69th Ohio Infantry).

Wilson, M.C. "Chickamauga: The Third Brigade of the Third Division, Fourteenth Army Corps," September 18, 1884. (38th Indiana Infantry).

Woodruff, C. "Chickamauga," December 11, 1890. (64th Ohio Infantry).

Woodruff, C. "Chickamauga," December 3, 1891. (64th Ohio Infantry).

Woodruff, C. "Wide of the Mark," January 28, 1892. (64th Ohio Infantry).

Work, J. B. "At Chickamauga," September 28, 1893. (52nd Ohio Infantry).

Wright, W. H. "Steedman at Chickamauga." May 18, 1916. (98th Ohio Infantry).

Yoe, W. H. "Chickamauga," November 21, 1889. (40th Ohio Infantry).

Young, Isaac K. "Chickamauga: The Battle as I Saw It," April 22, 1886. (89th Illinois Infantry).

Young, Isaac K. "Chickamauga," March 29, 1888. (89th Illinois Infantry).

Young, Isaac K. "Chickamauga," August 9, 1888. (89th Illinois Infantry).

Yunker, George. "Bradley's Brigade at Chickamauga," August 30, 1883. (51st Illinois Infantry).

Zehring, S. P. "Chickamauga," October 13, 1887. (35th Ohio Infantry).

Zehring, S. P. "Chickamauga Again," December 15, 1887. (35th Ohio Infantry).

Zehring, S. P. "Chickamauga," October 23, 1890. (35th Ohio Infantry).

Articles appearing in the *Southern Historical Society Papers*

Most of the articles that appeared in the *SHSP* were reprints of reports found in the *Official Records*. For brevity's sake, they are not included in this list.

Anderson, Archer. "Address of Col. Archer Anderson on the Campaign and Battle of Chickamauga," vol. IX, no. 7 (July, 1881), 386-418. (D. H. Hill Staff).

Anonymous. "The Battle of Chickamauga. An Eyewitness' Thrilling Story of the Great Conflict, as Seen from the Federal Side." vol. XXX (January to December, 1902), 178-188. (Reprint of article from New Orleans Picayune, November 9, 1902, in turn reprinted from Cincinnati Commercial, September 28, 1863.).

Anonymous. "An Important Dispatch from Lieutenant General N. B. Forrest. Did it Determine the Fate of the Confederacy?" vol. XXIV (January to December, 1896), 92-98.

Benning, Henry L. "Notes by General Benning on Battle of Chickamauga," vol. XIII, (January to December, 1885), 375-376.

Boynton, Henry Van Ness, "The Chickamauga Memorial Association," vol. XVI (January to December, 1888), 339-349.

Carnes, William W. "Chickamauga," vol. XIV (January to December, 1886), 398-407. (Carnes's Battery. Reprint of Atlanta Constitution letter, see below).

Dinkins, James. "The Battle of Chickamauga," vol. XXXII (January to December, 1904), 299-310.

Goggin, James M. "Chickamauga - A Reply to Major Sykes," vol. XII, no. 5 (May, 1884), 219-224. (McLaws's Division).

Jones, Joseph. "The Medical History of the Confederate States Army and Navy," vol. XX (January to December, 1892), 139-166. (Confederate casualties at Chickamauga).

Martin, William T. "A Defense of General Bragg's Conduct at Chickamauga," vol. XI, no. 4 (April, 1883), 201-206.

Palmer, Joseph. "Corrections concerning the Battle of Chickamauga," vol. XII, no. 5 (May, 1884), 239-240. (Confederate artillery formations present at the battle).

Polk, Capt. W. M. "The Battle of Chickamauga," vol. X, nos. 1-2 (January and February, 1882), 1-25.

Polk, Capt. W. M. "Roster of troops at the Battle of Chickamauga," vol. X, no. 5 (May, 1882), 236-238.

Polk, Capt. W. M. "General Bragg and the Chickamauga Campaign-A Reply to General Martin," vol. XII, nos. 7, 8, 9 (July, August, September, 1884), 378-390. (Polk's Staff),

West, Douglas. "'I am Dying, Egypt, Dying!' Touching Account of the Death of its Gallant Author, Gen. W. H. Lytle," vol. XXIII, (January-December, 1895), 82-94.

Articles appearing in *The Sunny South* (Atlanta)

Anonymous, "The first gun at Chickamauga and its opening scenes," June 29, 1895.

Cabot, G.W.G. "Chickamauga Heroism," September 18, 1897 (25th Arkansas Infantry).

Calhoun, Maj. Alfred R. "At the Battle's Close," December 11, 1897.

Consford, J. T. "A Drink of Water," March 19, 1898. (Co. C, 9th Georgia Artillery).

J.C.M. "A Story of the War," August 15, 1896. (3rd Tennessee Infantry).

Richardson, B.N. "Battle of Chickamauga," March 25, 1893. (1st Tennessee Infantry).

Ridley, B.L. "Field of Chickamauga," April 1, 1899. (A. P. Stewart's Staff).

Roberts, Claude. "Incidents of the Civil War," March 11, 1899. (15th Alabama Infantry).

Articles appearing in *The Zouave Gazette* (Chicago)

Anonymous. "To Mark the Field," January 31, 1894. (19th Illinois Infantry).

Young, John. "Recollections of Chickamauga," January 31, 1894. (19th Illinois Infantry).

Turchin, John B. "From Col. Turchin," January 31, 1894.

Articles appearing in other publications

Abrahams, John H. "Twenty-First Wisconsin Volunteer Infantry," *Cump and Company*, July/August, 1999, 4-15.

Agar, Waldemar. "The Fifteenth Wisconsin," *The American-Scandinavian Review*, vol. III, no. 6 (November/December, 1915), 325-333.

Alderson, William T. Ed. "The Civil War Diary of James Litton Cooper, September 30, 1861, to January, 1865," *Tennessee Historical Quarterly*, vol. XV, no, 1 (March, 1956), 141-161. (20th Tennessee Infantry).

Allen, William Gibbs. "Questionnaire," McKenzie's Fighting Fifth: Questionnaires of Veterans of the 5th Tennessee Cavalry Regiment, Confederate States of America. *Rhea County Historical and Genealogical Society*, 2001.

Anonymous. "The Battle of Chickamauga: Letter of October 14, 1863," *Lacrosse Area Genealogical Quarterly*, November, 1979, 26-28. (1st Wisconsin Infantry).

Anonymous. "the Autauga Guards in the Civil War," *Prattville Progress*, August 8, 1928. (24th Alabama Infantry).

Anonymous, "Historical Sketch of the 98th Illinois," *Robinson Argus*, September 20, 1882.

Anonymous. "The Second Tennessee Regiment at Chickamauga," in Edwin L. Drake, ed. *The Annals of the Army of Tennessee and Early Western History*. Jackson, TN: Guild Bindery Press, n.d., reprint of 1878 edition.

Anonymous. "In Memoriam: Brevet Major General Gordon Granger," *Society of the Army of the Cumberland, Fifteenth Reunion*. Chicago: 1883. 209-225.

Anonymous. "In Memoriam: Brigadier General Walter C. Whitaker," *Society of the Army of the Cumberland, Nineteenth Reunion*. Chicago: 1888.

Anonymous. "Reminiscence," *Confederate Reminiscences and Letters, 1861-1865, Volume X*. Atlanta: Georgia Division of the United Daughters of the Confederacy, 1999.

Anonymous. "The First Battalion Hilliard's Legion at Chickamauga," *Montgomery Advertiser*, May 5, 1907.

Anonymous. "Reminiscences of War Times," *The Hartford (KY) Herald*, June 7, 1911.

Anonymous. "Rosecrans' Removal," *Indianapolis Times*, March 13, 1882.

Anonymous. "Garfield and Rosecrans: Mr. J. W. Schuckers's contribution to the history of the controversy," *New York Times*, June 12, 1882.

Anonymous. "Stager Denies," *Chicago Daily Tribune*, June 15, 1882.

Anonymous. "Stager's Statements," *Rock Island Argus*, June 15, 1882.

Anonymous. "Rosecrans receives another facer from General Stager," *Sacramento Daily Record-Union*, June 16, 1882.

Anonymous. "Garfield-Rosecrans," *Chicago Daily Tribune*, June 17, 1882.

Avery, Judge A. C. "Farthest at Chickamauga," *Five Points in the Record of North Carolina in the Great War of 1861-65*. Daleville, VA: Schroeder Publications, 2001. Reprint of 1904 edition. (29th & 39th North Carolina Infantry).

Bade, Jim. "Bloodiest Battle of the War, Story of the 96th and Chickamauga," *Waukegan News-Sun*, May 22, 1961. (96th Illinois Infantry).

Beatty, John. "The Diary of John Beatty," *Ohio History*, vol. 58, no. 4 (October, 1949), 390-427.

Benham, Calhoun. "Major General Patrick R. Cleburne. A Biography, Chapter V," *The Kennesaw Gazette*, March 15, 1889.

Blevens, Clark. "Letter from Civil War Solder Clark Blevens To Wife Melinda," *The Heritage Genealogical Society Quarterly of Wilson County, Kansas*, vol. 15, no. 4 (1985-1986), 8. (125th Illinois Infantry).

Blevens, Clark. "Letter from Civil War Solder Clark Blevens to Wife Melinda." *The Heritage Genealogical Society Quarterly of Wilson County, Kansas*, vol. 16, no. 3 (1986-1987), 3-4. (125th Illinois Infantry).

Booth, John T. "A Night March from Pond Spring to Crawfish Spring on Night of September 18 and 19, 1863," *The Ohio Soldier and National Picket Guard*, January 4, 1890. (36th Ohio Infantry).

Boynton, Henry V. "The Chickamauga Campaign," in Campaigns in Kentucky and Tennessee. *Papers of The Military Historical Society of Massachusetts*, 1908.

Bright, Thomas R. "Yankees in Arms: The Civil War as a Personal Experience." *Civil War History*, vol. 19, no. 3 (September 1973), 197-218. (19th U.S. Infantry).

Brown, Theophilis. "What a Solder Saw and Knows," *Southern Bivouac, September 1882-August 1883*. 6 vols. Wilmington NC, Broadfoot Publishing, 1993. vol. 1, 355-358. (Davidson's Brigade).

Brown, Virginia Pounds. "I. W. McAdory and The Jonesboro Volunteers, Company H, 28th Alabama Regiment, Confederate States Army," *Journal of The Birmingham Historical Society*, vol. III no. 1 (January, 1962), 1-13.

Bunnell, Jesse H. "General Thomas and the Telegraph Operator," in Tim Goff, ed., *Under Both Flags: Personal Stories of Sacrifice and Struggle During the Civil War*. Guilford, CT: The Lyons Press, 2003. Reprint of 1896 edition. 451-455.

Burr, Frank A. "Chickamauga," *Cincinnati Enquirer*, April 1, 1883. (Interview with James Longstreet)*.

Caldwell, Martha B. ed. "Some Notes on the Eighth Kansas Infantry and the Battle of Chickamauga; Letters of Col. John A. Martin." *Kansas Historical Quarterly*, vol. XIII, no. 2 (May, 1944), 139-45.

Carl, Edward. "Stories of the Civil War," *Kewaunee Enterprise*, January 10, 1908. (24th Illinois Infantry).

Carden, Robert C., "The Old Confederate's Story," Boone Independent, April 5, 1912. (16th Tennessee Infantry).

Carnes, William W. "Flight from Shelbyville–an old Letter." *Bedford County Historical Quarterly*. Fall, 1982, 81-82. (Carnes's Battery).

Carnes, William W. "Chickamauga: A Battle of Which the Half Has Not Been Told." *Atlanta Constitution*, April 8, 1883. (Carnes's Battery).

Carter, Tod. "Chickamauga, A Deadly Embrace" *The Civil War Courier*, February, 2005. (20th Tennessee Infantry).

Cates, C. Pat. "From Santa Rosa Island to Bentonville: The First Confederate Regiment Georgia Volunteers." *Civil War Regiments*, vol. 1, no. 4 (1991), 42-63.

Chapin, John. "At Chickamauga," *Reunions of the First Ohio Volunteer Cavalry*. Columbus, OH: Landon Printing Co., 1891, 14-23.

Chalaron, Joseph E. "Memories of Major Rice E. Graves, C.S.A.," *Daviess County Historical Quarterly*, vol. 3, no. 1 (January 1985), 11-13.

Clark, William Allen., with Margaret Black Tatum, ed. "Please Send Stamps: The Civil War Letters of William Allen Clark," *Indiana Magazine of History*, vol. 3 (September, 1995), 288-320. (72nd Indiana Mounted Infantry).

Cole, P. P. "Wrote letter in Year 1863." *The Belleville Semi-Weekly Advocate*, September 21, 1910. (96th Illinois Infantry).

Connolly, James A. "Major James Austin Connolly," *Transactions of the Illinois State Historical Society for the Year 1928*. Springfield: Phillips Brothers, 1928. (123rd Illinois Mounted Infantry).

Cox, Jacob D. "the Chickamauga Crisis," *Scribner's Magazine*. vol. 28, no. 1 (July, 1900), 329-339.

Crenshaw, Edward. "Diary of Captain Edward Crenshaw," *Alabama Historical Quarterly*, Winter, 1930, 438-49. (17th Alabama Sharpshooters).

Dana, Charles A., "Reminiscences of the Civil War," *New York Sun*, November 26, 1879.

Davis, Robert Scott. "The Eyes of Chickamauga: General George H. Thomas as a Civil War Spymaster," *The Chattanooga Regional Historical Journal*, vol. 7, No. 1 (July, 2004), 73-92.

Davis, Stephen. "A Georgia Firebrand: Major General W. H. T. Walker, C. S. A." *Confederate Historical Institute Journal*, vol. II, no. 3 (Summer, 1981), 1-15

Dodge, Joseph B., "The Story of Chickamauga, as told by an eyewitness, part one," *Northern Indianian*, February 4, 1875.

Dodge, Joseph B., "The Story of Chickamauga, as told by an eyewitness, part two," *Northern Indianian*, February 11, 1875.

Dugger, J. W. and William Thomas, "A Diary kept by J. W. Dugger and William Thomas While in the Confederate Service, and Members of the 58th N. C. Reg. Part one," *Watauga Democrat*, May 21, 1891.

Dugger, J. W. and William Thomas, "A Diary kept by J. W. Dugger and William Thomas While in the Confederate Service, and Members of the 58th N. C. Reg. Part two," *Watauga Democrat*, May 28, 1891.

Fendley, Joseph H. "Fendley's Civil War Letter." *Clarke County Historical Society Quarterly*, vol. 7, no. 4 (Spring,1983), 107-108. (38th Alabama Infantry).

Fraser, James H. "September 26, 1863," *Montgomery Daily Advertiser*, October 8, 1905. (50th Alabama Infantry).

Fugitt, Gregg. "Reliable but Never Flashy, the 35th Ohio Infantry Regiment Took Pride in its Indomitable Performance at Chickamauga," *America's Civil War*, vol. 13, no. 1 (March, 2000), 8-12.

Fullerton, J. S. "Reinforcing Thomas at Chickamauga," in *Battles and Leaders of the Civil War*, 4 vols. New York, Thomas Yoseloff Inc., 1956. vol. 3, 665-7. (Gordon Granger's Staff).

Furqueron, James R. "The Bull of the Woods: Longstreet and the Confederate Left at Chickamauga," in DiNardo, R. L. and Albert A. Nofi, *James Longstreet: The Man, The Soldier, The Controversy*. Conshohocken PA: Combined Publishing, 1998.

Gilmore, James R. "Garfield's Ride at Chickamauga" *McClure's Magazine*, vol. 4 (1895), 357-360.

Gilmore, James R. "Rosecrans's Removal," *Norfolk Virginian*, November 22, 1895.

Gilmore, James R. "Why Rosecrans was removed," *Atlanta Constitution*, December 22, 1895.

Gilmore, James R. "The Relief of Rosecrans." *The Burial of General Rosecrans*, Cincinnati, OH: The Robert Clarke Co., 1902.

Glenn, D. L. "Indiana Veteran Saw Much Action in Campaign around Chattanooga." *Washington Times*, December 29, 1938. (82nd Indiana Infantry).

Graham, David. "A Fight for a Principle: The 24th Illinois Volunteer Infantry Regiment," *Journal of the Illinois State Historical Society*, vol. 104, nos. 1-2 (Spring-Summer, 2011), 38-55.

Griffith, Joe. "Smashed Against 'The Rock of Chickamauga'" *North Georgia Journal*, (Spring, 2000), 21-25. (46th Georgia Infantry).

Harrison, Jon. "Tenth Texas Cavalry, C.S.A." *Military History of Texas and the Southwest*, vol. 12, no. 2, 93-107; and vol. 12, no. 3, 172-183.

Harrison, Lowell H. "The Diary of an 'Average' Confederate Soldier." *Tennessee Historical Quarterly*. vol. XXIX, no. 3 (1970), 256-271.

Henig, Gerald S., ed. "'Soldiering Is One Hard Way of Serving the Lord.' The Civil War Letters of Martin D. Hamilton," *Indiana Military History Journal*, vol. 2, no. 3 (October, 1977), 5-11. (17th Indiana Mounted Infantry).

Hightower, Harvey Judson. "Letters from Harvey Judson Hightower, A Confederate Soldier, 1862-1864." *Georgia Historical Quarterly*, vol. 40 (1956), 174-189. (20th Georgia Infantry).

Hill, Andrew Malone. "Personal Recollections of Andrew Malone Hill" *Alabama Historical Quarterly*, vol. XX, no. 2 (Spring, 1958), 85-91. (16th Alabama Infantry).

Hill, Daniel H. "Chickamauga: The Great Battle of the West," *Battles and Leaders of the Civil War*, 4 vols. New York, Thomas Yoseloff, Inc., 1956. vol. 3, 638-662.

Hoole, Stanley, ed. "The Letters of Captain Joab Goodson 1862-64." *The Alabama Review*, vol. 10, no. 1 (April, 1957), 149-153. (44th Alabama Infantry).

Ikard, Robert W. "Lieutenant Thompson Reports on Chickamauga: A Comparison of Immediate and Historical Perspectives of the Battle." *Tennessee Historical Quarterly*, vol. XXXXIV, no. 4 (Winter, 1985) 417-438. (3rd Tennessee Infantry).

James, Alfred P. "General James Scott Negley," *Western Pennsylvania Historical Magazine*, vol. 14, no. 2 (April, 1931), 69-91.

Jaquess, Mrs. Arthur S. ed. "Account of my Experience in, and Capture, in the Battle of Chickamauga September 1863, William G. Jaquess," *Southwestern Illinois Genealogical Society Annals*, 1920-25. Read on May 25, 1925. (73rd Illinois Infantry).

Jennings, B. E. "War Diary of B.E. Jennings," *Historic Maury*, vol. 6, No. 2 (April, 1970), 21-24. (3rd Tennessee Infantry).

Johansson, M. Jane, "Brig. Gen. Daniel Weisiger Adams." *In Kentuckians in Gray, Confederate Generals and Field Officers of the Bluegrass State*. Edited by Bruce S. Allardice and Lawrence Lee Hewitt. Lexington: University Press of Kentucky, 2008.

Johnson, J. Stoddard. "A Personal Reminiscence of Chickamauga," *Montgomery Daily Advertiser*, October 1, 1905. (Buckner's Staff).

Johnson, Mark W. "Holding the Left of the Line: The Brigade of United States Regulars at Chickamauga," *Civil War Regiments*, vol. 7, no. 1, (Spring, 2001), 33-74.

Johnson, William L. "Diary of Sergeant W. L. Johnson of Company C, 33d Regiment Ohio Volunteer Infantry," in *Fifth Annual Report of the Chief of the Bureau of Military Statistics*. Albany, NY: Van Benthuysen & Sons, 1868.

Johnston, John M. "At Chickamauga. A Soldier's Story of the Battle." *The Lancaster New Era*, September 10, 1892. (79th Pennsylvania Infantry).

Jones, Charles T. Jr. "Five Confederates: The Sons of Bolling Hall in the Civil War." *Alabama Historical Quarterly*, vol. XXIV (1962), 134-186. (Hilliard's Legion).

Joyce, Fred. "Kentucky's Orphan Brigade at The Battle of Chickamauga," *The Kentucky Explorer*, April 1994, 27-29. (4th Kentucky Infantry CS).

Keller, Dean H., ed. "A Civil War Diary of Albion W. Tourgee," *Ohio History*, vol. 74, no. 2 (Spring, 1965), 120-124. (105th Ohio Infantry).

Kelly, Dennis. "Back in the Saddle: The War Record of William Bate." *Civil War Times Illustrated*, vol. XXVII, no. 8 (December, 1988), 27-33.

Kepler, Virginia. "My God, We Thought you had a Division Here!" *Civil War Times Illustrated*, vol. 5, no. 9 (January, 1967), 4.

Kerner, Robert J. Ed. "The Diary of Edward W. Crippin, Private 27th Illinois Volunteers, War of the Rebellion, August 7, 1861, to September 19, 1863," *Transactions Of The Illinois Historical Survey*, Springfield: 1909. 220-282.

Kimberly, Robert L. "At Chickamauga," *Lippincott's Magazine*, vol. XVII, no. 6 (June, 1876), 713-722. (41st Ohio Infantry).

Kinney, Shirley. "Mac at Chickamauga," *Northwest Georgia Historical and Genealogical Quarterly*, vol. 13 (Winter, 1990), 13. (6th Georgia Cavalry).

Kirk, William T. "Civil War Letters," *Reno County Genealogical Society Newsletter*, vol. IV, no. 2 (May, 1982), 18-20. (M, 1st Illinois Artillery).

Klement, Frank L. "I Whipped Six Texans: A Civil War Letter of an Ohio Soldier" *Ohio History*, vol. 73, no. 3 (Summer, 1964), 181-3. (4th Ohio Cavalry).

Labenski, Deanne, ed. "Jim Turner Co. G, 6th Texas Infantry, C.S.A. from 1861 to 1865," *Texana*, vol. 12, no. 1, (Spring, 1974), 149-178.

Long, Daniel E., with Ken Wollenberg, ed. "My War Recollections from 1862-1865." *Indiana Journal of Military History*, vol. 12, no. 1 (January, 1987), 24-29 (88th Indiana Infantry).

Mangham, Dana M. "Cox's Wild Cats: The 2nd Georgia Battalion Sharpshooters at Chickamauga and Chattanooga," *Civil War Regiments*, vol. 7, no. 1 (Spring, 2001), 91-128.

Mann, Charles B. "Anniversary of Chickamauga," *Muskegon Daily Chronicle*, September 19, 1908. (74th Indiana Infantry, Croxton's Staff).

Marchman, Watt P. "The Journal of Sergt. Wm. J. McKell," *Civil War History* vol. 3, no. 3 (September, 1957), 315-339. (89th Ohio Infantry).

Marks, Paula Mitchell. "The Ranger Reverend," *Civil War Times Illustrated*, vol. 24, no. 5, (December, 1985), 40-45. (8th Texas Cavalry).

Marriner, W. M. "Chickamauga: The Opening," *Southern Bivouac, September 1882-August 1883*, 6 vols. Wilmington, NC: Broadfoot Publishing, 1993, vol. III, no. 1 (September, 1884), 11. (Rucker's Legion).

Marsh, Bryan. "The Confederate Letters of Bryan Marsh," *Chronicles of Smith County, Texas*, vol. 14 (Winter, 1975), 9-30, 43-55. (17th Texas Dismounted Cavalry).

Mayfield, Leroy S., with John D. Barnhardt, ed. "A Hoosier Invades the Confederacy: Letters and Diaries of Leroy S. Mayfield," *Indiana Magazine of History*, vol. 39, no. 2, (June, 1943), 144-191. (22nd Indiana Infantry).

McLaws, Lafayette. "After Chickamauga," *Addresses Delivered before the Confederate Veteran Association of Savannah, Georgia, to Which is Appended the President's Annual Report*, Savannah: Braid and Hutton, Printers, 1898.

McDowell, William P. "The Fifteenth Kentucky," *Southern Bivouac*. New Series II (1886-7), 251.

McElroy, Rev. Thomas, "The War Letters of Father Peter Paul Cooney of the Congregation of Holy Cross," *American Catholic Historical Society Record*, vol. 44 (1933), 47-69, 151-169 and 220-237. (35th Indiana Infantry).

McGlachlin, Edward. "Reminiscences of Two Days at Chickamauga and Fifteen Months in Rebel Prisons," *Pedigree Pointers: Newsletter of the Historical and Genealogical Society of Steven's Point, Wisconsin*, vol. 12, no. 3 (Fall, 1989), 23-25 (1st Wisconsin Infantry).

Midgette, Nancy Smith. "Forgotten Hero," *Our State*. May, 1999, 87-91. (David Coleman, 39th North Carolina Infantry).

Mims, William J. "Letters of Major W. J. Mims, C.S.A," *Alabama Historical Quarterly*, vol. III, no. 2 (Summer, 1941), 203-215. (43rd Alabama Infantry).

Miner, Mike. "A Brave Officer: The letters of Richard Saffell, 26th Tennessee, C.S.A" *Military Images*, vol. XII, no. 2 (September-October, 1990), 16-18.

Minnich, John W. "Reminiscences of J. W. Minnick," *Northwest Georgia Historical and Genealogical Society Quarterly*, vol. 29, No. 3 (Summer, 1997), 19-28. (6th Georgia Cavalry).

Mitchell, Enoch L. "Letters of a Confederate Surgeon in the Army of Tennessee to his Wife," *Tennessee Historical Quarterly*, vol. 10, no. 1 (March, 1946), 142-151. (Cheatham's Division).

Mitchell, Enoch L. "The Civil War Letters of Thomas Jefferson Newberry," *Journal of Mississippi History*, vol. 10, no. 1 (January, 1948), 44-75. (29th Mississippi Infantry).

Mohon, James L. "Defending the Confederate Heartland: Company F of Henry Ashby's 2nd Tennessee Cavalry," *Civil War Regiments*, vol. 4, no. 1 (1994), 1-43.

Moore, William. "Writing Home to Talladega," *Civil War Times Illustrated*, vol. XXIX, no. 5 (November/December, 1990), 56, 71-4, 76-8. (25th Alabama Infantry).

Moorman, Lt. Hiram Clark, with R. W. Rosser, ed. "Memorandum," *Confederate Chronicles of Tennessee*. vol. 3 (December, 1989), 53-142.

Morelock, Jerry D. "Ride to the River of Death: Cavalry Operations during the Chickamauga Campaign," *Military Review*, October, 1984, 3-21.

Morgan, John M. "Old Steady: The Role of General James Blair Steedman at the Battle of Chickamauga," *Northwest Ohio Quarterly*, vol. XXII, no. 2 (Spring, 1950), 73-94.

Morris, Roy, Jr. "I Am Dying, Egypt, Dying," *Civil War Times Illustrated*, vol. 25, no. 10 (October, 1986), 24-31. (William H. Lytle).

Morris, Roy, Jr. "The Sack of Athens," *Civil War Times Illustrated*, vol. XXV, no. 2 (February, 1986), 26-32. (John B. Turchin).

Morris, Roy, Jr. "That Improbable, Praiseworthy Paper: The Chattanooga Daily Rebel," *Civil War Times Illustrated*, vol. XXIII, no. 7 (November, 1984), 21-25.

Mosser, Jeffrey S. "Commands: 5th Georgia Infantry," *America's Civil War*, March, 2002, 12, 52-3.

Neace, James C. & Edgar P. Harned. "Colonel John William Caldwell, Logan County's Civil War Hero," *The Kentucky Explorer*, January, 1999, 36-38. (9th Kentucky Infantry, CS).

Neel, Thomas Stephan. "Two Days Make a Hero: The Story of George P. Coleman," *Ohio Civil War Genealogy Journal*, vol. III, no. 1 (Spring, 1999), 15-17. (101st Ohio Infantry).

Nichols, James L., ed. "Reminiscing from 1861 to 1865; An 'Ex Confed', H. P. Morrow." *East Texas Historical Journal*, vol. 9, no. 1 (March, 1971), 5-19. (16th Louisiana Infantry).

O'Neal, Bill, ed. "The Civil War Memoirs of Samuel Alonza Cooke." *Southwestern Historical Quarterly*, vol. LXXIV, no. 4 (April, 1971), 535-548. (17th Texas Dismounted Cavalry).

Oates, William C. "General W. F. Perry and Something of his Career in War and Peace," *Montgomery Advertiser*, March 2, 1902.

Opdycke, Emerson. "Notes on the Chickamauga Campaign," *Battles and Leaders*, 4 vols. New York: Thomas Yoseloff, 1956. vol. 3, 670.

Palmer, John B. "The 58th North Carolina at the Battle of Chickamauga" *Our Living and Our Dead*. vol. 3 (1875), 454-455.

Park, Josiah B. "The Story of the Illinois Central Lines during the Civil Conflict 1861-5," *Illinois Central Magazine*, June, 1916, 11-22. (4th Michigan Cavalry).

Partridge, Charles A. "The Ninety-Sixth Illinois at Chickamauga," *Transactions of the Illinois State Historical Society for the Year 1910*. Springfield: Phillips Brothers, 1910. 72-80.

Pavelka, Greg. "Where Were You Johnny Shiloh?" *Civil War Times Illustrated*, vol. XXVII, no. 1 (January, 1989), 35-41. (22nd Michigan Infantry).

Peacock, Jane Bonner, ed. "A Wartime Story: The Davidson Letters," *The Atlanta Historical Bulletin*, vol. XIX, no. 1, (Spring, 1975), 9-75. (39th North Carolina Infantry).

Perry, William F. and Curt Johnson, eds. "A Forgotten Account of Chickamauga." *Civil War Times Illustrated*, vol. XXXII, no. 4 (September/October, 1993), 53-6. (Law's Brigade).

Peterson, Thomas G. "Civil War Letters" *Cenotaph*, vol. 5, no. 2 (Summer, 1969), 16-17. (Hutchinson County Texas Genealogical Society).

Polk, William M. "General Polk at Chickamauga," *Battles and Leaders of the Civil War*, 4 vols. New York, Thomas Yoseloff, Inc., 1956. vol. 3, 662-663.

Popowski, Howard. "Opportunity: Clash at Dug Gap." *Civil War Times Illustrated*, vol. XXII, no. 4 (June, 1983), 16-18, 35.

Powell, David A. "The Battles for Horseshoe Ridge." *North & South*, vol. 8, no. 2 (March, 2005), 48-59.

Prindle, Horace H. "Civil War Letter." *Bulletin of the California Central Coast Genealogical Society*, vol. 7, no. 4 (April, 1974), 72. (22nd Michigan Infantry).

Provenmire, H.M. "Diary of Jacob Adams, Private in Company F, 21st O.V.V.I.," *Ohio Historical Quarterly*, vol. XXXVIII, no. 4 (October, 1929), 650-4.

Ranson, A. R. H. "Reminiscences of the Civil War by a Confederate Staff Officer (Fourth Paper)" *The Sewanee Review*, vol. 22, no. 7 (July 1914), 298-308. (Pegram's Staff).

Reynolds, Donald E, and Max H. Kele, eds. "With the Army of the Cumberland in the Chickamauga Campaign: The Diary of James W. Chapin, Thirty-Ninth Indiana Volunteers," *Georgia Historical Quarterly*, vol. 59, no. 2 (Summer, 1975), 222-237.

Robertson, William Glenn. "The Chickamauga Campaign: The Fall of Chattanooga," *Blue & Gray Magazine*, vol. XXIII, no. 4 (Fall, 2006), 6-26, 43-50.

Robertson, William Glenn. "The Chickamauga Campaign: Bragg's Lost Opportunity," *Blue & Gray Magazine*, vol. XXIII, no. 6 (Spring, 2007), 6-26, 42-50.

Robertson, William Glenn. "The Chickamauga Campaign: The Armies Collide," *Blue & Gray Magazine*, vol. XXIV, no. 3 (Fall, 2007), 6-29, 40-50.

Robertson, William Glenn. "The Chickamauga Campaign: Chickamauga, Day1," *Blue & Gray Magazine*, vol. XXIV, no. 6 (Spring, 2008), 6-28, 40-52.

Robertson, William Glenn. "The Chickamauga Campaign: The Battle of Chickamauga Day 2, September 20, 1863," *Blue & Gray Magazine*, vol. XXV, no. 2 (Summer, 2008), 6-31, 40-50.

Rosecrans, William Starke. "The Mistakes of Grant," *The North American Review*, vol. 141, issue 349 (December, 1885), 580-600.

Rosecrans, William Starke. "The Campaign for Chattanooga," *The Century*, May, 1887, 129-135.

Ross, Julie M. "Civil War Casualties: The 6th Ohio Volunteer Infantry at Chickamauga," *The Tracer*, September, 1999, 79-82.

Sawyer, Benjamin F. "Chickamauga," *Battles and Leaders*, Volume 5, Urbana, IL: University of Illinois Press, 2002, 422-29. (24th Alabama Infantry).

Shaw, Arba F. "My Experiences," *Walker County Messenger*, April 3, 1902. (4th Georgia Cavalry)

Shaw, Arba F. "My Experiences," *Walker County Messenger*, April 10, 1902. (4th Georgia Cavalry).

Shaw, Frank. "A Journal Kept by John A. Clements–July 1, 1862, Resaca, Georgia." *Walker County Georgia Historical Newsletter*, October 15, 1987, 8-19.

Shelly, Joseph Frederick, Fanny Anderson, eds.; Sophie Gemant, trans.; "The Shelly Papers," *Indiana Magazine of History*, vol. 44 no. 2 (June, 1948), 181-198. (2nd Indiana Cavalry).

Shewmon, Joe. "The Amazing Ordeal of Private Joe Shewmon." *Civil War Times Illustrated*, vol. 1, no. 1 (April, 1962), 45-49. (93rd Ohio Infantry).

Skoch, George. "A test of Rebel Rails" *Civil War Times Illustrated*, vol. XXV, no. 8 (December, 1986), 12-19.

Smith, John Abernathy, ed. "Letters to Mary: The Civil War Diary of John Kennerly Farris." *Franklin County Historical Review*, vol. XXV (1994), 1-140. (41st Tennessee Infantry).

Smith, Lynn Therese Miller. "Eyewitness to War," *America's Civil War*, vol. XX, no. 3 (July, 2007), 19-20. (96th Illinois Infantry.).

Stevenson, William Robert. "Robert Alexander Smith: A Southern Son," *Alabama Historical Quarterly*, vol. XX (1958), 35-60. (3rd Alabama Cavalry).

Sunderland, Glenn W. "The Battle of Hoover's Gap." *Civil War Times Illustrated*, vol. VI, no. 3 (June, 1967), 34-41.

Sunseri, Alvin R., ed. "Transient Prisoner: The Reminiscences of William H. Gilbert." *Journal of the Illinois State Historical Society*, vol. LXXIV, no. 1 (Spring, 1981), 41-50. (19th Illinois Infantry).

Sykes, Edward T. "Walthall's Brigade, a Cursory Sketch with Personal Experiences of Walthall's Brigade, Army of Tennessee, C.S.A., 1862-1865." *Publications of the Mississippi Historical Society, Centenary Series 1*, (1916), 477-623.

Suppinger, Joseph E. Ed. "From Chickamauga to Chattanooga, The Battlefield Account of Sergeant John M. Kane," *East Tennessee Historical Society Publications*, no. 45, 1973. (101st Indiana Infantry).

Thruston, Gates P. "The Crisis at Chickamauga." *Battles and Leaders of the Civil War*, 4 vols. New York: Thomas Yoseloff, Inc., 1956. vol. 3, 663-665. (XX Corps Staff).

Tidball, John C. "The Artillery Service in the War of the Rebellion, 1861-65. Part vii, Chickamauga (first day)," *Journal of the Military Service Institution*, vol. XIII, no. 11 (November, 1892), 1085-1109.

Tidball, John C. "The Artillery Service in the War of the Rebellion, 1861-65. Part viii, Chickamauga (second day)," *Journal of the Military Service Institution*, vol. XIV, no. 1 (January, 1893), 1-29.

Tucker, Glenn. "The Battle of Chickamauga." *Civil War Times Illustrated*, vol. 8, no. 2 (May, 1969), 1-50.

Uhler, Margaret Anderson, ed. "Civil War Letters of Major General James Patton Anderson." *Florida Historical Quarterly*, vol. XVI, no. 2 (October, 1977), 150-175.

Vance, Wilson J. "Chickamauga," *Cincinnati Commercial Gazette*, May 25, 1889. (21st Ohio Infantry).

Vance, Wilson J. "On Thomas' Right at Chickamauga." *Blue and Gray*, vol. 1, no. 2. (February, 1893), 87-99. (21st Ohio Infantry).

Vaughn, Turner. "Diary of Turner Vaughn," *Alabama Historical Quarterly*, vol. XVII, no. 2 (Spring, 1956), 596-597. (4th Alabama Infantry).

Walker, Robert Sparks. "The Pyramids of Chickamauga: Peyton H. Colquitt," *Chattanooga Sunday Times*, October 4, 1936.

Watson, James Monroe." *The Permian Historical Annual*, vol. 18 (December,1978), 33-44. (10th Texas Dismounted Cavalry).

Wells, E. T. "The Campaign and Battle of Chickamauga" *United Service Journal*, September, 1896, 205-33.

Williamson, James A. "Civil War Letters" *Hempstead Trails*, April, 1995, 4-8. (Hempstead County Genealogical Society, Hope, Arkansas. 2nd Arkansas Mounted Rifles).

Williams, Robert Leo. "Letters of Wilbur M. Williams, Co. D. 18th Ohio Voluntary Infantry." *Ohio Civil War Genealogy Journal*, vol. III, no. 3 (Fall, 1999) 153-155.

Wilson, James Harrison. "Alexander McDowell McCook," *Thirty-Fifth Reunion of the Association of Graduates of the United States Military Academy*, Saginaw MI: Seeman and Peters, 1904, 38-100.

Wood, Thomas J. *"The Gaps at Chickamauga." New York Times*, November 19, 1882.

Wright, T. J. *"Battle of Chickamauga," Estill County Historical and Genealogical Society Newsletter*, vol. XVII, no. 1 (May, 1997), 5. (8th Kentucky Infantry US).

Personal narratives, primary sources, and unit histories

Adamson, A. P. *Sojourns of a Patriot: The Field and Prison Papers of an Unreconstructed Confederate. Edited by Richard Bender Abell and Fay Adamson Gecik.* Murfreesboro, TN: Southern Heritage Press, 1998. (30th Georgia Infantry)

Adamson, A.P. *Brief History of the 30th Georgia Regiment.* Rex, GA: The Mills Printing Co., 1912.

Ager, Waldemar. *Chickamauga: Colonel Heg and His Boys.* Northfield, MN: Norwegian-American Historical Society, 2000. Translation of Norwegian edition. (15th Wisconsin).

Allen, Robert D., and Cheryl J. Allen, eds. *A "Guest" of the Confederacy: The Civil War Letters & Diaries of Alonzo M. Keeler, Captain Company B, Twenty-Second Michigan Infantry including letters & diaries written while a prisoner of war.* Nashville, TN: Cold Tree Press, 2008.

Allen, William G. *Reminiscences of William G. Allen: McKenzie's 5th Tennessee Regiment.* Rhea County Historical and Genealogical Society, 2000. (Confederate).

Andes John W., and Will A. McTeer. *Loyal Mountain Troopers: The Second and Third Tennessee Volunteer Cavalry in the Civil War.* Maryville, TN: Blount County Genealogical and Historical Society, 1992. (Union).

Anonymous. *The Rear Guard of Company H: 39th Regiment of Indiana Volunteers Infantry and 8th Veteran Cavalry.* n.p., n.d.

Anonymous. *Ninety-Second Illinois Volunteers.* Freeport, IL: Journal Steam Publishing House and Bookbindery, 1875.

Anonymous. *Dedication of the Wilder Brigade Monument on Chickamauga Battlefield.* The Herald Press, 1900.

Anonymous. *Proceedings of the Thirtieth Annual Reunion, 1st O.V.V.C.* n.p., 1909.

Aldrich, C. Knight. *Quest for A Star: The Civil War Letters And Diaries of Colonel Francis T. Sherman Of The 88th Illinois.* Knoxville, TN: University of Tennessee Press, 1999.

Alexander, Edward Porter. *Military Memoirs of a Confederate.* New York: Charles Scribners' Sons, 1907.

Anderson, James H, ed. *Life and Letters of Judge Thomas J. Anderson and Wife.* Columbus, OH: Press of F. J. Heer, 1904. (21st Ohio Infantry).

Anderson, John Q. Editor. *Campaigning with Parsons' Texas Cavalry Brigade, CSA.* Hillsboro, TX: Hill Junior College Press, 1967 (includes letters from Henry G. Orr, 17th/18th/24th/25th Texas Dismounted Cavalry).

Andrew, A. Piatt. *Some Civil War Letters.* Gloucester, MA: privately printed, 1925. (21st Indiana Battery).

Association of the Regiment. *Roster of the Survivors of the Twenty-Sixth Ohio Veteran Volunteer Infantry.* Chilicothe, OH: The office of the Ohio Soldier, 1888.

Aten, Henry J. *History of the Eighty-Fifth Regiment, Illinois Volunteer Infantry.* Hiawatha, KS: Regimental Association, 1901.

Athearn, Robert G. ed. *Soldier In The West: The Civil War Letters Of Alfred Lacey Hough.* Philadelphia, PA: University of Pennsylvania Press, 1957. (19th U.S. Infantry and Negley's Staff).

Atkins, Smith. *Chickamauga. Useless, Disastrous Battle.* Talk by Smith D. Atkins, Opera House, Mendota, Illinois, February 22, 1907, At Invitation Of Women's Relief Corps. G.A.R. n.p. 1907.

Atkins, Smith. *Remarks by Smith D. Atkins, Late Colonel of the 92nd Illinois Volunteer Infantry (Mounted.)* Wilder's Brigade Reunion, Effingham, Illinois, September 17, 1909.

Albertson, Joan W. *Compiler. Letters Home to Minnesota: Cpl D. B. Griffin, 2nd Minnesota Volunteers.* Seattle, WA: P.D. Enterprises, 1992.

Bailey, Chester P. *Mansfield Men in the Seventh Pennsylvania Cavalry 1861-1865.* Mansfield, PA: Published by the author, 1986.

Barnes, James A., James R. Carnahan, and Thomas H. B. McCain. *The Eighty-Sixth Regiment, Indiana Volunteer Infantry. A narrative of its Services in the Civil War of 1861-1865.* Crawfordsville, IN: The Journal Company Printers, 1895.

Barnhill, Floyd R. Sr. and Calvin L Collier. *The Fighting Fifth. Pat Cleburne's Cutting Edge: The Fifth Arkansas Regiment, C.S.A.* Jonesboro, AR: Published by the Authors, 1990.

Bass, Ronald R. *History of the Thirty-first Arkansas Confederate Infantry.* Conway, AR: Conway Research, 1996.

Baumgartner, Richard A. and Larry M. Strayer. *Ralsa C. Rice: Yankee Tigers Through the Civil War with The 125th Ohio.* Huntington, WV: Blue Acorn Press, 1992.

Baumgartner, Richard A., ed. *Yankee Tigers II: Civil War Field Correspondence from the Tiger Regiment of Ohio.* Huntington, WV: Blue Acorn Press, 2004. (125th Ohio Infantry).

Baumgartner, Richard A. *Blue Lightning: Wilder's Mounted Infantry Brigade in the Battle of Chickamauga.* Huntington, WV: Blue Acorn Press, 1997. Revised edition, 2007.

Baumgartner, Richard A., Ed. *The Bully Boys: In Camp and Combat with the 2nd Ohio Volunteer Infantry Regiment 1861-1864.* Huntington, WV: Blue Acorn Press, 2011.

Beach, John M. *History of the Fortieth Ohio Volunteer Infantry.* London, OH: Shepard & Craig, Publishers, 1884.

Beatty, John. *The Citizen-Soldier: The Memoirs of a Civil War Volunteer.* Lincoln, NE: University of Nebraska Press, 1998. Reprint of 1879 edition.

Beaudot, William J. K. *The 24th Wisconsin Infantry in the Civil War: The Biography of a Regiment.* Mechanicsburg, PA: Stackpole Books, 2003.

Beers, Fannie A. *Memories, a Record of Personal Experience and Adventure During Four Years of War.* Philadelphia: J. B. Lippencott Company, 1894. (14th Louisiana Battalion).

Belcher, Dennis W. *The 10th Kentucky Volunteer Infantry in the Civil War: A History and Roster.* Jefferson, NC: McFarland & Co., 2010.

Benefiel, W. H. H. *History of Wilder's Lightning Brigade During the Civil War 1861 to 1865.* Pendelton, IN: The Times Print, n.d.

Benefiel, W. H. H. *Souvenir of the Seventeenth Indiana Regiment: A History from its Organization to the End of the War, Giving a Description of Battles, etc. Also, List of the Survivors, their Names; Ages; Company, and P. O. Address. And Interesting Letters from Comrades who were not present at the Regimental Reunions.* Elwood, IN: Model Printing and Litho Co., 1913.

Bennett, Charles W. *Historical Sketches of the Ninth Michigan Infantry.* Coldwater, MI: Daily Courier Print, 1913.

Bennett, Lyman G. and William M Haigh. *History of the Thirty-Sixth Regiment Illinois Volunteers During the War of the Rebellion.* Aurora, IL: Knickerbocker and Hodder, 1876.

Bergemann, Kurt D. *Brackett's Battalion Minnesota Cavalry 1861-1866.* Minneapolis: Adeniram Publications, 1996.

Berkenes, Robert E., ed. *Private William Boddy's Civil War Journal: Empty Saddles. . .Empty Sleeves. . .* Altoona, IA: TiffCor Publishing, 1996. (92nd Illinois Infantry).

Berry, Thomas F. *Four Years with Morgan and Forrest.* Oklahoma City: The Harlow-Ratliff Co., 1914 (Morgan's Detachment Cavalry)

Bevens, William E. *Reminiscences of a Private: Company "G" First Arkansas Regiment Infantry.* Fayetteville, AR: University of Arkansas Press, 1992. Reprint of 1913 edition.

Bierce, Ambrose. *Ambrose Bierce's Civil War.* Chicago: Gateway Press, 1956. (Hazen's Staff).

Bircher, William. *A Drummer Boy's Diary: Comprising Four Years of Service with the Second Regiment Minnesota Veteran Volunteers, 1861 To 1865.* St. Paul, MN: St. Paul book and Stationary Company, 1889.

Bird, Edgeworth, with John Rozier, Ed. *The Granite Farm Letters: The Civil War Correspondence of Edgeworth & Sallie Bird.* Athens, GA: University of Georgia Press, 1988. (15th Georgia Infantry).

Bishop, Judson W. *The Story of a Regiment, Being a Narrative of the Service of the Second Regiment, Minnesota Veteran Volunteer Infantry, in the Civil War of 1861-1865.* St. Cloud, MN: North Star Press, 2000. Reprint of 1890 edition.

Bishop, Judson W. *Van Derveer's Brigade at Chickamauga.* St. Paul, MN: n.p. 1903.

Bitter, Rand K. *Minty and his Cavalry: A History of the Saber Brigade and its Commander.* Self-published, 2006.

Blackburn, J. K. P., L. B. Giles, and E. S. Dowd. *Terry Texas Ranger Trilogy.* Austin, TX: State House Press, 1996. (8th Texas Cavalry).

Blackburn, John. *A Hundred Miles, A Hundred Heartbreaks.* n.p., Reed Printing Company, 1972. (17th Kentucky Infantry).

Blackburn, John W. Gray. *Jackets with Blue Collars.* Beaver Dam, KY: The Embry Newspapers, 1963. (Co. C, 9th Kentucky Infantry CS).

Blackburn, Theodore W. *Letters from the Front, A Union "Preacher" Regiment (74th Ohio) in the Civil War.* Dayton, OH: Press of Morningside House, Inc., 1981.

Blegan, Theodore C., ed. *The Civil War Letters of Colonel Hans Christian Heg.* Northfield, MN: Norwegian-American Historical Association, 1936. (15th Wisconsin Infantry).

Bobrick, Benson. *Testament: A Soldier's Story of the Civil War.* New York: Simon and Schuster, 2003. (includes letters of Benjamin W. Baker, 25th Illinois Infantry).

Boggs, Samuel S. *Eighteen Months a Prisoner under The Rebel Flag: A Condensed Pen Picture of Belle Isle, Danville, Andersonville, Charleston, Florence and Libby Prisons from Actual Experience.* Lovington, IL: S. S. Boggs, 1887. (31st Illinois Infantry).

Bond, James O. *Chickamauga and The Underground Railroad: A Tale of Two Grandfathers.* Baltimore: Gateway Press, 1993. (75th Indiana Infantry).

Bond, Natalie Jenkins and Osmun Latrobe Coward, eds. *The South Carolinians: Colonel Asbury Coward's Memoirs.* New York: Vantage Press, 1968. (5th South Carolina Infantry).

Bone, Harriet Phillips, comp. *Civil War Diary & Letters of James Martin Phillips, Company G, 92nd Illinois Volunteers*. St. Louis: Robert F. Parkes Genealogical Research & Productions, 1984.

Booth, John T. with Marie Mollohan, Ed. *Another Day in Lincoln's Army: The Civil War Journals of Sgt. John T. Booth*. Lincoln, NE: iUniverse, 2007. (36th Ohio Infantry).

Booth, Louise. *The Beleaguered Forty-First Tennessee*. Villa Park, CA: D.R. Booth Associates, 1996.

Botsford, T. F. *Memories of the War of Secession*. Montgomery, AL: Paragon Press, 1911. (47th Alabama Infantry).

Bowers Jr., William A. *The 47th Georgia Volunteer Infantry Regiment*. Global Author Press, 2013.

Boynton, Henry Van Ness. *Chattanooga and Chickamauga*. Reprint of Gen. H. V. Boynton's Letters to the *Cincinnati Commercial Gazette*, August 1888. Washington, DC: Gray and Clarkson, Printers, 1888.

Bradshaw, Wayne. *The Civil War Diary of William R. Dyer, A Member of Forrest's Escort*. n.p., 2009.

Bradt, Hiram Henry Gillespie, *History of the Services of the Third Battery Wisconsin Light Artillery in the Civil War of the United States 1861-65*. Berlin, WI: Courant Press, 1902.

Bragg, William Harris, *Joe Brown's Army: The Georgia State Line, 1862-1865*. Macon, GA: Mercer University Press, 1987.

Bratton, John. *Letters of John Bratton to His Wife*. n.p. 1942. (6th South Carolina Infantry).

Braun, Mark S. *The North Shore Soldiers of Chicago in the American Civil War*. North Shore Network Publications, 1997. (Various Illinois regiments).

Briant, Charles C. *History of the Sixth Regiment Indiana Volunteer Infantry, of both Three Months' and Three Years' Services*. Indianapolis: Wm. E. Burford, 1891.

Broadwater, Robert P. *Chickamauga, Andersonville, Fort Sumter and Guard Duty at Home: Four Civil War Diaries by Pennsylvania Soldiers*. Jefferson, NC: McFarland & Co., 2006. (William R. Glisan, 6th Ohio Infantry).

Brown, Campbell H., ed. *The Reminiscences of Sergeant Newton Cannon: From Holograph Material Provided by his Grandson, Samuel M. Fleming, Jr*. Franklin, TN: Carter House Association,1963. (11th Tennessee Cavalry).

Brown, Dee Alexander. *The Bold Cavaliers: Morgan's 2nd Kentucky Cavalry Raiders*. Philadelphia and New York: J.B. Lippincott & Company. 1960.

Brown, Norman D. ed. *One of Cleburne's Command: The Civil War Reminiscences and Diary of Captain Samuel T. Foster, Granbury's Texas Brigade, CSA*. Austin: University of Texas Press, 1980. (24th Texas dismounted Cavalry).

Brown, Robert Carson., with Charles G. Brown, ed. *The Sherman Brigade Marches South: The Civil War Memoirs of Colonel Robert Carson Brown*. Washington, DC: Charles G. Brown, 1995. (64th Ohio Infantry).

Brown Russell K. *Augusta's "Pet Company" The Washington Light Artillery of Augusta Georgia*. Clearwater, SC: Eastern Digital Resources, 2001.

Brown Russell K. *Our Connection with Savannah: A History of the 1st Battalion Georgia Sharpshooters*. Macon, GA: Mercer University Press. 2004.

Buck, Irving A. *Cleburne and His Command*. New York: Walter Neale Publishing, 1908.

Buckner, Allen. *The Memoirs of Allen Buckner: Colonel of The 79th Illinois Volunteer Regiment in the Civil War. Edited by Allan Buckner Rice*. Lansing, MI: The Michigan Alcohol and Drug Information Foundation. 1982.

Burlingame, Michael, and John R. Turner Ettlinger, eds. *Inside Lincoln's White House: The Complete Civil War Diary of John Hay*. Carbondale, IL: Southern Illinois University Press, 1997.

Bush, Bryan. *My Dear Mollie: The Letters of Brig. Gen. Daniel Griffin, Commander of The 38th Indiana Volunteer Infantry*. Bedford IN: JoNA Books, 2003.

Bush, Bryan S. *Terry's Texas Rangers: The 8th Texas Cavalry*. Paducah, KY: Turner Publishing, 2002.

Buslett, O. A., translated by Barbara G. Scott. *The Fifteenth Wisconsin*. n.p., 1999.

Butler, Jay Caldwell. *Letters Home*. n. p., 1930. (101st Ohio Infantry).

Cabaniss, Jim R., ed. *Civil War Journal and Letters of Washington Ives 4th Fla. C.S.A*. Tallahassee, FL: Jim R. Cabaniss, 1987.

Cahnovsky, Tony, and D. Franklin Reister. *For Those Who Still Hear the Guns: History Of The 22nd Regiment Illinois Volunteer Infantry*. n.p. 1989.

Calkins, William Wirt. *The History of the One Hundred and Fourth Regiment of Illinois Volunteer Infantry. War of the Great Rebellion 1862-1865*. Chicago: Donohue and Hennenberry, 1895.

Campbell, Robert, with George F. Skoch, and Mark W. Perkins, eds. *Lone Star Confederate: A Gallant and Good Soldier of the Fifth Texas Infantry*. College Station: Texas A & M University Press, 2003.

Canfield, Silas S. *History of the 21st Regiment Ohio Volunteer Infantry, in the War of the Rebellion*. Toledo, OH: Vrooman, Anderson and Bateman, 1893.

Cannon, Robert K. *Volunteers for Union and Liberty, History of the 5th Tennessee Infantry, U.S.A. 1862-1865*. Knoxville: Bohemian Brigade Publishers, 1995.

Carlock, Chuck, with V. M. Owens. *History of The Tenth Texas Cavalry (Dismounted) Regiment 1861-1865. "If we ever got whipped, I don't recollect it."* North Richfield Hills, TX: Smithfield Press, 2001.

Carlson, Charlie C. *The First Florida Cavalry Regiment, C.S.A.* New Smyrna Beach, FL: Luther's Publishing, 1999.

Carnahan, James R. *Personal Recollections of Chickamauga*. Cincinnati: H. C. Sherrick and Co. 1886. (86th Indiana Infantry).

Carter, Howell. *A Cavalryman's Reminiscences of the Civil War*. New Orleans: The American Publishing Co., 1900. (1st Louisiana Cavalry).

Carter, Ruth C. Ed. *For Honor Glory & Union: The Mexican & Civil War Letters of Brig. Gen. William Haines Lytle*. Lexington: The University Press of Kentucky, 1999.

Carter, William Randolph. *History of the First Regiment of Tennessee Volunteer Cavalry in the Great War of the Rebellion, With the Armies of the Ohio and Cumberland, Under Generals Morgan, Rosecrans, Thomas, Stanley, and Wilson*. Knoxville, TN: Gaut-Ogden Company, 1902.

Castle, John Stiles. *Grandfather was a Drummer Boy: A Civil War Diary & Letters of Charles B. Stiles*. Solon, OH: Evans Printing Company, 1986. (36th Illinois Infantry).

Castleman, John B. *Active Service*. Louisville, KY: Courier-Journal Job Printing Co. 1917. (2nd Kentucky Cavalry CS).

Cater, Douglas John. *As It Was: Reminiscences of a Soldier of the Third Texas Cavalry and the Nineteenth Louisiana Infantry*. Austin, TX: State House Press, 1990.

Cathey, M. Todd, and Gary W. Waddey. *"Forward My Brave Boys!" A History of the 11th Tennessee Volunteer Infantry, CSA 1861-1865*. Macon, GA: Mercer University Press, 2016.

Cavender, Michael Bowers. *The First Georgia Cavalry in the Civil War: A History and Roster*. Jefferson, NC: McFarland & Company, Inc. Publishers, 2016.

Chadwick, Albert G. *Soldiers' Record of the Town of St. Johnsbury, Vermont*. St. Johnsbury, C.M. Stone & Co., 1883. (26th Pennsylvania Battery).

Chapman, Hank, ed. *The Letters of William S. McCaskey*. Infinity Publishing Group, 2008. (79th Pennsylvania Infantry).

Chapman, Harvey Amasa, with David Wesley Chapman, ed. *The Man Who Carried a Drum: 108 War Letters and Love Letters of a Civil War Medic*. New York: iUniverse, 2006. (121st Ohio Infantry).

Chase, John A. *History of the Fourteenth Ohio, Regiment O.V.V.I. From the beginning of the War in 1861 to its close in 1865*. Toledo, OH: St. John Printing House, 1881.

Christ, Mark K. Editor. *Getting Used to Being Shot At: The Spence Family Civil War Letters*. Fayetteville, AR: University of Arkansas Press, 2002. (1st Arkansas Infantry).

Cist, Henry M. *The Army of the Cumberland: Campaigns Of The Civil War, Vol. VII*. New York: Charles Scribner's Sons, 1882.

Clark, Charles T. *Opdyke Tigers: 125th O.V.I. A History of the Regiment and of the Campaigns and Battles of the Army of the Cumberland*. Columbus, OH: Spahr and Glenn, 1895.

Clary, James B. *A History of the 15th South Carolina Infantry 1861-1865*. Charleston, SC: South Carolina Department of Archives and History, 2008.

Coker, James Lide. *History of Company G, Ninth S. C. Regiment, Infantry, S. C. Army, And of Company E, Sixth S. C. Regiment, Infantry, S. C. Army*. Greenwood, SC: The Attic Press, 1979.

Cole, Elias. *Journal of Three Years' Service with the Twenty-Sixth Ohio Volunteer Infantry in the Great Rebellion. . . 1861-1864.* n.p. 1897.

Collier, Calvin L. *The War Child's Children: The Story of the Third Regiment, Arkansas Cavalry, Confederate States Army.* Little Rock, AR: Pioneer Press, 1965.

Collier, Calvin L. *First In-Last Out: The Capitol Guards, Ark. Brigade.* Little Rock, AR: Pioneer Press, 1961. (6th Arkansas Infantry).

Collier, Calvin L. *"They'll Do to Tie To!" The Story of the Third Regiment, Arkansas Infantry, C.S.A.* Little Rock, AR: Pioneer Press, 1959.

Collins, R. M. *Unwritten Chapters of the War Between the States.* Dayton, OH: Morningside House, 1988. Reprint of 1892 edition. (15th Texas Infantry).

Confederate. *The Grayjackets: And How They Lived, Fought, and Died, For Dixie with incidents & sketches of life in the Confederacy, comprising narratives of personal adventure, army life, naval adventure, home life, partisan daring, life in the camp, field and hospital: together with the songs, ballads, anecdotes and humorous incidents of the war for Southern independence.* Richmond, VA: Jones Brothers and Co., 1867.

Connolly, James A. *Three Years in the Army of the Cumberland.* Bloomington, IN: Indiana University Press, 1987. Reprint of 1959 edition. (123rd Illinois Mounted Infantry).

Cooper, Edward S. *The Brave Men of Company A: The Forty-First Ohio Volunteer Infantry.* Madison: Fairleigh Dickenson University Press, 2015.

Cope, Alexis. *The Fifteenth Ohio Volunteers and its Campaigns War of 1861-5.* Columbus, OH: Published by the Author, 1916.

Cornue, Virginia, and William R. Trotter, eds. *So Much Blood: The Civil War Letters of CSA Private William Wallace Beard, 1861-1865.* Montclair, NJ: Creative Books, 2015. (18th Mississippi Infantry).

Cotten, Michael. *The Williamson County Cavalry: A History of Company F, Fourth Tennessee Cavalry Regiment, CSA.* Published by the Author, 1994.

Cotton, John W., with Lucille Griffith, ed. *Yours Till Death: Civil War Letters Of John W. Cotton.* University, AL: University of Alabama Press, 1951. (10th Confederate Cavalry).

Cox, Jacob Dolson. *Military Reminiscences of the Civil War,* 2 vols. New York: Charles Scribner's Sons, 1900.

Cozzens, Peter. ed. *Battles & Leaders of the Civil War, Volume 5.* Urbana, IL: University of Illinois Press, 2002.

Cozzens, Peter. ed. *Eyewitnesses to the Indian Wars: Volume Four, The Long War for the Northern Plains,* Mechanicsburg, PA: Stackpole Books, 2004.

Crissey, Elwell. *A Methodist Circuit Rider on the Illinois Frontier In the 1830's And His Later History.* Bloomington, IL: privately printed, 1981. (115th Illinois Infantry).

Crofts, Thomas. *History of the Third Ohio Cavalry, 1861-1865.* Toledo, OH: Stoneman Press, 1910.

Crook, George, with Martin F. Schmitt, ed. *General George Crook: His Autobiography.* Norman: University of Oklahoma Press, 1946.

Cross, Frederick C. *Nobly They Served the Union.* Published by the author, 1976. (includes letters of Henry G. Stratton, 19th Ohio Infantry).

Cross, Rev. Joseph. *Camp and Field: Papers from the Portfolio of an Army Chaplain.* Columbia, SC: Evans and Cogswell, 1864. (Buckner's Staff).

Cumming, Kate. *Gleanings from Southland, Sketches of Life and Manners of the People of the South Before, During and After the War of Secession, With Extracts from the Author's Journal and an Epitome of the New South.* Birmingham, AL: Roberts and Son, 1895.

Cumming, Kate, with Richard Barksdale Harwell, ed. *Kate: The Journal of a Confederate Nurse.* Baton Rouge: Louisiana State University Press, 1998.

Cumming, Katharine H., with W. Kirk Wood, ed. *A Northern Daughter and A Southern Wife: The Civil War Reminiscences of Katharine H. Cumming 1860-1865.* Augusta, GA: Richmond County Historical Society, 1976.

Cunningham, Sumner A. *Reminiscences of the 41st Tennessee.* Shippensburg, PA: White Mane Books, 2000.

Curry, William L. *Four Years in the Saddle: History of the First Regiment Ohio Volunteer Cavalry. 1861-1865.* Jonesboro, GA: Freedom Hill Press, 1984. Reprint of 1898 edition.

Cutrer, Thomas W., ed. *Oh, What A Loansome Time I had: The Civil War Letters of Major William Morel Moxley, Eighteenth Alabama Infantry, and Emily Beck Moxley.* Tuscaloosa, AL: University of Alabama Press, 2002.

Cutrer, Thomas W. ed. *Longstreet's Aide: The Civil War Letters of Major Thomas J. Goree.* Charlottesville: University Press of Virginia, 1995.

Cutter, O. P. *Our Battery; Or The Journal of Company B, 1st O.V.A.* Cleveland: Nevins' Book and Job Printing Establishment, 1864.

Daffan, Kate. *My Father as I Remember Him.* Houston: Press of Gray and Dillaye, 1907. (Autobiographical sketch of Lawrence A. Daffan, 4th Texas Infantry).

Dameron, Dave. *Benning's Brigade, Vol. I: A History and Roster of the Fifteenth Georgia.* Spartansburg, SC: The Reprint Co. 1997.

Dana, Charles A. *Recollections of the Civil War.* New York: Collier Books, 1963 edition. Reprint of 1902 edition.

Davidson, Henry M. *History of Battery A, First Regiment of Ohio Vol. Light Artillery.* Milwaukee: Daily Wisconsin Steam Printing Office, 1865.

Davis, Sam B. *A History of the 3rd South Carolina Volunteer Infantry Battalion (James Battalion): 1861-1865.* Wilmington, NC: Broadfoot Publishing Company, 2009.

Davis, William C., ed. *Diary of a Confederate Soldier: John S. Jackman of the Orphan Brigade.* Columbia, SC: University of South Carolina Press, 1990.

Davis, William C. *The Orphan Brigade.* New York: Doubleday, 1980.

Day, L. W. *Story of the One Hundred and First Ohio Infantry.* Cleveland, OH: The W. M. Bayne Printing Co. 1894.

Demoret, Alfred. *A Brief History of the Ninety-Third Regiment Ohio Volunteer Infantry: Recollections Of A Private.* Ross, OH: Graphic Printing, 1898.

Denslinger, C. W., ed. *Civil War Diary of James Wesley Riley Who Served with the Union Army in the War Between the States, April 22, 1861-June 18, 1865.* n.p., 1960. (42nd Illinois Infantry).

DeVelling, Charles T. *History of the Seventeenth Regiment, First Brigade, Third Division, Fourteenth Corps, Army of the Cumberland, War of the Rebellion.* Zanesville, OH: E. R. Sullivan, Printer and Binder, 1880. (17th Ohio Infantry).

Devol, Hiram F. *Biographical Sketch.* Kansas City: Hudson Kimberly Publishing Co., 1903. (36th Ohio Infantry. Includes marginalia by John Booth, copy from Abraham Lincoln Presidential Library, Springfield, IL).

DeWees, Joseph W., ed. *Joshua Dewees: His Civil War Diary.* n.p., n.d. (97th Ohio Infantry).

Dickert, D Augustus. *History of Kershaw's Brigade, with a complete roll of companies, biographical sketches, incidents, anecdotes, etc.* Newberry, SC: Elebert H. Aull Co., 1899.

Doan, Isaac C. *Reminiscences of the Chattanooga Campaign: A Paper Read at the Reunion of Company B, Fortieth Ohio Volunteer Infantry, at Xenia, O., August 22, 1894.* Richmond, IN: J. M. Coe's Printery, 1894. (40th Ohio).

Dodd, Ephraim Shelby *Dairy of Ephraim Shelby Dodd* Austin: 1914 (8th Texas Cavalry).

Dodge, William Sumner. *History of the Old Second Division Army of the Cumberland.* Chicago: Church & Goodman, 1864.

Dodge, William Sumner. *A Waif of the War; Or, The History of the Seventy-Fifth Illinois Infantry, Embracing the Entire Campaigns of the Army of the Cumberland.* Chicago: Church and Goodman, Publishers, 1866.

Dodson, W. C. *Wheeler and His Cavalry, 1862-1865.* Memphis, TN: E.F. Williams and J. J. Fox, 1997. Reprint of 1899 edition.

Doll, William H. *History of the Sixth Regiment Indiana Volunteer Infantry in the Civil War.* Indianapolis: 1903.

Dolton, George E., with Theodore A, Dolton, ed. *The Path of Patriotism: Civil War Letters of George Edwin Dolton.* Palo Alto, CA: Booksurge, 2005. (M, 1st Illinois Artillery).

Donald, David. *Inside Lincoln's Cabinet, The Civil War Diaries of Salmon P. Chase.* New York: Longmans Green, and Co., 1954.

Dornblaser, T. F. *Sabre Strokes of the Pennsylvania Dragoons, in the War of 1861-1865.* Philadelphia: Lutheran Publication Society, 1884. (7th Pennsylvania Cavalry).

Dougles, James Postell. *Douglas's Texas Battery, CSA.* Edited by Lucia Rutherford Douglas. Tyler, TX: Smith County Historical Society, 1966.

Doyle, Julie, John David Smith, and Richard M. McMurray, eds. *The Wilderness of War: The Civil War Letters of George W. Squier, Hoosier Volunteer.* Knoxville, TN: University of Tennessee Press. 1998. (44th Indiana Infantry).

Drake, Julia A. ed. *The Mail Goes Through, or the Civil War Letters of George Drake (1846-1918): Over Eighty Letters Written from August 9, 1862 to May 29, 1865 by 85th Illinois Vol.* San Angelo, TX: Anchor Publishing, 1964.

Drake, Edwin L. Ed. T*he Annals of the Army of Tennessee and Early Western History, Including A Chronological Summary of Battles and Engagements in the Western Armies of the Confederacy.* Jackson, TN: Guild Bindery Press. reprint of 1878 edition.

Duke, Basil W. *A History of Morgan's Cavalry.* West Jefferson, OH: Genesis Publishing, 1997. Reprint of 1867 edition.

Duncan, Thomas D. *Recollections of Thomas D. Duncan. Confederate Soldier.* Nashville: McQuiddy Printing Company, 1922. (Forrest's Escort).

Dyer, John Will, *Reminiscences; or Four Years in the Confederate Army. A History of the Experiences of the Private Soldier in Camp, Hospital, Prison, on the March, and on the Battlefield.* Evansville, IN: Keller Printing and Publishing Co., 1898. (1st Kentucky Cavalry, CS).

Early, Jacob F. *Letters Home, The personal side of the American Civil War.* Edited by Robert A. and Gloria S. Driver. Roseberg, OR: 1992. (99th Ohio Infantry).

Eby, Henry H. *Observations of an Illinois Boy in Battle, Camp, and Prisons–1861 to 1865.* Mendota, IL: Published by the author, 1910. (Palmer's Escort).

Emanuel, S. *A Historical Sketch of the Georgetown Rifle Guards and of Co. A of the 10th Regiment, So. Ca. Volunteers, in the Army of the Confederate States.* n.p., n.d.

Emerson, Samuel Henry. *History of the War of the Confederacy, 61 to 65.* Malvern, AR: n.p., 1918. (3rd Arkansas Infantry).

Evans, Paul L. *96th Volunteer Infantry: Jo Daviess and Lake Counties.* Baton Rouge: Land and Land, Printers, 1999. (96th Illinois Infantry).

Everson, Guy R, and Edward H. Simpson, Jr. *"Far, Far from Home" The Wartime Letters of Dick and Tally Simpson Third South Carolina Volunteers.* New York and Oxford: Oxford University Press, 1994.

Faust, Eric R., ed. *Conspicuous Gallantry: The Civil War and Reconstruction Letters of James W. King, 11th Michigan Volunteer Infantry.* Kent, OH: Kent State University Press, 2015.

Figg, Royall. Memoir of Royall W. Figg, in *Where Men Only Dare to Go! Or The Story of a Boy Company.* Richmond: Whitter & Shepperson, 1885. (Jordan VA Artillery).

Fisher, Horace Cecil. A Staff Officer's Story: The Personal Experiences of Colonel Horace Newton Fisher In The Civil War. Boston: 1960. (Rosecrans's Staff).

Fisher, John E. *They Rode with Forrest and Wheeler: A Chronicle of Five Tennessee Brothers' Service in the Confederate Western Cavalry.* Jefferson, NC: McFarland and Co., 1995. (4th and 11th Tennessee Cavalry).

Fitch, John. Chickamauga, *The Price of Chattanooga.* Philadelphia: J. B. Lippincott, 1864.

Fitch, Michael H. *Echoes of the Civil War as I Hear Them.* New York: R. F. Fenno and Company. 1905. (21st Wisconsin Infantry).

Fitch, Michael H. *The Chattanooga Campaign, With especial reference to Wisconsin's participation therein.* Madison, WI: Democrat Printing Co. 1911.

Fleming, James R. *Band of Brothers: Company C, 9th Tennessee Infantry.* Shippensburg, PA: White Mane Publishing, 1996.

Floyd, David Bittle. *History of the Seventy-Fifth Regiment of Indiana Infantry Volunteers, its Organization, Campaigns, and Battles (1862-1865).* Philadelphia: Lutheran Publication Society, 1893.

Fontaine, Lamar. *My Life and My Lectures.* New York: Neale Publishing Company, 1908. (Kershaw's Brigade).

Foote, Henry S. *Recollections of the Chickamauga Campaign.* n.p., n.d. (Buckner's Staff).

Foraker, Joseph Benson. *Notes of A Busy Life*. Cincinnati: Stewart & Kidd Company, 1916. (89th Ohio Infantry).

Ford, Thomas J. *With the Rank and File. Incidents and Anecdotes of the War of the Rebellion, as Remembered by One of the Non-Commissioned Officers*. Milwaukee: Press of the Evening Wisconsin Co., 1898. (24th Wisconsin Infantry).

Fowler, John D. *Mountaineers in Gray: The Nineteenth Tennessee Volunteer Infantry Regiment, C.S.A.* Knoxville: University of Tennessee Press, 2004.

Fradenburgh, J. N. *In Memoriam: Henry Harrison Cummings and Charlotte J. Cummings*. Oil City, PA: The Derrick Publishing Company, 1913. (105th Ohio Infantry).

Frano, Elizabeth C., ed. *Letters of Captain Hugh Black to his Family in Florida During the War Between the States, 1862-1864*. Evansville, IN: Evansville Bindery, 1998. (6th Florida Infantry).

Fugitt, Greg. *Fantastic Shadows Upon the Ground: The Thirty-Fifth Ohio Volunteer Infantry in the Civil War*. Milford, OH: Little Miami Publishing Co. 2011.

Funk, Arville L. *A Hoosier Regiment in Dixie: A History of the Thirty-Eighth Indiana Volunteer Infantry Regiment*. Chicago: Adams Press, 1978.

Gardner, William. *Some Footprints of the Army of the Cumberland, From The Private's Standpoint*. Washington, IL: Press of the Herald, 1883. (51st Illinois Infantry).

Gammage, W. L. *The Camp, The Bivouac, and The Battlefield, being a history of the Fourth Arkansas Regiment from its first organization down to the present date; its campaigns and its battles, with an occasional reference to the current events of the times, including biographical sketches of its field officers and others of the "old brigade."* Little Rock, AR: Southern Press, 1958. Reprint of 1864 Edition.

Gancas, Ron, and Dan Coyle, Sr. *Dear Teres: The Civil War Letters of Andrew Joseph Duff and Dennis Dugan of Company F, The Pennsylvania Seventy-Eighth Infantry*. Chicora, PA: Mechling Bookbindery, 1999.

Gancas, Ron. *The Gallant Seventy-Eighth: Stones River to Pickett's Mill*. Colonel William Sirwell and the Pennsylvania Seventy-Eighth Volunteer Infantry. Murraysville, PA: Mark V Enterprises, 1994.

Garrett, Grover S. *The Civil War Diary of Franklin G. Black*. Danville, IL: Faulstich Printing Co., 1998. (125th Illinois Infantry).

Gates, Arnold, ed. *The Rough Side of War: The Civil War Journal of Chesley A. Mosman 1st Lieutenant, Company D 59th Illinois Volunteer Infantry Regiment*. Garden City, NJ: Basin Publishing, 1987.

Genco, James G. To *The Sound of Musketry and the Tap of the Drum: A History of Michigan's Battery D Through the Letters of Artificer Harold J. Bartlett 1861-1865*. Detroit: Detroit Book Press, 1990.

Genco, James G. *Into the Tornado of War: A History of the Twenty-First Michigan Infantry in the Civil War*. Bloomington, IN: Abbott Press, 2012.

Gibson, J. T. *History of the Seventy-Eighth Pennsylvania Volunteer Infantry*. Pittsburgh: Pittsburgh Printing Company, 1905.

Gillum, Jamie. *The History of the Sixteenth Tennessee Volunteer Infantry Regiment, Volume II: No Hope of Getting Out Alive. Perryville, Murfreesboro, Chickamauga and Chattanooga. September 1862-December 1863*. Spring Hill, TN: James F. Gillum, 2012.

Girardi Robert I., and Nathaniel Cheairs Hughes, Jr., eds. *The Memoirs of Brigadier General William Passmore Carlin, U.S.A.* Lincoln, NE: University of Nebraska Press, 1999.

Gleeson, Ed. *Rebel Sons of Erin: A Civil War Unit History of the Tenth Tennessee Infantry Regiment (Irish) Confederate States Volunteers*. Indianapolis: Guild Press of Indiana, 1993.

Grebner, Constantine. *Translated and edited by Frederic Trautmann. We Were the Ninth: A History of the Ninth Regiment, Ohio Volunteer Infantry April 17, 1861 to June 7, 1864*. Kent, OH: Kent State University Press, 1987. reprint of 1897 German edition.

Green, Arthur E. *Southerners at War. The 38th Alabama Infantry Volunteers*. Shippensburg, PA: Burd Street Press, 1999.

Green, C. R. *Volunteer Service in the Army of the Cumberland*. Olathe, KS: 1913-14. (101st Ohio Infantry).

Gremillion, Nelson. *Company G, 1st Regiment Louisiana Cavalry, CSA: A Narrative*. Lafayette, LA: University of Southwestern Louisiana, 1986.

Grose, William. *The Story of the Marches, Battles, and Incidents of the 36th Regiment Indiana Volunteer Infantry.* New Castle, IN: The Courier Company Press, 1891.

Guild, George B. *A Brief Narrative of the Fourth Tennessee Cavalry Regiment.* Franklin, TN: Cool Springs Press, 1996. reprint of 1913 edition.

Hale, Douglas *The Third Texas Cavalry in the Civil War.* Norman, OK: University of Oklahoma Press, 1993.

Hall, J.N. *Prison Life: A Story of Capture, Imprisonment and Suffering in Rebel Prisons of the South.* Columbus, OH: Charles M. Cott, 1884. (113th Ohio Infantry).

Hallock, Judith Lee, ed. T*he Civil War Letters of Joshua K. Calloway.* Athens, GA: University of Georgia Press, 1997. (28th Alabama Infantry).

Hamer, John E. *The Saga of the three Lowry brothers of Three Creeks, Arkansas, Robert James, John Furniss, and Samuel Maxwell, and of Company G, Third Arkansas Infantry Regiment, Confederate States Army.* Alexandria, VA: 1965.

Hamilton, D. H. *History of Company M, First Texas Volunteer Infantry.* Waco, TX: W. M. Morrison, 1962.

Hampton, Noah J. *An Eyewitness to the Dark Days of 1861-1865, or a Private Soldier's Adventures and Hardships During the War.* Nashville: Privately printed, 1898. (18th Tennessee Infantry).

Hanks, O.T. *History of Captain B.F. Benton's Company, Hood's Texas Brigade, 1861-65.* Austin: Morrison Books, 1984. (Co. K, 1st Texas Infantry).

Hannaford, Ebenezer. *The Story of a Regiment: A History of the Campaigns, and Associations in the Field, of the Sixth Regiment Ohio Volunteer Infantry.* Cincinnati: Published by the author, 1868.

Hardin, Henry O. *History of the 90th Ohio Volunteer Infantry in the War of the Great Rebellion in the United States, 1861 to 1865.* Stoutsville, OH: Press of Fairfield-Pickaway News, 1902.

Hardy, Michael C. *The Fifty-Eighth North Carolina Troops: Tar Heels in the Army of Tennessee.* Jefferson, NC: McFarland & Company, Inc., 2010.

Hay, John Milton. *Letters of John Hay and Extracts from Diary.* Washington, DC: Privately Published, 1908. (Lincoln's Secretary).

Hay, John Milton, with Michael Burlingame and John R. Turner Ettlinger, Eds. *Inside Lincoln's White House, The Complete Civil War Diary of John Hay.* Carbondale, IL: Southern Illinois University Press, 1997.

Haynie, J. Henry. *The Nineteenth Illinois: A Memoir of a Regiment of Volunteer Infantry Famous in the Civil War of Fifty Years Ago for Its Drill, Bravery, and Distinguished Services.* Chicago: M.A. Donahue, 1912.

Hazen, William B. *A Narrative of Military Service.* Boston: Ticknor and Co, 1885.

Head, Thomas A. *Campaigns and Battles of the Sixteenth Regiment, Tennessee Volunteers, in the War Between the States, with Incidental Sketches of the Part Performed by Other Tennessee Troops in the Same War, 1861-1865.* Nashville: Cumberland Presbyterian Publishing House, 1885.

Heartsill, William W. *Fourteen Hundred and Ninety-one Days in the Confederate Army.* Wilmington, NC: Broadfoot Publishing, 1992. (6th/10th/15th Texas).

Hechler, Ken. *Soldier of the Union: Private George Hechler's Civil War Service.* Charleston, WV: Pictorial Histories Publishing Co., 2011. (36th Ohio Infantry).

Hern, Thomas A. *Devon to Andersonville, Four Hern Brothers in the American Civil War, Compiled and Written on the Occasion of the War's Sesquicentennial.* Perrysburg, OH: Thomas A. Hern, 2014. (excerpts of Jesse McClave diary, 89th Ohio Infantry).

Herr, George W. *Episodes of the Civil War, Nine Campaigns in Nine States: Fremont in Missouri - Curtis in Missouri and Arkansas - Halleck's Siege of Corinth - Buell in Kentucky - Rosecrans in Kentucky and Tennessee - Grant at the Battle of Chattanooga - Sherman from Chattanooga to Atlanta - Thomas in Tennessee and North Carolina - Stanley in Texas - In Which is Comprised the History of the Fifty-Ninth Regiment Illinois Veteran Volunteer Infantry - Together With Special Mention of the Various Regiments With Which it was Brigaded from 1861 to 1865.* San Francisco: The Bancroft Company, 1890.

High, Edwin W. *History of the Sixty-Eighth Regiment Indiana Volunteer Infantry, 1862-1865, with a Sketch of E. A. King's Brigade, Reynolds' Division, Thomas' Corps, in the Battle of Chickamauga.* Matamora, IN: n.p., 1902.

Hight, John J, and Gilbert R. Stormont. *History of the Fifty-Eighth Regiment of Indiana Volunteer Infantry, Its Organization, Campaigns, and Battles from 1861 to 1865.* Princeton, IN: Press of the Clarion, 1895.

Hill, Jeffrey A. *The 26th Ohio Veteran Volunteer Infantry, The Groundhog Regiment, Second Edition.* Bloomington, IN: Authorhouse, 2010.

Hinckley, Lucius Dwight. *Fourth Annual Reunion of the Tenth Wisconsin Infantry held at Tomah Wis., July 21 and 22, 1898.* Waupun, WI: Oliver Bros., Printers, 1898.

Hinman, Wilbur F. *The Story of the Sherman Brigade. The Camp, The March, The Bivouac, The Battle, and How "The Boys" Lived and Died During Four Years of Active Service.* Alliance, OH: Press of the Daily Review, 1897. (65th Ohio).

History of the Eighty-Eighth Indiana Volunteers Infantry: Engagements, Chronology, Roster. Fort Wayne, IN: W.D. Page, Printer, 1895.

History of the Twenty-Seventh Illinois Volunteers with a Roster of Surviving Members. Winchester, IL: Standard Steam Printing House, 1892.

Historical Sketch of the Chicago Board of Trade Battery, Horse Artillery, Illinois Volunteers. Chicago: The Henneberry Co., Printers, 1902.

Hoffman, Mark. *"My Brave Mechanics": The First Michigan Engineers and Their Civil War.* Detroit: Wayne State University Press, 2007.

Holland, Katherine S., ed. *Keep All My Letters: The Civil War Letters of Richard Henry Brooks, 51st Georgia Infantry.* Macon, GA: Mercer University Press, 2003.

Holmes, Henry McCall, with Alester G. Holmes, ed. *Diary of Henry McCall Holmes, Army of Tennessee.* State College, MS: Mississippi State College, 1968. (Trigg's Brigade).

Holmes, J. T. *52nd O.V.I.: Then and Now.* Columbus, OH: The Berlin Printing Company, 1898.

Hood, John Bell. *Advance and Retreat: Personal Experiences in the United States and Confederate States Armies.* Secausus, NJ: Blue and Grey Press, 1985. Reprint of 1880 edition.

Horrall, S. F. *History of the Forty-Second Indiana Volunteer Infantry.* Chicago: Donohue and Henneberry, Printers, Engravers and Binders, 1892.

Horton, Joshua H. and Teverbaugh. *A History of the Eleventh Regiment, (Ohio Volunteer Infantry) Containing the Military Record, So Far as ts Possible to Obtain it, of Each Officer and Enlisted Man of the Command - A List of Deaths - An Account of the Veterans - Incidents of the Field and Camp - Names of the Three Months" Volunteers, Etc., Etc.* Dayton, OH: W. J. Shuey, 1866.

Houghton, William R and M. B. *Two Boys in the Civil War and After.* Montgomery, AL: Paragon Press, 1912. (15th Alabama Infantry).

Howe, Daniel Wait. *Civil War Times 1861-1865.* Indianapolis: The Bowen-Merrill Company, 1902. (79th Indiana Infantry).

Hughes, Nathaniel Cheairs, Jr., ed. *Liddell's Record: St. John Richardson Liddell.* Baton Rouge: Louisiana State University Press, 1985. (Liddell's Autobiography).

Hughes, Nathaniel Cheairs, Jr. *The Pride of the Confederate Artillery.* Baton Rouge: Louisiana State University Press, 1997. (Slocomb's Battery).

Hunter, Alfred G. *History of the Eighty-Second Indiana Volunteer Infantry, its Organization, Campaigns and Battles.* Indianapolis: Wm. B. Burford, Printer and Binder. 1893.

Hunter, Edna, and J. Shank. *One Flag, One Country, and Thirteen Greenbacks a Month: Letters from a Civil War Private and His Colonel.* San Diego, CA: Hunter Publications, 1980. (125th Illinois).

Hyde, Solon, with Neil Thompson, ed. *A Captive of War.* Shippensburg, PA: Burd Street Press, 1996. (17th Ohio Infantry.

Jacobs, Lee, Comp. *Cry Heart: Stories and Memoirs from the Confederacy.* Shippensburg, PA: Burd Street Press, 2000. (Various).

Jackson, Alto Loftin, ed. *So Mourns the Dove: Letters of a Confederate Infantryman and his Family.* New York: Exposition Press, 1965. (33rd Alabama Infantry).

Jenkins, Kirk C. *The Battle Rages Higher: The Union's Fifteenth Kentucky Infantry.* Lexington: University Press of Kentucky, 2003.

Johnson, Adam Rankin. *The Partisan Rangers of the Confederate States Army.* Austin: State House Press, 1995. Reprint of 1904 Edition. (Morgan's Cavalry).

Johnston, Adam S. *The Soldier Boy's Diary Book; or, Memorandums of the alphabetical first lessons of military tactics, kept by Adam S. Johnson, from September 14, 1861 to October 2, 1864.* Pittsburgh: n.p., 1866. (79th Pennsylvania Infantry).

Johnson, Amasa. *The Ninth Indiana Regiment at Chickamauga: An Address Given August 25th, 1887, during the Fifth Annual Reunion of the Ninth Indiana Veteran's Association.* Watseka, IN: Watseka Republican Book Print, 1888.

Johnson, I. N. *Four Months in Libby, And The Campaign Against Atlanta.* Cincinnati: Methodist Book Concern, 1893. (6th Kentucky Infantry US).

Johnson, Mark W. *That Body of Brave Men: The U.S. Regular Infantry and the Civil War in the West.* Cambridge, MA: Da Capo Press, 2003.

Johnson, Robert Underwood and Clarence Clough Buel, eds. *Battles and Leaders of the Civil War.* 4 Vols. New York: Thomas Yoseloff, Inc., 1956.

Johnson, Robert W. *A Soldier's Reminiscences in Peace and War.* Philadelphia: J.P. Lippincott Company, 1886.

Johnston, Joseph E. *Narrative of Military Operations during the Civil War.* New York: De Capo Press, 1990. Reprint of 1874 edition.

Jones, Eugene, W. *Enlisted for the War: The Struggles of the Gallant 24th Regiment, South Carolina Volunteers, Infantry, 1861-1865.* Hightstown, NJ: Longstreet House, 1997.

Jones, J. Keith., ed. *The Boys of Diamond Hill: The Lives and Civil War Letters of the Boyd Family of Abbeville County, South Carolina.* Jefferson, NC: McFarland & Company, Inc., 2011. (letters of John Calvine Alewine, 19th South Carolina Infantry).

Jordan, Thomas, and J. P. Pryor. *The Campaigns of General Nathan Bedford Forrest and of Forrest's Cavalry.* New York: De Capo Press, 1996. Reprint of 1868 edition.

Jordan, William C. *Some Events and Incidents During the Civil War.* Montgomery, AL: The Paragon Press, 1909. (15th Alabama Infantry).

Keil, Frederick W. *Thirty-Fifth Ohio: A Narrative of Service from August, 1861 to 1864.* Fort Wayne, IN: Archer, Housh and Co. 1894.

Kelly, Gene. Compiler. *Collection of Civil War Letters written by Mercer County Soldiers.* n.p. n.d. (27th Illinois Infantry).

Kelly, Weldon. *A Historic Sketch, Lest We Forget - Company "E" 26th Ohio Infantry in the War for the Union 1861-65.* Osborn, MO: n.p., 1909.

Kempfer, Lester L., comp. *The Salem Light Guard: Company G 36th Regiment, Ohio Volunteer Infantry, Marietta, Ohio, 1861-65.* Chicago: Adams Press, 1973.

Kern, Albert. *History of the First Regiment Ohio Volunteer Infantry in The Civil War 1861-1865.* Dayton, OH: n.p., 1918.

Kerwood, Asbury L. *Annals of the Fifty-Seventh Regiment Indiana Volunteers.* Dayton, OH: W. J. Shuey, Printer and Publisher, 1868.

Kiene, Ralph E., Jr., ed. *The Journal of Francis A. Kiene: A Civil War Diary.* Privately published. 1974. (49th Ohio Infantry).

Kimberly, Robert L. and Ephraim S. Holloway. *The Forty-First Ohio Veteran Volunteer Infantry in the War of the Rebellion 1861-1865.* Cleveland, OH: W.R. Smellie, 1897.

Kinnear, J.R. *History of the Eighty-Sixth Regiment Illinois Volunteer Infantry During its Term of Service.* Chicago: Tribune Company, 1866.

Kirk, Charles H. *History of the Fifteenth Pennsylvania Volunteer Cavalry which was Recruited and Known as the Anderson Cavalry in the Rebellion of 1861-1865.* Philadelphia: n.p. 1906.

Kirkpatrick, George Morgan. *The Experiences of a Private Soldier of the Civil War.* Indianapolis: Hoosier Bookshop, 1973. Reprint of 1924 edition. (42nd Indiana Infantry).

Kirkwood, Asbury L. *Annals of the Fifty-Seventh Regiment Indiana Volunteers: Marches, Battles and Incidents of Army Life.* Dayton, OH: 1868.

Laine, J. Gary; and Morris M. Penny. *Law's Alabama Brigade in the War Between the Union and the Confederacy.* Shippensburg, PA: White Mane Publishing, 1996.

Lambert, Lois, J. *Heroes of the Western Theater: 33rd Ohio Veteran Volunteer Infantry*. Milford, OH: Little Miami Publishing Co., 2008.

Landers, Eli Pinson. *Weep Not for Me, Dear Mother*. Edited by Elizabeth Whitley Robertson. Washington, NC: Vantage Press, 1991. (16th Georgia Infantry).

Landt, Sophronius Stocking. *Your Country Calls*. Edited by Margaret J. Somers. Friendship, WI: New Past Press, 2003. (10th Wisconsin Infantry).

Lane, Mills. *"Dear Mother: Don't Grieve About Me. If I Got Killed, I'll Only Be Dead."* Savannah, GA: The Beehive Press, 1977. (Benning's Brigade).

Larson, James. *Sergeant Larson, 4th Cav*. San Antonio, TX: Southern Literary Institute, 1935. (4th US Cavalry).

Larson, Richard N., Ed. *Sergeant Major Charles Perry Goodrich: Letters Home to Francis Bowen Goodrich in Cambridge, Wisconsin from her Husband, Charles Perry Goodrich, Sergeant-Major in the First Wisconsin Cavalry 1862/1865*. Oregon, WI: Published by the author, 1990.

Lasswell, Mary, ed. *Rags and Hope: The Recollections of Val. C. Giles, Four Years with Hood's Texas Brigade, Fourth Texas Infantry 1861-65*. New York: Coward-McCann Inc. 1961.

Lathrop, D. *The History of the Fifty-Ninth Regiment Illinois Volunteers*. Indianapolis: Hall and Hutchinson, 1865.

Lavender, John W. *They Never Came Back: The Story of Co. F. Fourth Arks. Infantry C.S.A (Originally Known as the Montgomery Hunters) as Told by Their Commanding Officer*. Pine Bluff, AR: The Perdue Co., 1956.

Lee, J. Edward, and Ron Chepesiuk, eds. *South Carolina in the Civil War: The Confederate Experience in Letters and Diaries*. Jefferson, NC: McFarland and Co., 2000.

Leeper, Wesley Thurman. *Rebels Valiant: Second Arkansas Mounted Rifles (dismounted.)* Little Rock, AR: Pioneer press, 1964.

Lewis, George W. *The Campaigns of the 124th Regiment Ohio Volunteer Infantry with Roster and Roll of Honor*. Akron, OH: The Werner Company, 1894.

Lewis, Richard. *Camp Life of a Confederate Boy of Bratton's Brigade, Longstreet's Corps, C.S.A*. Charleston, SC: News and Courier Book Press, 1883. (4th South Carolina Infantry).

Linville, Dale Edward. *Battles, Skirmishes, Events and Scenes: The Letters and Memorandum of Ambrose Remley*. Crawfordsville, IN: Montgomery County Historical Society, 1997. (72nd Indiana Infantry).

Little, George. *A History of Lumsden's Battery, C.S.A*. Tuscaloosa, AL: R. E. Rhodes Chapter, United Daughters of the Confederacy, 1905.

Longacre, Glenn V. and John E. Haas, eds. *To Battle for God and the Right: The Civil War Letterbooks of Emerson Opdyke*. Urbana, IL: University of Illinois Press, 2003.

Longstreet, James. *From Manassas to Appomattox, Memoirs of the Civil War in America*. Philadelphia: P. J Lippincott, 1896.

Lord, Walter. *The Fremantle Diary, Being the Journal of Lieutenant Colonel James Arthur Lyon Fremantle, Coldstream Guards, on his Three Months in the Southern States*. Boston: Little, Brown and Company, 1954.

Lyon, William Penn. *Reminiscences of the Civil War*. San Jose, CA: Press of Muirson and Wright, 1907. (13th Wisconsin Infantry).

Magee, Benjamin F. *History of the 72nd Indiana Volunteer Infantry of the Mounted Lightning Brigade*. Lafayette, IN: S. Vater and Co. 1882.

Manigault, Arthur Middleton, with R. Tower Lockwood, ed. *A Carolinian Goes to War: The Civil War Narrative of Arthur Middleton Manigault*. Charleston, SC: University of South Carolina Press, 1983.

Mann, Richard F. *The Buckeye Vanguard: The Forty-Ninth Ohio Veteran Volunteer Infantry*. Milford, OH: Little Miami Publishing, 2010.

Marcoot, Maurice. *Five Years in the Sunny South, Reminiscences of Maurice Marcoot*. n.p., n.d. (15th Missouri Infantry).

Martin, John A. *Addresses: By John A. Martin delivered in Kansas*. Topeka, KS: Kansas Publishing House, 1888. (8th Kansas Infantry).

Mason, Thomas R. Letter. *Records of Middle Tennessee: Civil War Records, Volume 3*. Nashville: Historical Records Survey, 1939. (Morgan's Cavalry).

Mauk, Gilbert B. A *Few Reminiscences of a Civil War Veteran*. Fort Dodge, KS: December 25, 1921. (123rd Illinois Infantry).

Mauzy, James H. *Historical Sketch of the Sixty-Eighth Regiment Indiana Volunteers*. Rushville, IN: The Republican Company Printers, 1887.

McAdams, Francis M. *Our Knapsack. Sketches for the Boys in Blue*. Columbus, OH: Charles M. Cott & Co., 1884. (113th Ohio Infantry).

McAdams, Francis M. *Everyday Soldier Life, or a History of the One Hundred and Thirteenth Ohio Volunteer Infantry*. Columbus, OH: Charles M. Cott & Co., 1884.

McBride, James *A History and Biographical Cyclopaedia of Butler County Ohio*. Cincinnati: Western Biographical Publishing Company, 1882. (Letter of Surgeon Abraham H. Landis, 35th Ohio Infantry).

McCaffery, James M. *This Band of Heroes: Granbury's Texas Brigade, C.S.A.* College Station, TX: Texas A & M University Press, 1996.

McCain, Thomas Hart Benton, with Richard K. and Geraldine Rue, eds. *In Song And Sorrow: The Daily Journals of Thomas Hart Benton McCain, 86th Indiana Volunteer Infantry*. Carmel, IN: Guild Press of Indiana, 1998.

McCammon, Charles S., ed. *Loyal Mountain Troopers: The Second and Third Tennessee Volunteer Cavalry in the Civil War, Reminiscences of Lieutenant John W. and Major Will A. McTeer*. Maryville, TN: Blount County Genealogical and Historical Society, 1992.

McClendon, W. A. *Recollections of War Times*. Montgomery, AL: Paragon Press, 1909. (15th Alabama Infantry).

McClure, Judith Watson, ed. *Confederate from East Texas: The Civil War Letters of James Monroe Watson*. Quanah, TX: Nortex Press, 1976. (10th Texas Dismounted Cavalry).

McCray, Kevin B. *A Shouting of Orders: A History of the 99th Ohio Volunteer Infantry Regiment*. Xlibris, 2003.

McDonald, Andrew. *Daily Diary of Andrew McDonald During Civil War Years*. Edited by Niels T. Anderson. Cedar Springs, MI: Cedar Springs Rotary Club, 1987. (21st Michigan Infantry).

McFarland, Bill. *Keep The Flag to the Front: The Story of the Eighth Kansas Volunteer Infantry*. Overland Park, KS: Leathers Publishing, 2008.

McKee, Sarah Gouge, and John Silver Harris, eds. *The Civil War Letters of the Gouge Family of Mitchell County, N.C.* Kingsport, TN: S. G. McKee, 2000. (58th North Carolina Infantry).

McLaughlin, Josie Armstrong, ed. *Cherished Letters of Thomas Wayman Hendricks*. Birmingham, AL: Birmingham Publishing Co., 1947. (1st Alabama Cavalry).

McManus, Christopher, Thomas H. Inglis, Otho James Hicks, eds. *Morning to Midnight in the Saddle: Civil War Letters of a Soldier in Wilder's Lightning Brigade*. XLibris Corp., 2012. (Letters of Otho James McManus, 123rd Illinois Mounted Infantry).

McMurray, W. J. *History of the Twentieth Tennessee Regiment Volunteer Infantry, C.S.A.* Nashville: The Publication Committee, 1904.

McNeil, Samuel A. *Personal Recollections of Service in the Army of the Cumberland and Sherman's Army from August 17, 1861 to July 20, 1865*. Richwood, OH: n.p., 1910. (31st Ohio Infantry).

McPherson, Lucy Harmon. *Life and Letters of Oscar Fitzalan Harmon*. Trenton, NJ: MacCrellish & Quigley Co., Printers, 1914. (125th Illinois Infantry).

Memorial of Lieutenant Howard M. Burnham, United States Army, Who Fell in the Battle of Chickamauga, Tenn., September 19th, 1863. Springfield, MA: Samuel Bowles and Company, Printers. 1864. (H, 5th US Artillery).

Miller, Gerald J. *Middletown Yank's "Journey to War and Back."* Champaign, IL: n.p., 1985. (Diary of James G. Watson, 25th Illinois Infantry).

Miller, J. B. *The Watauga Boys in the Great Civil War*. Boone, NC: Watauga County Library, 1984. Reprint of 1900 edition. (58th North Carolina Infantry).

Miller, Rex. *Wheeler's Favorites, 51st Alabama Cavalry*. Austin, TX: Patrix Press, 1994, reprint of 1991 edition.

Mills, Anson. *My Story*. Edited by C. H. Claudy. Washington, DC: Press of Byron S. Adams, 1918. (18th U.S. Infantry).

Mims, Wilbur F. *War History of the Prattville Dragoons*. Autauga County, AL: n.d. (3rd Alabama Cavalry).

Minty, R.H.G. *Remarks of Brevet Major General R.H.G. Minty made September 18th, 1895 at the Dedication of the Monument Erected to the Fourth Michigan Cavalry at Reed's Bridge, Chickamauga National Park.* Ogden, UT: n.p., 1896.

Montgomery, George F. Jr. ed. *Georgia Sharpshooter: The Civil War Diary and Letters of William Rhadamanthus Montgomery, 1839-1906.* Macon, GA: Mercer University Press, 1997. (Kershaw's brigade and 3rd Georgia Battalion Sharpshooters).

Moor, Martin. *Diary of Martin Moor, Co. H, 37th Indiana Volunteers 1861-1864.* n.p. n.d.

Moore, Robert A. *A Life for the Confederacy.* Jackson, TN: McCowat-Mercer Press, 1959 (17th Mississippi Infantry).

Morales, Colonel William R. *The 41st Alabama Infantry Regiment Confederate States of America: A Narrative History of a Civil War Regiment from West Central Alabama.* Wyandotte, OK: The Gregath Publishing Co., 2001.

More, Betty E. *SOLDIER BOY: Letters and history of an Illinois Union soldier who left his family and farm and fought in Sherman's destructive army from Tennessee through Atlanta to the Carolinas.* Heritage Books, 2000. (92nd Illinois Mounted Infantry).

Morgan, O. H. and E. R. Murphy. *History of the 7th Independent Battery Indiana Light Artillery.* Bedford, IN: 1895.

Morgan, Vinton Lee and Peggy Dugger Morgan. *Darke County Recruit.* Lewisburg, TN: Published by the Authors, 1996. (40th Ohio Infantry).

Moriarty, Donald Peter II. *A Fine Body of Men, the Orleans Light Horse Louisiana Cavalry, 1861-1865.* New Orleans: The Historic New Orleans Collection, 2014.

Morris, George W. *History of the Eighty-First Regiment of Indiana Volunteer Infantry in the Great War of the Rebellion 1861 to 1865.* Louisville: Franklin Printing House. 1901.

Morrow, John Anderson. *The Confederate Whitworth Sharpshooters.* Published by the author, 1989.

Morse, Loren J., ed. *Civil War Diaries of Bliss Morse.* Pittsburg, KS: Pittcraft, Inc. 1964. (105th Ohio Infantry).

Morton, John Watson. *The Artillery if Nathan Bedford Forrest's Cavalry.* Marietta, GA: R. Bemis Publishing, 1995. Reprint of 1909 edition.

Moseley, Ronald H. ed. *The Stilwell Letters: A Georgian In Longstreet's Corps' Army of Northern Virginia.* Macon, GA: Mercer University Press, 2002. (53rd Georgia Infantry).

Mosgrove, George Dallas. *Kentucky Cavaliers in Dixie.* edited by Bell Irvin Wiley. Jackson, TN: McCowat-Mercer Press. 1957. (4th Kentucky Cavalry CS).

Munhall, L. W. *The Chattanooga Campaign.* n.p. n.d. (79th Indiana).

Munhall, L. W. *Leander Whitcomb Munhall's Letters Home 1862-1865.* Edited by George A. Smyth, III. n. p., 1992.

Myres, Sandra L., ed. *Force Without Fanfare: The Autobiography of K. M. Van Zandt.* Fort Worth: Texas Christian University Press, 1968. (7th Texas Infantry).

Niver, Edwin W. *Reminiscences of the Civil War and Andersonville Prison.* n.p., n.d. (3rd Ohio Cavalry).

Newlin, William H. *A History of the Seventy-Third Regiment of Illinois Infantry Volunteers.* Springfield, IL: The Regimental Association, 1890.

Noe, Kenneth W. ed. *A Southern Boy in Blue: The Memoir of Marcus Woodcock, 9th Kentucky Infantry, U.S.A.* Knoxville: University of Tennessee Press, 1996.

Noll, Arthur Howard, ed. *Doctor Quintard, Chaplain C.S.A. And Second Bishop of Tennessee: Being His Story of the War.* Harrisonburg, VA: Sprinkle Publications, 1999.

Oates, William C. *The War between the Union and the Confederacy and its Lost Opportunities with a History of the 15th Alabama Regiment and the Forty-eight Battles in which it was Engaged.* New York: Neale Publishing Company, 1905.

Obreiter, John. *The Seventy-Seventh Pennsylvania at Shiloh. History of the Regiment.* Harrisburg, PA: Harrisburg Publishing Company, 1905. (Includes Chickamauga).

Oeffinger, John C., ed. *A Soldier's General: The Civil War Letters of Major General Lafayette McLaws.* Chapel Hill, NC: University of North Carolina Press, 2002.

Oliphant, William J. *Only A Private: A Texan Remembers the Civil War*. Edited by James M. McCaffrey. Houston: Halcyon Press, 2004. (6th Texas Infantry).

Olson, Morgan. *Rollin Olson: 15th Regiment Wisconsin Volunteer Infantry, Civil War Letters*. Minneapolis: n.p., 1981.

Otto, John. *History of the 11th Indiana Battery*. n.p. 1894.

Otto, John Henry. *Memoirs of a Dutch Mudsill. Edited by David Gould and James B. Kennedy*. Kent, OH: Kent State University Press, 2004. (21st Wisconsin Infantry).

Overmeyer, Jack L. *A Stupendous Effort: The 87th Indiana in the War of the Rebellion*. Bloomington, IN: Indiana University Press, 1997.

Owen, William Miller. *In Camp and Battle with the Washington Artillery of New Orleans*. Gretna, LA: Pelican Publishing Co., 1998. Reprint of 1885 edition.

Owen, Urban Grammer. *Letters to Laura: A Confederate Surgeon's Impressions of Four Years of War*. Edited by Sadye Tune Wilson, Nancy Tune Fitzgerald, and Richard Warwick. Nashville: Tunstede Press, 1996.

Palmer, Beverly Wilson and Holly Byers Ochoa, eds. *The Selected Papers of Thaddeus Stevens*. 2 vols. Pittsburgh: University of Pittsburgh Press, 1997.

Palmer, John M. *Personal Recollections of John M. Palmer: The Story of an Earnest Life*. Cincinnati: The Robert Clarke Co., 1901.

Palmer, William J., with Isaac H. Clothier, Compiler. *Letters, 1853-1868, Gen'l Wm. J. Palmer*. Philadelphia: Ketterlinus, 1906.

Parker, George W. *History of the Seventy-Ninth Regiment Indiana Volunteers Infantry in the Civil War of Eighteen Sixty-One in the United States*. Indianapolis: The Hollenbeck Press, 1899.

Partridge, Charles. *History of the Ninety-Sixth Regiment Illinois Volunteer Infantry*. Chicago: Brown, Pettibone and Company, 1887.

Patrick Jeffrey L., and Robert J. Willey, eds. *Fighting for Liberty and Right: The Civil War Diary of William Bluffton Miller, 1st Sergeant, Company K, 75th Indiana Volunteer Infantry*. Knoxville: University of Tennessee Press, 2005.

Patterson, William Elwood, with Lowell Wayne Patterson, ed. *Jasper County Yankee: Campaigns of the 38th Regiment, Illinois Volunteer Infantry, Company K, 1861-1863*. Bowie, MD: Heritage Books, 2011.

Patton, Joseph T. *Personal Recollections of Four Years in Dixie*. Detroit: Winn and Hammond, 1892. (93rd Ohio Infantry).

Peddycord, William F. *History of the Seventy-Fourth Regiment Indiana Volunteer Infantry. A Three Years' Organization*. Warsaw, IN: Smith Printery, 1913.

Pendergast, T.H. *Pen Pictures from the Second Minnesota: "Personal Recollections by a Private Soldier" and "Marching Thro' Georgia"*. Roseville MN, Park Genealogical Books, 1998.

Perry, Henry Fales. *History of the Thirty-Eighth Regiment Indiana Volunteer Infantry: One of the Three Hundred Fighting Regiments of the Union Army*. Palo Alto, CA: F. A. Stuart, the Printer, 1906.

Phillips, Alfred R. *Fighting with Turchin*. Privately printed, 1924. (36th Ohio Infantry).

Pike, James. *The Scout and Ranger: Being the Personal Adventures of Corporal James Pike of the Fourth Ohio Cavalry*. Cincinnati and New York: J.R. Hawley and Co., 1865.

Polk, J. M. *The North and South American Review*. Austin, TX: Press of Von Boeckmann-Jones Co., 1914 (4th Texas Infantry).

Polley, J. B. *Hood's Texas Brigade: Its Marches, Its Battles Its Achievements*. Dayton, OH: Press of the Morningside Bookshop, 1988. Reprint of 1910 edition.

Polley, J. B. *A Soldier's Letters to Charming Nellie*. New York: Neale Publishing Company, 1908. (Hood's Texas Brigade).

Poole, John Randolph. *Cracker Cavaliers: The 2nd Georgia Cavalry under Wheeler and Forrest*. Macon, GA: Mercer University Press, 2000.

Prickitt, Daniel J., *Daniel J. Prickitt, Sergeant, Company H, Third Ohio Volunteer Cavalry*. Edited by Col. E. D. Stoltz. Archbold, OH: E. D. Stoltz, 1988.

Priest, John Michael. *Stephen Elliott Welch of the Hampton Legion*. Shippensburg, PA: Burd Street Press, 1994.

Puntenney, George H. *History of the Thirty-Seventh Regiment of Indiana Infantry Volunteers: Its Organization, Campaigns, and Battles-Sept., '61-Oct., '64.* Rushville, IN: Jacksonian Book and Job Department, 1896.

Putney William G. *Behind the Guns: The History of Battery I 2nd Regiment, Illinois Light Artillery.* Edited by Thaddeus C. S. Brown and Samuel J. Murphy. Carbondale, IL: Southern Illinois University Press, 1969.

Quinlin, Bradley, and Joshua Haugh. *Duty Well Performed, the Twenty-First Ohio Volunteer Infantry in the Civil War.* Milford, OH: Little Miami Publishing Co., 2001.

Quinlin, Brad. *"Good Night from Your Soldier Son" Letters from Tullahoma, Chickamauga, and Chattanooga.* n.p., n.d. (Various).

Ramsey, J. G. M. *Dr. J.G.M. Ramsey, Autobiography and Letters.* Edited by William B. Hasseltine. Knoxville: University of Tennessee Press, 2002. Reprint of 1954 edition. (Confederate Civilian).

Ratchford, James Wylie. *Some Reminiscences of Persons and Incidents of the Civil War.* Richmond, VA: Whittet & Shepperson, 1909. (staff of D. H. Hill).

Ratchford, James Wylie. *Memoirs of a Confederate Staff Officer from Bethel to Bentonville.* Edited by Evelyn Sieburg and James E. Hansen II. Shippensburg, PA: White Mane Publishing, 1998. (staff of D. H. Hill).

Raymond, Steve. *In the Very Thickest of the Fight: The Civil War Service of the 78th Illinois Volunteer Infantry Regiment.* Guilford, CT: Globe Pequot Press, 2012.

Regimental Committee. *Record of the Ninety-fourth Regiment, Ohio Volunteer Infantry, in the War of the Rebellion.* Cincinnati: Ohio Valley Press., n.d.

Reid, Richard J. *Fourth Indiana Cavalry Regiment: A History.* Fordsville, KY: Sandefur Offset Printing, 1994.

Reinhart, Joseph R. *A History of the 6th Kentucky Volunteer Infantry U.S.* Louisville: Beargrass Press, 2000.

Rennolds, Edwin H. *A History of the Henry County Commands Which Served in the Confederate States Army.* Jacksonville, FL: Sun Publishing Company, 1904. (5th Tennessee Infantry).

Rerick, John H. *The Forty-Fourth Indiana Volunteer Infantry: History of its Services in the War of the Rebellion and a Personal Record of its Members.* Lagrange, IN: Published by the Author, 1880.

Richards, Henry. *Letters of Captain Henry Richards of the Ninety-Third Ohio Infantry.* Cincinnati: Wrightson and Co., 1883.

Ridley, Bromfield L. *Battles and Sketches of the Army of Tennessee.* Mexico, MO: Missouri Printing and Publishing Co, 1906. (A.P. Stewart's Staff).

Robbins, Edward M. *Civil War Experiences, 1862-1865.* Carthage, IL: n.p., 1919 (78th Illinois Infantry).

Rogers, Robert M. *The 125th Regiment Illinois Volunteer Infantry. Attention, Battalion!* Champaign, IL: Gazette Steam Print, 1881.

Rowell, John W. *Yankee Cavalrymen: Through the Civil War with the Ninth Pennsylvania Cavalry.* Knoxville: University of Tennessee Press, 1971.

Rowell, John W. *Yankee Artillerymen: Through the Civil War with Eli Lilly's Indiana Battery.* Knoxville: University of Tennessee Press, 1975.

Royce, Isaac Henry Clay. *History of the 115th Regiment Illinois Volunteer Infantry.* Terre Haute, IN: Published by the author, 1900.

Ruddick, Roger D. *From the Hayfields to the Battlefields.* n.p., 1986. (Letter from A. W. Brown, 82nd Indiana).

Rude, Beverly A., ed. *Tas: The Civil War Experiences of Captain Tacitus T. Clay.* St. Paul, MN: Edit Write, Inc., 1992. (5th Texas Infantry).

Rugley, H.J.H. *Batchelor-Turner Letters 1861-64: Written by Two of Terry's Texas Rangers.* Austin, TX: Steck Co. 1961. (8th Texas Cavalry).

Salling, Stuart. *Louisianans in the Western Confederacy: The Adams-Gibson Brigade in the Civil War.* Jefferson, NC, McFarland Publishing Co., 2010.

Satterlee, John L. *The Journal and the 114th, 1861-1865.* Springfield, IL: Phillips Brothers, 1979. (Letters to the Illinois State Journal from men in the XIV and XX Corps).

Savage, John H. *The Life of John H. Savage.* Nashville: n.p., 1903. (16th Tennessee Infantry).

Schwartz, Ezekiel Koehler. *Civil War Diary of Ezekiel Koehler Schwartz, March 1863 To June 1865 and History of the E. K. Schwartz Family.* Shelbyville, IL: Shelby County Historical & Geneological Society, 1989. (115th Illinois Infantry).

Scribner, Benjamin F. *How Soldiers Were Made; Or The War as I Saw It under Buell, Rosecrans, Thomas, Grant, and Sherman.* Huntington, WV: Blue Acorn Press, 1995. Reprint of 1887 edition.

Schein, Connie, ed. *Diary of Nicholas Hiegel.* n.p. 2001. (27th Illinois Infantry).

Shanks, William F. G. *Personal Recollections of Distinguished Generals.* Huntington, NY: Harper and Brothers, Publishers, 1866.

Shaver, Lewellyn A. *A History of the Sixtieth Alabama Regiment, Gracie's Alabama Brigade.* Montgomery, AL: Barrett and Brown, 1867.

Shaw, James Birney. *History of the Tenth Indiana Volunteer Infantry, Three Months and Three Years Organizations.* Lafayette, IN: Burt-Haywood Co., 1912.

Sheppard, Jonathan C. *By the Noble Daring of her Sons: The Florida Brigade of the Army of Tennessee.* Tuscaloosa, AL: University of Alabama Press, 2012.

Sheridan, Philip H. *Personal Memoirs of P. H. Sheridan.* 2 vols. Wilmington, NC: Broadfoot Publishing Company, 1992. Reprint of 1888 edition.

Shook, Hezekiah. *Address delivered on the occasion of the 2nd annual reunion of the 37th Indiana Vols. Infty. at Greensburg, Ind., Sept. 19, 1878.* Indianapolis: Central Print. Co., 1879.

Simmerling, Jack, and Wayne Wolf, eds. *Capture at Missionary Ridge.* New York: McGraw-Hill, 1996. (Letters of Simon Wilkerson, 18th Alabama Infantry).

Simmons, Louis A. *The History of the 84th Reg't Ill. Vols.* Macomb, IL: Hampton Brothers Publishers. 1866.

Simpson, Harold B., Editor. *The Bugle Softly Blows: The Confederate Diary of Benjamin M. Seaton.* Waco, TX: Texian Press, 1965 (6th/10th/15th Texas Infantry).

Simpson, Col. Harold B. *Hood's Texas Brigade: A Compendium.* Hillsboro, TX: Hill Junior College Press, 1977.

Simpson, Col. Harold B. *Hood's Texas Brigade: Lee's Grenadier Guard.* Hillsboro, TX: Landmark Publishing, 1999. Reprint of 1970 edition.

Sipes, William B. *The Saber Regiment, History of the 7th Pennsylvania Veteran Volunteer Cavalry, 1861-1865.* Huntington, WV: Blue Acorn Press, 2000. Reprint of 1906 edition.

Skoch, George F. and Mark W. Perkins, eds. *Lone Star Confederate: A Gallant and Good Soldier of the Fifth Texas Infantry.* College Station, TX: Texas A & M University Press, 2003.

Smith, Benjamin T., with Clyde Walton, ed. *Private Smith's Journal, Recollections of the Late War.* Chicago: R. R. Donnelly, 1963. (51st Illinois Infantry).

Smith, Rev. E. A. *Records of Walthall's Brigade of Mississippians.* Brewton, AL: n.p. 1904.

Smith, Harry Virgil, ed. *The Life and Letters of PVT. Samuel Thomas Smith, Fifteenth Indiana Regiment Volunteers Civil War.* Bloomington, IN: Monroe County Historical Society, 1976.

Smith, Louis R. and Andrew Quist, eds. *Cush: A Civil War Memoir by Samuel H. Sprott.* Livingston, AL: Livingston Press, 1999. (40th Alabama Infantry).

Smith, John C. *Oration at the Unveiling of the Monument Erected to the Memory of Maj. Gen. James B. Steedman.* Chicago: Knight & Leonard Co. 1887.

Smith, John C. *The Right of the Federal Army at Chickamauga.* Chicago: Knight & Leonard Co. 1894.

Smith, John Thomas. *A History of the Thirty-First Regiment of Indiana Volunteer Infantry in the War of the Rebellion.* Cincinnati: n.p., 1900.

Snetsinger, Robert J. Ed. *Kiss Clara for Me: The Story of Joseph Whitney and his Family, Early Days in the Midwest, and soldiering in the American Civil War. A collection of Letters.* State College, PA: Carnation Press, 1969. (96th Illinois Infantry).

Society of the Seventy-Fourth Illinois Volunteer Infantry. *Reunion Proceedings and History of the Regiment.* Rockford, IL: W.P. Lamb, 1902.

Society of the Army of the Cumberland, *Reunions of the Army of the Cumberland.* 42 vols. Cincinnati, OH: Robert Clarke & Co., 1868-1914.

Sorrel, G. Moxley. *At The Right Hand of Longstreet: Recollections of a Confederate Staff Officer.* Lincoln, NE: University of Nebraska Press, 1999. Reprint of 1905 edition.

Spurlin, Charles D. Ed. *The Civil War Diary of Charles A. Leuschner.* Austin, TX: Eakin Press, 1992. (6th Texas Infantry).

Stanley, David S. *Personal Memoirs of Major General D. S. Stanley, U.S.A.* Cambridge, MA: Harvard University Press, 1917.

Stephenson, Philip Daingerfield. *The Civil War Memoir of Philip Daingerfield Stephenson, D. D. Private, Company K 13th Arkansas Volunteer Infantry, Loader, Piece No. 4, 5th Company, Washington Artillery, Army of Tennessee, CSA.* Baton Rouge: Louisiana State University Press, 1995.

Stevens, C. A. *Berdan's United States Sharpshooters in the Army of the Potomac, 1861-1865.* Dayton, OH: Press of Morningside Bookshop, 1984.

Stevens, Jno. W. *Reminiscences of the Civil War.* Hillsboro, TX: Hillsboro Mirror Print, 1902. (Texas Brigade).

Stewart, Nixon B. *Dan McCook's Regiment, 52nd O.V.I. A History of the Regiment, its Campaigns and Battles.* From 1862 to 1865. Alliance, Ohio: Review Print, 1900.

Stiles, Rev. Joseph C. *Captain Thomas E. King, or, a Word to the Army tnd The Country.* Charleston, SC: The South Carolina Tract Society, 1864. (Digital version available at: http://docsouth.unc.edu/imls/stiles/stiles.html).

Stockton, William T. *The Correspondence of Will and Ju Stockton, 1845-1869.* Edited by Herman Ulmer. Jacksonville, FL: published by H. Ulmer, 1989. (1st Florida Dismounted Cavalry).

Stout, L. H. *Reminiscences of General Braxton Bragg.* Hattiesburg, MI: The Book Farm, 1942. Reprint of 1876 edition.

Strong, Benjamin T., and Charles R. Green. *3 Years, or, During the War. Sergeant Benj. T. Strong's biography, late of Oberlin, Ohio: Reminiscences of his in Co. A, 101st O.V.I. . . . prefaced by his short story of the Battle of Chicamauga.* Olathe, KS: Charles R. Green, 1913.

Stroud, David V. *Ector's Texas Brigade and the Army of Tennessee, 1862-1865.* Longview, TX: Ranger Publishing, 2004.

Summers, Alexander. *Gone to Glory at Farmington.* Mattoon, IL: Mattoon Historical Society, 1963. (123rd Illinois Mounted Infantry.)

Sunderland, Glenn W. *Wilder's Lightning Brigade - And Its Spencer Repeaters.* Washington, IL: The Book Works Press, 1984.

Sutton, Verle Procter, ed. Benjamin Benn Mabrey, Yankee Soldier. San Bernardino, CA: Crown Printers, 1978. (82nd Indiana Infantry).

Swedberg, Claire E. ed. *Three Years with the 92d Illinois: The Civil War Diary of John M. King.* Mechanicsburg, PA: Stackpole Books, 1999.

Switzer. Charles I., Ed. *Ohio Volunteer: The Childhood & Civil War Memoirs of Captain John Hartzell, OVI.* Athens, OH: Ohio University Press, 2005. (105th Ohio Infantry).

Tarbell, Eli, ELI: *War of the Rebellion, October 10, 1861 to October 20, 1864.* n.p. 1992. (Headquarters, 1st Division, XIV Corps).

Taylor, John C. *Lights and Shadows: In the Recollections of a Youthful Volunteer in the Civil War.* Ionia, MI: Ionia Sentinel-Standard n.d. (21st Michigan Infantry).

Thatcher, Marshall P. *A Hundred Battles In The West. St. Louis to Atlanta, 1861-65. The Second Michigan Cavalry with the Armies of the Mississippi, Ohio, Kentucky and Cumberland, under Generals Halleck, Sherman, Pope, Rosecrans, Thomas and others; with mention of a few of the famous regiments and brigades of the west.* Detroit: Published by the author,1884.

Thompson, Ed Porter. *History of the Orphan Brigade.* Louisville: Lewis N. Thompson, 1898.

Todd, George T. *First Texas Regiment.* Waco, TX: Texian Press,1963.

Tomlinson, Helyn W. "Dear Friends" *The Civil War Letters and Diary of Charles Edwin Cort.* n.p.1962. (92nd Illinois Infantry).

Toney, Marcus. *Privations of a Private.* Nashville: Publishing House of the M.E. Church, South, 1907. (1st Tennessee Infantry).

Tourgee, Albion W. *The Story of a Thousand: Being a History of the Service of the 105th Ohio Volunteer Infantry, in the War for the Union from August 21, 1862 to June 6, 1865.* Buffalo, NY: S. McGerald and Son, 1896.

Tremewan, Paul G. ed. *As Near Hell as I Ever Expect To Be...: The Civil War Letters Of Lieutenant John V. Patterson Of The 21st Regiment, Ohio Volunteer Infantry.* XLibris, 2011.

Turchin, John B. *Chickamauga.* Chicago: Fergus Printing Company, 1888.

Twelfth Annual Reunion of the Tenth Wisconsin Infantry. Tomah, WI: n.p.,1906.

Vale, Joseph G. *Minty and the Cavalry: A History of Cavalry Campaigns in the Western Armies.* Harrisburg, PA: Edwin K. Meyers, 1886.

Van Eldik, James. *From the Flame of Battle to the Fiery Cross: the 3rd Tennessee Infantry.* Las Cruces, NM: Yucca Tree Press, 2001.

Van Horne, Thomas B. *The Army of the Cumberland.* New York: Smithmark Publishers, 1996. Reprint of 1875 edition. (13th Ohio, XIV Corps).

Van Vleck, Carter. *Emerging Leader, The Letters of Carter Van Vleck to his wife Patty, 1862-1864.* Edited by Theresa K Lehr and Philip L. Gerber. Bloomington, IN: iUniverse, 2012. (78th Illinois Infantry).

Varnon, R. Andrew. *Grandpa and the Alabama 28th Regiment.* n.p., 1988.

Vaughan, Alfred J. *Personal Record of the Thirteenth Regiment, Tennessee Infantry, by Its Old Commander.* Parsons WV: McClain Printing Co., 1975. Reprint of 1897 edition.

Vaughan, Alfred J. *A Brief Biographical Sketch, Gen. Alfred Jefferson Vaughan and His Family, for His Children and Grandchildren.* Memphis: S. C. Toof, 1896.

Villard, Henry. *Memoirs of Henry Villard, Journalist and Financier, 1835-1900.* 2 vols. New York: Houghton Mifflin and Co. 1904.

Virdin, Donald Odell. *The Civil War Correspondence of Judge Thomas Goldsborough O'Dell.* Bowie, MD: Heritage Books, 1992. (78th Illinois Infantry).

Waddle, Angus. *Three Years with the Armies of the Ohio and the Cumberland.* Chillicothe, OH: Scioto Gazette Book and Job Office, 1889. (33rd Ohio Infantry).

Waggoner, Clark. *Honors at Chickamauga—The Claim of "Hero" at that Battle—Delayed Justice to the Memory of a Brave and Gallant Soldier.* Toledo, OH: n.p., 1883. (Union Reserve Corps Staff).

Wagner, William. *History of the 24th Illinois Volunteer Infantry Regiment.* Chicago: n.p., 1911. Reprint of 1864 edition.

Walker, C. I. *The Rolls and Historical Sketch of the 10th Regiment So. Ca. Volunteers in the Army of the Confederate States.* Charleston, SC: Walker, Evans and Cogswell, 1881.

Walker, James A., and Robert Curren. *Those Gallant Men of the Twenty-Eighth Alabama Confederate Infantry Regiment.* Heritage Books, 1997.

Walker, Robert E. *Old Sorrel: The Life of Gilbert Moore.* n.p., 1994. (101st Indiana Infantry).

Ward, Elizabeth Probasco. *Life, Speeches and Orations of Durbin Ward of Ohio.* Columbus, OH: Hann and Adair, 1888. (17th Ohio Infantry).

Watford, Christopher M. *The Civil War in North Carolina: Soldiers' and Civilians' Letters and Diaries, 1861-1865.* Jefferson, NC: McFarland & Co. 2003. (6th North Carolina Cavalry).

Watkins, Sam R. *Co. Aytch: Maury Grays, First Tennessee Regiment, or A Side Show of the Big Show.* Edited by Ruth Hill Fulton McCallister. Franklin, TN: Providence House Publishers, 2007.

Watson, Robert K. *Service on Land and Water: My Confederate War Diary.* n.p. n.d.. (7th Florida Infantry).

Weatherbee, F. W. *The 5th (1st Middle) Tennessee Cavalry.* Carrollton, MS: Pioneer Publishing, 1992. (Union).

Weaver, Bryan P. and H. Lee Fenner. *Sacrifice at Chickamauga: A History of the 89th Ohio Volunteer Infantry Regiment.* Palos Verdes Peninsula, CA: MoyWeave Books, 2003.

Weaver, Jeffrey C. *63rd Virginia Infantry.* Lynchburg, VA: H. E. Howard, 1991.

Weaver, Jeffrey C. *54th Virginia Infantry.* Lynchburg, VA: II. E. Howard, 1993.

Weaver, Jeffrey C. *The Nottoway Artillery and Barr's Battery Virginia Light Artillery.* Lynchburg, VA: H. E. Howard, 1994.

Weaver, Jeffrey C. *The Confederate Regimental History Series: The 5th and 7th Battalions North Carolina Cavalry and the 6th North Carolina Cavalry (65th North Carolina State Troops).* Lynchburg, VA: H. E. Howard, 1995.

Welles, Gideon. *Diary of Gideon Welles, Secretary of The Navy Under Lincoln And Johnson.* 3 vols. New York: Houghton Mifflin Co. 1909.

Welshimer, Philip. *A Brief Sketch of Prison Life of Captain Philip Welshimer.* n.p. 1908. (21st Illinois Infantry)

Werrell. Kenneth P. *Crook's Regulars: The 36th Ohio in the War of the Rebellion.* Christiansburg, VA: KPW, 2012.

West, John C. *A Texan in Search of a Fight, Being the Diary and Letters of a Private Soldier in Hood's Texas Brigade.* Waco, TX: Press of J.S. Hill & Co., 1901. (4th Texas Infantry).

White, William Lee and Charles Denny Runion, eds. *Great Things Are Expected of Us: The Letters of Colonel C. Irvine Walker, 10th South Carolina Infantry, C.S.A.* Knoxville: University Of Tennessee Press, 2009.

Wilkinson, Warren, and Steven E. Woodworth *A Scythe of Fire: A Civil War Story of the Eighth Georgia Infantry.* New York: William Morrow, Division of Harper Collins, 2002.

Willett, Charles E. *A Union Soldier Returns South: The Civil War Letters and Diary of Alfred E. Willett 113th Ohio Volunteer Infantry.* Johnson City, TN: Overmountain Press, 1994.

Williams, Edward P. *Extracts from Letters to A.B.T. From Edward P. Williams During His Service in the Civil War, 1862-1864.* New York: n.p., 1903. (Turchin's Staff).

Williams, Frederick D., ed. *The Wild Life of the Army: Civil War Letters of James A. Garfield.* East Lansing, MI: Michigan State University Press, 1964.

Williams, John A.B. *Memoir of John A.B. Williams, or Leaves from a Trooper's Diary.* Philadelphia: Privately published, 1869. (15th Pennsylvania Cavalry).

Wills II, Ridley. *Old Enough to Die.* Franklin, TN: Providence House Publishers, 2006. (Letters of J.L. Bostick and Bostick Family, Liddell's Staff).

Wilson, James H. *Under the Old Flag: Recollections of Military Operations in the War for the Union, the Spanish War, the Boxer Rebellion, etc.* New York: D. Appleton and Co., 1912.

Wilson, Sadye Tune, Nancy Tune Fitzgerald, and Richard Warwick, eds. *Letters to Laura: a Confederate Surgeon's impressions of four years of war.* Nashville: Tunstede Press, 1996. (Cheatham's Division).

Wilson, Suzanne Colton. *Column South with the Fifteenth Pennsylvania Cavalry from Antietam to the Capture of Jefferson Davis.* Philadelphia: J. F. Colton & Co., 1960.

Winkler, A. V. *The Confederate Capital and Hood's Texas Brigade.* Austin, TX: Eugene Von Boeckmann, 1894

Womack, J. J. *The Civil War Diary of Capt. J. J. Womack.* McMinnville, TN: Womack Printing Company, 1961. (16th Tennessee Infantry).

Wood, C. J. *Reminiscences of the War, Biography and Personal Sketches of All the Commanding Officers of the Union Army: Narrative of the Morgan Raid in Indiana and Ohio, pursuit, capture, imprisonment and escape of Morgan from the Ohio Penitentiary, his last fight and tragic death of the renowned cavalier: fall of Richmond and surrender of Gen'l Lee: flight of Jeff. Davis from the rebel capital, pursuit and final capture of the rebel chief in the jungles of a dismal swamp in southeastern Georgia: capture, court-martial, conviction and hanging of Col. Orton and Major Dunbar, two rebel spies at Franklin, Tenn. in 1863.* n.p. 1880.

Woodruff, George H. *Fifteen Years Ago: Or the Patriotism of Will County.* Joliet, IL: Joliet Republican Book and Job Steam Printing House, 1876. (100th Illinois Infantry).

Woods, Joseph T. *Steedman and his Men at Chickamauga.* Toledo, OH: The Blade Printing Co., 1876.

Worsham, William J. *Old Nineteenth Tennessee Regiment, C.S.A., June 1861–April 1865.* Oxford, MS: Guild Bindery Press. 1992 reprint of 1902 edition.

Wright, Thomas J. *History of the Eighth Regiment Kentucky Volunteer Infantry During Its Three Years Campaigns Embracing Organization, Marches, Skirmishes, and Battles of the Command, With Much of the History of the Old Reliable Third Brigade, Commanded by Hon. Stanley Matthews, and Containing Many Interesting and Amusing Incidents of Army Life.* St. Joseph, MO: St. Joseph Steam Printing Co., 1880.

Wulsin, Lucien. *The Story of the Fourth Regiment Ohio Veteran Volunteer Cavalry.* Cincinnati OH: n.p.,1912.

Wyckoff, Mac. *A History of the Third South Carolina Infantry 1861-1865.* Fredericksburg, VA: Sgt. Kirkland's Museum and Historical Society, 1994.

Wyckoff, Mac. A History of the 2nd South Carolina Infantry 1861-65. Fredericksburg, VA: Sergeant Kirklands Museum and Historical Society, 1994.

Wyeth, John A. With Sabre and Scalpel: The Autobiography of a Soldier and Surgeon. New York: Harper 1914.

Yeary, Mamie, compiler. *Reminiscences of the Boys in Gray, 1861-1865*. Dallas, TX: Smith & Lamar, 1912.

Young, L.D. *Reminiscences of a Soldier of the Orphan Brigade*. Paris, KY: n.p., 1918. (4th Kentucky Infantry CS).

Published secondary sources, reference, and overview works

Abbazia, Patrick. *The Chickamauga Campaign, December 1862–November 1863*. Bryn Mawr, PA: Combined Books, 1988.

Addison, Stephen O., *Seen The Glory: Mark Thrash buried the dead at Chickamauga, The story of the oldest person of our country 1820-1943*. Cleveland, TN: Stephen O. Addison, Publisher, 1991.

Album of Genealogy and Biography, Cook County, Illinois with Portraits. Chicago: Calumet Book & Engraving Co., 1895.

Allardice, Bruce S. *Confederate Colonels: A Biographical Register*. Colombia, MO: University of Missouri Press, 2008.

Allardice, Bruce S. and Lawrence Lee Hewitt, eds. *Kentuckians in Gray. Confederate Generals and Field Officers of the Bluegrass State*. Lexington: University Press of Kentucky, 2008.

Ambrose, Stephen E. *Halleck, Lincoln's Chief of Staff*. Baton Rouge: Louisiana State University Press, 1982. Reprint of 1961 edition.

Anders, Curt. *Henry Halleck's War: A Fresh Look at Lincoln's Controversial General-in-Chief*. Carmel, IN: Guild Press of Indiana, 1999.

Anonymous. *Synopsis of the Military Career of General Joseph Wheeler*. Birmingham, AL: Birmingham Public Library Press, 1988. Reprint of 1865 Edition.

Ashdown, Paul, and Edward Caudill. *The Myth of Nathan Bedford Forrest*. Lanham, MD: Rowman & Littlefield, 2005.

Baird, John A. Jr. *Profile of a Hero: The Story of Absalom Baird, His Family, and the American Military Tradition*. Philadelphia: Dorrence & Co. 1977.

Baldwin, James J. *The Struck Eagle: A Biography of Brigadier General Micah Jenkins, and a History of the Fifth South Carolina Volunteers and the Palmetto Sharpshooters*. Shippensburg, PA: Burd Street Press, 1996.

Ballard, Michael B. *Vicksburg: The Campaign that opened the Mississippi*. Chapel Hill: University of North Carolina Press, 2004.

Bergeron, Arthur W. Jr., *Guide to Louisiana Confederate Military Units, 1861-1865*. Baton Rouge: Louisiana State University Press, 1989.

Bigger, David Dwight, *Ohio's Silver-Tongued Orator, Life and Speeches of General William H. Gibson*. Dayton, OH: United Brethren Publishing House, 1901.

Bilby, Joseph. *Civil War Firearms*. Conshocken, PA: Combined Books, 1996.

Bonds, Russell S. *Stealing the General, the Great Locomotive Chase and the First Medal of Honor*. Yardley, PA: Westholme Publishing, 2007.

Bridges, Hal. *Lee's Maverick General, Daniel Harvey Hill*. New York: McGraw-Hill, 1961.

Bradley, Michael R. *Tullahoma: The 1863 Campaign for the Control of Middle Tennessee*. Shippensburg, PA: Burd Street Press, 2000.

Bragg, C. L. *Distinction in Every Service: Brigadier General Marcellus A. Stovall, C.S.A.* Shippensburg, PA: White Mane Books, 2002.

Brown, Russell K. *To The Manner Born: The Life of General William H. T. Walker*. Athens, GA: University of Georgia Press, 1994.

Buell, Thomas B. *Warrior Generals: Combat Leadership in the Civil War*. New York: Crown Publishers, 1997.

Burnette, Patricia B. *James F. Jacquess: Scholar, Soldier and Private Agent for President Lincoln*. Jefferson, NC: McFarland & Co., 2013. (73rd Illinois Infantry).

Busey, John W. and David G. Martin. *Regimental Strengths and Losses at Gettysburg*. Hightstown, NJ: Longstreet House, 1986.

Cabell, Sears Wilson. *"The Bulldog" Longstreet at Gettysburg and Chickamauga*. Atlanta: Ruralist Press, 1938.

Carter, Robert L. *The Battle of Chickamauga: The Fight for Snodgrass Hill and the Rock of Chickamauga. A History and Walking Tour.* Carrollton, GA: Melica Books, LLC, 2012.

Carter, Robert L. *Longstreet's Breakthrough at Chickamauga: Accidental Victory. A History and Walking Tour.* Carrollton, GA: Createspace Independent Publishing, 2014.

Chicoine, Stephen. *John Basil Turchin and the Fight to Free the Slaves.* Westport, CT: Praeger Press, 2003.

Cisco, Walter Brian. *States Rights Gist: A South Carolina General of the Civil War.* Shippensburg, PA: White Mane Publishing, 1991.

Civil War Centennial Commission. *Tennesseans in the Civil War: A Military History of Union and Confederate Units with Available Rosters of Personnel.* 2 vols. Nashville: Civil War Centennial Commission, 1964.

Clark, Walter, ed. *Histories of the Several Regiments and Battalions from North Carolina in the Great War, 1861-'65.* 5 vols. Wilmington NC: Broadfoot Publishing Co., Reprint of 1901 edition.

Clayton, W. W. *History of Davidson County, Tennessee.* Philadelphia: J. W. Lewis & Company, 1880.

Cleaves, Freeman. *Rock of Chickamauga: The Life of General George H. Thomas.* Westport CT: Greenwood Press, 1974. Reprint of 1948 edition.

Connelly, Thomas L. *Autumn of Glory: The Army of Tennessee, 1862-1865.* Baton Rouge: Louisiana State University Press, 1986. Reprint of 1971 edition.

Connelly, Thomas L., and Archer Jones. *The Politics of Command: Factions and Ideas in Confederate Strategy.* Baton Rouge: Louisiana State University Press, 1973.

Cozzens, Peter. *This Terrible Sound.* Urbana: University of Illinois Press, 1992.

Cozzens, Peter. *No Better Place to Die: The Battle of Stones River.* Urbana: University of Illinois Press, 1997.

Crawley, Laura *Civil War Medicine at Chickamauga Battlefield.* Rossville, GA: Delta Genealogical Society, 1986.

Crute, Joseph H., Jr. *Units of the Confederate States Army.* Midlothian, VA: Derwent Books, 1987.

Cummings, Charles M. *Yankee Quaker, Confederate General: The Curious Career of Bushrod Rust Johnson.* Columbus, OH: The General's Books, 1993. Reprint of 1971 edition.

Cunningham, O. Edward. *Shiloh and the Western Campaign of 1862.* Edited by Gary D. Joiner and Timothy B. Smith. New York: Savas Beatie, 2007.

Dameron, Dave. *General Henry Lewis Benning: "This Was a Man."* Athens, GA, Iberian Publishing Co., 2000.

Daniel, Larry J. *Soldiering in the Army of Tennessee.* Chapel Hill: University of North Carolina Press, 1991.

Daniel, Larry J. *Cannoneers in Gray, The Field Artillery of the Army of Tennessee, 1861-1865.* Tuscaloosa: The University of Alabama Press, 1989. Reprint of 1984 edition.

Daniel, Larry J. *Shiloh, The Battle that Changed the Civil War.* New York: Simon & Schuster, 1997.

Daniel, Larry J. *Days of Glory: The Army of the Cumberland, 1861-1865.* Baton Rouge: Louisiana State University Press, 2004.

Daniel, Larry J. *Battle of Stones River: The Forgotten Conflict between the Confederate Army of Tennessee and the Union Army of the Cumberland.* Baton Rouge: Louisiana State University Press, 2012.

Daniell, Lewis E. *Types of Successful Men of Texas.* Austin: Eugene von Boeckmann, Printer and Bookbinder, 1890.

Davis, William C. *Breckinridge: Soldier, Statesman, Symbol.* Baton Rouge: Louisiana State University Press, 1974.

Davis, William C., ed. *The Confederate General.* 6 vols. Harrisburg, PA: National Historical Society, 1991.

DiNardo, R. L. and Albert A. Nofi, *James Longstreet: The Man, The Soldier, The Controversy.* Conshohocken, PA: Combined Publishing, 1998.

Dubose, John Witherspoon. *General Joseph Wheeler and the Army of Tennessee.* New York: Neale Publishing Co. 1912.

Dyer, John P. *"Fightin' Joe" Wheeler.* University, LA: University of Louisiana Press, 1941.

Easton, Loyd D. *Hegel's First American Followers.* Athens: Ohio University Press, 1966.

Eddy, Thomas M. *The Patriotism of Illinois.* Chicago: Clarke and Co., 1865.

Eicher, David J. *The Longest Night: A Military History of the Civil War.* New York: Simon and Schuster, 2001.

Elliott, Mark. *Color-Blind Justice, Albion Tourgee and the Quest for Racial Equality from the Civil War to Plessy V. Ferguson.* Oxford: Oxford University Press, 2006.

Elliott, Sam Davis. *Soldier of Tennessee: General Alexander P. Stewart and the Civil War in the West.* Baton Rouge: Louisiana State University Press, 1999.

Elliott, Sam Davis. *Isham G. Harris of Tennessee.* Baton Rouge: Louisiana State University Press, 2010.

Ellis, B.G. *The Moving Appeal: Mr. McClanahan, Mrs. Dill, and the Civil War's Great Newspaper Run.* Macon, GA: Mercer University Press, 2003.

Evans, E. Raymond. *Chickamauga: Civil War Impact on an Area: Tsikamagi, Crawfish Springs, Snow Hill, and Chickamauga.* Chickamauga, GA: City of Chickamauga, 2002.

Fanebust, Wayne. *Major General Alexander M. McCook, USA: A Civil War Biography.* Jefferson, NC: McFarland and Co., 2013.

Fitch, John. *Annals of the Army of the Cumberland.* Mechanicsburg, PA: Stackpole Books, 2003. Reprint of 1864 edition.

Fox, William F. *Regimental Losses in the Civil War.* Dayton, OH: Morningside press, 1985. Reprint of 1898 edition.

Freeman, Douglas Southall. *Lee's Lieutenants: A Study in Command.* 3 vols. New York: Charles Scribner's Sons, 1971.

Fry, James B. *Official Register of the Officers and Cadets of the U.S. Military Academy, West Point, New York.* James F. Baldwin, Printer, 1858.

Gorin, Betty J. *"Morgan Is Coming!" Confederate Raiders in the Heartland of Kentucky.* Louisville, KY: Harmony House Publishers, 2006.

Gott, Kendall D. *Where the South Lost the War: An Analysis of the Fort Henry-Fort Donelson Campaign, February 1862.* Mechanicsburg, PA: Stackpole Books, 2003.

Gracie, Archibald. *The Truth About Chickamauga.* Dayton: Morningside Press, 1987. Reprint of 1911 edition.

Green, Francis A. *The Witness of a House.* Chickamauga, GA: Gordon-Lee House, 1984.

Griggs, Walter S. *General John Pegram C.S.A.* Lynchburg, VA: H. E. Howard, 1993.

Govan, Gilbert E., and James W. Livingwood. *A Different Valor, General Joseph E. Johnston, C.S.A.* Indianapolis: The Bobbs-Merrill Company, Inc., 1956.

Hafendorfer, Kenneth A. *Mill Springs: Campaign and Battle of Mill Springs, Kentucky.* Louisville, KY: KH Press, 2001.

Hafendorfer, Kenneth A. *The Battle of Richmond, Kentucky: August 30, 1862.* Louisville, KY: KH Press, 2006.

Hallock, Judith Lee. *Braxton Bragg and Confederate Defeat: Volume II.* Tuscaloosa, AL: University of Alabama Press, 1991.

Hallock, Judith Lee. *General James Longstreet in the West: A Monumental Failure.* Fort Worth, TX: Ryan Place Publishers, 1995.

Haughton, Andrew. *Training, Tactics and Leadership in the Confederate Army of Tennessee.* London: Frank Cass Publishers, 2000.

Heidler, David S. and Jeanne T., Eds. *Encyclopedia of the American Civil War,* 5 vols. Santa Barbara, CA: ABC-CLIO, 2000.

Hughes, Nathaniel Cheairs, Jr., and Gordon D. Whitney. *Jefferson Davis in Blue: The Life of Sherman's Relentless Warrior.* Baton Rouge: Louisiana State University Press, 2002.

Hughes, Nathaniel Cheairs, Jr., and Roy P. Stonesifer, Jr. *The Life & Wars of Gideon J. Pillow.* Chapel Hill: University of North Carolina Press, 1993.

Hughes, Nathaniel Cheairs, Jr. *General William J. Hardee: Old Reliable.* Baton Rouge: Louisiana State University Press, 1992. Reprint of 1965 edition.

Hurst, Jack. *Nathan Bedford Forrest.* New York: Alfred A. Knopf, 1993.

Keefer, Bradley S. *Conflicting Memories on the "River of Death," the Chickamauga Battlefield and the Spanish-American War, 1863-1933.* Kent, OH: Kent State University Press, 2013.

Johnson, Kathy. *Colonel Frederick Bartleson.* Joliet, IL: The Will County Historical Society, 1983. (100th Illinois Infantry).

Jones, Evan C., and Wiley Sword, eds. *Gateway to the Confederacy: New Perspectives on the Chickamauga and Chattanooga Campaigns, 1862-1863.* Baton Rouge: Louisiana State University Press, 2014.

Kundahl, George G. *Confederate Engineer: Training and Campaigning With John Morris Wampler.* Knoxville: University of Tennessee Press, 2000.

LaFantasie, Glenn W. *Gettysburg Requiem: The Life and Lost Causes of Confederate Colonel William C. Oates.* New York: Oxford University Press, 2006.

Lamers, William M. *The Edge of Glory: A Biography of General William S. Rosecrans, U.S.A.* Baton Rouge: Louisiana State University Press, 1999. Reprint of 1961 edition.

Lee, Dan. *Kentuckian in Blue: A biography of Major General Lovell Harrison Rousseau.* Jefferson, NC: McFarland & Co, 2010.

Lewis, William Terrell. *Genealogy of the Lewis Family in America.* Louisville: Courier-Journal Job Printing Co., 1893.

Lindsley, John Berrien. *The Military Annals of Tennessee. Confederate. First Series: Embracing a Review of Military Operations, with Regimental Histories and Memorial Rolls.* 2 vols. Wilmington, NC: Broadfoot Publishing, 1995. Reprint of 1886 edition.

Linton, Roger C. *Chickamauga: A Battlefield History in Images.* Athens, GA: University of Georgia Press, 2004.

Livermore, Thomas L. *Numbers and Losses in the Civil War in America, 1861-1865.* Dayton, OH: Morningside Press, 1986. Reprint of 1900 edition.

Longacre, Edward G. *A Soldier to the Last, Maj. Gen. Joseph Wheeler in Blue and Gray.* Washington, DC: Potomac Books, 2007.

Longacre, Edward G. *Cavalry of the Heartland, the Mounted Forces of the Army of Tennessee.* Yardley, PA: Westholme Publishing, 2009.

Losson, Christopher. *Tennessee's Forgotten Warriors: Frank Cheatham and His Confederate Division.* Knoxville: University of Tennessee Press, 1989.

Lutzke Mitch. *The Life and Times of Kimber M. Snyder.* Bloomington, IN: Authorhouse, 2006. (78th Pennsylvania Infantry).

Mackall, William W. *A Son's Recollections of His Father.* New York: E. P. Dutton & Co. 1930.

Maness, Lonnie E. *An Untutored Genius: The Military Career of General Nathan Bedford Forrest.* Oxford, MI: Guild Bindery Press, 1990.

Martin, Samuel J. *General Braxton Bragg, C. S. A.* Jefferson, NC: McFarland & Co., 2012.

Marvel, William. *Burnside.* Chapel Hill: University of North Carolina Press, 1991.

Marvel, William. *Lincoln's Autocrat, the Life of Edwin Stanton.* Chapel Hill: University of North Carolina Press, 2015.

McArthur, Dr. Elizabeth Hoole, *The Sword Returns to Chickamauga: A True Chronicle of the Sword of Lieutenant Colonel Axalla John Hoole, 8th South Carolina Infantry, C. S. A.* Indianapolis: Dog Ear Publishing, 2010

McBride, Mary Gorton. *Randall Lee Gibson of Louisiana: Confederate General and New South Reformer.* Baton Rouge: Louisiana State University Press, 2007.

McKinnon, John L. *History of Walton County.* Gainesville, FL: Palmetto Books, 1968.

McKinney, Francis E. *Education in Violence: The Life of George H. Thomas and the History of the Army of the Cumberland.* Chicago: Americana House, 1991. Reprint of 1961 edition.

McMurry, Richard M. *John Bell Hood and the War For Southern Independence.* Lincoln, NE: University of Nebraska Press, 1982.

McWhiney, Grady. *Braxton Bragg and Confederate Defeat, Volume I.* Tuscaloosa, AL: University of Alabama Press, 1991. Reprint of 1969 Edition.

Mendoza, Alexander. *Confederate Struggle for Command: General James Longstreet and the First Corps in the West.* College Station, TX: Texas A & M University Press, 2008.

Mendoza, Alexander. *Chickamauga 1863: Rebel Breakthrough.* Santa Barbara, CA: Praeger Publishing, 2013.

Miles, Jim. Paths to Victory: *A History and Tour Guide of the Stone's River, Chickamauga, Chattanooga, Knoxville, and Nashville Campaigns.* Nashville: Rutledge Hill Press, 1991.

Moore, David G. *William S. Rosecrans and the Union Victory, a Civil War Biography.* Jefferson, NC: McFarland and Company, 2014.

Morris, Roy, Jr. *Sheridan: The Life & Wars of General Phil Sheridan.* New York: Crown Publishers, 1992.

Mulhane, L. W. *Major General William Stark Rosecrans: Hero of Iuka, Corinth and Stone River, and Father of the Army of the Cumberland.* Mount Vernon, OH: 1898.

Nash, Charles Edward. *Biographical Sketches of Gen. Pat Cleburne and Gen. T. C. Hindman Together with Humorous Anecdotes and Reminiscences of the Late Civil War.* Dayton, OH: Morningside Press, 1977. Reprint of 1898 Edition.

Neal, Diane, and Thomas W. Kremm. *Lion of the South: General Thomas C. Hindman.* Macon, GA: Mercer University Press, 1993.

Neff, Robert O. *Tennessee's Battered Brigadier: The Life of General Joseph B. Palmer, CSA.* Franklin, TN: Hillsboro Press, 2000.

Nicely, Maury. *Chattanooga Walking Tour & Historic Guide.* Chattanooga: Stillhouse Hollow Press, 2002.

Noe, Kenneth. *Perryville: This Grand Havoc of Battle.* Lexington: The University Press of Kentucky, 2001.

Northen, William J. *Men of Mark in Georgia, Vol. 3.* Spartanburg, SC: The Reprint Company, 1974.

O'Conner, Richard. *Sheridan the Inevitable.* New York: Konecky and Konecky, 1994. Reprint of 1953 edition.

O'Conner, Richard. *Hood: Cavalier General.* New York: Prentice-Hall, Inc., 1949.

Owen, Thomas McAdory. *History of Alabama and Dictionary of Alabama Biography*, 4 vols. Chicago: S. J. Clarke Publishing Co. 1921.

Palmer, George Thomas. *A Conscientious Turncoat: The Story of John M. Palmer 1817-1900.* New Haven, CT: Yale University Press, 1941.

Parks, Joseph H. *General Leonidas Polk, C.S.A. The Fighting Bishop.* Baton Rouge: Louisiana State University Press, 1992. Reprint of 1962 edition.

Partridge, Warren Graham *Life of Frederick H. Alms.* Cincinnati: Free Press of Jennings and Graham, 1904. (6th Ohio Infantry).

Perrin, William H., Ed. *History of Fayette County, Kentucky.* Chicago: O.L. Baskin, 1882.

Peterson, Lawrence K. *Confederate Combat Commander: The Remarkable Life of Brigadier General Alfred Jefferson Vaughan, Jr.* Knoxville: University of Tennessee Press, 2013.

Piatt, Donn, and Henry Van Ness Boynton, *General George H. Thomas, A Critical Biography.* Cincinnati: Robert Clarke & Co, 1893.

Piston, William Garrett, *Lee's Tarnished Lieutenant, James Longstreet and His Place in Southern History.* Athens, GA: The University of Georgia Press, 1987.

Plum, William R., *The Military Telegraph During the Civil War in the United States, with an Exposition of Ancient and Modern Means of Communication, and of the Federal and Confederate Cipher Systems; also a Running Account of the War Between the States.* 2 vols. Chicago: Jansen, McClurg & Company, Publishers, 1882.

Polk, William. *Leonidas Polk, Bishop and General.* 2 vols. New York: Longmans, Green, 1893.

Pollard, Edward A., *The Lost Cause.* New York: E. B. Treat & Co., 1866.

Powell, David A. and David A. Friedrichs. *The Maps of Chickamauga: An Atlas of the Chickamauga Campaign, Including the Tullahoma Operations, June 22-September 23, 1863.* New York, Savas-Beatie, 2009.

Powell, David A. *Failure in the Saddle: Nathan Bedford Forrest, Joseph Wheeler, and the Confederate Cavalry in the Chickamauga Campaign.* New York, Savas Beatie, 2010.

Powell, David A. *The Chickamauga Campaign. A Mad Irregular Battle: From the Crossing of the Tennessee River Through the Second Day, August 22 - September 19, 1863.* New York, Savas-Beatie, 2014.

Powell, David A. *The Chickamauga Campaign. Glory or the Grave: The Breakthrough, The Union Collapse, and the Defense of Horseshoe Ridge, September 20, 1863.* New York, Savas-Beatie, 2015.

Preskin, Allan. *Garfield, A Biography.* Norwalk, CT: Easton Press, 1987.

Prokopowicz, Gerald J. *All for The Regiment: The Army of the Ohio, 1861-1862.* Chapel Hill, NC: University of North Carolina Press, 2001.

Purdue, Howell and Elizabeth. *Pat Cleburne, Confederate General*. Hillsboro, TX: n.p., 1973.

Quiner, E. B. *The Military History of Wisconsin in the War for the Union*. Chicago: Clark and Co., 1866.

Raab, James W. J. *Patton Anderson, Confederate General*. Jefferson, NC: McFarland and Co., 2004.

Rafuse, Ethan S. *McClellan's War: The Failure of Moderation in the Struggle for the Union*. Bloomington, IN: Indiana University Press, 2005.

Reaves, Stacy W. *A History & Guide to the Monuments of Chickamauga National Military Park*. Charleston, SC: The History Press, 2013.

Reid, Whitelaw. *Ohio in the War: Her Statesmen, Her Generals, and Soldiers*. 2 vols. Cincinnati: Moore, Wilstach and Baldwin, 1868.

Robarts, William Hugh *Mexican War Veterans: A Complete Roster of the Regular and Volunteer Troops in the War Between the United States and Mexico, From 1846 to 1848*. Washington, DC: Brentano's, 1887.

Rodenbough Theophilus F., and William L. Haskin, eds. *The Army of the United States: Historical Sketches of Staff and Line with Portraits of Generals-In-Chief*. New York: Maynard, Merrill & Co., 1896

Roland, Charles P. *Albert Sidney Johnston: Soldier of Three Republics*. Austin, TX: University of Texas Press, 1987. Reprint of 1964 edition.

Roman, Alfred. *The Military Operations of General Beauregard*. 2 vols. New York: De Capo Press, 1994. Reprint of 1884 edition.

Rowland, Dunbar. *Mississippi, Comprising Sketches of Counties, Towns, Events, Institutions, and Persons, arranged in Cyclopedic Form*. 2 vols. Atlanta: Southern Historical Publishing Association, 1907.

Sanger, Donald Bridgman, and Thomas Robson Hay. *Longstreet: I. Soldier, II. Politician, Officeholder, and Writer*. Baton Rouge: Louisiana State University Press, 1952.

Sartain, James Alfred. *History of Walker County, Georgia*. 2 vols. Carrollton, GA: Thomasson Printing, 1972. Reprint of 1932 edition.

Saunders, James Edmunds. *Early Settlers of Alabama*. New Orleans: Graham and son, Printers, 1899.

Scott, William Forse. *Philander P. Lane Colonel of Volunteers in the Civil War, Eleventh Ohio Infantry*. n.p., 1920.

Sehlinger, Peter J. *Kentucky's Last Cavalier: General William Preston 1816-1887*. Lexington: Kentucky Historical Society, 2004.

Seigler, Robert S. *South Carolina's Military Organizations during the War Between the States: The Low Country & Pee Dee*. Charleston, SC: The History Press, 2008.

Seigler, Robert S. *South Carolina's Military Organizations during the War Between the States: The Midlands*. Charleston, SC: The History Press, 2008.

Seitz, Don C. *Braxton Bragg: General of The Confederacy*. Columbia, SC: The State Company, 1924.

Sheppard, Captain Eric William. *Bedford Forrest: The Confederacy's Greatest Cavalryman*. London: H. F. & G. Witherby, 1930.

Smith, Theodore Clarke. *The Life and Letters of James Abram Garfield*. 2 vols. New Haven CT, Yale University Press, 1925.

Smith, Timothy B. *Champion Hill: Decisive Battle for Vicksburg*. New York, Savas Beatie LLC, 2004.

Smith, Timothy B. *The Untold Story of Shiloh: The Battle and the Battlefield*. Knoxville: University of Tennessee Press, 2006.

Smith, Timothy B. *The Golden Age of Battlefield Preservation, The Decade of the 1890s and the Establishment of America's First Five Military Parks*. Knoxville: University of Tennessee Press, 2008.

Smith, Timothy B., *A Chickamauga Memorial, The Establishment of America's First Civil War National Military Park*. Knoxville: University of Tennessee Press, 2009.

Spruill, Matt. *Guide to the Battle of Chickamauga, Second Edition, Revised and Expanded*. Lawrence, KS: University Press of Kansas, 2017. Update of 1993 edition.

Stewart, Bruce H., Jr. *Invisible Hero, Patrick R. Cleburne*. Macon, GA: Mercer University Press, 2009.

Stickles, Arndt M. *Simon Bolivar Buckner: Borderland Knight*. Chapel Hill: University of North Carolina Press, 1940.

Symonds, Craig L. *Stonewall of the West: Patrick Cleburne & The Civil War*. Lawrence, KS: University of Kansas Press, 1997.

Symonds, Craig L. *Joseph E. Johnston, a Civil War Biography.* New York: W. W. Norton, 1992.

Tatum, Georgia Lee. *Disloyalty in the Confederacy.* Lincoln: University of Nebraska Press, 2000. Reprint of 1934 edition.

Thomas, Wilbur. *General George H. Thomas, the Indomitable Warrior.* New York, Exposition Press, 1964.

Tucker, Glenn. *Chickamauga, Bloody Battle in the West.* Dayton, OH: Press of the Morningside Bookshop, 1981. Reprint of 1961 edition.

Van Horne, Thomas B. *The Army of the Cumberland.* New York: Smithmark Publishers, 1996. Reprint of 1875 edition.

Varney, Frank P. *General Grant and the Rewriting of History.* New York: Savas Beatie Publishing, 2013.

Vermilya, Daniel J. *James Garfield & the Civil War: For Ohio and the Union.* Charleston, SC: The History Press, 2015.

Walker, C. Irvine. *History of South Carolinians in the Confederate War.* n.p. n.d.

Warner, Ezra J. *Generals in Blue: Lives of the Union Commanders.* Baton Rouge: Louisiana State University Press, 1991. Reprint of 1964 edition.

Warner, Ezra J. *Generals in Gray: Lives of the Confederate Commanders.* Baton Rouge: Louisiana State University Press, 1991. Reprint of the 1959 edition.

Welsh, Jack D. M.D. *Medical Histories of the Confederate Generals.* Kent: Kent State University Press, 1995. Kindle Edition.

Wert, Jeffry D. *General James Longstreet, The Confederacy's Most Controversial Soldier-A Biography.* New York: Simon and Schuster, 1993.

Westrate, E. V. *Those Fatal Generals.* Port Washington, NY: Kennikat Press, Inc., 1936.

Whalen, Charles and Barbara. *The Fighting McCooks: America's Famous Fighting Family.* Bethesda, MD: Westmoreland Press, 2006.

White, William Lee. *Bushwacking on a Grand Scale, The Battle of Chickamauga, September 18-20, 1863.* El Dorado Hills, CA: Sava-Beatie, 2013.

Wills, Brian Steel. *George Henry Thomas, as True as Steel.* Lawrence: University Press of Kansas, 2012.

Woodworth, Steven E. *Jefferson Davis and his Generals, the Failure of Confederate Command in the West.* Lawrence, KS: University Press of Kansas, 1990.

Woodworth, Steven E. *Six Armies in Tennessee: The Chickamauga and Chattanooga Campaigns.* Lincoln, NE: University of Nebraska Press, 1998.

Woodworth, Steven E. *A Deep Steady Thunder: The Battle of Chickamauga.* Abilene, TX: McWhiney Foundation Press, 1998.

Woodworth, Steven E. *Chickamauga, A Battlefield Guide with a Section on Chattanooga.* Lincoln: University of Nebraska Press, 1999.

Woodworth, Steven E., ed. *The Chickamauga Campaign.* Carbondale, IL: Southern Illinois University Press, 2010

Wyeth, John Allen. *That Devil Forrest: Life of General Nathan Bedford Forrest.* Baton Rouge: Louisiana State University Press, 1989. Reprint of 1899 edition.

Wyeth, John Allen. *The Life of Lieutenant General Nathan Bedford Forrest.* New York: Harper & Brothers, Publishers, 1908.

Index

Note: The units and commanders listed in Appendices 3 through 7 are not indexed here.

David A. Powell graduated from the Virginia Military Institute (Class of 1983) with a BA in history. He has written many magazine articles and more than fifteen historical simulations of various battles. He is also the author of *The Chickamauga Campaign: A Mad Irregular Battle: From the Crossing of the Tennessee River Through the Second Day, August 22 - September 19, 1863* (Savas Beatie, 2014), and *Glory or the Grave: The Breakthrough, the Union Collapse, and the Defense of Horseshoe Ridge, September 20, 1863* (Savas Beatie, 2015), the first two volumes in his magisterial three-volume study; the current volume completes the trilogy.

Mr. Powell is also the author (with David A. Friedrichs, cartographer) of *The Maps of Chickamauga: An Atlas of the Chickamauga Campaign, Including the Tullahoma Operations, June 22-September 23, 1863* (Savas Beatie, 2009), and the ground-breaking cavalry command study *Failure in the Saddle: Nathan Bedford Forrest, Joseph Wheeler, and the Confederate Cavalry in the Chickamauga Campaign* (Savas Beatie, 2010). The latter title was awarded the Atlanta Civil War Round Table's 2010 Richard Barksdale Harwell Award, as was *Glory or the Grave* in 2016, making David the first two-time recipient of this prestigious award. He is currently working on other volumes for the Savas Beatie Military Atlas Series™ including the Chattanooga and Atlanta campaigns.

David enjoys leading tours to Civil War battlefields in general, and the epic field of Chickamauga in particular, and runs a popular blog on the Chickamauga Campaign (chickamaugablog.wordpress.com). He is married and lives and works in Chicago, Illinois.